Inside Windows,

Platinum Edition

Jim Boyce

Bruce Hallberg
Forrest Houlette

NRP
NEW RIDERS
PUBLISHING

New Riders Publishing, Indianapolis, Indiana

Inside Windows, Platinum Edition

By Jim Boyce, Bruce Hallberg, and Forrest Houlette

Published by:
New Riders Publishing
201 West 103rd Street
Indianapolis, IN 46290 USA

Printed in the United States of America   4 5 6 7 8 9 0

Library of Congress Cataloging-in-Publication Data:

```
Inside Windows, Platinum Edition / Jim Boyce ... [et al.].
       p.    cm.
    Includes index.
    ISBN 1-56205-328-0 : $39.99
    1. Windows (Computer programs)  2. Microsoft Windows
(Computer file)    I. Boyce, Jim, 1958-  .
QA76.76.W56I573  1994
005.4'3 — dc20                                   94-25472
                                                 CIP
```

Warning and Disclaimer

This book is designed to provide information about the Windows operating environment. Every effort has been made to make this book as complete and as accurate as possible, but no warranty or fitness is implied.

The information is provided on an "as is" basis. The author and New Riders Publishing shall have neither liability nor responsibility to any person or entity with respect to any loss or damages arising from the information contained in this book or from the use of the disks or programs that may accompany it.

Publisher	Lloyd J. Short
Associate Publisher	Tim Huddleston
Product Development Manager	Rob Tidrow
Marketing Manager	Ray Robinson
Director of Special Projects	Cheri Robinson
Managing Editor	Matthew Morrill

About the Authors

Jim Boyce is a contributing editor of *WINDOWS Magazine,* and a regular contributor to *CADENCE Magazine* and other computer publications. He has been involved with computers since the late seventies, and has used computers in one way or another as a structural designer, production planner, systems manager, programmer, and college instructor. He has a wide range of experience in the DOS, Windows, and UNIX environments. Jim is the author and coauthor of numerous books published by New Riders Publishing. You can send e-mail to Mr. Boyce at the Internet address 76516.3403@compuserve.com.

Bruce Hallberg is the director of information systems for Genelabs Technologies, Inc., a biotechnology company located in Redwood City, California. He has been heavily involved with PCs since 1980 and has specialized in accounting and business control systems for the past eight years. He has consulted with a large number of local and national companies in a variety of areas and has expertise in networking, programming, and system implementations. He works with a wide variety of PC platforms, including DOS, Windows, OS/2, UNIX, and Macintosh. Mr. Hallberg is the author or a contributing author of numerous books from New Riders Publishing, including *OS/2 for Non-Nerds, WordPerfect for Wimps, Inside OS/2,* and *Inside Microsoft Office Professional.*

Forrest Houlette began programming in 1979 when he took a course in FORTRAN as part of his M.A. Since then, he has developed software in BASIC, C, CH, and Visual Basic. He has authored two books for New Riders Publishing and worked on eight jointly authored books. Mr. Houlette holds a Ph.D. in linguistics and rhetoric, does research on artificial intelligence and the writing process, and teaches English at Ball State University.

Trademark Acknowledgments

All terms mentioned in this book that are known to be trademarks or service marks have been appropriately capitalized. New Riders Publishing cannot attest to the accuracy of this information. Use of a term in this book should not be regarded as affecting the validity of any trademark or service mark. Windows is a trademark of Microsoft Corporation.

Product Director
MICHAEL GROH

Production Editor
JOHN KANE

Editors
AMY BEZEK
LAURA FREY
CLIFF SHUBS
JOHN SLEEVA

Acquisitions Editor
STACEY BEHELER

Technical Editors
ROBERT L. BOGUE
BRAD DEW

Editorial Assistant
KAREN OPAL

Publisher's Assistant
MELISSA LYNCH

Cover Designer
JAY CORPUS

Book Designer
ROGER S. MORGAN

Production Imprint Manager
JULI COOK

Production Imprint Team Leader
KATY BODENMILLER

Graphics Image Specialists
TERESA FORRESTER
CLINT LAHNEN
TIM MONTGOMERY
DENNIS SHEEHAN
SUSAN VANDEWALLE

Production Analysts
DENNIS CLAY HAGER
MARY BETH WAKEFIELD

Production Team
DON BROWN
ELAINE BRUSH
CHERYL CAMERON
KIM COFER
AMY CORNWELL
ELAINE CRABTREE
LISA DAUGHERTY
STEPH DAVIS
CHAD DRESSLER
TERRI EDWARDS
ROB FALCO
GREG KEMP
BETTY KISH
AYANNA LACEY
STEPHANIE J. MCCOMB
JAMIE MILAZZO
STEPHANIE MINEART
WENDY OTT
CHAD POORE
CASEY PRICE
RYAN RADER
BETH RAGO
CLAIR SCHWEINLER
KIM SCOTT
MARC SHECTER
SA SPRINGER
MARCELLA THOMPSON
SCOTT TULLIS
DENNIS Z. WESNER

Indexer
BRONT DAVIS

Contents at a Glance

Table of Contents

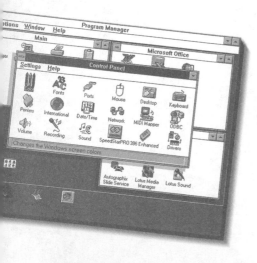

INTRODUCTION

In April 1992, Microsoft introduced version 3.1 of Windows, the most popular graphical user environment available for personal computers. With version 3.1, Windows provided enhanced features that changed the way people used computers. Windows has emerged as a platform on which tightly integrated applications can dynamically exchange data in a seamless fashion.

The new Windows environment also provides a more colorful interface, with proportionally spaced fonts, a wider range of video and printer drivers, and updated screen graphics. Through these enhancements, Windows 3.1 made powerful personal computers more accessible than ever to unskilled users.

Windows 3.11 is a minor upgrade to Windows 3.1. Windows 3.11 fixes a few minor bugs and adds a selection of new drivers. Windows for Workgroups 3.11, however, includes significant performance improvements over Windows 3.11 and Windows for Workgroups 3.1, including 32-bit file access and improved networking.

To date, more than 50,000,000 people have adopted Windows as their preferred working environment, and Microsoft promises that Windows will make a substantial impact on personal computing for years to come. Every Windows user will benefit from truly powerful memory-management features, the potential for integrated multimedia capabilities, and advanced object-oriented data management. These advanced capabilities enable you to become productive with all the applications you run under Windows—whether they are Windows-specific applications or older DOS programs.

Inside Windows, Platinum Edition is designed to address the needs of the advanced Windows user. This complex environment challenges even the most PC-literate user with its wealth of features and capabilities. Often the solution to some vexing problem or concern can only be discovered by hunting through books, magazines, and product documentation in search of some elusive tip or expert recommendation.

The authors and editors of *Inside Windows, Platinum Edition* have compiled the most comprehensive reference to Windows available in print. Between the covers of this book you will find good, solid, information on topics ranging from installation options to selecting a CD-ROM for your computer.

How This Book Is Different from Most Windows Books

Inside Windows, Platinum Edition is not meant to be read from cover to cover. Although, like most other Windows books, the material in *Inside Windows, Platinum Edition* is arranged in a methodical, logical manner, each chapter is a complete discussion of the subject matter. With few exceptions, you will not have to jump from chapter to chapter to find the information you need.

Each chapter introduces you to an important group of related Windows concepts and functions and quickly shows you how to apply new techniques to your use of Windows. The chapters lead you through basic steps you must follow to incorporate new techniques that enhance your own computing work. The extensive index enables you to locate information and answers to your questions quickly.

Inside Windows, Platinum Edition, therefore, is designed and written to accommodate the way you work. The authors and editors at New Riders Publishing know that you probably do not have a great deal of time to read books. You probably are anxious to get the answers you need as quickly as possible so that you can be as productive in your work as possible.

Later in this Introduction you will find descriptions of each of the parts in *Inside Windows, Platinum Edition.*

Who Should Read This Book?

Inside Windows, Platinum Edition is written for the experienced Microsoft Windows user who wants to learn more about Windows. This book assumes you have some Windows experience and want to know more about Windows' internal functions.

You can learn how to apply Windows' latest enhancements to your own computing work without relearning Windows concepts and functions you already know through your own experience. Specifically, this book makes the following assumptions about your Windows skill level:

✔ You are familiar with the mouse and mouse actions

✔ You know how to use dialog boxes and selection lists

✔ You understand the concept of windowed applications, and you know how to use Windows' maximize and minimize buttons

✔ You are familiar with the Windows Program Manager, program groups, and icons

✔ You know how to start and run applications under Windows

The Benefits of This Book to Experienced Windows Users

In contrast to many books on Windows, *Inside Windows, Platinum Edition* does not over-state the obvious. This book, for example, does not explain what Windows is or how to use a mouse. The book emphasizes practical information that explains the subject material without belaboring the point. You should read as many chapters and parts of chapters as you like, and feel free to experiment. As you already know, Windows keeps you from damaging anything in the process.

As an experienced Windows user, you probably will not read this book from start to finish. Instead, use the table of contents and index to find the information most interesting to you and go directly to the pages or chapter containing that information. When you have learned what you need to know, put the book away (or continue reading if you want!) until the next time you need to refer to this book's subject material.

How This Book Is Organized

Inside Windows, Platinum Edition is designed as a reference to help experienced Windows users find information quickly. To make finding the information easier, the book is divided into parts, each of which covers a specific group of Windows concepts and functions.

Part One: Understanding Windows

Part One introduces the Windows environment. Although you probably already know most of this material, this section forms the basis for many of the chapters that follow. Within the six chapters in this part are discussions of file management, navigating through Windows applications, customization, understanding how Windows uses fonts, and printing in Windows.

Part Two: Optimizing Windows

The latest release of Windows provides a much more stable environment than earlier versions, but you still can do many things to ensure the high integrity of your applications and their data. More than ever, the informed user is concerned about viruses, backups, and resolving system breakdowns as quickly as possible.

The chapters in Part Two provide coverage of a wide range of topics, including input and storage devices, performance tuning, and troubleshooting. Do not neglect to read Chapter 13, "Preventing and Overcoming Viruses," which explains how to protect your computer and its precious data from virus attacks.

Part Three: Putting Windows to Work

Even the most sophisticated user needs help now and then or can benefit from new ideas. Part Three condenses the aggregate learning of the authors of *Inside Windows, Platinum Edition* and explores important new topics such as image processing and communications.

Chapter 19, "Using and Building Windows Help," is unique among all Windows books because it explains how you can build your own on-screen help for your applications. This information is sure to appeal to system administrators, consultants, and other professionals charged with supporting Windows end users.

Part Four: Integrating Applications

Although macros and DDE (dynamic data exchange) have been around since Windows 3.0, not many users fully exploit these capabilities. In addition, OLE (object linking and embedding) has added to the complexity and richness of the Windows environment and to the capabilities of Windows applications.

A thorough understanding of the principles underlying data sharing are necessary before you can successfully exploit these capabilities. The chapters in Part Four provide you with everything you need to know to integrate seamlessly all your Windows applications.

In Chapter 25, "Data Exchange with DOS Applications," you even learn how to exchange data with DOS applications running under Windows.

Part Five: Networking and Windows

More and more often, Microsoft Windows is being installed in multiuser environments. In all business environments, ranging from small offices to huge corporations, networked systems have become the norm rather than the exception. The chapters in Part Five explain networking in general terms and offer tips on using Windows and Windows for Workgroups in a networked environment. Part Five also examines e-mail, scheduling, and other workgroup topics. Chapters in Part Five offer tips on integrating Windows in a Novell NetWare environment, using Remote Access Services (RAS), and integrating Windows with Windows NT.

Part Six: Applying Multimedia

Finally, *Inside Windows, Platinum Edition* explores the exciting field of Windows multimedia. Rather than just glance at this topic, chapters in Part Six explore the concepts, technologies, and products that make up multimedia video and sound.

Conventions Used in This Book

Throughout this book, certain conventions are used to help you distinguish the various elements of Windows, DOS, their system files, and sample data. Before you look ahead, you should spend a moment examining the following conventions:

- ✔ Shortcut keys normally are found in the text where appropriate. As an example, Shift+Ins is the shortcut key for the <u>P</u>aste command.

- ✔ Key combinations appear in the following formats:

    Key1+Key2. When you see a plus sign (+) between key names, you should hold down the first key while pressing the second key, then release both keys.

    Key1,Key2. When a comma (,) appears between key names, you should press and release the first key and then press and release the second key.

- ✔ On-screen, Windows underlines the letters of some menu names, file names, and option names. The underlined letter is the letter you can type to choose that command or option. In this book, such letters are displayed in bold, underlined, blue type, such as <u>F</u>ile.

- ✔ Information you type is in **boldface**. This applies to individual letters and numbers, as well as to text strings. This convention does not apply to special keys, such as Enter, Esc, or Ctrl.

- ✔ New terms appear in *italics*.

- ✔ Text that is displayed on-screen but which is not part of Windows or a Windows application—such as DOS prompts and messages—appears in a `special typeface`.

Notes, Tips, and Stops

Inside Windows, Platinum Edition features many special sidebars, which are set apart from the normal text by icons. Three different types of sidebars are used—Notes, Tips, and Stops.

Notes include extra information that you should find useful, but which complements the discussion at hand instead of being a direct part of it.

Notes might describe special situations that result from unusual circumstances. These sidebars tell you what to expect or what steps to take when such situations occur. Notes also might tell you how to avoid problems with your software and hardware.

Tips provide you with quick instructions for getting the most from your Windows system. A Tip might show you how to conserve memory in some setups, how to speed up a procedure, or how to perform one of many time-saving and system-enhancing techniques.

A Stop is a warning telling you when a procedure might be dangerous; that is, when you run the risk of losing data, locking your system, or even damaging your hardware. Stops generally tell you how to avoid such losses or describe the steps you can take to remedy them.

These sidebars enhance the possibility that *Inside Windows, Platinum Edition* will be able to answer your most pressing questions about Windows use and performance. Although Notes, Tips, and Stops do not condense an entire section into a few steps, these snippets will point you in new directions for solutions to your needs and problems.

New Riders Publishing

The staff of New Riders Publishing is committed to bringing you the very best in computer reference material. Each New Riders book is the result of months of work by authors and staff who research and refine the information contained within its covers.

As part of this commitment to you, the NRP reader, New Riders invites your input. Please let us know if you enjoy this book, if you have trouble with the information and examples presented, or if you have a suggestion for the next edition.

Please note, though: New Riders staff cannot serve as a technical resource for Windows or for related questions about software- or hardware-related problems. Please refer to the documentation that accompanies your Windows package or to the applications' Help systems.

If you have a question or comment about any New Riders book, there are several ways to contact New Riders Publishing. We will respond to as many readers as we can. Your name, address, and phone number will never become part of a mailing list or be used for any purpose other than to help us continue to bring you the best books possible. You can write us at the following address:

> New Riders Publishing
> Attn: Associate Publisher
> 201 W. 103rd Street
> Indianapolis, IN 46290

If you prefer, you can fax New Riders Publishing at (317) 581-4670.

You can send e-mail to New Riders from a variety of sources. NRP maintains several mailboxes organized by topic area. Mail in these mailboxes will be forwarded to the staff member who is best able to address your concerns. Substitute the appropriate mailbox name from the list below when addressing your e-mail. The mailboxes are as follows:

ADMIN	Comments and complaints for NRP's publisher
APPS	Word, Excel, WordPerfect, and other office applications
ACQ	Book proposals, inquiries by potential authors
CAD	AutoCAD, 3D Studio, and AutoSketch and CAD products
DATABASE	Access, dBASE, Paradox, and other database products
GRAPHICS	CorelDRAW!, Photoshop, and other graphics products
INTERNET	Internet
NETWORK	NetWare, LANtastic, and other network-related topics
OS	MS-DOS, OS/2, all operating systems except UNIX and Windows
UNIX	UNIX
WINDOWS	Microsoft Windows (all versions)
OTHER	Anything that does not fit the previous categories

If you use an MHS e-mail system that routes through CompuServe, send your messages to:

mailbox @ NEWRIDER

To send NRP mail from CompuServe, use the following to address:

MHS: *mailbox* @ NEWRIDER

To send mail from the Internet, use the following address format:

mailbox@newrider.mhs.compuserve.com

NRP is an imprint of Macmillan Computer Publishing. To obtain a catalog or information, or to purchase any Macmillan Computer Publishing book, call (800) 428-5331.

Thank you for selecting *Inside Windows, Platinum Edition*!

Part One

Understanding Windows

Chapter Snapshot

The first step in taking advantage of the Windows operating environment is, obviously, to install Windows on your system. This chapter explains the installation process and the Windows Setup program. It also explains how you can use the Windows Setup program to remove from your system the parts of Windows you do not use. You also learn how to add parts of Windows you did not install during the initial setup. This chapter covers:

If you are experienced with Windows but have never installed it, the installation is simple and highly configurable. If you are in charge of setting up Windows on a number of different systems or are just interested in modifying Setup, skip to the section "Examining Network Issues."

CHAPTER

Configuring Windows

Windows is a complex operating environment with many options. In addition to specifying which Windows components to install, you also must specify the types of hardware installed in your system. Every installation of Windows therefore involves a number of steps. The first step is to understand the function and operation of the Windows Setup program.

Installing Windows with the Setup Program

Windows uses a program called Setup to install Windows on your system. Setup is two programs in one: the first is a DOS-based program, and the second is a Windows-based program. In Windows for Workgroups 3.11, the Setup program actually is two physically separate programs, SETUP.EXE and WINSETUP.EXE. Regardless of whether you are installing Windows 3.1, Windows 3.11, or Windows for Workgroups 3.11, however, the DOS portion of Setup is what you see first when you install Windows.

Understanding DOS-Based Setup

The DOS portion of Setup is straightforward. Its purpose is to install enough of the Windows environment to enable the Windows portion of Setup to run on your system. Figure 1.1 shows one of the screens from the DOS Setup program.

Figure 1.1
DOS-based Setup is the first step toward installing Windows.

```
Windows Setup

     If your computer or network appears on the Hardware Compatibility List
     with an asterisk next to it, press F1 before continuing.

     System Information
         Computer:              MS-DOS System
         Display:               VGA
         Mouse:                 Whiskers SuperMouseDriver
         Keyboard:              Enhanced 101 or 102 key US and Non US keyboards
         Keyboard Layout:       US
         Language:              English (American)
         Codepage:              English (437)
         Network:               No Network Installed

         Complete Changes: Accept the configuration shown above.

     To change a system setting, press the UP or DOWN ARROW key to
     move the highlight to the setting you want to change. Then press
     ENTER to see alternatives for that item. When you have finished
     changing your settings, select the "Complete Changes" option
     to quit Setup.

  ENTER=Continue   F1=Help   F3=Exit
```

The DOS portion of Setup creates your Windows directory and copies essential Windows files such as GDI.EXE and USER.EXE to the system. These files, and a handful of others that the DOS portion of Setup copies to your system, form just enough of the Windows environment to run a Windows program (Setup). After these files are installed, the DOS portion of Setup starts the Windows portion of Setup.

Tip

After Windows is installed, you can use the DOS mode of Windows Setup when you want to make multiple changes to your Windows environment, such as changing two or more hardware selections.

Understanding Windows-Based Setup

The Windows-based portion of Setup enables you to select which parts of the Windows operating environment will be installed on your system. It also enables you to select a printer for Windows to install and, in the case of Windows for Workgroups, to install additional networking support. Figure 1.2 shows one of the Windows Setup screens.

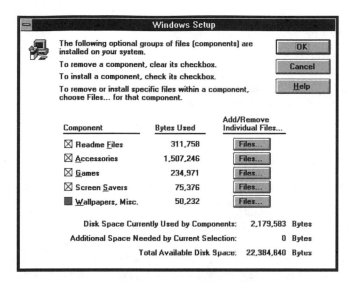

Figure 1.2
The Windows portion of Setup continues the installation process.

After Windows-based Setup completes its part of the installation process, it gives you the option to restart your system to take advantage of all the features Setup and Windows have added.

Choosing a Location for Windows

Windows must be installed in its own directory. Setup by default recommends the directory \WINDOWS on your local hard disk. You can change the name of the directory if you want.

The \WINDOWS directory (or whatever directory you specify) is used to store the majority of the Windows program files. Setup creates, in addition to the \WINDOWS directory, a directory called \WINDOWS\SYSTEM. This directory is used to hold Windows driver files, font files, and other system-specific files. You generally should not delete or otherwise manipulate any files in the \WINDOWS\SYSTEM directory. If you do, you might prevent Windows from functioning properly.

You do not have to use WINDOWS as the name of the directory in which you install Windows, but instead can use any valid directory name. Setup creates the SYSTEM directory under the directory you specify to contain Windows. If you specify WIN as the directory to contain Windows, for example, Setup creates \WIN\SYSTEM to contain the system files.

You should not erase or otherwise change files in the \WINDOWS\SYSTEM directory, because it contains font files and device driver files that are required for Windows to operate properly.

The important point to remember in deciding where to install Windows is that the Windows directory must be right beneath the root directory of the disk on which Windows is installed. You cannot install Windows in the directory \APPS\WINDOWS, for example.

Upgrading Your Copy of Windows

If you are upgrading to a new version of Windows, you should direct Setup to install Windows in the same directory as your existing copy of Windows. Setup replaces all your old Windows files with new ones and retains all your program groups and any settings appropriate to your installation.

Whenever possible, you should use the most recent copy of any device drivers included with the new version of Windows you are installing. Allow Setup to update the printer driver for your printer, for example, to ensure that you have under Windows all the new capabilities of your printer. You also should use the most up-to-date display driver for Windows.

The display drivers in Windows 3.1 enable you to use the mouse in a DOS window, enable you to display DOS graphics applications in a window, and provide other features not available with pre-3.1 drivers. Setup will update printer and display drivers by default.

If you are installing Windows for Workgroups 3.11 over an existing copy of Windows for Workgroups 3.1, Setup will attempt to modify your system's CONFIG.SYS file to remove references to network drivers. This is because the network drivers are loaded by Windows at run time rather that at system start-up. If your system uses a multiboot configuration, Setup will recognize that fact and will not attempt to modify CONFIG.SYS. Instead, Setup will create a new file called CONFIG.WIN in the Windows directory. This CONFIG.WIN file will contain the settings required in your system's CONFIG.SYS file. After you have completed Setup, open both CONFIG.SYS and CONFIG.WIN and merge them to form a proper CONFIG.SYS file. You will find additional tips on installing Windows for Workgroups 3.11 later in this chapter.

Preparing Your System for Windows— the Hard Disk and TSRs

Before you install Windows, you should perform a few steps to ensure that Windows installs properly on your system and that it functions optimally after it is installed. First, you should prepare your system's hard disk.

Before you even begin to use the Setup program to install Windows, you should take an hour or so to clean up and optimize your system's hard disk. Because Windows is a disk-intensive program, it makes extensive use of the hard disk. If you improve the performance of the disk, you improve not only Windows' performance but also the performance of DOS applications you run outside of Windows.

Eliminating Unused Files To Free Hard Disk Space

The first step in preparing the hard disk for Windows is to make as much space as possible available on the disk. To increase the amount of free disk space on your system, consider eliminating a few files:

✔ **Eliminate BAK files.** Many applications create backup files you can eliminate. When you save changes to a file with these programs, the program stores the new version of the document in a new file and places the old document in a backup file, which usually has a BAK file extension. Search your hard disk to locate these backup files. If you are sure you don't need them, delete them.

✔ **Eliminate log files.** Some applications create log files while they run. Many communications programs, for example, capture all your communications sessions to a file. Other programs use log files to store error or status messages that occur while the program is running. These files typically take up a lot of disk space that Windows can put to better use. Check your applications to see whether they create log files, and delete the log files if you no longer need them.

✔ **Eliminate mail and fax files.** E-mail and fax messages can use many megabytes of disk space if you do not regularly remove these files from your system. On a periodic basis, back up the e-mail and fax messages you no longer require on the system to floppy disk or tape.

✔ **Remove unused program files.** If you no longer use programs on your system, move them off the disk to make more free space available. If you are upgrading from Windows 3.0 to Windows 3.1 and you do not use some of Windows' accessories, such as Write, Cardfile, or Terminal, delete these programs and their Help files from the disk. When you upgrade to Version 3.1, you can omit these programs from the installation.

I

Understanding Windows

Eliminating Unnecessary DOS Files

You might be able to delete a number of DOS files that you probably never use. Table 1.1 lists these files and explains their use.

The disk space recovered by deleting the files listed in table 1.1 is not very large. It is worthwhile to delete these files only if you are very low on disk space and will not be using these files.

Table 1.1
Seldom Used DOS Files

File Name	Description
APPEND.EXE	Enables you to append a drive or directory to another directory. Delete this file if you do not use the APPEND command.
NLSFUNC.EXE, KEYB.COM, *CPI, COUNTRY.SYS, DISPLAY.SYS, KEYBOARD.SYS	Provide support for the international character sets. You can delete these files if you don't use foreign language support.
RAMDRIVE.SYS	Device driver used for setting up a RAM drive. Delete it if you do not use a RAM drive.
DOSSHELL.*, *.VID	Files for the MS-DOS Shell. Delete them if you do not use the MS-DOS Shell.
POWER.EXE	Works in conjunction with your laptop or notebook computer's power-saving feature to extend battery life. Delete it if you are installing Windows on a desktop computer running MS-DOS 6.0.
INTERLNK.*, INTERSVR.*	The MS-DOS 6.0 Interlink program files. Delete them if you don't plan to use Interlink.
4201.CPI, 4208.CPI, 5202.CPI, LCD.CPI, PRINTER.SYS	Provides international and character-set support for a handful of IBM ProPrinter and QuietWriter printer models. Delete them if you are not using these types of printers.
GRAFTABL.COM	Delete this file if you do not need to provide international support on a CGA monitor.

File Name	Description
ASSIGN.COM	This command redirects disk requests from one drive to another. If you currently use ASSIGN.COM, delete this file and use SUBST instead.
CV.COM, EXE2BIN.EXE, GWBASIC.*, BASICA.*, LINK.EXE, *.BAS	You can delete these files if you're not a programmer. Delete these BASIC programming language files if you don't program in BASIC or use any of the sample program files supplied with DOS, but do not delete them if you use the MS-DOS Editor (EDIT.EXE).
EDLIN.EXE	This is DOS's original line editor. Delete it if you use EDIT or Notepad to edit text files.
HDBKUP.EXE, HDRSTORE.EXE	These files were used to back up files during MS-DOS 5.0 installation and no longer are needed. You can delete them.
JOIN.EXE	This file joins a drive with a directory on a different drive. Delete it if you don't use JOIN.
MSHERC.COM	Supports Hercules monitors when you run the MS-DOS Editor or QBasic. Delete this utility if you don't have a Hercules monitor.
PRINTFIX.COM	This utility disables verification of a printer's status. You can delete it if you can print successfully from your computer.

Note International support refers to special character sets required by languages other than English.

Defragmenting the Hard Disk

After you find and delete unnecessary files from DOS and other programs, you should defragment your hard disk. As files are modified during regular use, they become broken up and scattered (fragmented) across the disk in noncontiguous areas of the disk. DOS and Windows have no problems reading the files, but it takes longer to do so than if the files were located in a single contiguous area. The reason: DOS and Windows must jump around the disk to read the entire file. When the files are placed in contiguous areas, disk access improves. When you improve disk access, you improve overall system performance.

The other benefit of defragmenting the disk is that it makes a much larger amount of contiguous free disk space available on the disk. When you have the largest possible contiguous free space available, you can have a much larger permanent Windows swap file than would be possible otherwise. Defragmenting the disk also makes more contiguous disk space available for new program and document files.

Windows uses a swap file to store temporary information and to simulate memory, which improves Windows' performance.

Delete the Windows Swapfile Before You Defragment

If you are upgrading from Windows 3.0 to Windows 3.1 and are using a permanent Windows swap file, delete it before defragmenting the disk. To do so, start Windows 3.0 in real mode by typing **WIN /R** at the DOS prompt. Then run the Swapfile program as follows:

1. From Program Manager's **F**ile menu, choose **R**un.

2. Type **SWAPFILE** in the Run dialog box and choose OK.

3. When the Swapfile dialog box appears, choose the radio button labeled **D**elete the current swap file, and then click on OK.

4. After you have deleted the swap file, exit from Windows to continue the disk defragmenting process.

You should defragment your system's hard disk regularly (monthly, for example) for continued optimum performance. Before defragmenting your drive, always delete the permanent Windows swap file, then defragment the drive and re-create the swap file.

Defragmenting the Drive

If you are using MS-DOS 6, follow these steps to optimize your hard disk (fig. 1.3 shows the MS-DOS 6 Defrag program window):

1. At the DOS prompt, type **DEFRAG** and press Enter.

2. After the Defrag program analyzes your hard disk, choose the Configure button when Defrag displays it.

3. From the Optimize menu, choose Optimization Method.

4. Choose Full Optimization and then choose OK.

5. From the Optimization menu, choose Begin Optimization.

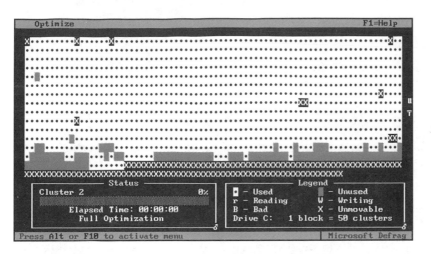

Figure 1.3
The MS-DOS 6 Defrag program window.

If you are using MS-DOS 5.0 or an earlier version, you can use a third-party disk-defragmenting utility to defragment the drive (or upgrade to MS-DOS 6.0). Both Symantec's Norton Utilities and Central Point Software's PC Tools, for example, include disk-defragmenting utilities.

Avoiding TSR Problems

TSRs, or *terminate-and-stay-resident programs*, are device drivers or utility programs that perform special-purpose functions. TSRs generally are loaded in AUTOEXEC.BAT. Some TSRs cause problems with Setup. If you have any of the TSRs in this list, follow these steps to avoid problems when you run Setup:

✔ **ASP Integrity Toolkit Version 3.7.** Remove during Setup. You should be able to run this TSR after installing Windows.

✔ **Data Physician Plus Version 2.0 (VirAlert).** Upgrade to version 3.0 or higher.

✔ **Norton AntiVirus Version 1.0.** Upgrade to version 1.5 or higher.

✔ **PC-Kwik Version 1.59.** Upgrade to version 2.0 or higher.

✔ **SoftIce Debugger.** Remove during Setup. You should be able to run this TSR after Setup is complete.

✔ **Vaccine.** Remove during Setup. You should be able to run this TSR after Setup is complete.

✔ **VDefend.** Remove during Setup. You should be able to run this TSR after Setup is complete.

✔ **Virex-PC Version 1.11.** Remove during Setup. You should be able to run this TSR after Setup is complete.

✔ **ViruSafe Version 4.0.** Upgrade to version 4.5 or higher and run with the /C switch.

If you want to disable a TSR temporarily while you run Setup, edit the AUTOEXEC.BAT and CONFIG.SYS files and add a REM statement at the beginning of every line that loads one of the TSRs in question. Then reboot the system. After running Setup, edit the files again to remove the REM statements.

Using Express Setup

The DOS-based portion of Setup offers two methods for running Setup—Express Setup and Custom Setup. The Express Setup mode enables you to install Windows on your system with virtually no input from you, other than to specify a directory in which to put Windows and to select a printer for installation.

 If you choose the Express Setup option, you need approximately 10 MB of free disk space in which to install Windows.

If you want to install all the Windows components, choose the Express Setup option after you begin the Setup program. After you specify a directory in which to install Windows, Setup continues to install all the Windows components on your system.

Using Custom Setup

Windows has a number of small accessory applications, such as Write, Paintbrush, and Cardfile, and a number of bitmap images, reference files, and other files you might not want Setup to install on your system because of limited disk space. In this case, choose Custom Setup after you have started the Setup program. Setup prompts you for a directory in which to install Windows and then continues to install as much of Windows as necessary to start the Windows-based portion of Setup. After Windows Setup begins, you see the dialog box shown in figure 1.4. This dialog box enables you to select which Windows components to install.

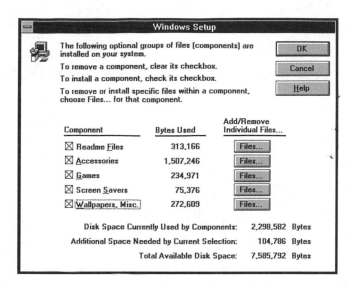

Figure 1.4
The Windows Setup dialog box enables you to specify which components of Windows to install.

The Component check boxes list each part of Windows you can affect during installation. If you do not want to install any of the files from a particular component, clear the component's check box. If you do not want to install any of the games supplied with Windows, for example, clear the Games check box. The Bytes Used column indicates the amount of disk space necessary for each component. Lists at the bottom of the dialog box indicate the amount of free disk space available, the total amount required by all your selections, and how much additional space is required by the selected component. These status indicators help you determine whether you have enough free disk space to add the selected component.

If you prefer to install only some items in a particular component, click on the Files button beside the component and select the features you want to include in the installation. If you want to install only a select few Windows Accessories, for example, click on the Files button beside the Accessories check box. This displays the Accessories dialog box, as shown in figure 1.5.

If you do not need them, a few accessories you might consider omitting are Character Map, Media Player, Recorder, Sound Recorder, and Terminal. For information on what these Accessories are for, consult your Windows User's Guide. Many applications rely on Notepad or Write to display reference files, so you should consider installing them on your system.

At the right side of the dialog box is the list of files that will be installed if you do not make any changes. To remove an item from the list so that it does not install, click on it in the list at the right and then choose the Remove button. This step moves the item to the list at the left of the dialog box and removes it from the installation process. When you are selecting items to remove from installation, remember that you often can remove a

Help file associated with the item. If you remove Write from installation, for example, you also can eliminate Write Help to save additional disk space.

Figure 1.5
The Accessories
dialog box
enables you to
choose which
Windows
accessories to
install.

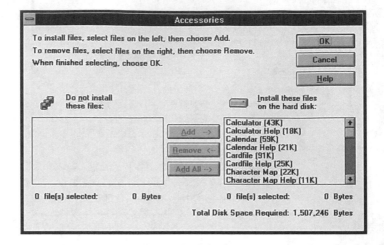

When you have finished specifying the components you want Setup to install, return to the Windows Setup dialog box and click on the OK button. Setup begins installing the components you have selected.

If you want to conserve disk space, consider eliminating all wallpaper, sound, and screen saver files you will not be using. Remember to eliminate Help files for any applications that you choose not to install.

Examining Network Issues

If you are installing Windows on a network, you should consider a number of additional issues besides those for installing Windows on a stand-alone workstation. The first issue is licensing.

Licensing Windows

Although you can install any number of copies of Windows from a single set of disks, it violates both the software license agreement and the law. When you install Windows on a network server or on a network node (workstation), you should verify that you have purchased a license for every station on which Windows will run.

Considering Where To Install Windows on a Network

The next Windows networking issue to consider is where you want to install Windows. You essentially have two options: install a shared copy of Windows on a network server or install a full local copy of Windows on the workstation. A local copy of Windows requires from 8 to 10.5 MB of free disk space on each workstation. If Windows is installed on the server and users work with a shared copy, you need only about 300 KB of free disk space per workstation but as much as 16 MB or more of disk space on the server. Diskless workstations obviously require Windows to be on the server.

The installation of Windows locally on each workstation can eliminate considerable network traffic and improve overall network performance. It requires much more local free hard disk space, however, than does a shared network installation.

Consider also how you want to install Windows on each workstation. You can choose to run Setup from across the network or from a floppy disk. If your network software provides a connection to the server from DOS, you can install Windows across the network and not use the Windows distribution disks.

Using the Setup /A Switch

To set up a shared copy of Windows on a network server, log in to the network server with administrator privileges. Then type **SETUP /A** at the DOS prompt. The /A switch causes Setup to expand all the Windows files from the distribution disks to the server, but it does not set up a usable Windows installation. Its only purpose is to place all the Windows files on the server on which they will be available for setup on each workstation.

After placing the files on the network server, make the directory read-only. Make sure that all users who need to access the Windows files on the server have access to the directory.

Using the Setup /N Switch

To install a shared copy of Windows in which only a few files reside on every workstation's hard disk, log in to the network server from the workstation on which you want to install Windows. Then type **SETUP /N** at the DOS prompt. The /N switch directs Setup to install a shared copy of Windows on the workstation. Only a few files are placed on the local hard disk; the rest remain in the shared Windows directory on the server.

If you are installing Windows on a diskless workstation, you also should use the /N switch. Setup places the node's Windows files in the user's personal directory on the network server.

Determining the Location of the Swap File

The Windows swap file for each workstation should be located, if at all possible, on the workstation's local hard disk. The placement of a swap file on a network server can reduce network performance significantly because of excessive network traffic. If you must place a node's swap file on a network server, use a temporary swap file—you cannot use a permanent swap file.

Looking At Setup Options

The Setup program supports a number of command-line switches, all of which are discussed in the following sections.

Using the Setup/? Switch

The Setup switch /? does not start Setup; rather, it lists all the possible switches you can use with Setup and provides a brief description of each.

Using the Setup/I Switch

Normally, Setup automatically detects the hardware installed in your system to configure Windows for that hardware. An item of hardware in the system occasionally can conflict with Setup. The /I switch prevents Setup from detecting your system's hardware. The use of the /I switch often can overcome problems with Setup hanging the system during the hardware-detection phase. With this switch you will have to tell Setup what hardware you have.

Using the Setup /A Switch

The /A switch copies and expands all the Windows files from the Windows distribution disks to the hard disk. The hard disk can be a local directory, but more often it is a network server. Enter **SETUP /A** when you want to install all the Windows files on a network server for access by the network's nodes.

Using the Setup /N Switch

The /N switch is used to install a shared copy of Windows on a network node. The /N switch directs Setup to copy to the node's local hard disk only a handful of files, such as initialization files and WIN.COM. If you do not use the /N switch, Setup installs a full copy of Windows to the node's hard disk.

Using the Setup /B Switch

The /B switch sets up Windows for a monochrome display. If you are installing on a system that has a monochrome monitor, or on a notebook computer, you might want to use this switch.

Using the Setup /T Switch

The /T switch forces Setup to search for currently running TSRs that are not compatible with Setup. In general, you should not need to use this switch because Setup usually detects these TSRs by default.

Using the Setup /H:*filename* Switch

The /H switch is particularly useful for installing Windows on a number of different workstations from a shared copy on a network server. This switch directs Setup to perform an automatic installation based on configuration information found in the file specified with the /H switch.

SETUP.INF and SETUP.SHH are ASCII files much like Windows initialization (INI) files. Each contains sections that define hardware options or operating options for Windows and for Setup. By modifying these two files, you can customize the way Setup installs Windows.

Using the Setup /O:*filename* Switch

This switch specifies the SETUP.INF file Setup will use. This capability is useful when you are installing Windows on a network node and you want to specify a custom configuration file from a selection of configuration files contained on the server. /O:*filename* also is useful if you want to add a device driver from an OEM floppy disk. You can use the /O switch and specify the SETUP.INF file on the floppy disk.

Using the Setup /S:*filename* Switch

The /S switch specifies a path to the Windows installation disks. If you have placed disk images of the installation disks on a network drive that is mapped as drive F, for example, and you want to use a SETUP.INF file located on drive G, use a Setup command similar to the following:

```
SETUP /O:G:\SETUP.INF /S:F:\
```

A *disk image* is an exact duplication of the distribution disks onto a hard disk. You can copy each distribution disk to a subdirectory on a network server, for example, and leave all the files in their compressed form. This conserves disk space, but is useful only when you intend to install local copies of Windows from these Windows source files. If you want to be able to install a shared copy of Windows from the server, however, you must expand all of the files to the server disk by running SETUP /A.

Installing Windows for Workgroups

If you have installed Windows 3.0 or 3.1 in the past, then you already know nearly all the installation process for Windows for Workgroups. When you install Windows for Workgroups, the only additional steps you must take (besides installing the software) are to install the workstations' network adapter cards, connect the cabling, and configure the adapters. The process is simple enough even for a novice computer user to perform, given a good set of instructions and a screwdriver. This section supplies the instructions; you supply the screwdriver.

Network adapter cards receive signals from the network cable and translate the signals into a format that the network software can interpret. This section provides you with information about a typical network adapter card, including methods for determining its base address, interrupt, and RAM address. The examples show you how to configure these options for a typical network adapter (the Intel EtherExpress 16 Ethernet card), how to install the card, and how to connect the cables.

The sections on software installation and setup cover both Windows for Workgroups and Workgroup Connection. Workgroup Connection—which is available from Microsoft as a separate product—is a DOS-based network interface that enables your non-Windows PCs to access resources on a Windows for Workgroups server. Workgroup Connection runs on all types of PCs (8088, 8086, 80286, 80386, 80486, and Pentium), enabling you to tie your older XT and 286 systems into the network along with your newer, more powerful workstations.

This chapter assumes you are somewhat familiar with PCs and their operation but are not necessarily an expert user. If you know your way around the inside of a PC, you probably will not need any help installing the network adapters and performing other hardware setup tasks. You can skip to the sections that cover software installation. If you are not comfortable working inside a PC, don't worry; contrary to popular belief, computers are not all that delicate. By following a few simple precautions, you can ensure a trouble-free installation. These precautions are noted in this chapter where appropriate.

Previewing the Installation Process

The amount of time you must spend setting up and configuring your network depends on the number of workstations you must install. If you are setting up only two or three workstations, you can complete the entire process in a few hours. Beyond that, you should need 30 minutes or an hour to set up each additional workstation, depending on how much of the workstation hardware already is set up.

The first step is to get the computers assembled and functioning as stand-alone work stations. If the workstations already are set up and running and you are just installing Windows for Workgroups, then much of the physical network setup is already done. If the workstations are still in their boxes and awaiting assembly, you have a little more physical labor ahead.

When the workstations are assembled, you might need to install DOS on them. The DOS installation process includes formatting each computer's hard disk. If your vendor already has installed DOS and other software on the workstations, a great deal of work has been done for you.

When the systems are functioning properly as stand-alone workstations (that is, if you can turn on the system, boot DOS, and see a C:> prompt), you are ready to install the network hardware. This installation involves opening each computer, configuring the network adapter card, and plugging in the card. When the card is installed and the machine is closed up again, you can connect the network cables.

The next step is to install either Windows for Workgroups or Workgroup Connection on each system, depending on what type of access you want each workstation to have to the network. When the software has been installed, you can configure and use the network. This last step includes setting up additional workgroups, installing the mail system and applications, and configuring shared resources.

The following list summarizes the installation process:

1. Unpack and set up all your computers as stand-alone workstations.

2. Install DOS and prepare each computer's hard disk.

3. Install and configure the network adapters.

4. Install Windows for Workgroups or Workgroup Connection.

5. Configure the network (Mail, workgroups, resources, and so on).

6. Get the system's users involved and trained.

The first few steps—assembling the workstations and installing the operating system—might already have been done for you. If you are adding networking capability to your existing installation by installing Windows for Workgroups, for example, your systems probably are already set up, configured, and functioning. If you are adding Windows for Workgroups to your existing network environment, you also have no need to install hardware.

If your workstations are not already assembled and set up, consult your workstation documentation for instructions on assembling the system and connecting the monitor, keyboard, mouse, and other devices. Consult your DOS manual for instructions on installing the operating system. Although you can install the network adapter card before you install DOS, it is a good idea to install DOS first. This ensures that the workstations are functioning properly before you add the network card, and will simplify network troubleshooting later.

Before opening and working inside a computer, always turn off the computer and unplug it. You also should take precautions to prevent damaging its components or the adapter card with static electricity. When you install an adapter card, avoid touching electronic components on the card or touching the card's connectors. Handle the card by its edges. Touch the computer's metal chassis to discharge any static buildup before you pick up the adapter card or touch the computer's motherboard.

When the workstations are assembled and you can boot them as stand-alone systems, you are ready to install the network adapter cards.

Installing Network Adapter Cards

The type of network adapter you install depends on the network topology you have chosen for your network (see Chapter 26, "Understanding Networks and Workgroups," for a discussion of network topology). Regardless of the topology, however, all network adapters are installed and configured in much the same manner.

The most important aspect of installing the network adapter card is to identify the proper base address, IRQ, and RAM address settings for each workstation (these settings are described in detail later in this chapter). If you want your installation to be trouble-free, you must coordinate the proper settings of new workstations with those already in use by the system. Configuring these settings on the card generally requires changing jumpers or setting switches on the board, so you first need to be familiar with the network card.

This chapter's examples assume that you are using the Intel EtherExpress 16 network interface card. If you are using a different type of card, do not worry. Be sure to check your card's documentation to find its correct settings for use with your system. If you cannot find this information, contact your card's vendor for assistance.

You change the settings for the EtherExpress 16 card by using a software configuration program that comes with the card; such is the case with many newer network adapters. In addition, Windows for Workgroups can automatically choose settings for many network adapter cards (including the EtherExpress 16). If your network adapter card uses a software configuration program to specify settings, consult the card's documentation for instructions on using the setup program supplied with the card. If you are installing the EtherExpress 16, you do not have to run the setup program; instead, you can allow Windows for Workgroups to set up the card's configuration for you.

If you are using a card that does not include a configuration program, you must configure the card manually. The following section provides an overview of this process.

Recognizing Jumpers and DIP Switches

Many network adapters use devices called jumpers and DIP switches on the card to specify IRQ address, I/O base address, and RAM address settings. These jumpers and DIP switches are used rather than a software configuration program to set the card's configuration. Some cards use a combination of jumpers, DIP switches, and software setup to configure the card.

Jumpers are small rectangular plugs that fit onto pin connectors on the adapter card. The jumper makes electrical contact between two connector pins, much like a switch makes a connection between switch poles. On adapter cards, jumpers commonly are used to specify various options. To change a jumper setting, simply pull the jumper off its current pin location and insert it snugly onto the new pins. Usually, pins are labeled to help you locate the proper jumper configuration. Figure 1.6 shows an example of a jumper.

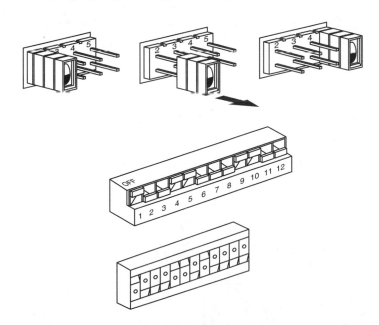

Figure 1.6
Jumpers and DIP switches.

DIP (Dual In-line Package) switches are small rectangular switch blocks that contain varying numbers of small switches. These on/off switches work in combination to specify options for the adapter. To change a DIP switch's setting, use the tip of a pencil or a ballpoint pen to move each switch to the proper orientation (on, off, closed, or open). Note that a 1 is often used on DIP switches to indicate On, and a 0 (zero) is used to indicate Off. Figure 1.6 shows an example of a DIP switch.

After you set a jumper or DIP switch, double-check your setting to make sure that it is correct before you continue with the installation process.

Setting the Base I/O Address

The CPU does not directly recognize other devices in the system. Instead, it communicates with these devices by placing data in specific locations in memory. The network adapter card and other devices in your workstation use a base I/O address as a means to communicate with the CPU. This base I/O address corresponds to the memory location that the CPU uses to communicate with the device. The base I/O address is something like mail slots at a hotel; when the desk clerk needs to leave a message for a guest, he places it in that guest's mail slot. When the CPU needs to communicate with a device, it copies the instruction or data to the device's base I/O address, where the device can retrieve it.

Remember that many of your computer's devices require base I/O addresses. If two or more devices use the same addresses, those addresses conflict, preventing your system from functioning properly. For this reason, you must choose an unused address for your network adapter. Table 1.2 shows the base addresses used by many systems. Note that your system may differ. Also note that the address ranges in table 1.2 are general, not specific. The address LPT1, for example, actually uses a starting I/O base address of 378. Table 1.2 provides a general address range in which common devices place their base I/O addresses.

Table 1.2
Common Base I/O Address Ranges

Base Address	Device	Base Address	Device
200 - 20F	Game port	300 - 30F	Unused
210 - 21F	Unused	310 - 31F	Unused
220 - 22F	Unused	320 - 32F	Hard disk (PS/2 Model 30)
230 - 23F	Bus mouse	330 - 33F	Unused
240 - 24F	Unused	340 - 34F	Unused
250 - 25F	Unused	350 - 35F	Unused

ress	Device
	Unused
	LPT2
	LPT1
	Unused
	Unused
	Unused
	EGA/VGA
	CGA/MCGA
	COM3
	COM1/floppy controller

addresses are available. Consult the
/O addresses, or run the Microsoft
d with MS-DOS and with Windows to
by your system. (The Microsoft Diagnostic
is chapter.) Using table 1.2, eliminate
those addresses that are being used by common devices such as the parallel ports (LPT1,
LPT2, and LPT3) and the serial ports (COM1, COM2, and so on).

Many network adapters use the addresses 280 or 300 as their default base I/O address. If
the workstation has no other adapter cards in it except for the video, disk controller(s),
and serial/parallel port, base addresses 280 and 300 probably are available. If the workstation has a special-purpose card, such as a fax card, check the card's documentation to
determine its base I/O address. If you can use the default address, do so to simplify the
installation procedure.

If you are using the Intel EtherExpress 16, be aware that the card uses a software configuration program to set the base I/O address. Windows for Workgroups, however, can
automatically set the base I/O address for you. You do not need to run the card's
configuration program before you install Windows for Workgroups.

If you are installing an EtherExpress 16 card in a workstation that will run
Workgroup Connection rather than Windows for Workgroups, you must use
the configuration program to set the card's base I/O address.

I

Understanding Windows

If your network adapter requires that you manually set the base I/O address by using a jumper, you must determine which pins to place the jumper on. Then carefully slide a jumper onto the pins, making sure to align the jumper on the correct pins, and press it firmly into place. If you must use a DIP switch to set the address, use a ballpoint pen to set the switches as described in the card's documentation. Double-check your settings before you continue.

After you have selected a base I/O address for your network adapter and configured the card, write it down for future reference. You might want to add it to table 1.2, along with the addresses of any other devices you add to the system.

Setting the IRQ

Many of the workstation's devices use a hardware event called an *interrupt* to inform the CPU that they need attention. The device sends the interrupt to the CPU through an interrupt request line (IRQ). With some exceptions, each device in the system must use a unique IRQ so that it does not conflict with interrupts from other devices. Like many other devices, the network adapter requires a unique IRQ to function properly.

Like base I/O addresses, IRQ assignments generally are standard among PC manufacturers. Table 1.3 shows common IRQ assignments for the various devices in a typical PC.

Table 1.3
Common IRQ Assignments

IRQ	Device
NMI	Non-Maskable Interrupt, reports parity errors
0	System timer
1	Keyboard
2	EGA/VGA, and cascade interrupt for second IRQ controller
3	COM2, COM4
4	COM1, COM3
5	LPT2
6	Floppy disk, or hard disk/floppy disk controller
7	LPT1
8	Real-time clock interrupt

IRQ	Device
9	Software redirected to IRQ2
10	Available
11	Available
12	Available
13	Coprocessor (FPU)
14	Hard disk controller
15	Available, or hard disk controller

Use table 1.3 to determine which IRQs are available in your system. "Available" IRQs generally are available unless they already have been assigned to other devices.

If you have only one serial and one parallel port (COM1 and LPT1), you should at least have IRQ3 and IRQ5 available. In addition, IRQ10, IRQ11, and IRQ12 probably are available. In table 1.3, cross out those items that are installed in your system to determine which IRQs you can assign to the network adapter.

Many network adapters use either IRQ3 or IRQ5 as defaults. If the default IRQ for your network adapter is available, use it to avoid having to change its jumper or switch setting on the card.

The Intel EtherExpress 16 uses its software configuration program to specify the adapter's IRQ. If you are installing the card in a computer that will run Workgroup Connection, run the setup program that came with your card to set the card's IRQ. If you are installing Windows for Workgroups, you do not need to specify an IRQ; Setup automatically specifies an available IRQ for you.

If your network adapter requires that you manually set the IRQ using jumpers or a DIP switch, consult the card's documentation to determine the correct settings to specify the IRQ you need. Then follow the procedure described previously to set the jumper or DIP switch.

After you set your network card's IRQ, write it down for future reference. You might want to add it to table 1.3.

Setting the Base Memory Address

Most network adapters also use a block of the PC's memory to buffer the data between the network and the CPU. The data resides in the buffer until the network adapter is ready to process it. (Some network adapters include onboard RAM that serves the same purpose.) This address range is referred to as the adapter's *base memory address*.

The buffer generally is located in the computer's *upper memory area* (UMA), which is the range of memory between 640–1,024 KB. Figure 1.7 shows a map of memory allocation in the UMA. The map shows hexadecimal memory values at the left (hex values are explained a little later), the decimal equivalent in the second column, and a description of devices and software that commonly use specific memory blocks in the rightmost column. On the left side of the map, each horizontal block represents a 16 KB block, or page, of memory. Each 16 KB memory page comprises 16 1 KB blocks, which are called *upper memory blocks,* or UMBs.

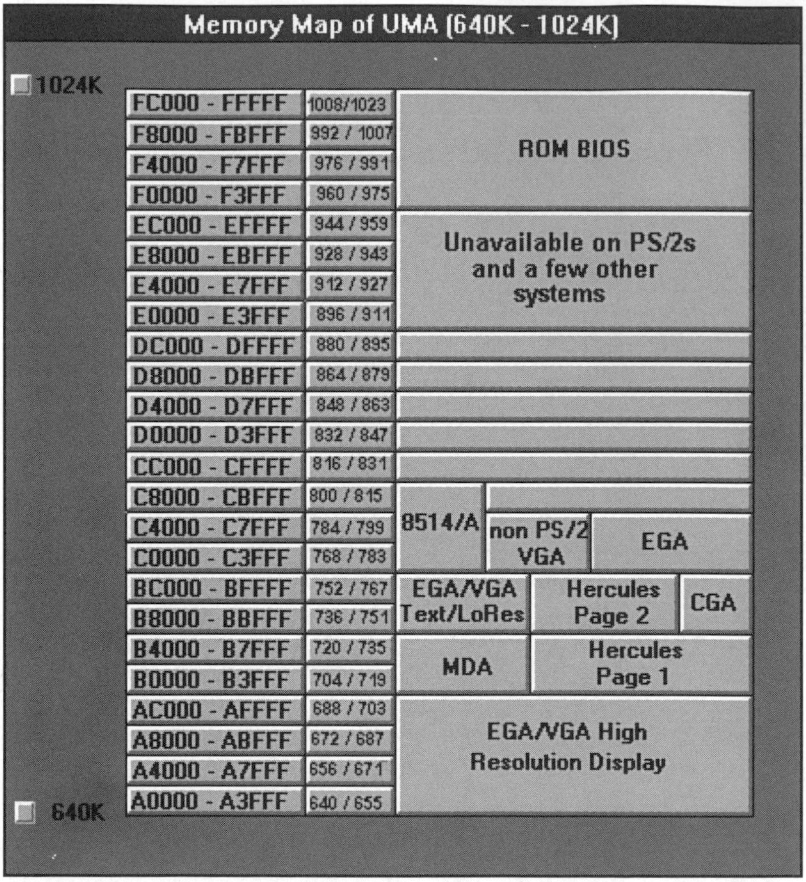

Figure 1.7
A map of the UMA, showing memory allocation.

Memory Map of UMA (640K - 1024K)		

□ 1024K

Hex	Decimal	Description
FC000 - FFFFF	1008/1023	ROM BIOS
F8000 - FBFFF	992 / 1007	
F4000 - F7FFF	976 / 991	
F0000 - F3FFF	960 / 975	
EC000 - EFFFF	944 / 959	Unavailable on PS/2s and a few other systems
E8000 - EBFFF	928 / 943	
E4000 - E7FFF	912 / 927	
E0000 - E3FFF	896 / 911	
DC000 - DFFFF	880 / 895	
D8000 - DBFFF	864 / 879	
D4000 - D7FFF	848 / 863	
D0000 - D3FFF	832 / 847	
CC000 - CFFFF	816 / 831	
C8000 - CBFFF	800 / 815	
C4000 - C7FFF	784 / 799	8514/A / non PS/2 VGA / EGA
C0000 - C3FFF	768 / 783	
BC000 - BFFFF	752 / 767	EGA/VGA Text/LoRes / Hercules Page 2 / CGA
B8000 - BBFFF	736 / 751	
B4000 - B7FFF	720 / 735	MDA / Hercules Page 1
B0000 - B3FFF	704 / 719	
AC000 - AFFFF	688 / 703	EGA/VGA High Resolution Display
A8000 - ABFFF	672 / 687	
A4000 - A7FFF	656 / 671	
A0000 - A3FFF	640 / 655	

□ 640K

Memory addresses often are expressed in hexadecimal values, which are also called hex values. *Hex values* are numbers expressed in the base-16 numbering system. Base-16 uses the following number set:

0,1,2,3,4,5,6,7,8,9,A,B,C,D,E,F

The letters A–F represent the decimal numbers 10–15. In the UMA, a memory block's hex address is expressed as a combination of letters and numbers, such as A0000, D8000, and E3FFF.

You do not need to know how to convert hex values to decimal equivalents to assign a memory address to your network adapter. You need only identify a free block of memory and assign it by using its hex value. (For an in-depth discussion of memory and hex notation, see *Keeping Your PC Alive,* also from New Riders Publishing.) Using the memory map shown in figure 1.7, you should be able to identify a free block quickly.

Viewing Your System's Memory

A map of common memory allocation in the UMA is helpful, but it also helps to have a map of the specific memory allocations that have been made in your PC. For this reason, Windows for Workgroups includes the Microsoft Diagnostic application (MSD), which enables you to view memory allocations in the UMA. The program file, MSD.EXE, is contained on Disk 4 of the Windows for Workgroups distribution disks (in the 3 ½-inch, 1.44 MB format). The file is not compressed, so you can copy it directly from the floppy disk to your hard drive. MSD is a standard DOS program, which you can execute by typing **MSD** at the DOS prompt. Figure 1.8 shows the main MSD menu.

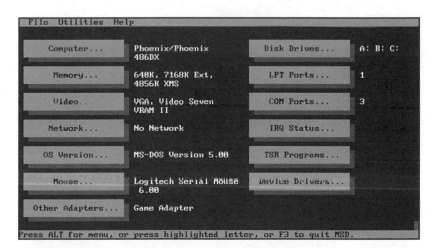

Figure 1.8
The main MSD menu.

If you have a previous version of Windows or another Microsoft application installed on your system, you might have a copy of an earlier version of MSD. MSD has been updated for Windows for Workgroups, so you should copy the file from your Windows for Workgroups Disk 4 even if you already have an earlier version.

The program's Memory option enables you to view a graphical representation of memory allocations in the UMA. MSD displays UMBs as being in one of the following states:

✔ **Available.** Memory not currently controlled by an upper memory manager (such as EMM386.EXE) or which is available to the operating system.

✔ **RAM.** Memory in use by applications, such as device drivers.

✔ **ROM.** Memory mapped to ROM on adapter cards (such as the ROM on disk controllers and video adapters) or to the system's ROM.

✔ **Possibly Available.** Memory that may or may not already be in use (indeterminable).

✔ **EMS Page Frame.** Memory allocated for an expanded memory page frame.

✔ **Used UMBs.** UMBs under the control of a UMA memory manager such as EMM386.EXE, but which have been allocated to another program or device.

✔ **Free UMBs.** UMBs that are under the control of a UMA memory manager, but which are not yet allocated to a program or device.

Figure 1.9 shows MSD's memory map of the UMA.

Figure 1.9
A memory map of the UMA, generated by the Microsoft Diagnostic application.

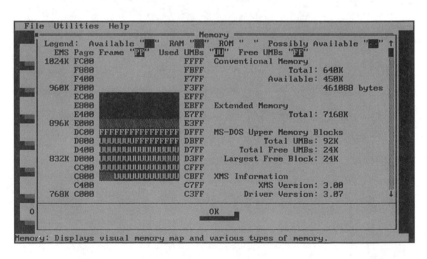

After you copy MSD to your hard disk, you can use the program to view your system's UMA and locate an available memory block for your network adapter. If you are not using EMM386.EXE or another UMA memory manager to provide memory access in the UMA to DOS, the memory range from C8000 to EFFFF probably will be listed as available by MSD (all black). If you are using a UMA memory manager to provide access by DOS to the UMA, look for memory ranges marked as Free (FF).

Assigning a RAM Address

Some network adapters require only 8 KB of RAM for their buffers, while others use 16 KB or 32 KB. A larger buffer provides better performance, but leaves less memory available in the UMA for applications and other devices.

If your computer has no other adapter cards beyond the typical disk controllers, serial/ parallel ports, and video card, you should have no trouble finding a free base memory address. Much of the UMA will be available.

In general, most video adapters use memory in the range from A0000 to C8000. The range from F0000 through FFFFF is reserved for the ROM BIOS on most systems. This leaves the memory range from C8000 to EFFFF available on most systems. If you have a PS/2 (or a few other select systems), the memory range E0000 through EFFFF is not available.

Check the other devices that are installed in the system to determine which memory ranges they use in the UMA. Make a copy of figure 1.7 and mark off these used ranges. Next, use MSD to check the availability of free memory, making sure that no conflicts exist with other devices or programs. When you have identified the appropriate memory block for the network adapter, you can set the adapter's jumpers or DIP switches accordingly.

The Intel EtherExpress 16 uses its software configuration program to specify its base address. If you are installing the card in a machine that will run Workgroup Connection, run the configuration program to set the card's base address range. If you are installing the EtherExpress 16 in a Windows for Workgroups workstation, you do not need to run the configuration program; Windows will choose an address range for you.

If your network adapter requires that you specify its RAM address range by setting jumpers or DIP switches, refer to the adapter's documentation to determine the correct settings. Then follow the procedure described previously to set the DIP switches or jumpers.

If you are using a UMA memory manager such as EMM386, you must take an additional step in allocating the selected memory address to the network adapter. That is, you must make sure that the address is not allocated to another device or program after the system boots and device drivers are installed, or that Windows does not allocate this segment of RAM for its own use when you start Windows. The following section shows you how to do this.

Excluding the RAM Base Address

By default, UMA memory managers such as EMM386 scan the UMA for available memory at boot, and add all the available memory to a pool of free UMBs. The memory manager then can provide UMBs to applications and devices from this pool. To protect the network adapter's RAM block, you must direct your memory manager (if you are using one) to exclude the network adapter's memory range from its pool.

If you use EMM386, you can use the X switch (which stands for exclude). The following statement, which you add to your system's CONFIG.SYS file, prevents EMM386 from using the 16 KB range D0000 through D3FFF:

```
C:\WINDOWS\EMM386.EXE noems X=D000-D3FF
```

If you have allocated a different memory block to the network adapter, change the X parameter accordingly. In addition, note that even though a memory location is represented by five digits, as in *D3FFF*, you need to specify only the first four digits with the X switch, as shown in the preceding example.

In the preceding example, notice that EMM386 is loaded from the C:\WINDOWS directory (the Windows for Workgroups directory). You might already be using a different version of EMM386 (such as from MS-DOS 5 or a stand-alone version of Windows). If so, install Windows for Workgroups as directed in the following sections, then edit CONFIG.SYS to exclude the network adapter's memory. When you edit CONFIG.SYS, make sure that the entries for EMM386.EXE and HIMEM.SYS point to the directory in which you installed Windows for Workgroups. This step ensures that you are using the latest version of these two memory managers.

Now that the network adapter is configured, you are ready to install it in the system.

Installing the Network Adapter

To install the network adapter, make sure the system is turned off and unplugged, then remove the computer's cover. Touch the metal chassis to ground yourself and discharge any static electricity that has built up in your body. Locate the bus slot into which you are installing the network adapter and remove the slot's cover (the metal bracket that covers the corresponding slot in the back of the computer). Keep the screw; you will need it to secure the network adapter in place.

When you are deciding which bus slot to use, you need to consider only whether your adapter card is an 8-bit or 16-bit card. If it is an 8-bit card, it has only one edge connector. If it is a 16-bit card, is has two edge connectors that are separated from each other by a narrow gap. If it is an 8-bit card, you can install it in either an 8-bit slot or a 16-bit slot. This is because 8-bit slots have a single connector on the motherboard, and 16-bit slots use two connectors. Identify an available 8-bit slot and install the card in it. If you have no available 8-bit slots, install the card in any of the available 16-bit slots.

If your network adapter is a 16-bit card, you must install it in a 16-bit slot. A 16-bit card cannot function in an 8-bit slot. Locate an available 16-bit slot and install the card.

Insert the network adapter into the slot, pressing down firmly to seat it in the socket. Screw it in place with the screw you removed from the slot cover. Check the installation one last time, then close and secure the cover on the chassis.

If you need additional help installing the card, consult your network adapter's documentation and Chapter 2 of the Windows for Workgroups *Getting Started* guide.

Connecting the Cables

The method of cabling you use depends on the type of network topology you have selected. If you are using Ethernet topology and Thin-Ethernet cable, use figure 1.10 as a guide to connecting the cables between computers. Remember to install a cable terminator at each end of the cable bus (at the first and last computers on the cable).

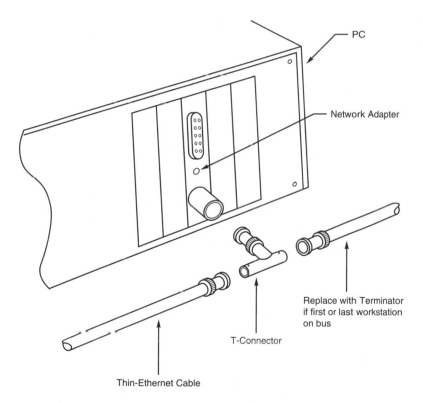

— PC

Figure 1.10
Thin-Ethernet
cable connections.

— Network Adapter

Replace with Terminator
if first or last workstation
on bus

T-Connector

Thin-Ethernet Cable

If you are using a different type of cabling and network topology, consult the network adapter's documentation or the Windows for Workgroups *Getting Started* guide for additional help. Chapter 26, "Understanding Networks and Workgroups," also includes information on different network topologies.

Complete the hardware setup tasks described in the previous sections for each workstation on the network. When all the workstations and the cables are connected, you are ready to install Windows for Workgroups.

Understanding Windows

Installing Windows for Workgroups

The Windows for Workgroups *Getting Started* guide includes instructions on installing Windows for Workgroups. If you follow the instructions in the *Getting Started* guide and the prompts in the Setup program itself, you should have no trouble installing Windows for Workgroups. Instead of detailing the installation process, therefore, this section offers some tips on optimizing your Windows for Workgroups installation and installing Windows for Workgroups over an existing copy of Microsoft Windows.

If your systems are new, the hard disk should be performing optimally. If your systems have been in use for some time, and you have not maintained the hard drives recently, you should do so before installing Windows for Workgroups. Refer to the section "Preparing Your System for Windows" earlier in this chapter for tips on optimizing each system's hard disk.

Installing Windows for Workgroups over an Existing Copy of Windows

If you install Windows for Workgroups over an existing copy of Windows 3.0 or Windows 3.1, Windows for Workgroups maintains your existing program groups and settings. Your new Windows environment will be very much like it was before, but with the addition of new networking features.

If you want to maintain your existing Windows environment under Windows for Workgroups, you must install Windows for Workgroups into the same directory as Windows 3.0 or 3.1.

Whenever possible, use the new device drivers that are shipped with Windows for Workgroups rather than those that came with your copy of Windows 3.0 or Windows 3.1. The device drivers in Windows for Workgroups have been updated to add new features and to correct problems that might have existed in previous versions.

Video drivers are a good example of drivers you should use when you install Windows for Workgroups over an existing copy of Windows 3.0 or 3.1. Many of the new video drivers include additional support for running DOS applications in a window and for using the mouse with your DOS applications. The new Super VGA display driver included with Windows 3.1 and Windows for Workgroups supports most of the major video adapters at 800x600 resolution in 16 colors.

If you have a compatible third-party driver installed for Windows 3.0 or 3.1, Windows for Workgroups keeps and uses the driver.

Installing Windows for Workgroups across the Network

If you are installing Windows for Workgroups on a system that currently uses Microsoft LAN Manager or Novell NetWare as its network operating system, you can install Windows for Workgroups across the network. You do not need to use the distribution disks to install it at each workstation.

To enable installation of Windows for Workgroups on your workstations across the network, first install Windows for Workgroups on a network file server. This installation usually requires that you have network administrator access rights to the server (depending on the way your network is set up).

To install Windows for Workgroups on the server, log in with administrator-level access privileges. Then insert Disk 1 of the distribution disks in the appropriate floppy disk drive, make the drive active, and enter **SETUP /A**. The /A option directs Setup to copy all files from the distribution disks to the specified directory on the server and to assign the files read-only status. The complete file set requires just under 21 MB of disk space.

When you have copied all the files to the server, you can begin setting up Windows for Workgroups on the workstations. To install Windows for Workgroups on a workstation across the network, first log in from the workstation and attach to the file server that contains the Windows for Workgroups files. Change to the directory that contains the Windows for Workgroups files.

Next, enter **SETUP /N** to install a shared version of Windows for Workgroups on the workstation. When prompted to do so, specify the name of a local directory in which to place the Windows for Workgroups files. If Windows 3.0 or 3.1 is installed on the workstation, specify the directory that contains the existing copy of Windows.

The benefit to using SETUP /N is that only a few of the Windows for Workgroups files are copied to the local workstation. This type of installation requires only about 900 KB on the local workstation's hard disk for Windows for Workgroups. The following list identifies the files that are placed on the local workstation when you run SETUP /N to install a shared copy of Windows for Workgroups:

File Name	Description
ACCESSOR.GRP	Accessories group file
BOOTLOG.TXT	Error log file used during boot
CONTROL.INI	INI file for Control Panel
DOSPRMPT.PIF	PIF for the MS-DOS item in the Main group

continues

File Name	Description
EMM386.EXE	UMA memory manager and EMS provider
GAMES.GRP	Games group file
HIMEM.SYS	Extended memory manager
IFSHLP.SYS	Installable file system driver
MAIN.GRP	Main group file
NCDINFO.INI	INI file listing previous network connections
NDISHLP.SYS	NDIS network driver
NET.EXE	Network redirector
NET.MSG	Network redirector message file
NETH.MSG	Network redirector help message file
NETWORK.GRP	Network group file
PROGMAN.INI	Program Manager INI file
PROTMAN.DOS	Protocol manager file
PROTMAN.EXE	Protocol manager TSR
PROTOCOL.CLN	Copy of last good PROTOCOL.INI file
PROTOCOL.INI	Protocol manager INI file
RAMDRIVE.SYS	RAMDrive utility
REG.DAT	Registration database
SERIALNO.INI	User and registration information
SHARES.PWL	Password list file for shared resources
SMARTDRV.EXE	SmartDrive utility (disk cache program)
SMCMAC.DOS	Network adapter driver (varies by NIC)
SPART.PAR	Pointer file to swap file
STARTUP.GRP	StartUp group file

File Name	Description
SYSTEM.CLN	Copy of last good SYSTEM.INI file
SYSTEM.INI	Windows INI file
WFWSYS.CFG	Network driver support file
WIN.INI	Windows INI file
WIN.CLN	Copy of last good WIN.INI file
WIN.COM	Windows start-up file
WININIT.EXE	Initializes network services
WINFILE.INI	File Manager INI file
WINVER.EXE	Windows version program
_DEFAULT.PIF	Default PIF for DOS applications

All other files remain in the shared Windows directory on the server. When Windows runs on the local node, it accesses these files from the network server.

If you prefer to reduce network traffic at the expense of local disk space, you can install a complete local copy of Windows for Workgroups. Instead of using the /N switch with Setup, just enter **SETUP**. This command performs a complete local installation across the network.

Installing Windows for Workgroups without an Existing Network

If Windows for Workgroups is your only network environment (that is, if you have no other network operating system already in place), you can use the DOS network capability provided by Workgroup Connection to install Windows for Workgroups on your workstations. Workgroup Connection is a DOS-based client facility Microsoft offers as a separate product from Windows for Workgroups. Workgroup Connection enables your DOS PCs to access a Windows for Workgroups server, and is fully compatible with Windows for Workgroups.

If you want to use Workgroup Connection to install Windows for Workgroups across the network, you first must install Workgroup Connection on each machine. You also must install a copy of Windows for Workgroups on at least one machine, using SETUP/A on that machine to copy all the Windows for Workgroup files to the system. Figure 1.11 illustrates the concept.

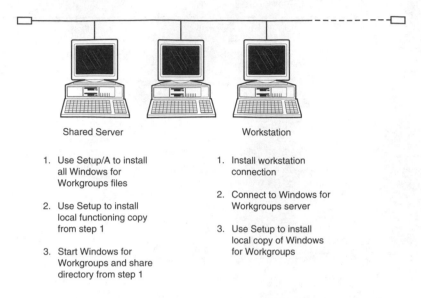

Figure 1.11
Installing
Windows for
Workgroups
across the
network.

Shared Server   Workstation

1. Use Setup/A to install   1. Install workstation
   all Windows for   connection
   Workgroups files
                                   2. Connect to Windows for
2. Use Setup to install   Workgroups server
   local functioning copy
   from step 1   3. Use Setup to install
                                      local copy of Windows
3. Start Windows for   for Workgroups
   Workgroups and share
   directory from step 1

If Windows for Workgroups is your only network operating system, however, you should install a full local copy of Windows for Workgroups on each workstation, even if you install across the network. This type of installation saves memory when you run Windows for Workgroups on the workstation. To run Windows for Workgroups from a shared directory across the network, you first must load Workgroup Connection to access the shared server. Windows for Workgroups duplicates the features in Workgroup Connection, so you do not need to run both.

To speed the installation process, you can install Windows for Workgroups from a shared server by using Workgroup Connection. This way, you do not need to install Windows for Workgroups from floppy disks at each workstation.

You must take the following steps to install Windows for Workgroups across the network by using Workgroup Connection:

1. Install Windows for Workgroups on one system by typing **SETUP/A** to copy all the Windows for Workgroups files to a directory on the server, such as C:\WINSHARE. Return to the DOS prompt when Setup is finished.

2. Install a local configuration of Windows for Workgroups on the server. From the root directory of drive C on the server, enter *share***SETUP**, replacing *share* with the name of the directory that contains the Windows for Workgroups files. Enter a new destination directory for your Windows for Workgroups installation, such as **C:\WINDOWS**.

3. Start Windows for Workgroups on the server, open File Manager, and share the directory that contains the Windows for Workgroups files. (See Chapter 2, "Navigating in Windows," for assistance with sharing and File Manager.)

4. Install Workgroup Connection at each workstation. You must install the program from a local floppy disk at each workstation. Installation of Workgroup Connection is explained later in this chapter.

5. Start Workgroup Connection on the workstation by entering **NET START WORKSTATION** at the DOS prompt.

6. Connect to the Windows for Workgroups server that contains the shared Windows for Workgroups files. Do so by typing **NET USE** *d:\\servername\share*. In this generic syntax, *d:* is the next available drive ID on the workstation, *servername* is the computer name for the Windows for Workgroups directory (which you supplied when installing the local copy of Windows for Workgroups on the server), and *share* is the name of the shared directory that contains the Windows for Workgroups files (such as WINSHARE).

7. Run Setup at the workstation by typing *d:***SETUP**. In this generic syntax, *d:* is the drive ID you assigned to the shared Windows directory in the previous step.

If many of your workstations share a common hardware configuration, consider customizing Setup to install and configure the necessary Windows drivers automatically. This enables you to set up Windows for Workgroups on the workstations with little or no intervention on your part. For more information on customizing Setup, consult *Maxmizing Windows 3.1* (New Riders Publishing), the Microsoft Windows 3.1 Resource Kit, or the Microsoft Windows for Workgroups Resource Kit.

Installing Workgroup Connection

Workgroup Connection is a DOS-based network client facility that enables DOS PCs to access a Windows for Workgroups server and use its resources (disks and printers), as well as send and receive mail on the network. Workgroup Connection is an excellent means for connecting your non-Windows workstations to the network. Network nodes running Workgroup Connection cannot share their local resources; they can access only those resources that are connected to a Windows for Workgroups server (or another network server). If you want to share local resources, you must run Windows for Workgroups on the workstation.

You also might want to install Workgroup Connection on each workstation to simplify the installation process for Windows for Workgroups as described in the previous section.

To install Workgroup Connection, insert the Workgroup Connection disk into the workstation's floppy drive. Make the drive active, then enter **SETUP**. The Workgroup Connection Setup program executes and installs Workgroup Connection for you. Follow the prompts to supply a computer name, workgroup name, and other information requested by Setup.

Troubleshooting the Installation

If everything is connected and configured properly, you should have no trouble installing, configuring, and using the network. To correct any problem that does arise, you primarily need to localize the problem.

Start with a simple setup at first. Configure one workstation on the network to act as a server. Start Windows for Workgroups on this workstation, open File Manager, and share the root directory (with a name such as ROOT, for example). Then attempt to connect to the server from each of the other workstations by using either Workgroup Connection or Windows for Workgroups at the workstation.

If you cannot access the server from any workstation, make sure that you have specified the correct computer name on the server. To check the computer name, open Control Panel on the server and double-click on the Network icon. The computer name is listed in the Computer Name edit box in the Microsoft Windows Network dialog box, as shown in figure 1.12. Verify that the server name you specified from the workstation matches exactly the computer name you assigned to the server. You also should verify that the share name to which you are trying to connect is correct.

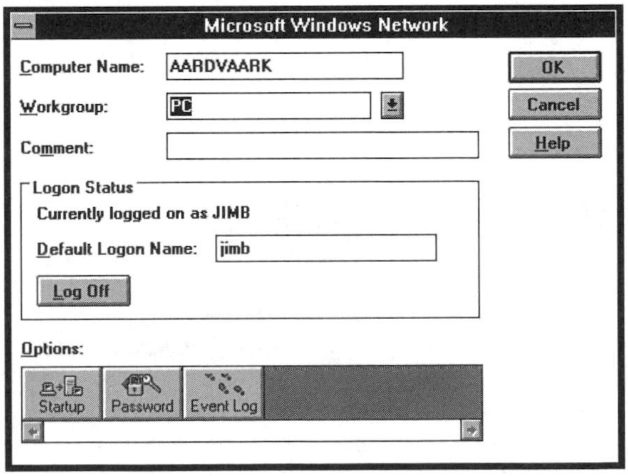

Figure 1.12
The Microsoft
Windows Network
dialog box.

If the problem persists, check the network cabling. A missing cable terminator or loose connection can prevent the network from functioning at all.

If you can connect from some workstations but not others, the problem probably is in the network adapter configuration at these workstations. Make sure that each network adapter's base I/O address, IRQ, and RAM base address do not conflict with another device or program in the workstation. Then make sure that you made the correct settings in Windows for Workgroups by running Network Setup from the Network group. Choose the Drivers button to open the Network Drivers dialog box, then choose Setup to view the driver's configuration (see fig. 1.13).

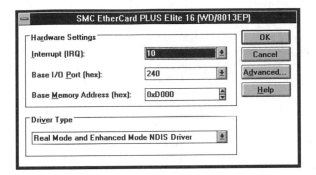

Figure 1.13
The network adapter configuration dialog box.

If the settings do not match the settings you physically configured on the card, change them in the network adapter configuration dialog box. If the dialog box contains the words Automatic or Unused rather than actual values, the network adapter you are using either contains the settings in ROM, configures them by using software at boot, or does not require the given setting.

If the configuration is correct, make sure you are using the correct driver for the network card. Windows for Workgroups supports a wide array of network adapters, and you might have selected a similar but incompatible driver.

If the adapter configuration and driver are correct and you still cannot connect from a workstation, return to the DOS prompt to check the network adapter's operation. The adapter probably includes a diagnostic program to test the adapter. Use the diagnostic program to determine whether the card is defective. If the card checks out, determine whether the diagnostic program enables you to send and receive test information between two workstations. If you have a functioning card in another workstation, you should be able to test the adapter's capability to send and receive across the network. If the card cannot send and receive data, contact the manufacturer for assistance in locating the problem.

Making Changes to Your Network

After installation, you might decide to change each workstation's configuration. The Setup program enables you to change your Windows for Workgroups setup on each workstation. If you run Setup from within Windows for Workgroups (Setup resides in the Main program group), you can change drivers for the video adapter, keyboard, and mouse.

If you need to change other hardware parameters, run Setup from DOS. The DOS-based version of Setup enables you to change settings for the computer type, display, mouse, keyboard, keyboard layout, language, and code page.

To change the network configuration, use the Network Setup icon in the Network group. Network Setup enables you to control resource sharing, add or delete network support, and modify adapter configuration. If you change an adapter's hardware configuration for some reason, remember to coordinate the change with other devices in the workstation and with your UMA memory manager (if you are using one). If you move the adapter's RAM base address from D0000 to E0000 to make room for another device that requires the D0000 page, for example, remember to exclude the E0000 page from the UMA memory manager's use.

Chapter Snapshot

As a user environment, Windows provides several advantages. One of the most convenient and important features is that Windows applications are consistent—the way you work with your spreadsheet is much the same way you work with your word processor. As a user of Windows, you probably find it difficult to remember everything about using Windows. This chapter provides a convenient guide to Windows navigation; all you need to know but might not remember at the time you need it.

To use the common user interface successfully in Windows, you need to be familiar with these actions:

As a Windows user, you might find it convenient to review the sections of this chapter frequently just to keep your Windows skills sharp. No one remembers the entire Windows interface 100 percent of the time. An occasional glance at this chapter can help you remember the less frequent keystrokes and mouse actions that make you more productive.

Navigating in Windows

To help new users become familiar with Windows and to refresh the memories of frequent users, Windows provides a tutorial program. To access it, use the File, Run option on the Program Manager's menu. When the Run dialog box appears, type **wintutor** in the Command Line text box and click on OK (see fig. 2.1). After the tutorial starts, follow the on-screen directions.

Figure 2.1
Starting the
Windows Tutorial.

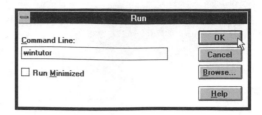

The Windows Tutorial provides two paths. The first path shows you how to use the mouse. The second path teaches Windows basics. If you feel uncomfortable with the mouse, begin with the mouse path and then follow the Windows path. If you are skilled with the mouse, skip the mouse portion of the tutorial.

Comparing the Screen to a Desktop

Windows is built around the metaphor of a *desktop;* that is, Windows acts as if your computer screen were the flat surface of a desktop. The application programs are like the tools you might have on your desk. The Cardfile program can serve as your Rolodex, for instance, and the Calendar program can be your appointment book. Just as you can have several tools laid out on your desk, you can have several application programs running on the Windows desktop.

Windows divides the desktop into layers, graphically represented in figure 2.2.

✔ **Background layer.** Represents the surface on which the other two layers rest. In the default Windows setup, the background layer appears as a light gray. Typically, you interact with this layer very little. If you double-click on this layer, however, the Task List appears, giving you control over the other programs running on the desktop.

✔ **Wallpaper layer.** Lies on top of the background layer. A wallpaper is a picture created by a paint program. Such pictures can be placed on the wallpaper layer to provide a graphical background for the desktop. If the wallpaper is large enough, it completely covers the background layer. (You also can tile smaller wallpapers so that they cover the entire background layer.) Usually your only interaction with this layer is to change the wallpaper.

✔ **Application layer.** Lies on top of the wallpaper layer. It contains the windows and icons that represent the programs that are running on your system. This is the layer in the desktop with which you normally interact as you work. The application layer contains application windows, document windows, and icons.

✔ **Mouse pointer.** Floats over these three layers of the desktop, providing you with a means of interacting with the layers. It indicates the point on the screen at which the next mouse action will take place. The hot spot for the mouse pointer is usually the tip of its shape.

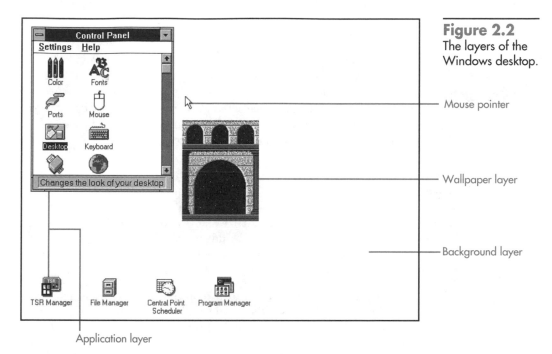

Figure 2.2
The layers of the Windows desktop.

Mouse pointer

Wallpaper layer

Background layer

Application layer

The most common mouse pointer is an arrow. However, the mouse pointer changes shapes to tell you which functions are currently available and to provide you with information about system status. If the mouse pointer is over an editable workspace, for example, it becomes an I-beam selection cursor to inform you that you can edit with the mouse. If a long operation is running, the mouse pointer becomes an hourglass to inform you that you must wait for the operation to finish before you can continue work.

Understanding the Application Window

In Windows, each application runs in a window called an *application window.* Application windows have several parts, each with its own function. Not all application windows have all the components shown in figure 2.3. The components appear as they are required by the application program. Nevertheless, any application window can display any of the following 12 components:

✔ **Control menu box.** Activates the Control menu, which is explained in the section "Understanding the Control Menu."

✔ **Menu bar.** Presents the application's selection of commands and functions. To select a menu item, click on it with the mouse. Either the action named by the menu item takes place, or a list of additional menu items appears.

The menu bar is organized so that the File pull-down menu is always first on the left (assuming the application enables file operations). The next menu is Edit, if editing functions are allowed. The menu item on the far right is always Help. If the application uses document windows, the Window pull-down menu is immediately to the left of Help. The other menu items provided by the application appear in between Edit and Help on the menu bar.

✔ **Title bar.** Displays the name of the application. If a document window completely fills the workspace, the title bar also displays the name of the file associated with the document. (If the application does not use document windows, the name of the file loaded appears on the title bar.) To move a window, drag on the title bar with the mouse. Double-clicking on the title bar maximizes the window to full-screen size. Double-clicking on the title bar of a maximized window restores it to its previous size.

✔ **Minimize button.** Shrinks the window to an icon after you click on it. The application's icon usually appears at the bottom left side of the background layer. However, if you moved the icon to another location and then restored the application to its normal size, the icon appears where you last placed it on the desktop.

✔ **Maximize button.** Expands the window to full-screen size when you click on it. If the window is maximized, this button changes to a double arrow. Clicking on the double arrow restores the window to its previous size, shape, and position.

✔ **Workspace.** The area of the application window in which you work. If the application is a word processor, for example, you type and edit in this area.

✔ **Vertical scroll bars.** Indicate that additional information exists that is not displayed within the vertical area of the workspace. You can use the scroll bar to move the visible workspace up or down to reveal the hidden information. Clicking on the arrows at the end of the scroll bar moves the workspace one line at a time. (Holding the mouse button down repeats the scrolling, one line at a time.)

Clicking in the scroll bar, but not in the scroll box, moves the equivalent of one window at a time. (Holding the mouse button down repeats the scrolling, one window at a time.) Dragging the scroll box repositions the information displayed in the workspace quickly.

✔ **Horizontal scroll bars.** Indicate that additional information exists that is not displayed within the horizontal area of the workspace. You can use the scroll bar to move the visible workspace right or left to see this information. Clicking on the arrows at the end of the scroll bar moves the workspace one column at a time. (Holding the mouse button down repeats the scrolling, one column at a time.)

Clicking in the scroll bar but not in the scroll box moves the workspace the equivalent of one window at a time. (Holding the mouse button down repeats the scrolling, one window at a time.) Dragging the scroll box right or left repositions the information displayed in the workspace quickly.

✔ **Scroll boxes.** Serve as dragging points for scrolling several lines or columns at a time. The scroll box always indicates your relative position in the file by its relative position on the scroll bar.

✔ **Window border.** The boundary of the application window. If it is over the window border, the mouse pointer becomes a double arrow that indicates you can resize the window by dragging. Dragging the horizontal border changes the vertical dimension. Dragging the vertical border changes the horizontal dimension.

✔ **Window corner.** A special section of the window border. You can change both the horizontal and vertical dimensions of the window at the same time by dragging the corner.

✔ **Selection cursor.** Shaped like an I-beam. The mouse pointer becomes the selection cursor whenever it is over an editable workspace, indicating that you can edit with the mouse.

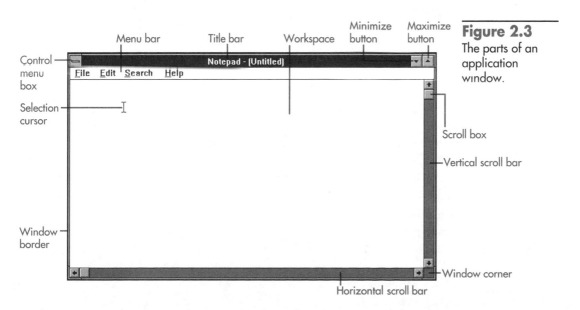

Figure 2.3
The parts of an application window.

Understanding the Document Window

Applications use document windows to present several different workspaces, each containing a single document. A *document* is the information processed by the application. In a word processor, the term "document" makes the most sense—each document window presents a document (or "file") created and saved with the word processor. Each spreadsheet document window presents a different sheet. A document window in Program Manager presents a program group.

Document windows always appear within the workspace of an application window. They might slide under the edge of the application window's border, but the area past the border remains hidden.

Document windows contain many of the same parts as application windows; however, some of the parts behave differently. The following list explains the parts, shown in figure 2.4, that behave differently from document windows:

- ✔ **Control menu.** The document window has the same options as the application window, but adds the Next option. Selecting Next passes the focus to the next document window on the list maintained by the application window.

- ✔ **Title bar.** Displays the name of the file presented in that window. Double-clicking on the title bar expands the document window to fill the workspace of the application window. The document window's title bar then slides under the application window's menu bar.

  The application window's title bar displays the name of the file represented by the maximized document window. The document window's Control menu appears at the left edge of the application window's menu bar. The document window's maximize button appears at the right edge of the application window's menu bar.

- ✔ **Minimize button.** Shrinks the document window to an icon that appears at the bottom of the application window's workspace.

- ✔ **Maximize button.** Expands the document window to fill the workspace of the application window. The document window's title bar then slides under the application window's menu bar. The application window's title bar displays the name of the file represented by the maximized document window. The document window's Control menu appears at the left edge of the application window's menu bar. The document window's maximize button appears at the right edge of the application window's menu bar.

- ✔ **Window border.** The boundary of the document window. It operates like the application window border; however, you cannot resize the document window past the border of the application window.

✔ **Window corner.** Operates similar to the application window corner; however, you cannot resize the document window past the border of the application window.

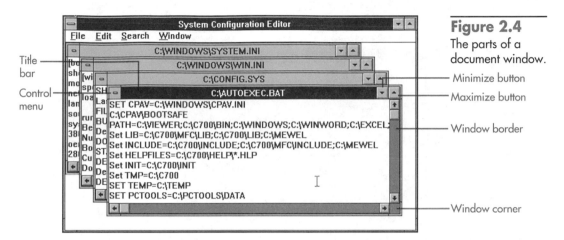

Figure 2.4

The parts of a document window.

Comparing Icon Types

Icons represent applications that are available, running applications that have been minimized, or documents that have been minimized. Clicking on an icon displays the associated application's Control menu, if it is available. Double-clicking on an icon either starts the associated application or returns the application to its previous size, shape, and position on the screen.

Tip

A minimized window helps to unclutter both your screen and your computer's memory. Minimized applications require much less memory to run.

Windows uses four types of icons (see fig 2.5):

✔ **Application icons.** Represent windows that have been minimized. They appear along the lower edge of the desktop.

✔ **Document icons.** Represent document windows that have been minimized. They appear along the lower border of an application window.

✔ **Group icons.** Represent the document windows that contain program items in Program Manager. They appear along the lower border of the Program Manager application window.

  ✔ **Program item icons.** Appear in the document windows within Program
    Manager. They represent applications available in Windows.

Figure 2.5
The different icon
types available in
Windows.

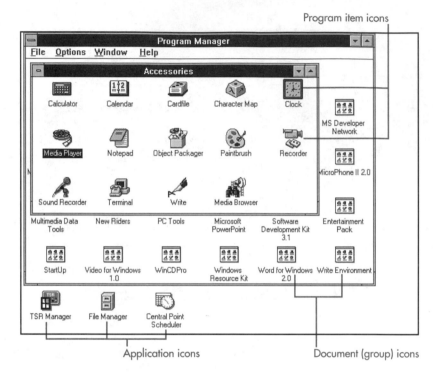

Programs can use icons in other ways. File Manager, for instance, attaches an icon to each
file name, directory name, and drive letter. The icons change shape and character to
provide information about the status of the files, directories, and drives.

Understanding the Control Menu

Clicking on the Control menu box of an application window or document window opens
the Control menu (see fig. 2.6). You can specify different actions by selecting options on
the Control menu:

Command	Result
Restore	Returns the window to its previous size, shape, and position.
Move	Repositions the window. This option enables you to move a window using the arrow keys.

Command	Result
Size	Resizes the window. This option enables you to resize a window using the arrow keys.
Mi**n**imize	Shrinks the window to an icon.
Ma**x**imize	Expands the window to full-screen size. In some applications, maximizing the window changes the action of the positioning keys.
Close	Closes the window.
S**w**itch To	Activates the Task List, enabling you to move among applications.
Edit	Appears only for DOS applications. Enables you to highlight (or mark) information for copying or pasting, copy information from, paste information to, and scroll within the DOS window. Basically, this option mimics the standard Edit menu for DOS applications.
Se**t**tings	Appears only for DOS applications. This command displays a dialog box that enables you to set the options for the DOS window.
Fonts	Appears only for DOS applications. This command displays a dialog box that enables you to set the font for the DOS window.
Nex**t**	Appears only for document windows. Changes the focus to the next document window on the list maintained by the application window.

Figure 2.6
The Control menu.

A Control menu is available for every window. It is attached to the Control menu box in the upper left corner of the window. Some applications display all the commands in the Control menu and dim the commands that are not currently available. Others display only the commands available within the current window.

Press Alt+spacebar to open the Control menu of an application window. Press Alt+hyphen to open the Control menu of a document window. If you have trouble remembering these shortcuts, Windows provides visual mnemonics to help you. The long dash of the application window control box looks like a spacebar. The short dash of the document window control box looks like a hyphen.

Arranging the Desktop

You can arrange your desktop using the Cascade, Tile, and Arrange Icons buttons presented by the Task List application (see fig. 2.7). Start the task list by selecting the Switch To option from the Control menu of any application or by double-clicking on the background layer.

Figure 2.7
The Task List with its Cascade, Tile, and Arrange Icons buttons.

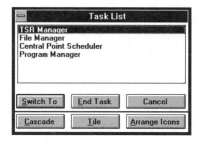

The Cascade button arranges the windows on the desktop so that they overlap one another with their title bars showing, starting at the upper left corner of the screen and descending (or cascading) to the right, as shown in figure 2.8. The Tile button arranges the windows on the desktop like the tiles on a wall, as figure 2.9 shows. If for some reason the icons on your desktop are in disarray, the Arrange Icons button places them in a straight line starting at the lower left corner of your screen.

Arranging Multiple Document Windows

Use the Cascade and Tile commands on an application's Window menu to arrange document windows within the workspace of the application window (figure 2.10 shows these commands). The result of using these commands is exactly like that of cascading or tiling windows on your desktop, except that the cascade or tiling stays within the border of the application window. You can use the Arrange Icons command on the Window menu to make sure all document icons are arranged in a line across the bottom of the application window's workspace.

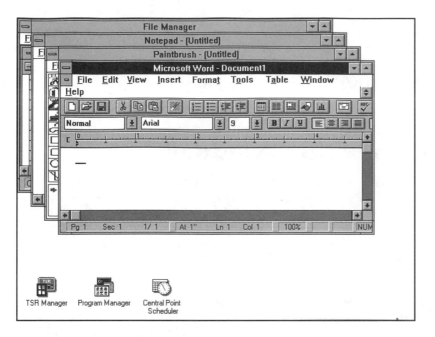

Figure 2.8
Cascaded
windows on the
desktop.

Understanding Windows

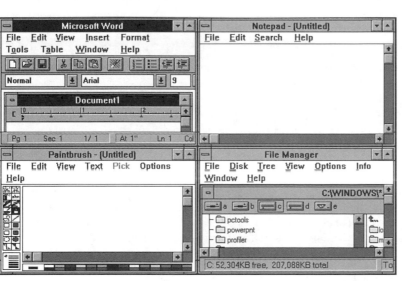

Figure 2.9
Tiled windows on
the desktop.

Figure 2.10
The Window
menu, with the
Cascade, Tile, and
Arrange Icons
commands.

Window	Help	
New Window		
Cascade		Shift+F5
Tile		Shift+F4
Arrange Icons		
Refresh		F5
√1 C:\WINDOWS*.*		

Navigating within Windows

To navigate in Windows, you must master the notion of focus. The *focus* is what the currently active window or control possesses. Visually, it is represented at the application-window or document-window level by a highlighted title bar. Within the workspace, the focus is represented by the flashing insertion point, the vertical line that shows where your next action will have effect. Within a dialog box, the focused area is highlighted or outlined by a dotted box.

Navigating within Windows is a matter of moving and controlling the focus. The object that has the focus is the object on which you can take action. Windows automatically sets the focus to the workspace of an application or document window. The following sections describe the most common methods for moving and controlling the focus to accomplish tasks in a Windows application.

Some DOS applications have actions defined for the Windows movement keys described in the following sections, and conflicts might occur. Use the DOS application's PIF to reserve a key combination for the active DOS application rather than Windows.

Activating the Menu

To activate an application window's menu, click on a menu title or press the Alt key (see fig. 2.11). With the mouse action, the pop-up menu named by the menu title appears (or the action named by the menu title takes place if no pop-up menu is associated with the title). With the keyboard action, a highlighter appears on the menu bar. You must press the underlined letter in a menu title to make the pop-up menu appear. If you decide not to select a menu item, you must press Alt to remove the focus from the menu bar.

Moving among Menus

To move among the menus on a menu bar, click on the menu title you want. You can also use the left- and right-arrow keys to move from one menu title to another or from one open pop-up menu to another. To close the current menu, click on the workspace or press Esc. If you press Esc, the menu bar remains active, enabling you to select another menu title by pressing the underlined letter, or *hot key*. To remove the focus from the menu bar, click on the workspace or press Alt.

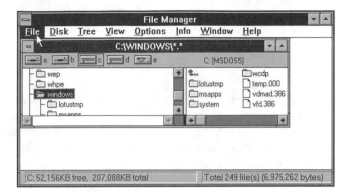

Figure 2.11
Activating the menu bar.

Understanding Types of Menu Items

You can interact with four types of menu items, as figure 2.12 shows:

- ✔ **Standard.** Menu items that appear as a word or phrase in which there is one underlined letter. This type of item initiates an action.

- ✔ **Dialog box.** Menu items that have ellipsis points following the word or phrase. These menu items bring up a dialog box that enables you to take further action within the application.

- ✔ **Cascading.** Menu items followed by a triangular pointer. These items bring up a cascading pop-up menu that enables you to make further choices.

- ✔ **Check.** Menu items that enable you to set a characteristic of your application. A check mark precedes the item if the characteristic it describes is set. No check mark indicates the characteristic is not set.

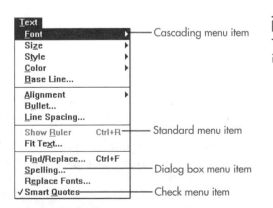

Figure 2.12
Types of menu items.

Selecting a Menu Item

To select a menu item with a pop-up menu displayed, click on the item or press its hot key. Selecting a menu item executes the command associated with the item, brings up the associated dialog box, brings up the associated cascading menu, or sets the associated characteristic, depending on the type of menu item. This is the most common way to issue commands to a Windows application.

If a menu item appears dimmed, it is not currently available for use and cannot be highlighted or chosen. Applications use this technique to inform you of which options are available at any given time. The available options often change when a different action is selected. As a result, an item might be dimmed at one time and active at another.

Moving among Application Windows

To move among application windows and icons, click on the application window or application icon you want in focus. You can also press Alt+Tab to move among application windows and application icons. Windows presents a panel that shows you the name of the application window or icon that will come into focus after you release the Alt key. If a full-screen DOS application is in the foreground, the item title displays in a banner across the top of the screen. The application window or icon with the focus moves to the top position on the desktop and is often called the current or active application.

Moving among Document Windows

To move among document windows and document icons, click on the document window or document icon you want to be in focus. You also can press Ctrl+Tab to move among document windows and icons. The item title of the document window or icon that has the focus becomes highlighted. If Program Manager has the focus, Ctrl+Tab enables you to switch among the group windows and group icons. (In some applications, especially word processors, Ctrl+Tab might have another purpose. In such cases, use the mouse or Ctrl+F6.)

Moving within the Workspace

To move within the workspace, click with the mouse at the point to which you want to move the insertion point. Use the scroll bars to scroll the workspace to the information you desire, if necessary. You also can use the positioning keys (PgUp, PgDn, Home, and End) and the arrow keys to move the insertion point. In some applications, scrolling with a scroll bar does not move the insertion point but scrolling with the positioning keys does. This difference enables you to scroll with the scroll bars and return to your previous place by typing a character at the keyboard.

Moving the Focus in a Dialog Box

To move the focus in a dialog box, click on the dialog control that you want to bring into focus. You also can use the Tab key to move the focus to the appropriate dialog control. When you use the Tab key, the focus is represented by a dotted outline box, shown in figure 2.13.

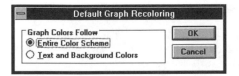

Figure 2.13
The dotted outline box showing focus in a dialog box.

Using the Task List

To display the Task List application (shown in fig. 2.14), double-click on the desktop or press Ctrl+Esc. The Task List contains a list of the active applications. Double-click on an application's name to give it focus, or use the arrow keys to scroll through the list, and then press Enter to switch to the appropriate application. (You also can click on the Switch To button after the application's name is highlighted.)

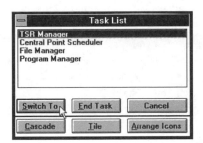

Figure 2.14
The Task List application.

Learning Common Keystrokes

Windows provides common keystrokes that affect applications in identical ways. These keys serve as shortcuts for experienced typists who prefer to keep their fingers on the keys. They also can be faster than the related mouse action because you do not have to waste time reaching for the mouse. The following tables provide a convenient reference guide for the common Windows keystrokes. The tables group the keystrokes by function.

System Keys

Key or Key Combination	Function
Ctrl+Esc	Starts the Task List.
Alt+Esc	Switches to the next application window or icon.
Alt+Tab	Switches to the last application window you used, or switches to the next application window. Applications running as icons are restored.
PrScr	Copies the current screen to the Clipboard.
Alt+PrScr	Copies the current application window to the Clipboard.
Alt+spacebar	Activates the Control menu for an application window.
Alt+hyphen	Activates the Control menu for a document window.
Alt+F4	Quits the current application.
Ctrl+F4	Closes the current document window.
Alt+Enter	Switches the execution of a DOS program from windowed to full screen.
Arrow keys	Moves or resizes a window after you have selected **M**ove or **S**ize from the Control menu.

Cursor Movement Keys

Key or Key Combination	Function
Up arrow	Moves the insertion point up one line.
Down arrow	Moves the insertion point down one line.
Right arrow	Moves the insertion point right one character.
Left arrow	Moves the insertion point left one character.
Ctrl+right arrow	Moves the insertion point right one word.
Ctrl+left arrow	Moves the insertion point left one word.

Key or Key Combination	Function
Home	Moves the insertion point to the beginning of the line.
End	Moves the insertion point to the end of the line.
PgUp	Moves the insertion point up one screen.
PgDn	Moves the insertion point down one screen.
Ctrl+Home	Moves the insertion point to the beginning of the document.
Ctrl+End	Moves the insertion point to the end of the document.

Dialog Box Keys

Key or Key Combination	Function
Tab	Moves the focus from option to option.
Shift+Tab	Moves the focus from option to option in reverse order.
Alt+hot key	Moves to the option or group identified by the underlined letter.
Arrow key	Moves the focus from option to option within a group of options.
Home	Moves to the first item in a list box or to the first character in a text box.
End	Moves to the last item in a list box or to the last character in a text box.
PgUp	Scrolls up a list box one screen at a time.
PgDn	Scrolls down a list box one screen at a time.
Alt+down arrow	Opens a list in a drop-down list box.
Spacebar	Selects an option button or cancels a selection. Places or removes a check in a check box.
Ctrl+slash (/)	Selects all the items in a list box.

continues

Key or Key Combination	Function
Ctrl+backslash (\)	Cancels the selection in a list box, but leaves the item that currently has the focus selected.
Shift+arrow key	Extends or cancels the selection in a text box, one character at a time.
Shift+Home	Extends or cancels the selection in a text box to the first character.
Shift+End	Extends or cancels the selection in a text box to the last character.
Enter	Executes a command. If the focus is on an item in a list, the item is selected and then the command is executed.
Esc or Alt+F4	Cancels the dialog box without executing any commands.

Editing Keys

Key or Key Combination	Function
Backspace	Deletes one character to the left of the insertion point or deletes the selected text.
Del	Deletes one character to the right of the insertion point or deletes the selected text.
Shift+Del Ctrl+X	Deletes the selected text and places it on the Clipboard.
Shift+Ins Ctrl+C	Pastes the text from the Clipboard to the place indicated by the insertion point.
Ctrl+Ins Ctrl+V	Copies the selected text to the Clipboard.
Alt+Backspace	Undoes the last editing keystroke.

Help Keys

Key or Key Combination	Function
F1	Starts the Help window and displays the Help Contents for the application. If the Help window is already active, displays the Help Contents for How to Use Help. In some applications, displays a Help topic for the selected command.
Shift+F1	Causes the mouse pointer to become a question mark. Click on an object with this cursor to get help for it. To get help for a keystroke, press Shift+F1 and type the keystroke. (Might not be active in all applications.)

Menu Keys

Key or Key Combination	Function
Alt or F10	Activates the menu bar and selects the first item, or removes the focus from the menu.
Underlined	Selects the command indicated by the underlined letter (also called a *hot key*).
Left arrow	Moves to the next menu on the left.
Right arrow	Moves to the next menu on the right.
Up arrow	Moves up to the next menu command.
Down arrow	Moves down to the next menu command.
Enter	Opens the selected menu or executes the selected command.
Esc	Closes an open menu or removes the focus from the menu bar.

Selection Keys

Key or Key Combination	Function
Shift+left arrow	Extends or cancels a selection one character to the left.
Shift+right arrow	Extends or cancels a selection one character to the right.
Shift+up arrow	Extends or cancels a selection one line up.
Shift+down arrow	Extends or cancels a selection one line down.
Shift+PgUp	Extends or cancels a selection one screen up.
Shift+PgDn	Extends or cancels a selection one screen down.
Shift+Home	Extends or cancels a selection to the beginning of the line.
Shift+End	Extends or cancels a selection to the end of the line.
Ctrl+Shift+left arrow	Extends or cancels a selection one word to the left.
Ctrl+Shift+ right arrow	Extends or cancels a selection one word to the right.
Ctrl+Shift+Home	Extends or cancels a selection to the beginning of the document.
Ctrl+Shift+End	Extends or cancels a selection to the end of the document.

Mastering Common Mouse Operations

Windows uses common mouse operations to make the operation of Windows applications consistent and convenient. The following table provides a convenient reference guide to Windows mouse actions.

Term	Action	Response
Click	Press the mouse button once	Moves the focus to the object clicked upon.
Double-click	Press the mouse button twice rapidly	Moves the focus to the object clicked upon and executes the action associated with the object. (Example: double-click on an icon to expand it into a window.)

Term	Action	Response
Drag	Hold the mouse button down and move the mouse	Moves the object on the screen or creates and extends a selection.
Drag-and-drop	Drag an object and release the mouse button	Moves the object on the screen and causes an action to take place after the button is released. If the object is dropped on a second object, the action that takes place is defined by the second object. (Example: Drag a file icon from File Manager and drop it on a program item icon in Program Manager to open the related application and load the file.)

Learning Common Windows Controls

Windows uses controls as a means for you to interact with the command structure of your application. Instead of issuing commands by typing them at the keyboard, you manipulate Windows' controls in a dialog box or in the application's workspace using a number of different objects (see figs. 2.15 and 2.16).

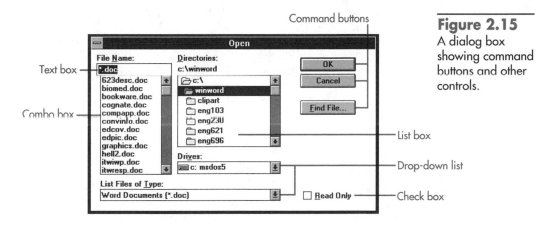

Figure 2.15
A dialog box showing command buttons and other controls.

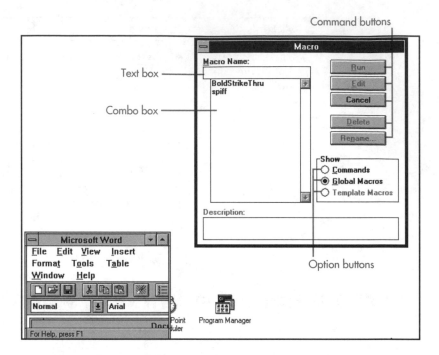

Figure 2.16
A dialog box
showing combo
box and other
controls.

✔ **Command buttons.** Cause immediate execution of a command or cancellation of a command. The nature of the command or action is described by the button's text. Click on a button, or press its hot key (Alt+*underlined letter*).

✔ **Text boxes.** Enable you to enter text for the current application to use (see fig. 2.16). Type the text you want in the box. Press a control button to make your application take action with the text.

✔ **List boxes.** Present lists of options from which you can select. Click on an option (or press Enter when it is highlighted) to select it. Use the scroll bar (or the arrow and position keys) to scroll through the list. To scroll the list to an item beginning with a specific letter, type that letter key.

✔ **Combo boxes.** Combine a list box and a text box. You can enter the text you need in the text box, or select it from the list box. Each portion of this combined control behaves like its separate counterpart; however, when you select an item in the list box portion, it is entered into the text box portion.

✔ **Drop-down list boxes.** Present a list of options and show you the current choice in a rectangular box. Click on the arrow (or press Alt+down arrow) to open the list. The list works exactly like a list box.

✔ **Option buttons.** Visually present a list of mutually exclusive items. Click on an option button (or press the spacebar when it is in focus) to darken the button. The darkened button shows that the associated option is selected. Click (or press the spacebar when it is in focus) again to clear the button. This shows that the associated option is no longer selected. In some sets of option buttons, one option must always be selected. In other sets, however, either one or none of the options can be selected.

✔ **Check boxes.** Present options that you can turn on or off. Click on the check box (or press the spacebar when it is in focus) to place a check in the box. The check indicates that the option has been selected. Click on the check box again (or press the spacebar when it is in focus) to remove the check. An empty check box indicates that the option has not been selected.

Chapter Snapshot

Windows 3.1 provides a revised File Manager for manipulating files and directories. To use File Manager effectively, you must learn how to use the File Manager interface and learn how File Manager manipulates files, directories, and drives. This chapter discusses things you can do within File Manager, including:

When you have completed this chapter, you should be comfortable managing files under Windows with File Manager. In addition to managing files locally, you also will learn how to work with network connections in File Manager.

CHAPTER

Managing Files

Disk and file management are tasks that most users perform regularly. Windows provides an application called File Manager to simplify the task of managing disks and files. File Manager provides all the same capabilities offered by the wide range of DOS file system commands, and also adds new capabilities.

Using File Manager

The File Manager application window gives you access to almost all the file and disk management capabilities of DOS. The File Manager menu lists almost all the DOS commands by name, and its dialog boxes enable you to set switches you would normally type on the command line. File Manager's workspace always contains at least one document window called a directory window. (File Manager is, in fact, a classic example of the Windows multiple document interface. Each drive and its contents is represented in a document window dedicated to that drive.)

File Manager offers almost all the capabilities of DOS commands. Notable absences are CHKDSK and FDISK. You can manage files from the File Manager, but you cannot partition or repair a disk drive as you can with these DOS commands. Although you can use CHKDSK and FDISK on your system, you cannot do so while running Windows. If you must run CHKDSK or FDISK, first exit Windows.

The directory window is split between a window that displays a visual representation of the directories on a disk (a directory tree) and a window that displays the contents (files and subdirectories) of the directory highlighted on the directory tree. File Manager also contains a drive bar with icons for each available drive. A few features of this interface—commands for manipulating file and disk operations—are shown in figure 3.1.

Figure 3.1
The File Manager interface.

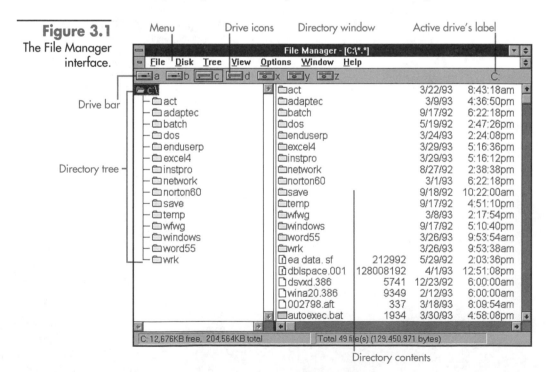

Directory contents

One useful feature of File Manager is that it uses graphical objects to communicate information to you. If you look at the drive icons in figure 3.1, you will notice that each type of drive is represented by a different icon:

- ✔ **Floppy drive.** Shows the opening where you would insert a disk.

- ✔ **Hard drive.** Shows a typical faceplate and drive light.

- ✔ **Network drive.** The X, Y, and Z drives show a cable with a connector.

Windows 3.1 includes drive icons for any type of drive, including RAM drives and CD-ROM drives, that you might use in the course of working with the Windows operating system. File Manager uses graphical objects to communicate which type of drive you are working with.

Even though the File Manager interface is useful, it can take several seconds to load directory information from a large, full hard drive. If you use File Manager frequently, you can avoid this delay by loading File Manager from the StartUp program group and checking the **R**un Minimized box in the Program Item Properties dialog box for the File Manager's program icon.

As an application that is started from the StartUp program group, File Manager loads the directory information once and provides it instantly whenever you need it. If you feel the directory information is old (you might have changed something in the past few minutes), use **W**indow, **R**efresh (or press the F5 key) to update the directory and contents windows.

Opening a Directory Window

One of the most common operations in File Manager is opening a directory window. A directory window is always open, but to copy or move files efficiently, a directory window for each drive you are working with needs to be open. **W**indow, **N**ew Window on the menu (see fig. 3.2) creates a new window identical to the directory window that currently has the focus. You then can click on the appropriate drive icon to fill the directory window with the appropriate contents.

Another way to fill a new directory window with information is to press Ctrl+*drive letter* to give the drive icon the focus. To arrange multiple directory windows in the File Manager workspace, use **W**indow, **C**ascade and **W**indow, **T**ile.

Figure 3.2

Opening a new
directory window
with the New
Window option.

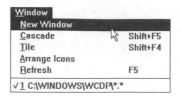

Arranging the Document Windows within File Manager

The Window, Cascade option causes the directory windows to overlap each other from the upper left corner of the File Manager window towards the lower right corner (see fig. 3.3).

Figure 3.3

Cascaded
document
windows in the
File Manager
window.

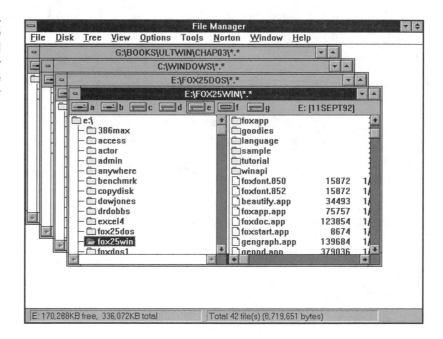

The Tile option arranges the document windows in a pattern that maximizes the space available within the File Manager window. In figure 3.4 there are only two document windows open, so File Manager automatically arranges the document windows in a horizontal fashion.

To tile directory windows vertically (see fig. 3.5) rather than horizontally, hold down the Shift key when you select Window, Tile.

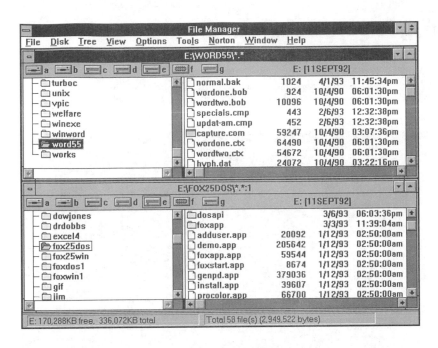

Figure 3.4
Horizontally tiled document windows in the File Manager window.

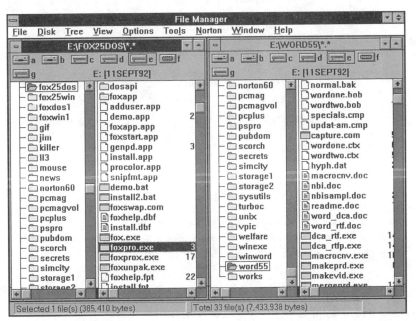

Figure 3.5
Vertically tiled document windows in the File Manager window.

Although the display in figure 3.5 might look rather awkward, this arrangement can be useful for copying files from one directory to another or even from one disk to another.

Indicating Expandable Branches

The file-folder icons on the directory tree indicate whether the branch of the tree is expandable—whether a directory on the tree has subdirectories. When a directory has subdirectories under it, a tiny plus sign (+) appears on the directory folder icon. To activate this feature, select Tree, Indicate Expandable Branches, as shown in figure 3.6.

Figure 3.6
Indicating
expandable
branches.

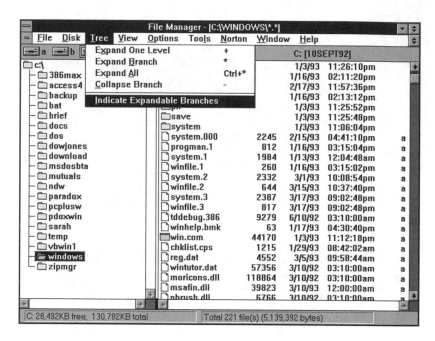

File-folder icons for expandable branches appear with a plus sign that changes to a minus sign if you expand the branch. The minus sign reverts to a plus sign when you collapse the branch, as shown in figure 3.7

To deactivate this feature, select Tree, Indicate Expandable Branches again.

File Manager's expandable branches feature is extremely useful, but it increases the amount of time File Manager takes to load and refresh directory information. Leave this feature turned off if speed is critical.

Expanding the Directory Tree

You can expand your view of the directory tree using three commands, all found on the Tree menu (see fig. 3.8).

Expandable branches   Unexpandable branches

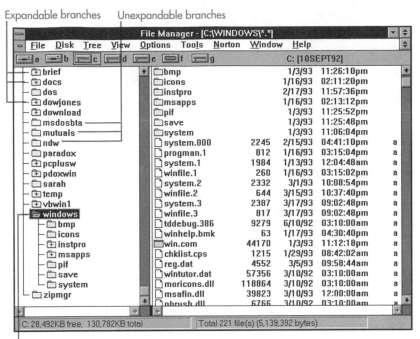

Expanded branch

Figure 3.7
A File Manager display with expandable branches indicated.

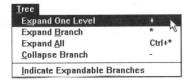

Figure 3.8
The menu commands for expanding the directory tree.

✔ **Expand All.** Fully expands all directory branches. You see the full extent of the directory structure for the drive in question (see fig. 3.9).

✔ **Expand One Level.** Reveals the group of subdirectories that branch from the highlighted parent, but does not show any subdirectories that might branch from the children. This is the default expansion when you double-click on a directory icon.

✔ **Expand Branch.** Fully expands the branch represented by the highlighted parent, showing all the subdirectories that branch from the parent and all the subdirectories that might branch from those children (see fig. 3.10).

Figure 3.9
A File Manager document window with Expand All turned on.

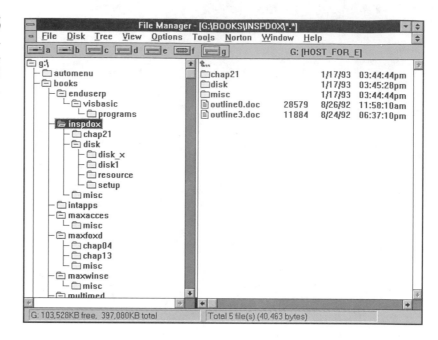

Figure 3.10
A File Manager document window with only the DOWJONES branch expanded.

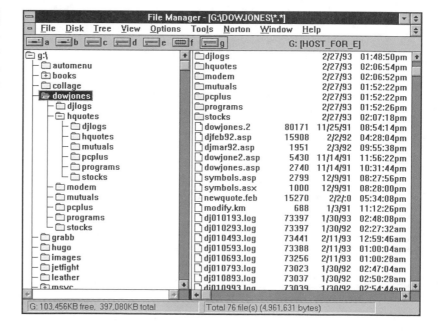

Double-click on a directory in the directory tree to expand it one level. Press the plus key (+) to expand a highlighted directory one level, and press the asterisk key (*) to expand the branch completely. Ctrl+* completely expands all directories in the tree.

Collapsing a Branch

To collapse a branch in the directory tree, select the branch and choose Tree, Collapse Branch (see fig. 3.11). All subdirectories to the right of the parent disappear. The action affects only the highlighted parent subdirectory and its children.

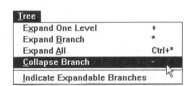

Figure 3.11
Collapsing a directory branch from the menu.

To navigate the directory tree from the keyboard, press Tab until the directory tree has the focus. Then use the arrow keys to move the highlighter. To collapse a branch, press the minus key (-) on the keyboard when the parent is highlighted.

Including Files in a Directory Window

You can determine which files File Manager displays in a directory window using View, By File Type. The By File Type dialog box (see fig. 3.12) provides check boxes for specifying whether you want directories, programs, documents, other files, or hidden/system files to appear in the directory contents window.

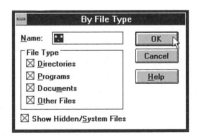

Figure 3.12
The By File Type dialog box.

When you check the Show Hidden/System Files check box (near the bottom of the By File Type dialog box in figure 3.12), files with the hidden attribute set will appear with exclamation marks in their icons (see fig. 3.13).

Understanding Windows

Figure 3.13
Hidden files are indicated by exclamation marks in their icons.

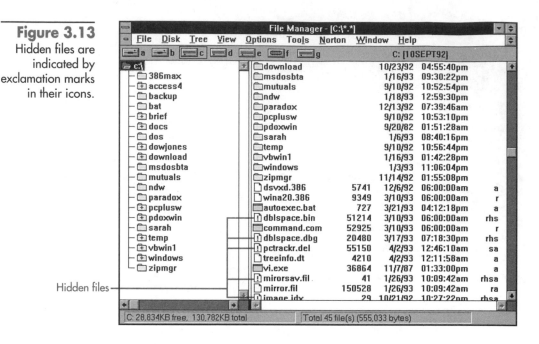

Hidden files

You can use the <u>N</u>ame text box in the By File Type dialog box to limit the files that appear by name (the standard DOS wild-card characters ? and * also work in this text box). By default, the <u>N</u>ame text box contains *.*, signifying that all file names should be shown. You could limit the display to help files, for example, by entering *.HLP.

Viewing File Information

The third section of the <u>V</u>iew menu displays only selected information about a file. This section provides three options:

✔ **Name.** Permits only a file's name to be displayed.

✔ **All File Details.** Presents the name, size, last modification date, last modification time, and attributes for each file.

✔ **Partial Details.** Presents the Partial Details dialog box (see fig. 3.14), which enables you to select any or all of four pieces of information about your files.

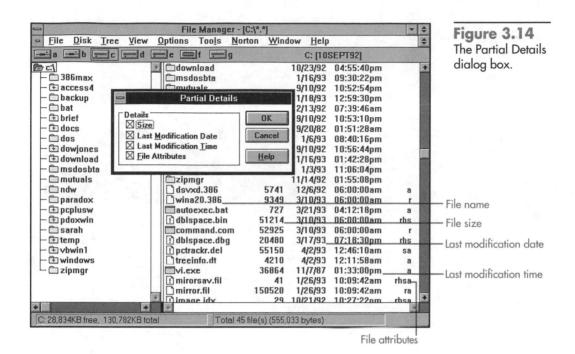

Figure 3.14
The Partial Details
dialog box.

File name

File size

Last modification date

Last modification time

File attributes

Selecting Files

When you want to modify a file or a group of files, you first must select the files. File
Manager provides three ways to select files:

✔ For a single file, click on its name.

✔ For a contiguous group of files, click on the first file, press and hold down the
Shift key, then click on the last file (see fig. 3.15).

✔ For a noncontiguous group of files, press and hold down the Ctrl key and click on
the files you want to select (see fig. 3.16).

Rather than highlight a noncontiguous group of files individually, it might be easier to
select an entire group of files and then deselect unwanted files from the group by holding
down the Ctrl key and clicking on the unwanted files.

Tip

To select files using the keyboard, press Tab until the directory contents window
has the focus; then use the arrow keys to move the highlighter.

The spacebar turns on and off the selection of an individual file. Select
contiguous groups of files by holding down the Shift key while moving the
focus with the arrow keys. You can select all files by pressing Ctrl+/.

Figure 3.15
A contiguous
group of files.

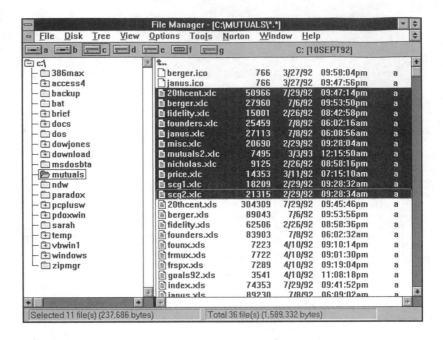

Figure 3.16
A noncontiguous
group of files.

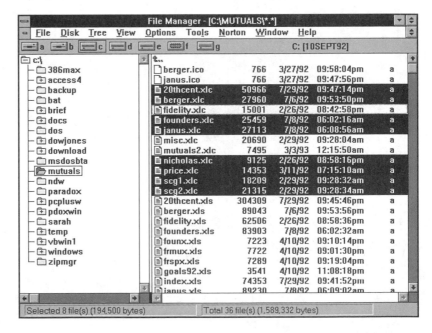

Selecting the View of the Directory Tree and Files

The File Manager's **V**iew menu provides several options that adjust the way you see the information in the directory tree window and the directory contents window. The tree section of the menu, shown in figure 3.17, determines what you see in the workspace of the directory window.

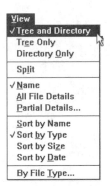

Figure 3.17
The tree portion of the View menu.

Tree and Directory, the default view, places a directory tree window and a directory contents window in the workspace of the directory window. The Tree Only and Directory Only views can be seen in figures 3.18 and 3.19.

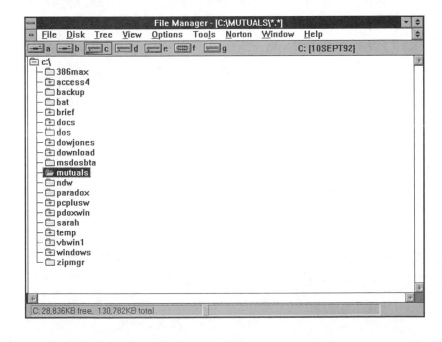

Figure 3.18
The Tree Only view.

Figure 3.19
The Directory
Only view.

```
─                        File Manager - [C:\MUTUALS\*.*]              ▼ ▲
─  File  Disk  Tree  View  Options  Tools  Norton  Window  Help        ▲
🖫a  🖫b  🖫c  🖫d  🖫e  🖫f  🖫g                     C: [10SEPT92]
▲
t..
  🗎berger.ico        766     3/27/92  09:58:04pm      a
  🗎janus.ico         766     3/27/92  09:47:56pm      a
  📄20thcent.xlc    50966     7/29/92  09:47:14pm      a
  📄berger.xlc      27960      7/6/92  09:53:50pm      a
  📄fidelity.xlc    15001     2/26/92  08:42:58pm      a
  📄founders.xlc    25459      7/8/92  06:02:16am      a
  📄janus.xlc       27113      7/8/92  06:08:56am      a
  📄misc.xlc        20690     2/29/92  09:28:04am      a
  📄mutuals2.xlc     7495      3/3/93  12:15:50am      a
  📄nicholas.xlc     9125     2/26/92  08:58:16pm      a
  📄price.xlc       14353     3/11/92  07:15:10am      a
  📄scg1.xlc        18209     2/29/92  09:28:32am      a
  📄scg2.xlc        21315     2/29/92  09:28:34am      a
  📄20thcent.xls   304309     7/29/92  09:45:46pm      a
  📄berger.xls      89043      7/6/92  09:53:56pm      a
  📄fidelity.xls    62506     2/26/92  08:58:36pm      a
  📄founders.xls    83903      7/8/92  06:02:32am      a
  📄founx.xls        7223     4/10/92  09:10:14pm      a
  📄frmux.xls        7722     4/10/92  09:01:30pm      a
  📄frspx.xls        7289     4/10/92  09:19:04pm      a
  📄goals92.xls      3541     4/10/92  11:08:18pm      a
  📄index.xls       74353     7/29/92  09:41:52pm      a
  📄janus.xls       89230      7/8/92  06:09:02am      a
▼
─Selected 1 file(s) (27,113 bytes)      ─Total 36 file(s) (1,589,332 bytes)
```

T̲ree Only places only a directory tree window in the workspace, as shown in figure 3.18. This view can be useful if you want to concentrate only on directory names, rather than the contents of the highlighted directory.

The Directory O̲nly view (see fig. 3.19) places only the contents of the highlighted directory in the document window's workspace. Notice that File Manager's title bar contains the directory name, so you still know which directory you are viewing.

You can set the view of the tree and directory separately for each directory window. If you have a complex directory tree on a drive, you might want to have one window just for viewing the tree alone. If you have a bunch of files in several subdirectories, you might want a window just for viewing the files.

If you are moving files from a full subdirectory to another location, you can use one window for selecting the files. With the drag-and-drop feature of File Manager, you can drag the files to move and drop them on the appropriate branch of the directory tree in the other window.

Adjusting the Split between the Directory Tree and Directory Contents

The V̲iew, S̲plit option enables you to adjust the split between the directory tree window and the directory contents window. Select this option to attach the mouse cursor to the split line (see fig. 3.20). Roll the mouse until the split is where you want it and click. The split between the two windows adjusts to the new position.

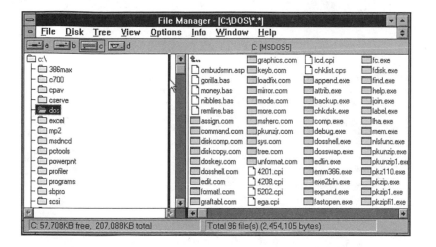

Figure 3.20
Adjusting the split between the directory tree and directory contents.

Tip

After selecting **V**iew, Sp**l**it, you can use the arrow keys to adjust the position of the split line. Esc makes the split adjust to the new position. You also can drag the split line with the mouse to readjust its position.

Sorting File Information

The fourth section of the **V**iew menu enables you to determine how files are sorted for display in the directory contents window. This section offers four options:

- ✔ **Sort by Name.** Causes the files to be presented alphabetically by name. Figure 3.21 shows files arranged alphabetically.

- ✔ **Sort by Type.** Presents the files alphabetically by file extension. Figure 3.22 shows this arrangement.

- ✔ **Sort by Size.** Presents the files by size (see fig. 3.23).

- ✔ **Sort by Date.** Presents files by date (see fig. 3.24).

Figure 3.21
Files sorted by name.

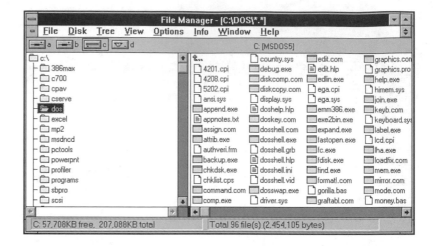

Figure 3.21
Files sorted by name.

Figure 3.22
Files sorted by type.

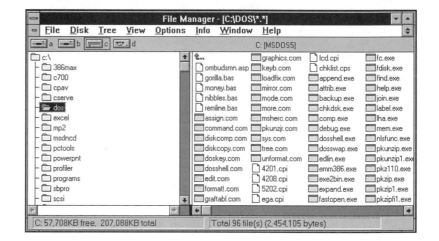

Arrange files by type if you want to copy or move a group of files with the same extension. Arrange files by name if you want to operate on files that all begin with the same root name.

Refreshing the File Manager Screen

Use **W**indow, **R**efresh to refresh the File Manager screen whenever you think an application has modified a file or directory but has not caused File Manager to update the directory window (see fig. 3.25). Press the F5 shortcut key to make File Manager refresh its screen.

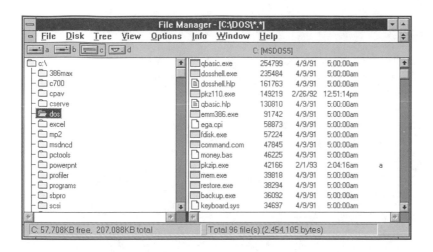

Figure 3.23
Files sorted by
size.

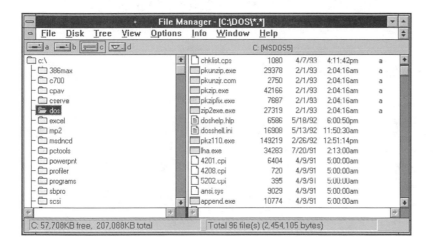

Figure 3.24
Files sorted by
date.

Figure 3.25
Refreshing the File
Manager screen.

A Note from the Author

Windows applications are supposed to notify File Manager that they have changed the file system, and File Manager is supposed to update the screen automatically. These updates do not always happen, however. Word for Windows backup files, for example, do not always appear in the File Manager directory window if you have just saved for the second time and then switch to File Manager to do some directory work. This absence is especially apparent when the Winword directory is the active directory.

DOS programs are notorious for not updating File Manager. You often have to mess with INI switches to force File Manager updates.

Windows applications automatically notify the File Manager of any changes they make to the file structure. You can force DOS applications to notify the File Manager if they change file information by including `FileSysChange=TRUE` in the `[386enh]` section of the SYSTEM.INI file. This setting might slow system performance, however.

File and Disk Operations

File Manager enables you to perform almost all the disk, file, and directory operations you can perform under DOS. (The last section of this chapter shows you how to overcome the minor limitations that you might encounter.) In addition, you can perform fast searches for files—something that is difficult to do under DOS. File Manager also enables you to manage connections to network drives as easily as you manage local drives. These file and disk operations are covered in the next few sections.

Formatting a Floppy Disk

To format a floppy disk in File Manager, insert the disk in the drive and select the Disk, Format Disk option in the disk menu. The dialog box shown in figure 3.26 appears, with options for selecting the drive and disk capacity of the format operation. You can choose to give the disk a label by typing up to 11 characters in the Label box. You can make a bootable floppy by checking the Make System Disk box.

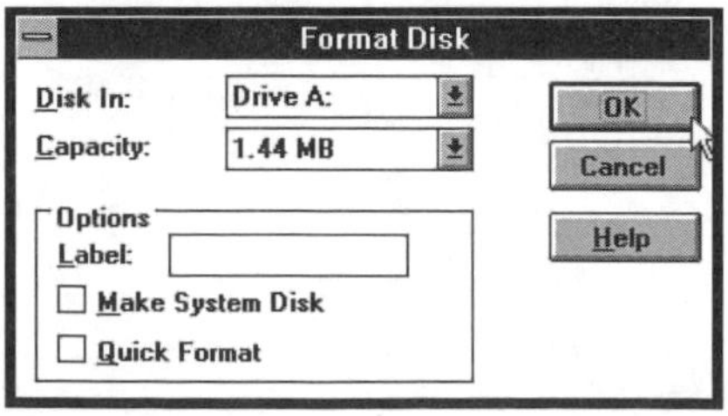

Figure 3.26
The Format Disk
dialog box.

If your disk has already been formatted and you want only to remove information from it, check the Quick Format box. If you press OK, File Manager warns you (unless you have turned format confirmation off using the Options, Confirmation command) that the impending operation will destroy all data on the disk.

You also can format a disk by inserting it into the drive and clicking on the icon for that drive in File Manager. If the disk has not been formatted, File Manager asks if you want to format it.

The File Manager Format option has some advantages over the DOS FORMAT command. File Manager does not force you to enter a volume name the way the DOS FORMAT command does. In addition, when formatting several disks, File Manager's Format option prevents you from using a volume label for more than one disk. File Manager "forgets" the volume label after its initial use so that subsequent floppies do not accidentally receive duplicate labels. These features make using File Manager superior to using DOS for disk activities.

Labeling a Floppy Disk

To label a disk that has already been formatted, select the drive containing the disk you want to label. Choose the Disk, Label Disk option, which displays the dialog box shown in figure 3.27. Enter up to 11 characters to identify the disk in the Label text box and click on OK. Make sure your label does not contain spaces or punctuation marks. Although the label input box appears to give you more space than necessary, it allows you to enter only the 11 characters permitted in a volume label.

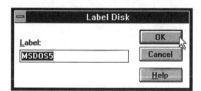

Figure 3.27
The Label Disk
dialog box.

Use disk labels to identify the contents of your disks. The label for the drive with focus appears on the drive bar of the directory window on the right side (see fig. 3.28).

Figure 3.28
The label for a
drive as it appears
on the drive bar.

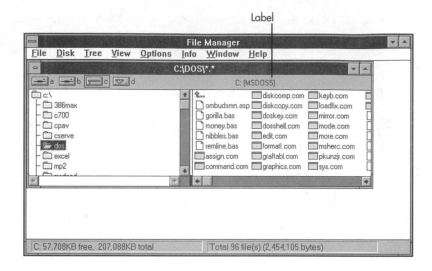

Copying a Disk

Copying a disk under File Manager is easy: simply place the disk in a drive and select **D**isk, **C**opy Disk. If you have two floppy disk drives, a dialog box appears from which you can enter the letters for the source and destination drives. (If you have only one floppy drive, this dialog box does not appear.) When you click on OK, File Manager displays the Confirm Copy Disk dialog box, which warns you that the copy operation will destroy all data on the destination disk (see fig. 3.29). Click on **Y**es to confirm the operation.

Figure 3.29
Press Yes to begin
the copy process.

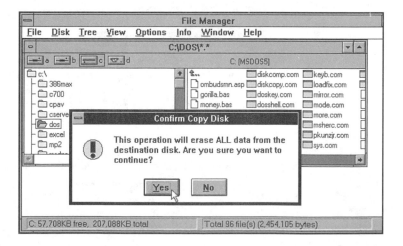

File Manager does not enable you to use the **D**isk, **C**opy operation to copy between disks of different sizes. Your source and destination disks must be of the same size. If you have a 5.25-inch disk that must be copied to a 3.5-inch disk (or vice versa), use **F**ile, **C**opy to accomplish the task. Select the files that you need to copy, including hidden and system files. Choose <u>F</u>ile, <u>C</u>opy from the menu. Specify the destination disk as the destination for the copy operation. You can also use File Manager's drag-and-drop feature to accomplish this operation. Drag the selected files and drop them on the icon for the destination drive.

The disk copying process is easier the more memory you have. When memory is tight and your source and destination drives are the same, such as when you have only one disk drive, you have to swap disks more often. When memory is free, File Manager copies the source image to memory, and then copies the image from memory to the destination drive. The only time you change disks is when you switch from source disk to destination disk.

Making a System Disk

To make a previously formatted floppy disk bootable, use the <u>D</u>isk, <u>M</u>ake System Disk command. If your system has two disk drives, a dialog box appears asking you which drive contains the disk. When you press OK, File Manager displays a dialog box asking you to confirm the operation.

When you want to create a system disk, use drive A, whether it is a 5.25-inch or 3.5-inch drive. Some motherboard BIOSs (Basic Input Output Systems) do not enable you to boot from drive B.

Selecting a Drive

File Manager provides a menu command that enables you to select the active drive. To select a drive, use the <u>D</u>isk, <u>S</u>elect Drive menu option. The Select Drive dialog box appears (see fig. 3.30), which enables you to choose from the available drives presented in a list box. Click on the desired drive and then click on OK.

A quicker way to display the Select Drive dialog box is to double-click on the drive bar background. This operation is the equivalent of clicking on a drive icon or pressing Ctrl+*drive letter*.

If you can just click on the desired drive, why even have a Select Drive dialog box? Because some users don't have a mouse! One of the basic rules of CUA is that all mouse actions have keyboard equivalents. The seemingly redundant Select Drive dialog box also is helpful if you have shoved part of File Manager off the screen while you are working and want to select a drive.

Figure 3.30
The Select Drive
dialog box.

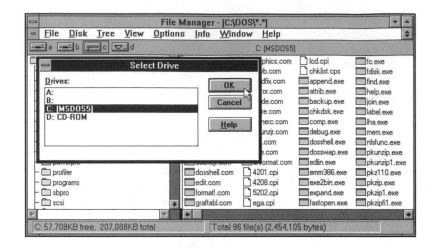

Copying Files and Directories

To copy files or directories, select the files or directories in either the directory tree window or the directory contents window. Then select **F**ile, **C**opy to display the dialog box shown in figure 3.31. Enter a destination in the **T**o text box and click on OK. File Manager asks you to confirm the operation unless you have turned off confirmation for the copy operation. If you want to copy the file to the Clipboard, click on the **C**opy to Clipboard button.

Figure 3.31
Copying files
under File
Manager.

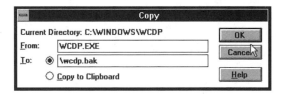

You can also use File Manager's drag and drop feature to copy files and directories. After you select your files and directories, hold down the Ctrl key and drag the files with the mouse and drop them on the destination drive icon or destination directory branch on the directory tree. You can also drop them into the directory contents window of another directory window. As you drag files for copying, the mouse pointer changes into a files icon and displays a plus sign to indicate the files are being duplicated.

Be wary of turning off the **O**ptions, **C**onfirmation, File **R**eplace check box. When this check box is cleared, you can accidentally copy over a file with the same name or copy an earlier version of a file over a later version.

Deleting a File or Directory

To use File Manager to delete files or directories, select the file or directory you want to delete, then choose File, Delete (or press Del). File Manager displays the Delete dialog box, which asks you to okay the list of files or directories to be deleted (see fig. 3.32). Unless you have turned off delete confirmation, File Manager presents a Confirm File Delete dialog box in which the Yes and Yes to All buttons finish the job.

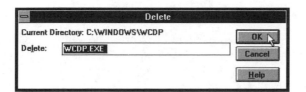

Figure 3.32
Deleting files with File Manager.

You cannot delete files marked with the Read Only or Hidden attributes. You must change these attributes before you attempt to delete them. See the section "Setting File Attributes or Properties" later in this chapter.

Moving a File or Directory

Moving a file or directory is the equivalent of first copying the file or directory to a new location and then deleting the file or directory at the old location. To move files or directories in File Manager, select the file or directory and then choose File, Move. File Manager presents the Move dialog box, shown in figure 3.33, which asks you to enter a destination in the To text box.

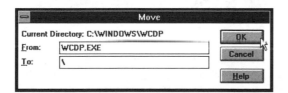

Figure 3.33
Moving a file or directory in File Manager.

You also can move files or directories using File Manager's drag-and-drop feature. Simply drag the selected files and drop them on their new destination. Unless you have turned off mouse action confirmation, you will be prompted to confirm the operation.

If you use **F**ile, **M**ove, you will not be asked to confirm your move after you press OK in the Move dialog box. For this reason, double-check the entry in the **T**o field before you press OK.

If you use the mouse to drag and drop a moved file, make sure a plus sign does not appear during the move—+ indicates the file is being copied.

Renaming a File or Directory

To rename files or directories, select the files or directories you want to rename, then choose **F**ile, **R**ename. In the Rename dialog box, enter the new name in the **T**o text box (see fig. 3.34). You can use standard DOS wild-card characters to rename several files at once, as when changing the extension of several files.

Figure 3.34
Renaming files in
File Manager.

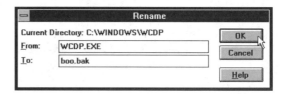

Use **F**ile, **M**ove to rename a file and move it from one directory to another in a single operation.

Confirming File Actions

File Manager attempts to protect you from accidental disaster by asking you to confirm actions that could result in loss of data, such as deleting a file, replacing a file, or formatting a disk. You can control which actions require confirmation by choosing **O**ptions, **C**onfirmation. The Confirmation dialog box (see fig. 3.35) contains check boxes for several File Manager operations that could possibly lose data.

Figure 3.35
File Manager's
confirmation
options.

Be very wary of turning off any of the confirmation options, because you can easily become confused in the middle of an operation. Even with confirmation turned on, you can accidentally delete important files. You could also rename a file with the same name as an existing file and overwrite the existing file, an error that no undelete program can correct. If several people use your computer, you most likely will want to leave all confirmation options on.

The DOS 5.0 UNDELETE command and DOS 6.0 Undelete utility provide extra protection against accidental loss of data. If you accidentally delete a file, you have a good chance of recovering it. With DOS 6.0, the best choice is to use the Delete Sentry method of protection. This method preserves an image of the file on your disk for a specified number of days, giving you the best chance of recovering from accidental data loss.

DOS 6.0 adds a Tools menu to the File Manager menu bar. This menu gives you access to the DOS 6.0 Undelete, Compression, Anti-virus, and Backup utilities.

Setting File Attributes or Properties

DOS files can be configured with any or none of the following attributes:

✔ **Read Only.** Prevents changes from being saved to the file.

✔ **Archive.** Marks the file as having been changed since the last backup.

✔ **Hidden.** Does not display the file in the standard directory list.

✔ **System.** Enables the operating system to use the file.

File Manager provides switches for changing the attributes for any file or group of files. Select the desired files and choose File, Properties. The Properties dialog box (see fig. 3.36) contains check boxes for setting the attributes of files.

Properties for WCDP.EXE
File Name: WCDP.EXE
Size: 188,928 bytes
Last Change: 3/14/93 3:30:58PM
Path: C:\WINDOWS\WCDP
Attributes
☐ Read Only   ☐ Hidden
☒ Archive   ☐ System
OK   Cancel   Help

Figure 3.36
The Properties dialog box.

I

Understanding Windows

Choose **V**iew, **A**ll File Details to see all file details, including the attributes. Choose **V**iew, **P**artial Details and check the **F**ile Attributes box to see only the file attributes. If a file is marked as Hidden or System, you cannot see it in the File Manager unless you select Show Hidden/**S**ystem Files in the **V**iew, By File **T**ype menu option.

Creating Associations

File Manager enables you to associate a document (or file) extension with the application that created the document or file. After a document is associated with an application, double-clicking on the file automatically starts the associated application and loads the file. You also can add the document as an item within a Program Manager group and activate both the file and the application by double-clicking on its icon.

You can associate any document file with any appropriate application. You can associate PCX files with any application that is capable of opening and displaying the file, for example. More than one type of file can be associated with an application. If you are using Word or a similar word processor, for example, you can associate TXT and other types of document files with the word processor.

The help files installed as program items in Program Manager by most applications are help files that have been associated with the Windows Help application. The file listed in the **C**ommand Line text box is actually the HLP file. Windows Help starts and loads the file because HLP files have been associated with the Windows Help executable file, WINHELP.EXE.

To associate a file with an application, use the **F**ile, **A**ssociate command. File Manager displays the Associate dialog box, as shown in figure 3.37. Choose the application you want to associate with the file extension in the **A**ssociate With combination box. Type the extension you want to associate with the application in the **F**iles with Extension text box. To cancel an association, type the extension in the text box and choose (None) in the pull-down menu box.

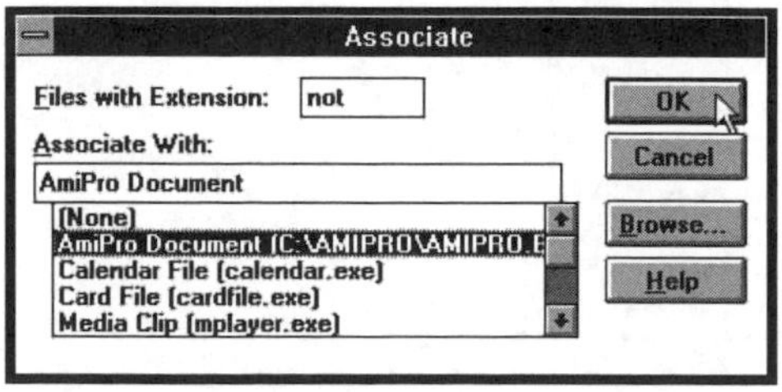

Figure 3.37
Associating a file
with an
application.

Associate

Files with Extension: | not |

Associate With:

AmiPro Document

(None)
AmiPro Document [C:\AMIPRO\AMIPRO.E
Calendar File [calendar.exe]
Card File [cardfile.exe]
Media Clip [mplayer.exe]

OK

Cancel

Browse...

Help

Tip

If an application is included in the **A**ssociate With combination box, you can print an associated file by dragging the file name from File Manager and dropping it on the Print Manager icon. During installation, applications with this capability install themselves in the Registration Database, the file Windows uses to keep track of applications that can take advantage of features such as associated files and drag-and-drop. They appear automatically in the **A**ssociate With combination box as a result.

If the application you want to associate with a file extension does not appear in the **A**ssociate With combination box, use the **B**rowse button to locate it; then create the association. Each document extension can be associated with only one application, but many extensions can be associated with a single application. If you change the association for an extension from one application to another, the previous association is automatically canceled without warning. You cannot accidentally associate an extension with more than one application. All associations for DOS applications are based on PIFs rather than actual application files.

Creating a Directory

To create a directory using File Manager, select the directory in the directory tree window where you want to create the new subdirectory. Select **F**ile, **C**reate Directory to display the Create Directory dialog box, shown in figure 3.38. Enter the directory name and click on OK.

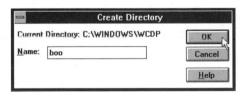

Figure 3.38
Creating a new directory.

Note

You can name a directory to include an extension, but the name must be eight characters or fewer in length and contain no spaces or punctuation other than the period that starts the extension. You can create only one level of directory at a time; you cannot create a parent directory and a child subdirectory in a single operation. If the parent directory does not exist for a new subdirectory, Create Directory aborts and an error message appears.

Searching for Files

File Manager enables you to search for files by name. Choose the **F**ile, Sear**c**h menu option to display the Search dialog box, as shown in figure 3.39. Type the file specification you want to find in the **S**earch For text box. (You can use the standard DOS wild-card characters.) Type the directory you want to begin searching from in the Start From text box. Check the Search All Subdirectories box to search all child subdirectories of the directory named in the Start From text box.

Figure 3.39
Searching for files
using the Search
dialog box.

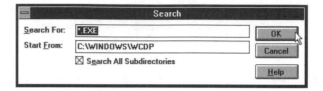

File Manager performs the search and displays the contents in a document window titled Search Results (see fig. 3.40). This window contains a list of the located files. You can select these files and perform file operations on them just as you would if they appeared in the directory contents window in a directory window.

Figure 3.40
The Search Results
window, showing
the result of a
search for BAK
files.

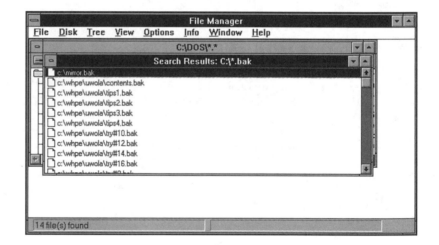

To help maintain the performance of your hard drive, periodically search for BAK and TMP files that might have been left behind by applications. Most of these files can be deleted safely, freeing up drive space.

Establishing a Network Connection

File Manager enables you to manage connections to your network. If you are connected to a network, the Disk menu contains the Network Connections option. This command displays the Network—Drive Connections dialog box. The controls that appear in this dialog box vary according to the type of network you are using. You specify the name of the network drive, the drive letter, and the password, if required. Some networks present a **B**rowse button that enables you to bring up a list of possible connections. After you have specified your connection, use the **A**ttach or **C**onnect button to complete the connection.

Before you start Windows, your network shell must have successfully been loaded for File Manager to recognize possible network connections. You then can use File Manager to perform all permitted file and drive operations on your network, just as you would on a local drive.

Removing a Network Connection

To remove a network connection, select the **D**isk, **N**etwork Connections menu option. Most networks present you with a list of current connections; others might ask you to use a **B**rowse button to identify current connections. Click on **D**etach to break a connection.

Disconnecting breaks all links you have with print queues, shared files, or applications provided to your workstation by the network connection.

Using Recorder Macros To Compensate for File Manager's Missing Features

File Manager offers you most of the advantages of DOS commands under Windows. Some features, however, are missing, particularly printing file and directory information. You can get around these problems so that the function of any DOS command can be performed in Windows.

The next two sections describe solutions for the two most pressing needs felt by most users—printing directory lists and printing directory trees. Keep in mind that you can use the general process for almost any DOS command. These sections also show how to use Recorder macros to make these commands available to you at the double-click of your mouse.

The Windows Recorder application enables you to record keystrokes for later playback to an application. Sets of keystrokes, or *macros,* can be stored in a file. The file can be loaded into the Recorder any time you need to replay such commonly used keystrokes. Macros are useful to Windows users when they perform repeated actions frequently. When you want to create supplements to File Manager to compensate for a feature that is not present, the Recorder is a natural choice.

Creating a macro has only a few steps:

1. Start the Recorder application.

2. Use the <u>M</u>acro, Re<u>c</u>ord menu option to initiate the recording process.

3. Perform the keystrokes and mouse actions that you want to replay.

4. Double-click on the Recorder icon to end the recording process.

5. Choose the <u>S</u>ave Macro option in the dialog box that appears and click on OK.

After you have created the macros you need, you can save them in a file using <u>F</u>ile, <u>S</u>ave. (Several macros can be saved in a single file.) When you load the file, the workspace of the Recorder window shows you a list of the available macros. You run a macro by double-clicking on its name in the list.

If you are using macros to enhance File Manager, chances are you will want the macros available all the time. Add the Recorder to your StartUp group, and place the file name to be loaded as an argument following the executable file name on the command line using the Program Manager's Properties dialog box. (You access it using <u>F</u>ile, <u>P</u>roperties.) Your extensions to File Manager are always at your fingertips. The following sections demonstrate two extensions you might want to have ready as macros.

Printing Directory Lists

To print a directory list, choose <u>F</u>ile, <u>R</u>un. In the Command Line text box, enter the following command:

```
COMMAND.COM /C DIR > LPT1
```

This command starts a new copy of COMMAND.COM, the DOS command file that initiates any DOS session under Windows. The /C switch directs COMMAND.COM to perform the command after it on the command line and then to stop running. The command DIR > LPT1 displays the DOS directory and redirects it to the printer port, providing a printout of directory contents. When it runs, your screen blanks for a moment as the DOS session starts, the command runs, and the DOS session exits.

You can use redirection in this DOS command to reroute the directory list to any DOS device capable of accepting it, including a file. To print the directory contents to a file, enter the following in the Run dialog box:

```
COMMAND.COM /C DIR > DIR.TXT
```

If you reroute the output to a file, you can load the directory list into an application for viewing or printing. (The TXT extension associates the file with Notepad, for instance.) You can use File Manager's drag-and-drop feature to print such a file when you want a printout.

Some printers may not respond to redirected output from a DOS command immediately. If this happens, the printer probably is waiting for a linefeed character to begin printing. Take the printer offline, press the line feed or form feed button on the front panel (whichever is available), and place the printer back online. It should begin printing.

To automate the process of printing directory lists, follow the procedure outlined earlier in this chapter. Start the Recorder application. Select Macro, Record, then enter a macro name in the Record Macro Name field. Assign a keystroke to the macro using the controls in the Shortcut Key group, and enter a description in the Description text box (see fig. 3.41). Click on OK to initiate the recording process. Repeat the steps described for printing a directory list described earlier, using the variation on the command you prefer. Then double-click on the Recorder macro. When the dialog box appears, choose Save Macro and click on OK. You then can perform the directory print operation from the Recorder by loading the file containing the macro and double-clicking on its name in the Recorder's workspace. You might want to load such a file of useful macros from your StartUp group.

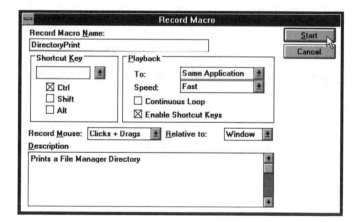

Figure 3.41
Recording a macro to print a directory.

Printing Directory Trees

Another common disk operation missing from File Manager is the capability to print directory trees. You can compensate for this missing feature by creating a macro with the following command:

```
COMMAND.COM /C TREE /A> LPT1
```

This command uses the DOS TREE command to produce a directory tree, which then is rerouted to the printer. The /A switch on tree directs it to use text characters to show the lines in the tree rather than graphics characters. This enables the tree to print on printers that might have trouble interpreting graphics characters. If you want, this macro can redirect output to a TXT file that you can view with Notepad. Simply substitute a file name for the device name on the command line.

Aside from the visually welcome interface, File Manager's benefits are helpful, but can take time to learn. If you are a seasoned DOS user, you probably know the shortcomings of c:\ and the DOSSHELL and recognize the advantages of File Manager's graphical drag-and-drop features. If you are new to PCs, File Manager is the obvious choice for learning how to control and work with files and directories. Every type of user can benefit from File Manager's features, even those who swear by DOS.

Chapter Snapshot

If you think back to earlier versions of Windows, recall that it has always been a much friendlier environment in which to manage fonts than DOS. Fonts are dealt with at the operating-environment level rather than the application level. With third-party font managers, such as Adobe Type Manager (ATM), users work with text that looks the same on-screen as when printed out.

Windows 3.1, however, has become much more sophisticated than earlier versions of the graphical environment by seamlessly integrating a scalable font technology into Windows. This chapter looks at the world of fonts in Windows 3.1 by focusing on the following topics:

Managing fonts on your Windows desktop has never been easier than in Windows 3.1. You can create and print professional-looking documents using the fonts included with Windows on virtually any output device.

Working with Fonts

s you work in Windows 3.1, you will become acquainted with the following four distinct groups of fonts:

✔ **Bitmap or raster fonts.** These fonts are created by arranging pixels in a particular pattern to display and print in a fixed point size. A unique bitmap must be created for each character, point size, and type style. Windows 3.0 fonts, such as Helvetica and Times Roman, are bitmap fonts that come in 8-, 10-, 12-, 14-, 18-, and 24-point sizes. A separate file is needed for each point size and style (normal, bold, italic, and bold italic). These screen fonts cannot be downloaded to printers; as a result, these screen fonts usually are different from what is printed by the printer.

✔ **TrueType fonts.** These fonts are known as outline fonts, generated using mathematical calculations. An *outline font* is a set of mathematical instructions for each character that contain a series of points to form an outline. An outline font is scalable because you can increase or decrease the point size of a font by multiplying or dividing by the desired factor. An outline font can be scaled in a wide range of sizes, from 2 to nearly 700 points (although many Windows applications limit this actual range). All mathematical instructions for a font can be stored in a single file rather than in multiple bitmap files. TrueType fonts are compatible with all devices except plotters.

✔ **Device-specific fonts.** These fonts are either installed on the printer or downloaded, and are controlled more by the device than by Windows. Windows does not map device-specific fonts; instead, it relays the logical font request to the device—printer or software (such as ATM or FaceLift)—whose job it is to map the fonts properly. PostScript fonts are considered device-specific fonts.

✔ **Vector fonts.** These fonts are scalable fonts consisting of tiny dots and line segments. *Vector fonts* typically are used only when outputting to a plotter, although a few dot-matrix printers support vector fonts. Windows comes with three vector fonts: Modern, Roman, and Script. Because of their makeup, vector fonts do not have the same quality as the other types of fonts. Thus, most Windows applications do not even display vector fonts in their font lists.

Although *typeface* and *font* are used interchangeably in PC circles, a distinct difference exists between the two. A *typeface* is the basic design of characters; a *font* is the complete set of characters for a given typeface at a particular point size and style.

Exploring TrueType

Windows 3.1 introduced a breakthrough in font technology on the PC platform. Before Windows 3.1, you had to purchase a third-party font manager, such as ATM, to achieve identical screen and printer output. Without ATM, you probably worked with Helvetica and Times Roman on-screen, and found your documents looking quite different when you printed them. Not so in Windows 3.1, which integrated the scalable font technology known as TrueType into the operating environment.

TrueType was developed jointly by Apple and Microsoft. The TrueType fonts included with Windows 3.1 match those of Apple System 6.0.5 or later, and can be used on the Macintosh without conversion. The basic TrueType fonts included with Windows 3.1 (see fig. 4.1) are designed to match the core PostScript fonts.

The 14 standard TrueType fonts in Windows were made by Monotype, one of the major font foundries. These fonts have been widely praised for their outstanding quality; in fact, many consider them to be unequaled by their PostScript Type 1 counterparts.

Although TrueType is the new kid on a block traditionally dominated by PostScript, its acceptability has been widespread. This acceptability centers on four factors, which can be summarized as follows:

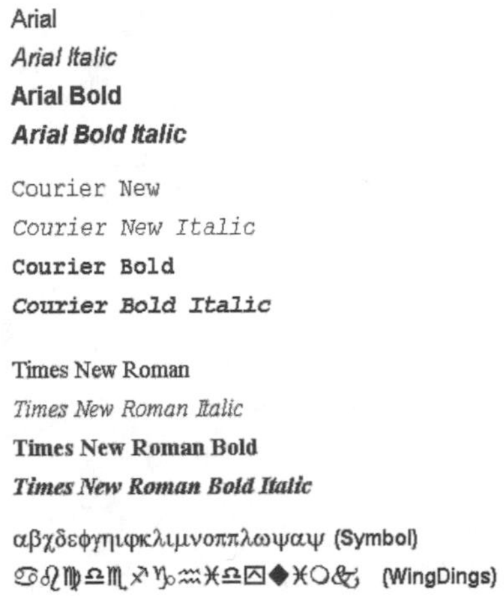

Arial

Arial Italic

Arial Bold

Arial Bold Italic

Courier New

Courier New Italic

Courier Bold

Courier Bold Italic

Times New Roman

Times New Roman Italic

Times New Roman Bold

Times New Roman Bold Italic

αβχδεφγηιφκλιμνοππλωψαψ (Symbol)

♈♌♏♓☝♍⚹♓≈✳⌂▣◆✳○♋ (WingDings)

Figure 4.1
TrueType fonts included with Windows 3.1.

✔ **Ease of use.** One of the greatest strengths of TrueType is that it is closely integrated in the Windows environment. In fact, the Windows Graphical Device Interface (GDI) was redesigned specifically for this purpose. No other font manager is as easy to use. Installing, removing, and working with TrueType fonts is effortless. Even applications designed for Windows 3.0 can use TrueType fonts because of the way Microsoft integrated TrueType into the GDI. Moreover, new TrueType application programming interface functions give applications greater control over placement and manipulation of characters.

TrueType can be used in Windows 3.0 applications, but the printed document might not be exactly WYSIWYG (What You See Is What You Get) in the same way that Windows 3.1 documents are.

✔ **Identical screen and printer output.** TrueType enables you to work with fonts that appear the same on-screen as they will on the printer.

TrueType is almost WYSIWYG. Because of the differences in dots-per-inch between your monitor (usually around 96–120 dpi) and printer (usually 300–600 dpi), no font technology is absolutely identical.

✔ **Scalable.** No longer do you need to design your document around the sizes of the Windows bitmap fonts (8, 10, 12, or 14). If you use bitmap fonts with point sizes other than the built-in ones, they look jagged as they are resized. TrueType fonts are scalable fonts that can be displayed and printed in virtually any size above two points. Figure 4.2 shows the letter *Q* in Arial typeface at 12 and 82 points. As you can see, the two are directly proportional.

Figure 4.2
TrueType fonts are
scalable.

✔ **Portable.** TrueType fonts are printer portable, meaning that a TrueType document prints identically on any output device, regardless of the printer's page description language (PDL), such as PostScript or Hewlett-Packard's PCL. TrueType also is portable across platforms so that a document created in Windows can be moved seamlessly to a Macintosh.

How Windows Handles TrueType Fonts

Although TrueType looks identical on the screen and printer, the processes Windows goes through to display TrueType on these various devices is much different. Suppose you start Word for Windows and begin typing an office memo. Based on the character specifications—such as font, point size, and style—Word asks the Windows GDI for the appropriate bitmap to represent each character in the document.

The GDI finds the appropriate TrueType font file, based on the information provided by Word, and sends it to the TrueType rasterizer. The TrueType rasterizer converts the outline instructions into a bitmap, and returns the bitmap to the GDI to display. This bitmap then is sent to the device driver for displaying on-screen. This process is shown in figure 4.3.

Figure 4.3
The process of
displaying a
TrueType font.

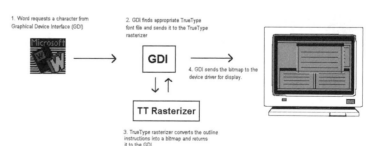

TrueType outlines are device-independent, and thus are an ideal representation of the font. However, 96-dpi screens and even 300-dpi laser printers do not have enough resolution to display or print the character properly because the size of a pixel is too large. Diagonal lines and curves within a font outline sometimes look jagged because the optimum outline of a character cannot always be represented accurately by a set of pixels. A diagonal line, for example, might need only part of a pixel to represent it, but because the pixel is the smallest unit of measure, the pixel either needs to be on or off. If the pixel is on, the line looks too wide; if the pixel is off, the line is too narrow.

To prevent this from happening, before TrueType creates the bitmap, it first optimizes the bitmap by using *hints*—instructions that optimize the look of the scaled outline character by changing its outline to produce a better-looking character. For example, without hints, a lowercase *m* or *n* might have different widths for each of its legs. Hinting distorts the original outline characters so that the *m* and *n* bitmaps displayed do, in fact, have identical legs, regardless of the number of pixels available.

Hints are less important when the font is larger and the resolution is greater on the output device. Although hints are needed when printing or displaying on devices below 800-dpi, new 600-dpi laser printers, such as the HP LaserJet IV, can produce the desired results with fewer hints.

A Note from the Author

Both TrueType and PostScript support hinting, but they use different techniques. PostScript Type 1 hints are a set of instructions given to the rasterizer, telling it how the character can be modified. The PostScript rasterizer is then responsible for carrying out these instructions. In contrast, TrueType hints are carried out by the font itself rather than the TrueType rasterizer.

The significance of this difference might not be immediately obvious, but it can affect the performance and quality of the hint. First, TrueType hints are faster because they are performed by the font producer during the development of the font, instead of at run time by the rasterizer. Second, built-in hints can improve the quality of the generated TrueType font because the font designer, not the rasterizer, is in control of the final appearance of the font. Third, potential hinting problems can be resolved during the development process instead of at run time. As a result, the TrueType font rasterizer is quicker and more efficient in executing the font code.

A PostScript rasterizer *interprets* PostScript hints; a TrueType rasterizer simply *processes* the TrueType font's hints. PostScript can be thought of as a high-level interpreted language; TrueType can be considered a low-level assembler-like language.

When you print your TrueType document, the way the fonts are dealt with is based on the type of printer being used. On LaserJet and compatible printers, TrueType generates LaserJet soft fonts, and downloads only the characters needed by the printer to print the text, instead of entire font files being sent. (Typical soft fonts require downloading entire character sets.) Characters are printed as text, not as graphics.

On PostScript printers, TrueType downloads smaller characters (14-point characters and below) as Type 3 fonts (bitmap), which is faster than downloading an outline font. For larger fonts, TrueType sends a Type 1 outline for each size that needs to be rasterized by the PostScript printer.

On dot-matrix printers, TrueType sends text as graphics for each pass of the printhead. Although printing TrueType on a dot-matrix printer is slow, the quality is remarkably good.

Embedding TrueType Fonts in Documents

TrueType solves the problem of transferring Windows documents between computers. Before TrueType, a document created on a computer with a specific set of fonts could not be properly displayed or printed on a second computer without the same set of fonts being installed. As a result, document sharing within an office environment was limited to those workstations that were equipped with identical fonts and font managers. When sending a document to a typesetter, you also had the legal dilemma of whether to include copyrighted font files on the disk to ensure that their output was identical to that of the service bureau.

TrueType eliminates these problems through a technology called *font embedding*, which embeds the fonts in the document so that they still can be displayed and/or printed when opened on a computer without those fonts installed. A font is specifically coded by the developer to have one of the following three embedding qualities:

✔ **No embedding.** If a font allows no embedding capabilities, the source application will not embed the font in a document when it is saved. The receiving computer is forced to make a font substitution when the document is opened on the computer. PostScript and most other current non-TrueType fonts are in this class.

✔ **Read-only.** If a document contains one or more read-only fonts, you can read and print the document, but the receiving application does not enable you to edit it until every read-only embedded font has been removed.

✔ **Read/write.** The read/write option enables you to read, modify, and print the document with the embedded TrueType fonts. Moreover, the application in which you open the embedded document asks you whether you want the font installed permanently. The standard TrueType fonts that come with Windows 3.1 all are read/write fonts (as are the fonts that come in the TrueType Font Pack). If a font is read/write enabled, you can distribute an embedded document to whomever you choose; there are no copyright restrictions placed on you.

Windows 3.1 Font Mapping

Windows 3.1 enables you to substitute fonts not found on your system with installed fonts. This process is known as *font mapping*. When you open an existing document or create a new one, an application requests a font from Windows by listing its face name and other characteristics. If there is no exact match with a physical font (a font that can be transferred to the printer and screen), Windows must try to map that request to the closest possible physical font.

Windows 3.1 advanced font-mapping capabilities are available in Windows 3.0. Both Windows 3.0 and 3.1 have a core-mapping facility, which selects the physical font that most closely matches the requested font. Windows 3.0 requires that all font requests go to the core mapper—even when a font request has a match. Windows 3.1 speeds up the process considerably by making an end-around the core mapper when an exact match is found (that is, the core mapper is not even accessed).

When Windows maps a font, it first looks at its own internal font-substitution table in the GDI. This list includes, among other substitutions, several PostScript font mappings to their TrueType equivalents. You can amend or override this list by modifying the entries to the [Font Substitutes] section of WIN.INI. The section normally includes the following entries:

```
[FontSubstitutes]
Helv=MS Sans Serif
Tms Rmn=MS Serif
```

As an application requests the Helv (Helvetica) or Tms Rmn (Times Roman) font (used in Windows 3.0), Windows looks at the font-mapping section of WIN.INI and substitutes the bitmap MS Sans Serif or MS Serif fonts instead. You can modify these entries. Suppose you want to use all TrueType fonts. Change the WIN.INI section to the following:

```
[FontSubstitutes]
Helv=Arial
Tms Rmn = Times New Roman
```

You can alias any font, but TrueType and bitmap fonts are the only fonts that can act as substitutes. In the following example, *FontA* can be any type of font; *FontB* must be TrueType or bitmap:

FontA=FontB

If you have worked with fonts for any length of time, you know that a vast number of fonts are available that are virtually identical in appearance, but which have copyrighted face names. Font mapping eliminates any possible confusion by Windows when it searches for exact face names.

When an application requests a font from Windows, Windows has to decide which font to use, based on the following conditions:

✔ **Font does not exist.** If the name of the font does not exist, Windows always selects the appropriate TrueType font by matching the font characteristics (point size, serif/sans serif, monospaced/proportional).

✔ **Font matches a bitmap font.** To ensure compatibility with Windows 3.0, a bitmap font is used and stretched when needed for displaying at all point sizes if the name of a font matches only a bitmap font.

✔ **Font matches a bitmap and TrueType font.** If the name of a font matches a bitmap and TrueType font, the bitmap font is used at the point sizes for which there is a bitmap; the TrueType font is used at the remaining point sizes.

✔ **Font has a duplicate face name.** If two or more fonts have the same name, most applications list only the first occurrence of that font; other fonts with the same name are ignored. TrueType fonts are always listed first.

✔ **Font does exist.** If the name of the font does exist, Windows ignores the substitution table and uses the specified font. This action might seem obvious, but it is very useful. Suppose you often exchange documents with a coworker who always uses PostScript Type 1 fonts. Using the font substitution, you have two options: map the Type 1 fonts to TrueType equivalents and turn ATM off, or leave ATM on to use the Type 1 fonts.

Comparing TrueType and PostScript Type 1

PostScriptis a page description language (PDL) developed by Adobe and Apple in the mid-1980s that quickly became the standard PDL used by serious typographers. Type 1 fonts are the industry standard and are used by every service bureau. PostScript printers have a set of Type 1 fonts built into them—often Helvetica, Times Roman, Palatino, and Avant Garde, to name a few. There are two major types of PostScript fonts: Type 1 is a set of scalable typefaces, and Type 3 fonts typically are bitmap fonts used primarily for printing text at small sizes. You can change this threshold by adding or modifying the MinOutlineppem= line in your WIN.INI file.

A *page description language,* such as PostScript or Hewlett-Packard's PCL, is a set of instructions used to manipulate fonts, graphics, and color, and to set printer options. PDLs are resident in a printer or printer cartridge.

The debate now rages over which scalable font technology you should use—TrueType or PostScript. Table 4.1 lists the major differences between the two font technologies. PostScript still is the best choice for desktop publishing and graphics design because of its universal support by service bureaus. TrueType is the best choice for normal use and in standard business communications. Thus, if your chief concern is to produce professional-quality documents without hassle, you cannot go wrong with TrueType.

Table 4.1
TrueType vs. PostScript Type 1

Category	TrueType	PostScript
Scalable font technology	Yes	Yes
Universally available for all Windows users	Yes	No
Hinting instructions carried out by rasterizer	Font	Font
Industry standard for typesetters/service bureaus	No	Yes
Estimated number of fonts available	2,500	Over 20,000
Overall level of typeface sophistication	Mixed	High
Printer portability	Virtually any printer	With ATM, virtually any printer
Platform portability	PC, Mac platforms	All major

Although PostScript has a much richer library of available fonts, the number of quality TrueType fonts is growing rapidly with the success of Windows 3.1. Microsoft introduced the TrueType Font Pack for Windows, which contains 44 typefaces. These fonts are designed to be combined with the standard TrueType typefaces to make an equivalent to the standard set of PostScript fonts. Many new CD-ROMs also contain TrueType fonts.

Tip

One of the best sources for free or shareware fonts is the DTPFORUM on CompuServe. You can find hundreds of TrueType (and PostScript Type 1) fonts in Library 9. Although some are of dubious quality, there are many decorative fonts that can enrich your font library.

Looking At Adobe Type Manager

Adobe Type Manager (ATM) is the PostScript equivalent to TrueType. It acts as a PostScript font rasterizer and enables you to print PostScript fonts on LaserJets and other non-PostScript printers. It is by far the most popular third-party font manager for Windows. You can buy ATM separately, but it often is bundled with other Windows applications, such as Ami Pro or Aldus PageMaker.

After you install it, ATM loads automatically when you start Windows. In fact, just as you never have to think about the TrueType font manager, you can forget that ATM is even on your system unless you want to install or remove PostScript fonts.

In the past, TrueType held a performance advantage over ATM. ATM versions 2.0 and earlier were noticeably slower because they downloaded characters as bitmaps rather than as text. If you used a character multiple times, ATM was forced to send it multiple times. However, beginning with version 2.5, ATM now sends characters the same way TrueType does to eliminate the speed advantage held by TrueType.

When you install ATM, the ATM fonts are installed only on the port(s) that is currently connected to a PostScript printer(s). If you change the ports on your printer, ATM no longer works for that printer until you modify your WIN.INI file by cutting the `softfont` lines from the old `[PostScript, port]` section, and pasting them to the new `[PostScript, port]` section.

Managing Fonts

Windows provides the Font section of the Control Panel to enable you to install and remove TrueType, bitmap, and vector fonts. It also enables you to set TrueType options. The Fonts dialog box is shown in figure 4.4.

Figure 4.4
The Control
Panel's Fonts
dialog box.

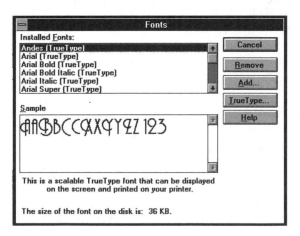

Installing Fonts

The process of installing fonts in Windows is straightforward. To install TrueType, bitmap, or vector fonts, click on the Fonts icon in the Control Panel to display the Fonts dialog box. Click on the <u>A</u>dd button to display the Add Fonts dialog box, as shown in figure 4.5. Use the Dri<u>v</u>es and <u>D</u>irectories controls to select the path that contains the font files you want to install. When you change directories, Windows looks for font files located in the path and lists the font names in the List of <u>F</u>onts box. You have a choice of the following fonts to install:

✔ **Single font.** Select a single font from the fonts list by clicking on it with your mouse.

✔ **Group of fonts.** Select a group of fonts by clicking on each font while holding down the Ctrl key. You also can select a range of fonts by dragging your mouse down the list.

✔ **All fonts.** Select all fonts by clicking on the <u>S</u>elect All button.

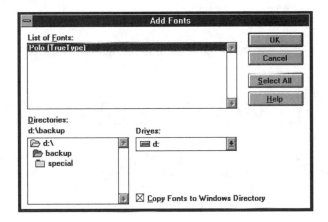

Figure 4.5
The Add Fonts dialog box.

By default, the <u>C</u>opy Fonts to Windows Directory box is checked. With this option checked, Windows copies each font to the WINDOWS\SYSTEM directory. It usually is best, from a font management point of view, to centralize all your fonts into a single location. However, if you have large numbers of fonts located on a CD-ROM or network drive, you can save space on your hard drive by keeping the fonts at the other location. Remember, though, if you do not copy the file to the WINDOWS\SYSTEM directory, Windows needs to access the CD-ROM or network to use it. Windows prompts you to insert the disk containing the fonts when required.

Avoid using fonts stored on a network disk because you add to the network traffic each time Windows accesses that font.

When you are ready to add the selected fonts, click on the OK button. The fonts are added to Windows, and new entries are made in the [fonts] section of the WIN.INI file.

Although it is nice to have as many fonts as possible available to you when you are working, installed fonts slow the time it takes to load Windows and most applications. They also use some of the system's memory even when the fonts are not being used. You probably will not notice much of a difference unless you have at least 100 fonts installed. The general rule of thumb is to install only the fonts you use regularly. You can remove a font from Windows without deleting the font file, then add the font if you need it later.

Removing Fonts

To remove a TrueType, bitmap, or vector font from Windows, click on the Fonts icon in the Control Panel to display the Fonts dialog box (refer to figure 4.4). Select the font(s) from the Installed **F**onts list and click on the **R**emove button. The Remove Font dialog box appears (see fig. 4.6), asking you to confirm your action. You also have the option of deleting the font file from your hard drive by checking the **D**elete Font File From Disk box. Click on the **Y**es button to remove the specified font, or, if you are deleting a group of fonts, click on the Yes to **A**ll button to avoid confirming the removal of each font.

Figure 4.6
The Remove Font
dialog box.

You also can remove a font by commenting out its entry in the [fonts] section of the WIN.INI file (place a semicolon at the beginning of the line). For example, the following three plotter fonts are commented out:

```
[fonts]
;Modern (Plotter)=MODERN.FON
;Script (Plotter)=SCRIPT.FON
;Roman (Plotter)=ROMAN.FON
Arial (TrueType)=ARIAL.FOT
Arial Bold (TrueType)=ARIALBD.FOT
Arial Bold Italic (TrueType)=ARIALBI.FOT
Arial Italic (TrueType)=ARIALI.FOT
Courier New (TrueType)=COUR.FOT
Courier New Bold (TrueType)=COURBD.FOT
Courier New Bold Italic (TrueType)=COURBI.FOT
Courier New Italic (TrueType)=COURI.FOT
Times New Roman (TrueType)=TIMES.FOT
```

```
Times New Roman Bold (TrueType)=TIMESBD.FOT
Times New Roman Bold Italic (TrueType)=TIMESBI.FOT
Times New Roman Italic (TrueType)=TIMESI.FOT
```

You then can reenable a font by taking out the semicolon. Some users find this easier than using the Font section of the Control Panel. Restart Windows for changes to take effect.

Setting TrueType Options

The Font section of the Control Panel enables you to set some global TrueType options. If you want to work with TrueType exclusively or not at all, click on the TrueType button in the Fonts dialog box. The TrueType dialog box appears (see fig. 4.7), and displays the following check boxes:

- ✔ **Enable TrueType Fonts.** By default, this option is checked. By unchecking it, you disable the use of TrueType fonts and free memory normally used by Windows for them. If you work with Type 1 fonts exclusively, you will find this option helpful. This option does not take effect until after you restart Windows.

- ✔ **Show Only TrueType Fonts in Applications.** If you work with TrueType exclusively, you can restrict applications from listing all other available fonts.

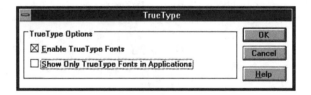

Figure 4.7
The TrueType
dialog box.

These options apply to all TrueType fonts. You cannot, for example, use these options to enable some but not all TrueType fonts.

To make it easier to distinguish between TrueType and non-TrueType fonts, you can force Windows to display all non-TrueType fonts in font lists in all capital letters. To do this, make the nonTTCaps= entry in the [TrueType] section of your WIN.INI equal to 1, as follows:

```
[TrueType]
nonTTCaps=1
```

Changes take effect when you restart Windows.

Looking At Bitmap Fonts

Windows 3.1 includes five bitmap fonts available for screen use (see table 4.2). These are essentially the same set of bitmap fonts from Windows 3.0, although Windows 3.1 has different names for two of them—Helv became MS Sans Serif and Tms Rmn became MS Serif.

Table 4.2
Windows 3.1 Screen Fonts

Font	Point Sizes Supported	Font File Name (? = A–F)
Courier	10, 12, 15	COUR?.FON
MS Sans Serif	8, 10, 12, 14, 18, 24	SSERIF?.FON
MS Serif	8, 10, 12, 14, 18, 24	SERIF?.FON
Small	2, 4, 6	SMALL?.FON
Symbol	8, 10, 12, 14, 18, 24	SYMBOL?.FON

These fonts are not listed in all your applications, such as Word for Windows. Many applications list only those fonts that can be printed to the default printer. Consequently, they are listed if you have a dot-matrix printer as the default, but not if a laser printer is set as the default printer. Some applications, such as ObjectVision or Paradox for Windows, enable you to design a document for either the screen or printer; their font lists can vary.

Understanding System Fonts

The next group of fonts used in Windows is the system fonts. These are the fonts used in various parts of the Windows interface, such as dialog boxes and menus. All of the fonts discussed in the following three sections are required by Windows.

System Font

The System font is the default font used by Windows in menus, dialog boxes, window titles, and caption bars. The System font is proportional, and it is based on the type of display you are running. It is specified in the [boot] section of the SYSTEM.INI file. If, for example, you are running Windows in 1,024 × 768 resolution, its entry looks like the following:

```
FONTS.FON=8514SYS.FON
```

The System font varies, depending on the display at which you run Windows. Table 4.3 lists the system font files that normally are used at the corresponding resolutions.

Table 4.3
System Fonts

Font File Name	Display Resolution
EGASYS.FON	EGA 640 × 350
CGASYS.FON	CGA 640 × 200
VGASYS.FON	VGA 640 × 480
8514SYS.FON	8514/a 1,024 × 768

You can change the default system font by modifying the FONTS.FON= line of the SYSTEM.INI file. The results can be interesting. If you use 8514SYS.FON on a VGA display, for example, a Windows dialog box takes up most of the screen.

You can change the default system font to a bitmap font. If you are running Windows on a 8514/a display, for example, and want to change the system font to MS Sans Serif, first change the FONTS.FON line of the [boot] section of SYSTEM.INI to look like the following:

```
FONTS.FON = SSERIFF.FON
```

Next, add the following line to the [windows] section of WIN.INI:

```
SystemFont=SSERIFF.FON
```

Be sure you change both the WIN.INI and SYSTEM.INI entries; otherwise, Windows does not load properly. A TrueType font cannot be used as the system font.

Fixed Font

The fixed font is a monospaced font, and it is the default font for Windows versions prior to 3.0. Some applets (Notepad, for example) and applications that require a monospaced font use the fixed font. It is based on the FIXFONTS.FON line of the [boot] section of SYSTEM.INI. If no font is specified, the system font is substituted and used as the fixed font. Table 4.4 lists available fixed-screen fonts.

Table 4.4
Fixed Fonts

Font File Name	Display Resolution
EGAFIX.FON	EGA 640 × 350
CGAFIX.FON	CGA 640 × 200
VGAFIX.FON	VGA 640 × 480
8514FIX.FON	8514/a 1,024 × 768

OEM Font

The OEM font is a monospaced font based on the code page by the system. The OEM font plays several roles. It determines the height of dialog boxes, and is used by the Clipboard Viewer to display OEM Text. The OEM font is based on the OEMFONTS.FON line of the [boot] section of SYSTEM.INI. If no font is specified, the system font is substituted and used as the OEM fixed font. Table 4.5 lists available OEM screen fonts.

Table 4.5
OEM Fonts

Font File Name	Display Resolution
EGAOEM.FON	EGA 640 × 350
CGAOEM.FON	CGA 640 × 200
VGAOEM.FON	VGA 640 × 480
8514OEM.FON	8514/a 1,024 × 768

Understanding DOS Session Fonts

When Windows 3.1 is running in 386 Enhanced mode, it enables you to change the fonts of your DOS applications that run in a windowed DOS session. Variable-sized fonts enable you to customize the size of the text and window to a size that is suitable for you. DOS session fonts are based on the code page of the computer. Table 4.6 lists the font files for a standard U.S. configuration.

Table 4.6
DOS Font Files for Code Page 437 (Standard U.S.)

Font File Name	Display
DOSAPP.FON	VGA
CGA40WOA.FON	CGA 40-column
CGA80WOA.FON	CGA 8-column
EGA40WOA.FON	EGA 40-column
EGA80WOA.FON	EGA 80-column
HERCWOA.FON	Hercules

To change the font in your DOS-based application, open the program in a window and choose the Fonts command from the window's control menu. In the Font Selection dialog box (see fig. 4.8), select the appropriate font size from the Font list: 4×6, 5×12, 6×8, 7×12, 8×8, 8×12, 10×18, 12×16, 16×8, or 16×12. Use the Window Preview and Selected Font boxes to see what the window and font will look like. If you want every windowed DOS session to have the same configuration, check the Save Settings on Exit box, and click on OK.

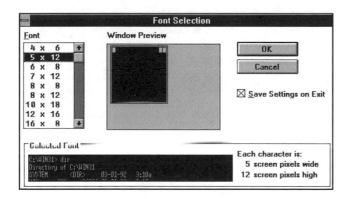

Figure 4.8
The Font Selection dialog box.

Chapter Snapshot

Windows 3.1 makes printing easier, more seamless, and more painless than previous versions of Windows or DOS. In fact, after you get your printer configured the way you want it, Windows will free you from worrying about the printing process. Instead, you will be able to think about the quality of your printer's output.

Be aware, however, that Windows 3.1 is not perfect when it comes to printing. You need to configure your printer carefully to get the best possible output quality and performance. In that light, this chapter examines the following topics:

Configuring a printer is not a difficult process, but you must follow certain steps to ensure that the printer will work properly. This chapter will not only help you configure your printer, but also provides tips on printing from Windows applications.

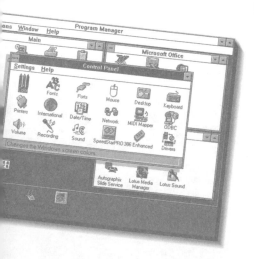

CHAPTER

Printing in Windows

T he first step in configuring a printer to work with Windows is to verify that it is connected properly with the PC. If you have not already done so, refer to your printer manual to verify that it is connected properly. If you are installing a printer driver for a printer that is located on your network and not on your PC, you can begin configuring the printer as described in the following section.

Installing and Configuring Printers

When you are ready to install or configure a printer, open the Printer section of the Control Panel. You can access this facility by opening the Control Panel and clicking on the Printers icon. The Printers dialog box appears, as shown in figure 5.1.

Figure 5.1
The Printers dialog box.

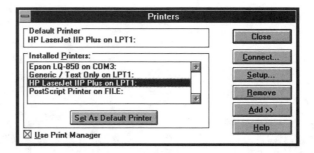

The Printers dialog box shows the default printer as well as the list of printers you have installed on your system. In addition to displaying printers, the Printers dialog box enables you to perform a number of operations, including configuring your printer connection, setting up your printer options, and installing and removing a printer.

Notice that you can have more than one printer assigned to a given port, such as LPT1 shown in figure 5.1. However, keep in mind that only one of these printers associated to the same port can be active at one time.

Adding a Printer

If you want to install a new printer, click on the Add button in the Printers dialog box. A list of available printers appears, as shown in figure 5.2, from which you can select the desired printer. To install the printer, simply double-click on its name, or click once on the name to highlight it and then click on the Install button to add the printer driver to your configuration.

When you add a new printer driver, Windows copies the driver file from your driver disk into the Windows SYSTEM directory. The driver then is used to communicate between Windows and your printer.

If the printer driver is not already on your system, Windows prompts you to insert the appropriate disk (one of the Windows distribution disks or an updated driver on a separate disk) into a floppy drive. After it is installed, you need to configure its appropriate port and other settings.

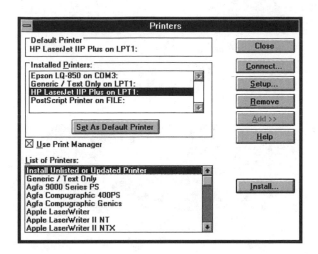

Figure 5.2
The list of
available printers.

When you insert the disk and click on OK, the driver file is copied onto your system.

Windows enables you to install the same printer multiple times. Multiple configurations of the same printer are helpful if you frequently change the port to which your printer is attached or if you frequently need to print to both a printer and a file using the same printer.

Suppose you desktop publish frequently and use a PostScript printer in your office. You also need to print to a file when you take a job to your typesetters. Although you can use a single installed PostScript printer and change port settings between printer and file output, a much easier solution would be to install two instances of the same printer. Configure one to your printer port, such as LPT1, and the second to a file. You then can switch between the two printers.

If you install a printer more than once, Windows does not need to reinstall the printer driver. Instead, Windows uses the printer driver installed the first time.

The Generic/Text only driver can be useful if you have problems with another printer driver. It enables you to print unformatted text to virtually any printer. This driver also is useful if you want to print a document to a text-only file.

Setting a Default Printer

You also can use the Printers dialog box to specify or change the default printer. You can select the desired printer from the Installed Printers list by double-clicking on its name, or by clicking once on the name and then clicking on the Set As Default Printer button. You also can set the default printer in the Printer Setup dialog box of many Windows applications.

Connecting a Printer

When you install a new printer, Windows automatically assigns it to the LPT1 port. If you want to connect the printer to a different port (such as LPT2 or a COM port), click on the Connect button in the Printers dialog box to display the Connect dialog box (see fig. 5.3).

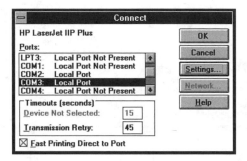

Figure 5.3
The Connect
dialog box.

Selecting a Printer Port

The Ports list box in the Connect dialog box enables you to specify a different port for the printer. You can choose one of the following ports:

✔ **LPT1–LPT3.** These names identify your computer's parallel ports. Most printers use LPT1.

✔ **COM1–COM4.** These names identify your computer's serial ports. If you select a COM port, you can click on the Settings button to specify additional information in the Settings for COM*x* and Advanced Settings for COM*x* dialog boxes, shown in figures 5.4. and 5.5. (In these illustrations, the COM3 port has been selected.) Most printers support the default settings; if yours does not, refer to your printer manual to determine the correct configuration for the COM port.

Figure 5.4
The Settings for
COM3 dialog
box.

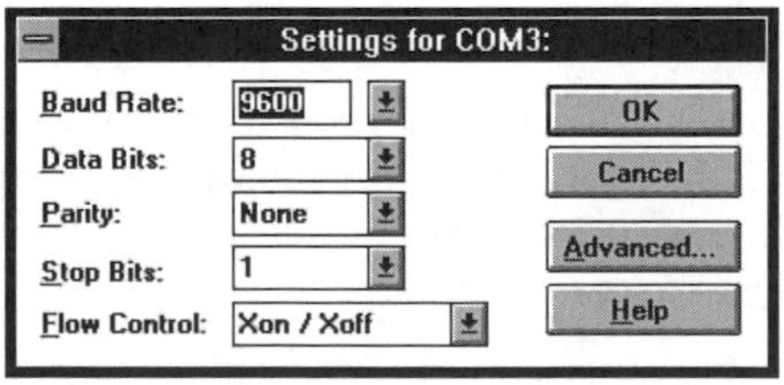

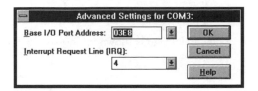

Figure 5.5
The Advanced Settings for COM3 dialog box.

In the Setting for COM3 dialog box, you need to configure five settings. Most printers support the default settings; if yours does not, refer to your printer manual to determine the correct configuration for the COM port.

✔ **Baud Rate.** Determines the speed at which characters are sent through the port.

✔ **Data Bits.** Determines the number of data bits used to represent each character.

✔ **Parity.** Determines the method used for error checking. Parity checks to ensure that the correct number of bits have been received.

✔ **Stop Bits.** Determines the time between transmitted characters.

✔ **Flow Control.** Determines the handshaking method used by the receiving device to control the flow of data. Handshaking refers to the method by which the sending and receiving devices communicate with one another.

In the Advanced Settings dialog box, two additional settings appear:

✔ **Base I/O Port Address.** Determines the address used by the port in your computer's I/O address space.

✔ **Interrupt Request Line (IRQ).** Determines the interrupt used by the COM port.

Under most circumstances, do not make any changes to the default settings configured by Windows. If you have problems, first try to change your hardware configuration to match the defaults used by Windows.

✔ **EPT.** This selection identifies an enhanced parallel port on an IBM system or a special port on an expansion card. Some printers, such as the IBM Personal Pageprinter, use this port.

✔ **FILE.** This selection tells Windows that print jobs will be sent to a file rather than a printer. You can name the default file to print to by modifying the FILE:= setting in the [ports] section of WIN.INI. If you do not specify a default print file, Windows will prompt you for a file name whenever you start a print job.

The process of modifying INI files is shown in Chapter 7, "Enhancing Windows Performance."

✔ **LPT1.DOS–LPT2.DOS.** These selections enable you to route Windows printing through DOS. This option is used in some network configurations.

Setting Print Job Time-Outs

When you print to a port, Windows enables you to specify the time-out settings for a print job. These settings ensure that if an error occurs or a printer is not able to print, you are prompted of the problem. In the Timeouts box of the Connect dialog box, you can set two options:

✔ **Device Not Selected.** Identifies the amount of time Windows waits for the printer to acknowledge that it is online. After the designated time period, a dialog box appears to prompt you that your printer is offline. The default time-out is 15 seconds.

✔ **Transmission Retry.** Identifies the amount of time the Print Manager waits for a printer to come back online and accept information. A printer cannot accept transmissions following an error condition or during a large print job. The defaults are 45 seconds and 90 seconds for PostScript printers. If you are using a PostScript printer, you might want to increase the default by 90 seconds during large print jobs.

If you normally don't remember to turn on your printer until *after* you send a print job, Windows probably will display a message stating that the printer is offline. To avoid the message, increase the **D**evice Not Selected number to 30 seconds.

The **F**ast Printing Direct to Port check box is checked by default. This option tells Windows to access the designated port directly instead of using DOS interrupts, thus getting your jobs to the printer in less time. This setting works well under most conditions. If you are having problems printing correctly from an application, however, try unchecking this box.

Removing a Printer

If you no longer are using a printer and want to remove it from your printer list, select the printer from the installed printers dialog box and then click on the **R**emove button from the Printers dialog box. Click on Yes when Windows verifies that you want to remove the printer.

When you use the **R**emove button, Windows does not actually delete the printer driver file. Instead, it only removes the printer's name from the list of available printers. Later, if you want to re-add the printer to the list, you can simply click on the **A**dd button and reinstall the same printer driver. Because the driver still resides on your hard disk, you do not have to use the Windows distribution disk to copy the driver file onto your computer.

Setting Up a Printer

After you install and connect a printer, you still might need to set up some settings specific to your particular printer. You have two ways to set up a printer depending on where you are working within Windows:

- ✔ **Control Panel.** In the Printers dialog box, select a printer from the Installed **P**rinters list and click on **S**etup.

- ✔ **Windows applications.** Virtually all Windows applications enable you to print text or graphical data. If so, then they also should have a **F**ile, P**r**int Setup command that displays installed printers. Click on the **S**etup button in that application's dialog box.

The exact setup options depend on the type of printer you are using. The most popular printer options include LaserJet and PostScript laser printers and dot-matrix printers.

Configuring a LaserJet Printer

The most popular laser printers available today are HP LaserJet or compatible printers. If you have a LaserJet, configuring it is a relatively straightforward process. Click on the **S**etup button in the Printers dialog box when your PostScript printer is selected in the installed printers list, or choose **F**ile, P**r**int Setup from most Windows applications to display the LaserJet dialog box, as shown in figure 5.6.

In this dialog box, you can specify the following:

- ✔ Resolution

- ✔ Paper size

- ✔ Paper source

- ✔ Memory

✔ Page orientation

✔ Number of copies

✔ Two printer cartridges

Figure 5.6
The HP LaserJet
dialog box.

You need a LaserJet Series IIP Plus or later model if you want to download TrueType fonts as PCL fonts.

Even though most laser printers print at 300 dpi, more advanced printers, such as the LaserJet series, have resolution enhancement capabilities. With special software, LaserJet printers can vary the size of the ink dots printed on a page. The LaserJet 4 uses Resolution Enhancement Technology in addition to printing at 600 dots per inch. These features improve dramatically the grayscale output and sharpness of photos and art.

To set one of these options, click on the Options button. The Options dialog box appears, as shown in figure 5.7.

Setting LaserJet Options

The Options dialog box enables you to specify the way graphics are printed, through the Dithering and Intensity Control options. Generally, the Print TrueType As Graphics box should be checked only under special conditions (these are discussed later in this chapter, in the section "Troubleshooting TrueType Printing") because it slows down printing considerably.

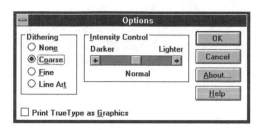

Figure 5.7
The Options
dialog box.

If you try to print a grayscale graphic, the image might print as black if **I**ntensity Control is set toward Darker on the slider bar. Move the **I**ntensity Control toward the Lighter side to correct this problem. This problem can occur on any printer using the UNIDRV.DLL driver.

Adding HP Soft Fonts

If you want to use any HP or third-party soft fonts with the LaserJet, click on the **F**onts button in the HP LaserJet dialog box to display the HP Font Installer dialog box (see fig. 5.8). In this dialog box, click on the **A**dd Fonts button to add a font; Windows prompts you to insert the disk that contains the font files. After the Font Installer gathers a list of available fonts on the disk, you can select the desired fonts from the source box and click on the **A**dd button.

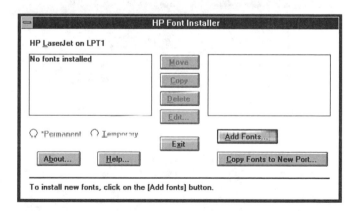

Figure 5.8
The HP Font
Installer dialog
box.

After the new fonts are added to your configuration, you can specify whether a font is a permanent or temporary font. A permanent font, once downloaded, is available until you turn the printer off. A temporary font is not downloaded until the printer requires it. Thus, while permanent fonts are quicker to print, they take up more memory in the printer.

Configuring a PostScript Printer

Chapter 4 compared PostScript and TrueType fonts. To print PostScript fonts, you need a PostScript-compatible printer. PostScript printers involve more options than any other type of printer. To set these options, your PostScript driver dialog boxes can lead you through as many as four levels of nested dialog boxes. To display the initial setup dialog box, click on the Setup button in the Printers dialog box after you select your PostScript printer, or choose File, Print Setup.

The initial dialog box, shown in figure 5.9, provides the basic paper source, size, and orientation, as well as the number of copies. Click on the Options button to display the Options dialog box, as shown in figure 5.10.

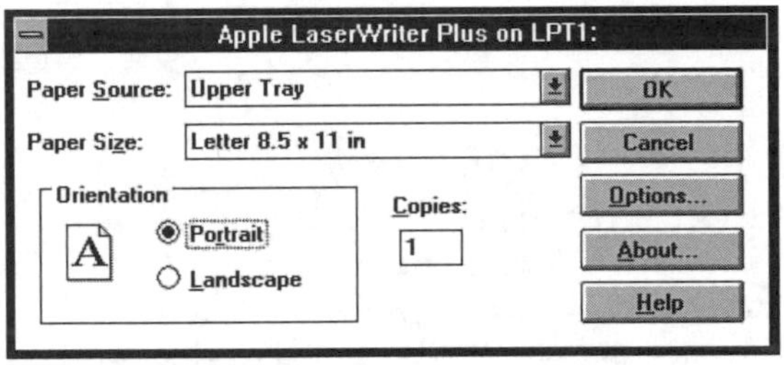

Figure 5.9
The default
PostScript setup
dialog box.

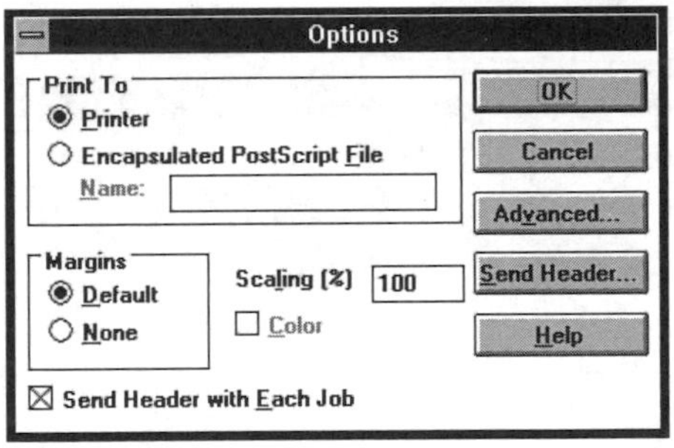

Figure 5.10
The Options
dialog box for
PostScript printer
drivers.

The Options dialog box contains the following options:

✔ **Print To.** Enables you to print directly to the attached printer or to an Encapsulated PostScript (EPS) file. An EPS file—the name of which you enter in the Name text box—contains commands in PostScript command language that specify the contents of the print job. If you select the EPS option, it remains active only during the current Windows session.

An EPS file is not the same thing as a document printed to a file using the PostScript driver. An EPS file cannot be sent to a printer directly because it does not contain the header needed to print on a PostScript printer.

✔ **Scaling.** This setting enables you to specify the scale at which a page is printed. The default setting of 100 can be changed to an integer value between 10 and 400.

✔ **Margins.** If you are printing to a laser printer, be sure this option is set to <u>D</u>efault. If this is set to <u>N</u>one, margin settings from your application are ignored.

✔ **Color.** If you have a color PostScript printer, this box enables you to print in color if checked, or in grayscale if unchecked.

✔ **Send Header with Each Job.** Whether you are sending your print jobs to a printer or file, this box typically is checked. A *header* is a series of PostScript commands that set up fonts, page layout, and other specifications. You can click on the <u>S</u>end Header button to specify whether to send the header to the printer or to a separate file.

Setting Advanced Options for PostScript Printers

In the Options dialog box, you can click on the Ad<u>v</u>anced button to display yet another dialog box, as shown in figure 5.11. This dialog box provides advanced settings options. The default settings generally are the fastest.

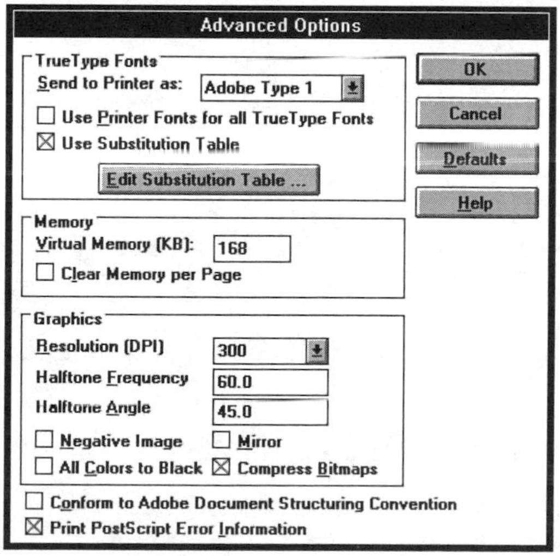

Figure 5.11
The Advanced Options dialog box for PostScript printer drivers.

Understanding Windows (vertical side text)

You do not have to have a PostScript printer to use the PostScript printer driver. You can set up the PostScript settings as usual and print the job to a file. This can be extremely useful if you want to print a PostScript file on a printer not attached to your system, or if you need to submit a PostScript file to a service bureau for typesetting.

If you want to print a PostScript document to a file, choose <u>F</u>ile as your port when you connect your printer (explained in the "Connecting a Printer" section earlier in this chapter).

Using the TrueType Fonts Options Box

When you print TrueType fonts on a PostScript printer, Windows automatically sends either a PostScript Type 1 or Type 3 font (depending on the point size) to the printer. If you would like to control the way TrueType fonts are sent to the printer, you can specify the following options in the TrueType Fonts box of the Advanced Options dialog box:

✔ **Send to Printer as.** Enables you to specify whether to send TrueType fonts as Type 1 outline fonts or Bitmap (Type 3) fonts.

✔ **Use Printer Fonts for all TrueType Fonts.** If this box is checked, the PostScript printer substitutes resident fonts for all TrueType fonts used in a print job.

✔ **Use Substitution Table.** If this box is checked, you can customize the TrueType/PostScript substitution table. Click on the <u>E</u>dit Substitution Table button to view the Substitution dialog box, as shown in figure 5.12. Select a font from the TrueType font list and then pick the Type 1 font you want to map to in the Printer Font list box. Click on the <u>D</u>efault button to reset your changes.

Figure 5.12
The Substitution
dialog box.

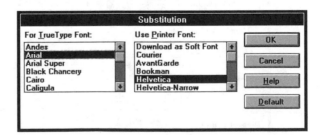

Using the Memory Options Box

The Memory box in the Advanced Options dialog box enables you to specify the amount of virtual memory available for your printing. To determine the amount of memory available on your printer, print the TESTPS.TXT file residing in the WINDOWS\SYSTEM directory.

If you have problems printing a large document with TrueType fonts, check the Clear Memory per Page box. This option clears the printer memory after each page is sent. Although it takes longer to print (the fonts must be resent after each page), this option ensures the page prints correctly.

Using the Graphics Options Box

The Graphics box in the Advanced Options dialog box enables you to specify the following options regarding the output of graphics:

- ✔ **Resolution.** Determines the output resolution of your document. For best quality, use the highest number available.

- ✔ **Halftone Frequency.** Determines the lines per inch for halftone screens.

- ✔ **Halftone Angle.** Determines the angle used for halftone screens.

- ✔ **Negative Image.** Causes the document to print as an inverted grayscale image.

- ✔ **Mirror.** Causes the document to print as a mirror image.

- ✔ **All Colors to Black.** Causes all colors (except white) to print as black.

- ✔ **Compress Bitmaps.** Causes all graphics to compress before being sent to the printer. If this box is checked, your application becomes available more quickly, but it also makes the job take longer to print.

Two additional options are at the bottom of the Advanced Options dialog box:

- ✔ **Conform to Adobe Document Structuring Convention.** If you are printing to a file, check this box to print to a file that adheres to the Adobe Document Structuring Conventions (DSC).

- ✔ **Print PostScript Error Information.** If you have problems printing a PostScript document, check this box to print error information, which can help determine the cause of the problems.

Configuring a Dot-Matrix Printer

A dot-matrix printer has fewer available options to configure. If you have a dot-matrix printer, click on the Setup button in the Printers dialog box when your printer is selected in the installed printers list, or choose File, Print Setup from most Windows applications to display the print setup dialog box. Figure 5.13 shows a dialog box for an Epson 24-pin dot-matrix printer. Windows enables you to control the following aspects of a dot-matrix printer:

✔ Resolution

✔ Paper size

✔ Paper source

✔ Orientation

✔ Font cartridges

Figure 5.13
The Epson LQ-850
dialog box.

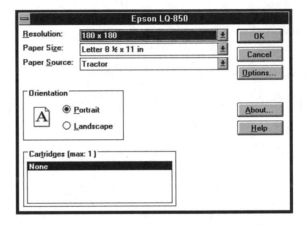

Click on <u>O</u>ptions to display the Options dialog box, as shown in figure 5.14. This box enables you to set dithering, intensity control, and print quality.

Figure 5.14
The Options
dialog box for the
Epson LQ-850.

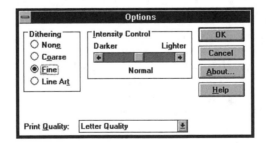

Using Print Manager
To Control Print Jobs

Although installing and configuring printers is done using the Printers section of the Control Panel, the actual management of Windows print jobs is through the Print Manager. Print Manager is a print-spooling utility that, when activated, receives print jobs from all Windows applications, logs them into a queue, and sends the jobs to one or more printers at the appropriate time.

The Print Manager icon is located in the Main group of Program Manager, but you do not have to run it to be able to use it. When you print a document from an application, Print Manager automatically opens until the print job is over; then it closes automatically. Print Manager stays open only if a printer needs your attention.

Depending on your system configuration, you can speed up printing to a local printer by disabling the Print Manager. Remember, however, that you can print only one file at a time when the Print Manager is off. By disabling the Print Manager, you can save memory as well as the disk space needed to create temporary files.

To disable Print Manager, open the Printers dialog box by clicking on the Printer icon in Control Panel. Clear the **U**se Print Manager check box and click on the Close button. Additionally, if you are printing to a network printer with its own print-spooling facility, having the Print Manager on is redundant. Turn off Print Manager and save time.

You can, however, use the Print Manager to view the print queue and perform other print management tasks. Figure 5.15 shows the Print Manager window with a print queue.

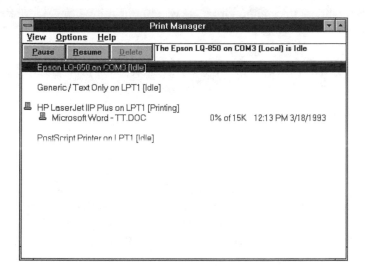

Figure 5.15
The Print Manager window.

Windows 3.1 Print Manager has a queue limit of 100 print jobs.

Changing the Print Queue Order

You can change the order of files in the print queue. This capability is helpful if you are printing a number of documents and you want to print a lower-priority document first. To move a print job, select the desired job with your mouse, then drag and drop it into a new position.

There are two limitations to changing the queue order. First, you cannot move a job that is currently being printed. Second, you cannot move a print job from one printer to another.

Deleting a Print Job

If you want to cancel a pending or current print job, select the job from the print queue and choose <u>D</u>elete at the top of the Print Manager menu. A message box confirms your action.

Prioritizing Windows Printing

You can prioritize the amount of processing time Windows devotes to printing by selecting one of the following three menu items from the <u>O</u>ptions menu:

✔ **High Priority.** Gives the maximum amount of CPU time to the printing of your documents. Choose this option for the fastest printing using Print Manager. Other tasks you are trying to perform in Windows are slower while the job is printing.

✔ **Medium Priority.** Divides CPU time evenly between the print job and the tasks you are performing. Medium is the default setting.

✔ **Low Priority.** Gives the least amount of CPU time to printing so that you can work in an application with minimal delays. Printing takes longer with this option.

Does Windows 3.1 seem to take less time printing than Windows 3.0? In fact, the actual time to print a document is unchanged, but Windows 3.1 returns control of the cursor to you sooner (the hourglass is replaced by the pointer). The reason is that Windows 3.0 tries to spool and print files simultaneously, but Windows 3.1 waits for the spooling to finish before trying to print.

Troubleshooting TrueType Printing

TrueType is an innovative font technology, but inevitably as any new technology is introduced, there are bound to be compatibility problems with the scores of printers and printer drivers available today. In time, these problems will be solved by Microsoft and the printer manufacturers. Until that day arrives, however, if you have problems printing with TrueType, use this section as a guide. Overall, the single best thing you can do with a printer problem under Windows is to get the latest driver available. The best resource for this is in the printer manufacturer's forum, the Microsoft Software Library on CompuServe, or the Microsoft Download Service (MSDL) at (206) 936-6735.

General Problems

Windows 3.0 printer drivers. Printer drivers written for earlier versions of Windows are not compatible with TrueType fonts. You need updated drivers to print TrueType fonts.

Printing TrueType as graphics. If the Print TrueType as Graphics check box in the Options dialog box of your printer setup is grayed out, you might have to adjust your Graphics Resolution setting. Some Windows drivers only enable this capability at higher resolutions, such as 300 dots per inch.

HP LaserJet Problems

No soft font support (PCL III). You cannot download TrueType fonts as PCL fonts to the PCL III printers (HP LaserJet, LaserJet Plus, and LaserJet 500+). Instead, TrueType fonts must be printed as bitmap graphics. You can select this option by checking the Print TrueType as Graphics box in the Advanced Options dialog box for your printer driver configuration. Additionally, the printer resolution must be set to 300 dots per inch.

Maximum number of TrueType fonts (PCL IV). PCL IV printers (LaserJet Series II, IIP, IID) can download a maximum of 16 fonts per page. If you have more than 16 fonts, select the Print TrueType as Graphics option.

White on black text (PCL IV). PCL IV printers cannot print white TrueType downloaded fonts on a black background. The workaround is to print TrueType fonts as graphics. This option can be selected by checking the Print TrueType as Graphics box in the Advanced Options dialog box.

Grayscale or colored TrueType fonts (PCL V). You cannot print colored or grayscale TrueType fonts on any PCL V printer (such as models III, IIID, IIIP, or IIISI) using the HPPCL5A.DRV version 3.89 printer driver. The only workaround is to print TrueType as graphics. This option can be selected by checking the Print TrueType as Graphics box in the Advanced dialog box of the printer driver configuration.

No WYSIWYG. Mixing TrueType fonts and graphics on a page can cause LaserJet II and LaserJet III series printers to print differently from what appears on-screen. If the hard copy does not match the screen, check the Print TrueType as Graphics box in your printer setup dialog box.

Understanding Windows

PostScript Problems

TrueType printing Courier. TrueType fonts can default to Courier when printing to a PostScript printer. This situation occurs if you uncheck the Use Substitution Table box and check the Clear Memory per Page box in the printer setup dialog box. In a multiple-page document, any TrueType font coming after a PostScript font on the second or later page will print as Courier. To fix the problem, either check the Use Substitution Table box or uncheck the Clear Memory per Page box in the Advanced Options dialog box. This problem can occur on Windows PostScript driver versions 3.5, 3.51, 3.52, and 3.53.

QMS-PS 815 PostScript printer. TrueType fonts will not print correctly on QMS-PS 815 PostScript printers that were manufactured before TrueType was introduced. If you encounter this problem, you need to upgrade the printer BIOS. The QMS BIOS that supports TrueType fonts is version 2.9.

Panasonic KX-P 4450 Problems

TrueType as graphics. You must print TrueType fonts as graphics if you are using the Panasonic KX-P 4450 version 1.1 printer driver. This option can be selected by checking the Print TrueType as Graphics box in the Advanced Options dialog box.

DeskJet 500 Printer Problems

TrueType fonts in graphs. Graphs generated by Microsoft Excel or Graph that contain TrueType fonts might print incorrectly on an HP DeskJet 500 printer that uses the HPDSKJET.DRV printer driver version 1.1 or 1.2. To correct this problem, get version 2.0 of the printer driver.

Novell Networks Problems

Printing TrueType. The PRINTCON.DAT file should be located in the SYS directory of your Novell network for TrueType fonts to print correctly. To fix this problem, run PRINTCON to generate a PRINTCON.DAT file with a default data stream of "BITSTREAM." Upon completion, the fonts should print as expected.

If you still have trouble printing TrueType fonts to your HP III or IIIsi printers with PostScript installed, turn off Adobe Type Manager. ATM might be the problem.

With the integration of TrueType technology into Windows 3.1, printing is even easier and more seamless than ever before. The type quality of TrueType is matched only by PostScript and other advanced font technologies. Although the recent release of the font technology has caused some problems (described in the preceding section), most of these have workarounds and will be eliminated by Microsoft and hardware manufacturers. Even though Windows printing is not entirely pain free, it is well on its way to becoming the easiest printing method.

Understanding Windows

Chapter Snapshot

You can make many changes to your Windows environment that control the way Windows looks and functions. Some changes are purely aesthetic; others provide a definite performance improvement. This chapter explains techniques you can use to customize your Windows environment, including:

You can make many changes to the Windows environment directly from Windows through the Control Panel and other utilities. Other changes require third-party applications and utilities. This chapter begins with an overview of changes that you can make to Windows without any special software.

6

CHAPTER

Customizing Windows

Many Windows users find that customizing their system is one of the more enjoyable aspects of Windows. Whereas DOS provides only a few minor ways to customize the DOS environment, Windows offers many. The first change you might want to make, for example, is to change the way Windows starts.

Controlling Windows Start-Up

Three primary changes affect the way Windows starts on your system. These include controlling the graphics screen that appears when Windows starts; starting applications automatically with the StartUp group; and starting applications by placing entries for them in the WIN.INI file.

These three changes are some of the modifications that can make Windows a more productive tool. In particular, the capability to start applications automatically can speed up the process of opening applications when Windows starts, which helps you get to work more quickly.

Bypassing the Start-Up Screen

If you type **WIN** and press Enter at the DOS prompt to start Windows, the Windows logo displays for a few seconds during the start-up process (see fig. 6.1). You can prevent it from displaying or replace it with one of your own bitmaps, such as your company logo.

Figure 6.1
The standard Windows 3.1 start-up logo.

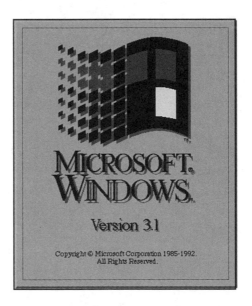

A number of command-line switches used with the WIN command control the operating mode in which Windows starts. These command-line switches are listed in table 6.1.

Table 6.1
Windows Operating Mode Switches

Switch	Mode
(No switch)	Starts Windows in the default mode for your system.
/S	Starts Windows in Standard mode. This is the default mode when starting Windows on a 286 system, or on a 386 or 486 system with less than 2 MB of RAM.
/2	Starts Windows in Standard mode (identical to the /S switch).
/3	Starts Windows in 386 Enhanced mode. This is the default Windows operating mode on a 386 or 486 system with at least 2 MB of RAM.

When you include one of the three switches listed in table 6.1 on the WIN command line, or do not include a switch with the WIN command, Windows displays the Windows start-up logo.

To prevent Windows from displaying the start-up logo, include a colon as the last character on the WIN command line. The following are examples:

```
WIN :
WIN /S:
WIN /2:
WIN /3:
```

Modifying the Start-Up Screen

Instead of simply bypassing the start-up screen (by entering **WIN:**), you can create your own logo and have it appear each time you start Windows. You might want to have your company's logo or a favorite image appear rather than the Windows logo.

Changing the start-up screen is a simple, two-step process. First, you must create or already have the image to be used for the start-up screen. Then, you must create a new WIN.COM file. Although WIN.COM is a binary file and contains the Windows start-up logo, you can easily create your own WIN.COM file using the DOS COPY command.

When you enter WIN at the DOS prompt to start Windows, you are executing the program file WIN.COM, which is located in your Windows directory. WIN.COM performs a couple of functions:

✔ WIN.COM analyzes your system's hardware to determine in which operating mode Windows should start.

✔ WIN.COM displays the Windows start-up logo before it starts Windows.

The Setup program creates WIN.COM when you install Windows on your system or change from one video resolution to another (such as changing from VGA to Super VGA). Setup combines three files to form WIN.COM. On a VGA system, for example, these three files are WIN.CNF, VGALOGO.LGO, and VGALOGO.RLE. The WIN.CNF file is the same on all systems; the last two files vary according to the display driver used.

If you choose to modify the RLE file for your video display rather than create a new one, you should make a backup of the original file (such as copy VGALOGO.RLE to MYLOGO.RLE) and then modify the backup copy. Also, you cannot modify WIN.CNF or VGALOGO.LGO.

WIN.CNF is the part of WIN.COM that is responsible for sensing your system's hardware and determining the proper Windows operating mode. VGALOGO.LGO switches your display into the proper mode and displays the logo file, which is VGALOGO.RLE. The file VGALOGO.RLE is the Windows start-up logo in Run Length Encoded (RLE) file format.

Create Your Own Logo RLE File

The new file you want to use as your Windows start-up screen must be a graphics file in Run Length Encoded (RLE) format. Windows Paintbrush will not store files in RLE format, so you will need either a graphics editor that can save the file in RLE format, or a graphics conversion program such as WinGIF or PaintShop. Graphics conversion programs convert the file from its native format (such as BMP) to RLE format.

A typical graphics file, such as a BMP file, generally stores information about each pixel in the image. RLE files, however, provide extra data compression in the file by storing data about groups of pixels rather than individual pixels. If many pixels of the same color are side-by-side in a single scan line of the image, for example, these same-color pixels are stored as a single data item in the RLE file.

As you are creating the image to use as the RLE logo file, keep in mind that COM files such as WIN.COM can be no larger than 64 KB in size. To create a WIN.COM file that is small enough to load properly, keep the RLE file to a maximum of about 50 KB. To keep the size of the RLE file to a minimum, use a solid background and keep the number of colors in the image to a minimum.

Protect Your Original Files

Although you will not be doing anything that will damage your original CNF, LGO, or RLE files, you should protect them in case you mistakenly type something that can damage them while you are creating your new WIN.COM file. Use the following commands to make your three original start-up files read-only:

```
CD \WINDOWS\SYSTEM
ATTRIB +R WIN.CNF
ATTRIB +R *.LGO
ATTRIB +R *.RLE
```

The preceding example assumes that \WINDOWS is the name of the directory on your system in which Windows is installed. If Windows is installed in a different directory on your system, substitute its name in place of \WINDOWS in the previous example.

Next, you might also want to make your original WIN.COM file read-only. Instead of creating a new WIN.COM file to replace the original, you will be creating a new file with a new name. To make WIN.COM read-only, enter the following:

```
CD \WINDOWS
ATTRIB +R WIN.COM
```

Now you are ready to create a new file that starts Windows. The following commands combine the CNF and LGO files into a new COM file, and include your new logo image in the file:

```
CD \WINDOWS\SYSTEM
COPY /B WIN.CNF+VGALOGO.LGO+YOURLOGO.RLE \WINDOWS\GO.COM
```

In the preceding example, VGALOGO.LGO and WIN.CNF are the standard Windows files described earlier in this chapter. The file YOURLOGO.RLE is your custom start-up screen image file in RLE format. If your RLE file is named something other than YOURLOGO.RLE, substitute the correct name in the COPY command line.

The COPY command in the preceding example creates a new file called GO.COM in the Windows directory. When you want to start Windows with your new start-up logo, just type **GO** at the DOS prompt and press Enter. Your logo image will appear rather than the standard Windows start-up logo. In the preceding COPY command example, substitute the correct *.LGO and *.RLE file names for your system.

If you receive the error `Program too big to fit in memory` when you attempt to start Windows, your RLE file is too large. Edit the file with your favorite graphics editor as necessary to make it smaller (in bytes), then reissue the COPY command (as described earlier) to create the file GO.COM. Afterward, retest the GO command to see if it works.

If your graphics editor will not write a file in RLE format, you can use a number of shareware applications to convert the file from one format to another. WinGIF and PaintShop Pro, both available on the WINADV forum on CompuServe, will enable you to convert a graphics file to RLE format.

The StartUp Group

Windows 3.1 includes a group called StartUp, which the Setup program creates when it installs Windows on your system. By default, the StartUp group is empty. Figure 6.2 shows a StartUp group with a few items in it.

Figure 6.2
Items in the
StartUp group
start automatically
when Windows
starts.

Any program items contained in the StartUp group are started automatically when Windows starts. If you have programs that you want to start automatically when Windows starts, create program items for them in the StartUp group, or copy their icons from their existing Program Manager groups. If you are not familiar with how to create a program item, refer to the section later in this chapter titled "Creating and Changing Program Items."

To copy a program icon from one Program Manager group to another, hold down the Ctrl key and then drag the icon from its original group to the group in which you want it copied. Release the mouse button and the Ctrl key, and the icon will be copied to the group.

The StartUp group can be used to start a program with special command-line switches or with a document file, set a special working directory for the program, or set a special hot key for the program. None of these options is possible with the WIN.INI settings. The StartUp group makes it much easier to control which applications execute when Windows starts, and also simplifies changes to StartUp items.

If you want to prevent Windows from starting the programs located in the StartUp group, press and hold down the Shift key while Windows starts. This is useful when you are experiencing a problem with a program that is located in the StartUp group, or when you do not want the programs to start for the current Windows session, and do not want to remove them permanently from the StartUp group.

Creating a StartUp Group

If (for some reason) your Program Manager environment does not include a StartUp group, creating one is simple:

1. In Program Manager choose <u>F</u>ile, <u>N</u>ew.

2. In the New Program Object dialog box, choose the Program <u>G</u>roup radio button, then click on OK.

3. In the Program Group Properties dialog box, type the word **Startup** in the <u>D</u>escription edit box.

4. Click on OK. Program Manager will define its own name for the StartUp group file.

The process described here is the same one you use to create any program group. The only difference between the StartUp group and other groups is the name StartUp.

After you create the StartUp group, you can add program items to it. The section later in this chapter titled "Customizing Program Manager" explains how to create new program items.

Although Windows looks for a group named StartUp to start programs automatically, you can use any group as the start-up group. In the file PROGMAN.INI, change or add the setting `startup=` to the `[settings]` section. Enter the name of your new start-up group after the setting name, such as the following:

```
startup=accessories
```

Note that the name you specify is the name located in the program group's <u>D</u>escription field, not its group file name.

Initialization File Settings

As an option to starting applications by placing items for them in the StartUp group, you instead can add entries in WIN.INI for each program you want to start automatically when Windows starts. The `load=` and `run=` lines in the `[windows]` section of WIN.INI can be used to start applications automatically when Windows starts.

✔ `run=`. Program entries on this line start in their normal windowed state when Windows starts. Here is an example:

```
run=notepad.exe c:\excel\excel.exe d:\plugin\plugin.exe
```

✔ `load=`. Program entries on this line start as icons. This is similar to starting a program by means of the StartUp group with the Run Minimized property checked. Here is an example:

```
load=notepad.exe c:\excel\excel.exe
```

The StartUp group has advantages over the other method for starting applications automatically—adding entries for the programs on the run= or load= lines of WIN.INI (explained later).

The StartUp group is much more versatile for starting applications than either of these [windows] settings. You can include the following with StartUp program items:

✔ Command-line switches

✔ Optional document files

✔ A startup directory

You also can assign a shortcut key to the program. None of these options is possible with the run= or load= lines. The Windows INI files are discussed in more detail in Chapter 7, "Enhancing Windows Performance."

Using the Control Panel To Customize Windows

The Control Panel is located in Windows' Main program group. When you open the Control Panel, you see a selection of icons. The number of icons displayed depends on the mode in which Windows is running. If Windows is running in 386 Enhanced mode, the 386 Enhanced icon appears in the Control Panel. If Windows is running on a network, a Network icon appears. Other icons might also appear that have been added by third-party applications.

Each of the icons in the Control Panel enables you to control or customize a particular aspect of Windows. Rather than describe in detail how to use the Control Panel to change the Windows environment, this section outlines what you can control with the Control Panel. If you need help with a particular option, the Help buttons and menus in the Control Panel should provide the information you need.

Control Panel's different controls include the following:

✔ **Color.** Controls the colors of the Windows interface, including the workspace, background, border, and buttons.

✔ **Fonts.** Enables you to view, install, and delete fonts.

✔ **Ports.** Contains settings for baud rate and other parameters for each of the system's COM ports.

✔ **Mouse.** Enables you to swap the function of the left and right mouse buttons and adjust mouse sensitivity.

✔ **Desktop.** Controls desktop features such as wallpaper, screen saver, background pattern, icon spacing, and window border width.

✔ **Printer.** Enables you to add, configure, and delete printer drivers, and to set global printing parameters.

✔ **International.** Controls many features that vary by country, including date, time, currency, and units of measure.

✔ **Keyboard.** Controls the keyboard's repeat rate and sensitivity.

✔ **Date/Time.** Sets the system date and time.

✔ **Sound.** Assigns sounds to various events for systems with sound hardware; turns on and off generic warning beep for all systems.

✔ **386 Enhanced.** Controls contention by applications for use of LPT and COM ports, specifies disk-swapping method, and sets priorities for multitasking under Windows.

✔ **Network.** Controls network features of Windows.

✔ **Drivers.** Used to install, configure, and remove drivers for multimedia.

Changing Interface Colors

Selecting the Color icon in the Control Panel displays the Color dialog box shown in figure 6.3. This initial Color dialog box enables you to select and preview a predefined color scheme for the Windows interface. You also can save a color scheme by name.

Figure 6.3
The Color dialog box.

Windows includes 23 predefined color schemes from which to choose. In addition to using predefined color schemes, you also can define your own color schemes. By clicking on the Color Palette button, you can expand the Color dialog box to include controls for setting the color of individual display components and defining custom colors. This expanded dialog box is shown in figure 6.4.

Figure 6.4
The expanded
Color dialog box.

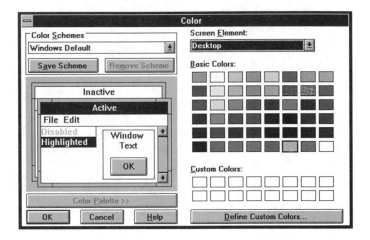

With the expanded Color dialog box, you can change 21 different Windows interface components. These Windows components include the following:

✔ **Desktop.** The background that appears behind all program windows, and the current wallpaper.

✔ **Application workspace.** The area inside a program's window (for MDI applications, the parent-window background color).

✔ **Window background.** The background for each program window (for MDI applications, the child-window background color).

✔ **Window text.** The text inside a window.

✔ **Menu bar.** The menu bar that appears at the top of each program window.

✔ **Menu text.** The text in each menu bar.

✔ **Active title bar.** The active program window's title bar.

✔ **Inactive title bar.** All inactive program windows' title bars.

✔ **Active title bar text.** The text that appears in the active window's title bar.

✔ **Active border.** The border around the active window.

✔ **Inactive border.** The borders of all inactive windows.

✔ **Window frame.** All window frames.

✔ **Scroll bars.** All horizontal and vertical scroll bars.

✔ **Button face.** The top face of control buttons.

✔ **Button shadow.** The shadow around the bottom and right edges of control buttons.

✔ **Button text.** Text on the face of control buttons.

✔ **Button highlight.** The highlight color at the left and upper edges of control buttons.

✔ **Disabled text.** The dimmed text in menus.

✔ **Highlight.** The highlighted item in a menu.

✔ **Highlighted text.** The text of a highlighted menu item.

✔ **Inactive title bar text.** All inactive windows' title bar text.

If you want to create custom colors, choose the Define Custom Colors button. This displays the Custom Color Selector dialog box shown in figure 6.5.

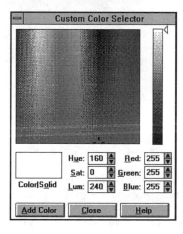

Figure 6.5
The Custom Color Selector dialog box.

You can use the Custom Color Selector dialog box to define custom colors quickly for use for various Windows components. This is particularly useful with 256-color displays.

Tip

You might want to try using black for the Windows desktop. This helps your program windows stand out, makes the icons easier to recognize, and generally cuts down on eyestrain. Also, if you are used to the DOS world, a black background will make you feel right at home.

The easiest way to define new colors is to approximate the color using the crosshair tool, then fine-tune the color using the H<u>u</u>e, <u>S</u>at, and <u>L</u>um spin buttons in the Custom Color Selector dialog box (choose Colors from the Control Panel).

A Note from the Author

Don't get too crazy with wild color schemes; they cause eyestrain. Those fairly muted color defaults in Windows are there for a reason: you don't want to have a brain hemorrhage after an hour at your PC.

Colors sometimes appear different from what you expect because of a particular Windows component you're using. This probably can't be helped.

Remember, changing a color's RGB (red-green-blue) value affects that color's HSL (hue-saturation-luminosity), and vice versa. We live in a hopelessly interconnected universe.

The subtle difference between two colors adjacent to one another in the color spectrum might not be apparent because of limitations in your video adapter and video driver.

For fine-tuning colors, use the cross for approximate setting, and then the scrolling method for color tweaking.

Controlling Fonts

The Fonts icon in the Control Panel enables you to view installed fonts, add new fonts, and remove fonts. Click on the Fonts icon to display the Fonts dialog box shown in figure 6.6. To view an example of a font, simply click on a font name in a dialog box's list.

The Fonts dialog box includes a <u>T</u>rueType button that displays the TrueType fonts dialog box, which is used to specify options for using TrueType fonts in Windows.

For extended coverage of fonts and the ways they are used in Windows, refer to Chapter 4, "Working with Fonts."

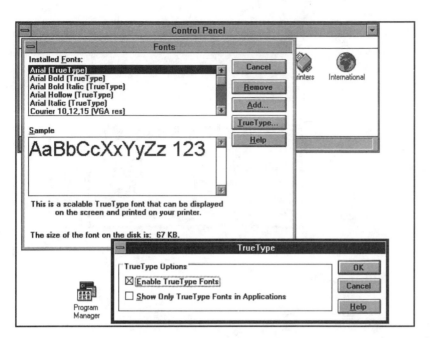

Understanding Windows

Figure 6.6
The Fonts and
TrueType fonts
dialog boxes.

Tip

You can use a TrueType font for the descriptions under icons by adding the setting IconTitleFaceName= to the [desktop] section of WIN.INI. To use Arial, for example, include the setting IconTitleFaceName=arial. You can control the size of the icon description's font with the IconTitleSize= setting (specify the font point size to be used, such as IconTitleSize=10).

Controlling Ports

The Ports icon in the Control Panel enables you to set operating parameters for your system's serial (COM) ports. You can set baud rate, number of data bits, parity, number of stop bits, and flow control method. Choosing the Ports icon displays the Ports and Settings dialog boxes shown in figure 6.7.

In addition to setting these general parameters, you also can set the base I/O port address and interrupt request line (IRQ) for each COM port. Clicking on the Advanced button in the Settings for COM*x* dialog box displays the Advanced Settings for COM*x* dialog box shown in figure 6.8.

Use this dialog box to specify the base I/O address and IRQ for the selected port. You should leave these settings as is to avoid problems with modems and serial mice, unless you are sure of the correct settings.

Figure 6.7
The Ports and
Settings for COMx
dialog boxes.

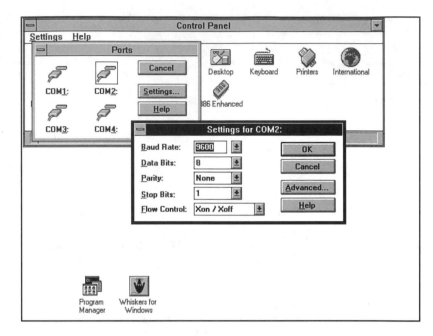

Figure 6.8
The Advanced
Settings for COMx
dialog box.

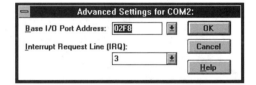

Controlling the Mouse

The Mouse icon in the Control Panel displays the Mouse dialog box shown in figure 6.9.

Figure 6.9
The Mouse dialog
box.

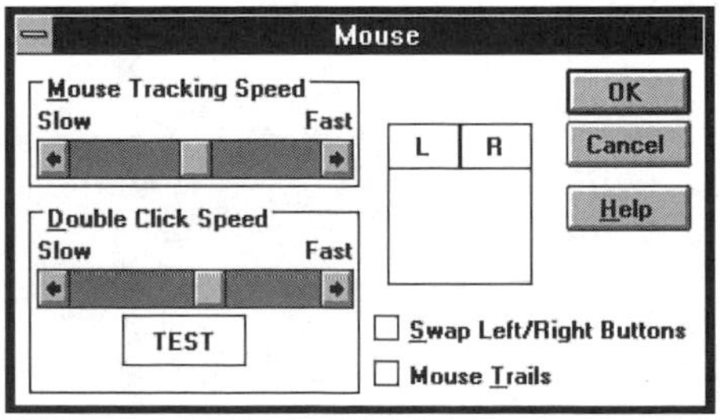

The Mouse controls in this dialog box include the following:

✔ **Mouse Tracking Speed.** Controls the speed at which the mouse moves across the Windows desktop when you move the mouse. Microsoft mice have separate horizontal and vertical tracking speeds.

✔ **Double Click Speed.** Sets the relative amount of time that must pass between two clicks of the mouse button for it to be recognized by Windows as a double-click.

✔ **Swap Left/Right Buttons.** Swaps the function of the left and right mouse buttons.

Tip

In addition to being a good alternative for left-handed users, swapping mouse buttons from left to right and using the mouse with your left hand can be useful when entering numbers in a spreadsheet. You can move the mouse with your left hand to select cells, and enter numbers with your right hand, making it unnecessary to move your hand repeatedly from the mouse to the numeric keypad.

✔ **Mouse Trails.** When checked, this option causes a ghost image to follow the mouse pointer on the display. This makes the cursor more visible on liquid crystal displays (LCDs). If your selected video driver does not support mouse trails, this option is dimmed.

✔ **TEST.** The TEST area in the Mouse dialog box enables you to test double-click speed. When you successfully double-click inside the Test box, its background switches between white and black.

For additional information on mice and other pointing devices, refer to Chapter 10, "Input Devices: Keyboards and Mice."

Controlling the Desktop

The Desktop icon in the Control Panel enables you to control a wide range of parameters that determine the way the Windows environment appears. The Desktop icon also includes a few options for controlling the way the Windows environment operates. The Desktop icon in the Control Panel displays the Desktop dialog box shown in figure 6.10.

The Pattern group box enables you to specify a pattern to cover the Windows desktop. The pattern appears behind any wallpaper you configure Windows to display. Figure 6.11 shows the Weave pattern.

Understanding Windows

Figure 6.10
The Desktop
dialog box.

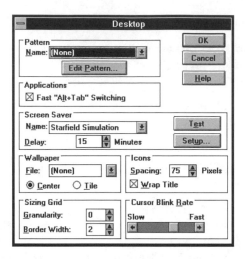

Figure 6.11
The Weave
pattern.

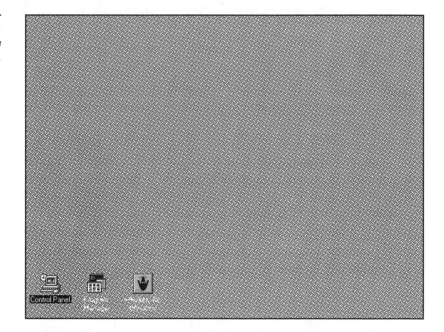

Windows includes 13 predefined patterns. If you want to create your own
pattern, click on the Edit **P**attern button in the Desktop dialog box.

The Wallpaper group box contains controls for specifying a wallpaper pattern. The wallpaper pattern is a bitmap that appears on top of the desktop pattern, if any is selected. Figure 6.12 shows a bitmap used as a wallpaper image.

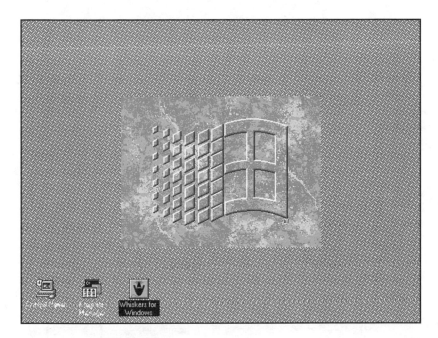

Figure 6.12
A wallpaper bitmap.

Windows includes a selection of bitmaps you can use for wallpaper. You also can use any Windows bitmap file (BMP format) as a wallpaper image.You will find that a darker background and wallpaper will cause the least amount of eyestrain if you use Windows for extended periods. This is particularly true if your video adapter and monitor use interlaced display mode. For best results, use a black background with no wallpaper.

A Note from the Author

Have fun with all of this, but don't go overboard—a cluttered, gaudy desktop scheme is confusing and causes eyestrain.

Messing around with custom wallpaper can use too much memory for some systems. You can, however, compress bitmap files to save memory. This can free up that all-important wallpaper power.

You can create and save a number of different desktop schemes at once and access them whenever you wish.

Understanding Windows

Normally, wallpaper files must be located in the Windows directory. You can, however, directly edit the `wallpaper=` setting in the `[desktop]` section of WIN.INI to specify a file in a different directory, such as `wallpaper=c:\images\bmps\panic.bmp`.

In addition, you can specify the name of an RLE file instead of a BMP file. Because they use a compression technique, RLE files generally are smaller in size than BMP files. You might want to use a utility such as WinGIF or PaintShop Pro to convert your BMP wallpaper files to RLE format.

The Applications group box contains the Fast "Alt+Tab" Switching check box. This item provides a quick method for switching between applications using Alt+Tab. When this feature is turned on and you press Alt+Tab, Windows displays a dialog box containing an icon of the application that will become active when you release the Alt key. You can continue to hold the Alt key down and cycle through the running programs by pressing Tab.

The Screen Saver group box includes controls that specify and configure your Windows screen saver. The screen saver can be used to password protect your workstation. After the screen saver is activated, you must provide the password to regain access to the Windows display. This enables you to leave your workstation unattended and unavailable to other users. Note that a password is optional. Figure 6.13 shows the configuration dialog box for one of Windows' screen savers.

Figure 6.13
The Mystify Setup
dialog box.

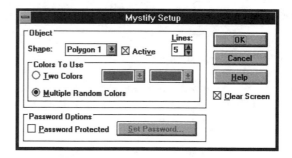

The Sizing Grid group box in the Desktop dialog box includes controls that enable you to control the way windows are positioned on the Windows desktop and the width of window borders.

The Icons group box enables you to specify the horizontal spacing between icons in program groups. It also controls whether icon descriptions wrap to multiple lines or appear as a single line.

To change the vertical spacing between icons, use the `IconVerticalSpacing=` setting in the `[desktop]` section of WIN.INI. Here is an example:

```
IconVerticalSpacing=75.
```

The Cursor Blink **R**ate group box enables you to control the speed at which the cursor blinks. This controls the blink rate for Windows programs and for windowed DOS programs.

Controlling the Keyboard

The Keyboard icon in Control Panel enables you to control the key repeat rate for the keyboard. It also enables you to specify the amount of time a key can be depressed before Windows begins repeating the key's character. Choosing the Keyboard icon displays the Keyboard dialog box shown in figure 6.14.

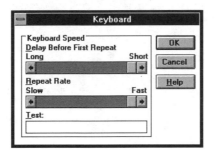

Figure 6.14
The Keyboard dialog box.

To improve key response time, increase the values as desired.

Tip

For the keyboard, you can switch to the ever-popular Dvorak system (which is easy to use, especially for keyboard beginners) by using the Keyboard layout option.

Controlling Printers

The Printers dialog box, shown in figure 6.15, is used to add, configure, and remove printer drivers. In addition, the Printers dialog box contains the **U**se Print Manager check box. When checked, printing is processed by Print Manager. When this check box is cleared, printing goes directly to the printer driver, bypassing Print Manager. You can clear this check box and improve printing speed in many cases.

Note

You might attempt to install a printer driver for your printer but not see it in the list when you click on the **A**dd button. Check your printer's manual to determine if it emulates another type of printer (many laser printers emulate the HP line of laser printers, for example). If you determine that your printer emulates another, choose the printer driver for the printer that your printer will emulate.

Figure 6.15
The Printers dialog
box.

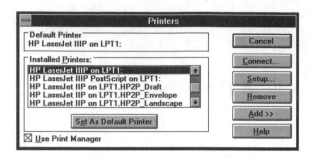

For more information on configuring printers with the Printers dialog box and printing from Windows, refer to Chapter 5, "Printing in Windows."

Controlling International Settings

The International icon displays the International dialog box shown in figure 6.16. This dialog box provides controls that specify country-specific settings for Windows. These settings include language, keyboard layout, date format, time format, currency format, and number format.

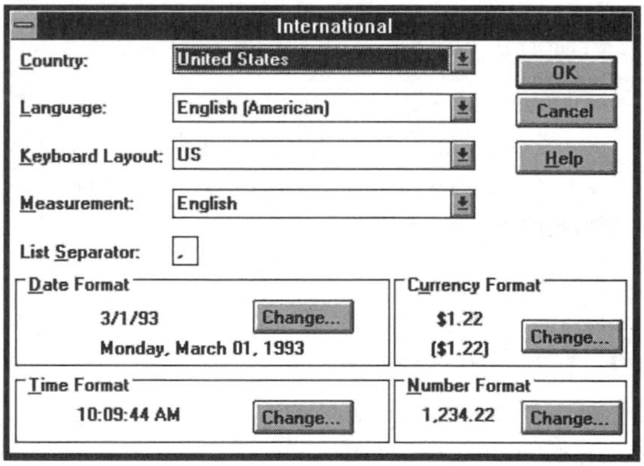

Figure 6.16
The International
dialog box.

Selecting a country setting from the Country list box changes other settings within the dialog box automatically.

Setting the System Date and Time

The Date/Time icon displays the Date & Time dialog box shown in figure 6.17. Use this dialog box to set your computer's system date and time. This is equivalent to using the CMOS setup routine for your workstation to set the CMOS time and date.

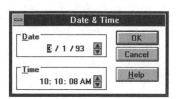

Figure 6.17
The Date & Time
dialog box.

The system's date and time are stored in a ROM chip, called a *CMOS chip*. PCs have a system setup utility that enables you to set the date and time, as well as specify hardware items such as the type of floppy drives and hard drive in the system. Using the Date/Time icon is much simpler than attempting to change the date and time through the CMOS setup program.

Setting 386 Enhanced Mode Options

If you are running Windows in 386 Enhanced mode (which requires a 386 or better processor), the Control Panel includes an icon labeled 386 Enhanced. Double-clicking on the 386 Enhanced icon displays the 386 Enhanced dialog box shown in figure 6.18. This dialog box enables you to control a number of operating parameters for Windows running in 386 Enhanced mode.

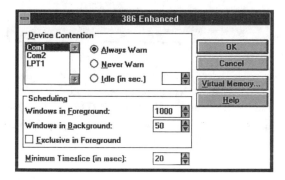

Figure 6.18
The 386 Enhanced
dialog box.

The Device Contention group box controls the way Windows handles contention between applications that attempt to access the same COM port. The Always Warn option causes Windows to display a warning message whenever a program attempts to access the associated COM port when it is already in use by another program. The Never Warn options causes Windows to ignore these types of conflicts when they occur (which could result in a loss of data or hardware not functioning properly). The Idle option enables you to specify an amount of time in seconds that the associated COM port must be idle before another program can use it.

The Scheduling group box controls priority values Windows uses for multitasking Windows and DOS programs. The **E**xclusive in Foreground check box enables you to specify that Windows applications will have 100 percent of the CPU's time when Windows programs are in the background, which effectively disables multitasking of DOS programs. The **M**inimum Timeslice control specifies the amount of time allocated to each process when multitasking.

The **V**irtual Memory button displays the Virtual Memory dialog box shown in figure 6.19. This dialog box enables you to change the type and size of swap file that Windows uses in 386 Enhanced mode. You also use it to turn on and off Windows' 32-bit disk access.

Figure 6.19
The Virtual
Memory dialog
box.

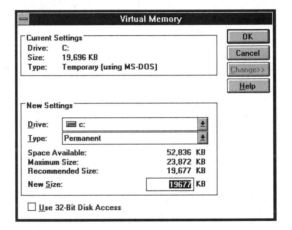

32-bit disk access refers to the optional Windows virtual disk access driver, called FastDisk. If your system contains an IDE hard drive subsystem or a drive subsystem that is compatible with the WD1003 controller, you should consider using FastDisk. Chapter 11, "Optimizing Data Storage Space," explains FastDisk in detail. Chapter 11 also explains 32-bit file access, a feature that is new in Windows 3.11.

Controlling Multimedia Drivers

The Drivers icon displays the Drivers dialog box (see fig. 6. 20) you can use to add, configure, and remove various device drivers for multimedia equipment. Multimedia equipment includes sound boards, MIDI devices, and audio CDs.

For more information about installing device drivers for multimedia, refer to Chapter 35, "Working with Multimedia in Windows." For information on multimedia audio, see Chapter 36, "Using Multimedia Audio." For information on multimedia video, see Chapter 37, "Using Multimedia Video."

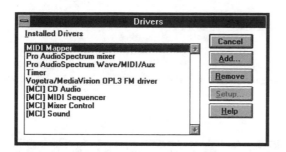

Figure 6.20
The Drivers dialog box.

The installation program for a new multimedia device usually updates the multimedia drivers for you automatically. You seldom, if ever, have to use the Drivers icon to make changes to your multimedia drivers.

Controlling Sounds

The Sound icon in the Control Panel displays the Sound dialog box shown in figure 6.21. If your system contains a sound adapter, such as Media Vision's Pro AudioSpectrum or Creative Labs' SoundBlaster Pro, the Sound dialog box enables you to assign digitized sounds to various Windows events. If your system does not include a sound adapter, the Sound dialog box enables you to turn on and off Windows' standard warning beep.

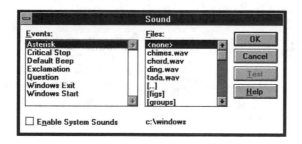

Figure 6.21
The Sound dialog box.

If you want to add limited sound capability to your system without adding a sound adapter, you can use a special driver—SPEAKER.EXE—for your PC's speaker (you can find this driver on the WINADV forum on CompuServe, the WDL [Windows Device Library], and the Microsoft Download Service). SPEAKER.EXE uses the standard PC speaker to play WAV files such as those you assign to various Windows events through the Sound dialog box. The speaker driver provides much poorer sound than an audio adapter, but at least you can interpret a few of the sounds and experiment with multimedia audio. Voice reproduction is particularly poor, especially if the voice is low-pitched. For a detailed discussion of sound applications in Windows, see Chapter 36, "Using Multimedia Audio."

Modifying the Network

Depending on your system, your Control Panel may include additional items or controls. One of these is the Network icon, which provides options for changing various settings that control your workstation's network access. The controls in the Network dialog box vary according to the network you are using. Figure 6.22 shows the Network dialog box for Windows for Workgroups.

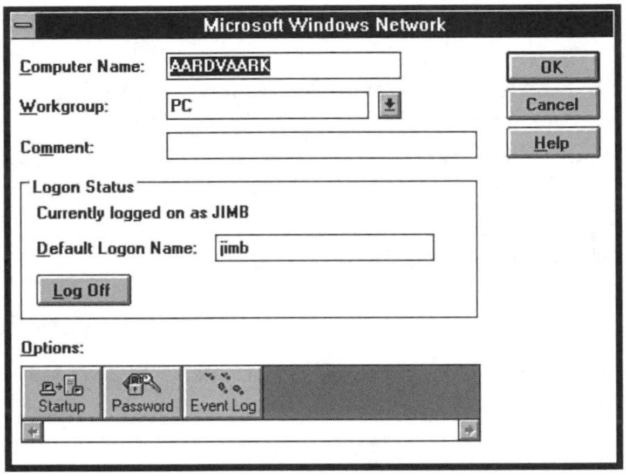

Figure 6.22
The Windows for Workgroups Network dialog box.

Customizing Program Manager

You can make a handful of changes to Program Manager to change the way it functions. The most obvious changes are adding or deleting program groups or items. Before adding these items, however, you should have an understanding of what they are and what purpose they serve in Windows.

> **Note** A number of utilities are available that either replace Program Manager as the Windows shell or supplement its functions. Norton Desktop for Windows, Hewlett-Packard's Dashboard, and Plannet Crafters' Plug In are three such utilities you might want to investigate.

Understanding Groups and Items

Program Manager's primary purpose is to make it easy to start applications. To that end, Program Manager provides document windows called *group windows* within its main program window. Group windows provide a mechanism for grouping your programs together in a logical way.

Inside each group window are program items. A program item is represented in the group window by an *icon*, or simple picture. Under each icon is a description of the program item.

You can create new program groups to contain program items, delete groups you do not use or need, and copy or move items from one group to another. The following section explains how to create a new group.

Creating Program Groups

Windows Setup creates four standard groups when you install Windows: Main, Accessories, Games, and StartUp. You also can create your own program groups. To create a program group, follow these steps:

1. In Program Manager, choose File, New.

2. In the New Program Object dialog box, choose the Program Group radio button, then click on OK.

3. In the Program Group Properties dialog box, enter a name for the group in the Description edit box. This name will appear in the group window's title bar and under its icon when it is minimized.

4. In the Group File edit box, enter the file name under which you want the group to be stored. This step is optional. If you omit a file name, Program Manager will come up with a file name on its own.

 If you have a program group file that has already been created, and simply want to add it to your Program Manager environment, leave the description blank in the previous set of steps and specify the name of the existing group file in the Group File edit box. After you click on OK, Program Manager will read the existing group file and add it to the Program Manager window.

5. Click on OK.

After you have created a new group, you can begin adding program items (icons) to it.

Deleting a Program Group

To delete a program group, perform the following steps:

1. Minimize the program group to an icon.

2. Select the group's icon by clicking on it once.

3. Press Del, or from Program Manager's File menu, choose the Delete command.

4. When Program Manager prompts you with a confirmation dialog box, choose Yes to delete the group, or No to abort the operation.

If a group is empty (contains no icons), you do not have to minimize it to delete the group. With the empty group window open in Program Manager, simply press Del. Program Manager will prompt you to confirm deletion of the group.

Note that when you delete a program group, the programs contained within the group are not deleted. The programs' files still reside on the hard drive. The group file, however, is deleted from the disk.

Creating and Changing Program Items

A program item is represented in a group window by an icon. Double-clicking on the program item's icon starts the program associated with the item. Program items can be associated with programs or with document files. Double-clicking on a document item in a group window generally opens the document's source application and places the document in the program for editing.

If the document type is not associated with a program, you cannot start the application by double-clicking on the document item's icon. Generally, programs associate their document types with the application automatically when you set them up.

To set up an association manually, open File Manager, select an appropriate document file, then choose the Associate command from File Manager's File menu. Follow the directions in the Associate dialog box to complete the file association.

To create a program item, perform the following steps:

1. Open and make active the program group (for example, Main, Games, Accessories) into which you want to place the new program item.

2. From Program Manager, choose File, New.

3. In the New Program Object dialog box, choose Program Item, then click on OK.

4. In the Program Item Properties dialog box, enter the **D**escription, **C**ommand Line, **W**orking Directory, and **S**hortcut Key properties (explained in table 6.2).

5. If you want the program to start as an icon, check **R**un Minimized.

6. To change the icon associated with the item, choose Change **I**con, then follow the directions in the dialog box to select an icon.

7. Return to the Program Item Properties dialog box and click on OK to create the program item.

Table 6.2
Program Item Properties

Property	Description
Description	This description appears underneath the item's icon. The text will wrap to a maximum of three lines under the icon.
Command Line	This is the command that is executed to start the program. Usually, the path to the program and its executable file name are used as the command-line entry, such as: C:\EXCEL\EXCEL.EXE. You also can add optional command-line switches for the program or the name of a document file, such as: C:\EXCEL\EXCEL.EXE REPORT.XLS.
Working Directory	This is the directory that will be made current when the application starts. If you omit an entry, the Windows directory will be the current directory.
Shortcut Key	Use this property to assign a shortcut key to the program. When the program is running and you press the assigned shortcut key, the application becomes active (receives focus).
Run Minimized	If checked, this causes the program to start as an icon, rather than in its normal windowed state.

Tip

You can drag files from File Manager into Program Manager to create program items without going through Program Manager's **F**ile menu. To do so, simply open File Manager and Program Manager and position them so you can see both program windows. Then, select the application or document file in File Manager, drag it to the Program Manager window, and drop it into whichever group window you want.

Adding Restrictions

If you are responsible for setting up and maintaining Windows for other users, such as on a network, you can make a number of changes to control the features that users have when running Program Manager. All these features are controlled through Program Manager's initialization file, PROGMAN.INI. PROGMAN.INI resides in the Windows directory.

 Adding restrictions to Program Manager is generally useful only in a business environment when you want to restrict a user's ability to change existing program groups and items. It also can be useful at home, however, to prevent children who use your computer from making changes to the Windows desktop (either purposely or accidentally).

PROGMAN.INI contains three sections labeled [settings], [groups], and [restrictions]. The settings in the [settings] and [groups] sections are set by manipulating the Program Manager window or setting options using the Program Manager menu. The [restrictions] section, however, is optional. To add or make changes to the [restrictions] section, you must edit PROGMAN.INI. (You can edit PROGMAN.INI with Notepad or with the DOS EDIT program.)

The settings in the [restrictions] section control the menu options and functions available in Program Manager. You might want to add a [restrictions] section and modify its settings to control the way Program Manager functions on your workstation, or restrict the ability of other users who want to access certain Program Manager functions on their workstations. The following sections assume that you are responsible for managing your Windows network and are making changes to PROGMAN.INI to restrict other users' access to Program Manager functions.

The following list describes the settings that can be added to the [restrictions] section of PROGMAN.INI:

✔ norun=. Disables the <u>R</u>un command in Program Manager's <u>F</u>ile menu. If norun= is set to 1, the <u>R</u>un command is dimmed and cannot be accessed. When norun= is set to 0 (the default), the <u>R</u>un command is available.

✔ noclose=. Disables the E<u>x</u>it Windows command in Program Manager's <u>F</u>ile menu. When this setting is set to 1, the E<u>x</u>it Windows command is dimmed. When this setting is 0, the E<u>x</u>it Windows command is available.

✔ nosavesettings=. Disables the <u>S</u>ave Settings on Exit command in Program Manager's <u>O</u>ptions menu. If set to 1, nosavesettings= causes the <u>S</u>ave Settings on Exit command to be dimmed, making it unavailable. Specifying a setting of 0 causes the command to be available as normal.

✔ nofilemenu=. When set to 1, this setting removes the File menu from Program Manager's menu bar. Removing the File menu makes its commands unavailable. A setting of 0 makes the File command available.

✔ editlevel=. Controls the ability of a user to modify items in the Program Manager environment. editlevel= can have a value from 0 to 4. These settings are described in detail a little later in this section.

Disabling the Run Command

If you add the setting norun=1 to the [restrictions] section of a user's PROGMAN.INI file, the Run command still appears in Program Manager's File menu, but the menu item is dimmed and cannot be selected (see fig. 6.23). This prevents the user from executing a program using the Run command, and helps restrict the user to executing only those programs that are contained in program groups on the user's desktop.

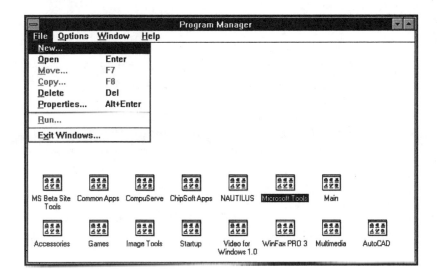

Figure 6.23
The Run command dimmed in Program Manager's menu.

Even with the Run command dimmed, however, the user still can use the Run command in File Manager or double-click on program files in File Manager to execute applications. The user also can add the program to a program group and execute it.

If File Manager is available to the user, the norun= setting in the [restrictions] section will provide only limited security against the user executing restricted programs. To ensure better security, place applications in shared remote directories protected by passwords.

Preventing Exit from Windows

The noclose= setting in the [restrictions] section of PROGMAN.INI can prevent a user from exiting the Windows environment (assuming Program Manager is the user's shell). When set to 1, noclose= disables the Exit Windows command in the File menu (see fig. 6.24), the Close command in Program Manager's control menu, and the Alt+F4 shortcut key for closing Program Manager. This setting effectively prevents the user from exiting Windows, short of rebooting with Ctrl+Alt+Del or turning off the power.

Figure 6.24
The Exit Windows command dimmed.

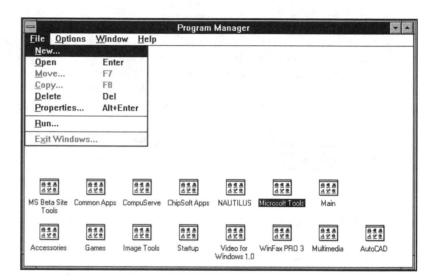

Disabling the Capability To Change Program Manager

The setting nosavesettings=1 in the [restrictions] section disables the Save Settings on Exit command in Program Manager's Options menu. This prevents the user from saving any changes that have been made to the Windows desktop during the current session. This includes such changes as moving group windows or changing the state of a group (whether it is displayed as a window or an icon).

This setting is most useful for preventing inexperienced users from making accidental changes to their Program Manager environment.

Restricting Group and Program Item Features

In addition to controlling user functions for some of the menu items in Program Manager, you also can control the user's ability to create and edit program groups and program items. These capabilities are controlled by the value of the editlevel= setting in the [restrictions] section of PROGMAN.INI.

The possible values for editlevel= include the following:

✔ editlevel=0. The default value. The user can make any change to the desktop, including creating and deleting program groups and items.

✔ editlevel=1. Disables the user's ability to create, delete, and rename groups. This setting dims the New, Move, Copy and Delete items from the File menu when a group is selected. A setting of editlevel=1 does not affect the user's ability to perform these same types of functions on program items within a group.

This setting also disables shortcut methods for deleting groups, such as pressing Del when a group icon is selected.

✔ editlevel=2. Incorporates the same restriction level as a setting of 1, but also prevents the user from creating or deleting program items (icons in a program group). This setting dims the New, Move, Copy, and Delete menu items in the File menu at all times. Shortcut methods for corresponding commands also are disabled.

✔ editlevel=3. Includes all restrictions present in level 2, and also prevents the user from changing a program's Command Line entry property. The user can still view the item's properties by selecting the item's icon, then choosing Properties from the File menu or by pressing Alt+Enter. All other properties, including the item's Description, can still be edited by the user.

✔ editlevel=4. Includes all the restrictions of level 3 and prevents the user from making any changes to a program item's properties. The user can still view the item's properties, but all fields in the Program Item Properties dialog box are read-only.

Using Plug In

One shareware program that has been well received by the Windows community is Plug In, from Plannet Crafters, Inc. Plug In enables you to specify different icons for each program group and create your own Program Manager menu of commands for quick access, and also provides many other features that make Program Manager easier and more useful. Figure 6.25 shows Program Manager with Plug In being used to change program group icons.

Plug In does not have its own icon. Instead, it replaces the Program Manager icon with one of your choosing. If you prefer, you can continue to use the standard Program Manager icon.

Figure 6.25
In this figure, Plug
In has changed the
standard group
icons to custom,
user-defined icons.

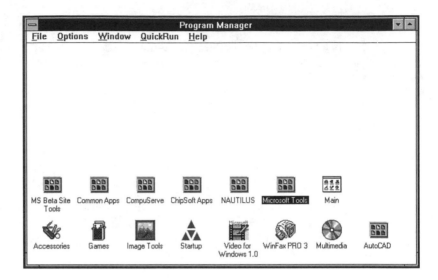

Plug In's major features include the following:

✔ **Icon support.** Plug In enables you to specify a different icon for each program group. You can use one of the icons that is included with Plug In, or create your own using an icon editing program. Plug In also simplifies the task of assigning an icon to a program item.

✔ **Improved Run command.** Plug In provides an improved Run command dialog box that includes a command-line history and the capability to execute individual DOS commands quickly.

✔ **QuickRun Menu.** Plug In provides a customizable menu called QuickRun that resides in Program Manager's menu bar. You can add your own program items to the menu, which simplifies the process of starting a program. You can select a program from the QuickRun menu rather than hunting through a group window for the program's item.

✔ **System information.** Plug In provides a function for viewing detailed information about your system. This information includes memory usage, hardware information, and a list of all programs currently running under your Windows session.

To obtain a copy of Plug In, check the ZIFFNET forum on CompuServe or contact Plannet Crafters, Inc. at (404) 740-9821.

Customizing Application EXE Files

With the proper tools, you can customize a program's executable (EXE) file, its associated DLL (dynamic link library), or other files to change its appearance. The software that enables you to edit these files is called a resource editor.

Before attempting to change resources in an EXE or DLL file, you should make a backup copy of the file or files you will be editing. In addition, never attempt to modify a file that is in use. If you want to modify Program Manager (PROGMAN.EXE), for example, make a copy of PROGMAN.EXE and modify the copy, and then replace the original with the modified version. Maintaining a backup is essential in the event that the file becomes unusable. Attempting to edit a file that is in use can cause erratic behavior of the system, which could lead to a loss of data.

Resource Editors

A *resource editor* is a program that enables you to create and modify Windows program resources. Program resources include bitmaps, icons, menus, accelerator tables, cursors, and dialog boxes. Some resource editors only enable you to work with individual resource files—they do not enable you to work with resources already embedded in a program's EXE or DLL files. Other resource editors enable you to edit resources contained in an EXE or DLL file. One such editor is the Whitewater Resource Toolkit (WRT). Figure 6.26 shows the main resource browse window for the Whitewater Resource Toolkit.

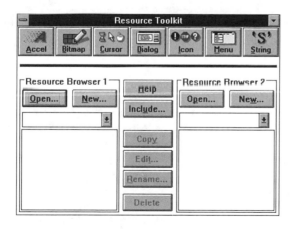

Figure 6.26

The main resource browse window for the Whitewater Resource Toolkit.

The Whitewater Resource Toolkit includes editors you can use to edit icons, bitmaps, cursors, menus, string tables, accelerator tables, and dialog boxes. These resources can be new or contained in a program's EXE or DLL files.

Changing Resources

A few important points about editing resources in an existing EXE file need to be mentioned:

- ✔ **Make a backup of the EXE file.** If you are editing an EXE file, always make a backup copy of it in case your editing damages the file to the point where it can no longer be used. After you make a backup, edit the original. If you have problems running the program after editing it, replace it with the backup copy.

- ✔ **The program should not be running.** You should not attempt to edit resources in a program that is running. If you want to make some changes to Program Manager, for example, copy its executable file to another file, such as to PROG.EXE. Then, edit the file PROG.EXE and change whatever resources you like. When you are finished, exit Windows, make a backup copy of PROGMAN.EXE, then copy PROG.EXE to replace PROGMAN.EXE.

- ✔ **Editing limitations.** Limitations exist to the successful changes you can make to a particular program. For example, you cannot add new menu items to a program's menu because that would also require adding program code and recompiling the program. You can, however, change the names of existing menu items.

Changing Icons

One change you might want to make to one of your existing applications is to change one or more of the icons it uses. A program's icons usually are located in its EXE file; sometimes additional icons will be included with one of the program's DLL files (if it has any). You can replace the program's standard icon with your own using an icon editor such as WRT's (see fig. 6.27).

 If you are interested in new icons but don't want to go through the trouble of creating them yourself, you can download literally thousands of icons from the various Windows forums on CompuServe and other information services. On CompuServe, for example, check the WINADV and WINNEW forums for icons and icon editors.

Changing Cursors

Cursors are the graphical images associated with the screen pointer. The hourglass, arrow pointer, and resize pointers are typical of standard Windows cursors. Applications sometimes include their own cursors.

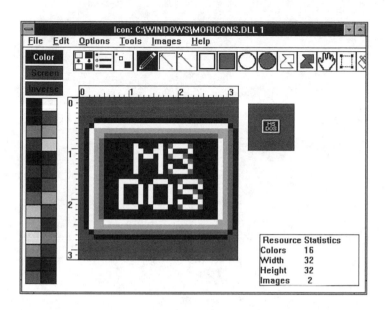

Figure 6.27
The Whitewater
Resource Toolkit's
icon editor.

With a resource editor similar to the WRT, you can load an existing cursor from a
program's EXE file and change it to suit your preferences.

Other Resource Changes

Other resource changes you can make with the Whitewater Resource Toolkit and with
other resource editors include modifying bitmaps, menus, accelerator tables, and other
Windows program resources. The usefulness of changing these resources, however, is
limited. They often also require modifying program code, something you cannot do with
a resource editor.

Other Resource Editors

The Whitewater Resource Toolkit is just one of the resource editors currently available.
All the program development environments for developing Windows applications from
Microsoft, Borland, and other companies also include resource editors. The Whitewater
Resource Toolkit, however, is one of the few that is available as a separate product without
the programming tools.

Although modifying the resources in existing EXE and DLL files is certainly useful for
some users, the majority of Windows users find general changes to Program Manager, the
start-up screen, and the other changes described in the earlier parts of this chapter to be
most useful.

Part Two

Optimizing Windows

Chapter Snapshot

Many factors determine how well Windows will perform on your system. Some relate directly to the type of hardware that is installed in your system. Others can be controlled by changes to the software's configuration, either in DOS or in Windows. This chapter examines many factors that affect Windows' performance, and covers the following topics:

Although some of the performance enhancements described in this chapter require upgrading your system's hardware, many changes require only modifying one or two configuration files. This chapter examines both types of changes.

CHAPTER

Enhancing Windows Performance

I f you are buying a new system for Windows, there are many hardware issues to consider to ensure that the system will provide the best possible performance. Upgrading an older system also requires some consideration and planning. This section of the chapter explains some common hardware issues, beginning with processor type.

Powering Up for Windows

Your system's processor is one of the most important factors affecting Windows' performance. The model of processor, however, is not the only important thing; so is the processor's type and speed.

Processor Type

Four types of microprocessors are commonly available for today's PCs in various clock speeds and configurations. Table 7.1 lists these microprocessors and their many variations.

Table 7.1
PC Microprocessor Types

Processor	Description
80286	The 286 is used in AT-class systems. Although Windows 3.1 runs on the 286, future versions of Windows will not. Furthermore, Windows' performance is quite limited on a 286-based system.
80386-SX	The 386-SX should be considered the very minimum entry-level system for Windows. The 386-SX is capable of running 32-bit software, but uses 16-bit I/O, making it a poorer performer than the 386-DX.
80386-DX	The 386-DX implements full 32-bit internal and external architecture, making it faster than the SX. Systems based on the 386-DX processor are good Windows systems for the average user.
80486-SX	The 486-SX is a full 32-bit chip that performs from two to four times faster than an equivalent 386-DX chip. The 486-SX, unlike the 486-DX, does not have an internal math coprocessor.
80486-DX	The 486-DX is identical to the 486-SX, but the DX model includes a built-in math coprocessor.
80486-DX2	The 486-DX2 is a clock-doubled version of the 486. If your system's BIOS is compatible with the DX2, you can remove your existing 486 chip and replace it with a DX2 version, nearly doubling your system's speed.
80486-DX4	The 486-DX4 is a clock-tripled version of the 486. The DX4 is available in 75 and 99 MHz versions (tripled versions of the 25 and 33 MHz CPUs, respectively).

Processor	Description
Pentium	The Pentium is the CPU that would have become the 586 had Intel stuck with the same product-naming scheme it used with its other CPUs. The Pentium generally is available in clock speeds as high as 66 MHz, although higher clock-speed Pentium processors should be available soon. The Pentium processor generally provides double the performance of a 486 CPU of the same clock speed.

Except in the case of the 486-DX2, 486-DX4, and Pentium CPUs, selection is relevant only when you are either buying a new system or upgrading your existing system with a completely new motherboard. You cannot upgrade a 386-SX, for example, to a 386-DX just by replacing the CPU. Depending on motherboard design, however, you might be able to add a 486-DX2, 486-DX4, or Pentium to your existing 486-based system to improve its performance.

Selecting a CPU

If you plan to buy a new system or to upgrade your existing system by installing a new motherboard, the following tips should help you pick the system that is right for you:

✔ **Don't buy a 286 or 386 system.** Although Windows 3.1 runs on 286 systems, the performance usually is poor. Future versions of Windows will not run on a 286 system, so you should not buy a 286 system to run Windows.

Although 386-based systems run Windows, the performance of a 486-based system is much more desirable for running Windows. Few manufacturers offer 386-based systems, and the price of 486-based systems has dropped considerably, making a 486-based system an ideal entry point for Windows.

✔ **486 systems are the minimum.** Any 486 system is an excellent choice for a Windows system. If you are running a peer-to-peer network such as Windows for Workgroups, or computation-intensive programs such as AutoCAD for Windows, you should opt for a 486-DX2 or 486-DX3 system if cost is not a major factor. When shopping for a system, keep in mind that the 486-SX does not include a built-in math coprocessor. If you run applications that require or can use a math coprocessor, or you will be running these types of applications in the future, buy a DX system to get the built-in math coprocessor.

✔ **A DX2 is great if it will work with your system.** If you are considering buying a DX2 chip to install in your existing 486 system, first make sure that your system's BIOS supports it. Then take into account the DX2's price; a 486-DX2 that brings your system's speed up to 66 MHz will cost around $500.

✔ **Pentium systems are the next wave.** Pentium systems offer the best performance of all the PC systems. Although they are more expensive than 486 systems, Pentium systems generally provide at least twice the performance of a 486 system. Prices are coming down now on Pentium systems, making them an attractive option.

Clock Speed

The CPU's clock speed is just as important as the model of CPU in your system. The *clock speed* determines how fast the chip performs, and is expressed in megahertz (MHz). The higher the number, the faster the chip. A 486 chip running at 66 MHz, for example, is faster than a 486 chip running at 33 MHz.

When considering what type of system to buy, always buy the fastest system you can afford. Also remember that clock speed is only half of the equation; a Pentium is faster than a 486, even when both chips are running at the same clock speed.

Memory

When evalutating new systems for Windows, memory is just as important as CPU type and clock speed. Optimum performance in Windows requires lots of memory. Consider 4 MB (megabytes) of RAM to be a minimum. If the cost does not overwhelm you, install 8 MB or more of RAM in the system.

Math Coprocessors

A *math coprocessor* is a special-purpose microcircuit that performs extensive math operations more quickly than a system's CPU. On 386 systems, the math coprocessor is a separate chip from the 386 CPU. The same is true on 486-SX systems. On 486-DX systems, however, the math coprocessor is built into the CPU itself. Pentium chips also have built-in math coprocessors.

Unfortunately, Windows does not take advantage of a math coprocessor, even if one is installed in the system. Some applications, however, do take advantage of a math coprocessor. These generally are spreadsheet, CAD (computer-aided design), and other math-intensive programs. Check your application's manual to determine if it will make use of a math coprocessor.

Examining System Buses

An additional consideration when evaluating a Windows system is the bus type the system uses. The *bus* provides input/output (I/O) services between the system's CPU and its adapter cards and memory. To a large degree, the system's bus is the weak link in any PC. A slow bus speed becomes a bottleneck to performance even on systems with very fast processors.

As with CPU type and speed, however, the question of which bus to use is relevant only when you are upgrading your system with a new motherboard or if you are buying a new system. You cannot change bus types in an existing system without replacing the entire motherboard.

A *motherboard* is the main printed circuit board inside the PC. The motherboard contains the CPU, bus slots, and support circuitry for the PC. Everything in the PC connects to the motherboard in one way or another.

Today's PCs make use of the following five primary bus designs:

✔ **Industry Standard Architecture (ISA).** The ISA bus is the traditional AT-class bus, which grew out of IBM's original PC bus (the one used on the original IBM PC). The ISA bus is by far the most common in PCs today.

✔ **Micro Channel Architecture (MCA).** IBM developed the MCA bus to provide a new standard for 32-bit systems based on CPUs like the 386 and 486. Cards designed for the ISA bus are not compatible with the MCA bus.

✔ **Extended Industry Standard Architecture (EISA).** The EISA is an extension of the standard ISA bus. The EISA bus provides many of the same design improvements as the MCA bus, but is compatible with ISA bus cards.

✔ **VESA local bus.** Systems that incorporate a VESA local bus typically contain two local bus slots, and the rest of the slots are standard ISA bus slots. Local bus adapters for video and disk subsystems can significantly improve the performance of the system.

✔ **PCI local bus.** The PCI local bus is relatively new, and offers some advantages over the VESA local bus in terms of performance. Most Pentium systems include a PCI bus, and some 486 systems also are now available with PCI bus.

As it relates specifically to Windows' performance, the selection of the ISA, MCA, or EISA bus is only marginally important. Local bus technology is perhaps more important specifically to Windows (as you will read later). The question of bus type is important, however, to overall system performance. As you improve your system's overall performance, you also improve Windows' performance.

ISA

By far the most common bus in use today is the ISA bus, which arose from the IBM AT class of systems. One of the primary drawbacks of the ISA bus is its lack of speed. The typical ISA bus operates at 8.33 MHz, or roughly one-fourth the speed of a 33 MHz CPU. Another drawback to the ISA bus is that it does not allow for the concurrent sharing of interrupts. You usually cannot have two devices sharing IRQ 3, for example. In some situations, two devices can share an interrupt in the system, but only if you do not try to use the two devices at the same time.

The vast majority of adapter cards manufactured today are designed for the ISA bus. If you currently have an ISA-bus system and you want to buy a new system, your existing adapter cards will be compatible with the new system. You will not have to purchase a new internal fax modem, for example, if you already have one. This compatibility is perhaps the most important issue surrounding the selection of an ISA bus system.

MCA

The Micro Channel Architecture (MCA) bus was developed by IBM to address, IBM claims, the many shortcomings of the ISA bus. Because it is not compatible with the ISA bus, and adapter cards designed for the ISA bus cannot function in an MCA system, many in the computer industry feel IBM developed the MCA bus to leverage its own position in the industry.

Although the MCA bus is technically a good design, it has not been very successful, primarily because most users are not willing to give up compatibility with their existing ISA adapter cards.

EISA

The Extended Industry Standard Architecture (EISA) bus is just what its name implies: an extension of the ISA bus standard. The EISA bus provides all the design improvements inherent in the MCA bus, but also provides compatibility with adapter cards that are designed for the ISA bus. If you have an ISA system and purchase a new EISA system, you can use all the existing adapter cards from your ISA system in your new EISA system.

Even though the EISA bus is more powerful than the ISA bus while maintaining ISA compatibility, it has not been a big success. The primary reason for this is that the EISA bus adds $800–$1,000 to a system's cost. Most users feel the added performance gain is not worth the additional cost.

Local Bus: The Real Answer for Windows?

Local bus is the newest design craze in today's PCs. A local bus system bypasses the system's primary bus and connects certain devices more directly to the CPU. In many ways, local bus technology is decades old, but it promises very substantial improvement in system performance for Windows.

By coupling a device directly to the CPU, local bus technology potentially puts a much higher load on the CPU than does a typical AT bus design. In recent years, CPU speeds and capability have increased dramatically, enabling the CPU to handle the increased load without degrading overall system performance.

Local bus technology has become most prevalent in video and hard disk I/O, the two resources on which Windows relies the most. (The video and hard disk subsystems, which have onboard caching, each use their own local bus.) Video and the hard disk perform much better on a system that uses a local bus for each of those items than a typical ISA, EISA, or MCA bus alone. If you are considering buying a new system, take a close look at local bus systems for use with Windows, but keep these tips in mind:

✔ **Local bus and EISA.** The performance improvements in the EISA bus and local bus are not mutually exclusive. A local bus system that utilizes an EISA bus still performs better than a local bus system that utilizes an ISA bus.

✔ **Video accelerators.** Many video systems now are available that make use of video coprocessors, also called video accelerators. The video speed improvements provided by a video coprocessor are not exclusive to the benefits provided by local bus video. If you can find a system that provides for local bus video and accelerated graphics, the performance will be better than performance on a system that uses only one of those two technologies.

✔ **PCI and Pentium.** If you are buying a Pentium system, buy one that provides at least two PCI local bus slots; one for video and the other for the disk subsystem. Configure the system with a PCI local bus video adapter and PCI local bus disk host adapter.

For a more in-depth evaluation of local bus video, accelerated video, and other video system topics, refer to Chapter 8, "Enhancing Windows Video."

Using Windows Setup
To Change Configuration

Windows automatically takes advantage of such things as your system's bus type or local bus. You do not need to configure anything to make Windows use these items. You can make other hardware configuration changes, however, through the Windows Setup program. If you have changed your display, keyboard, mouse, or network, Setup is the program you use to make those changes effective under Windows. Figure 7.1 shows the Windows Setup dialog box.

II

Optimizing Windows

Figure 7.1
The Windows
Setup dialog box.

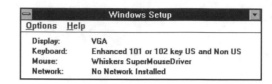

Changing System Settings

The icon for the Windows Setup program usually is located in your Main group. When you run Windows Setup, one of the items in the Options menu is Change System Settings. This command enables you to change your system's display, keyboard, mouse, and network configurations. When you choose Change System Settings, the Change System Settings dialog box appears, as shown in figure 7.2.

Figure 7.2
The Change
System Settings
dialog box.

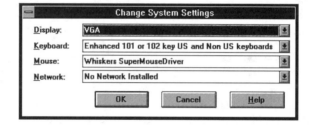

Selecting a New Video Driver

To change the driver that Windows uses for your video adapter, choose the appropriate driver from the Display drop-down list in the Change System Settings dialog box. If the needed driver files are not already on the system, Setup prompts you to insert one or more of your Windows distribution disks. When prompted to do so, insert the requested disk. If you are inserting the disk in a drive other than the one Setup is specifying in its dialog box, change the drive letter in the dialog box and click on OK.

If you want to use a driver that is supplied with your video adapter and is not included with Windows, choose the option labeled Other display (requires disk from OEM) in the Display drop-down list. Setup prompts you to insert the disk that came with your video adapter. Follow the instructions in the dialog box to provide the disk needed by Setup.

After changing your system's video configuration, Setup gives you the option of restarting Windows or continuing to work with the existing configuration. If you have other configuration changes to make with Setup, choose Continue. If you have finished your changes, choose Restart Windows to make your changes take effect.

For more information on video adapters, monitors, and driver selection, see Chapter 8, "Enhancing Windows Video."

Selecting a New Keyboard Driver

If you change keyboards on your system, or your system's keyboard was not properly configured for Windows when you first installed Windows, you can use Setup to change the keyboard driver Windows uses. If you are replacing an existing 84-key keyboard with a 101-key enhanced keyboard, for example, use Setup to select the appropriate driver.

To choose a different keyboard driver, choose the Options menu in Setup, then choose Change System Settings. In the Change System Settings dialog box, choose the required driver from the Keyboard drop-down list and click on OK. Setup might prompt you to insert one of the Windows distribution disks. Insert the required disk and click on OK.

If you want to use a driver that is supplied on a disk that comes with your keyboard, choose the option Other keyboard (requires disk from OEM) from the Keyboard drop-down list. When prompted to do so, insert the disk containing the driver and click on OK.

When Setup has completed the keyboard driver change, you will be given the option of restarting Windows or continuing with the current configuration. If you have other configuration changes to make with Setup, choose Continue. If you have finished your changes, choose Restart Windows to make your changes take effect.

For additional information on keyboard types and keyboard drivers, refer to Chapter 10, "Input Devices: Keyboards and Mice."

Selecting a New Mouse Driver

You might want to change the driver Windows uses for your mouse. This will be the case when you buy a new mouse and want to use it with Windows, or if your mouse was not properly configured when Windows was installed.

To change mouse drivers, click on the Mouse drop-down list from Setup's Change System Settings dialog box. Then choose the desired mouse driver from the list. As with other hardware changes, Setup might prompt you to insert one of the Windows distribution disks. Insert the disk when requested. To use a driver that is supplied with your mouse, choose the option labeled Other mouse (requires disk from OEM). When prompted to do so, insert the disk containing the mouse drivers that came with your mouse.

One point to note is that some mouse utilities such as genSoft Development Corporation's program Whiskers for Windows are not installed through Setup, even though they replace any other Windows mouse driver you might be using. These utilities come with their own installation and setup programs. Run the installation program to install the new driver and utility.

For a more detailed discussion of mice and other input devices, refer to Chapter 10, "Input Devices: Keyboards and Mice."

II

Optimizing Windows

Selecting a New Network Driver

One additional change you can make to your Windows environment through Setup is to change the network driver that Windows uses. This is necessary when you add a network to your system or change from one network to another.

To change network drivers, click on the Network drop-down list and choose the appropriate network. If you are adding a network that is not listed, choose the option labeled Other network (requires disk from OEM). After you have installed your new network driver, you will find additional network configuration options by choosing the Network icon in the Control Panel.

Your network software probably will require settings in CONFIG.SYS or AUTOEXEC.BAT to start the network prior to starting Windows. Consult your network manuals or ask your network administrator for help if your system is not yet set up.

For a more detailed discussion of networks, refer to Part Five.

Changing Multiple Items from DOS-Based Setup

Each time you make a change to one item in Setup, Windows prompts you to either continue or restart Windows to make the change take effect. If you prefer to make all changes at once, run Setup from DOS. This configuration method enables you to change any combination of the four items listed in the previous sections, as well as other changes to your hardware configuration.

To run Setup from DOS, first exit from Windows. Then type **setup** at the DOS prompt to start DOS-based Setup. Although the screen is different from the one you see in Windows-based Setup, the two Setup modes function in much the same manner.

Setting Up Applications

Another change you can make to your Windows system with Windows-based Setup is to add applications to your Program Manager desktop. Setup enables you to add DOS and Windows application items to Program Manager groups with little intervention from you. Setup can install an application you specify, or can search your hard disk for applications to set up.

To set up applications, start Setup from within Windows. Then choose the Set Up Applications item from Setup's Options menu. The Setup Applications dialog box appears, as shown in figure 7.3.

To search your hard disk for one or more applications, click on the radio button labeled Search for applications, then click on OK. Setup displays a new dialog box that you can use to specify the drives to be searched (see fig. 7.4).

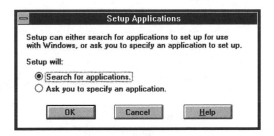

Figure 7.3
The Setup
Applications
dialog box.

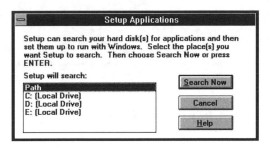

Figure 7.4
Specifying the disk
or directories to
search.

You can choose any combination of the disks listed in the dialog box. You also can choose the Path option to have Setup search all the directories on your system's path. The Path option is highlighted by default when the dialog box appears. To select a different option, simply click on it. To deselect an item, click on it while it is highlighted. When your selection is complete, choose **S**earch Now.

If Setup is not sure of a program's name (a program name might be duplicated between two different applications), Setup displays a dialog box similar to the one shown in figure 7.5. This dialog box prompts you to verify the program's name so that Setup can configure it properly.

Figure 7.5
Setup prompting
you to confirm an
application's
name.

After Setup's search is complete, it displays the results in the dialog box shown in figure 7.6. At the left side of the dialog box is a list of all the applications Setup located in its search. To add one or more of the applications to your Program Manager environment, choose them in the list and click on the **A**dd button. If you want to remove an item from the list at the right side of the dialog box, choose it and click on the Remove button. To add all the applications in the list to your Program Manager environment, click on the Add All button.

Figure 7.6
Selecting the applications to set up.

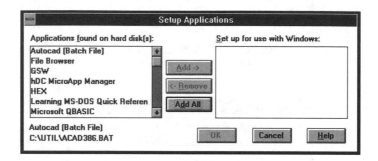

When you have finished your selections, click on OK to set up the applications. In the case of DOS applications, Setup creates a PIF for the application. Refer to Chapter 15, "Integrating Windows and DOS," for a detailed discussion of PIFs and how they are used.

If you want to set up only one application, click on the radio button labeled Ask you to specify an application in the first Setup Applications dialog box. Doing so displays the dialog box shown in figure 7.7.

Figure 7.7
Setting up a single application.

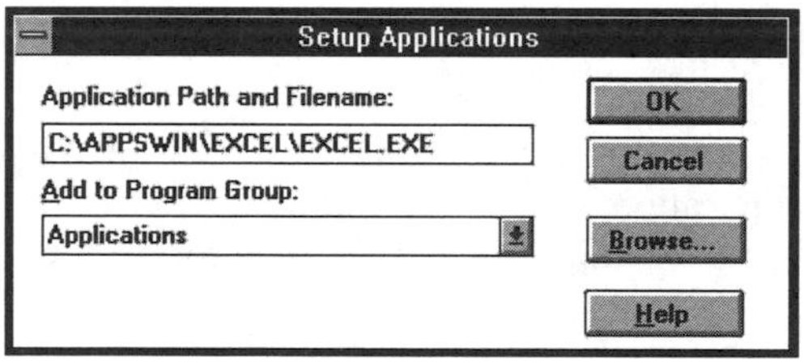

In the Application Path and Filename edit box, enter the drive, path, and file name for the application, such as C:\APPSWIN\EXCEL\EXCEL.EXE. If you prefer, you can choose Browse to browse through the file system for the program's file.

By default, Setup places the new program item in the Applications group. If an Applications group does not exist, Windows creates it. To select a different group, click on the Add to Program Group drop-down list box and select the group into which you want the new program item placed.

When your selections are complete, click on OK. Setup sets up the program in the group you specified. If the program is a DOS program, Setup creates a PIF for the program.

Adding or Removing Windows Components

You also can use Setup to add or remove Windows components from your workstation. If you want to delete the games, for example, you can use Setup to do so. If you installed only some of the Windows components when you installed Windows on your system, you can use Setup to add some of the items you did not originally install.

To add or remove Windows components, start Setup. Then, from Setup's Options menu, choose Add/Remove Windows Components. A dialog box appears, as shown in figure 7.8.

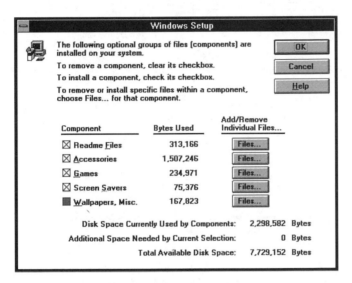

Figure 7.8
This Windows Setup dialog box enables you to add or remove Windows components.

The dialog box organizes the Windows components into different categories and shows you which items currently are installed on the system. If all the items for a particular category already are installed, the component's check box is checked. If none of the component's files are installed, its check box is clear. If only some of the component's files are installed, the check box is shaded.

To add all the files for a particular component, check its check box. To remove all the files for a particular component, clear its check box. If you want to add or remove individual files for a component, click on the Files button beside the appropriate component. Setup displays another dialog box, like the one shown in figure 7.9, in which you can select or remove specific files.

As you make selections to add and remove components, the status lines at the bottom of the Windows Setup dialog box change to indicate how much disk space will be required to install the new items or how much space will be freed by removing items. This is a good gauge to help you decide which items to add or remove if free disk space becomes low.

Figure 7.9
This dialog box
enables you to
add or remove
specific files for a
component.

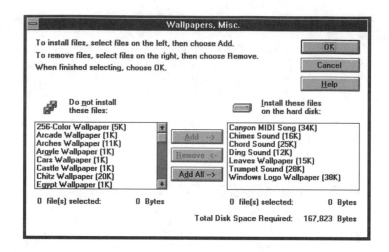

When you have finished making your changes, click on OK. Setup then adds or removes items as you have specified. If you are adding components, Setup prompts you to insert one or more of the Windows distribution disks.

Modifying Configuration Files

Much of the fine-tuning you perform for Windows requires that you directly edit some of your system's configuration files. These files include the system files CONFIG.SYS and AUTOEXEC.BAT, as well as the Windows initialization files WIN.INI and SYSTEM.INI. Although you can edit these files from DOS by using the EDIT program or some other text editor, you probably will find it easier to use a Windows program to edit the files. One of the programs you can use is the System Editor, or SysEdit.

Using the System Editor

SysEdit is located in the \WINDOWS\SYSTEM directory. Its executable file is SYSEDIT.EXE. To run SysEdit, open Program Manager's File menu and choose Run. Then type **sysedit** in the edit box and click on OK. If you prefer, you can add SysEdit to one of your program groups and run it by double-clicking on its icon. SysEdit resembles figure 7.10.

SysEdit consists of a main program window where you can see child or document windows. Each document window displays one of your system's configuration files. SysEdit displays windows for AUTOEXEC.BAT, CONFIG.SYS, WIN.INI, and SYSTEM.INI.

When you need to make changes to one of these files, run SysEdit and select the appropriate window. Make the changes to the file in the window. Then, with the same window active, open SysEdit's File menu and choose Save. To edit a different file, switch to its window and repeat the same process. The important point to note is that choosing File, Save does not save all four of the files. It saves only the file in the active window.

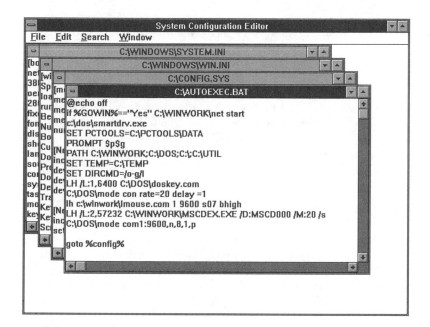

Figure 7.10
Configuration files
loaded in SysEdit.

Optimizing Windows

Tip

If you are running Windows for Workgroups, SysEdit enables you to edit other files in addition to the four files supported by the Windows 3.1 version of SysEdit. These additional files include SCHDPLUS.INI, MSMAIL.INI, and PROTOCOL.INI.

Editing Configuration Files in Notepad

If you prefer not to use SysEdit, or if you need to edit one of Windows' other initialization files, you can use Notepad to do so. Like SysEdit, Notepad is an ASCII text editor (ASCII files are unformatted alphanumeric files).

To edit one of your system's configuration files with Notepad, simply start Notepad and load into it the file you want to change. Make the changes, then use the Save command in Notepad's File menu to save the changes.

Making Changes Take Effect

Simply making changes to your system or Windows configuration files does not make the change take effect. When you make changes to AUTOEXEC.BAT and CONFIG.SYS, you must reboot the system to make the changes effective. When you make changes to the Windows INI files, you must restart Windows to make the changes take effect (with a few exceptions).

To restart Windows, simply exit from Windows, then type **win** again at the DOS prompt to restart it. If you are using Plug In to enhance Program Manager (see Chapter 6), open Program Manager's File menu, then choose Exit Windows. In the Plug-In/Exit Windows dialog box, choose the Restart Windows radio button, then click on OK.

To reboot your system, first exit from Windows to ensure that you do not lose any data. Then, press Ctrl+Alt+Del at the DOS prompt to reboot. You also can press your computer's Reset button to reboot the system. Using Ctrl+Alt+Del is faster, however, because it does not cause the system to run through its diagnostic routines.

Examining the AUTOEXEC.BAT File

The most important change you can make to AUTOEXEC.BAT to improve your system's performance is to limit the number of TSRs (terminate-and-stay-resident programs) and device drivers that are started by AUTOEXEC.BAT. Limiting these to a minimum makes more memory available to Windows, and particularly improves the performance of DOS applications you run under Windows.

The following list summarizes the main changes you might want to consider making to your system's AUTOEXEC.BAT file:

✔ **Reduce TSRs.** If you have DOS TSRs loaded by AUTOEXEC.BAT and you seldom use those TSRs, remove them from AUTOEXEC.BAT. Instead, create a batch file that loads the TSRs. Whenever you want to use these TSRs, open a DOS session in Windows by double-clicking on the MS-DOS Prompt icon in the Main program group. Then execute your TSR batch file. This prevents the TSRs from being duplicated in the environments of each of the DOS programs you run under Windows.

✔ **Combine a TSR with a program.** If you run any DOS programs that require a particular TSR, you also can remove the TSR from your AUTOEXEC.BAT file. Create a batch file that first loads the TSR, then loads the program. Then, create a program item for this batch file in Windows. Whenever you need to run the program, simply select its icon. A DOS session is created, the TSR is loaded, and then the program starts. This prevents the TSR from being duplicated for other DOS programs you run under Windows.

✔ **Use WINSTART.BAT.** If you use a TSR that is specifically for Windows or for a Windows program, you may be able to move it from AUTOEXEC.BAT to WINSTART.BAT. When you start Windows in 386 Enhanced mode, Windows executes the commands contained in WINSTART.BAT. By moving your Windows

TSRs to WINSTART.BAT, you prevent them from being loaded until you start Windows. This makes more memory available to the DOS environment before you start Windows.

✔ **Eliminate a mouse driver.** If you do not use the mouse with DOS applications, and you currently have a mouse driver installed by AUTOEXEC.BAT, you can eliminate the mouse driver from your AUTOEXEC.BAT file.

✔ **Start Windows automatically.** If you want Windows to start automatically when you turn on your computer, add a new line to the end of the AUTOEXEC.BAT file that contains only the WIN command (the WIN command must be the last line of the file).

Exploring the CONFIG.SYS File

Some of the most common changes you can make to your CONFIG.SYS file to make Windows perform better are identical to changes you make to AUTOEXEC.BAT. Primarily, these changes include eliminating as many device drivers and TSRs from memory as possible, optimizing some standard CONFIG.SYS settings, changing your DOS environment size, and adding a STACKS= setting.

Reduce TSRs and Device Drivers

You should keep the number of drivers and TSRs loaded by CONFIG.SYS to a minimum to make the most memory possible available to the system and to Windows. If you have a mouse driver loaded by CONFIG.SYS, for example, and you do not use a mouse in the DOS applications you run under Windows, remove the mouse driver from CONFIG.SYS. If you use the mouse in DOS applications that you run outside of Windows, and the mouse driver includes a COM or EXE version, start the driver when you need to use the DOS program by typing the driver's executable file name (such as MOUSE for MOUSE.COM).

BUFFERS and FILES

Two settings in CONFIG.SYS help control, at least to a small extent, your hard disk's performance. The BUFFERS= setting sets aside a certain number of memory buffers for disk I/O. *Buffers are blocks of memory set aside for moving information between the disk and memory.* If you are using a disk cache such as SmartDrive, use a maximum setting of 10 for BUFFERS=. If you are not using a disk cache, set BUFFERS=20. Increasing the setting beyond that point can improve performance (only if you are not using a cache), but will use up some of your system's conventional memory. In general, you should use a cache such as SmartDrive and set BUFFERS=10.

The FILES= setting controls the number of files that can be open at one time. The optimum setting for a non-networked Windows system is 30. If your workstation is running on a network, or you work with a very large number of programs at once, you might need to increase the FILES= setting. A higher FILES= setting uses a small amount of conventional memory.

DOS Environment Size

Another change you might want to make in CONFIG.SYS, particularly if you use few or no DOS programs, is to minimize your DOS environment size. Global settings such as BUFFERS, FILES, PATH, and others are stored in the DOS environment space.

The /E switch is used with the SHELL command to specify the DOS environment size. If you do not specify an environment size with the SHELL command in CONFIG.SYS, the default environment size is 256 bytes. The following example of the SHELL command specifies an environment size of 1,024 bytes (1 KB):

```
SHELL=C:\DOS\COMMAND.COM /P /E:1024
```

The COMMAND.COM entry specifies the command interpreter, and the /P switch places COMMAND.COM permanently in memory. Both are required (it is assumed that COMMAND.COM is in a directory called \DOS on your system). The /E switch in this example specifies an environment size of 1,024 bytes. If you have a larger setting, or simply want to specify a small setting, change the SHELL= line accordingly. To specify an environment size of 384 bytes, for example, use the following line:

```
SHELL=C:\DOS\COMMAND.COM /P /E:384
```

Generally, the only reason to specify a SHELL= statement in CONFIG.SYS is to change the environment size. If you want to use the minimal default 256-byte environment, omit the SHELL= setting from CONFIG.SYS altogether.

Other Changes

There are a handful of other settings you might want to modify in CONFIG.SYS. Changing these settings requires an understanding of your system's memory and disk cache. These settings are discussed in Chapters 9, "Optimizing Memory," and 11, "Optimizing Data Storage Space."

Understanding Windows Initialization Files

Just as DOS has its initialization files CONFIG.SYS and AUTOEXEC.BAT, Windows also uses initialization files. Windows initialization files generally are referred to as INI files because of their file extensions. The primary INI files on a typical Windows 3.1 system are WIN.INI, SYSTEM.INI, PROGMAN.INI, CONTROL.INI, and WINFILE.INI. Modifying these files can be an important part of fine-tuning Windows' performance.

INI files are ASCII files, meaning that they contain only printable alphanumeric characters. Generally, INI files contain only letters and numbers, with a few punctuation marks and other special characters, such as square brackets [ ], commas, and semicolons.

A Windows INI file is divided into sections, with each section containing a certain number of settings that apply to a particular option or category of options. Each section has a section header as the first line of the section, with the section name contained in square brackets, as in the following example:

```
[windows]
```

Settings in each section usually consist of a setting name followed by an equal sign (=), which is then followed by the value of the setting. The following is an example:

```
[386Enh]
FileSysChange=Off
```

The value of a setting depends on the type of setting. Settings can be alphanumeric, numeric, or Boolean. *Boolean settings* are essentially toggle settings that have an On or Off value. In addition to On and Off, however, Boolean settings also can be set to 1 or 0, or True or False. A 1 or True represents On, and a 0 or False represents Off.

Most changes you can make to your Windows environment are accomplished through the Control Panel or other Windows utilities. Occasionally, however, you must directly edit an INI file to make certain changes. You can edit an INI file in Notepad, or use SysEdit, which was discussed earlier.

Understanding the WIN.INI File

The first of the Windows INI files is WIN.INI. The WIN.INI file contains settings that control Windows at an operating level. In other words, WIN.INI primarily controls the way Windows appears and interacts with the user. Typical settings in WIN.INI define the fonts that are installed, the colors used for the desktop, communication port settings, document and program file associations, and so on. Figure 7.11 shows a portion of WIN.INI displayed by SysEdit.

By default, WIN.INI contains the following sections:

✔ `[windows]`. Contains entries that control the mouse, keyboard, and sound as well as the programs that Windows recognizes and loads automatically. Most of these settings can be modified from the Control Panel; those that cannot are entries that control, recognize, or load programs.

Figure 7.11

A portion of
WIN.INI displayed
in SysEdit.

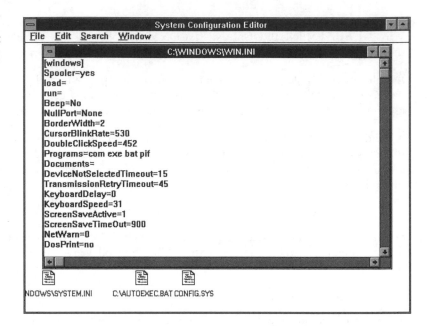

✔ [Desktop]. Includes the current wallpaper used for Windows' background and other entries that control spacing of icons and visual attributes of the Windows interface. It is easiest to change these settings through the Desktop icon in the Control Panel.

✔ [Extensions]. Lists all the file extensions that Windows recognizes as being associated with specific applications. For example, one entry tells Windows to associate TXT file extensions with the Notepad application. When you install a new application, it might alter this section to include its file types.

✔ [intl]. Specifies the way items are displayed according to the country setting you choose. This section controls currency, time, date, and other country-specific settings. These are mostly controlled by the International icon in the Control Panel.

✔ [ports]. Lists all the I/O ports that are available on your computer system. If you include an entry in the form of FILENAME.PRN=, the file name you enter for FILENAME.PRN is found in the selection of ports in the <u>C</u>onfigure menu when you set up a printer. If you configure a printer using that name, print output is redirected to the file.

✔ [fonts]. Lists the screen font files that are loaded by Windows. If you add new font files to the system, this entry can be used to load the new files automatically. Use the Fonts dialog box in the Control Panel to add a new font.

✔ [fontsubstitutes]. Contains a list of fonts that are recognized by Windows as being interchangeable.

✔ [TrueType]. Specifies options that determine how TrueType fonts are used and displayed.

✔ [mci extensions]. Contains settings that associate file types with multimedia devices.

✔ [networks]. Defines various network settings and previous network connections.

✔ [embedding]. Specifies client/server associations for OLE (object linking and embedding).

✔ [Windows Help]. Includes settings that determine colors used to display Help text, as well as the size and position of Help windows and dialog boxes.

✔ [sounds]. Associates a sound file with a Windows system event, such as the TADA.WAV sound with Windows start-up. Note that systems without a sound card cannot play sounds.

✔ [PrinterPorts]. Lists the printers and ports you have installed for Windows. Each entry includes a time-out setting, a port setting, and other printer-specific settings for each printer. The default values for each of the settings are located in the [windows] section.

✔ [devices]. Nearly identical to the [PrinterPorts] section, this section is used only by Windows 2.*x* applications. If you have entries for a printer in both [PrinterPorts] and [devices], make sure that the entries for the printer are the same.

✔ [programs]. Specifies additional paths that Windows searches, in addition to the system path, to locate program files when you open an associated document file.

✔ [colors]. Defines colors used to display the Windows screen interface. These settings can control the color of the menu border, menu bar, and other desktop graphics.

An explanation of the most common settings for WIN.INI is contained in the file WININI.WRI, which Setup places in your Windows directory during installation. The WININI.WRI file contains explanations of the settings as well as examples that show you how to change them.

Editing WIN.INI Settings

The following list summarizes the most common settings in WIN.INI that you must edit manually if you want to implement or change them:

✔ DoubleClickHeight=*number*
  DoubleClickWidth=*number*

These settings specify the height and width (in pixels) that the mouse can move between the two clicks of a double-click. If the mouse moves more than the specified distance during the event, the clicks are recognized as single clicks. The default for both settings is 4. Raise this setting if you have problems keeping the mouse still during a double-click. Here's an example:

    DoubleClickWidth=10

This setting is found in the [windows] section.

✔ MenuDropAlignment=*Boolean*

Specifies how drop-down menus are aligned with their menu names. If the setting is 0 (the default), the menu is left-aligned. If the setting is 1, the menus are right-aligned. Here's an example:

    MenuDropAlignment=1

This setting is found in the [windows] section.

✔ NullPort=*string*

Specifies the name used for the null printer port entry that appears in the Printers Connect dialog box in the Control Panel. This name appears beside printers that are installed but not connected to any port. Here's an example:

    NullPort=No Port Specified

This setting is found in the [windows] section.

✔ IconTitleFaceName=*font name*

Specifies the font used to display titles under icons. The default is MS Sans Serif. If you change the setting, use a TrueType font for best results. Here's an example:

    IconTitleFaceName=Arial

This setting is found in the [desktop] section.

✔ IconTitleSize=*integer*

Specifies the size of the font used to display icon titles. The default is 8. Here's an example:

    IconTitleSize=12

This setting is found in the [desktop] section.

✔ IconVerticalSpacing=*integer*

Specifies the distance in pixels between icons. Here's an example:

    IconVerticalSpacing=75

This setting is found in the [desktop] section.

✔ JumpColor=*red green blue*

Specifies the color for text in a Help file that, when selected, causes Help to jump to the Help page that is associated with the jump word. Each of the three values is a number from 0 to 255, specifying increasing amounts of the associated color. Here's an example for an aqua color (equal parts blue and green, with no red):

    JumpColor=0 128 128

This setting is found in the [Windows Help] section.

✔ PopupColor=*red green blue*

Specifies the color for text in a Help file that, when selected, displays a pop-up definition of the colored term or word. Here's an example for purple (equal parts blue and red, no green):

    PopupColor=128 0 128

✔ This setting is found in the [Windows Help] section.

If you want a complete list of all the possible settings in the WIN.INI file, you can purchase the Windows Resource Kit from Microsoft. The kit includes full documentation of all INI settings. To order the Windows Resource Kit, contact Microsoft at (800) 426-9400.

The SYSTEM.INI File

Although the WIN.INI file primarily controls Windows' appearance and its use of resources, SYSTEM.INI defines your system resources. Basically, SYSTEM.INI specifies settings that control Windows at the hardware level. Settings in SYSTEM.INI include many that define the hardware drivers Windows uses, others that control hardware configuration, and many others that control the way Windows performs in either Standard mode or 386 Enhanced mode. Figure 7.12 shows a portion of SYSTEM.INI in SysEdit.

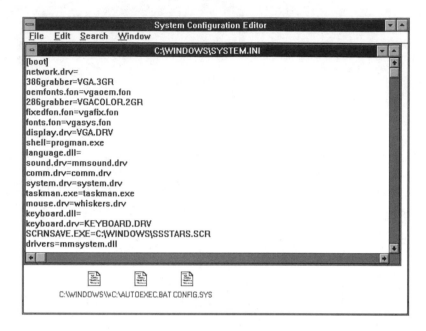

Figure 7.12
A portion of
SYSTEM.INI in
SysEdit.

As with WIN.INI, most of the settings in SYSTEM.INI are most easily set through options in the Control Panel. You can add or modify some settings, however, only by manually editing SYSTEM.INI.

Before you make changes to SYSTEM.INI, you should always make a backup copy of the file. Incorrect changes can sometimes prevent Windows from starting. If you experience such a problem, you can copy the backup file to replace the damaged SYSTEM.INI file and make it possible to restart Windows.

The following list describes the standard sections Setup creates in SYSTEM.INI during installation:

✔ [boot]. Contains a list of device drivers and program modules that Windows uses to configure itself each time it loads. All the entries in the [boot] section are required; do not delete any of these entries.

✔ [boot.description]. Contains a list of the devices you can change when using the Windows Setup program. Whereas the [boot] section contains the names of actual driver files, [boot.description] contains the description that is associated with each driver. Changing entries in this section can prevent you from changing drivers with Setup.

✔ [drivers]. Contains a list of alias names that are assigned to installable driver files. For example, the midimapper and timer drivers are associated in [drivers] with MIDIMAP.DRV and TIMER.DRV, respectively.

✔ [keyboard]. Contains configuration information about the keyboard, such as entries to identify nonstandard keyboards and different keyboard configurations. Do not change anything in this section; instead, make your changes through the Keyboard dialog box by choosing the Keyboard icon in the Control Panel.

✔ [mci]. Contains a list of Multimedia Command Interface (MCI) device drivers. As with the [drivers] section, lists in [mci] associate alias names with driver files.

✔ [NonWindowsApp]. Contains setup information that is used by DOS applications when you run them in Windows (the location of the application swap disk is a good example). Most of these settings refer to either memory concerns or features used for 386 Enhanced mode.

✔ [standard]. Contains a list of settings that Windows uses when running in Standard mode, including memory-management settings.

✔ [386Enh]. Contains a large number of settings that Windows uses when running in 386 Enhanced mode.

An explanation of the most common settings for SYSTEM.INI are contained in the file SYSINI.WRI, which Setup places in your Windows directory during installation. The SYSINI.WRI file contains explanations of the settings as well as examples that show you how to change them.

Editing SYSTEM.INI Settings

The following list summarizes the most common settings in SYSTEM.INI that must be edited manually to implement or change them.

✔ CachedFileHandles=*number*

Specifies the number of most recently used EXE and DLL files that can remain open at one time. The number can range from 2 to 12. The default is 12. Decrease this number if you have problems running Windows from a network server. Here's an example:

```
CachedFileHandles=2
```

This setting is found in the [boot] section.

✔ Shell=*filename*

Specifies the Windows program that Windows uses as your shell. The default is PROGMAN.EXE, which is Program Manager. If you want to use some other program, such as Excel, for example, specify it with this setting, as follows:

```
Shell=C:\APPSWIN\EXCEL\EXCEL.EXE
```

This setting is found in the [boot] section.

II

Optimizing Windows

✔ TaskMan.Exe=*filename*

Specifies the application that appears as the Task Manager when you double-click on the desktop or select S<u>w</u>itch To from a control menu. There is no entry by default; Windows uses TASKMAN.EXE. Here's an example:

```
TaskMan.exe=C:\APPSWIN\SIDEBAR\SIDEBAR.EXE
```

This setting is found in the [boot] section.

✔ CommandEnvSize=*bytes*

Specifies the environment size in bytes of DOS virtual machines (DOS sessions) that are created under Windows. This sets the environment size independently of the environment size that existed outside of Windows before Windows was started. Here's an example:

```
CommandEnvSize=1024
```

This setting is found in the [NonWindowsApp] section.

✔ MouseInDosBox=*Boolean*

Determines whether the mouse is available in DOS program windows. The default is 1 (on) if a mouse driver that supports the mouse in a DOS box under Windows is started before Windows is started. Here's an example:

```
MouseInDosBox=0
```

This setting is found in the [NonWindowsApp] section.

✔ ScreenLines=*integer*

Specifies the number of screen lines displayed for a DOS program. The default is 25. Using a higher number, such as 50, provides more lines. Note that many applications override this setting (it has no effect on such applications). Here's an example:

```
ScreenLines=50
```

This setting is found in the [NonWindowsApp] section.

✔ DOSPromptExitInstruc=*Boolean*

If the setting is On, a message appears explaining how to return to Windows when you open a DOS session under Windows. Turning this setting off disables this message. Here's an example:

```
DOSPromptExitInstruc=Off
```

This setting is found in the [386Enh] section.

✔ `FileSysChange=Boolean`

Determines whether File Manager receives notification when a DOS application creates, renames, or deletes a file. In general, you should leave this setting off for best performance in File Manager, as follows:

    FileSysChange=Off

This setting is found in the [386Enh] section.

✔ `MessageBackColor=VGA color value`

Specifies the background color for message screens, such as the message screen that appears when you press Ctrl+Alt+Del in Windows. The default value of 1 specifies a blue background. Use a base-16 number from 0 (black) through F (white) to specify one of the standard 16 VGA colors (note: valid color values are the numbers 0 through 9, and the letters A through F). Example:

    MessageBackColor=0

This setting is found in the [386Enh] section.

✔ `MessageTextColor=VGA color value`

Specifies the color of text that appears on message screens, such as the one that appears when you press Ctrl+Alt+Del in Windows. The default is F, for white. Enter a base-16 number from 0 to F to specify a color. Example:

    MessageTextColor=2

This setting is found in the [386Enh] section.

A number of SYSTEM.INI settings must be edited manually. Over 20 settings, for example, are associated with the system's COM ports. For a complete list of these settings, consult SYSTEM.INI or the Microsoft Windows Resource Kit.

The PROGMAN.INI File

Like many Windows programs, Program Manager uses an INI file to store its operating settings. The Program Manager INI file is PROGMAN.INI, and is located in the Windows directory. Figure 7.13 shows PROGMAN.INI loaded into Notepad for editing.

The settings in the PROGMAN.INI file control the size and position of Program Manager's window, store some of its operating options, specify the name of the Startup group, define the groups that Program Manager displays, and also can be used to set restrictions on Program Manager's features.

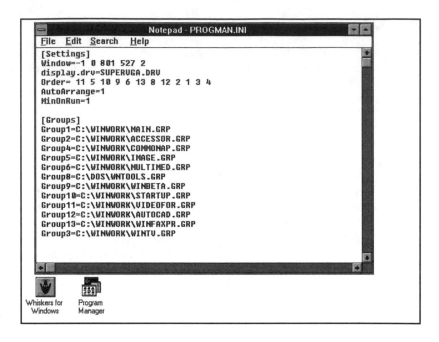

The following sections can appear in PROGMAN.INI:

✔ [settings]. Contains settings that define the position and size of Program Manager's window, set Program Manager options, and define the name of the Startup group.

✔ [groups]. Lists the groups that Program Manager displays. As you add and delete groups, their entries are added and deleted from this section.

✔ [restrictions]. This optional group can contain settings that limit or turn off features in Program Manager. For example, the [restrictions] sections can be used to disable the Exit Windows, Run, and Save Settings on Exit commands. Other settings can be added to control a user's ability to create and modify program groups and items.

Generally, the only settings that are worth changing manually are the Startup= setting and the settings in the [restrictions] section. These settings are discussed in Chapter 6, "Customizing Windows."

In addition to the INI files described previously, Windows also uses other INI files. Control Panel, for example, uses an INI file named CONTROL.INI, and File Manager uses an INI file name WINFILE.INI. Virtually all the settings in these two files are set through the Control Panel or through File Manager. It generally is not very useful to edit these files manually.

Using Multiple Configurations

It is sometimes useful or even necessary to run Windows under more than one hardware or software configuration. You may have your workstation connected to a network, but sometimes want to run Windows without the network drivers installed, for example. Or, perhaps you want to use two different environments: one in which your system loads a number of TSRs and device drivers at start-up, and another in which no TSRs or device drivers are loaded.

Although you can create and maintain separate CONFIG.SYS and AUTOEXEC.BAT files, and copy them into your root directory whenever you want to use a particular configuration, the new multiple boot feature in MS-DOS 6 is a much better alternative.

Using DOS 6's Multiboot Feature

MS-DOS 6 includes a new feature that makes it simple to create multiple configurations and select a configuration from a menu at boot time. By adding a few commands to your CONFIG.SYS file, you can custom-tailor any number of different configurations from which to choose when the system boots.

Defining CONFIG.SYS Menu Blocks

You create multiple configurations with MS-DOS 6 by defining menu blocks in CONFIG.SYS. *Menu blocks* are very much like the sections in a Windows INI file. Each has a header enclosed in square brackets, with commands contained underneath.

The first menu block in CONFIG.SYS is the [menu] block. The [menu] block defines the menu items that will appear at boot, and also can be used to specify other options. The following settings can appear in the [menu] block:

✔ MENUITEM=*menu block name, description*

Specifies the name of a menu block and an optional description. The description appears in the menu. Example:

```
menuitem=NetWin, Start Network and Windows
```

✔ MENUDEFAULT=*menu block name,time*

Specifies which item in the menu will be highlighted by default. The optional *time* variable specifies the amount of time in seconds the system will wait for a menu option to be selected. If none is selected in that time, the system uses the default menu item. Example:

```
menudefault=NetWin,10
```

✔ MENUCOLOR=*text,background*

Specifies the text and background colors for the boot menu. The values range from 0 (black) through 15 (bright white). Example for white text on blue background:

```
menucolor=15,1
```

✔ SUBMENU=*menu block name, description*

Specifies the name and description for a submenu block. The submenu block then contains the name of additional menu items. When the menu item associated with the submenu is selected, DOS displays the items specified by the submenu block's menu-item commands.

✔ NUMLOCK=*On or Off*

Turns Num Lock on the keyboard on or off at boot.

In addition to using those commands, you also can use two more commands to tailor your menu system:

✔ INCLUDE=*menu block name*

Directs DOS to include the commands from another menu block when processing the current menu block. You can create a [common] block, for example, then *include* it in another block called [net]. When DOS processes the [net] block, it first executes all the statements in the [common] block (including any include statements, as well), then processes the remaining statements in the [net] block. You can specify multiple INCLUDE commands in a menu block.

✔ SET *environment variable=value*

This sets an environment variable equal to some value. Example:

```
SET GOWIN="Yes"
```

GOWIN is the variable name, and "Yes" is its value.

The INCLUDE command is important because it enables you to include multiple menu blocks at boot with a single menu selection. The SET command is important because it enables you to control which commands will be executed in AUTOEXEC.BAT based on your menu selection in CONFIG.SYS.

The following example CONFIG.SYS file provides two main menu items. Selecting the first menu starts the system without loading any network drivers or starting Windows. Selecting the second item in the main menu displays a submenu with the options to start the network only, or start the network and start Windows.

```
[menu]
menuitem=common, Do not start network or Windows
submenu=Maybe, Network and Windows options
menucolor=15,0
numlock=Off
menudefault=1,10

[common]
device=c:\dos\himem.sys
device=c:\dos\setver.exe

[Maybe]
menuitem=NetOnly, Start network only
menuitem=NetAndWin, Start network and Windows

[Net]
include=common
device=c:\winwork\protman.dos /i:c:\winwork
device=c:\winwork\workgrp.sys
device=c:\winwork\smcmac.dos
set STARTNET="Yes"

[NetAndWin]
include=Net
```

Note that in the [NetAndWin] block, only one INCLUDE statement is listed. When [NetAndWin] is processed, however, the statements in the [common] block and [Net] block will be executed. The [NetAndWin] block INCLUDEs [NetOnly], which then INCLUDEs [common].

If you examine the file closely, you will realize that selecting the NetAndWin item ("Start network and Windows") is virtually the same as selecting the Net item ("Start network only"). This is because the [NetAndWin] block does not contain any additional commands besides its one INCLUDE command. There is a significant point to selecting the NetAndWin item, however. MS-DOS stores in an environment variable called CONFIG the name of whichever menu item you select. You then can use the CONFIG variable to provide conditional execution of statements in the AUTOEXEC.BAT file. The next section explains how.

Conditional Execution in AUTOEXEC.BAT

The capability to execute commands conditionally in AUTOEXEC.BAT based on your boot-up menu selection is important because it enables you to do such things as start a network, start Windows, or execute other commands that are required by your menu selection, but which cannot be included in CONFIG.SYS. Two methods enable you to

II

Optimizing Windows

execute commands conditionally in AUTOEXEC.BAT based on menu selections from CONFIG.SYS: use of the CONFIG environment variable and use of other environment variables.

The following AUTOEXEC.BAT file illustrates both methods. It is based on the CONFIG.SYS sample file discussed in the previous section (note the REM statements that explain the pertinent lines):

```
@echo off
REM  In the next line, the NET START command is executed
REM  if the environment STARTNET was set to "Yes" in
REM  CONFIG.SYS.

if %STARTNET%=="Yes" C:\WINWORK\net start

REM  The following commands are always executed.

c:\dos\smartdrv.exe
PROMPT $p$g
PATH C:\WINWORK;C:\DOS;C:\;C:\UTIL
SET TEMP=C:\TEMP

REM  The following statement branches execution to the
REM  :Net_Win label if the CONFIG environment variable
REM  equals "NetAndWin" (if the Net_Win menu item was
REM  selected at boot). If CONFIG does not equal
REM  "NetAndWin", REM  execution branches to the :end
REM  label.

goto %config%

:NetAndWin
WIN
goto end

:end
```

If you review the previous CONFIG.SYS sample, you will note that the STARTNET variable was set to "Yes" in the [Net] section. Therefore, selecting either the [Net] or [NetAndWin] items will set the STARTNET variable to "Yes". This is because the commands in the [Net] section are executed when you select the [NetAndWin] item (because of the INCLUDE command in [NetAndWin]). When STARTNET is set to "Yes", the NET START command is executed in AUTOEXEC.BAT. If STARTNET has not been set to "Yes" (no network-related item was selecting from the boot menu), the NET START command is not executed.

Note also that if the [NetAndWin] item was selected from the boot menu, execution in AUTOEXEC.BAT will jump to the NetAndWin label and execute the WIN command.

Using Dual Video Displays

If you have an application that you run in Windows that can take advantage of dual displays (two video adapters and two monitors in the same system), or if you have a DOS program that can use two displays (such as AutoCAD), there are some special setup considerations for making the adapters work properly with Windows.

First, one of the two adapters must be a Monochrome Display Adapter (MDA). The second must be a VGA adapter or a similar adapter. You cannot have two MDA adapters in the system, and you cannot have two VGA adapters in the system. This is because the duplicate adapters would attempt to share the same memory space, causing a memory conflict.

Generally, Windows detects an MDA if it is installed. If you experience strange problems with your displays, try adding the DualDisplay= setting to SYSTEM.INI, as in the following example:

```
[386Enh]
DualDisplay=On
```

Although this configuration works on many systems, you should note that some VGA adapters (and other adapters) use the area of memory that normally is set aside for the MDA. Therefore, you might experience problems when you try to use dual display adapters in such a system.

II

Optimizing Windows

Chapter Snapshot

The graphical nature of the Windows environment makes video a primary component of your Windows system. In fact, the quality of the video subsystem is one of the most important factors of Windows performance and usability. If your video subsystem displays slowly or with poor quality, Windows will not be too usable. On the other hand, if your Windows video is adequately fast and of acceptable image quality, Windows becomes a worthwhile environment in which to work. For this reason, local bus video has become common in many PCs.

This chapter looks at your Windows video system and helps you optimize Windows performance by examining:

Optimizing your video system is one of the least expensive ways to run Windows faster and more efficiently. An accelerated video card or updated display driver, for example, can make more of a difference than additional RAM or a faster hard drive.

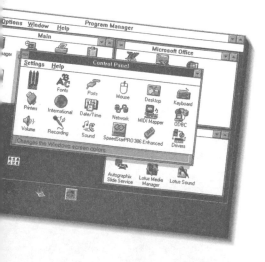

Enhancing Windows Video

The Windows video system actually is three different pieces of hardware and software working together, as shown in figure 8.1. The video card and display driver are responsible for video performance; the video card and monitor are responsible for the image quality of the video.

✓ **Video driver.** The video driver is the software component of the video system. Although the video driver often is overlooked, an optimized video driver can improve considerably the speed at which Windows runs. Always make sure you are using the latest available drivers.

Keep in touch with your video card manufacturer to ensure that you are using the latest available Windows drivers for your card. You will find that you often can increase the performance of Windows just by installing a new driver.

Several resources are available on CompuServe that you can use to get the latest drivers. The Graphics Vendors forum (Go GRAPHVEN) is the home of several video card manufacturers, such as ATi. In addition, the Microsoft Software Library (Go MICROSOFT) and WUGNET forum (Go WUGNET) both contain a library of driver updates.

✓ **Video adapter.** A video adapter can be either a separate 16-bit expansion card or an integrated part of the PC's motherboard. The display adapter is responsible for converting video instructions from the CPU into a form the monitor can understand and display.

✓ **Monitor.** The monitor receives the information from the video adapter and displays it.

Figure 8.1
The video
subsystem.

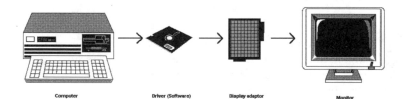

Computer   Driver (Software)   Display adaptor   Monitor

Exploring Display Standards

As you begin to look at video, you easily can become confused with the terminology used. Gaining an inside understanding of such terms as *resolution, color, scanning frequency, and noninterlaced mode* will enable you to maximize your video system and the way you work with Windows.

Optimizing Your PC's Video Resolution

When you work in Windows, one of the most important physical considerations is *resolution,* which refers to the number of pixels displayed on-screen. Table 8.1 lists the major video resolution standards for the PC. The popularity of VGA in the late 1980s and the advancements of Super VGA have made earlier video technologies obsolete for running Windows.

Table 8.1
Major PC Video Displays

Video Display	Pixel Resolution
Enhanced Graphics Adapter (EGA)	640×350
Hercules	720×348
Video Graphics Array (VGA)	640×480
Super VGA	800×600
Extended VGA	$1,024 \times 768$
Very High Resolution (VHR)	$1,280 \times 1,024$

Of these six resolutions, three are popular for running Windows: Standard VGA, Super VGA, and Enhanced VGA.

✔ **Standard VGA 640 × 480.** VGA (Video Graphics Array) was introduced by IBM in 1987 with the PS/2. VGA has a resolution of 640 pixels by 480 pixels and is the de facto minimum standard for running Windows. The problem with Standard VGA is the screen is not wide enough for many tasks you need to perform in Windows. Figures 8.2 and 8.3 illustrate the amount of space you have to work in a spreadsheet and the Windows desktop.

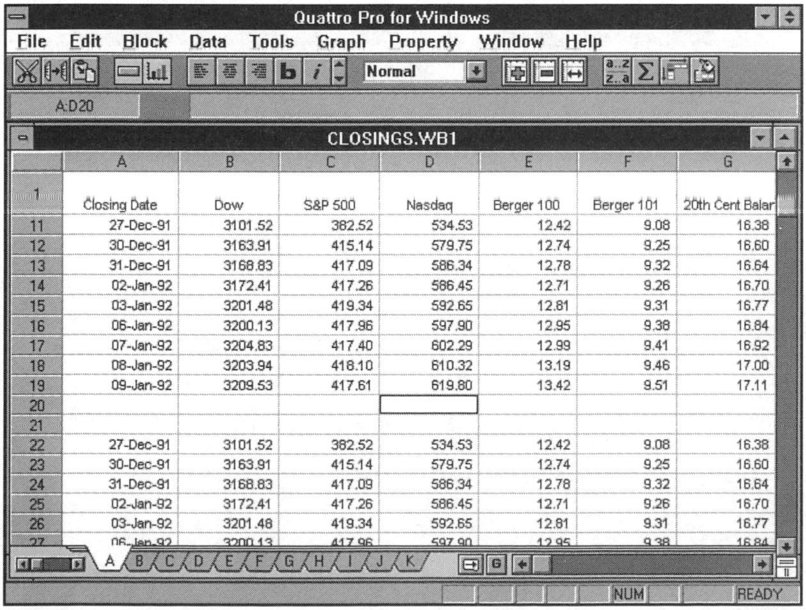

Figure 8.2
Working with a spreadsheet at 640 × 480.

II

Optimizing Windows

Figure 8.3
Working on the
Windows desktop
at 640 × 480.

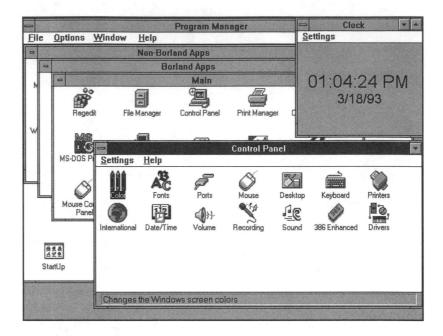

✔ **Super VGA 800 × 600.** Super VGA at 800 × 600 pixels is the preferred resolution for many Windows users. It enlarges the Windows desktop, but not so much that the text is hard to read (see figs. 8.4 and 8.5). 800 × 600 is ideal for 14- and 15-inch monitors.

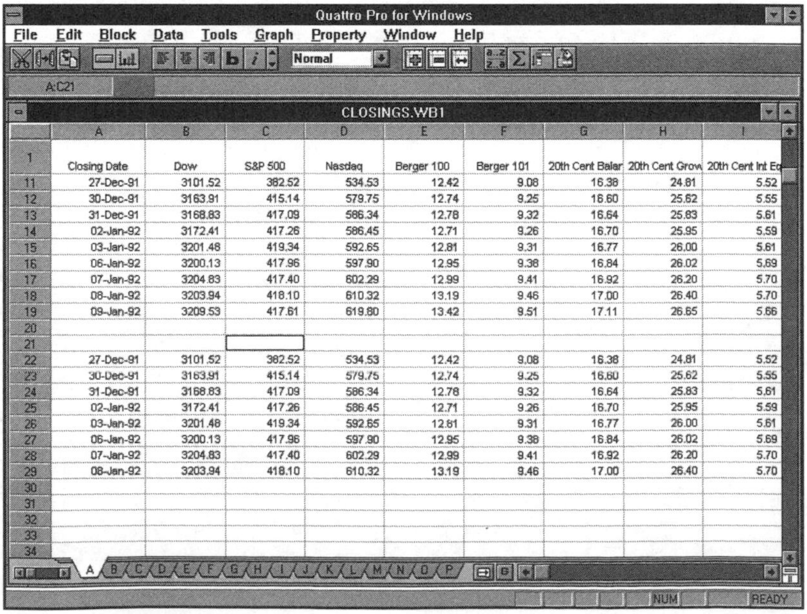

Figure 8.4
Working with a
spreadsheet at
800 × 600.

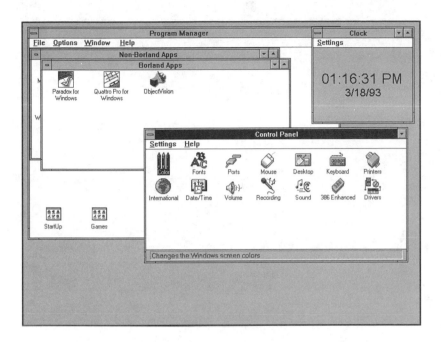

Figure 8.5
Working on the
Windows desktop
at 800 × 600.

✔ **Enhanced VGA 1,024 × 768.** Enhanced VGA at 1,024 × 768 gives you the most real estate for your desktop (see figs. 8.6 and 8.7). As the resolution gets higher, the objects on your desktop get smaller, which can make it difficult to read menus, dialog boxes, and on-screen text. To offset this, many display drivers also have a large font driver that enables you to substitute a larger set of fonts than normal. As a result, 1,024 × 768 with large fonts is an excellent environment in which to work (see figs. 8.8 and 8.9). This resolution is easiest to use on a 17-inch screen, although it is becoming more popular on 15-inch monitors.

If you plan on running windowed DOS applications under Windows, you probably will want to adjust the DOS font size depending on the resolution for which you are working. The following DOS font sizes are recommended for the given resolutions.

Font Size	Resolution
7 × 12	640 × 480
8 × 12	800 × 600
10 × 18	1,024 × 768

Figure 8.6
Working with a
spreadsheet at
1,024 × 768 small
font.

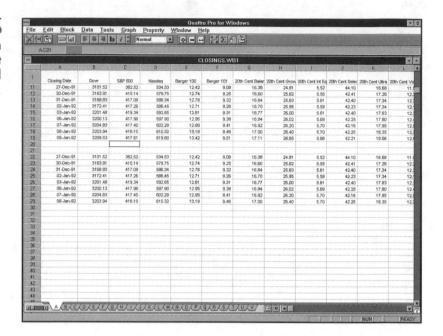

Figure 8.7
Working on the
Windows desktop
at 1,024 × 768
small font.

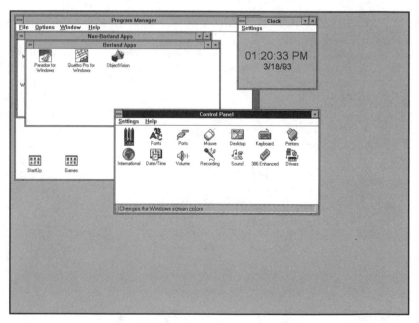

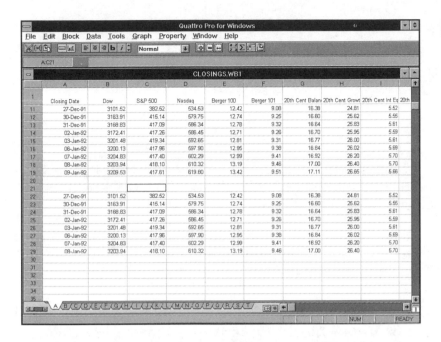

Figure 8.8
Working with a spreadsheet at 1,024 × 768 large font.

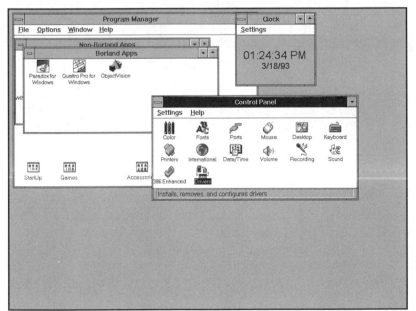

Figure 8.9
Working on the Windows desktop at 1,024 × 768 large font.

II

Optimizing Windows

Taking Advantage of Windows' Vibrant Colors

The world of Windows is becoming more colorful and is a far cry from the amber monitors of just a few years ago. Color might have been considered a luxury in the past, but now a colored display is a virtual necessity for Windows computing. Most people use 16- or 256-color mode. If you are working with high-resolution graphics or photographs, however, you need a true-color display of up to 16.8 million colors.

Most video cards today contain 256 KB, 512 KB, or 1 MB of video RAM, and thus are designed primarily to display up to 256 colors. For high-end layout and prepress separation, you will need to upgrade your video memory to at least 2 MB of video RAM.

The capability to display colors is based on the amount of memory of the video adapter, as shown in Table 8.2. Most high-quality video adapter cards enable you to add additional RAM to produce higher resolutions and colors.

Table 8.2
Amount of Video Memory Required To Display Colors

Resolution	4-bit (16 colors)	8-bit (256 colors)	24-bit (16.8 million colors)
640 × 480	154 KB	308 KB	922 KB
800 × 600	240 KB	480 KB	1.44 MB
1,024 × 768	394 KB	787 KB	2.4 MB
1,280 × 1,024	656 KB	1.32 MB	3.93 MB

Scanning Frequencies

Inexpensive VGA monitors available today are known as *fixed-frequency monitors*; they cannot display using frequencies other than the one for which they were designed. With the popularity of higher resolutions, however, the new standard is quickly becoming the multifrequency or multiscan monitor. A *multiscan monitor* can operate at more than one frequency. In practical terms, a multiscan monitor enables you to work in Windows at Super VGA and shell to a full-screen DOS mode automatically.

When configuring your video adapter card, be sure the frequency settings correspond to the limits of your multiscan monitor. If a video adapter outputs higher frequency rates than the monitor can handle, you could stress the internal video circuitry of your monitor and ultimately damage your monitor.

Video frequency is made up of two frequencies—horizontal and vertical scan rates. *Horizontal frequency* measures the length of time in kilohertz (KHz) that it takes to draw one horizontal line across the screen. *Vertical frequency* (also called *refresh rate*) measures how many times per second the monitor repaints the screen. The higher the number, the clearer the screen, because the screen is drawn more times per second.

A Note from the Author

A sure way to ruin your eyes and drive yourself crazy is to work with a monitor that has a low scan rate. Never compromise on monitor quality. Windows is a great test for seeing whether you can work with a particular monitor. If the dialog boxes and background are shaking, and you can see the entire screen shake when you look at it in your peripheral vision, find a better monitor.

Vertical frequency is the key factor in screen flicker. Your monitor flickers when the refresh rate is too low, which can cause considerable eye stress and headaches. VESA (Video Electronics Standards Association) has set minimum refresh rate standards for VGA at 72 Hz and SVGA at 70 Hz. Note that the higher the number, the faster the refresh rate.

A monitor must be capable of handling the frequencies sent to it by the video adapter, or the monitor can be damaged.

Windows in Noninterlaced and Interlaced Modes

Although you may be comfortable with the video settings you have configured for Windows, look closely at your screen. Does it jitter when you look out of the corner of your eye, or is there a noticeable shake when viewing dialog boxes? If so, you are probably using an interlaced monitor. An *interlaced* display repaints the screen by drawing every other line in one pass, then drawing the remaining lines in a second pass. Noninterlaced displays, however, paint the entire image in one pass, reducing (and generally eliminating) flicker.

As you select video components, try to get a video adapter and monitor capable of a noninterlaced display at higher resolutions (see fig. 8.10). The alternative is an interlaced display, which repaints the screen by drawing every other line on the screen (lines 1, 3, 5, 7, 9, and so on) and then returning to the top to draw the empty lines (lines 2, 4, 6, 8, 10, and so on). An interlaced system is cheaper, but it produces a flickered image that is quite noticeable to the human eye. Over time, it can cause eye strain and headaches.

Figure 8.10
Noninterlaced
displays paint the
image in one
pass; interlaced
displays require
two passes to
complete the
image.

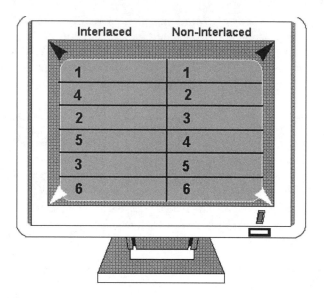

Understanding Physical Considerations for Windows Monitors

The quality of your Windows display also is affected by the size of the monitor and the monitor's dot pitch. These physical elements are two more variables you need to consider when optimizing your Windows video system.

Dot Pitch

Dot pitch refers to the size of the monitor's pixels displayed on-screen. Each pixel consists of a group of three dots—red, green, and blue. The spacing of the holes between these dots determines the dot pitch. Figure 8.11 shows how dot pitch is measured.

For 14- and 15-inch monitors, a dot pitch of .28 mm or smaller is a healthy eye-saving characteristic; quality 17-inch and larger monitors use a .31 or smaller dot pitch. Note that the smaller the number, the sharper the screen.

The dot pitch of your monitor plays an important part in how well you can view and manipulate objects on your Windows desktop. If you have a 14-inch monitor with a .31 or higher dot pitch, for example, you will have a harder time reading text and working with Windows icons than on a .28 dot pitch (or lower) monitor.

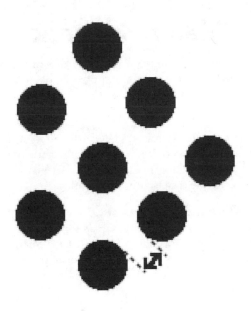

Figure 8.11
Dot pitch indicates
the distance
between holes in
the grid mask.

Monitor Size

Monitor size usually is a personal choice. Good 14-inch monitors, which are cheap and plentiful, are fine for most Windows work. The ideal Windows monitor, however, is a 17-inch monitor. These monitors are much more expensive, but are required if you plan to do page layout or technical drawing. Another popular size is the 15-inch monitor. The size of your monitor is directly related to the resolution in which you can run comfortably. A 14-inch monitor is ideal for 640 × 480, sufficient for 800 × 600, but probably too small for most people to run 1,024 × 768. A 15-inch monitor is ideal for 800 × 600 and marginally acceptable at 1,024 × 768.

The way in which monitors are measured can be confusing. The actual size (14, 15, 17 inches, for example) refers to the diagonal dimensions of the cathode ray tube (CRT) inside the monitor, not the actual size of the screen. In general, the actual screen size can be up to .5–2.0 inches smaller than the number given.

Even after you determine the actual size of the screen, you still need to consider the black borders that surround the display image, taking up valuable display space. Consider a flat-screen monitor to minimize black borders. The screen on a flat-screen monitor is not perfectly flat (it's actually slightly cylindrical), but it provides less distortion and reduces the amount of black matte around the display area.

II

Optimizing Windows

Opening the Video Bottleneck

The video adapter market is rapidly changing, primarily because of Windows. Windows places demands on the video subsystem of a computer that the older VGA video cards cannot handle. New types of graphics acceleration cards have been developed to manage Windows video. Their purposes differ considerably:

✔ **Dumb frame buffer cards.** Standard VGA cards and many low-priced Super VGA cards are often referred to as *dumb frame buffers* because they cannot do anything by themselves. They simply manage the display memory; the CPU is responsible for moving all the data to the frame buffer.

✔ **Coprocessed video cards.** A coprocessor video card is much faster than a frame buffer card because it is designed to offload some of the work of the CPU. A coprocessor card receives raw information from the CPU, such as bit-block transfers (BitBlts), that it processes to generate an image. A coprocessor card is programmable, which makes it flexible in a variety of environments. This flexibility, however, is expensive.

✔ **Accelerated video card.** An accelerated video card is similar to a coprocessor card except an accelerated card is hard-coded to perform a specific task—speed up Windows graphics. Accelerated cards are less expensive than coprocessor cards because they are not programmable. Nevertheless, they perform as well as or better than coprocessor boards in Windows. The downside is that because they are optimized for Windows, they often perform worse than frame buffer cards in DOS applications.

Accelerated cards are much more popular today than coprocessor cards. Among the leaders are the ATI Graphics Pro, Diamond Stealth, and Fahrenheit 1280. If you plan to do much serious work in Windows, the addition of an accelerated video card makes a tremendous difference in Windows' video performance.

✔ **Local bus cards.** A local bus card currently is the state-of-the-art card and is based on 32-bit local bus technology. A local bus is integrated into the motherboard and connected to the CPU, essentially providing a direct connection between the display adapter and the CPU, bypassing the bus. Because it avoids the 16-bit bottleneck of the expansion bus (see fig. 8.12), a local bus video card can run at 32-bit speed.

Many local bus cards combine an accelerated chipset with the local bus to gain significant improvements in video speed. The ATI Graphics Ultra VLB with the Mach32 chipset is among the industry leaders in local bus video. Local bus is an expensive investment if you already have a system; to take advantage of local bus technology, you must get a new local bus computer system.

The Video Bottleneck

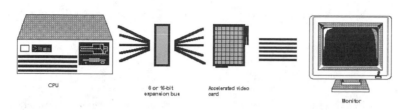

CPU   8 or 16-bit   Accelerated video   Monitor
expansion bus   card

Figure 8.12
The video bottleneck: too much information trying to fit into too small a door.

II

Optimizing Windows

In the past, local bus technology was plagued by the lack of a standard. Many proprietary local bus implementations were available, but you always had to risk buying into the wrong system. Although standards still are changing, there are two well-defined local bus standards. The first is called VL-Bus (also called VESA local bus), a standard put forth by the Video Electronics Standards Association (VESA) committee. The second standard is known as the Peripheral Component Interconnect (PCI) bus.

VESA local bus is found in many 486-based systems, and PCI local bus is found in most Pentium-based systems (and a small selection of 486-based systems). Both bus types offer good performance, but the PCI architecture does have some structural advantages over VESA and is better overall in terms of performance. The decision between buying VESA or PCI is really not very difficult; if you buy a 486-based system, it probably will use VESA local bus. If you buy a Pentium-based system, it probably will have a PCI local bus.

A second factor to consider in speeding up your video adapter is whether the video adapter memory is DRAM (dynamic RAM) or VRAM (video RAM). DRAM is used on most standard VGA cards; it can only read or write, but not both, at any given moment because of a single port. VRAM, however, provides a second port to enable concurrent reads and writes. VRAM chips are double the cost of DRAM chipsets, but they also are twice as fast.

Chapter Snapshot

Windows' use of your system's memory is one of the most important factors that affects your system's performance under Windows. Windows uses the system's memory in unique ways, and understanding how Windows uses memory will help you make Windows perform better.

This chapter explains the different types of memory and how Windows uses them, including the following topics:

The first requirement for understanding how Windows uses memory is to understand the types of memory in your system.

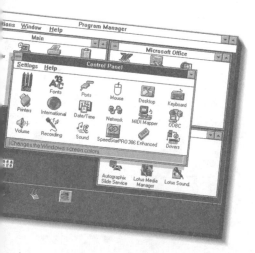

9

CHAPTER

Optimizing Memory

Your system does not have one large block of memory, all the same type and all accessed by Windows and by DOS in the same way. For many reasons this is unfortunate, because it makes for cumbersome memory management by DOS and Windows. The memory structure used by today's PCs is virtually identical to the structure used by the original IBM PC, now over a decade removed.

Understanding the different types of memory in your PC, however, requires that you have a minimal understanding of such things as memory addresses.

Understanding Memory

Computers need a means of storing information such as programs and data internally so they can use that information. The system's memory provides that storage.

Data is stored in a computer's memory using bits. Bits technically are high or low voltages, but to make them understandable, think of a bit this way: Imagine that inside the computer are thousands of small *memory cells,* each one being a bit. In each cell you can store one of two things: a one or a zero.

Storing a one or a zero in a cell is not very useful for storing information. But, if you collect a certain number of bits together, you can use them in combination with one another to represent information. That's where bytes come into the picture.

Data is generally organized into bytes. A *byte* is a collection of eight bits. The byte does nothing except store a number in binary form (a series of data locations that store either a one or zero). The computer can recognize that number as representing all types of data, including program code, test, numbers, and any other type of data.

A byte is enough data space to hold one character, such as a letter or number. So, a byte really does not represent much storage space.

Bits, Bytes, Kilobytes, Megabytes, and Gigabytes

The relationship between bits, bytes, kilobytes, megabytes, and gigabytes is really very simple. They really are nothing but multiples of one another. You already have read that a bit is the smallest data unit, and that there are eight bits in a byte. To understand the rest, you just have to remember the number 1,024.

There are 1,024 bytes in one kilobyte, or 1 KB. So, 1,024 bytes = 1 KB. There are 1,024 kilobytes in one megabyte (1 MB), so 1,024 KB = 1 MB. There are 1,024 megabytes in one gigabyte (1 GB), so 1,024 MB = 1 GB. Gigabytes are a bit more than the average user has to deal with, so concentrate on megabytes. How many bytes are there in one megabyte? Just take 1,024 bytes per kilobyte times 1,024 kilobytes per megabyte (1,024×1,024), and you have the answer: 1,048,576 bytes in one megabyte. So, 1 MB of memory will hold the equivalent of just over one million characters.

Memory Addresses and Hexadecimal Numbers

Each memory location in a typical PC contains 1 byte. In a typical PC that has 8 MB of memory, there are over 8.3 million bytes. To make it possible for the computer to keep track of all of those memory locations, each one is assigned a memory address. Just as the street address of a house helps you locate the house, a *memory address* helps the computer locate a particular memory location. The computer stores and retrieves data in memory by the data's memory address.

It is no surprise that humans use a base-10 numbering system (based on 1s, 10s, 100s, and so on) in everyday life—most of us have 10 fingers on which to count. Computers do not have fingers, so they are much more adaptable to different numbering systems. In fact, PCs use base-16.

 For a more detailed discussion of hexidecimal numbers and memory addresses, refer to *Maximizing Windows 3.1,* from New Riders Publishing.

Whereas memory capacity is usually expressed in some multiple of bytes, memory addresses are usually expressed as hexadecimal numbers. Hexadecimal numbers are base-16 numbers. Base-10 numbers, which we deal with every day, can be made up of any combination of 10 numerals, 0 through 9. Hexadecimal numbers, however, are made up of combinations of as many as 16 different numerals. These numerals are:

$$0,1,2,3,4,5,6,7,8,9,A,B,C,D,E,F$$

In this number set, the letters A–F represent the decimal numbers 10–15. Each hexadecimal digit represents a four digit binary number. The hexadecimal digit 0h, for example, equals the binary number 0000, and the hexadecimal digit 9h equals 1001. Most of the addresses discussed in this chapter are above 640 KB, so 640 KB is a good example to use to illustrate hex values.

To understand how hexadecimal addresses work, step back and review how decimal base-10 numbering works. When you write the number 1,234 you are really writing $1\times10^3 + 2\times10^2 + 3\times10^1 + 4\times10^0$. The result is the table shown here:

1×10^3	1,000
2×10^2	200
3×10^1	30
4×10^0	4
Total	1,234

Each column in a number really tells you what power to raise the number to. For each column you must multiply the number by 10^{c-1}; c is the column number. For the third column in the preceding example, you raise 10 to the second power (10^2). You raise 10 to a certain power because 10 is the *base* for our numbering system.

A number in hexadecimal has a base of 16. In that environment each column is the number 16 raised to a certain power. The following table shows a typical hexadecimal number, 1,234, and its decimal equivalent:

Hexadecimal Number	Decimal Equivalent
1×16^3	4,096
2×16^2	512
3×16^1	48
4×16^0	4
Total	4,660

The value 640 KB is A0000 in hexadecimal; 20 binary digits are needed to express the value 640 KB. In a hexadecimal number, the first digit to the right represents 16^0, and the digits to the left represent 16^1, 16^2, 16^3, and so on. With A (which represents the value 10) in the fifth place, multiply 10×16^4 and you get 655,360, which is a value in bytes. Divide that by 1,024 bytes per kilobyte, and the result is 640 KB (655,360/1024=640), which is the *decimal,* or base-10 equivalent, of A0000.

Another common address is C8000. On many systems, C8000 is the starting address of the first free memory block in the UMA (upper memory area). The letter C represents the value 12, so the hex value C8000 can be converted as follows:

$$(12 \times 16^4) + (8 \times 16^3) = 819,200$$

$$819,200 / 1,024 = 800 \text{ KB}$$

Although an understanding of memory addresses is important if you want to manipulate your system's memory, most memory-management tasks do not require an extensive knowledge of the subject. The following section includes a memory map to help you equate hex memory addresses to their decimal equivalents.

Note that by convention, the last digit often is dropped from a hexadecimal memory address. C7FFF, for example, becomes simply C7FF. This is because the last digit is understood to be the same as the fourth digit.

Conventional Memory

The first type of memory that today's PCs have (and they all have this type) is called conventional memory. *Conventional memory* is the memory in your system that is mapped into the first megabyte of memory. In other words, conventional memory is the memory range between 0 KB and 1,024 KB—the first 1 MB of memory.

The block of memory addresses from 0 KB to 640 KB is called *system memory.* Often, the term conventional memory is used to describe only the first 640 KB of memory, although that is not fully correct. Conventional memory is the full first megabyte of memory from 0 KB to 1,024 KB.

The UMA

The upper portion of conventional memory from 640 KB to 1,024 KB is called the upper memory area, or UMA. Whereas programs run in the memory range below 640 KB, the memory in the UMA is generally reserved for the video display, the system's BIOS, and often for device drivers. Figure 9.1 shows a memory map of the UMA. Blocks of memory in the UMA are called upper memory blocks, or UMBs.

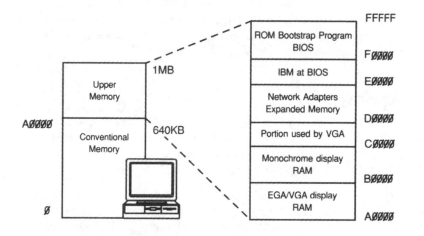

Figure 9.1
A memory map of the upper memory area.

The areas in the memory map that are designated for specific uses—such as the area between F0000 and FFFFF, which is designated for the BIOS—represent blocks of memory addresses that are allocated to the listed device or use. These devices are mapped into the address ranges listed, as explained in the next section.

ROM Shadowing

One of the functions for which the system uses the UMA is to map the BIOS. *BIOS* is an acronym for basic input/output system. The BIOS is a set of software program routines that perform very basic input/output functions to control video, disk access, and so on. In addition to the system BIOS, many devices such as hard disk controllers have their own onboard BIOS chips.

The system's BIOS is actually located in a read-only memory (ROM) chip contained on the computer's motherboard. To enable the system to reference code in the BIOS by a memory address, the system maps the BIOS into a range of memory locations in the UMA, usually between F0000 and FFFFF. This is called *ROM shadowing*. ROM shadowing also is performed for other devices that contain their own BIOS.

It is important to understand that the UMA does not have to be made up of physical memory locations in the first 1 MB of memory on the motherboard. Earlier systems had only 640 KB of memory in the system, so there was no physical memory above 640 KB. What ROM shadowing does is simply assign a range of addresses to a device such as the system BIOS or a BIOS on a hard disk controller.

When the system accesses the device by one of those addresses, the access might actually take place on the device, not in the computer's memory. So, you should think of the memory map shown in figure 9.1 as a map of *potential memory addresses,* not a map of physical memory.

RAM Shadowing

Reading from ROM is slower than reading from the system's RAM (random access memory). On today's systems that generally have a full 1 MB of conventional RAM physically located on the motherboard, it is possible to improve performance by copying a device's ROM into RAM. This is called *RAM shadowing.*

In RAM shadowing, the system copies a device's BIOS into the physical memory locations to which it has been mapped. For example, the system BIOS might be physically copied from the BIOS chip into physical memory locations F0000 through FFFFF. Or, the system's video BIOS may be copied from the BIOS chip on the video adapter to a range such as C0000 through C7FFF. Copying the device's BIOS to RAM in this way can significantly improve the system's performance.

Device Drivers and the UMA

Even with the system's BIOS and a handful of other devices being mapped into the UMA, there usually is plenty of room left (memory addresses available) in the UMA for other devices or TSR programs. Often, you can increase available conventional memory by loading these devices and TSRs into the UMA. Loading these device drivers and TSRs makes more conventional memory available, which is particularly important if you run DOS programs in Windows. A section later in this chapter ("Examining Memory Device Drivers") explains how to load device drivers and TSRs into the UMA.

Extended Memory

Most of today's PCs include a second kind of memory in addition to conventional memory. This additional memory is called *extended memory.* Extended memory is very much what its name implies: an extension of the system's conventional memory. Extended memory is the memory in the system that is mapped to memory addresses above 1,024 KB.

DOS is limited to accessing memory addresses in the range of 0–1,024 KB. DOS cannot directly access memory above 1,024 KB. Therefore, DOS cannot access extended memory directly. Instead, an *extended memory manager* is used to control the extended memory and provide DOS with access to it. The standard Microsoft extended memory manager is the device driver HIMEM.SYS (discussed later in this chapter).

The system can access extended memory linearly, which provides a faster alternative to expanded memory, which you will read about shortly. Windows can use your system's extended memory to hold data, programs, and its own program code. The more extended memory available in your system, the better Windows will perform.

Expanded Memory

In the 1980s, before extended memory was available (the limited-memory 1 MB Intel 8086 microprocessor was all they had), Lotus Development Corp., Intel Corp., and Microsoft joined together to develop a standard method of overcoming DOS's inability to access memory beyond the 1 MB mark. The standard that emerged from this consortium was called the *Lotus-Intel-Microsoft Expanded Memory Specification* (LIM EMS). Memory that used the methods defined in the standard became known simply as *expanded memory*.

DOS accesses all memory, regardless of whether it is conventional, extended, or expanded memory, by its address. Although DOS does not normally make use of memory in the UMA to run programs, there is nothing to prevent it from doing so. Expanded memory works by mapping memory from an add-in card into an area in the UMA. An expanded memory manager and special hardware are used to map a 64 KB block of memory on an expanded memory card into a 64 KB block of memory addresses in the UMA.

The 64 KB block in the UMA is called an *expanded memory page frame*. The memory manager maps different 64 KB blocks of memory from the memory card into the page frame, making a potentially large amount of memory on the card available to DOS, although only in 64 KB chunks at a time.

Because expanded memory requires swapping memory in and out of the page frame, it is slower than extended memory. Although many earlier DOS programs were designed to use expanded memory, few do so today. Windows does not use expanded memory even if it is present in the system. It can, however, emulate expanded memory for applications that request it. It does this by making some of the system's extended memory function like expanded memory.

If you are planning on adding more memory to your system, add extended memory. Do not add expanded memory.

Virtual Memory

The 386, 486, and Pentium CPUs can address up to 4 GB (gigabytes) of memory, equivalent to 4,096 megabytes of RAM. It is unlikely that PCs will even come remotely close to having that much RAM installed in them any time in the foreseeable future. Besides, your memory requirements are more modest.

Assume that you are running a handful of programs which together are using 6 MB of RAM. Your system has 8 MB of RAM in it, so there still is a comfortable margin. What if you start another program that is particularly memory hungry? Assume that it needs another 6 MB to run. Your system now is 4 MB short to make up the total of 12 MB that your applications are requesting.

To solve the problem, Windows uses part of the space on your hard disk to simulate memory—in other words, to create virtual memory. When memory runs low, Windows swaps the contents of some of the system's memory to the hard disk to make more physical memory available. If the memory that was swapped to disk is needed again, Windows moves something else from memory to disk, and brings the original data back into physical memory. Virtual memory makes it theoretically possible for Windows to make use of up to 4 GB of memory on a PC that has far less (assuming there is sufficient disk space to make up the difference).

Deciding How Much RAM Is Enough

To run in Standard mode, Windows requires a minimum 256 KB of free conventional memory and at least 192 KB of free extended memory. Because memory is installed in a system in 1 MB increments, this translates into a minimum requirement of 2 MB of RAM in the system. To run in 386 Enhanced mode, Windows requires at least 256 KB of free conventional memory and at least 1,024 KB of free extended memory. Although a minimum configuration of 2 MB can enable Windows to run in 386 Enhanced mode, performance will be poor.

Table 9.1 lists the relationships between CPU, memory, and Windows operating modes.

Table 9.1
CPU, Memory, and Windows Operating Modes

CPU	Memory	Operating Mode
286	1 MB plus 192 KB of free ext. memory	Windows will run on a 286 system only in Standard mode, but it must have at least 192 KB of free extended memory. Additional memory will improve performance, but not let Windows run in 386 Enhanced mode.

CPU	Memory	Operating Mode
386/486/ Pentium	2 MB (with at least 1 MB of free ext. memory)	Windows will run in Standard mode.
386/486/ Pentium	More than 2 MB (with at least 1 MB of free ext. memory)	Windows will run in 386 Enhanced mode.

 Windows for Workgroups runs only in 386 Enhanced mode. It does not support Standard mode.

The minimum RAM amounts described in table 9.1 do not take into account the memory required by your applications and data. Although Windows can take advantage of virtual memory in 386 Enhanced mode—thus making the system seem as if it has more memory than it really does—the disk-swapping involved with virtual memory bogs down performance. Having plenty of free physical RAM is a much better alternative to virtual memory.

For stand-alone Windows 3.1, consider 4 MB to be the minimum amount of RAM that still will provide good performance in either Standard or 386 Enhanced mode. If you run large applications or work with large data files, consider a minimum of 6 MB to 8 MB. Some applications, such as AutoCAD Release 12 for Windows, require even larger amounts. The base requirement for AutoCAD is 8 MB, but 12–16 MB or more is a more realistic amount.

Also, if you are running Windows for Workgroups, you will need more memory than if you were running Windows 3.1. Windows for Workgroups requires a minimum of 3 MB, and will perform sluggishly with only 4 MB. Therefore, consider 6–8 MB to be a good starting point for systems running Windows for Workgroups.

Optimizing DOS 6 Memory with Memmaker

If you have upgraded to MS-DOS 6, you can use its memory optimization program called Memmaker to fine-tune your system's use of memory. Memmaker evaluates your CONFIG.SYS and AUTOEXEC.BAT files, examines the device drivers and programs you are starting from both files, then makes use of new features of the DEVICEHIGH and LOADHIGH command to rearrange these device drivers and programs into specific memory blocks in the UMA. This makes better use of the UMA and usually results in more free memory below 640 KB.

To use Memmaker, exit Windows and type **MEMMAKER** at the DOS prompt. Memmaker will run three times to configure and test your system's memory, rebooting the system after each time. The first time Memmaker runs, you specify options for how Memmaker will optimize your system's memory. (You have to start Memmaker only the first time—Memmaker reboots the system and starts itself automatically the second and third times.)

When the first Memmaker window appears, press Enter to access the first configuration screen. Memmaker then will display a succession of screens that prompt you to specify options. To switch between options on a screen, press the spacebar. The following lists the options you should select to optimize your system for Windows:

- ✔ **Express Setup or Custom Setup.** Choose Custom Setup to enable you to set special options for Windows.

- ✔ **Do you use any programs that need expanded memory (EMS).** Choose No, unless you have DOS programs that require expanded memory and you run those DOS programs outside of Windows. If you run those programs inside of Windows, answer No. Windows will simulate expanded memory if needed.

- ✔ **Specify which drivers and TSRs to include in optimization.** Answer No, unless you have a driver that you know specifically cannot be loaded into the UMA.

- ✔ **Scan the upper memory area aggressively.** Answering Yes causes Memmaker to scan the range of addresses between F000 through F7FF for free UMBs. If your system shadows the system BIOS in the memory range F000 through F7FF, leave this setting at No.

- ✔ **Optimize upper memory for use with Windows.** Answer Yes if you run DOS programs in Windows. Answer No if you do not run DOS programs in Windows (or run very few).

- ✔ **Use monochrome region (B000-B7FF) for running programs.** No, unless your video adapter does not use this range of memory (many EGA and VGA adapters do not use this memory range, but some do).

- ✔ **Keep current EMM386 memory exclusions and inclusions.** Yes, unless you know that some of the inclusions or exclusions are not necessary, or you want Memmaker to rescan and respecify your inclusions and exclusions.

- ✔ **Move Extended BIOS Data Area from conventional to upper memory.** No. Setting it to Yes will gain only 1 KB of conventional memory.

After setting the options specified above, press Enter. Memmaker prompts you to enter the directory where Windows is located. Specify the directory, then press Enter. Follow the prompts Memmaker provides to complete the optimization process.

Examining Memory Device Drivers

Windows uses a number of device drivers to provide access to your system's memory. These device drivers support extended memory and expanded memory (simulated), provide access to the UMA, enable you to set up a RAM drive, and provide for improved disk performance through disk caching. The most important of these device drivers is HIMEM.SYS.

HIMEM.SYS

The device driver HIMEM.SYS provides access to extended memory and to the HMA, or high memory area, which is the first 64 KB block of memory above 1 MB. In almost all cases, a simple entry in CONFIG.SYS, such as the following, is enough to set up HIMEM.SYS properly:

```
device=c:\windows\himem.sys
```

In the vast majority of cases, HIMEM.SYS does not require that any special command-line switches be added for it to function properly or at its optimum. In a few rare instances, you might need to add some command-line switches to the command in CONFIG.SYS that loads HIMEM.SYS. The following list summarizes the possible HIMEM.SYS settings (current to the MS-DOS 6 version):

✔ /A20CONTROL:*ON or OFF*   Controls whether Himem takes control of the A20 line, which gives your system access to the HMA. If set to ON, Himem takes control of the A20 line even if it is on when Himem was loaded. If set to OFF, Himem will take control of the A20 only if it was off when Himem was loaded. The default is ON.

✔ /CPUCLOCK:*ON or OFF*   Controls whether or not Himem will affect your system's clock speed. You should need to set this option only if your system clock speed changes after Himem is installed. The default is OFF.

✔ /EISA   This switch directs Himem to allocate all available extended memory, and is necessary only on EISA systems that have more than 16 MB of memory.

✔ /HMAMIN   By default, Himem gives control of the HMA to whichever application requests it. This setting specifies the amount of memory in the HMA an application must request before Himem will grant the HMA to the application.

✔ /INT15=*xxxx*   Specifies an amount of memory to be allocated for access through the Interrupt 15h interface. Most applications use the method defined by the XMS (Extended Memory Specification). Some older applications, however, use Int 15h. If you have applications that require Int 15h access to memory, specify a value in kilobytes (KB) from 64 through 65,535 that is 64 KB larger than the amount required by the application.

II

Optimizing Windows

✔ /NUMHANDLES=*n*   Sets the number of EMB (extended memory block) handles that can be used simultaneously. This setting has no effect when Windows is running in 386 Enhanced mode.

✔ /MACHINE:*machine name*   Used to specify the system type. Currently, only the Acer 1100, IBM 7552, and Wyse systems require this setting. The settings are *acer1100*, *ibm7552*, and *wyse*.

✔ /SHADOWRAM:*ON or OFF*   Controls whether Himem disables shadowing of ROM in RAM. On a Windows system (which must have at least 2 MB of RAM), Himem will not attempt to disable shadowing. Because you generally can control whether the system sets up shadowing by changing its CMOS setup, you should not need to use this setting.

✔ /VERBOSE   If this switch is present, Himem displays status and error messages as it is loading. You also can cause Himem to display status and error messages by holding down the Alt key while Himem is loading.

For additional information on Himem switches, type **HELP HIMEM** at the DOS prompt.

EMM386.EXE

The device driver EMM386.EXE, which is installed by your system's CONFIG.SYS file, also controls memory access. EMM386 simulates expanded memory for applications that request it (outside of Windows only), and also provides access to the UMA for use by TSRs, device drivers, and programs. If you want to make as much conventional memory available below 640K as possible for DOS applications you run under Windows, you should use EMM386. The following example, which would be added to CONFIG.SYS, sets up EMM386 to manage the UMA, but to not provide expanded memory support:

```
device=c:\windows\emm386.exe noems
```

The NOEMS switch directs EMM386 not to provide expanded memory simulation. The reason you should disable EMM386's EMS support in this way when using Windows is that Windows will provide EMS memory simulation on its own, taking over the job from EMM386. Therefore, simulating EMS memory with EMM386 wastes extended memory that Windows could put to better use. The only time to enable EMM386's EMS memory support is when you are running applications outside of Windows that require EMS memory support. If this is the case, use a multiboot configuration (described in Chapter 7, "Enhancing Windows Performance") to provide a separate boot configuration that supports EMS memory with EMM386.

Supporting the UMA

EMM386 also can be used to provide support in the UMA for device drivers, TSRs, and other programs. EMM386 takes memory supplied by Himem and maps these types of programs into it, freeing conventional memory below 640 KB that might otherwise be used by the programs.

To provide support for the UMA by EMM386 on a Windows system, simply add the NOEMS switch, as described in the previous EMM386 example. If you need to supply EMS memory support for DOS applications running outside of Windows, omit the NOEMS switch and specify the amount of extended memory in kilobytes that EMM386 is to make available as EMS memory:

```
device=c:\windows\emm386.exe 2048
```

Supporting UMA and EMS Memory

If you want EMM386 to provide UMA support as well as EMS memory support, also include the RAM switch as follows:

```
device=c:\windows\emm386.exe 2048 ram
```

This example configures EMM386 to provide 2 MB of RAM as EMS memory and directs it to provide access to the UMA. Note that you can specify a specific range with the RAM switch and restrict UMA access only to a specific range. This option of the RAM switch is covered in the next section.

Controlling UMA Access

You can use a few switches with EMM386 to control the amount of memory it makes available in the UMA, and which ranges of memory will be available. It is important to be able to control how EMM386 allocates memory in the UMA to prevent conflicts between two applications or devices that attempt to use the same block of memory.

Take the example of a network interface card (NIC). Most NICs require a block of memory in the UMA to transfer data between the computer and the NIC. A NIC might use the range D000–D3FF, for example, and no other device or program can use that same range of memory. Although EMM386 often can detect when a device is using a block of memory in the UMA, there are times when it cannot. In these instances, EMM386 will make that range of memory available. A conflict will occur if another application tries to use that memory range, thus preventing the workstation's network software (or other device) from functioning properly.

The I and X switches are used with EMM386 to include (I) and exclude (X) ranges of memory from EMM386's use. The following example excludes the range D000–D3FF, and includes the range B000–B7FF:

```
device=c:\windows\emm386.exe i=b000-b7ff x=d000-d3ff
```

Setting EMM386.EXE Switches

A number of additional switches can be used with EMM386. The following list describes all of them (current to MS-DOS 6):

- ✔ MIN=*size in KB*   Specifies the minimum amount of EMS/VCPI (Virtual Control Program Interface) memory EMM386 will make available. The default is 0.

- ✔ W=*ON or OFF*   Turns on or off support for the Weitek math coprocessor.

- ✔ FRAME=*address*   Specifies the starting address for the EMS memory page frame. Valid entries are 8000h–9000h and C000h–E000h.

- ✔ /P*nnnn*   Specifies the starting address of the first page of the EMS page frame. Use this switch instead of FRAME if you want to break up the four 16 KB pages that make up the page frame into noncontiguous memory blocks.

- ✔ P*n*=*address*   Specifies the location of one page of the EMS page frame. Use four P switches to specify the locations of all four pages. The value *n* can be from 0 to 3. The four page frames must be contiguous to be compatible with the LIM 3.2 specification, but can be noncontiguous for LIM 4.0.

- ✔ X=*address range*   Specifies a range of addresses for EMM386 to exclude from its use in the UMA.

- ✔ I=*address range*   Specifies a range of addresses for EMM386 to include for its use in the UMA.

- ✔ B=*address*   Specifies the lowest address that can be used for swapping EMS memory. Valid entries are in the range 1000h–4000h (the default is 4000h).

- ✔ l=*minimum XMS in KB*   Specifies a minimum amount of XMS extended memory that still will be available when EMM386 is installed.

- ✔ A=*alternate registers*   Controls how many alternate register sets will be allocated by EMM386. The default is 7, but you can specify from 0 to 254.

- ✔ H=*memory handle*   Specifies the number of memory handles EMM386 can use. The default is 64, but you can specify a value from 2 to 255.

- ✔ D=*kilobyte*   Specifies the amount of memory in kilobytes that will be reserved for buffered DMA (direct memory access). If you have applications that use DMA, you might need to increase this setting. The default is 16; valid entries are from 16 to 256.

- ✔ RAM=*nnnn-nnnn*   Turns on EMS support and also specifies a range of addresses EMM386 will make available in the UMA. If no range is specified, all the unused memory in the UMA is made available.

✔ `NOEMS` Turns off support for EMS, but enables UMA memory support.

✔ `NOVCPI` Disables support for applications that request memory through the VCPI specification. You can recover a little additional extended memory by adding this switch.

✔ `HIGHSCAN` Causes EMM386 to scan the UMA aggressively for available memory blocks. This can potentially make a little more UMA memory available, but in some cases can cause EMM386 to recognize a block of memory in the UMA as being free when it is not.

✔ `VERBOSE` Causes EMM386 to display status and error messages while it is loading.

✔ `WIN=nnnn-nnnn` Reserves the specified memory range in the UMA for use by Windows instead of by EMM386.

✔ `[NOHI]` This switch prevents EMM386 from installing itself in the UMA, and instead installs itself in conventional memory below 640 KB. This makes additional memory available in the UMA for other programs.

✔ `[ROM=nnnn-nnnn]` Specifies a memory range that EMM386 will use for shadowing ROM in RAM. Valid entries are in the range of A000h–FFFFh.

✔ `[NOMOVEXDBA]` This switch prevents EMM386 from relocating the extended BIOS data into upper memory.

✔ `[ALTBOOT]` Add this switch if you cannot reboot the system with Ctrl+Alt+Del with EMM386 running.

Use the following switches to optimize your system's memory for Windows, assuming you do not use applications that require EMS/VCPI memory support:

```
device=c:\windows\emm386.exe noems novcpi highscan win=cd00-cfff
```

Change the value of the `WIN` switch according to your system's configuration and use of memory in the UMA. If you do not use the UMA for device drivers and TSRs, specify the entire range of available UMBs for the `WIN` switch. Add other settings to the line as necessary for your system's configuration.

RAMDRIVE.SYS

A *RAM drive* is an area of memory that has been configured to perform as a virtual disk drive. After a RAM drive has been created, you can copy files to it, delete files from it, and perform almost any other disk-related operation on the RAM disk. The RAM disk does not, however, provide long-term storage. When the computer is rebooted or turned off, the contents of the RAM drive are lost.

II

Optimizing Windows

The TEMP Directory

Windows creates temporary files as it runs. Many Windows applications, as well as Print Manager, create temporary files. Usually, these temporary files are stored on the hard disk in the directory pointed to by the TEMP environment variable.

You can improve the performance of programs that use temporary files by creating a RAM drive and using it, instead of the hard disk, for the TEMP directory.

The following list summarizes the situations in which it is useful to use a RAM drive with Windows and set it up as the TEMP directory:

> ✔ **You are running Windows on a diskless workstation that has at least 6 MB of RAM.** You can create a 1 MB RAM drive and use it as the Windows TEMP directory, improving printing performance and the performance of programs that create temporary files.

> ✔ **You are running applications on a workstation with a local hard disk, and those applications create many temporary files.** You can improve the performance of these applications by configuring a RAM drive and using it as the Windows TEMP directory.

> ✔ **Your computer contains physical expanded memory that cannot be configured as extended memory.** You can set up a RAM drive to use the expanded memory and configure it as the Windows TEMP directory. (If the expanded memory can be configured as extended memory, do that instead.)

> ✔ **Your computer contains plenty of RAM (more than 8 MB) and you want to improve printing performance through Print Manager.** Create a 2 MB or larger RAM drive and use it as your TEMP directory. If you have a considerable amount of memory in the system (16 MB or more), consider copying some of your Windows or program files to the RAM drive for faster performance.

RAM Drive Parameters and Switches

The device driver RAMDRIVE.SYS, which is included with MS-DOS, enables you to set up a RAM drive. There are a handful of switches that can be included on the command line that configures RAMDRIVE.SYS. They are as follows (switches are listed in the order in which they must appear on the RAMDRIVE command line):

> ✔ `disk size`   Specifies the size of the RAM drive in K. A setting of 2048, for example, creates a 2 MB RAM drive.

> ✔ `sector size`   Specifies the sector size, in bytes, for the RAM drive. The default is 512 bytes. You should not need to change this parameter.

✔ `number of entries` Specifies the number of file entries that can be contained in the RAM drive's root directory. The default is 64. Increase this if you create a combination of more than 64 files and subdirectories in the root directory of the RAM drive.

✔ `/e` Specifies that the RAM drive be set up in extended memory. If this switch is omitted (and the /a switch is not included), the RAM drive will be set up in conventional memory.

✔ `/a` Specifies that the RAM drive be set up in expanded memory.

Setting Up a RAM Drive

If you want to use the default values for your system's RAM drive and specify only the size of the drive, you need only include one parameter on the RAMDRIVE.SYS command line. The following command in CONFIG.SYS will create a RAM drive of 2 MB, and the RAM drive is assigned the next available drive ID:

```
device=c:\windows\ramdrive.sys 2048
```

If you want to change any of the other default parameters, you must include all parameters that precede it on the command line, even if you are not changing them from their defaults (except for the /e and /a switches). If you want to specify a different number of directory entries, for example, you must also include the sector size parameter as a "placeholder" in the command line.

The following example sets up a RAM drive of 2 MB with the default 512-byte sector size and 128 directory entries, and places the RAM drive in extended memory:

```
device=c:\windows\ramdrive.sys 2048 512 128 /e
```

Setting Up RAMDRIVE for Windows

In addition to configuring RAMDRIVE in CONFIG.SYS, you also must set it up for use by Windows, which includes directing Windows to use the RAM drive for its TEMP directory. In your system's AUTOEXEC.BAT file, include the following command:

```
temp=f:\
```

The preceding example assumes that the RAM drive is using drive ID F. Substitute the correct drive ID for your system.

If you want to create a directory in RAM drive for the TEMP directory, add entries similar to the following:

```
md f:\temp

temp=f:\temp
```

You must reboot your system after making these changes for them to take effect.

Figure 9.2
The About dialog box for Program Manager displays the percentage of free resources.

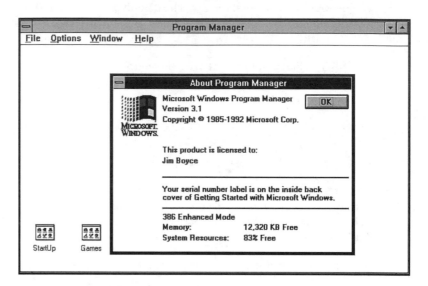

Understanding Memory and Windows Resources

Windows uses a fixed amount of your system's RAM for resource memory. You might have seen the term *free resources* in Windows. If not, choose Program Manager's <u>H</u>elp menu, then choose <u>A</u>bout Program Manager. The dialog box is shown in figure 9.2.

In addition to displaying the current Windows run mode and amount of memory free (including virtual memory), the dialog box displays as a percentage the amount of system resources that are free. The term *system resources* refers to the amount of memory used by the core Windows components GDI.EXE and USER.EXE, as well as the Windows kernel. The following list explains these Windows components:

> ✔ **The Windows kernel.** Either KRNL286.EXE or KRNL386.EXE, depending on your system. The kernel handles loading and executing Windows programs, and also handles memory use by Windows programs.

> ✔ **GDI.EXE.** Manages general Windows functions such as graphics (controlling the display) and printing.

✔ **USER.EXE.** This component handles user I/O (input and output), such as for the keyboard and mouse. It also controls the sound driver, system timer, COM ports, and the display and management of program windows.

GDI uses a single 64 KB memory storage area called a *local heap*. USER uses two 64 KB heaps, called the *menu heap* and *user heap*. The amount of free system resources your system has is a percentage of the free memory available in these heaps.

As you open more applications, a greater amount of resource memory is required to manage the programs. When the amount of free resource memory drops below a certain point, you are unable to open additional programs, even if you still have plenty of memory left in the system.

The following tips will help you conserve resource memory and overcome the problem of not having enough resource memory to start another program:

✔ **Keep Program Manager groups to a minimum.** Although icons in Program Manager do not use heap space, group windows do. The more group windows you have open in Program Manager, the more resource memory will be required to support them. Keep all your most-used programs in a single group, and keep only this one group open. Open other group windows only when you need to access an item in them.

✔ **Close applications when memory runs low.** If you receive a not enough memory error when you attempt to start a new application, close some of the applications currently running and try again.

Another cause for the not enough memory error is the lack of available selectors (memory pointers). If a program allocates many small data objects, it can use up all the available selectors. There is little you can do about the problem except contact the software developers to see if they can supply a fix for the problem.

Understanding Memory in Standard Mode

Windows in Standard mode uses conventional and extended memory exclusively; it does not use expanded memory. Standard mode uses the total of available conventional and extended memory as one contiguous block of memory.

Standard Mode and Extended Memory

HIMEM.SYS provides access to extended memory for Windows running in Standard mode. Himem provides all free conventional and extended memory to Windows applications. Windows in Standard mode also can support extended memory requests by DOS programs.

HIMEM.SYS automatically handles memory management for Standard-mode Windows. You can do very little to optimize Standard mode's use of extended memory.

Extended Memory and DOS Programs in Standard Mode

If you run DOS programs in Windows' Standard mode that need to use extended memory, you must specify each program's extended memory requirements in its PIF. Figure 9.3 shows the Standard mode PIF Editor.

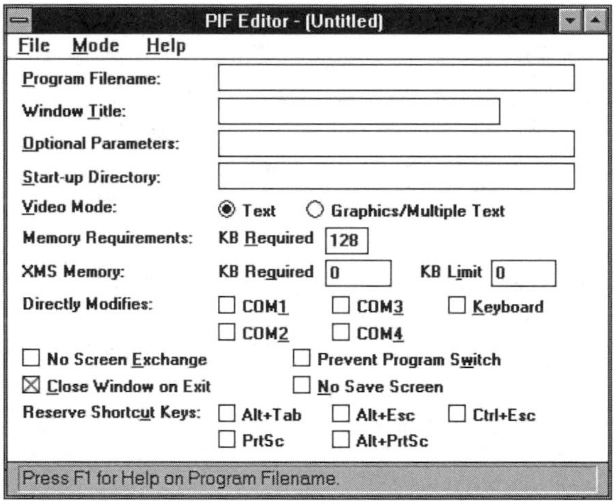

Figure 9.3
The Standard-mode PIF Editor.

In the KB Required box of the XMS Memory settings, specify the minimum amount of extended memory required by the program. In the KB Limit box, specify the maximum amount of extended memory to which you want the program to have access.

Standard Mode and Expanded Memory

Windows does not use expanded memory in either Standard or 386 Enhanced modes. DOS programs that require expanded memory, however, can use expanded memory when they are run under Windows. The restriction, however, is that the expanded memory must be physical expanded memory managed by an EMS memory manager supplied with the physical memory card. EMS memory simulators such as EMM386 cannot provide EMS memory support to DOS programs in Standard mode.

EMM386 can, however, provide EMS memory support for DOS programs that are run outside of Windows. Therefore, if you want to support EMS memory for DOS programs with EMM386, run the DOS programs outside of Windows. To optimize your system's memory use, use multiple CONFIG.SYS files or MS-DOS 6's multiple boot capability to define two configurations: one in which EMM386 provides EMS memory support and another for which EMM386 does not provide EMS memory support. Use the configuration that supports EMS only when you need to run the DOS programs that require it (run them outside of Windows).

For more information on MS-DOS 6's multiple boot capability, refer to Chapter 7, "Enhancing Windows Performance."

Understanding Memory in 386 Enhanced Mode

Memory use in 386 Enhanced mode is similar to memory use in Standard mode, although there are a few exceptions, particularly concerning expanded memory and DOS programs. Extended memory use, however, is very similar to Standard mode.

386 Enhanced Mode and Extended Memory

In 386 Enhanced mode, Windows takes available conventional memory, adds extended memory and virtual memory, and uses that combination for total system memory. When you start Windows in 386 Enhanced mode, it loads itself and its drivers into extended memory. This is why Windows 386 Enhanced mode requires that an extended memory manager (such as HIMEM.SYS) be loaded in the CONFIG.SYS file. Windows then takes over memory management from HIMEM.SYS.

If you run DOS applications in a virtual machine, they also can access extended memory in 386 Enhanced mode. Windows' internal extended memory manager becomes a part of each virtual machine's environment (a *virtual machine* is the virtual DOS session in which the DOS program is running). As with Standard mode, you should specify the amount of extended memory a DOS program requires in its PIF. Figure 9.4 shows the 386 Enhanced mode PIF Editor.

In the KB Required box of the XMS Memory section, specify the minimum amount of extended memory the program will need. Specify the maximum amount of extended memory to which the program should have access by setting the KB Limit value. To prevent a program from using any extended memory, set the KB Limit value to 0. To give a DOS program all the extended memory it requests, set KB Limit to -1.

The device driver WINA20.386, which was required to resolve conflicts between MS-DOS 5 and Windows 3.0, is not required with Windows 3.1. If you are running Windows 3.1, you can delete this file if it still resides on your system.

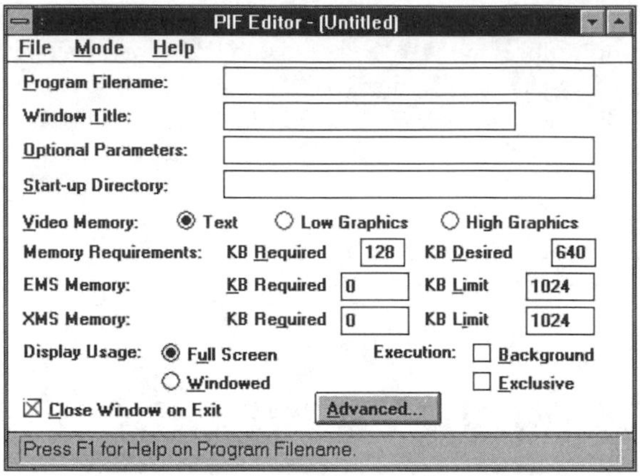

Figure 9.4
The 386 Enhanced
mode PIF Editor.

386 Enhanced Mode and Expanded Memory

As with Standard mode, Windows in 386 Enhanced mode does not use expanded memory at all. It can, however, provide expanded memory emulation for DOS programs that request it. Although Windows provides its own EMS memory simulation and management separate from EMM386, Windows cannot support EMS memory if EMM386 has been installed with the NOEMS switch, because no page frame will have been allocated.

To set up Windows to support EMS memory when running in 386 Enhanced mode, use the RAM switch with EMM386 to allocate an EMS page frame. The following example assumes that you have a network adapter in your system that uses the memory range D000–D3FF, so the page frame is located starting at E000. If this is not the case, you probably can specify a different page frame location.

```
device=c:\windows\emm386.exe ram frame=e000
```

Understanding Memory Use and DOS

If you run Windows in 386 Enhanced mode and run DOS applications as tasks under Windows, conserving conventional memory below 640 KB is important. Each new virtual machine (DOS session) created under Windows inherits the DOS environment that was in place before Windows was started. The more conventional memory below 640 KB that is available before Windows starts, the more memory will be available for DOS programs that you later run under Windows. This section examines some methods for freeing additional conventional memory.

Loading DOS High

You can cause DOS to load part of itself into the high memory area (HMA), which is the first 64 KB block of memory above 1,024 KB. Placing DOS in the HMA frees the conventional memory that otherwise would be used to contain DOS.

To place DOS in the HMA, add the following line to CONFIG.SYS (if it is not already present):

```
dos=high
```

If you want EMM386 to be able to provide access to the UMA for device drivers and TSRs, add the UMB switch to the line, as follows:

```
dos=high,umb
```

It is important to note that only one application can use the HMA. If you have another program, such as network software, that requires use of the HMA, do not load DOS into the HMA.

Using WINSTART.BAT

Another technique you can use to make more memory available under DOS before Windows is started is to reduce the number of TSRs that are loaded by AUTOEXEC.BAT. If you have Windows TSRs (TSRs that support Windows and Windows programs, but not DOS programs) and you run Windows in 386 Enhanced mode, you can place the commands that load these TSRs into the WINSTART.BAT file rather than AUTOEXEC.BAT.

Create a file in your Windows directory with the name WINSTART.BAT, then place in it all the commands previously in AUTOEXEC.BAT that loaded the Windows TSRs. These TSRs will not be duplicated in each virtual machine Windows creates, but will only be available to Windows.

Conserving Memory through Batch Loading

If a DOS program that you use under Windows requires a device driver or TSRs, you might be able to load that device driver or TSR only in that application's virtual machine. To do so, create a batch file that loads the needed TSR or device driver, and then start the program. Next, create a PIF for the batch program (as described in Chapter 11, "Optimizing Data Storage Space"), then create a program item for the PIF. When you need to run the program, double-click on its icon. Windows will create a virtual machine, load the TSR or device driver into it, and then load the program. When you exit the program, the TSR or device driver will be removed from memory. This prevents it from being duplicated in all other virtual machines.

Chapter Snapshot

Windows, like any operating system, requires the use of input devices. To communicate with your programs, you must have a means of sending signals. In a multitasking operating system, the operating system captures these signals, processes them, and routes them to the appropriate program. In Windows, the two devices that enable you to send such signals to programs by means of the operating system are the keyboard and a pointing device.

This chapter describes typical keyboards and pointing devices that you might want to use with your system. It covers the following topics:

In addition to covering hardware and driver issues, this chapter examines techniques and software you can use to automate much of your work through keyboard and mouse macros.

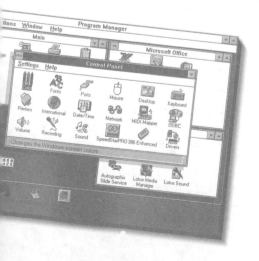

10

CHAPTER

Input Devices: Keyboards and Mice

lthough the connection of a keyboard and pointing device to your computer might seem like a simple mechanical and electrical connection, getting these devices to communicate with Windows is not so simple. Because Windows provides a hardware-independent computing platform, it must provide a means of connecting any keyboard and pointing device to your computer in a way that enables application programs to receive input, regardless of which keyboard and pointing device you choose. Windows accomplishes this task through small programs called *device drivers,* or simply, *drivers.* The purpose of input device drivers is to collect input from the hardware and deliver it to Windows in a usable form. As a result, in addition to connecting the standard keyboard and mouse to your computer, you also must install the appropriate keyboard driver and mouse driver for your system to accept input.

The following sections describe the options you have in selecting input devices and the means for selecting and installing the appropriate device drivers.

Exploring Keyboards

Choosing a keyboard for your system might seem like an easy task. A keyboard usually is included with a system. The one that comes with the system, however, might not be comfortable to you. You might not like the feel of the keys or the tactile feedback you receive through your fingers, the clicking sound emitted with each keypress, or the angle at which the keyboard rests. You also might not find the layout of the keys comfortable.

In addition to the feel and layout of the keys, you might have some special requirements for the keyboard you use. If you use a calculator often, you might want a keyboard with a built-in numeric keypad. If you are a touch typist, you might not want to reach to your right or left to use a pointing device; you might rather have a pointing device built into your keyboard. If you work in a cramped space, you might want a keyboard with a small footprint. If you type repetitive key sequences often, you might prefer a keyboard that enables you to store keystrokes in a memory buffer and send them to the operating system at the touch of a single key; such keyboards are said to have macro capabilities. You also might prefer a keyboard that enables you to redefine keys so that you can easily reach the keys you need.

> *Footprint* refers to the size of an object, or the amount of space it takes up on a surface when the object is at rest on the surface. The footprint of a keyboard, for example, is the amount of space it takes up on your desk.

These kinds of keyboards generally are available for purchase as accessories to your system. Sometimes you can substitute the keyboard of your choice for the keyboard that is advertised as a part of your system.

The keyboard you use is intimately tied to your productivity. You should use one that not only provides the options you need but also is comfortable. Try out the different keyboards available on the systems that others use in your office and at local computer outlets. If you order a keyboard for your system, order it from a dealer who offers a trial period guarantee. (You don't want to be stuck with a keyboard that sounded good in the catalog but feels awful.)

The following sections describe some of the most common choices available, each readily obtained through any of several catalog dealers. Use these descriptions as a guide to think about the possibilities.

> Most keyboards that advertise improved speed and feel use key switches of the same type, most of them from the same manufacturer. Your sense of the keying action might depend on other factors in the design of the keyboard. Your choice of keyboard should depend on how the keying action feels to you.

Northgate Keyboards

Northgate offers a keyboard with the following features:

- ✔ Fast key switches that provide both tactile and audible feedback to speed your typing

- ✔ Numeric and cursor keypads

- ✔ Color-coded Ctrl, Alt, and Shift keys for use with WordPerfect

- ✔ Interchangeable Ctrl, Alt, and Caps Lock keys to enable you to choose the layout that best suits your keyboarding style

- ✔ A comma/period lock that prevents the shifting of the comma and period keys so that you can type without producing strings such as 8:00 A>M>

The Northgate keyboard is available in three different layouts. One is identical to the standard IBM 101-key keyboard, with the addition of the preceding features. The second offers function keys both across the top and down the left side. The third offers function keys down the left side only.

The Northgate keyboard easily attracts WordPerfect users and users who are most comfortable with touch typing on a typewriter. It also attracts those who want to place the Ctrl, Alt, and Caps Lock keys in places that will help them avoid mistakes.

Gateway 2000 AnyKey Keyboard

This keyboard ships with Gateway 2000 systems but is available separately if you already own a Gateway system (Gateway sells parts and peripherals only to existing Gateway customers). The principal advantage of this keyboard is the capability to redefine any key as any other key. You also can record several keystrokes as a macro and send them to an application with a single keystroke. This keyboard includes several special keys, most notably diagonal arrow keys on the keypad, which enable you to move the cursor diagonally in an application. The AnyKey keyboard also has two sets of function keys and includes an extra key in the center of the arrow keypad that you can define for any purpose.

When using the Gateway 2000 keyboard, be careful not to hit the macro recording keys. You can accidentally alter your keyboard macros by reaching too far and pressing one of the macro recording keys instead of the Enter key.

Chicony Keyboards

Chicony keyboards are IBM-style replacement keyboards that provide improved key switches for a better feel, and improved angle adjustment. One model is slightly smaller than the standard IBM keyboard and is aimed at smaller desktops. Another is the standard size with improved tactile feedback. The third includes a built-in, three-button trackball, eliminating the need for a separate pointing device. These keyboards appeal to users who want an improved feel in the touch of the keys.

Focus Keyboards

The Focus line of keyboards offers enhancements to the feel of the keys and several additional direction keys. One model offers 12 programmable function keys. All models include a built-in calculator with LCD display. These keyboards offer both improved functionality and improved tactile feedback. They especially appeal to users who need to integrate calculations into their keyboarding and who need some degree of programmability.

KeyTronic Keyboards

KeyTronic keyboards often receive reviewers' praise for a good feel. The key switches provide definite tactile feedback without an audible click. The keyboards also receive praise for the layout and shape of the keys. One model offers a built-in trackball instead of an arrow keypad. This line appeals primarily to users who want a standard-style replacement with improved feel characteristics.

Micro Type Space-Saver Keyboard

Micro Type offers a special-purpose keyboard for those who work in cramped spaces. This keyboard fits all the standard keys into a space just 10.75" × 6". Obviously the two-tiered layout, with function keys and keypad above the alphabetic keypad, takes some getting used to. For small work areas, however, this keyboard is the best choice.

Sejin J.M. Keyboard

The Sejin keyboard takes a different approach to integrating a pointing device in the keyboard. The J key can be held down and swiveled, which moves the mouse pointer on-screen. The spacebar serves as the left mouse button, enabling you to perform most Windows mouse actions from the keyboard without moving your fingers from the home keys. This keyboard appeals most to skilled typists who do not want to reach for a pointing device. A standard pointing device, however, can coexist with the Sejin keyboard without conflicts.

Exploring Pointing Devices

Your choice of a pointing device depends greatly on the kind of pointing you do. If you work with sophisticated drawing and drafting programs, you might need a mouse that works in conjunction with a digitizing tablet so that you can enter lines, points, and curves precisely on a grid. You also need to consider how the pointing device feels in your hand. Using Windows, you will spend a great amount of time holding the device. If it is tiresome or uncomfortable to hold, you will not want to use it. You need to choose a pointing device that you think will maximize your productivity.

Although most systems include a pointing device, you generally have some latitude as to which type of device you initially purchase with the system. It should be easy to substitute the device of your choice for the one offered with the package. Give some thought to the uses you have for the pointing device before you choose it or choose a new one, and use the following sections as a guide. All the products described in these sections generally are available from catalog dealers.

Mouse

A *mouse* typically includes two or three buttons that enable you to perform click, double-click, and drag actions. The mouse has the advantage of being an inexpensive and efficient pointing device. It works well for actions such as activating menus and dragging data from one location to another. It might, however, lack precision in detailed drawing applications.

Tip

The selection of mouse types is wide, as is the price range. You might want to look carefully at discount mice. A discount mouse might feel as good to you and offer the same features as a higher-priced alternative.

Microsoft Mouse

Perhaps the most famous mouse, the Microsoft Mouse, is included with many systems. It is comfortable in your hand and offers two buttons for mouse actions (this is not a good choice for applications that require a three-button mouse, such as CAD or drawing programs).

IBM PS/2 Mouse

The IBM PS/2 Mouse also is popular, because it ships with most IBM systems. This mouse has two buttons, and it represents a different approach to ergonomics. The mouse is longer so that your hand rests mainly on top of the mouse, not around it. The buttons also require more pressure to operate.

Logitech MouseMan

Logitech has long been known for its three-buttoned mice, so the MouseMan is a logical choice for three-button applications. The MouseMan, however, demonstrates a third approach to mouse ergonomics. It is shaped so that it has a thumbrest on the side, giving you an additional place to grab the mouse and, theoretically, greater control over its movement. The MouseMan, consequently, must be ordered in either a left- or right-handed version. An advantage of the MouseMan is the inclusion of ballistic drivers, which enable the mouse pointer to move greater or lesser distances across the screen depending on the speed with which you roll the mouse. This feature makes the MouseMan a good choice for applications that require fine movement of the mouse pointer.

Trackball

A *trackball* basically is a mouse turned upside down. The ball is on the top, and instead of moving the entire unit along your desktop, you roll the ball around in its housing. Trackballs are good for cramped working spaces. They also are excellent choices for users who do not feel comfortable moving their hands in the motions required by the mouse.

Mouse Systems PC Trackball

The Mouse Systems Trackball is a good example of the trackball concept. It provides a wide palm rest, a large ball, and three buttons arranged to either side of and below the ball. With the appropriate driver, the center button can be used to lock the left or right button down so that you can perform actions such as dragging an object or extending a selection more easily. The buttons are large and easy to operate, and the entire unit uses very little desk space. It is a typical choice for users who prefer a trackball.

Logitech TrackMan

The Logitech TrackMan looks like a MouseMan with the ball at the juncture of the palm rest and the thumb rest. It also must be ordered in a left- or right-handed version. It has three buttons that rest just under the fingertips when your palm is positioned on the palm rest. Your thumb rotates the ball, while your fingers control the buttons. Reviewers praise this trackball for its ergonomics. The TrackMan also comes in a portable version.

Microsoft Ballpoint Mouse

The Ballpoint Mouse is an example of a portable trackball designed to attach to the keyboard of a laptop or notebook computer. Your hand curls around it comfortably, and your fingertips rest upon two buttons. You use your thumb to control the ball. This pointing device has two sets of buttons. When you grasp it with either your right or left hand, one set of buttons always is under your fingertips.

Microsoft's Ballpoint Mouse earns praise for its ease of use on airline tray tables.

Mouse Alternatives

Some users do not like the feel of mice or trackballs, or they have specialized pointing needs. As a result, a variety of mouse alternatives are available. The following are some examples.

AceCAT Digitizer

The AceCAT is a 5" × 5" *digitizing pad,* an electrically sensitive surface on which you draw or write with a stylus. The motion of the stylus is translated into precise grid coordinates. As a result, the AceCAT is a useful alternative to a mouse for drawing. It is essential for pen computing and excellent for use with CAD programs.

MousePen Pro

The MousePen looks like a pen, but it has a small mouse ball at its tip. You hold it like a pen and move it like a pen to control the position of the mouse pointer. (You can use the MousePen on any surface.) Two buttons near the tip of the pen enable you to perform normal mouse operations. The MousePen is recommended for users who hate the feel of a standard mouse and prefer the familiar position of holding a pen. It also offers superior freehand drawing capabilities.

Understanding Input Drivers

Input devices require input drivers. Without an input driver, Windows cannot accept or use the input from the input device. Fortunately, Windows is packaged with several drivers for the most popular input devices. Input devices that require special drivers for Windows come packaged with the drivers. Whether your driver came with Windows or with your input device, you need to specify which drivers to use for Windows to communicate with your keyboard and your pointing device.

When you install Windows, either the Setup program senses your hardware devices and chooses the right devices, or you must select them from the menu provided early in the Setup screens. (See Chapter 1, "Configuring Windows," for more information about the actual installation procedure.) Once you approve the choice of hardware devices, you must select which drivers Windows installs to manage your hardware. After Windows has finished installation, it can communicate with your devices.

If your device does not appear on Windows' list of devices, you must choose the option on the menu for an unspecified device and insert into the drive the disk that came with your device. Setup reads the required manufacturer and driver information from a file called OEMSETUP.INF on the disk. It then copies the appropriate driver from the disk into the Windows system directory.

If you already have installed Windows and want to install a new hardware device not on the Windows standard list, you must go back to DOS Setup and use the hardware menus there to load the driver. At this time, Windows learns of the existence of the driver and adds it to its internal list of known drivers for input devices. Windows also copies any support files necessary for the driver's successful operation.

After you have installed an input device, you can run Windows Setup from the Main group in Program Manager to switch between the input devices you might attach to your system. Use the Options, Change System Settings menu command, and use the pull-down menu boxes to choose the new settings (see fig. 10.1). In this way, you can use multiple input devices with Windows and manage their drivers efficiently.

Figure 10.1
Choosing input device drivers using Windows Setup.

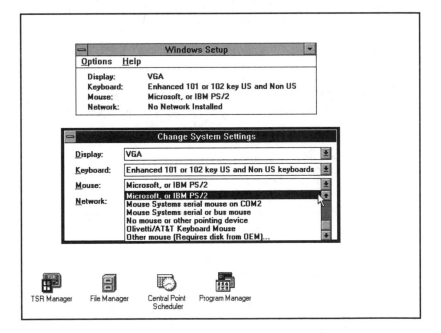

Windows programs no longer require you to install a DOS mouse driver. If you want to use your mouse with DOS applications that run under Windows, however, you must install the DOS mouse driver in your AUTOEXEC.BAT file.

Automating Your Mouse and Keyboard

A number of utility programs are now available that enable you to program your keyboard and mouse, adding the capability to execute complex macros with a few keystrokes or mouse clicks. Three such products are Whiskers (Numbers & Co.), Power Launcher (hDC Computer Corporation), and MouseWare (Logitech). Each of these three products offers a somewhat different approach to automating tasks through keyboard and mouse macros and user-defined custom menus. Products such as these can greatly improve your productivity by automating complex tasks.

Whiskers

Whiskers is a mouse and keyboard utility from Numbers & Co. This single application enables you to program virtually any key on your keyboard to automate keystrokes, execute macros, launch applications, or display user-defined menus. With Whiskers you also can assign these functions to a single mouse button or to combinations of mouse buttons (called mouse *chords*). Figure 10.2 shows the Whiskers configuration window that you can use to program your keyboard and mouse.

II

Optimizing Windows

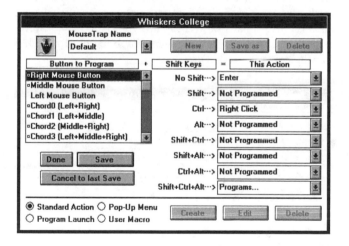

Figure 10.2
The Whiskers College window enables you to program the keyboard and mouse.

Whiskers provides support for many predefined actions, which include tasks such as minimizing and maximizing document and program windows, choosing various menu items, and other common Windows tasks. You also can create a program launcher to automatically start an application, create custom pop-up menus, and create macros, all of which can be assigned to a keystroke or to one or more mouse button combinations. You can associate a particular mouse/macro configuration with a specific program or make it global to all programs. This means that you can tailor the mouse and keyboard to specific applications.

One of the primary benefits of using Whiskers is that it supports three-button input devices. If you do not have a three-button mouse but want to provide the same level of features as you would have with a three-button mouse, Whiskers will optionally emulate a third button on a two-button mouse. In addition, Whiskers also supports button chording. You can, for example, cause a macro or other action to occur when you click the left and right mouse buttons simultaneously.

Whiskers is available as shareware on services such as CompuServe and America Online, and also is available in a more fully featured retail version directly from Numbers & Co. The retail version, which sells for $38, includes its own mouse driver that adds the button chording and the capability to simulate a three-button mouse with a two-button mouse. You can contact Numbers & Co. at (509) 476-2216.

Power Launcher

hDC Computer Corporation's Power Launcher is actually four programs in one: Power Launcher, Power Mouse, Power Toolbox, and Power Keyboard. These utilities work together to give you many different ways to automate tasks on your system. With Power Keyboard, for example, you can remap any or all of the keys on your system's keyboard. You also can use Power Keyboard to record and assign macros to keys and key combinations. Figure 10.3 shows Power Keyboard's interface. Like Whiskers, Power Keyboard enables you to create different key mapping and macro combinations for each program you use and to create a single one for global use.

Figure 10.3
Power Keyboard enables you to program your system's keyboard.

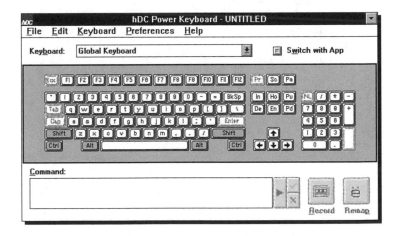

Power Launcher also includes a program called Power Mouse, which enables you to record and assign macros to mouse buttons and keyboard-mouse combinations (such as Ctrl+left click). Unlike Whiskers, however, Power Mouse does not support button chording. Figure 10.4 shows the Power Mouse interface.

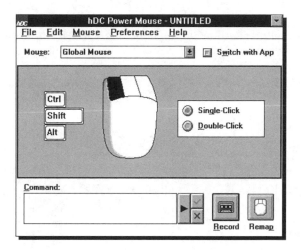

Figure 10.4
Power Mouse enables you to assign macros to mouse and keyboard combinations.

You also can create your own floating toolboxes with Power Toolbox, which is included with Power Launcher. You can create a global toolbox that you can use with all applications, or create toolboxes for specific applications. Power Toolbox offers a good way to automate tasks and provide quick access to functions that you use often in a program. Figure 10.5 shows the Power Toolbox interface.

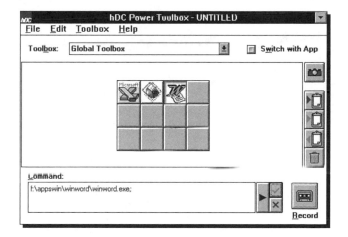

Figure 10.5
Power Toolbox enables you to create custom toolboxes.

Logitech MouseWare

If you already have a Logitech pointing device, you might have the capability to program your mouse without investing in any additional programs. Logitech now includes a utility called MouseWare (see fig. 10.6) with its pointing devices that enables you to program the device's buttons and control other mouse options. Unlike Whiskers and Power Mouse, however, Logitech's MouseWare does not enable you to program the left mouse button. It also does not support button chording or programming the keyboard. Nevertheless, MouseWare still can be a useful tool for automating mouse actions.

Figure 10.6
Logitech's
MouseWare
enables you to
program a
Logitech pointing
device.

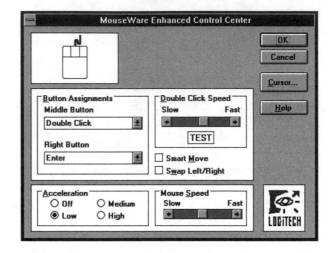

Chapter Snapshot

Your system's hard disk is a resource that Windows uses extensively, not only to store its files, but also to simulate memory and provide temporary storage for various working files. For this reason, your system's hard disk has a significant impact on how Windows performs. Using a number of techniques, you can ensure that your hard drive performs at its optimum with Windows.

This chapter examines not only hard disk topics that relate to Windows' performance, but also other mass storage issues, such as the use of tape drives in Windows. This chapter covers the following topics:

Optimizing your PC's hard disk and managing the file system are tasks you should perform often to ensure that your PC works to its optimum. This chapter provides background information that will help you understand how your hard disk functions, and also provides specific tips on optimizing its performance.

CHAPTER

Optimizing Data Storage Space

O ptimizing your hard disk and file system can be a relatively simple task, but it does require some background knowledge about hard disk technology. Before you can begin to optimize your system's hard disk, you need to understand the type of disk you have and what the other types offer.

Comparing Hard Drive Types

Although hard disk technology is relatively mature, a number of different types of hard drives are available today. Five basic types exist, each offering different levels of performance and cost.

MFM and RLL

If your PC is an older system, your hard drive may be an *MFM* (Modified Frequency Modulation) or *RLL* (Run Length Limited) hard drive. These two terms refer to the way information is written to and retrieved from the disk. Both these types of drives use an interface known as ST506. The ST506 uses two cables—one narrow cable and one wide cable—to connect the hard disk to the disk controller, which makes it easy to identify an MFM or RLL drive.

MFM and RLL drive performance is relatively poor compared to today's standards. Older MFM drives, for example, offered an access rate of around 65 ms (milliseconds). Today's drives offer much faster performance, often around 15 ms. If your system contains an MFM or RLL hard drive and you want to improve Windows' performance, consider installing a new IDE or SCSI drive in the system (IDE and SCSI are discussed later).

A fast hard disk will improve not only Windows' performance overall, but also the performance of your applications, particularly those that are disk-intensive (access the disk frequently). This performance gain also carries over into the DOS environment, making DOS applications perform better.

ESDI Drives

ESDI stands for *Enhanced Small Disk Interface*. The ESDI standard originated from the ST506 interface used in MFM and RLL drives. The primary change was an increase in speed of ESDI drives over ST506 drives. ESDI drives accomplish this by packing twice as much data into a single track as an ST506 drive.

The ESDI standard did not, however, enjoy much success. Although it provided better performance than earlier ST506 drives, users were not quick to adopt ESDI drives for use in their systems.

If you do have an ESDI drive, there is no reason to trade it in for a newer IDE or SCSI drive. ESDI drives provide very good performance for Windows, in particular when used with a caching ESDI disk controller.

IDE Drives

By far the most common type of hard disk interface used in PCs manufactured today is the IDE (Integrated Drive Electronics) interface. Unlike ST506 and ESDI drives, in which the hard disk controller is installed in one of the computer's bus slots with its other expansion cards, the controller circuitry in an IDE drive is mounted directly on the drive. If your system has an IDE drive in it and it connects to an adapter card installed in one of the system's bus slots, the adapter card is a host adapter that translates the signals going to and from the hard drive's controller circuitry. In some systems, the IDE host adapter circuitry is built into the system's motherboard.

IDE drives use a single 40-pin cable to connect the drive to the system—look at the cable to see if your hard drive is an IDE drive. Most host adapters support a maximum of two hard drives, but adapters are available that support up to four. As you will read later in this chapter, IDE tape drives now are available that can connect to your existing IDE host adapter.

IDE drives are somewhat less expensive than SCSI drives (discussed next). IDE drives offer excellent performance for any type of operating environment, including Windows. IDE drives also can take advantage of Windows' 32-bit disk access to speed up disk performance (32-bit access is covered later in this chapter). If you are looking to replace an older drive with a newer one, consider an IDE drive as your first option.

Tip

If you plan to upgrade your hard disk subsystem and replace your existing hard disk with an IDE drive, remember that you must also add an IDE host adapter to the system if it does not already contain one. You cannot, for example, run an IDE drive with an MFM, RLL, or ESDI controller.

If your system does not have any more available drive slots and you want to add another hard disk to the system, consider adding a *hardcard*—a hard disk on an adapter card that plugs into your system's expansion bus. Or, if you already have a SCSI host adapter in the system, you might consider adding an external SCSI drive to the system.

SCSI Drives

SCSI, which is pronounced "scuzzy," is the latest type of mass storage interface. Like IDE, SCSI places the controller circuitry on the storage device (such as a hard disk). Most PCs require a host adapter, installed in one of the system's bus slots, to translate data going to and from the drive.

The SCSI interface actually provides a sub-bus to which you can connect up to eight devices. The SCSI host adapter counts as one of those devices, leaving seven available for other devices. SCSI supports hard drives, CD-ROM drives, tape drives, scanners, and other types of hardware.

Two SCSI standards exist: SCSI-1 and SCSI-2. The SCSI-2 standard improves the data transfer speed and offers additional improvements over the SCSI-1 standard. If you are considering buying a SCSI host adapter, hard disk, or other SCSI device, you should make sure the device supports SCSI-2 for the best performance. In particular, the host adapter should support SCSI-2 so that you can use SCSI-2 devices. SCSI-2 host adapters are backward-compatible with SCSI-1 devices. A SCSI-1 device connected to a SCSI-2 host adapter functions properly.

CD-ROM XA drives, which are multisession drives, are supported by the SCSI-2 interface; older, less advanced Level 1 CD-ROM drives—also called Yellow Book, single-session, and MPC ROM drives—are not compatible with the SCSI-2 standard. This incompatibility is a good way to tell the difference between older, soon-to-be-outdated MPC drives and the newer CD-XA drives.

Windows 3.1 and 3.11 currently do not include 32-bit disk access for SCSI or ESDI devices, although future versions of Windows will support 32-bit access for these devices. Many third-party host adapter manufacturers, including Future Domain, UltraStor, Quantum, and Compaq, provide their own 32-bit disk access software as an enhancement to Windows.

If you are using SmartDrive with a SCSI device, you may need to enable double-buffering for the drive. Double-buffering is explained later in this chapter in the section on disk caching.

Improving Disk Performance with Fast 32-Bit Access

Windows 3.1 and 3.11 include a feature called FastDisk that can significantly speed up disk performance. FastDisk enables Windows to communicate directly with the system's hard disk controller, bypassing the system BIOS.

FastDisk works with any controller and drive combination that is fully compatible with the Western Digital 1003 controller. These include ST506-type controllers. Most hard disk controllers, including IDE drives, are compatible with FastDisk. Only ESDI and SCSI devices are not compatible with FastDisk.

Windows incorrectly senses a few types of hard disk subsystems as being compatible with FastDisk when they are not. For this reason, Windows does not automatically enable FastDisk. If you enable FastDisk on your system and notice hard disk errors or file corruption, disable FastDisk immediately and check with your hard disk subsystem's manufacturer to verify that your system is compatible with FastDisk.

Speeding Up Disk Access

Without FastDisk, the system must switch a number of times between protected mode and virtual mode to process disk I/O. FastDisk enables Windows to handle disk I/O through virtual device drivers in protected mode, reducing the number of times the system must switch into virtual mode to process the disk BIOS requests. Because mode switching is time-consuming, FastDisk can speed up disk activity considerably.

Early processors such as the 8088 and 8086 operated in what is called *real mode*. Real mode is limited to addressing 1 MB of memory. The 386 and newer CPUs can function in real mode, protected mode, and virtual mode. In *protected mode,* the CPU can address up to 4 GB of RAM. In *virtual mode,* a CPU can create an almost unlimited number of "virtual machines," or simulated 8086-based computers. Virtual mode is what enables Windows in 386 Enhanced mode to multitask DOS applications (wherein each runs in its own virtual machine).

Improving DOS Program Performance

When running DOS programs under Windows, you may receive an out-of-memory error even when the Help About dialog box shows that plenty of memory is still available. Because of the way DOS programs are structured, conflicts can occur if Windows pages part of a DOS program to disk. Windows might be unable to page a needed part of the DOS program back into memory because the DOS program might be waiting for disk access from the BIOS, preventing Windows from also accessing the BIOS to page the needed part of the program back into memory. To avoid this problem, Windows does not page an active DOS program to disk if FastDisk is not enabled.

With FastDisk enabled, Windows is able to handle disk I/O independent of the BIOS. If a DOS program is communicating with the BIOS for disk I/O and part of the DOS program needs to be paged back into memory, Windows can page the data from disk to memory without waiting for the DOS program to complete its BIOS calls. This means that Windows can page active DOS programs to disk, making more memory available to start additional DOS programs.

FastDisk also speeds up overall system response when using DOS programs. This is because DOS programs can be paged to disk, instead of completely swapped to disk. Windows needs to load into memory only those parts of the DOS program that are required at that moment, not the entire program.

Any DOS program that performs extensive disk access, such as database programs, will see significant benefits when FastDisk is enabled under Windows. Other DOS programs also will benefit, but the change may be less noticeable.

Setting Up FastDisk

FastDisk consists of four virtual device drivers, which are built into the file WIN386.EXE:

- ✔ **WDCtrl.** This supports WD1003 and ST506 controllers. Setup installs this device driver only if it detects that your system's hard disk is compatible with FastDisk.

- ✔ **Int13.** This traps and handles INT 13H BIOS calls that otherwise would be processed by the system BIOS. Int13 is installed by Setup only if Setup detects a FastDisk-compatible disk.

- ✔ **BlockDev.** This serves as an interface between FastDisk and devices that request block I/O services. Setup always installs this device driver.

- ✔ **PageFile.** This handles the virtual memory paging file. Setup always installs this device driver.

Installing FastDisk

Because there is a potential to lose data when using FastDisk with a controller that is not 100 percent compatible with FastDisk, Setup will not turn on FastDisk by default. To turn on FastDisk, open the Control Panel, double-click on the 386 Enhanced icon, then choose Virtual Memory. This displays the Virtual Memory dialog box. In the Virtual Memory dialog box, choose Change to expand the dialog box (see fig. 11.1).

The check box labeled Use 32-Bit Disk Access in the lower left corner of the Virtual Memory dialog box turns FastDisk on and off. To enable FastDisk, check this check box. After making this change, click on OK. Windows prompts you to restart Windows to make the change take effect.

Because there is a potential for loss of data if your disk subsystem is not compatible with FastDisk, you should back up your hard disk if you are unsure of its compatibility.

When you turn on FastDisk, Windows modifies your SYSTEM.INI file. The following lines are added or modified in the [386Enh] section of SYSTEM.INI:

```
device=*int13
device=*wdctrl
32BitDiskAccess=On
```

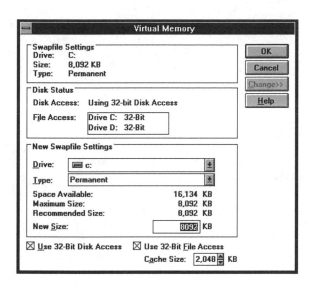

Figure 11.1
The expanded Virtual Memory dialog box enables you to turn on FastDisk.

Turning Off FastDisk

If you have enabled FastDisk and begin experiencing problems with disk access or other operations, your hard disk subsystem might not be compatible with FastDisk and might be causing the problem. To troubleshoot the problem, turn off FastDisk and restart Windows.

You can disable FastDisk in three ways:

✔ **Use the Virtual Memory dialog box.** Open Control Panel, click on the 386 Enhanced icon, then choose Virtual Memory. Choose Change, then clear the Use 32-Bit Memory Access check box. Click on OK and restart Windows.

✔ **Edit the 32BitDiskAccess= setting.** Open SYSTEM.INI in Notepad or in DOS EDIT, and change the 32BitDiskAccess= setting to read 32BitDiskAccess=**Off**.

✔ **Use the /D:F switch to start Windows.** Windows provides a debug switch that you can use to start Windows with FastDisk disabled. To do so, exit to DOS, then type **WIN /D:F**. Windows will start with FastDisk disabled.

Using 32-Bit File Access

Windows for Workgroups 3.11 includes a new feature called 32-bit file access. *32-bit file access* consists of two virtual device drivers, VFAT.386 and VCACHE.386, that extend Windows support for 32-bit file and disk access operations. 32-bit file access enables Windows for Workgroups 3.11 to support MS-DOS Int 21H services in protected mode, eliminating the need for the processor to switch to real mode to handle these interrupts. Int 21H services manipulate the File Allocation Table (FAT) and control the way data is written to and read from a FAT volume. The virtual device driver VFAT.386 provides these protected-mode Int 21H services. This 32-bit file access capability provides improved file access and, to a limited degree, better memory management.

Windows 3.11 and Windows for Workgroups 3.11 do not share the same non-network features, even though their version numbers are the same. Windows 3.11 is a minor upgrade that fixes a few bugs and includes a few new device drivers. Windows for Workgroups 3.11, however, includes significant general changes in addition to its networking features. One of these changes is 32-bit file access. Windows 3.11 does not include 32-bit file access. This feature is available only in Windows for Workgroups 3.11.

32-bit file access also provides a protected-mode replacement for the SmartDrive disk cache (explained in the next section of this chapter). Providing a protected-mode disk cache makes disk and file access in Windows more efficient and improves overall system performance. The virtual device driver VCACHE.386 handles protected-mode disk caching.

Examining the Requirements for 32-Bit File Access

The VFAT virtual device driver will only mount onto storage devices that it recognizes as being supported by 32-bit disk access. VFAT therefore functions automatically with devices that are supported by 32-bit disk access, such as WD1003-compatible drives. In addition, Windows includes a *real-mode mapper* that transfers protected-mode file I/O calls from VFAT to the real-mode MS-DOS device driver chain. The real-mode mapper supports 32-bit file access for devices that are not supported by 32-bit disk access, such as some SCSI and ESDI devices. The real-mode mapper also is required to support file access to and from compressed volumes (disks compressed using DoubleSpace or Stacker, for example). The virtual device driver RMM.D32 serves as the real-mode mapper.

RMM.D32 will not appear in your SYSTEM.INI file even if 32-bit file access is enabled. RMM.D32 is loaded by the VXDLDR.386 virtual device driver and supported by IOS.386. There will be entries for these two virtual device drivers in the [386Enh] section of SYSTEM.INI when 32-bit file access is enabled.

Using 32-Bit File Access

By default, 32-bit file access is turned off when you install Windows for Workgroups 3.11. To enable 32-bit file access, open the Control Panel and choose the 386 Enhanced icon, then choose the Virtual Memory button in the Enhanced dialog box to display the Virtual Memory dialog box. Choose the Change button to expand the dialog box as shown previously in figure 11.1.

To enable 32-bit file access, place a check in the Use 32-Bit File Access check box. Because 32-bit file access requires 32-bit disk access support, the check box labeled Use 32-Bit Disk Access should also contain a check.

After you have placed a check in the Use 32-Bit File Access check box, the Cache Size spin control below the check box will change to reflect a recommended virtual cache size for your system. You can accept the default or change the size of the cache. For most configurations, the default cache size will be acceptable. Refer to the section titled "Exploring Disk Caching" later in this chapter if you want to learn if changing the size of the virtual disk cache could improve your system's performance.

Enabling the 32-bit disk cache (by enabling 32-bit file access) will not automatically disable SmartDrive. The Control Panel will, however, modify the SmartDrive line in AUTOEXEC.BAT to reduce the size of the SmartDrive cache when Windows is running to a minimal size of 128 KB. Leaving SmartDrive enabled provides disk caching for applications that you might run outside of Windows. If you do not run applications outside of Windows, consider eliminating SmartDrive altogether.

Understanding the Installable File System Manager

The Installable File System Manager (IFS) virtual device driver (IFSMGR.386) provides overall management of 32-bit disk and file access. IFSMGR serves as an interface between applications' Int 21H calls and the other aspects of 32-bit disk and file access. When an application makes an Int 21H call for access to the FAT, IFSMGR intercepts the call and determines the status of the target disk. If the target disk is a network drive, IFSMGR passes the I/O request to the network redirector. If the target device is supported by VFAT, IFSMGR passes the request to VFAT. If the target device is not serviced by either VFAT or the network redirector, IFSMGR passes the disk request to MS-DOS to be handled by the DOS real-mode I/O services. IFSMGR is installed automatically when you install or update to Windows for Workgroups 3.11.

Exploring Disk Caching

Two physical factors limit hard disk performance: access speed and transfer rate. *Access speed* is the amount of time, expressed in milliseconds, required to move the disk's heads between disk tracks. *Transfer rate* is the rate at which data can be transferred between the disk and the PC's memory.

II

Optimizing Windows

Both transfer rate and access time are fundamental physical limitations; you cannot do anything to overcome them in an existing disk subsystem. You cannot force the heads to move any faster than they already move or change the system's bus rate to improve transfer speed.

Disk performance can be particularly troublesome with an environment such as DOS (upon which Windows relies). DOS is a single-threaded operating environment: it performs only one task at a time. DOS waits for each task to complete before it starts a new one. If DOS requests data from the hard disk, it does not begin a new operation until the data has been retrieved.

A disk cache overcomes this limitation by enabling DOS to retrieve the most recently used data from the cache, rather than retrieving it from the disk, which takes longer. Disk caching helps overcome the physical limitations of a hard disk's design and gives you a way to improve existing hard disk performance.

Checking Out a Disk Cache

A *cache* is a temporary storage area for data moving between the hard disk and memory. To illustrate how a cache works, suppose an application requests data from the disk. The request is intercepted by a cache manager, such as Windows' SmartDrive. The cache software checks the cache to determine if the requested data is already in the cache (which it is, if the data has been read recently). If the data is in the cache, the cache manager passes the data back to the requesting application as if it had come from the hard disk. The data comes from the cache RAM rather than the hard disk. The cache improves the apparent access time of the disk, because access to RAM is much faster than access to a hard disk.

If the data is not in the cache, the cache manager passes on the request and it is serviced by the hard disk subsystem. The data is transferred from the disk to the cache, and then passed on to the application. If the application requests the same data later, it is read from the cache. This describes a *read-only cache.* It applies only to requests to read data from the disk.

 Even though the system might have read certain data into the cache recently, there is no guarantee that data will still be in the cache because enough new data might have been read into the cache to overwrite the previous data. Even so, a disk cache still has a significant overall net benefit.

SmartDrive functions as a write-behind cache as well as a read cache. Not only does SmartDrive cache requests for data to be read from the disk, but it also caches requests for data to be written to the disk.

To illustrate a write-behind cache, suppose an application stores a file. The data goes into the cache, and the cache manager indicates to the application that the file transfer is complete. The application can then continue working. Later, while the system's CPU is idle, the cache manager uses small amounts of time to send the file to the disk. This process improves overall system performance because the application does not have to wait for the physical file transfer.

Hardware Caches

Disk caches take two forms: hardware and software. The most common type of hardware cache consists of RAM installed on the hard disk controller. Onboard cache circuitry on the controller manages the cache. A caching controller or host adapter is much more expensive than a hard disk controller with no cache. As an example, an IDE host adapter costs around $30; a typical caching IDE host adapter costs around $150.

Aside from adding cost to the system, controller-based caches have one other drawback: they cannot overcome the performance degradation caused by the system's bus. Data still must be transferred from the hardware cache on the controller, through the bus, to the CPU. The hardware cache improves performance, but in many cases better performance is possible with a software cache unless processor cycles are a primary concern.

If you are interested in implementing a hardware cache for your system, EISA and VESA motherboards are good choices for implementing hardware caching. If you want to add a hardware-based cache to an existing ISA system, consider a caching disk controller.

Software Caches

SmartDrive, which is included with Windows and MS-DOS, is a software cache. SmartDrive uses some of your system's RAM as a cache. It manages this memory, using it to process disk I/O requests. When an application requests data from the disk, SmartDrive intercepts the request and checks its cache to see if the data is already there. If it is, SmartDrive passes the data to the application as if it had been retrieved from the disk. If the data is not in the cache, SmartDrive passes the request to the disk. When the data is returned from the disk, SmartDrive intercepts it, places it in the cache, and then transfers it to the application.

Because SmartDrive is installed in the operating environment before Windows is started, DOS and DOS programs also benefit from SmartDrive, even when you are not running Windows. In addition, DOS programs that you run under Windows will benefit from SmartDrive's cache.

SmartDrive also functions as a write-behind cache. When an application sends data to the disk, SmartDrive intercepts it and places it in the cache. SmartDrive then uses small amounts of time when the CPU is idle to send the data to the drive. This improves performance because the application can continue to work without waiting for the slower hardware-based data transfer to occur.

When in DOS, allow a few seconds for the disk cache to be cleared after you exit an application before turning off the system. This ensures that any disk writes remaining in the cache will be transferred to disk before the system is shut down.

The primary benefit of a software cache is that it overcomes the system bus speed limitation of a hardware cache. When data needs to be moved from the cache to the CPU, data moves from the system's RAM to the CPU, which is much faster than moving the data from a hardware cache across the bus and to the CPU.

SmartDrive offers close integration with Windows. Windows often can write directly to the cache, further reducing disk I/O overhead.

Improving Performance with SmartDrive

If you are not yet using a cache, you can add one without any additional expense and with very little trouble. SmartDrive 5.0 is included with Windows 3.11, Windows for Workgroups 3.11, and MS-DOS 6.2. The file SMARTDRV.EXE, which is SmartDrive's executable file, is located in your Windows directory and in your DOS directory. Check the dates of the SMARTDRV.EXE files in your Windows and DOS directories to determine which is the most current file. Always use the most current copy of SmartDrive.

To install SmartDrive, you must add an entry to your AUTOEXEC.BAT file. The following syntax shows the format for the SmartDrive command line:

```
SMARTDRV.EXE /E:size /B:size DRIVE +¦- initsize WinSize
/R /L /Q /S /?
```

✔ /E. Element size specifies the amount of cached data in kilobytes that SmartDrive will move at one time. The default is 8 KB.

✔ /B. Buffer size specifies the size of the read buffer.

✔ /R. Clears the contents of the cache and restarts SmartDrive.

✔ /L. Prevents SmartDrive from loading into the UMA, even if UMBs are available.

✔ /Q. Suppresses display of SmartDrive status information on start-up.

✔ /S. Displays additional status information.

✔ /?. Displays a help screen listing the available parameters.

✔ `drive + or -`. Enables (+) or disables (-) read and write caching for the specified drive.

✔ `initsize`. Sets initial size of SmartDrive's cache prior to starting Windows.

✔ `WinSize`. Sets the size to which Windows reduces the cache when Windows starts.

Another parameter you can specify on the SmartDrive command line is the size of the cache in kilobytes. See the section "Controlling Cache Size" for more information.

Although you can install SmartDrive at the DOS command line before starting Windows, you should install it using AUTOEXEC.BAT to improve the performance of DOS applications you run outside of Windows.

If you are using 32-bit file access, which includes its own 32-bit protected mode disk cache, you do not need SmartDrive when running Windows for Workgroups 3.11. When you enable 32-bit file access, Control Panel will modify the SmartDrive line in AUTOEXEC.BAT, if it exists, changing the size of the SmartDrive cache when Windows is running. If you do not run applications outside of Windows and are using 32-bit file access, you do not have to use SmartDrive.

Installing SmartDrive

Usually, you can install SmartDrive without any of its optional parameters and have it work fine with your system. The following example, added to AUTOEXEC.BAT, installs SmartDrive:

```
C:\WINDOWS\SMARTDRV.EXE
```

Although you can change the way SmartDrive works by adding various switches to its command line, SmartDrive will perform well in most situations with its default settings.

You should always use the most up-to-date version of SmartDrive. If you have installed MS-DOS 6.2, you will have a more current version of SmartDrive than the one supplied with Windows 3.1. If so, change the SmartDrive line in AUTOEXEC.BAT to load SmartDrive from the DOS directory instead of from the Windows directory. If you have installed Windows 3.11 or Windows for Workgroups 3.11, the Windows directory will contain the most up-to-date version of SmartDrive.

Controlling Cache Size

When SmartDrive starts, it sets the cache to a specific size. When Windows starts, it can reduce SmartDrive's cache size to recover some of the memory SmartDrive is using. If SmartDrive later needs more memory, Windows enlarges SmartDrive's cache. You can change the size of SmartDrive's cache in two ways—change its initial size or its minimum size when Windows is running.

If no parameter is specified to set the initial cache size, SmartDrive chooses a default based on the amount of RAM in the system. Table 11.1 lists default initial cache sizes and Windows SmartDrive sizes according to memory size.

Table 11.1
Default Cache Sizes for SmartDrive

Extended Memory	Initial Size	Size in Windows
1 MB or less	All extended memory	0 (no cache)
Up to 2 MB	1 MB	256 KB
Up to 4 MB	1 MB	512 KB
Up to 6 MB	2 MB	1 MB
6 MB or more	2 MB	2 MB

To set either size, just add the appropriate values to the SmartDrive command line. The following example sets initial cache size (outside of Windows) to 2 MB and cache size in Windows to 1.5 MB:

```
C:\WINDOWS\SMARTDRV.EXE 2048 1536
```

For the best performance, do not set the initial cache size less than 512 KB. Specify as large a cache as possible according to how much memory you are willing to take from Windows to give to SmartDrive. In general, a maximum 1–2 MB cache will be sufficient for most systems.

If you are not running applications outside of Windows, and you can use 32-bit file access on your system, you do not have to use SmartDrive. The protected mode virtual cache that is part of the 32-bit file access services will provide better performance than SmartDrive. If you want to continue using SmartDrive because you run applications outside of Windows, reduce the size of the cache in Windows to a minimum of 128 KB.

Enabling and Disabling Caching

By default, Windows enables read- and write-caching for hard drives but only enables read-caching for floppy drives. Write-caching for floppy disks is not enabled because a floppy disk might be removed from the drive before all write-behind blocks have been cleared.

 If you want, you can enable write-caching of floppy disks. Just be sure to let the system sit idle for a few seconds to clear the cache before removing the floppy disk.

You can disable caching for one of your hard drives or enable write-caching for a floppy drive. Simply specify the drive letter and a plus (+) to enable read- and write-caching or a minus (-) to disable caching.

The following example disables caching for drive F, enables caching for drive B, sets the initial cache size to 2,048 KB, and sets the minimum Windows cache size to 1,024 KB:

```
SMARTDRV B+ F- 2048 1024
```

Disabling caching for a drive disables both read- and write-caching. If you enable write-caching on a floppy drive, for example, and then return to the original default of read-caching enabled and write-caching disabled, you must reboot the system. B- disables both read- and write-caching for the B drive.

Enabling Double Buffering

Some hard disk controllers use a technique called *bus mastering*, in which the disk controller takes control of the bus to transfer data between the CPU and the hard disk. This can lead to problems when the system switches to virtual mode, because the virtual memory addresses used to transfer data from the cache might not match the physical memory addresses of the cache. This can cause data to be incorrectly read from, or written to, the wrong area of memory. To overcome the problem, SmartDrive can create a secondary buffer in which virtual and physical addresses match. This is called *double buffering*.

SmartDrive is compatible with most hard disk controllers, including many ESDI and SCSI adapters. Setup can generally recognize incompatible adapters and then add the necessary entry to CONFIG.SYS to enable double buffering (explained later in this chapter). In fact, Setup usually errs on the side of safety and installs double buffering for SCSI devices even if it is not required.

To determine if your system's hard disk requires double buffering, first start the system and allow SmartDrive to load in AUTOEXEC.BAT. At the DOS prompt, type **SMARTDRV** and press Enter. You will see output similar to the following:

```
        Microsoft SMARTDrive Disk Cache version 5.0
        Copyright 1991,1993 Microsoft Corp.
        Cache size: 2,097,152 bytes
        Cache size while running Windows: 2,097,152 bytes
Disk Caching Status
        drive   read cache   write cache   buffering
        ------------------------------------------------------------
        A:         yes           no           no
        B:         yes           no           no
        C:         yes           yes          no
        D:         yes           yes          no
For help, type "Smartdrv /?".
```

If the buffering column in the output indicates no for the drive in question, the drive does not require double buffering.

SmartDrive is installed by the AUTOEXEC.BAT file or from the DOS command line. Double buffering, however, is installed by the CONFIG.SYS file. The following example enables double buffering (it must be included in CONFIG.SYS, but it does not take the place of the entry in AUTOEXEC.BAT):

```
DEVICE=C:\WINDOWS\SMARTDRV.EXE /DOUBLE_BUFFER
```

You can use the LOADHIGH command in AUTOEXEC.BAT to load SmartDrive into upper memory. You cannot, however, use the DEVICEHIGH= command in CONFIG.SYS to install double buffering in the upper memory area. Instead you must use the DEVICE= command, which sets up double buffering below 640 KB.

If your system contains an expanded memory board that cannot be configured as extended memory, contains plenty of extended memory (8 MB or more), or is a diskless workstation with more than 4 MB of RAM, you might want to consider using a RAM drive. A RAM drive can speed up printing and performance of some of your applications.

Because using a RAM drive requires use of some of your system's memory, RAM drives are explained in detail in Chapter 9, "Optimizing Memory."

Using Data Compression

Considering the amount of space required to hold today's applications and the possibility that you run many different applications on your system, the lack of available disk space can rapidly become a problem. Although you can add a bigger hard disk to your system or augment the existing disk with a second disk, many users are not able or willing to suffer the additional expense of a new drive.

Instead of buying a new hard drive, many Windows users take advantage of disk compression software or hardware, which reduces the size of files and programs.

Many files are made up of repetitive data that appear in the file in patterns. A disk compression algorithm can be used to scan files for these repetitive patterns and replace them with a small token of only a few bytes. Thus, a large amount of data can be reduced to only a few bytes, compressing the information into a smaller amount of disk space. When the data needs to be read from the disk, the compression hardware or software reads the token and replaces it with the original data.

Some types of files compress more readily than others because they are more repetitive in nature. Others cannot be compressed as much because fewer repetitive patterns are present in the file.

If there are many BMP files on your system and you use them for wallpaper, you should consider converting them to RLE format, instead. RLE files are encoded differently from BMP files in a way that requires less disk space. Even with the files in RLE format, you still can use them as wallpaper files. You can use a program such as Hijaak, WinGIF, or PaintShop Pro to convert the files.

Most files on a hard disk can be compressed by approximately 50 percent, which means that disk compression can effectively double the capacity of your system's hard disk. This is equivalent to converting a 100 MB hard disk to a 200 MB hard disk. If your hard disk is beginning to fill up, you can compress it and make more free space available, postponing the need to buy a new hard disk.

DoubleSpace (MS-DOS 6)

If you are using MS-DOS 6.0 or 6.2, you already have disk compression software—you do not need to buy additional software. MS-DOS 6 includes a feature called DoubleSpace that compresses your system's hard disk. DoubleSpace is integrated with the DOS BIOS, making it transparent to applications and to Windows. DoubleSpace can nearly double the effective capacity of your system's hard disk.

DoubleSpace was removed from MS-DOS 6.21 due to a lawsuit by Stac Electronics against Microsoft that claimed patent infringement by Microsoft. If you have MS-DOS 6.0 or 6.2, you can continue to legally use DoubleSpace. If you prefer, Microsoft will have an alternative disk compression technology available by the time this book goes to press. The new disk compression should be available as part of an interim DOS upgrade or as a stand-alone add-on. The MS-DOS 6.21 package includes a coupon for a free copy of the new disk compression utility.

If you are currently using MS-DOS 6.0 however, you should consider carefully whether or not to use DoubleSpace. The version of DoubleSpace that shipped with MS-DOS 6.0 caused data loss in a very limited number of situations. Although it is unlikely that you would experience problems using the MS-DOS 6.0 version of DoubleSpace, it is a possibility. DoubleSpace was modified in MS-DOS 6.2 to correct these potential problems.

 DoubleSpace does not offer an uninstall option. After your hard disk has been converted to DoubleSpace, the only way to convert it back to an uncompressed drive is to back up the files, remove the DoubleSpace logical disk, and restore the files. Therefore, you should definitely make a backup of your entire hard disk before converting to DoubleSpace.

Installing DoubleSpace

DoubleSpace includes an automated setup program that makes configuring DoubleSpace on your computer a relatively simple task. If you want to compress all the data on your hard drive, follow these steps to set up DoubleSpace on your MS-DOS 6 system:

1. Back up your hard disk. Although DoubleSpace will safely compress your hard disk, and compression can even be suspended and restarted, you still should create a backup of your important data.

2. Exit Windows, type **DBLSPACE** at the DOS prompt, then press Enter. The DoubleSpace Setup program starts. At the first screen, press Enter to begin configuring DoubleSpace.

3. If you want to compress your existing drive and have DoubleSpace automatically set all parameters for you, choose Express Setup. DoubleSpace Setup will compress all your existing data and set all operating parameters.

The Custom setup option enables you to specify which drive you want compressed and also enables you to create a new compressed drive using the free space on an existing drive. You can take a portion of the free space on drive C, for example, and create a new compressed drive D with that space. The new drive D will be twice as large as the amount of free space. With 20 MB of free space, for example, DoubleSpace creates a 40 MB drive D. If you still have plenty of free space on a drive and do not want to compress the existing data, use the following steps to install and configure DoubleSpace:

1. Back up your hard disk.

2. Type **DBLSPACE** at the DOS prompt and press Enter.

3. Select the Custom Setup option.

4. Select the option labeled Create a new empty compressed drive.

5. From the list of available drives supplied by DoubleSpace Setup, select the drive containing the free space from which you want to create a new compressed logical drive.

6. DoubleSpace Setup then prompts for three parameters:

```
Amount of free space to leave on the drive
Compression ratio
Drive letter to be assigned to the drive
```

Specify the amount of free space you want to leave on the existing drive and specify which drive ID to assign to the new drive. Changing the compression ratio value affects only the way DoubleSpace estimates free space on the new disk. It does not change the amount of storage space on the compressed drive. Leave it at its default of 2.0.

7. Follow the remainder of DoubleSpace Setup's prompts to create the new compressed drive.

DoubleSpace Setup creates a hidden file to contain the new compressed disk. It also adds a device driver line in CONFIG.SYS for the DoubleSpace device driver.

Using DoubleSpace Drives with Windows

After DoubleSpace has been installed, you use the compressed drive as you would any other disk drive. The compression is completely transparent to you. When you want to save a file on a compressed disk, simply select the drive's logical drive ID when saving the file. DoubleSpace will intercept the file operation, compress the document, and place it in the compressed drive. When you load a file from a compressed drive, MS-DOS intercepts the file operation, expands the file, and passes it to your application.

When you install MS-DOS 6, some new features are added to your Windows File Manager. You will find a new **T**ools menu that contains a command labeled **D**oubleSpace Info. Select a DoubleSpace drive from File Manager's drive bar or select the directory window for a DoubleSpace drive if one is already open. Choose **T**ools, **D**oubleSpace Info to display the DoubleSpace Info dialog box shown in figure 11.2.

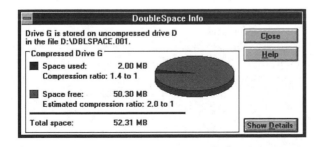

Figure 11.2

The DoubleSpace Info dialog box provides information about compressed drives.

The DoubleSpace Info dialog box shows the amount of free space on the disk (compressed), the amount of space used, and estimated compression ratios for each. Choose the Show **D**etails command to view information about specific files in the compressed

II

Optimizing Windows

drive. Figure 11.3 shows the expanded DoubleSpace Info dialog box with file status displayed.

Figure 11.3

Clicking on the Show Details button displays information about files in the compressed drive.

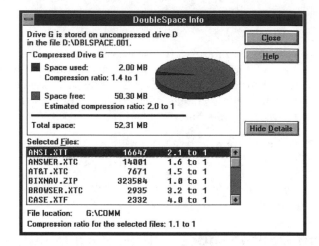

Other Disk Compression Software

A number of disk compression products are available in the market—Stacker and DoubleSpace are just two of them. If you are considering buying a disk compression product, take a close look at the product's integration with Windows. The disk compression/decompression should work seamlessly with Windows. A Windows-based disk management utility, such as is offered in DoubleSpace and Stacker, is a definite plus.

Setting Up a Swap File

In addition to using your system's hard disk to store files, Windows uses the hard disk for temporary storage, also called swap files. A *swap file* is a special file that Windows uses for virtual memory, swapping memory pages from RAM to the swap file as necessary to accommodate all the applications using system memory. Unlike a SmartDrive cache, which affects the system even in DOS when Windows is not running, swap files are used only by Windows. Windows offers three options for the use of swap files, and these options can be selected from the 386 Enhanced icon in Control Panel.

If you have a large amount of RAM in your system (16 MB or more), you can reduce swap file size to a minimum, but you should not remove the swap file altogether. Experiment with different sizes according to the amount of memory installed in the system. For example, try a 4 MB swap file if your system has 16 MB of RAM, 2 MB if it has 24 MB, and so on. For best results, do not reduce the swap file size below 2 MB.

Without a swap file, Windows is unable to accommodate many applications unless your system contains a large amount of RAM. Even with plenty of RAM, a swap file ensures plenty of space to accommodate your data and improve Windows' performance. Therefore, the type and size of swap file you use has a significant impact on Windows' performance.

Swap File Locations

Windows uses the directory defined by the TEMP environment variable in the SYSTEM.INI file to indicate where the swap files are created.

If you want to place the swap files elsewhere, such as to place the swap files on the faster of two hard disks, add the swapdisk= setting to the [NonWindowsApp] section of SYSTEM.INI:

```
[NonWindowsApp]
Swapdisk=d:\TEMP
```

Specify the disk ID and directory in which you want the swap files to be placed. The following tips can help you decide where your swap files should be located:

✔ **Ensure at least 1 MB of free space.** You should have at least 1 MB of free space available on the swap disk. For each additional DOS program you run, you should have a minimum of 512 KB additional free space on the disk.

✔ **Use the fastest drive.** If you have more than one hard drive in your system, and one is faster than the other, use the faster drive, if possible.

✔ **Use the disk with the most free space.** If you have more than one hard drive, use the one with the most free space, unless you plan to run few or no DOS programs.

Standard Mode Swap Files

When Windows runs in Standard mode, it creates a swap file shared by all Windows applications; Windows also creates a separate swap file for each DOS program currently running. Windows uses these swap files as necessary to manage the system's memory according to the applications that are active.

If you start a DOS program running in Standard mode, Windows swaps all Windows applications into their swap file. If you switch back to Windows from the DOS program, Windows swaps the DOS program into its swap file and restores the Windows environment from the Windows swap file.

The use of swap files in Standard mode is automatic. You do not need to do anything to take advantage of them. You can, however, control where the swap files are placed (see the section "Swap Files Locations").

386 Enhanced Mode Swap Files

In 386 Enhanced mode, Windows does not use application swap files as it does in Standard mode. Instead, Windows uses a single swap file to contain all applications, including Windows and DOS programs. Windows offers three options for a swap file in 386 Enhanced mode: no swap file, a temporary swap file, or a permanent swap file.

No Swap File

In 386 Enhanced mode you usually benefit from using a swap file; it improves performance and ensures that you have the capability to run as many applications as you need. Only three situations exist in which you would not want to use a swap file in 386 Enhanced mode: if your system has little free disk space, if the system has a large amount of RAM, or if you are running Windows on a diskless workstation.

If your system has little free disk space, scan the drive for files you no longer need. If you find files you no longer need, move them to floppy disks or tape, or delete them. If you are running Windows on a diskless workstation, you should avoid swapping to a network drive if at all possible. Swapping to a network drive creates an inordinate amount of network traffic. If you do have to swap to a network drive, use a temporary swap file.

 Ideally, your system's swap file should equal roughly one and one-half to two times the amount of RAM installed in the system. As the amount of installed memory increases, however, swap file size can decrease.

To specify no swap file for Windows in 386 Enhanced mode, open Control Panel and click on the 386 Enhanced icon. Select Virtual Memory, Change to display the Virtual Memory dialog box shown in figure 11.4.

From the Type pull-down menu, highlight None, then click on OK. Windows prompts you to continue or restart Windows. Allow the Control Panel to restart Windows to make the change take effect.

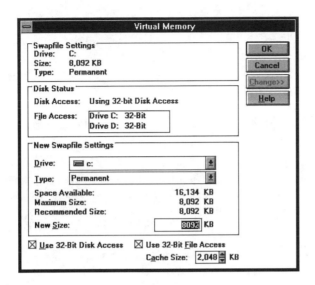

Figure 11.4
The Virtual
Memory dialog
box is used to
specify a swap
file.

Temporary Swap File

The second option for a swap file in 386 Enhanced mode is the temporary swap file. Windows dynamically resizes a temporary swap file as necessary. If Windows runs low on memory, it makes the file larger. If it does not need as large a swap file, it reduces its size. When Windows exits, it deletes the temporary swap file.

A temporary swap file offers one benefit over a permanent swap file: it does not take up disk space when you are not using Windows. When you exit Windows, the temporary swap file is deleted. If you always use Windows, however, this really is not an advantage. You should consider using a temporary swap file only if it is important to have the most free disk space available in DOS outside of Windows.

To set up a temporary swap file, double-click on the 386 Enhanced icon in Control Panel. Select Virtual Memory, Change. In the Type pull-down menu, choose Temporary. Then, in the New Size edit box, specify the maximum file size desired in kilobytes. To specify a maximum swap file size of 4 MB, for example, type **4096**.

Permanent Swap File

Instead of using a temporary swap file, you can create a permanent swap file. Unlike most files, which usually are fragmented across the disk, a permanent swap file is created in contiguous sectors. This makes access to the file much faster.

The drawback to a permanent swap file, however, is that Windows does not delete the swap file when you exit Windows. The permanent swap file stays on the disk even when you are not using Windows.

> You cannot create a permanent swap file on a network drive or on a compressed disk (such as a disk using Stacker or DoubleSpace).

Before you create a swap file, you first should defragment the hard disk on which the permanent swap file will be created. This makes the maximum amount of free contiguous disk space available for creating the swap file. (For more information on defragmenting a drive, refer to the section "Protecting Drive Performance" later in this chapter.)

To create a permanent swap file after defragmenting the drive, click on the 386 Enhanced icon in Control Panel. Select Virtual Memory, Change. In the Type pull-down menu box, choose Permanent. Then, in the New Size edit box, enter the size in kilobytes for the desired swap file.

> Use one and one-half to two times the amount of installed RAM for the size of your system's swap file, unless you have 16 MB or more of RAM. At 16 MB, try a swap file of 4–8 MB, according to the number of applications you run concurrently (for more applications, use a larger swap file). Above 16 MB, you can further reduce the size of the swap file, but do not reduce it below 2 MB.

Protecting Drive Performance

To keep Windows functioning best, you should perform periodic and regular maintenance on your hard disk. This does not mean cleaning the drive. In fact, if you can clean or repair anything on a hard disk, you will damage it beyond repair. Instead, routine maintenance means performing general housekeeping chores on the disk, such as eliminating old files, defragmenting the disk, and checking the integrity of the data on the disk.

Checking Disk Structure

You should periodically check the structural integrity of your hard disk's file system. Normally, the clusters on a disk (*clusters* are storage areas that make up sectors) are either allocated as being available or as belonging to a file. Occasionally, however, chains of clusters can end up in a state of limbo—neither allocated to a file nor allocated to the disk's available free space.

You can use the DOS CHKDSK command to recover these lost clusters. CHKDSK can either convert the lost cluster chains to files so that you can examine them, or it can add the clusters to the pool of available clusters, giving you more free space on the disk.

To recover lost cluster chains with CHKDSK, you must first exit Windows.

Never execute within Windows any program such as CHKDSK that modifies the disk structure. Doing so will result in a loss of data.

At the DOS prompt, type **CHKDSK /F** and press Enter. With this command CHKDSK scans the disk, and asks you whether you want CHKDSK to convert to files any lost cluster chains it finds. If you answer Yes, CHKDSK converts the lost cluster chains to files in the root directory of the disk with the file name FILE*nnnn*.CHK; *nnnn* is a number. You then can view the contents of the files to see if you need them.

The files created by CHKDSK /F from lost chains retain the file format they originally had. Therefore, you might have to use different applications to view the various files. To view a recovered Excel file, for example, you need to use Excel.

If you answer No to CHKDSK's prompt, CHKDSK places the lost cluster chains in the pool of available clusters, making more disk space available.

If you prefer to perform a more detailed scan of your system's hard disk, and you have MS-DOS 6 installed on your system, you can use ScanDisk to analyze the drive. To run ScanDisk, exit Windows and type **SCANDISK** at the DOS prompt. In addition to checking and fixing the same potential problems as CHKDSK, ScanDisk also can perform a surface analysis of the disk to locate bad sectors. ScanDisk is a menu-driven program and very simple to use.

Eliminating Cross-Linked Files

Cross-linked files are files or directories that use the same disk space, which indicates that one of the files is corrupted. CHKDSK reports the names and locations of cross-linked files, but it does not repair them. To repair cross-linked files, copy the cross-linked files to a new directory (which creates new copies of the files). Then check the files to see if they are corrupted. You might lose some data from one of the files.

An EXE or COM file that has become cross-linked might no longer function properly. If an EXE or COM file becomes cross-linked, reinstall the file from your application's source disks.

Defragmenting

As files are written to your disk, the amount of contiguous free space decreases. (*Contiguous disk space* refers to available sectors located side-by-side on the disk.) DOS attempts to place files in contiguous sectors whenever possible. If the disk does not have enough contiguous sectors to contain a file, however, DOS must scatter the file across the disk in any available sectors it can find. The result: files become fragmented.

Nothing is wrong with the fragmented files; DOS and Windows can retrieve them and put them back together without any problem. It just takes more time to hunt across the disk for all the sectors that make up a file.

 Because the heads on a fragmented drive must move more often than on a drive that has been recently defragmented, defragmenting your drive can increase the working life of the disk by reducing head movement and the mechanical wear associated with it.

By defragmenting your drive, you place all the files into contiguous sectors and lump together all the free space on the disk. This improves disk access time, which improves Windows' performance. A defragmented drive also is critical for swap files. A permanent swap file must be created in contiguous sectors; to create the largest swap file possible, you need the largest amount of contiguous free space possible.

If you are using MS-DOS 6, you can use the new DEFRAG command to defragment your system's hard disk. For more information on using DEFRAG or third-party utilities to defragment your system's hard disk, refer to Chapter 1, "Configuring Windows."

Understanding the Disk Interleave Factor

If yours is an older system, one of the first maintenance tasks you should perform is to check the drive's interleave. A disk's *interleave* factor is related to the way sectors are numbered in each disk track. An interleave of 1:1 indicates that the sectors are located sequentially on the track. Any other ratio indicates the sectors are scattered in the track in various patterns according to the interleave factor.

Disk interleave was used in the early days of PCs to eliminate the problem created when hard disks supplied data to the CPU faster than the CPU could accept it. By scattering the sectors around the track, the disk had to spin more than once to read all the sectors. This slowed down the effective transfer rate of the disk to a rate the CPU could handle. With an interleave of 1:1, the disk has to spin only once for all sectors in a track to be read, providing the fastest performance.

You probably will not have to change your system's interleave—your system probably uses a 1:1 interleave. If your system is old, however, and you suspect it is not using a 1:1 interleave, you can use a utility such as Norton Utilities or PC Tools to verify and change the interleave of the drive to 1:1. Note that you cannot change interleave on IDE or SCSI drives.

Protecting Data with Backups

One bad habit that many computer users share is inconsistently backing up their files. *Backups* are copies of files stored on floppy disks, network hard disks, or tape. If a file is lost or becomes corrupted, or if the hard disk suffers a catastrophic failure, the data can be recovered from the backup copy. Aside from this benefit, backups also make more disk space available. You can archive a set of files onto a floppy disk or tape and remove the originals from the hard disk.

Choosing a Backup Strategy

Only you can determine how often to back up your computer's files. Although some users can afford to back up files only once a month, other users' data changes so rapidly that backups twice a day are not unreasonable. To determine how often you should back up your system, consider how much time you are willing to spend re-creating lost data. If your data changes little in a week's time, weekly backups might be enough for you. It is more likely, however, that you will decide your system should be backed up once a day. Whatever backup frequency you choose, the way you structure the directories on each workstation can make backups easier to accomplish.

You should always separate applications from data whenever possible. After an application is installed and backed up, you should not have to back it up again unless the application has been customized or has had new features added. There is no point in backing up applications day after day if they do not change.

To make it easier to back up your document files, consider creating a logical drive to contain all your applications. For example, create drives C and D on your hard disk, and place all applications on C and all documents on D.

Data, however, is a very different matter. Your documents and other data probably change often. The most up-to-date backup is vitally important. Several options are available for ensuring that data is backed up.

Using Backup Utilities

A number of good utilities are designed with one purpose in mind—backing up your hard drive. These utilities generally support a wide range of backup media, including floppy drives, hard drives, and tape drives. Central Point Backup is just one example of a backup utility available for Windows. Figure 11.5 shows Central Point Backup being used to back up drive C to a cartridge tape.

Figure 11.5
Central Point
Backup being
used to back up a
disk.

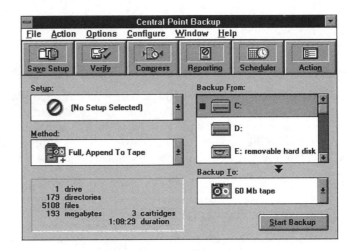

One of the primary benefits of backup utilities, such as Central Point Backup, is that much of the backup process is automated. Most utilities enable you to save and restore directory selections, making it easy to select files for backup. Also, most utilities include a scheduling facility for scheduling automatic backups. Backup utilities also can be configured to back up only the files that have changed since the last backup, speeding up the backup process.

Backing Up with MS-DOS 6

If you are using MS-DOS 6, you already have a limited backup utility. DOS 6 includes a Windows-based utility, called Microsoft Backup, which is a scaled-down version of Norton Backup for Windows. Although Microsoft Backup does not support tape drives, it does enable you to back up files to floppy disks and to local or remote networked hard disks.

When you install MS-DOS 6, its Setup program modifies File Manager's INI file, WINFILE.INI, to include support for the new DOS 6 features. One of these is Microsoft Backup. To run Microsoft Backup, open File Manager and choose Tools, Backup. If you prefer to start Microsoft Backup from Program Manager, add a program item for the file MWBACKUP.EXE, which should be located in your system's DOS directory.

Using Microsoft Backup

The first time you run Microsoft Backup, the program performs a compatibility test on your system: a small backup to one of your floppy drives. Microsoft Backup prompts you to perform the compatibility test automatically the first time it runs. Backup displays the dialog box shown in figure 11.6.

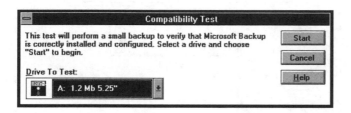

Figure 11.6
Backup performs a compatibility test the first time you run the program.

From the Compatibility Test dialog box, choose the floppy drive to use for the backup, even if you intend to back up to a network hard disk. Then, click on the Start button. Backup prompts you to insert one or two floppy disks in the drive during its test. Insert a blank disk or a disk that contains data you no longer need. After Backup completes its compatibility test, it displays the main Backup dialog box shown in figure 11.7.

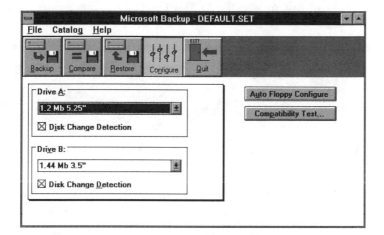

Figure 11.7
The Microsoft Backup program window.

To back up files, either to floppy disks or to a hard disk, choose the Backup button. The program window then changes to give you controls for selecting the files to be backed up, as well as the destination for the files (see fig. 11.8).

Figure 11.8
The Backup window enables you to select files to back up, as well as the destination.

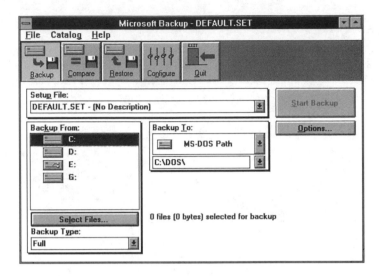

To choose the drive containing the files you want to back up, select the drive from the Backup From pull-down menu. To specify the destination for the backup, select the drive from the Backup To pull-down menu. To back up to a specific directory or to a network drive, choose the MS-DOS Path option from the Backup To list, then enter the required path in the edit box below the Backup To list. To select the files you want to back up, choose Select Files. Backup then displays the window shown in figure 11.9.

Figure 11.9
The file selection window in Backup is similar to File Manager.

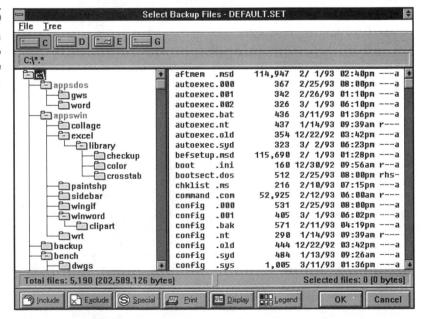

Select one or more directories by clicking on the directory's name. This selects all the files in the directory. To deselect a directory, click on it again. To select or deselect specific files, click on them in the files list.

At the bottom of the Select Backup Files window are six buttons that control Backup's options:

✔ **Include.** This enables you to provide a wild-card specification for files to include in the file selection list.

✔ **Exclude.** This enables you to provide a wild-card specification for files to exclude from the file selection list.

✔ **Special.** This enables you to select files whose dates match a specified range, exclude copy protected files, exclude read-only files, exclude system files, and exclude hidden files (such as a permanent swap file).

✔ **Print.** This enables you to print the current file selection.

✔ **Display.** This provides controls for defining the information that Backup displays about a file, including its size, date, and attributes. The Display button also enables you to specify how the file list is sorted and to specify other display-related options.

✔ **Legend.** This displays a dialog box that explains the different icons that can appear beside a directory to indicate which files in the directory have been selected for backup.

After you have selected the files you want to back up, click on OK to return to the main Backup program window. Then, choose Start Backup to begin the backup process.

After you have performed a backup, you might want to save the file selections to make it easier to perform a backup on the same files at a later date. To do so, choose File, Save Setup As. Specify a name by which you want the current file selection saved. Later, when you want to back up the same file set, choose File Open Setup to reload the setup file.

Restoring Files

When you need to retrieve one or more files from a backup set, open Microsoft Backup and select Restore. In the Restore window, select the disk that has the files you want to restore and select the location where you want the restored files to go. To place the files in their original locations, choose the Original Locations option in the Restore To pull-down menu. Choose Alternate Drives or Alternate Directories if you want to place the files in a drive or directory different from their original location. Next, choose Select Files to select the files you want to restore from the backup set. When your selections are set, choose $\underline{S}$tart Restore to begin restoring the files.

Other Backup Options

Microsoft Backup includes a number of different options for backing up and restoring files. These can be viewed and changed by choosing the $\underline{O}$ptions button from the Backup or Restore program windows. For more information on these options, consult the Backup Help file.

Exploring Tape Drives

The two primary backup storage media in use today are hard disks and magnetic tape. Hard disks, although convenient, often are not the best solution. It is unlikely that you will want to add another hard disk to your system just to back up the existing hard disk. (The exception is on a network, where a large hard disk on a server is dedicated as a backup storage device.)

Tape backup units offer a better solution. These units store data on magnetic tape, much like music is stored on an audio tape. The two most common tape media formats are $\frac{1}{4}$-inch cartridge tape and 4 or 8 mm DAT (Digital Audio Tape). Cartridge tape units vary in price and capability. A typical cartridge tape drive that can store 250 MB costs about $250, or about $1 per megabyte for the initial investment in hardware. Higher-performance units also are available, in the $600–$700 range. Newer models can connect to your existing IDE controller. Others connect to your system's floppy drive controller or require special controllers.

The benefit of using a cartridge tape system is that when a tape fills up, you can insert a new tape and continue backing up the system. If your backup hard drive fills up, you do not have that capability. Blank, unformatted $\frac{1}{4}$-inch tapes that can hold up to 300 MB cost about $20, or about 7 cents per megabyte.

DAT is another tape drive option to consider. DAT cartridges are smaller than $\frac{1}{4}$-inch cartridge tapes but hold more data because of differences in the DAT drive's read/write mechanisms. Typical DAT drives are available in 1, 2, and 4 GB capacities in both 4 mm and 8 mm formats. A typical 2 GB DAT drive costs about $1,200; 2 GB blank tapes cost about $14.

If you can afford the additional cost for a DAT drive, the difference is well worth it in capacity and speed. Not only is backup time quicker with a DAT drive, but restoring a file from tape often can be accomplished in seconds with a DAT drive. It can take minutes of searching for a cartridge tape drive to locate and retrieve a file.

Tape Controller Options

The most common type of tape drive for PCs has long been that which connects to the system's existing floppy disk controller. Today, however, a number of different types of tape drives are available that you can install in your system:

✔ **Floppy controller.** The most common, and generally the least expensive, type of tape drive in use in PCs today connects directly to your system's floppy drive controller, using the same type of cable as the floppy drives. A floppy controller is not recognized as an additional floppy drive, however. Instead, it is transparent to the system—the backup software you use recognizes the tape unit on its own.

This type of tape backup system is the most popular, primarily because it is the least expensive. SCSI and IDE tape drivers, however, offer better performance.

✔ **Dedicated controller.** To provide better performance than a floppy controller can provide, many tape drive manufacturers have models that include a dedicated controller. This controller's only function is to control the tape drive. Although dedicated controllers provide faster performance than floppy drive controllers, tape controllers require an additional bus slot and are more expensive.

✔ **IDE.** Tape drives now are available that can connect to your system's IDE host adapter along with your IDE hard drive. These drives offer excellent performance and do not require an additional bus slot (assuming you already have an IDE host adapter in the system).

✔ **SCSI.** Perhaps the best performance in tape drives comes from SCSI units. These tape drives connect to a SCSI host adapter. If you already have a SCSI hard drive or CD-ROM drive, you might want to consider a SCSI tape drive. Like IDE tape drives, SCSI tape drives offer excellent performance and do not need a separate adapter.

SCSI tape drives are not as popular currently as other types of tape systems because SCSI drives are more expensive. They often provide the best performance, however.

The choice between tape drive types boils down to two issues: cost and the type of controller you want to use. If you do not require fast backups (you can perform them at night, for example), you might want a less expensive (and slower) tape drive that connects to your system's floppy disk controller.

If you have an IDE or SCSI host adapter already in your system, and want faster performance and higher capacity, consider either an IDE or SCSI tape drive.

If you have a floppy-controller type of tape drive and want to increase performance without switching to an IDE or SCSI system, you might be able to purchase a dedicated controller for your existing tape unit and improve its performance. Check with your tape unit's manufacturer to find out.

Chapter Snapshot

As good as Windows is, sometimes it will cause you problems. No team of operating system designers can completely anticipate every possible hardware configuration, nor can it anticipate every combination of software packages that users will choose to run. Fortunately, you can easily resolve most of these problems. This chapter is designed to help you solve problems quickly. Each section addresses one of these problems:

Each section begins with general strategies that can help you quickly isolate the problem. You will find, after the general strategies, a list of problem conditions and solutions. If these strategies don't solve your problems, consult the resources listed in the section "Using Other Resources for Trouble-shooting."

This chapter also explains how to use Dr. Watson effectively. The section on Dr. Watson shows you how this diagnostic program (supplied with Windows) works, why you should run it, how to set it up for your computing context, and how to interpret a Dr. Watson log file.

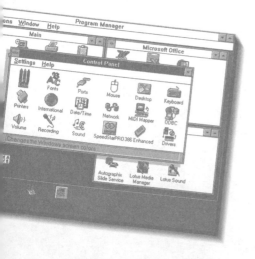

Troubleshooting Windows

S ome problems are easy to define. Others, however, are more difficult to identify and fix. This section describes problems that can occur with the Windows operating environment that cannot be subclassified effectively. These problems affect the entire system. This section also describes the following strategies, which you should apply to solving any type of problem:

✔ Back up your hard drive before you attempt troubleshooting so that you do not accidentally lose data.

✔ Copy your existing CONFIG.SYS file to CONFIG.BEF and your existing AUTOEXEC.BAT file to AUTOEXEC.BEF. (The file extension stands for "before.") Flag the files as read-only. Files with this extension are unlikely to be overwritten accidentally during the troubleshooting process by an editor that makes automatic backups.

✔ Create a CONFIG.SYS file with these lines:

```
files=40
buffers=20
device=c:\windows\himem.sys
```

```
device=c:\windows\ega.sys      ;for EGA monitors only
stacks=9,256                   ;for MS-DOS 3.3 and higher
shell=c:\dos\command.com c:\dos /p /e:256
;add any network commands here
```

✔ After creating the CONFIG.SYS file, create an AUTOEXEC.BAT file with these lines:

```
path=c:\;c:\dos;c:\windows
set temp=c:\windows\temp
prompt $p$g
;add any network commands here
```

✔ Make a bootable disk by using the DOS FORMAT command with the /S parameter.

✔ Copy your new CONFIG.SYS and AUTOEXEC.BAT files to the floppy disk.

✔ Copy the following files to the floppy disk:

```
\windows\win.ini
\windows\system.ini
\windows\progman.ini
config.bef
autoexec.bef
```

✔ Use the DOS DISKCOPY command to copy this floppy disk. Use one copy for troubleshooting and the other copy for protection.

You should substitute in these steps the names of your Windows and DOS directories if you did not use the default names during installation.

Use the floppy disk you have created to boot your machine if you suspect that the problem is related to the boot files on your hard drive, or if your system locks up while booting. Make changes in CONFIG.SYS and AUTOEXEC.BAT on the floppy disk one at a time to test for possible problems incrementally. After you have reproduced the problem, the last line you have added to a file is the problem. (Use the copy you have set aside for protection to boot your system if your system locked up while booting.) You also can use this disk to restore your configuration files to their pre-troubleshooting state.

If your problem is not related to booting or to Windows start-up, try changing Windows' operating mode. Sometimes software can contain mode-specific problems. In addition, try to re-create the problem by using one of the Windows applets. If you can do this, the problem might be in Windows rather than in your application software.

General Troubleshooting

Problem: Windows does not run when you type WIN and press Enter.

1. Check the `display.drv=` line in SYSTEM.INI to ensure that you have the correct display driver installed.

2. Run Setup again, and change the video adapter type.

3. Remove any TSRs and device drivers from AUTOEXEC.BAT and CONFIG.SYS that you do not need in Windows.

4. Add the line `EMMEXCLUDE=C000-D000` to SYSTEM.INI in the `[386Enh]` section.

Problem: Windows displays an Application Execution Error when you try to run an application from File Manager or Program Manager.

1. Add the application's directory to the PATH statement in the AUTOEXEC.BAT file.

2. Or, specify the full path to the application's executable file by using the Program Manager's File, Properties command (for a program item in Program Manager) or in the File, Run command dialog box when you attempt to start the application.

Problem: Program groups frequently become corrupted.

1. Check to ensure that your hard drive has sufficient spare disk space. You need at least 2 MB for temporary files.

2. Reduce the number of files in your Windows directory by deleting or moving unnecessary files.

3. Keep backup copies of your program group files to protect against further corruption. (They have a GRP extension.)

Problem: The mouse pointer jerks when you move it, or windows jerk when you move them.

Use the Desktop icon in the Control Panel to adjust the Grid Granularity setting to a lower value.

II

Optimizing Windows

Problem: Applications do not recognize the Alt key.

Two settings in SYSTEM.INI affect the way the Alt keypress is processed. `AltKeyDelay=` controls the amount of time Windows waits to process the keyboard interrupt when the Alt key is pressed. The default is .005 seconds. Try adjusting it to a higher value (.05, for example). `AltPasteDelay=` controls the amount of time Windows waits before pasting characters after the Alt key is pressed. The default value is .025 seconds. Try adjusting it to a higher value.

Problem: Applications respond sluggishly to the keyboard when other applications are running in the background.

Increase the value for `KeyBoostTime=` in the `[386Enh]` section of SYSTEM.INI. This setting determines how much time an application gains to run with higher priority with each keystroke it receives. The default is .001.

Problem: Cursor is distorted or garbage appears on-screen.

Try setting `MouseSofInit=false` in the `[386Enh]` section of SYSTEM.INI.

Problem: A `Sharing Violation` message appears.

Try installing SHARE.EXE in your AUTOEXEC.BAT file. If the problem persists, try using the /L parameter to increase the lock count. A sample line follows:

```
c:\dos\share.exe /l:500.
```

Setup Strategies

This section describes problems that can occur during Windows Setup. The Setup program runs in two stages. The first is a DOS program that copies Windows core files to your hard drive. The second is a Windows program that completes the process of copying files and configures your system. Problems can occur in both stages.

1. Remove all TSRs and device drivers from your system before attempting to run Setup. (You can add them again after Windows is installed.)

2. If you cannot remove all TSRs, run Setup with the /T switch to determine if incompatible TSRs and drivers are present.

3. Read the SETUP.TXT file to learn about any incompatible TSRs or device drivers not documented elsewhere.

4. Check the lines in the `[incompTSR1]` and `[incompTSR2]` sections of the SETUP.INF file for a complete list of known incompatible TSRs and drivers.

Setup Troubleshooting

Problem: DOS or Windows reports floppy drive errors.

1. If SHARE.EXE is installed in AUTOEXEC.BAT or CONFIG.SYS, use the /L parameter to increase the number of file-lock handles, as shown in these examples:

   ```
   share.exe /l:500 (for AUTOEXEC.BAT)

   install=c:\dos\share.exe /l:500 (for CONFIG.SYS)
   ```

2. Reboot without SHARE.EXE installed if the problem continues.

3. If SHARE.EXE is not installed by CONFIG.SYS or AUTOEXEC.BAT, check to see if the file is in the root directory. If it is, DOS installs it automatically. Move it to another directory.

Problem: Setup hangs or returns to the DOS prompt when it attempts to check your hardware configuration.

The autodetection routine is not compatible with your system. Try running Setup with the /I parameter. You must select your hardware settings manually.

Problem: Setup hangs when it gets to Disk 2.

1. Remove all TSRs and device drivers from AUTOEXEC.BAT and CONFIG.SYS, and then reboot. Try Setup again.

2. If Setup still hangs, remove SMARTDrive and RAMDrive from the CONFIG.SYS file. Reboot, and try Setup again.

3. If Setup still hangs, disable autoswitching on your display adapter and ROM shadowing, if either of these is supported in your CMOS. Reboot and try Setup again.

4. If Setup still hangs, try running it with the /I parameter. Be careful to set your hardware configuration correctly.

5. If you still encounter the problem, try installing Windows without a mouse or network. Run Setup from within Windows after installation is complete to add these features.

Problem: Windows mode Setup fails to start.

Either a TSR is causing a conflict or you selected the wrong display adapter in your hardware configuration. Rerun Setup and choose the correct display adapter. If all else fails, try the generic EGA or VGA setting.

II

Optimizing Windows

Hardware Strategies

This section describes problems that can occur with hardware devices.

1. Turn off all peripheral devices that can be powered down to see if the problem still occurs.

2. Use the Microsoft Diagnostics program (MSD.EXE) that ships with Windows to determine whether conflicts exist between devices over base port addresses, interrupt request lines (IRQs), or direct memory access (DMA) channels. If they do, change the jumpers, DIP switches, or software selectable settings on the devices to avoid these types of conflicts. As a general note, keep in mind that IRQ9 cannot be used—Windows uses it internally.

Hardware Troubleshooting

Problem: Cannot use COM1 and COM3 (or COM2 and COM4) at the same time.

1. Your hardware might not be capable of sharing the interrupts the serial ports use. Only Micro Channel and EISA computers have this capability.

2. If your hardware is capable, set `COMIrqSharing=true` in the `[386Enh]` section of SYSTEM.INI.

Problem: COM3 and COM4 do not work in standard mode.

You might have to use your serial ports in numeric order. COM3 might not work unless COM2 is active, for example. Always use the lowest-numbered available serial port for a serial peripheral device.

Problem: COM3 and COM4 work in standard mode but not in 386 Enhanced mode.

Make sure that you have a `COMnBase` and a `COMnIrq` setting for every port in the `[386Enh]` section of SYSTEM.INI, or check the port settings by using Control Panel's Ports icon. (*n* represents the port number.) Make sure that these settings identify the correct base address and interrupt request for each port.

Problem: Floppy drive access hangs the system, or floppy drive performance is degraded.

Add the line `IRQ9Global=true` to the `[386Enh]` section of SYSTEM.INI. Your system probably needs IRQ9 masks to be global rather than local.

Problem: Keystrokes are misinterpreted from a nonstandard keyboard.

Set `TranslateScans=yes` in the `[386Enh]` section of SYSTEM.INI. This setting causes Windows to translate your keyboard's scan codes into IBM standard scan codes.

Problem: The hard disk drive loses data.

Windows might be terminating the interrupts coming from your hard disk drive. Set `VirtualHDIrq=false` in the `[386Enh]` section of SYSTEM.INI.

Software Conflict Strategies

This section describes problems that can occur when software programs conflict with Windows.

1. Remove all TSRs from AUTOEXEC.BAT.

2. Remove all programs from the StartUp group in Program Manager.

3. Check the files indicated in the Setup section of this chapter for programs with known incompatibilities with Windows.

Software Conflict Troubleshooting

Problem: A TSR that uses INT2A does not perform properly.

Set `ReflectDOSInt2A=true` in the `[386Enh]` section of SYSTEM.INI.

Problem: Setup does not run correctly.

You might have a TSR conflict. Check the files noted in the "Setup Strategies" section of this chapter for the most recent list of known software conflicts and an explanation of how to resolve them.

Problem: Windows docs not run properly.

The following programs are known to cause problems:

Many of the problems in the following list have been overcome by updates to the applications or drivers listed. If you are still using the version specified in the following lists, check with the developer to determine if there is a more recent version that overcomes the problem.

ANARKEY Version 4.0

APPEND (an MS-DOS utility)

DOSCUE

GRAPHICS (an MS-DOS utility)

JOIN (an MS-DOS utility)

LanSight Version 2.0

Lockit Version 3.3

Mirror (an MS-DOS utility that cannot be unloaded if you run it by using the File, Run command in Standard mode)

Newspace Version 1.07

Norton Utilities Version 5.0, Diskreet and Ncache

Norton Utilities Version 6.01, DiskMon

Printer Assistant

XGAAIDOS.SYS

The following programs require special treatment:

✔ **BOOT.SYS.** You must modify all the sections in the configuration files after the first section. Windows Setup modifies only the first one.

✔ **Doubledisk Version 2.5.** You must use the DRVOFF utility.

✔ **FASTOPEN.** You must remove it in low-memory situations and when you are using disk-defragmenting utilities.

✔ **LaserTools Control Panel Version 2.2.** Load the TSR before starting Windows.

✔ **LANtastic KBFLOW.** Start the TSR after starting Windows.

✔ **Le Menu Version 1.0.** Run Windows from a batch file rather than directly from this menuing system.

✔ **Logitech Mouse Software Versions 5.0 and 6.0.** To use Click and Logimenu, load the TSRs after Windows starts.

✔ **Norton Utilities Ncache Version 6.01.** You cannot use a permanent swap file while you are using this utility.

✔ **PC Tools Deluxe Versions 6.0 and 7.0.** Run the Desktop from a PIF.

✔ **Pyro! Version 1.0.** Load the program after you start Windows.

✔ **SideKick Versions 1.0 and 2.0 and SideKick Plus.** Run the programs from a PIF.

✔ **SPEEDFXR.** Use the -X switch to run the program.

✔ **SUBST.** Do not change the state of the substituted drives while Windows is running.

✔ **Trantor T100 Host Adapter Driver.** Do not access the SCSI hard disk with File Manager.

Configuration Strategies

This section describes problems you might have with Windows configuration.

1. Before doing anything, back up your WIN.INI, SYSTEM.INI, CONFIG.SYS, and AUTOEXEC.BAT files. If you have backups, you always can return to the system configuration you had before you began.

2. Change one configuration setting at a time. Changing several settings at a time can confuse your situation. You might not be able to tell which change solved the problem. You also can solve one problem and introduce another and not be able to tell which setting has caused the new problem.

Configuration Troubleshooting

Problem: Windows gives an error message that a group file is missing or that damage occurred at start-up.

1. You might have moved the file to another directory. Return it to the Windows directory.

2. The file has been corrupted or accidentally deleted. Restore it from a backup or rebuild it by using the commands on the Program Manager's File menu.

3. If no groups appear in Program Manager, use the File, Run command to run Setup, and reinstall all the Windows components that were installed before the problem occurred.

Problem: Windows or Windows applications do not display correctly on-screen.

1. Reinstall your display driver. It probably has been corrupted. Make sure that you install the correct driver for your video card.

2. Your display driver uses nonmaskable interrupts. Either disable this option or install a display driver supplied by the manufacturer of the card.

II

Optimizing Windows

Problem: Data cannot be copied between Windows and DOS applications.

1. Reinstall your display driver, and make certain that grabber files (with GR in the extension) are copied.

2. Make sure that the grabber file is listed on the 286grabber= and 386grabber= lines in the [boot] section in SYSTEM.INI.

Problem: Either DOS applications do not start or an error message says that your display adapter is incompatible.

1. Reinstall your display driver. It has been corrupted or installed incompletely.

2. If reinstallation does not work, install the standard VGA driver shipped with Windows to see whether it works.

Problem: In 386 Enhanced mode, the initial logo appears and then disappears, leaving the screen blank.

Your display driver uses nonmaskable interrupts. Either disable this feature or install a driver supplied by the manufacturer.

Problem: An incorrect system version error message appears when you start a DOS application in 386 Enhanced mode.

The virtual display device and 386 grabber are mismatched. Edit SYSTEM.INI to include these lines:

```
[boot]
386grabber=vga.3gr
[386Enh]
display=*vddvga
```

Some adapters require the use of Windows 3.0 versions of these files. The lines for such cards are as follows:

```
[boot]
386grabber=vga30.3gr
[386Enh]
display=vddvga30.386
```

Problem: Windows has problems running in 386 Enhanced mode with your VGA display adapter.

Try adding the following line to the [386Enh] section of SYSTEM.INI:

```
emmexclude=C400-C7FF
```

Your display adapter needs this memory area to function, and Windows has been attempting to use it. This line tells Windows not to use this memory area.

Problem: Applications do not display properly on your VGA screen.

You might need to replace the digital-to-analog converter (DAC) chip on your display card. Contact the manufacturer.

Problem: You have display problems with your Super VGA adapter.

You probably need to update to a Windows 3.1-specific version of the display driver for your adapter. Contact the manufacturer.

Problem: You cannot load device drivers or programs in high memory.

You should be able to load drivers and programs in high memory on an 80386 computer with 350 KB of extended memory free. Make sure that HIMEM.SYS is installed and that you are using the appropriate dos=, devicehigh=, and loadhigh= commands in CONFIG.SYS and AUTOEXEC.BAT. Make sure that you have not inadvertently installed EMM386 with the RAM switch. Check the EMM386 documentation for information about increasing the space for UMBs if the problem persists.

Problem: A specific driver or TSR refuses to work when it is loaded in high memory.

Some drivers and TSRs do not work when they are loaded in high memory. Load these programs in conventional memory.

Problem: You get a Cannot find file error while APPEND is running.

The DOS APPEND utility is confusing Windows' capability to determine the correct path to files. Remove APPEND from your AUTOEXEC.BAT file.

Standard Mode Strategies

This section describes problems you might have while your system is running in standard mode.

1. Make sure that you have an XMS driver (such as HIMEM.SYS) installed.

2. Make certain that you have at least 256 KB of conventional memory free and 192 KB of extended memory free.

Standard Mode Troubleshooting

Problem: Windows refuses to start in standard mode, even when you are using the WIN /S command line.

1. RAMDrive or some other software is using the memory that Windows needs to run in standard mode. Reduce the memory allocated to such programs or do not load these types of programs.

2. XMS driver is not compatible with Windows. Use the version of HIMEM.SYS packaged with Windows.

3. HIMEM is not correctly identifying your computer. Try using the /M switch to identify your machine type. Check the README files and Windows documentation for the up-to-date list of machine types available.

4. Your computer might not have enough extended memory. Allocate as extended memory as much physical memory as possible, and reduce the amount of extended memory you allocate to individual programs.

386 Enhanced Mode Strategies

This section describes problems you might have while your system is running in 386 Enhanced mode.

1. Choose a computer with an 80386 microprocessor or higher.

2. Make sure that you have at least 256 KB of free conventional memory.

3. Make sure that an XMS driver (such as HIMEM.SYS) is installed.

4. Make sure that you have at least 1,024 KB of extended memory free.

386 Enhanced Mode Troubleshooting

Problem: Windows runs slowly when DOS applications and File Manager are running.

The DOS applications might be making changes to the file system and forcing File Manager to keep track of them on the fly, which slows down the system. Add the following line to the [386Enh] section of SYSTEM.INI:

```
FileSysChange=off
```

Problem: Windows runs in Standard mode but not in 386 Enhanced mode, even when you are using the WIN /3 command line.

You might have a UMB conflict. Try running Windows by using the /d:x switch on the command line. If Windows runs correctly in 386 Enhanced mode, you have this type of conflict. Use the Microsoft Diagnostics program to see whether you have a program or hardware device that is using the UMB area. If so, exclude that area from Windows' use by placing that memory range in the emmexclude= setting of the [386Enh] section in SYSTEM.INI, as follows:

```
[386Enh]
emmexclude=C000-C7FF
```

Problem: Windows crashes when you run it in 386 Enhanced mode.

You have a UMB conflict. Use the following line in the [386Enh] section of SYSTEM.INI:

```
emmexclude=A000-EFFF
```

If the problem is solved, you can isolate which areas of the UMB are used by other programs or hardware devices and exclude only those areas.

Problem: Running in 386 Enhanced mode causes hard drive problems.

1. If you do not have an ST506 or ESDI hard drive controller, you must install SMARTDrive to gain appropriate access to your hard drive.

2. If the problem still persists, add the following line to the [386Enh] section of SYSTEM.INI:

```
[386Enh]
VirtualHDirq=off
```

3. Try turning off fast 32-bit access. Your hard drive controller might not be capable of supporting it, even though Windows detects that it can.

4. If you experience further problems, you must contact your hard drive manufacturer for a solution, because no other Windows system settings will assist you.

Problem: You receive an internal stack overflow message.

If you have MS-DOS 3.2, add the following line in CONFIG.SYS:

```
stacks=9,192
```

If you have MS-DOS 3.3 or higher, add the following line to CONFIG.SYS:

```
stacks=9,256
```

Problem: Typing slows down when you run multiple applications, even though you have plenty of free memory.

1. Use the 386 Enhanced icon in the Control Panel to increase the foreground priority. (You can do the same thing in a DOS application's PIF.)

2. Increase the priority for the application running in the foreground with each keystroke it receives. Use the following line in the [386Enh] section of SYSTEM.INI:

```
KeyBoostTime=.005
```

To add more to the priority, increase the value.

DOS Application Strategies

This section describes problems you might have with DOS applications.

1. Make sure that every DOS application has a PIF tailored to its needs.

2. If you are starting the DOS application from a batch file, make sure that you do not load any TSRs or other programs that are causing conflicts from the batch file.

DOS Applications Troubleshooting

Problem: Mouse does not work with DOS applications.

Install the mouse driver by adding the following line to AUTOEXEC.BAT (add the appropriate driver for your mouse):

```
c:\windows\system\mouse.com
```

You must install the separate mouse driver for the mouse to work with DOS applications.

Problem: DOS batch files that are run in a DOS session under Windows run out of environment space.

Enter a larger value on the CommandEnvSize= line in the [NonWindowsApp] section of SYSTEM.INI. The following line sets the environment size to 512 bytes:

```
CommandEnvSize=512
```

Problem: Keyboard input is distorted when you run a DOS application in 386 Enhanced mode.

Two settings in the [386Enh] section of SYSTEM.INI might help. Try increasing the value for KeyBufferDelay=, the time Windows waits after the keyboard buffer is full before accepting more keystrokes. The default is .2 seconds. Reduce the setting for KeyIdleDelay=, the amount of time Windows ignores idle calls after sending a keystroke to a virtual DOS machine. The default is .5 seconds.

Problem: Your application provides an `Unexpected MS-DOS Error #11` message.

Your grabber file has been corrupted. In addition, WINOA386.MOD (386 Enhanced mode) or WINOLDAP.MOD (standard mode) might have been corrupted. Copy these files from the installation disks and expand them by using EXPAND.EXE.

Problem: Your applications have problems running in standard mode.

1. If the application does not run from the directory you expected, check for a conflict between the start-up directory specified in the program item properties and the start-up directory specified in the program's PIF. The one in the program item properties overrides the one in the PIF.

2. If data is lost, check the Directly Modifies settings in the PIF file that give the application exclusive control of the keyboard and COM ports. Also uncheck No Save Screen.

3. If screen captures do not paste, uncheck No Screen Exchange in the application's PIF.

4. If you cannot switch to Windows, uncheck Prevent Program Switch and Directly Modifies Keyboard in the application's PIF.

Problem: DOS applications have problems when Windows is in 386 Enhanced mode.

1. If you run out of memory when you are running high-resolution graphics in a DOS application, check High Graphics and Retain Video Memory in the application's PIF. If the problem persists, try using full-screen mode.

2. If the mouse does not work, make sure that the MS-DOS mouse drive is installed in AUTOEXEC.BAT.

3. If the display is garbled or improper in some way, check Monitor Ports and uncheck Emulate Text Mode in the application's PIF.

Problem: Running some DOS applications simultaneously causes problems, but they run okay alone.

One application probably is locking EMS or XMS memory that the others need. Clear the EMS Memory Locked and XMS Memory Locked settings in each application's PIF.

Memory Strategies

This section describes solutions to problems you might encounter with memory allocation under Windows.

Optimizing Windows

1. In general, configure all your memory above 640 KB as extended memory.

2. Load DOS, TSRs, and drivers in high memory if possible.

Memory Troubleshooting

Problem: An `Invalid path for EMM386` error message appears when Windows starts in 386 Enhanced mode.

1. Add the `/y=path` switch to the EMM386 statement in CONFIG.SYS, in which *path* is the full directory path and file name for EMM386, as shown in this example:

   ```
   device=emm386.exe /y=c:\dos\emm386.exe
   ```

2. Make sure that both EMM386.EXE and HIMEM.SYS are available on your system. Verify that they are working properly by booting from the clean boot floppy disk described in the section "Strategies for General Questions."

Problem: You experience a conflict between your third-party disk cache and EMM386.

Use SMARTDrive as your disk cache. It is designed to work with EMM386.

Problem: Your computer stops mysteriously, and nothing can make it work. (The UMB space needed by EMM386 probably is being used by another program or hardware device.)

1. Boot from your clean boot floppy disk (described in the section "Strategies for General Questions"). Edit AUTOEXEC.BAT and CONFIG.SYS, installing one program at a time until you reproduce the program. Load the offending program in conventional memory rather than in high memory.

2. If the preceding instruction does not solve the problem, the offender is probably a hardware device. Examine the documentation for the devices you have installed to see if they use UMB space. Use the `x=` switch to exclude that area of memory from use by EMM386, as shown in this example:

   ```
   device=emm386.exe noems x=d800-dfff
   ```

You might need to use the `noems` switch also with some devices.

Problem: DOS programs that require EMS give `Out of Memory` errors when they are started, or give these errors randomly after starting. Or, the program stops Windows from running, but you have no trouble running other DOS applications. (Windows is failing to provide expanded memory to a DOS application that needs it.)

1. Substitute the RAM switch for the noems switch in the command line for EMM386. If other drivers and TSRs fail to load high as a result, you might need to add more space for UMBs with the i= switch. Check your Windows, DOS, and hardware documentation to see if you can use this technique to add more space for UMBs.

2. If the preceding instruction fails, your computer hardware might be using the UMB area for system purposes. Check your hardware documentation for suggested solutions.

Fonts Strategies

This section describes problems you might have with fonts.

1. Make sure that you have properly installed the font you want to use from the Fonts dialog box in Control Panel.

2. If you recently have installed a new printer, make sure that you copied fonts to the new port.

Fonts Troubleshooting

Problem: You have system problems when you choose TrueType fonts.

Some display adapters have problems displaying TrueType fonts. If your adapter caches fonts in unused video memory, you might have difficulties. Contact the manufacturer for a solution.

Problem: You cannot print TrueType fonts with your third-party display driver.

Your driver probably is not compatible with Windows 3.1. Use a driver supplied with Windows, and contact the manufacturer for an update.

Problem: TrueType fonts cause problems with your font converter.

Contact the converter manufacturer for an update. The problem is in the converter's code.

Problem: You are having problems with TrueType fonts on your 2 MB computer.

You might have trouble using TrueType fonts in low-memory situations. Either acquire more memory or use non-TrueType fonts.

II

Optimizing Windows

Printing Strategies

This section describes problems you might have with printers and printing.

1. Make sure that your printer is powered on.

2. Make sure that the cables are seated properly in their receptacles.

3. Try printing from several different programs to see whether the problem is related to a single program or to a group of programs.

4. Try printing from DOS using a command such as the following:

    ```
    DIR > LPT1
    ```

5. Make sure that you have set the TEMP variable in AUTOEXEC.BAT and that the disk drive on which you have placed your \TEMP directory has at least 2 MB free. Make sure that the \TEMP directory exists. Set the TEMP variable with a command similar to the following:

    ```
    SET TEMP=C:\TEMP
    ```

6. Use the Printers icon in Control Panel to ensure that you are using the correct driver for your printer.

7. If you have a serial printer, check to see if you need to run the DOS MODE command from your AUTOEXEC.BAT file to configure the serial port. If you do, make sure that the command is correct in AUTOEXEC.BAT. Also check the COM port settings by using the Ports icon in Control Panel. Almost all printers require 9,600 baud, no parity, 8 bits, 1 stop bit, and hardware handshaking.

8. Try changing your port setting in the [ports] section of WIN.INI to enable direct DOS printing. Add the DOS extender to the [ports] line for your printer port, as shown in this example:

    ```
    LPT1.DOS=
    ```

    This line causes Windows to print to a file named LPT1.DOS, which DOS then reinterprets as the device LPT1 because DOS can interpret a file beginning with a port name only as output to that port. Use this method for printing on a network with a network driver.

9. Read the PRINTERS.WRI file to get the latest information about possible printer problems.

Printing Troubleshooting

Problem: The P̲rint command is dimmed on application menus.

1. Use the Printers icon in Control Panel to ensure a printer is installed.

2. Use the Printers icon in Control Panel to ensure you specified a default printer.

Problem: Output is garbled on the printer.

Use the Printers icon in Control Panel to ensure you are printing with the correct driver for your printer.

Problem: Printer is installed and configured correctly, but it does not print.

1. Check the power, paper, ribbon, toner cartridge, cables, access panels, and lids to ensure each one is positioned properly.

2. Double-check to ensure you have the correct driver installed and the correct printer selected, and that the print setup matches your printer's capabilities.

Problem: A Cannot Print error message appears.

1. If you are on a network, ensure you have the correct network driver installed. If the problem persists, try the lpt1.dos= method described under "Printing Strategies" in this section.

2. Check to ensure the printer is online, filled with paper, and not jammed. Check the cabling and all devices that mediate communication between your computer and printer, such as print-sharing devices. Make sure all access panels are closed.

3. If the problem persists, connect the printer directly to your computer and try printing. If you still cannot print, replace the cable and try again.

4. Reconnect each intervening device to determine which one has caused the problem, and have the device serviced.

5. If you still cannot print, ensure your \TEMP directory exists, that the TEMP variable is set, and that you have not run out of disk space.

Problem: A print error message appears.

Try using the Printers icon in the Control Panel to increase the setting for C̲onnect, T̲ransmission Retry. This setting determines how long Windows waits after sending a character before it posts an error message.

Problem: Your PostScript printer is missing print jobs or printing incomplete jobs.

1. Verify that the communications settings are correct and that the cable is okay.

2. Make sure your printer has enough memory to handle the print jobs.

3. Double-click on Printers in the Control Panel, choose the <u>A</u>dvanced options button, and check the Print PostScript Error Information option. Repeat the print job that caused the problem. If you see an error message, the problem is in either your application or your printer's level of compatibility.

Network Strategies

This section describes problems you might have when your system is attached to a network.

1. Read the NETWORKS.WRI file to get the latest information about possible network configurations and problems.

2. Use the Network selection in Windows Setup to ensure you have the correct network driver installed.

3. Use the Microsoft Diagnostics program to ensure you do not have any conflicting memory port addresses, UMB regions, or IRQs.

4. On a Novell network, use the version of NETX.COM that was supplied with your version of Windows.

Network Troubleshooting

Problem: The network hangs while you are using a TSR.

Both your network driver and the TSR probably are using INT28h. In the `[386Enh]` section of SYSTEM.INI, add `INT28Critical=true`.

Problem: A `Resource Busy` message appears.

1. If you are not running SHARE.EXE, try installing it in your AUTOEXEC.BAT file.

2. If SHARE.EXE is installed, try increasing the number of locks available with the /L parameter. A sample AUTOEXEC.BAT line follows:

```
c:\dos\share.exe /l:500
```

If you continue to have problems, try increasing the lock count to 1,000.

Multimedia Strategies

This section describes problems you might have with multimedia tools and applets.

1. Make sure the multimedia extensions (Display, Drivers, Joystick, MIDI Mapper, and Screen Saver) were installed in Control Panel when you ran Windows Setup. (If not, rerun Setup.)

2. Check all cables and connections in your multimedia hardware.

Multimedia Troubleshooting

Problem: You cannot play audio.

1. Make sure the speakers are plugged into the speaker port.

2. Make sure the speakers are receiving power, if they need to.

3. Verify that the volume control has not been turned down (if your sound card has software volume controls, make sure they are set to the maximum).

4. Make sure the audio driver is installed by using the Drivers icon in the Control Panel.

Problem: Audio plays at an inappropriate volume.

1. Check the volume control on the hardware.

2. Make sure that battery-operated equipment has battery power.

3. If your equipment provides software volume control, check to ensure the volume has not been turned down by the software.

Problem: DOS applications that support audio cannot play audio.

1. Run the application from DOS to ensure its audio setup is okay.

2. Run Windows in Standard mode when you want to use a DOS audio application within Windows. Windows takes control of the audio hardware in 386 Enhanced mode and does not yield control to DOS applications.

Problem: You cannot access your CD-ROM drive.

1. Check the cables and terminator (if your drive and adapter require one).

2. Make sure the device driver for the CD-ROM drive is installed.

3. Make sure MSCDEX.EXE is installed properly.

II

Optimizing Windows

4. Make sure MSCDEX.EXE is in a directory that is found in your PATH statement in AUTOEXEC.BAT.

Problem: Your CD drive cannot read a disc.

1. Make sure the disc is inserted properly in the drive caddy (if one is required), with the label side up.

2. Make sure all the hardware is configured to the manufacturer's specifications and all device drivers are installed.

3. Make sure you have used the correct type of disc. File Manager, for instance, cannot recognize audio CDs.

4. Make sure the disc has not been damaged. Wipe it clean with a soft cloth. Do not use cleaning solutions that contain alcohol.

Problem: Music Box does not play.

1. Place the disc in the drive before starting Music Box.

2. Make sure you inserted an audio disc.

3. Make sure you are using the most recent version of MSCDEX.EXE.

Problem: Sound Recorder does not record.

1. Make sure your microphone is plugged in and turned on. Also, make sure your drivers for your sound card are properly installed.

2. Speak directly and distinctly into the microphone.

3. Verify that you have enough free disk space for the Sound Recorder file.

4. Check both the hardware and software volume controls for your sound hardware to be sure the volume is not turned down.

Problem: Media Player does not play MIDI files.

1. Verify that you have installed the correct MIDI driver (use the Drivers icon in the Control Panel).

2. Use the Device menu to select MIDI files as the files to play.

3. Make sure the MIDI mapper is set up correctly by using the MIDI Mapper icon in the Control Panel.

Problem: Media Player does not play animation.

1. Verify that you have selected animation files by using the Device menu.

2. Verify that the correct animation driver is installed by using the Drivers icon in the Control Panel.

Problem: Media Player does not play audio files.

1. Verify that you have selected audio files from the Device menu.

2. Verify that the file you want to play is a WAV file or MIDI file.

3. Verify that the correct audio driver is installed by using the Drivers icon in the Control Panel.

Strategies for General-Protection Faults

This section describes how to troubleshoot general-protection faults.

1. Load Dr. Watson so that you can get more detailed information about what caused the general-protection (GP) fault.

2. Use Ctrl+Alt+Del to close an application that has hung (crashed) your computer. Generally, after a GP fault occurs, save your files, exit from Windows, and reboot your computer.

General-Protection Fault Troubleshooting

Are you running applications designed for Windows 2.*x*?

Applications designed for Windows 2.*x* cause a GP fault on execution. They cause Windows to display a dialog box reporting that they cannot run under Windows 3.1.

Are your hardware and network settings correct in Windows Setup?

You might have accidentally selected an incorrect setting, or Setup's auto-detection routine might have made an error.

Are you using incompatible TSRs or unsupported network drivers?

Use only compatible TSRs and supported network drivers. Contact the manufacturer for an update.

Do you have a page-mapping conflict?

Try running Windows in Standard mode or use the /D:X switch when you are starting your system in 386 Enhanced mode. If this method solves the problem, use the techniques described in the memory section to eliminate UMB conflicts.

II

Optimizing Windows

Are you running the correct version of DOS?

Do not use an OEM version of DOS on a machine made by another manufacturer. If this seems to be the problem, install the Microsoft MS-DOS 6.*x* upgrade.

An Inside Look: Deciphering Dr. Watson

Dr. Watson is an error-analysis tool that ships with Windows 3.*x* and is available for use by any Windows user. This program detects errors and then writes to a file called the Dr. Watson log file a report about the error that was detected. This report provides detailed information about what has caused the problem, including the exact program statement that caused the problem and a description of the error. Dr. Watson logs enable you to diagnose problem conditions precisely and to fix them if you have the tools to do so.

Not every user needs the Dr. Watson Windows application. Most users do not have the tools to fix the software problems that are detected. Most users also might not have the knowledge or expertise to understand the errors reported even if they know the names of the errors and their locations in the program. Under these circumstances, you might wonder why you should even bother loading Dr. Watson when Windows starts.

Generally, if you run only commercial software, and you do not experience frequent errors, especially general-protection faults, you probably do not need to load Dr. Watson. On the other hand, if you work with custom-developed software or software that is proprietary to your company, you probably should use Dr. Watson.

By providing Dr. Watson's information to the team that maintains your custom software, you easily can help avoid software-related problems. Dr. Watson can help your company efficiently detect problems at an early stage before they seriously threaten data. Especially if your custom software is mission critical, you should load Dr. Watson from your StartUp group and develop a mechanism for routinely returning log files to your software maintenance team.

Who the Good Doctor Is

Dr. Watson is a diagnostician for two kinds of programs: the Windows operating environment and Windows applications. It runs in either Standard or 386 Enhanced mode as an icon at the bottom of your screen (see fig. 12.1). You can run only a single instance of Dr. Watson. The program uses the special Windows routines included in the TOOLHELP.DLL file included with Windows to monitor the behavior of Windows and Windows applications. (As a result, TOOLHELP.DLL must be present in your \WINDOWS\SYSTEM directory for Dr. Watson to function.)

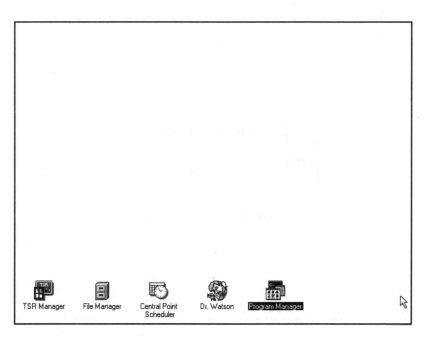

Figure 12.1
Dr. Watson
running as an
icon.

TSR Manager   File Manager   Central Point   Dr. Watson   Program Manager
                                Scheduler

II

Optimizing Windows

Tip   Dr. Watson can perform diagnostics for Windows and Windows applications
only. It cannot track errors for DOS sessions under Windows.

When Dr. Watson detects an error, it takes a snapshot of the system status. It also presents
a dialog box (called the Clues dialog box) that asks you to record what you were attempting to do. Dr. Watson records all this information for the first 3 errors in a log file. It
creates a shortened version of the report for the next 17 errors. Dr. Watson stops recording additional information after 20 errors have occurred. You can make Dr. Watson
resume its error report by closing the program and running it again.

To determine the number of errors currently logged during your Dr. Watson session,
double-click on the Dr. Watson icon. In response to this action, Dr. Watson displays a
dialog box containing the number of logged errors (see fig. 12.2).

If your log file grows to more than 100 KB, Dr. Watson displays a message that warns you
about this fact. At this point, you need to copy the file to a floppy disk and turn it over to
your software maintenance team. Then, you should delete the Dr. Watson log file.
Leaving it on your disk only wastes space.

Figure 12.2
Displaying the
number of faults
detected by Dr.
Watson.

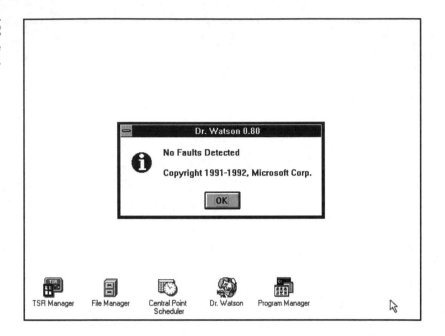

The default name for the Dr. Watson log file is DRWATSON.LOG. Dr. Watson writes this file to the Windows directory.

What the Good Doctor Does

When Dr. Watson detects an error, it collects the following information about your system:

✔ The values stored in the registers of your system's microprocessor

Registers are memory cells in the microprocessor in which data and instructions are stored while they await processing.

✔ The Windows version number, the type of microprocessor installed in your system, and the amount of memory (RAM) available

✔ The active memory segments containing your program's code and data, the base addresses of these segments, the lengths of these memory segments, and any processor flags that have been set

The design of the original 8088 microprocessor used in PCs required that memory be treated as 10 segments 64 KB long. Every segment had a beginning point (the base address) and an ending address (the limit). The limit defines the length of the segment. Windows 3.*x* continues to use this segmented approach to memory.

✔ A list of all the programs running at the time the error occurred

Dr. Watson converts this information to text and writes the text to its log file.

Windows NT abandons the segmented approach to memory. Windows NT sees your computer's memory as one continuous segment rather than a series of 64 KB segments.

You can control which information Dr. Watson places in its log file by creating a [Dr. Watson] section in your WIN.INI file and including as many as seven settings. The following sections describe the way each setting adjusts the information Dr. Watson includes in the log file.

When you create your [Dr. Watson] section, you must be certain to include the blank space between the two words that make up the program's name.

Adding *SkipInfo=* to *[Dr. Watson]*

Dr. Watson writes to disk only the portion of the error report you request. Dr. Watson by default writes the entire error report. You can disable different sections of the report, however, with the SkipInfo= entry. The following entry disables all sections of the error report:

```
[Dr. Watson]
SkipInfo=32b clu inf reg seg sta sum tas tim
```

The three-character SkipInfo= values govern the disabling of the sections of the error report (see table 12.1). Every value is a three-character abbreviation for the full name presented in the table.

Table 12.1
SkipInfo Values for Dr. Watson

Value	Disables
32bitregs	Contents of 32-bit registers (80386 and 80486 processors only)
clues	Dr. Watson Clues dialog box
information	Windows version number, microprocessor type, and RAM available
registers	Contents of 16-bit registers
segments	Contents of segments, base addresses, length of segments, and flags
stack	Stack backtrace
summary	Summary information at beginning of report
tasks	List of running applications (tasks)
time	Stop and start times for Dr. Watson

You would not generally choose to disable the entire error report. You should choose, from the sample entry provided here, only those values that do not seem relevant to the context in which your applications run. If you know in advance, for example, that your application runs on only 80486-based machines with 8 MB of memory under Windows 3.1, it makes sense to disable the information value. In this case, your entry for SkipInfo= would look like this:

```
[Dr. Watson]
SkipInfo=inf
```

Adding *ShowInfo* to *[Dr. Watson]*

Dr. Watson can collect information in addition to the information presented in the default error report. The ShowInfo= entry tells Dr. Watson to collect and include this additional information. The following entry calls for all the additional information:

```
[Dr. Watson]
ShowInfo=dis err loc mod par sou
```

The three-character ShowInfo values direct Dr. Watson to include additional information (see table 12.2). Every value is a three-character abbreviation for the full name presented in the table.

Table 12.2
The ShowInfo Values for Dr. Watson

Value	Enables
disassembly	Disassembly of the fault address separate from the disassembly of the stack frames
errorlog	Error logging
locals	Dump of local variable and parameter values from the stack
modules	List of modules that are loaded, including fonts and dynamic link libraries
paramlog	Parameter-validation logging
sound	Warning sounds

Adding *DisLen* to *[Dr. Watson]*

When an error occurs, Dr. Watson looks back into the *stack*, a segment of memory that holds instructions and data waiting to be processed by the CPU, to see which instruction might have caused the error. Because the instructions are in assembled code, Dr. Watson disassembles them so that they are readable as assembly language instructions. The DisLen= setting tells Dr. Watson how many instructions to pull off the stack and disassemble. If you provide no entry for this setting, Dr. Watson selects the last eight instructions for disassembly.

The following example decreases this trace into the stack to the last four instructions:

```
[Dr. Watson]
DisLen=4
```

This setting lets you narrow or expand your search for an offending instruction.

Adding *TrapZero* to *[Dr. Watson]*

When a divide overflow error occurs, Dr. Watson ignores it unless you provide an entry for the TrapZero= setting. Dr. Watson is set up to do this because most applications usually provide an error handler for this type of error. If you want Dr. Watson to trap such errors, however, include the following entry:

```
[Dr. Watson]
TrapZero=1
```

Adding *GPContinue* to *[Dr. Watson]*

If a general-protection fault occurs, Windows typically terminates the application that caused the fault. Windows takes this action because this type of error always indicates that a bug is present. Dr. Watson, however, can allow the offending application to continue. Even though continuing under these circumstances can be dangerous to the integrity of data and the stability of the system, some developers recover valuable information from the system as it continues to run.

A general-protection fault occurs when a program attempts to access memory outside the range the operating system allocates to it. These types of errors create problems by modifying memory that belongs to other programs or the operating system. As a result, both other programs and the Windows operating system can become unstable.

Dr. Watson permits an application to continue only if the following four tests yield a value of TRUE:

- ✔ Bit 0 of a variable named GPContinue=, which is maintained internally by Dr. Watson, is set.

- ✔ The instruction that produced the error is one that can continue. (A jump to an invalid address is an example of an instruction that cannot continue. There is no physical memory address to which the instruction can transfer control of the program.)

- ✔ The error was not produced by the Windows KERNEL or USER modules, or the appropriate bit is set in GPContinue= that enables KERNEL and USER to continue despite the danger.

- ✔ Continuation is agreeable to the user. Dr. Watson displays a dialog box that asks the user whether she wants to close the application or ignore the error. Dr. Watson then follows the user's instructions.

You can set the value of GPContinue= to enable continuation after a general-protection fault (see table 12.3).

Table 12.3
The Values of GPContinue= for Dr. Watson

Bit	Value	Permit Continuation
0	1	Yes (default)
1	2	Yes, but provide three-line reports

Bit	Value	Permit Continuation
2	4	Yes, even if KERNEL caused the error
3	8	Yes, even if USER caused the error

To choose more than one of these features, add the values and use the resulting sum as the setting for GPContinue=. The following entry, for example, enables continuation and the writing of three-line reports:

```
[Dr. Watson]
set GPContinue=3
```

Adding *DisStack* to *[Dr. Watson]*

Dr. Watson disassembles two levels back into the stack in search of an error unless you provide an entry for the DisStack= setting. This setting, like DisLen=, enables you to narrow or expand your search for the offending instruction. The following example increases to 100 the number of levels Dr. Watson disassembles:

```
[Dr. Watson]
DisStack=100
```

A *level* in the stack, also known as a *stack frame,* is the portion of the stack that contains a particular procedure's data and parameters.

Adding *LogFile* to *[Dr. Watson]*

If you include no entry for the LogFile setting, Dr. Watson places its report in a file called DRWATSON.LOG. You can place in this entry, however, any file name or device name to which your computer can write. When you do, Dr. Watson writes its information to that file or device. The following entry, for example, changes the name of the file to which Dr. Watson writes:

```
[Dr. Watson]
LogFile=MYLOG.LOG
```

Similarly, the following entry causes Dr. Watson's report to be written to the printer attached to LPT1:

```
[Dr. Watson]
LogFile=LPT1
```

The Complete *[Dr. Watson]* Section

If you were to include an entry for every one of Dr. Watson's initialization settings, your [Dr. Watson] section in WIN.INI would look like the following:

```
[Dr. Watson]
SkipInfo=inf
ShowInfo=dis err loc mod par sou
DisLen=4
TrapZero=1
set GPContinue=3
DisStack=100
LogFile=LPT1
```

What the Good Doctor Tells You

A Dr. Watson error report can be rather cryptic unless you are fluent in assembly language. After you know which key items to look for, however, you easily can spot the information that will help you understand what caused the error. The following Dr. Watson error log is annotated to explain what each entry means and how to search for the cause of an error.

```
Start Dr. Watson 0.80 - Mon Dec 7 23:38:41 1992
    ##This line announces the time and date on which
    ##Dr. Watson started the current session. A similar
    ##line is added to this file each time Dr. Watson
    ##ends a session.


*************************************************************
    ##This line of asterisks divides each error report
    ##from the rest. Such a line is inserted at the
    ##beginning of each new report.

Dr. Watson 0.80 Failure Report - Tue Dec 8 03:30:07 1992
    ##This line gives the version of Dr. Watson and the
    ##date and time the report was generated.

ABCWIN had a 'Exceed Segment Bounds (Read)' fault at
ABCWIN 3:083b
    ##The application ABCWIN experienced an 'Exceed
    ##Segment Bounds' error during a memory read
    ##operation. The code that failed was in the module
    ##ABCWIN 0x83 bytes past the instruction labeled '3.'
```

tagABCWIN$Exceed Segment Bounds (Read)$ABCWIN 3:083b$mov
ax, [si+6c]$Tue Dec 8 03:30:07 1992
>   ##This line provides the above information in a form
>   ##used for automatic code parsing. The actual
>   ##instruction that causes the error (a move
>   ##instruction) is provided for the first time in
>   ##this line.

$param$, Last param error was: Invalid handle passed to
USER 1:ac80: 0x0006
>   ##This line provides information about parameter
>   ##errors. In this case, a bad parameter (a handle)
>   ##was passed to the Windows USER module.

CPU Registers (regs)
ax=0465 bx=08f6 cx=0000 dx=0000 si=8ae0 di=399c
>   ##These are the values of the 16-bit registers on
>   ##the microprocessor. They contain the memory
>   ##addresses an instruction was modifying.

ip=083b sp=0d6c bp=0d78 O- D- I+ S+ Z- A- P- C-
>   ##These are the values of the instruction pointer
>   ##(IP), stack pointer (SP), and base pointer (BP).
>   ##The remaining items reveal the states of the
>   ##overflow, direction, interrupt, sign, zero,
>   ##auxcarry, parity, and carry flags. A minus (-)
>   ##indicates the flag is clear (0); a plus (+)
>   ##indicates the flag is set (1).

cs = 0b0f 809ebde0:3d1f Code Ex/R
>   ##This line identifies information about the code
>   ##segment. The selector is 0b0f, the linear address
>   ##is 809ebde0, and the limit is 3d1f. Accessing
>   ##segments beyond their limits is a common cause of
>   ##this type of error.

ss = 0087 804c6000:0fff Data R/W
>   ##This line provides information about the stack
>   ##segment. It is interpreted in the same way as the
>   ##code segment line.

ds = 0087 804c6000:0fff Data R/W
>   ##This line provides information about the data
>   ##segment. It is interpreted in the same way as the
>   ##code segment line.

II

Optimizing Windows

```
es = 055f 805e4660:0fbf Code Ex/R
        ##This line provides information about the extra
        ##segment. It is interpreted in the same way as the
        ##code segment line.


CPU 32 bit Registers (32bit)
eax = 00000465 ebx = 26d208f6 ecx = 00000000 edx = 00000000
esi = 00008ae0 edi = 0000399c ebp = 00000d78 esp = 80010d5c
fs = 0000   0:0000 Null Ptr
gs = 0000   0:0000 Null Ptr


eflag = 00000202
        ##This section provides the contents of the 32-bit
        ##registers. Note the selectors here (gs and fs) are
        ##0, indicating use of a null pointer. Use of a null
        ##pointer is another common cause of errors.


System Info (info)
        ##This section records information about the system.
Windows version 3.10
        ##The version of Windows.
Retail build
        ##The build of Windows, retail or debug.
Windows Build 3.1
        ##The internal Microsoft build number.
Username Gateway 2000
        ##The name of the user.
Organization Authorized License
        ##The name of the organization owning the license.
System Free Space 15650368
        ##The free RAM on the system.
Stack base 164, top 4062, lowest 4046, size 3898
        ##The stack size and stack parameters for the current
        ##task, the one that produced the error.
System resources: USER: 66% free, seg 06b7 GDI: 52% free,
seg 0507
        ##The current usage of system resources.
LargestFree 10416128, MaxPagesAvail 2543,
MaxPagesLockable 1028
TotalLinear 4924, TotalUnlockedPages 1035, FreePages 0
TotalPages 1423, FreeLinearSpace 2612, SwapFilePages 4496
Page Size 4096
        ##Various statistics about Windows memory usage and
        ##virtual memory usage. These are not too useful in
        ##debugging.
```

```
10 tasks executing.
      ##The number of tasks executing.
WinFlags -
 Math coprocessor
 80486
 Enhanced mode
 Protected mode
      ##These flags tell you whether a math coprocessor is
      ##present, which CPU is installed, and which mode
      ##Windows is running in.


Stack Dump (stack)
      ##Dr. Watson dumps the stack to reveal the
      ##instructions that might have caused the error.


Stack Frame 0 is ABCWIN 3:083b     ss:bp 0087:0d78
      ##We know from the lines above that the error
      ##occurred 0x83 bytes past the instruction labeled
      ##'3.' As a result, it will appear in this stack
      ##frame, because it carries the same 3:083b label.
0b0f:0834 eb 24      jmp short 085a
0b0f:0836 57         push di
0b0f:0837 0b f6      or si, si
0b0f:0839 74 05      jz short 0840
(ABCWIN:3:083b)
0b0f:083b 8b 44 6c    mov ax, [si+6c]
      ##Here is the line that produced the error. It is
      ##marked with a tag by Dr. Watson. You can move to
      ##this line using the assembly language view of your
      ##code in any debugger. You then can use the source
      ##view of your code to determine the exact program
      ##statement that caused the problem. From the
      ##information in the lines above, it appears that
      ##this instruction attempted to pass a bad function
      ##parameter to the USER module, which is the part of
      ##Windows that controls presentation function
      ##of the user interface. You should look for some kind of
      ##incorrect parameter in your code. Because you know the bad
      ##parameter was a handle, you should look for a
      ##parameter of the Windows data type HANDLE that is
      ##incorrectly specified. You might have passed a
      ##handle of the wrong type to a function.
```

```
0b0f:083e eb 02      jmp short 0842
0b0f:0840 8b c6       mov ax, si
0b0f:0842 50      push ax


Stack Frame 1 is USER 1:3ab4      ss:bp 0087:0d98
037f:3aaa 8e c1       mov es, cx
037f:3aac 8e d9       mov ds, cx
037f:3aae 8b dc       mov bx, sp
037f:3ab0 36 ff 5f 0a   callf     word ptr ss:[bx+0a]
(USER:1:3ab4)
037f:3ab4 83 c4 04     add     sp, 04
037f:3ab7 5f      pop     di
037f:3ab8 5e      pop     si
037f:3ab9 1f      pop     ds


      ##A list of the remaining stack frames appears below.
Stack Frame 2 is ABABCEXE 3:23ac    ss:bp 0087:0e6c
Stack Frame 3 is USER 1:3ab4      ss:bp 0087:0e8c
Stack Frame 4 is USER 1:7ae6      ss:bp 0087:0ea4
Stack Frame 5 is USER 1:7964      ss:bp 0087:0ebc
Stack Frame 6 is USER 1:7a4d      ss:bp 0087:0ed4
Stack Frame 7 is USER 1:7a4d      ss:bp 0087:0eec
Stack Frame 8 is USER 1:7a4d      ss:bp 0087:0f04
Stack Frame 9 is USER 7:0292      ss:bp 0087:0f1c
Stack Frame 10 is USER 7:035b      ss:bp 0087:0f2e
Stack Frame 11 is USER 7:0093      ss:bp 0087:0f44
Stack Frame 12 is AWIN2 103:011c    ss:bp 0087:0f5c
Stack Frame 13 is USER 1:8094      ss:bp 0087:0f7e
Stack Frame 14 is USER 1:0bfd      ss:bp 0087:0f8e
Stack Frame 15 is USER 1:09fe      ss:bp 0087:0f9e
Stack Frame 16 is KERNEL 1:5f48     ss:bp 0087:0fc8


System Tasks (tasks)
      ##The list of currently running tasks appears below.
Task NHOOKEXE, Handle 24c7, Flags 0001, Info 6144 03-27-92 2:00
 FileName C:\NORTONDW\NHOOKEXE.EXE
Task DRWATSON, Handle 255f, Flags 0001, Info 26864 03-10-92 3:10
 FileName C:\WINDOWS\DRWATSON.EXE
Task VISION, Handle 3797, Flags 0001, Info 987840 08-28-92 2:10
 FileName C:\VISION\VISION.EXE
Task MSWORD, Handle 214f, Flags 0001, Info 1273024 02-18-92 2:00
 FileName C:\WINWORD\WINWORD.EXE
Task  NDW, Handle 0547, Flags 0001, Info 8112 03-27-92 2:00
```

```
    FileName C:\WINDOWS\NDW.EXE
  Task CLOCK, Handle 249f, Flags 0001, Info 16416 03-10-92 3:10
   FileName C:\WINDOWS\CLOCK.EXE
  Task SYSMETER, Handle 18c7, Flags 0001, Info 36652 04-06-92 0:00
   FileName C:\WINDOWS\WRKIT\SYSMETER.EXE
  Task  AD, Handle 2867, Flags 0001, Info 253904 10-15-92 19:20
   FileName C:\AFTERDRK\AD.EXE
  Task NDWMAIN, Handle 158f, Flags 0001, Info 12256 03-27-92 2:00
   FileName C:\NORTONDW\NDWMAIN.EXE
  Task ABCWIN, Handle 67bf, Flags 0001, Info 112896 10-23-92 1:00
   FileName C:\ABCW\ABCWIN.EXE
          ##If the user explained what he tried to do, his
          ##comments would appear here. Obviously, this user
          ##made no comment.

Attempting to continue execution at user request,
Tue Dec 8 03:30:09 1992
          ##This line indicates that Dr. Watson inquired
          ##whether the user wished to continue execution, and
          ##the user asked to continue. GPContinue was set to
          ##allow this form of continuation.
```

Troubleshooting Windows for Workgroups

You read earlier in this chapter about some of the command-line switches you can use to start Windows to troubleshoot various types of problems. Windows for Workgroups 3.11 provides a few new command-line switches that are useful for troubleshooting networking and other problems. The following list summarizes these new command-line switches:

- ✔ **/N.** This switch starts Windows for Workgroups without protected-mode networking support. No protected-mode network drivers are loaded, and no network services will be available. Use this switch if you suspect a problem with the network. You also can use this switch when starting Windows on a PC that is not currently connected to the network (such as a notebook PC).

- ✔ **/D:T.** This switch starts Windows for Workgroups with no virtual device drivers (VXDs). When Windows is started with this switch, no MS-DOS or communications programs can run. Also, networking functionality is disabled unless the real-mode network drivers were loaded prior to starting Windows.

- ✔ **/D:C.** This switch starts Windows without 32-bit file access (VFAT). Use this switch if you suspect that 32-bit file access is causing the problem.

II

Optimizing Windows

Using CLN Files

Using debug switches to start Windows does not always overcome the problem. Some problems are caused by changes to the three Windows configuration files: WIN.INI, SYSTEM.INI, and PROTOCOL.INI. To help overcome problems with these files, Windows for Workgroups automatically creates backups of these files when you use Setup to modify your PC's configuration under Windows. These backup copies of the files have the same file name as the original files, but have the file extension CLN. The backup copy of WIN.INI, for example, is named WIN.CLN.

If you experience a problem with Windows and cannot determine the cause or correct the problem, you can replace the current system configuration files with the CLN backups. This is particularly helpful when you use Setup to change configuration and Windows ceases to function properly. It also is helpful when improper changes have been made to these three Windows INI files by an application, or you have edited the files yourself.

To restore these backup copies of your Windows configuration files, follow these steps:

1. Exit Windows.

2. Rename the files SYSTEM.INI and PROTOCOL.INI to SYSTEM.BAK and PROTOCOL.BAK, respectively.

3. Copy the file PROTOCOL.CLN to PROTOCOL.INI.

4. Copy the file SYSTEM.CLN to SYSTEM.INI.

5. Restart Windows for Workgroups and test its performance.

6. If Windows still does not run properly, rename the file WIN.INI to WIN.BAK, then copy WIN.CLN to WIN.INI and retest.

Testing the Network

Windows for Workgroups 3.11 provides a network diagnostic tool you can use to troubleshoot problems with network access. You can use this troubleshooting tool to isolate problems when a network node is not communicating with the network or when the network is functioning erratically. Although you can run the network diagnostic from within Windows, you should exit Windows before running the diagnostic to ensure accurate results.

To test the network, one node must be acting as a network diagnostic server. You then can run the network diagnostic software on the node that is experiencing problems. To test network connections, use the following procedure:

1. Exit Windows on the node that will act as the diagnostic server, and at the DOS prompt enter **NET DIAG**.

2. If you are running IPX and NetBIOS on the node, the diagnostic will prompt you to specify which protocol you want to use for the test. Press I to use IPX, or press N to use NetBIOS.

3. The diagnostic will search for a diagnostic server, and if no diagnostic server is running, will prompt you to determine if there are other nodes running the diagnostic. Answer no by pressing N. This will place the node in diagnostic server mode.

4. At the node that is experiencing the problem, exit Windows and at the DOS prompt enter **NET DIAG**.

5. The diagnostic program will determine if IPX and NetBIOS are both running on the machine. If both protocols are found, the diagnostic will prompt you to specify which protocol to use. Specify the same protocol that you used for the diagnostic server.

6. The diagnostic program will search the network for the diagnostic server and automatically begin testing, providing a status message when it has completed testing. If the node cannot locate the server, it is likely that you have a hardware or cabling problem. Begin troubleshooting the network interface card and cable.

You can use two command-line switches with the network diagnostic to control its operation. These switches are described in the following list:

✔ **NET DIAG /STATUS.** The STATUS switch causes the diagnostic to display the status of the network adapter since it was last initialized. This option is available only with a NetBIOS provider.

✔ **NET DIAG /NAMES.** This switch enables you to specify the names of the two nodes that will be communicating in the diagnostic session. This switch is useful when multiple nodes are acting as diagnostic servers. This switch is available only with a NetBIOS server.

✔ **NET DIAG /?.** This switch displays an explanation of the previous two command-line switches.

Troubleshooting Network Capability

If you are experiencing problems with network access and running the network diagnostic did not identify the problem, you can take specific steps to diagnose the problem. First, verify that the node has the proper hardware configuration to run Windows for Workgroups. The requirements are as follows:

II

Optimizing Windows

✔ 80386 or later processor

✔ Minimum of 3,072 KB of free XMS memory

✔ Network card, properly configured for I/O base address, IRQ, and RAM address range

If you determine that the node has the proper hardware configuration to run Windows for Workgroups, use the following procedure to troubleshoot the network:

1. Exit Windows, and at the DOS prompt start the real-mode network drivers by entering the command **NET START WORKSTATION**.

2. If the network starts without generating an error message, enter **NET STOP /Y**, which stops the network but leaves the real-mode network drivers loaded. Start Windows for Workgroups. If the network functions properly, there is a problem running the protected-mode network drivers on the node. Verify with the interface adapter's manufacturer or vendor that it will function properly with Windows for Workgroups' protected-mode network drivers. You might need to acquire updated drivers for the network adapter.

3. Run Windows by entering **WIN /N** at the DOS prompt. Check the configuration of the network driver (or drivers) to determine that it is properly installed.

4. Check the network adapter's IRQ, I/O base address, and RAM address to verify that these settings do not conflict with other devices in the PC.

5. Make backup copies of SYSTEM.INI and PROTOCOL.INI. Run Windows with the /N switch to disable network functionality, then use the Network Setup icon in the Network group to remove all protocols except NetBEUI. Restart the system and start Windows to determine if the network is functioning. If the network functions, begin adding the additional protocols one at a time.

You might receive the error message Not enough memory when attempting to browse for a network connection. This is a known bug and Microsoft is evaluating it. The only workaround is to use UNC naming to explicitly connect to a shared resource. UNC resource names have the form *server**sharename*. An example is \\\\SERVER1\\D, which specifies a disk resource shared as D on a machine named SERVER1.

Using Other Resources for Troubleshooting

If the information in this chapter has not solved your problem with Windows or with running applications under Windows, you should turn to other resources. Try your hardware and software manuals first. Be sure to check appendixes and chapters that discuss troubleshooting.

Perhaps the most useful publications containing information about troubleshooting are the *Microsoft Windows Resource Kit* and *Microsoft Knowledge Base on CD-ROM*, both available from Microsoft.

The *Resource Kit* contains the names, phone numbers, and addresses of all the user groups worldwide that can provide more information about problems. It also provides the same information for key hardware companies, and, of course, for Microsoft. The *Resource Kit* also provides a directory of bulletin board forums you can call for assistance, including vendor forums sponsored by hardware and software manufacturers.

The *Knowledge Base* is a list of articles that answer questions Windows users raise about its use. The CD provides information about a wide range of topics, and it can be searched efficiently by using the access software that comes with it. It is limited to Microsoft products, however; answers to questions about other vendors' products might not be available in that publication.

If you have exhausted these print resources and still have a problem, you can turn to customer support from either Microsoft or the third-party vendor that manufactured your hardware or software. You should also turn to the forums available through online services, especially Windows Users Group Network (WUGNET) and Microsoft Connection (MSCON) on CompuServe. Difficult problems almost always have solutions. They are difficult because only a few users have experienced the problem. To solve these types of problems, you should talk to one of the few people who knows the answer. By asking the question in an online forum, chances are you will meet someone who either knows the answer or who knows someone who does.

II

Optimizing Windows

Chapter Snapshot

Remember all the excitement in February 1992, when the media was predicting the impending disaster in the PC world from the so-called Michelangelo virus? On March 6, this virus was going to come alive and crash computers everywhere. Well, that day has come and gone and although many computers did fall prey to Michelangelo, it wasn't nearly as widespread as originally predicted.

This chapter discusses ways to prevent computer virus attacks, including steps you can take to keep your computer free from virus infection. Other types of preventative medicine include:

Michelangelo certainly was the most widely publicized virus, but thousands of others exist that can destroy data and programs and crash your computer. By recognizing that viruses exist and taking action to look for them and prevent your computer from becoming infected, you can help avoid unwanted headaches in the future.

13

CHAPTER

Preventing and Overcoming Viruses

A *computer virus* is a program written solely to cause something unexpected, unwanted, or destructive to happen to your computer and the data and programs contained within it. Viruses actually are programs written by individuals or groups of individuals intent on infecting your computer without your knowing about it (at least initially).

After your computer is infected with a virus, the virus usually replicates itself. At a later time, the virus causes something to happen, such as displaying a message on-screen, corrupting data and program files, or even reformatting your hard disk. These attacks might happen in the next five minutes or even the next five months. Some viruses, like Michelangelo, are programmed to activate on a certain date. Others attack as soon as your computer is infected.

Some viruses are identified by messages that they display on your screen. The popular Stoned virus, for example, displays a message on your screen that says, "Your computer is now stoned. Legalize marijuana." Most viruses do not display messages, however; they infect your computer and do their damage without announcing their presence.

Understanding the Different Types of Viruses

Many viruses exist, each one with its own bag of tricks and potentially destructive capabilities. Most viruses can be classified into three categories: boot sector viruses, file infectors, and Trojan horses.

Boot sector viruses infect the boot sector of your disk, replacing some of the program code in the boot sector with the virus's own code. When the computer boots, the virus is loaded from the boot sector into memory along with the rest of the operating system. After being loaded into memory, the virus can infect the boot sectors of other disks used in your computer, or it can perform some other action such as delete files on your hard disk.

Usually a computer virus infection isn't discovered until it is too late—the virus has already done its damage and probably spread to another computer. The secret to discovering if your computer or floppy disks have been infected by a virus is to have a plan for regularly scanning for viruses with antivirus software.

File infector viruses infect programs and data on your computer's hard disk or floppy drive. When an infected program runs, the virus is loaded into memory along with the program. After the virus is in memory, it infects other programs or performs other devious tasks.

File infector viruses stay in memory even after you exit the program. When another program runs, the virus infects the new program and the replication process continues.

Viruses typically have two primary purposes: to perform some destructive or annoying action (such as randomly trash data files), or to replicate and spread by infecting other programs so that when the newly infected program runs, the virus program also runs.

Any time an infected program runs, the virus program also runs; it doesn't matter whether the program was run from a floppy or hard drive. With the virus in memory, any program or file is fair game for infection or damage regardless of its location.

Trojan horse viruses look like legitimate programs. When the program is run, however, the virus performs some destructive action, such as corrupting files or formatting your hard drive.

As the name Trojan horse implies, Trojan horse viruses appear to be something they are not. You run what appears to be a legitimate program, but in reality its purpose is to perform a destructive action.

One example of a Trojan horse might be a program on your hard disk named FUN.EXE. When you type **fun** to run the program, all the programs on your hard disk are deleted.

Use caution when running any program unless you know exactly what it is. A program named "bugs" could be a virus that displays cute little insects on your screen and then starts deleting files on your hard disk. Always scan an unknown program with antivirus software before you run it.

Understanding What a Virus Can Do

The actions viruses can perform are almost unlimited because viruses are computer programs. Anything a computer program can be written to do, whether good or bad, a computer virus can do. Most computer viruses first try to spread or replicate themselves in other programs. Then, at some point in time or during a particular event, the virus performs a destructive action. Even viruses not intended to be destructive can cause many problems. Often when a virus infects a program, the program file becomes corrupted, leaving the program unstable or unusable.

Many antivirus programs can actually remove a virus from an infected program. Often, however, the program does not operate properly even after the virus has been removed because the program file is corrupted. In this situation, the only solution is to reinstall the program or to restore the program from a backup. If restoring from a backup, be sure to scan for viruses with antivirus software to make sure your backup was not infected as well.

The most common problem caused by computer viruses is damaged program and data files. This results from the virus infecting the program, modifying or deleting the contents of a file, or damaging the file allocation table or directory of the disk drive.

Some viruses write messages on-screen; others actually play music. Although the effects of these viruses may seem minor and humorous at worst, the very nature of computer viruses causes more and more files to become infected. An unexpected chuckle from a silly virus can quickly turn into a crashed computer.

In the case of the music virus, for example, the virus begins by playing a single note in a song. Each program that comes into contact with this virus is infected. The longer your computer has been infected, the more music is played. Eventually you come to a point where each time you press a key on your keyboard, a song is played. Imagine trying to type a letter to someone and being entertained with a six-minute song before the computer will accept another keystroke.

The most damaging viruses are those that actually make your hard disk unusable by reformatting the hard drive or corrupting the file allocation table (FAT) to a point at which retrieving data is almost impossible. In the same way you use DOS to delete unwanted files on your hard drive, a virus can randomly or selectively delete files on your hard disk. Also, a virus might destroy data on your hard disk by formatting it.

Understanding How Viruses Are Spread

Computer viruses usually are spread by running a program infected by a virus on your computer. When you run an infected program, the computer virus program also is run. You might not notice anything out of the ordinary at first because the virus operates in the background. Often a computer virus stays active in your computer's memory even after you have finished using the infected program. When you run another program, the computer virus infects that program, continuing the infection process.

Boot sector viruses work in much the same way. A boot sector virus often loads into memory as soon as the computer boots. Because the only way to run a program that is part of the boot sector is to boot from the disk, a boot sector virus runs by booting off a disk whose boot sector has been infected. From that point, it tries to infect the boot sector of your hard disk and any disk inserted into the floppy drive. The next time the computer boots, whether from the infected floppy disk or the infected hard drive, the virus becomes active and is ready to continue the infection process.

Not all boot sector viruses remain resident in memory. Some try to infect the boot sectors of other disks when your computer boots and then remain inactive until the next time your computer boots. It is just like loading a program that performs its task (in this case, the task is infecting the boot sectors of other disks) and then exits and performs no action until you run it again.

Even a floppy disk that is not bootable can contain a boot sector virus. The Michelangelo virus, for example, can infect the boot sector of your hard disk even if you leave the floppy disk in the hard drive when the computer boots. Even though the computer does not boot from this floppy, the infected disk transfers the virus when the boot process checks the disk drive.

A common way for your computer to become infected is by sharing infected programs and floppy disks with other computer users. Your computer also can become infected by using infected software downloaded from a BBS (bulletin board system) or other online service.

All the major online services and even most of the smaller BBSs scan their downloadable files for viruses. The chance always exists, however, that a virus will slip through without being checked or that the antivirus software will not catch a particular virus.

Although it is less likely, your computer can become infected from a program that you have purchased. Computer viruses have found their way into some software manufacturers' companies and have been shipped to customers in commercial software programs before being identified and removed.

Often it is difficult to pin down the source of a virus infection. Even original software disks could have been infected by your computer when you installed the software (unless the original disks had a write-protect tab on them).

Computer viruses also can be spread across networks. If your computer is part of a network, any program located on a different computer on the network potentially can infect your computer. When you run a program located on another computer in the network, that program actually is loaded into memory and executed on your computer. If you run an infected program, the virus is loaded into the memory on your computer where it can infect other programs, whether these programs are run from your local hard drive or the hard drive of another computer located on the network.

Understanding Antiviral Strategies

If you understand the way viruses spread and what they are capable of doing, you are on your way to preventing your computer from becoming infected. Your computer can become infected with a computer virus in only a few ways. As a result, you can take a few precautions to prevent virus infections from damaging your programs and data.

The most common way to infect your computer with a virus is by running an infected program on your computer. To prevent this, check all new programs for viruses before you run them. The best way to check for viruses is by scanning the program with antivirus software, which is discussed in detail later in this chapter.

A computer virus cannot spread unless some action is taken that enables the virus program to be run on your computer. The two ways this can happen are by running an infected program or by booting from a disk (floppy or hard drive) that contains a boot sector virus. Copying or scanning a disk or program for viruses does not cause the virus to execute or spread.

If you are going to use your floppy disk in someone else's computer, write-protect the disk. This way, if the computer you use is infected with a virus, it cannot write that virus to your floppy disk. Also remember that you cannot write other information to a write-protected floppy disk.

If your computer is on a network, make sure the programs located on the other computers you are using have been scanned for viruses. Also make sure that you scan your computer for viruses to prevent possible damage to programs and data on your hard drive, and to prevent spreading viruses that might exist on your computer to other computers in the network.

Exploring Software Protection

Many antivirus programs are available that detect, remove, and prevent infection from computer viruses. Many of these programs not only scan your disk for virus-infected programs, but also tell you if something suspicious occurs that might be caused by a virus.

Two of the most popular antivirus programs available for Windows are Central Point Anti-Virus and The Norton Anti-Virus. These programs include features that detect, remove, and prevent virus infections. To prevent virus infections, most programs incorporate a TSR that sits in memory looking for suspicious activity such as changing program files or writing information to the disk's boot sector.

The Microsoft Anti-Virus program included with DOS 6 is licensed from Central Point and is almost identical to the Central Point Anti-Virus.

Most antivirus programs scan your files for viruses by comparing a small amount of program code unique to each virus with the code in each program you are scanning. This is the most reliable technique for identifying viruses, but the antivirus software must have the viruses' signatures for all viruses it is capable of detecting.

Some antivirus software manufacturers offer a service you can use to update your antivirus software with the latest virus signatures (new viruses appear daily). Virus signature updates usually are provided on disk or can be downloaded from a BBS.

With the multitasking capabilities of Windows, implementing a regular routine for scanning for viruses can be almost effortless and can save you from data loss and damage from virus infections in the future.

By including your antivirus software in the Startup program group in Windows, your antivirus software will be started each time you start Windows. To take it one step further, many antivirus programs will enable you to specify an option on the command line to control the way the program searches for and handles viruses. To add a command-line parameter, choose File, Properties, Command Line while in Program Manager with your antivirus software icon highlighted.

Antivirus software also is being included in some communications software that, because of its very nature, could aid in the spread of computer viruses. Virus detection methods are being used to identify viruses when transferring programs and data over a modem. Central Point's Commute program scans for viruses as files are uploaded.

Because transferring programs to your computer with a modem is one way to obtain an infected program, in the future more communications software programs probably will include antivirus software bundled with the communications program or actually incorporated into the upload and download routines.

Another feature included in many antivirus software programs is the capability to detect and prevent a program from writing information to the boot sector of your hard drive or from overwriting a program file. This is important because viruses infect your computer by infecting either the boot sector on your hard drive or your program files.

If your computer has been infected with a virus, most antivirus software includes the capability to remove the virus from the infected programs or areas of your hard drive. Most programs do a good job of removing the virus. A virus can, however, damage a program file so badly that even after the virus is removed the program will not operate. If this is the case, you must restore the damaged program from a backup or reinstall the program from the original program disks.

The secret to avoiding damage from a computer virus is to catch it before it can do any damage. In addition to regular virus scans, you should scan any new program you have installed for viruses before you actually run the program.

Using Microsoft Anti-Virus for Windows

Included with MS-DOS 6 is a DOS and Windows version of Microsoft Anti-Virus. The Microsoft Anti-Virus software is a slightly modified version of the popular Central Point Anti-Virus software.

Microsoft Anti-Virus for Windows is located in the same directory as your DOS 6.0 files and can be started by executing the MWAV.EXE file while in Windows. If you upgraded to DOS 6.0 after installing Windows, choose the Anti-Virus icon in the Microsoft Tools program group to start the program.

When Microsoft Anti-Virus starts, you see the screen shown in figure 13.1. To select the drives you want to scan, click on the appropriate drive icon in the Drives box. The Status box displays the number of drives, directories, and files to be scanned.

Figure 13.1
Microsoft Anti-Virus for Windows initial screen.

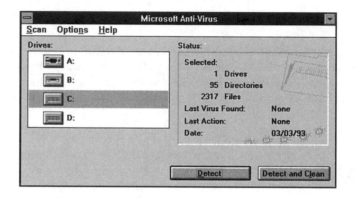

Click on the Detect button to scan your disk for viruses. The program notifies you if a virus is found. Anti-Virus first scans the PC's memory and then the selected drives (see fig. 13.2). While scanning, Anti-Virus displays the file that currently is being scanned and the progress of the operation. If a virus is found, you have the option to Clean, which removes the virus, Stop the scanning process, Delete the infected file, or Continue without taking any action.

Figure 13.2
Anti-Virus for Windows scanning for viruses.

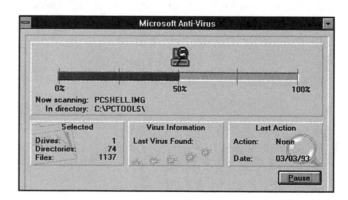

Anti-Virus also notifies you if any executable files have changed. The Verify Error dialog box (see fig. 13.3) displays the file that has been changed and enables you to prevent an error message from appearing for this file in future scans (Update), delete the file (Delete), proceed without any changes (Continue), or discontinue the scanning (Stop).

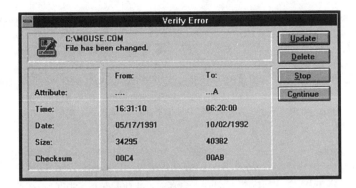

Figure 13.3
Anti-Virus for
Windows Verify
Error message.

When the scanning process is complete, Anti-Virus displays a Statistics screen (see fig. 13.4) that shows you the results of the scan, including the number of files scanned, the number of viruses found, and the number of viruses cleaned or removed.

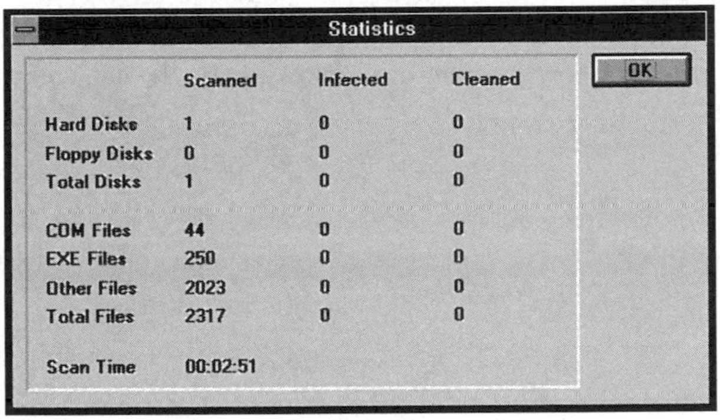

Figure 13.4
Anti-Virus for
Windows Statistics
screen.

Microsoft Anti-Virus for Windows has a number of options that can be changed to specify how the program operates. Also included is a virus list that shows the viruses for which Anti-Virus scans and some information about each one.

MS-DOS 6 also includes a program called VSAFE. This program remains resident in memory and notifies you of any activity that might indicate the presence of a virus, such as writing to the boot sector of the disk. If suspicious activity is detected, a `Virus Found` message appears that names the detected virus(es).

Understanding Hardware Protection

Hardware methods for preventing virus infections and easing the recovery of your programs and data if your computer becomes infected are becoming available. Unlike antivirus software programs, hardware virus protection devices cannot be infected by a virus.

II

Optimizing Windows

Many of the hardware devices available keep a copy of your hard drive's boot record and partition table information isolated from your hard drive. Often these devices also can store some critical program files and antivirus software. If the contents of your hard disk are damaged by a virus, these devices enable you to boot clean from the hardware device (similar to booting from a clean floppy boot disk), restore your boot record and critical files, and take the appropriate actions necessary to remove other virus infections that might exist on your hard drive.

Hardware virus protection schemes are relatively new and are implemented in a variety of different ways. Some manufacturers incorporate antivirus code into the system BIOS. Western Digital incorporates antivirus technology into one of its controllers that monitors write requests to the hard drive. Other manufacturers use a card that plugs into an expansion slot in your computer.

In the same way that using a write-protect tab protects your floppy disk from becoming infected with a virus, some hardware and software methods enable you to write-protect either your entire hard drive or selected areas on it. This way you can choose to write-protect those directories that contain program files and eliminate the chance of a virus infecting your program files.

Chapter Snapshot

Today, approximately one out of eight new computers purchased is a notebook PC or other type of portable. Within the next two years, notebook PCs could represent as much as half of all new computer purchases. Because of their fundamental differences from desktop PCs, notebook PCs require a few special considerations for running Windows. This chapter provides an overview of notebooks and offers tips on using Windows on a notebook PC. The chapter examines the following topics:

The first step in using Windows effectively on a notebook PC is choosing the right equipment.

14
CHAPTER

Using Windows on a Notebook PC

Today's notebook PCs are in most ways as powerful as desktop systems. There are some general trade-offs between portability and function, but on the whole, the added flexibility of a notebook PC overcomes the few trade-offs that do exist. With the addition of a docking station (explained later in the section "Other Useful Features"), a notebook PC gains all the benefits offered by a desktop system without giving up any inherent advantages.

Many of the issues related to selecting a notebook PC for Windows are the same as for choosing a desktop PC. There are, however, some specific considerations at which to look.

Buying a Notebook

One of the first issues to consider when shopping for a portable PC is whether to choose a notebook or a subnotebook. The following list describes the primary differences between notebooks and subnotebooks, and explains the advantages and disadvantages of each:

- ✔ **Size.** Notebooks and subnotebooks are roughly the same size in width and length (about 8 ½"×11"), although some subnotebooks are smaller. The size of notebooks and subnotebooks is unlikely to shrink much farther due to the space requirements for a typical keyboard and a practical display. The reduced size of subnotebooks makes them lighter, but results in smaller displays and fewer options.

- ✔ **Weight.** Because they are thinner and often do not have the same equipment as notebooks, subnotebooks generally are lighter than notebooks (approximately 3 ½ pounds versus 6 ½ pounds).

- ✔ **Display.** The displays on many subnotebooks are smaller than those found on notebooks. Color displays are less common on subnotebooks than on notebooks, although more subnotebooks now are available with color displays.

- ✔ **CPU.** Subnotebooks lag behind notebooks in raw CPU power, partly because the demand for high-end CPUs makes notebooks a more attractive alternative. Manufacturers, therefore, concentrate the majority of their efforts on notebook development. High-speed 486-DX3 and 486-DX4 notebooks now are common, and Pentium-based notebooks are just becoming available. Similar CPU power generally is not available in a subnotebook configuration.

- ✔ **Disk Storage.** Because of their larger size, notebooks typically offer better disk storage capacity than subnotebooks. Hard disk capacity often is greater on notebooks, and many subnotebooks do not include disk drives. However, you can get an optional external disk drive for most subnotebooks if you seldom use a disk drive.

- ✔ **Expandability.** Notebooks now include at least one PCMCIA slot for adding peripherals such as hard disks, modems, network adapters, and other devices to the notebook. Many notebooks include two PCMCIA slots, whereas subnotebooks generally provide only one.

When deciding whether to buy a notebook or subnotebook, you should consider all these options carefully. If you will be using the system extensively, buy a notebook PC. The larger and higher-quality display, additional storage space, and greater capability to add options to the system will make the added weight of a notebook worthwhile. If portability and weight are your main concerns, and you will not be using the system extensively, a subnotebook is a good alternative.

The Display

Three types of displays are used in today's notebook (and subnotebook) PCs: monochrome (backlit VGA), passive color (dual-scan color), and active matrix color. Currently, almost all notebook PCs support a maximum resolution of 640×480 (standard VGA resolution). No systems support higher resolution on the notebook's own display, although many systems will drive an external monitor at a resolution of 1,024×768.

As you might guess, monochrome displays are the least expensive. Not all monochrome displays are alike, however. Some of the newer monochrome displays provide image quality nearly as good as active matrix color displays. However, these types of monochrome displays generally are more expensive than the average monochrome display. If you are interested in saving money, consider a notebook with a monochrome display. If possible, examine the system beforehand to determine if you will be satisfied with the display quality.

The mid-range choice for notebook video is dual-scan, or passive, color. The image quality of most passive color displays is similar to the quality of today's monochrome displays. Monochrome and passive color do have two drawbacks, although they are the least expensive. First, the viewing angle of monochrome and passive color displays is somewhat limited. If you move more than 20° either side of center, the display fades and becomes difficult to read. These types of displays also suffer from ghosting—as objects (such as the pointer) move across the display, the objects generate ghost images. These are not major drawbacks, but many users dislike these characteristics, particularly when using the system for an extended period.

The best and most expensive display is the active matrix color display. Active matrix displays offer crisp, fast graphics without the problems of reduced viewing angle and ghosting. If you plan to use your notebook for extended periods, or you simply want the best display possible, consider buying a system with active matrix color.

Many notebook PCs use local bus video, which improves graphics performance. Because Windows is a graphics-intensive environment, video performance has a major impact on Windows' performance. If possible, buy a notebook that uses local bus video.

The Keyboard

Most PC buyers do not consider the keyboard when shopping for a new desktop PC, but the keyboard is one area to consider closely when shopping for a notebook PC. Keyboards on notebook PCs are the same basic size as keyboards on desktop PCs with a few exceptions. Although the character keys are the same, many of the other keys are smaller and positioned differently from a typical 101-key desktop keyboard. In addition, key travel typically is much less on a notebook keyboard than on a desktop keyboard.

After converting to a notebook, you might find that you prefer the notebook's keyboard over a desktop keyboard because of the reduced key travel (the distance the keys move when you press them). After you become accustomed to this change, you might be able to type a little faster on the notebook.

If possible, test the keyboard of the notebook you plan to buy before you actually buy the system. This will give you a feel for the keyboard and help you decide if the system is right for you.

Disks

Virtually all of today's notebook and subnotebook PCs include a hard disk. Most notebooks include an internal floppy drive, but some provide an external drive to reduce the weight of the system. Some, like the NEC UltraLite Versa, include removable drives that can be replaced with an optional second battery. Most subnotebooks also use external floppy disk drives. Whether a system uses an internal or an external floppy disk drive makes little difference. An external drive offers the advantage of reducing the system's weight, but you must pack and carry the drive when you take your notebook on the road. An internal drive is more convenient, but adds to the weight of the system (although not appreciably).

The most important consideration when buying a notebook is the system's hard disk. Windows requires approximately 10–15 MB of space depending on the options you install. Your applications will take considerably more disk space. Hard disk capacities of 80 MB and 120 MB are common in notebooks, but many vendors also offer systems with drives in the 250 MB range. These larger drives are expensive, however, when compared to similar capacity drives for desktop systems.

As when buying a desktop PC, buy the largest hard disk you can afford for your notebook, but base your decision on how you will use the system. If you will be using the notebook as your primary system, a large disk capacity is a necessity. If you will be using the notebook as a supplement to your desktop system, you might get by with a smaller hard disk. In either case, compressing the drive is a good idea to get the most from it. Read the section "Configuring Your System" later in this chapter for tips on maximizing the disk space on your notebook.

You can increase the hard disk capacity of a notebook or subnotebook by adding a removable PCMCIA hard disk to the system. PCMCIA devices are discussed in the next section.

PCMCIA Support

PCMCIA (Personal Computer Memory Card International Association) devices are credit card–sized adapters for notebook and desktop systems (see fig. 14.1). PCMCIA devices include memory modules, modems, network adapters, sound adapters, and hard disks. Most notebook PCs include one or two PCMCIA slots for adding these types of devices to the notebook. Subnotebooks typically have only one PCMCIA slot. Figure 14.2 shows two PCMCIA slots in a typical notebook.

Figure 14.1
A PCMCIA modem and network adapter.

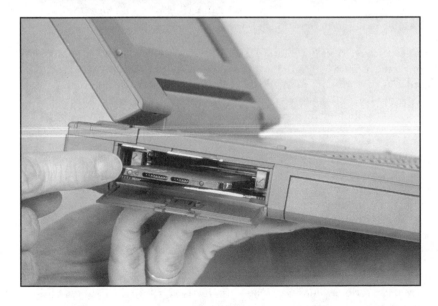

Figure 14.2
Two PCMCIA slots.

The capabilities of a system's PCMCIA slots are determined by the slot's type. Newer notebooks include PCMCIA slots that will accommodate Type I, Type II, and Type III adapters. The only difference between each slot type is the thickness of the adapters—the length and width are the same. Systems with two PCMCIA slots will accommodate two Type I or Type II adapters, or one Type III adapter. Systems with only one PCMCIA slot will accommodate one device of the highest type specified for the slot.

Most PCMCIA devices will fit into a Type II slot. The main exception is a removable PCMCIA hard disk, which generally requires a Type III slot. Inserting one of these drives into a system with two PCMCIA slots uses both slots (physically blocking the second slot, but not using its internal connector).

If you need to use two adapters at the same time, such as a modem and a network card, buy a system with two PCMCIA slots. If you also would like to use your PCMCIA adapters in a desktop system, you can buy a PCMCIA card deck that connects to your desktop system's bus and makes it possible to use the PCMCIA devices in the desktop PC. Internal card decks mount in an empty drive bay, just like a floppy drive. External card decks rest on the desktop and connect to the back of the PC. Both types of card decks include an adapter that plugs into the desktop PC's bus, so your system must have one free bus slot to accommodate the card deck.

Other Useful Features

The items discussed in the previous sections are some of the most important considerations when buying a notebook PC. The following list describes other features to look for when you are deciding which notebook PC to buy:

✔ **Docking stations.** Docking stations provide a "base of operations" for your notebook. You can install full-size hard disks, floppy disks, CD-ROM drives, sound cards, and other peripherals in the docking station. The notebook then plugs into the docking station, making these devices available to the notebook. A docking station is a good option if you are using the notebook as your primary system and want to expand.

✔ **Concurrent video.** Many notebooks support concurrent video, which enables you to use the notebook's display while also driving an external monitor. Concurrent video is a useful feature if you use the notebook for demonstrations, because you can use the notebook's display for yourself and an external monitor for your audience. Systems that do not support concurrent video generally have an external video port, but only one video device can be used at a time—using an external monitor disables the notebook's internal video.

✔ **Battery life.** Battery life of today's PCs is fairly standard. The type of notebook and how you use it determines how long it can be used before the battery requires recharging. Active color systems drain the battery faster than monochrome or passive color. Frequent use of the hard disk also drains the battery. Utilizing the notebook's built-in power management functions—which turn off the hard disk, display, and even CPU when the system is idle—significantly increases the length of time you can operate the notebook on a single charge.

✔ **Input device.** Many newer notebooks include a built-in trackball; others come with a clip-on trackball. Built-in trackballs can be awkward and difficult to use. Clip-on trackballs are a better alternative, but for most experienced Windows users, there is no substitute for a mouse. Fortunately, you can plug a mouse into virtually any notebook and use it just as you would on a desktop system.

After you decide which notebook is right for you, your next task is to configure the system, beginning with optimizing the system's disk space.

Configuring Your System

Most vendors sell their systems with DOS and Windows pre-installed, and notebooks are no exception. As with any new system, you likely will want to make changes to the system's configuration as soon as you receive it. There are special considerations for configuring your notebook to work with Windows. The first is to optimize the system's hard disk.

Optimizing Disk Space

Most notebooks have lower capacity hard disks than desktop systems. For this reason it often is useful to compress the notebook's hard disk to make more effective use of the space available on the disk. If you are using MS-DOS 6.2, you can compress your hard disk with DoubleSpace, which is included with DOS. If you are using MS-DOS 6.21, however, you will not be able to compress the drive with DoubleSpace, because DoubleSpace is not included with MS-DOS 6.21. (Microsoft was required to remove DoubleSpace due to a patent-infringement lawsuit by Stac Electronics.) As of this writing, Microsoft is developing a replacement for DoubleSpace that will be provided free of charge to registered MS-DOS users. This disk compression replacement should be available by third quarter 1994. Many third-party disk compression utilities also exist. Stacker, from Stac Electronics, is one of the most popular of these compression utilities.

Regardless of the compression utility you choose, you should maintain some uncompressed space on the hard disk. Although Windows can be placed on a compressed disk, the permanent Windows swap file must reside on a local, uncompressed disk. Installing Windows on an uncompressed disk also improves performance by a small amount. Because Windows probably will already be installed on your PC when you receive it, you can leave all your Windows and DOS files on the hard disk, create a permanent swap file on the uncompressed drive, then compress the majority of the remaining free disk space to create a new, compressed drive. The following steps suggest one method for compressing the hard disk on a new system:

1. If Windows is not yet installed on the PC, install it.

2. Open the Control Panel, choose the Enhanced icon, and choose the <u>V</u>irtual Memory button to display the Virtual Memory dialog box (see fig. 14.3).

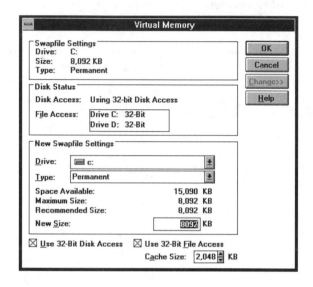

3. If the Swapfile Settings group box indicates that a permanent swap file already is in use, skip to step 4. If the Swapfile Settings group box indicates that a temporary swap file is being used, or that no swap file is being used, choose the <u>C</u>hange button. Select Permanent from the <u>T</u>ype drop-down list, then click on OK. Follow the prompts to restart Windows.

4. If Windows is running, exit to the DOS prompt. Create a new, uncompressed drive from the free space on the hard disk, leaving enough free space on drive C to accommodate whatever programs or document files you want to retain on the uncompressed drive C.

5. Install your applications on the new compressed drive.

The method that you use in step 4 to create the compressed drive will vary according to the disk compression utility you are using. Follow the instructions and prompts provided by your utility to create the new compressed drive.

Do not compress the existing drive C. Although Windows can run from a compressed drive, performance will be better if Windows runs from an uncompressed drive. Also, the permanent swap file cannot be compressed and must remain on the uncompressed drive C.

Even if you do not choose to compress the notebook's hard disk, you should check the type of swap file being used by the system. Use a permanent swap file for best performance. Follow steps 1–3 in the previous example to set up a permanent swap file.

If you have been using your notebook for an extended period and are just now compressing the drive, the hard disk might not have the maximum amount of contiguous disk space available. Use the Control Panel to set your swap file option to None, then exit Windows. Use DEFRAG or any other disk defragmenting utility to defragment the hard disk. This will make the most possible contiguous space available on the disk. Then create the permanent swap file using the Control Panel.

Using 32-Bit Disk and File Access

Windows 3.1 includes 32-bit disk access, which speeds access to the disk and can conserve memory when running DOS applications. Windows 3.11 adds 32-bit file access to speed up file access operations. 32-bit file access also includes a virtual disk cache that offers improved performance over the standard MS-DOS disk cache, SmartDrive.

Unfortunately, neither 32-bit disk access nor 32-bit file access is compatible with the power management features on most notebooks. Therefore, you cannot use either of these options on most notebooks. Doing so could result in lost or corrupted data. If you do not use the power management features of the notebook, however, you should be able to use both 32-bit file access and 32-bit disk access on the notebook. The following tips explain techniques for using 32-bit disk and file access on a notebook, even when you sometimes use power management:

✔ **No power management.** When the notebook is connected to AC power, there is no need to use power management. Therefore, you can use 32-bit disk access and 32-bit file access when the system is operating from AC power. Start the system without power management enabled, enter Windows, and use the Control Panel to turn on 32-bit disk and file access. Once you have configured Windows to use 32-bit disk and file access, you can simply start Windows by entering **WIN** at the DOS prompt, and Windows will automatically use 32-bit disk and file access.

✔ **Power management.** Virtually all notebooks that support power management provide special function keys on the keyboard that you can use to quickly change power management modes. Therefore, it is not necessary to configure the system to use power management at boot. Instead, you can change power management settings whenever necessary from the keyboard. When power management is enabled, however, you cannot use 32-bit disk and file access. Therefore, whenever power management is enabled, start Windows by entering **WIN /D:CF**. This starts Windows with 32-bit file and disk access disabled. If you prefer, you can create a multiboot configuration that offers two options: one that enables power management and starts Windows with 32-bit disk and file access disabled, and a second option that disables power management and starts Windows with 32-bit file and disk access enabled.

For more information on using multiboot configurations (available with MS-DOS 6.0 or later), consult Chapter 7, "Enhancing Windows Performance." For a more detailed description of 32-bit disk access and 32-bit file access, refer to Chapter 11, "Optimizing Data Storage Space."

Configuring Video

Today's notebook displays support a maximum resolution of 640×480, which is lower than the maximum resolution possible with many desktop PCs. You can use an external monitor with your notebook, however, and most notebooks support resolutions of up to 1,024×768 on their external monitor ports. Although it is possible on many notebooks to use the notebook's internal display at the same time as the external display (called *concurrent video*), the resolution of each display must be the same—640×480. When you are using just the external display, you can increase the resolution to the maximum supported by the notebook's graphics hardware and by the external monitor.

You can manually change video driver resolution, but you might find it more convenient to automate the process. One method to automate video driver configuration is to use DOS's multiboot capability, creating boot options for each of the video resolutions you want to use. A second option is to create a batch file that sets the resolution and then starts Windows. This second method is the most practical because you can use it to start Windows with a particular video resolution at any time, not just at system boot.

Automating the video configuration process requires that you maintain separate SYSTEM.INI files for each video configuration. You then can create a batch file that copies the appropriate SYSTEM.INI file into the Windows directory and starts Windows. The following steps will help you set up multiple video configurations on your system:

1. Exit Windows and change to the Windows directory.

2. Run Setup and configure Windows for the notebook's internal display (640×480).

3. After making this change, exit Setup and copy SYSTEM.INI to VGA.INI (verify that you do not have a VGA.INI file already located in the Windows directory; if you do, choose a different name for this INI file).

4. Run Setup again and configure Windows for the resolution you want to use on the external monitor.

5. Exit Setup and copy SYSTEM.INI to SUPERVGA.INI.

6. Create the following batch file and name it WINVGA.BAT (or a similar name of your choosing):

```
COPY \WINDOWS\VGA.INI \WINDOWS\SYSTEM.INI
WIN
```

7. Create the following batch file and name it SUPERVGA.BAT (or a similar name of your choosing):

```
COPY \WINDOWS\SUPERVGA.INI \WINDOWS\SYSTEM.INI
WIN
```

When you want to run Windows using the notebook's internal display, enter **WINVGA** at the DOS prompt. To run Windows using the external display, enter **SUPERVGA** at the DOS prompt.

If you make changes to your hardware configuration or install new software, update both copies of SYSTEM.INI (VGA.INI and SUPERVGA.INI) to ensure that all the necessary settings are duplicated in both files.

Configuring and Using PCMCIA Devices

Installing a PCMCIA adapter is simple: slide the device into an available slot and connect the cable to it (if applicable). Configuring and using the device, however, is often more difficult. You can overcome a majority of PCMCIA configuration problems by ensuring that your system uses the most up-to-date system PCMCIA drivers. These drivers are available from the notebook's manufacturer, usually through the manufacturer's BBS. Some manufacturers also provide support and driver updates through online services such as CompuServe and America Online. If you do not know how to locate the most recent PCMCIA drivers for your notebook, contact the manufacturer or vendor's technical support department and ask how you can obtain the most recent drivers. Driver installation varies, so you must follow the directions that come with the drivers to install them.

Updating the system PCMCIA drivers not only ensures easier configuration of the device, but also enables the device to perform better. If you are using the older PCMCIA drivers, for example, PCMCIA modems require a configuration utility program to make the system recognize the modem each time the system boots. Switching to the latest PCMCIA system drivers can eliminate the need to run the modem configuration program because the new drivers will properly recognize the modem without the configuration utility.

You should understand the following two terms to properly configure and use PCMCIA devices:

✔ **Socket Services.** The Socket Services driver enables the system to communicate with the PCMCIA sockets. This driver forms the lower software layer between the socket hardware and the rest of the system.

✔ **Card Services.** The Card Services driver enables applications to communicate with the PCMCIA cards that are installed in the slots. This driver forms the upper layer of software between the PCMCIA cards and the applications that must access the cards.

In addition to the two PCMCIA system drivers described previously, the devices you use in your notebook's PCMCIA slots might also require additional drivers. The actual requirements vary from card to card, as do configuration and installation procedures; therefore, it is not possible to cover all the possible devices in this chapter. The following general tips should help you configure and use your PCMCIA cards in your notebook:

✔ **Use current system drivers.** The first step in configuring a PCMCIA device is to verify that you are using the very latest PCMCIA Socket Services and Card Services drivers for your notebook. Check your vendor's or manufacturer's BBS or online service to determine if there are newer system PCMCIA drivers available for your system. Download these newer drivers and install them on your notebook.

✔ **Use special device drivers if necessary.** Your PCMCIA devices might require other drivers in addition to the Socket Services and Card Services drivers. Modems typically do not require any special drivers if you have the latest Socket Services and Card Services drivers. Devices such as network adapters and hard disks, however, generally require their own device drivers to function properly. When installing these support drivers, make sure they are added to CONFIG.SYS *after* the Socket Services and Card Services device drivers.

✔ **Follow installation instructions.** If you experience problems configuring and using the device, check the installation instructions that came with the adapter to verify that you have inserted, connected, and configured the device properly. You might have omitted some necessary command-line switches on the device's driver line in CONFIG.SYS, or you might need to use a configuration utility to set up the device each time the system boots (or you begin using the device).

✔ **Contact vendor/manufacturer technical support.** If you cannot configure and use the device, first contact the notebook manufacturer's technical support department and ask if they can provide you with specific tips or instructions on using the particular PCMCIA device on your notebook. If the notebook vendor's technical support staff cannot solve the problem, contact the PCMCIA card manufacturer's technical support staff for help in configuring and using the device.

When shopping for PCMCIA devices, consider whether the connectors on the devices' cables will conflict with one another. Although the jack on the Megahertz X-Jack modem is convenient, it might conflict with the connector for a device installed in the second PCMCIA slot. If you want to use a network adapter and modem at the same time, for example, you might not be able to connect both devices at the same time. Most PCMCIA devices, however, use a flat connector that is the same thickness as the card. These connectors do not conflict with one another.

Using Multiple Pointing Devices

Many notebooks include built-in trackballs, and some manufacturers provide clip-on trackballs with their notebooks. If you have been using a mouse for some time and are comfortable with it, the trackball can be a cumbersome input device, offering less control over the pointer. Most users find that the mouse provides the finest and smoothest control of the pointer. Because moving the pointer is such a major part of using Windows, using the right input device can make you much more productive when using Windows.

Because most notebooks include an external mouse port, you can connect a mouse to the system and use it instead of a trackball, even if the trackball is built into the notebook. Generally, if a mouse or other pointing device is connected to the notebook's external mouse port when the system is booted, that device will be used instead of the built-in trackball.

One solution to the problem of supporting two different mouse drivers is to use a mouse from the same manufacturer as the trackball. If the system includes a Logitech trackball, selecting and using a Logitech mouse with the notebook should enable you to simply plug in the mouse and reboot the system. The mouse should work properly with the drivers that are already installed on the system for the trackball. If your notebook's trackball is compatible with the Microsoft Mouse and uses the standard Microsoft mouse drivers, choose a mouse that is compatible with the Microsoft Mouse.

If the mouse you select is not directly compatible with the trackball, you must use multiple driver configurations. You can automate the selection and configuration of the drivers in much the same way you use multiple video resolutions, although you might need to add one step.

If you do not use the mouse or trackball outside of Windows (in DOS applications that you run outside of Windows), you probably do not need to load a mouse driver at boot in CONFIG.SYS. Instead, the device can use the mouse driver provided by Windows. If this is the case with your notebook, use the following steps to create two batch files to start Windows with the appropriate driver:

1. Exit Windows and change to the Windows directory.

2. Run Setup and configure Windows for the trackball.

3. Exit Setup and copy SYSTEM.INI to WINTRACK.INI (use a different file name if WINTRACK.INI already exists on your system).

4. Run Setup again and configure Windows for the mouse.

5. Exit Setup and copy SYSTEM.INI to WINMOUSE.INI (use a different file name if WINMOUSE.INI already exists on your system).

6. Create the following batch file and name it WINTRACK.BAT:

   ```
   COPY \WINDOWS\WINTRACK.INI \WINDOWS\SYSTEM.INI
   WIN
   ```

7. Create the following batch file and name it WINMOUSE.BAT:

   ```
   COPY \WINDOWS\WINMOUSE.INI \WINDOWS\SYSTEM.INI
   WIN
   ```

To use the trackball with Windows, start Windows by entering **WINTRACK** at the DOS prompt. To use the mouse with Windows, start Windows by entering **WINMOUSE** at the DOS prompt.

 As when using multiple video configurations, you must keep both the WINTRACK.INI and WINMOUSE.INI files up-to-date whenever you make other hardware changes or install new programs that modify SYSTEM.INI.

If your pointing devices require device drivers to be loaded in CONFIG.SYS before Windows starts, create a multiboot configuration that provides two options: one for loading the trackball driver and a second option for loading the mouse driver. For more information on creating multiboot configurations, consult Chapter 7, "Enhancing Windows Performance."

Part Three

Putting Windows to Work

Chapter Snapshot

Although Windows probably is your primary operating environment, it is likely that you still use a few DOS programs. You might not want to invest the additional money to switch from the DOS programs to Windows versions, or you simply might be satisfied with the DOS program's performance and do not want a Windows program to replace it.

This chapter examines a number of issues that relate to running DOS programs under Windows. The topics covered include the following:

Windows is an excellent environment for running DOS programs. Because of Windows' capability to multitask programs and its support for data exchange for DOS programs through the Clipboard, Windows offers a better DOS environment than DOS itself.

15

CHAPTER

Integrating Windows and DOS

Although most Windows users would agree that Windows offers a much broader range of features and capabilities than the DOS environment, Windows still provides excellent support for DOS and DOS programs. The capabilities you will have for using DOS programs under Windows depend primarily on the mode in which Windows is running.

Running DOS Programs in Standard Mode and 386 Enhanced Mode

Windows in Standard mode enables you to run DOS programs, although you do not have as many options for running them as you do in 386 Enhanced mode. The following list summarizes the way DOS programs run in Standard mode:

✓ **Full screen only.** DOS programs can run only as full-screen applications in Standard mode. Although you cannot run them in a window, you can switch back and forth between Windows and the DOS programs, or switch from one DOS program to another.

✓ **No multitasking.** Because Windows in Standard mode does not make use of the CPU's virtual mode, you cannot multitask DOS programs when running Windows in Standard mode. Starting a DOS program causes all Windows applications to be suspended and swapped to disk. In addition, DOS programs cannot run in the background when run under Standard mode.

✓ **Limited Clipboard support.** You can copy only full-screen text from a DOS program to the Clipboard—you cannot copy a selection of text from a DOS program to the Clipboard. You can, however, copy any amount of text from the Clipboard to the DOS program. You cannot copy graphics from DOS to the Clipboard.

Standard mode is not the best choice for running DOS programs under Windows. Standard mode in some situations provides slightly improved performance when running only Windows applications. 386 Enhanced mode offers the best performance for the vast majority of users, however. In addition, Windows for Workgroups 3.11 will run only in 386 Enhanced mode. It does not support Standard mode.

When you run Windows in 386 Enhanced mode, you have more options for running DOS programs. The following list summarizes the way DOS programs run in 386 Enhanced mode:

✓ **Multitasking.** You can run multiple DOS programs at the same time you run Windows programs. DOS programs can run in the background under 386 Enhanced mode.

✓ **Windowed support.** You can run DOS programs in a window, in addition to running them in full-screen mode (see fig. 15.1).

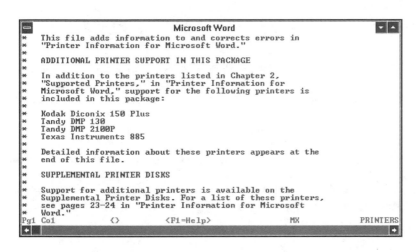

```
*  This file adds information to and corrects errors in
*  "Printer Information for Microsoft Word."
*
*  ADDITIONAL PRINTER SUPPORT IN THIS PACKAGE
*
*  In addition to the printers listed in Chapter 2,
*  "Supported Printers," in "Printer Information for
*  Microsoft Word," support for the following printers is
*  included in this package:
*
*  Kodak Diconix 150 Plus
*  Tandy DMP 130
*  Tandy DMP 2100P
*  Texas Instruments 885
*
*  Detailed information about these printers appears at the
*  end of this file.
*
*  SUPPLEMENTAL PRINTER DISKS
*
*  Support for additional printers is available on the
*  Supplemental Printer Disks. For a list of these printers,
*  see pages 23-24 in "Printer Information for Microsoft
*  Word."
Pg1  Co1          {}       <F1=Help>          MX          PRINTERS
```

Figure 15.1
A DOS program running in a window in 386 Enhanced mode.

✔ **Mouse support.** You can use the mouse in a windowed DOS program, just as you can when running the program from DOS.

✔ **Graphics applications.** Windows 3.1 now supports DOS programs running in a window in graphics modes.

✔ **Expanded Clipboard support.** When running DOS programs under Windows' 386 Enhanced mode, you can copy selected text from DOS programs to Windows and copy graphics from DOS to Windows.

DOS Prompt under Windows

The Setup program automatically creates a program item called MS-DOS Prompt in the Main program group. This program item starts a DOS session by executing COMMAND.COM. You can use the MS-DOS Prompt item to open a DOS session to execute DOS commands and run programs.

Although you can start a program with the MS-DOS Prompt item, doing so might mean that you are not using your system's resources—particularly memory—to their best advantage. To ensure that you get the most from the system's resources when you run DOS programs, use a custom program information file for each DOS program.

Understanding Program Information Files

Windows applications are written specifically to take advantage of the Windows environment. Because of this, Windows applications can coexist with one another in the Windows

III

Putting Windows to Work

environment without competing for resources such as video, memory, disk, and the printer.

DOS programs, however, are designed for DOS's single-tasking operating environment. They are not designed to coexist with other applications—DOS programs expect to have exclusive use of the system's resources. Windows therefore uses program information files (PIFs) to store information about the resources that a program uses, including video requirements, memory requirements, and more.

If you direct Setup to search for and install applications for you, Setup will create PIFs for any DOS programs that it finds. You can fine-tune these PIFs as much as you like to change the way the associated DOS program runs. In addition, you can create your own PIFs for DOS programs that you set up by yourself in Windows.

Examining PIFs

The information in a PIF includes the amount of memory the application needs, what type of video it requires, and other settings that tell Windows how the application should work. Figure 15.2 shows the Windows PIF Editor with a PIF loaded to illustrate some of the settings contained in a PIF.

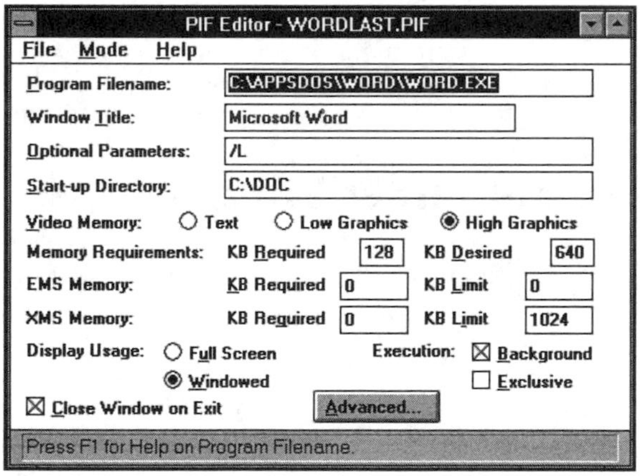

Figure 15.2
A PIF contains a wide range of information about its associated DOS program.

When you start a DOS application that does not have a PIF associated with it, Windows uses a default PIF to define the required settings. Unfortunately, the information in the default PIF might not be what your program needs.

The applications you want to add might already have their own PIFs. Some DOS applications include PIFs in case the user wants to run them under Windows. Check the application's documentation and directory to see if a PIF already exists for the program.

Creating a PIF

The best way to create a PIF is to let Setup create it for you. When you need to install a new DOS application under Windows, run Setup to see if Setup recognizes it. Besides ensuring that the PIF includes the correct settings, Setup creates the PIF much faster than you can. The following example uses Setup to create a PIF:

1. Open the Main program group and double-click on the Windows Setup icon.

2. Select the Options menu and choose Set Up Applications. The Setup Applications dialog box shown in figure 15.3 appears.

Figure 15.3
The Setup
Applications
dialog box.

3. In the Setup Applications dialog box, click on the radio button labeled Ask you to specify an application, and click on OK.

4. Enter the name of the application's executable file, including its path, in the Application Path and Filename text box.

5. Using the Add to Program Group list box, select the group to which you want to add the new DOS program.

6. Click on OK. Setup creates a PIF for the DOS application and places it in the Windows directory.

Setup creates not only a PIF, but also a program item for the new DOS application in the group you specify. If you examine the new item's properties, its Command Line entry references the PIF, not the executable file. By referencing the PIF, Setup ensures that the settings in the PIF are always used when the application is started from its icon.

Creating a PIF Manually

Windows provides a program called the PIF Editor to enable you to create and edit PIFs. The Windows PIF Editor usually is located in the Main group window. If you do not have a Main group, or if the PIF Editor is not part of it, the PIF Editor's executable file, PIFEDIT.EXE, should be on the hard drive in the Windows directory.

III

Putting Windows to Work

What you see in the PIF Editor dialog box depends on the mode in which Windows is running. The dialog box for Standard mode, shown in figure 15.4, is somewhat different from the 386 Enhanced mode PIF Editor dialog box. The 386 Enhanced mode PIF Editor dialog box, as shown in figure 15.5, is smaller, but it includes an **A**dvanced button that displays the Advanced Options dialog box for additional 386 Enhanced mode PIF settings.

Figure 15.4
Standard mode
PIF Editor dialog
box.

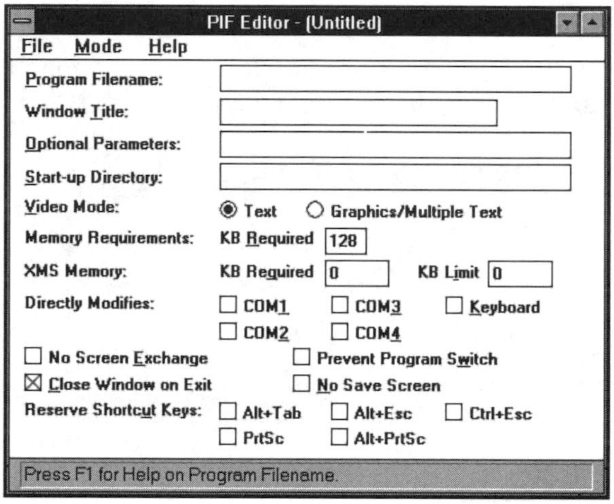

Figure 15.5
386 Enhanced
mode PIF Editor
dialog box.

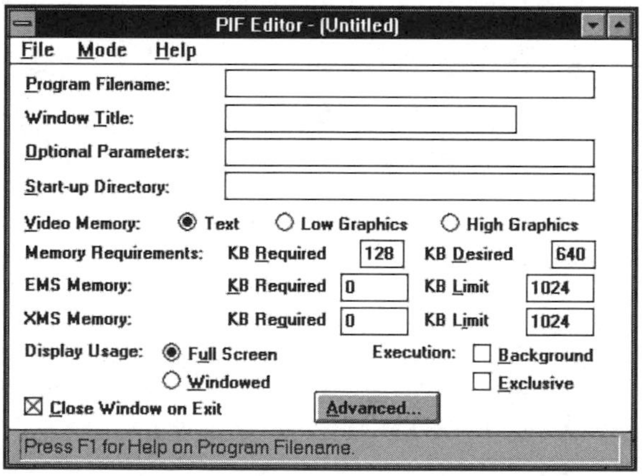

Regardless of the mode in which you create a PIF, many PIF parameters are the same. As shown in figures 15.4 and 15.5, the **P**rogram Filename, Window **T**itle, **O**ptional Parameters, and **S**tart-up Directory fields are the same.

Specifying the Executable File's Name

The Program Filename entry specifies the name of the program's executable file. The *executable file* is the file name you type at the DOS prompt to start a program. It is a good idea to include the drive letter and full path name, including the file extension. Most program file names have EXE, COM, or BAT extensions; the PIF Editor requires that you enter one of these three file types.

If you specify the name of the PIF in the Command Line field in the program item's properties, the specified PIF must have a valid Program Filename entry in the PIF. If no entry is included, Windows generates an error message saying it cannot find the file when you double-click on the program's icon in Program Manager.

Specifying a Window Title

The Window Title field in the PIF Editor's dialog box specifies the window title that appears when the program runs in a window. The Description field for the item in the Program Item Properties dialog box overrides this setting. The Description is used as the DOS program's window title, not the Window Title entry in its PIF, unless the Description property is left blank. The Window Title PIF entry is used, however, when you execute the PIF using the Run command from Program Manager's or File Manager's File menus.

It is not possible to eliminate an entry for the item's Description property and default to the PIF description because you cannot leave the Description field blank in the Program Item Properties dialog box. If you omit a description, Windows automatically uses the name of the item shown in the Command Line field for the Description. This then becomes the item's window and icon title. Therefore, the Window Title field has no effect in Windows 3.1 unless you launch the program by using the Run command.

Adding Optional Parameters

The third entry in the PIF Editor dialog box, Optional Parameters, enables you to pass command-line switches or other command arguments to the program each time you start it. Parameters can be file names, letters, numbers, or any other command-line switch the program accepts. If you use the same command-line parameter for the program each time you run it, place it in the Optional Parameters edit box. If you want Windows to prompt you for the parameter each time you start the program, enter a question mark (?) as an optional parameter. Windows then pauses and prompts you to enter the additional parameter(s) after you start the program (see fig. 15.6).

Figure 15.6
Windows prompts for command-line parameters with this dialog box.

III

Putting Windows to Work

The Optional Parameters field also is useful when used with replaceable parameters in batch files. Replaceable parameters are represented in a batch file by a percent sign (%) and a number from 0 to 9. Command-line options that you enter for the batch file are passed to it and replace the instances of the %n entries. Replaceable parameters are discussed in more detail later in this chapter.

As its name implies, the Optional Parameters entry is optional. For this reason, you can leave it blank if you do not need or want to supply command-line options with the program.

Specifying a Start-Up Directory

The Start-up Directory entry defines the drive and directory that are made current when you start the program. If you keep all your word processing document files in a directory called \MYDOCS on drive D, for example, and the word processor is on drive C, you might want the program to start from D:\MYDOCS. Enter the full path name of the drive and directory that you want Windows to make current. For this example, enter the following in the Start-up Directory box:

D:\MYDOCS

When you run a program by clicking on its icon, and a Working Directory entry exists in the program item's properties, the entry overrides the Start-up Directory setting in the PIF. If the program item's properties list C:\DOCS as the Working Directory, and the program's PIF specifies D:\OTHERDOC as the Start-up Directory, for example, C:\DOCS becomes the current directory when you start the program from the icon. If there is no entry for Working Directory in the item's properties, or if you start the program using the File, Run command, the entry for Start-up Directory in the PIF is used as the start-up directory.

If neither Working Directory nor Start-up Directory has an entry, the Windows directory becomes the active directory when the program is started. The order of precedence of the three settings is as follows:

1. Working Directory (Program Item Properties dialog box)

2. Start-up Directory (PIF)

3. Windows directory (no entry for either 1 or 2)

Exploring Standard Mode PIF Options

The Standard mode PIF Editor provides a single window you can use to specify settings for a PIF. These settings are used when running the program under Windows' Standard mode. If you run the DOS program under 386 Enhanced mode also, you can switch the PIF Editor to 386 Enhanced mode and specify additional settings there. This section examines the Standard mode PIF Editor settings. Figure 15.7 shows the Standard mode PIF Editor.

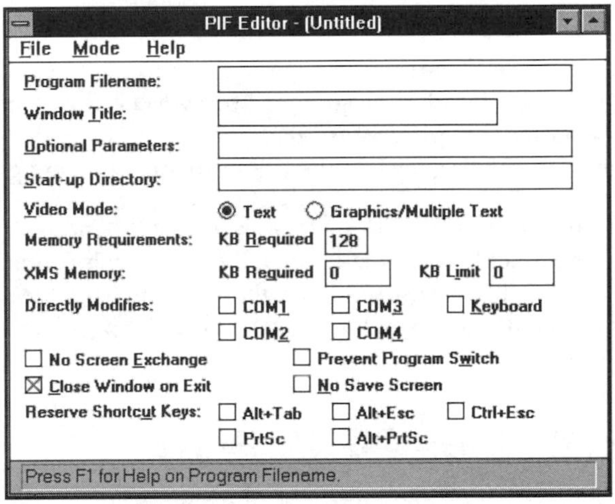

Figure 15.7
The Standard mode PIF Editor.

Standard Mode Video Options

When DOS programs run, they can use either text display mode or graphics mode. Windows always uses graphics mode because it is a graphical operating environment. Text mode is used by DOS programs such as word processing programs and spreadsheets that do not take advantage of the video adapter's graphics capabilities. Graphics mode is used by graphics-oriented programs, such as CAD and paint programs, and uses more memory than text mode. Some programs offer both modes. The MS-DOS Shell program in DOS 5 and 6, for example, offers three text modes and three graphics modes.

When you run DOS programs and switch from one program to another (or switch to Windows), the display must be saved so that the video can be restored when you later restore the program. If you use Video Mode's Text option, you ensure that the program uses only as much memory as necessary for its display in text mode. You still can run a graphics program if you specify Text mode in its PIF, but you might lose the display when the system's memory resources become low. In Standard mode, you might not be able to switch back to Windows without first terminating the program.

If your program uses graphics mode, select Graphics/Multiple Text in the program's PIF so that it operates properly. Specify Text mode only if your program does not use the graphics capabilities of your system's video adapter.

The No Save Screen check box controls whether Windows maintains a DOS program's display when you switch from the program back to Windows. Check this box only if the DOS program updates its own display when you switch back to it from Windows.

III

Putting Windows to Work

COM Port and Keyboard Settings

The Directly Modifies section of the PIF Editor controls the manner in which Windows handles the interaction of the program and the system's communication ports and keyboard.

Some DOS programs take exclusive control of the keyboard or a communication port, preventing them from being used by other programs. If you select one of the COM ports in the Directly Modifies section of the program's PIF, Windows monitors the port and prevents any other program from using it while the PIF's program is running.

If the Keyboard option in the Directly Modifies section is selected, Windows is prevented from responding to any keystrokes that are made while the program is running. This setting even prevents the use of the Alt+Esc sequence that switches from the program back to Windows. If this is set in the PIF, you have to terminate the program before you can switch back to Windows.

Other Standard Mode PIF Options

The No Screen Exchange option prevents you from being able to use the Print Screen key (Alt+PrtSc) for copying data from the program to the Windows Clipboard. If you do not plan to use this feature, you can gain extra memory for your program by selecting No Screen Exchange.

The Prevent Program Switch setting also conserves memory by preventing switching from the program back to Windows. You must exit the program to return to Windows.

Program Shortcut Keys

Windows uses shortcut keystrokes to perform certain operations. The Alt+Tab keystroke is a good example—it switches between active programs. Your DOS program, however, might also use the Alt+Tab sequence; when you use Alt+Tab within your program, you are switched into Windows instead of performing the program's Alt+Tab function. To use the shortcut key in the program instead of Windows, specify the shortcut keystroke in the program's PIF as a Reserved Shortcut Key.

The shortcut keys used by Windows in Standard mode are shown in the following table. These shortcut key options also appear in the Standard mode PIF Editor.

Table 15.1
Reserved Shortcut Key Settings (Standard Mode)

Option	Description
Alt+Tab	Switches between programs
Alt+Esc	Switches to the next program
Ctrl+Esc	Displays the Task List
PrtSc	Copies a full screen to the Clipboard
Alt+PrtSc	Copies a full screen to the Clipboard

Remember that if you reserve one of the above task-switching keystrokes for the program, you cannot use it to switch back into Windows. You can still use one of the alternate keystrokes, however, such as Alt+Esc or Ctrl+Esc.

Memory Settings for Standard Mode

The KB Required setting within the Memory Requirements option defines the amount of conventional memory that must be free to start the program under Windows. Specify the minimum amount of conventional memory the DOS program requires to run.

The KB Required setting in the XMS Memory option controls the amount of extended memory the DOS program requires. Specify the minimum required by the program to ensure that Windows has the most memory possible.

The KB Limit setting specifies the maximum amount of extended memory the program can use. Again, specify as small an amount as possible. If you want the program to have as much extended memory as it requests, set KB Limit to -1.

Exploring 386 Enhanced Mode PIF Options

The PIF Editor's 386 Enhanced mode options are somewhat different from those in the Standard mode PIF Editor; as well, there are more settings possible in 386 Enhanced mode, primarily to control multitasking (see fig. 15.8).

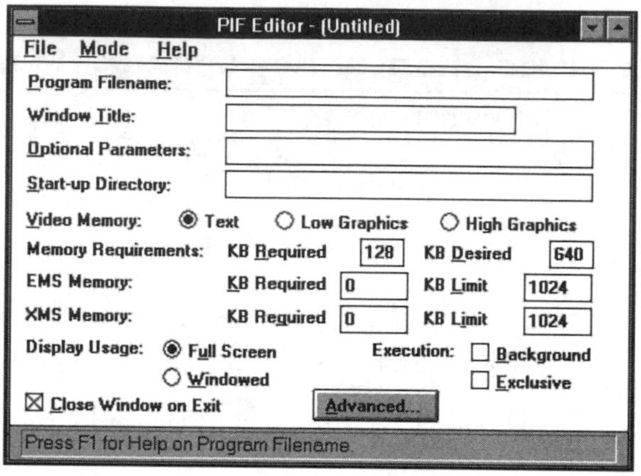

Figure 15.8
The 386 Enhanced
mode PIF Editor
dialog box.

Specifying Multitasking Options

Windows in 386 Enhanced mode is capable of multitasking DOS programs. The Multitasking Options part of the Advanced Options PIF Editor dialog box (see fig. 15.9) enables you to define the manner in which a program works when it multitasks. To display the Advanced Options, choose the Advanced button in the PIF Editor's main window.

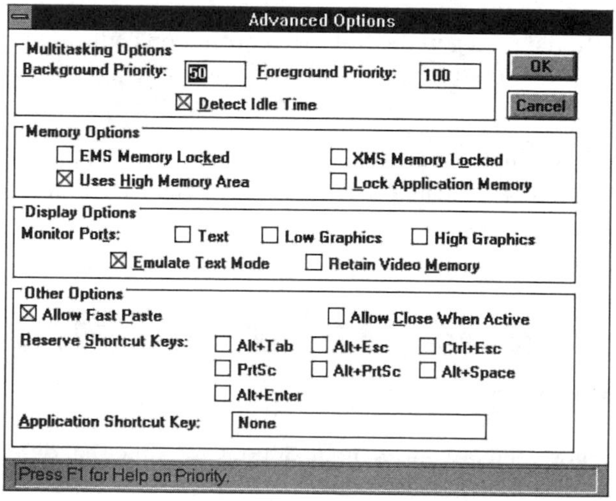

Figure 15.9
The Advanced
Options dialog
box in the PIF
Editor.

The Background Priority setting controls the amount of CPU time given to the program when it runs in the background. The default is 50. If you want to give the program more time, you can increase this number (valid entries range from 0 to 10,000).

The Foreground Priority setting controls the amount of CPU time given to the program when it runs as the foreground task. Like Background Priority, the setting can be any number from 0 to 10,000. For now, you should leave these settings at their defaults because the default values provide good performance in most situations.

If the Detect Idle Time option is checked, Windows detects periods when the program is idle and gives CPU time to other programs during this period. If this option is checked, other programs run faster because they receive more CPU time. Some programs, how-ever, do not function properly if this option is checked. Experiment to see if your DOS program works properly with this option.

Setting Memory Requirements

In 386 Enhanced mode, you have many of the same memory-control settings that appear in the Standard mode PIF Editor. The settings can be different in 386 Enhanced mode, although the setting names are virtually the same in both modes (refer to figures 15.7 and 15.8).

The first memory setting in the 386 Enhanced PIF Editor, KB Required, specifies the amount of memory required to start the program. This setting does not impose a limit, however, on the amount of memory available to the program.

The KB Desired setting does limit usable memory for the program by imposing a limit on the amount of conventional memory the program's environment can use. By default, the value is 640. However, you might want to decrease this amount if you want to conserve memory for other programs. When set at 512, for example, the program cannot use more than 512 KB of memory. This limits the amount of virtual conventional memory that the program can sense is available.

Extended and Expanded Memory Settings

The next group of memory settings can be found on the primary 386 Enhanced PIF dialog box. These settings control the use of extended (XMS) and expanded (EMS) memory used by the program when it runs in 386 Enhanced mode. Both extended and expanded memory have KB Required and KB Limit settings, and both mean the same for either type of memory.

KB Required specifies the amount of extended or expanded memory that must be free for the program to start. If it does not have the specified amount, Windows displays a message telling you that too little memory is available to start the program. Set KB Required at the true minimum that enables the program to work. The KB Required settings do not impose a limit on how much extended or expanded memory a program can use, only on whether you can start the program. If the program does not use either extended or expanded memory, leave these two settings at 0.

The KB Limit settings for extended and expanded memory impose a memory limit. If set to 0, KB Limit prevents Windows from allocating extended or expanded memory (depending on which setting is 0) to the program. Otherwise, a positive value can be used, and Windows allocates memory only up to the limit specified. Some programs take control of all extended or expanded memory. For this reason, use this setting to ensure that the other programs have extended or expanded memory available if they request it.

The Memory Options group of the Advanced Options dialog box also has two check boxes for locking expanded and extended memory (EMS Memory Locked and XMS Memory Locked). If checked, Windows does not swap the extended or expanded memory to the hard disk. If you lock a program's memory, its performance improves (because no time is lost for swapping), but overall system performance suffers because the locked memory is not available to the rest of the system until you quit the program.

A third check box in the Memory Options group, Lock Program Memory, causes the program's conventional memory to be locked and not swapped out to disk. Like extended- and expanded-memory locking, this can speed up the program's performance at the expense of overall system performance.

The Uses High Memory Area option specifies whether Windows enables the program to use the High Memory Area (HMA), which is the 64 KB block of memory between 1,024–1,088 KB. If checked, the program can use the HMA.

Using 386 Enhanced Mode Video Options

386 Enhanced mode provides video mode settings similar to those in Standard mode. The settings in the first group, Video Memory, are similar to the Video Mode settings in Standard mode. Text mode allocates approximately 16 KB of RAM to the program for storing its display. The Low Graphics radio button allocates approximately 32 KB for video and is used with programs that require low-resolution graphics mode (equivalent to CGA). The High Graphics option assigns approximately 128 KB of RAM and is used for high-resolution modes such as EGA and VGA (including SuperVGA).

If you run text-based programs on a VGA adapter, select Text mode in the Display Options group box of the Advanced Options dialog box. Graphics settings are necessary only if the program actually uses the graphics capabilities of the video adapter.

Another Advanced Options video setting is Emulate Text Mode. This setting forces the program to appear in 80-column by 25-line monochrome display adapter (MDA) mode. With some programs, this option has no effect; the program continues to run in its normal mode. Other programs, however, emulate MDA when this box is checked.

Emulate Text Mode can increase the speed at which the program displays text, and it can remain checked for most programs. If one of your programs is corrupted on-screen or if you have trouble running the program, clear the Emulate Text Mode option and restart the program to see if it solves the screen display problem.

Setting Ports

Some programs directly access the display adapter, bypassing the system's BIOS. This process is easy when you have only one program running outside of Windows (as with a typical DOS program). However, if the program is running from Windows, and you switch to Windows, Windows might not be able to restore the display when you switch back to the DOS program.

The Monitor Ports settings in the Display Options group tell Windows to monitor the program's use of video. Unfortunately, these options require a lot of system overhead and degrade system performance, and they should be unchecked unless you experience problems with the program's display after switching back to the program from Windows. Most programs run properly with these settings unchecked.

Looking At Other 386 Enhanced Mode Options

Also located in the 386 Enhanced mode Advanced Options dialog box is the Other Options group box. The settings in this section enable you to customize Windows even more. The first option that appears is Allow Fast Paste, which tells Windows to use either the fast-paste or the slow-paste method. If you have trouble pasting information into a program, clear the Allow Fast Paste option and restart the program. This forces Windows to use the slow-paste method.

The Other Options section also includes a check box for Allow Close When Active. Select this check box to close the program's window with the Close command in its Control menu, or to exit Windows without exiting the program (the program is automatically terminated). If you have files open, however, you might lose data if you close the program by using the Control menu (instead of using the program's commands to exit). Select this option only if the program does not use data files.

Shortcut Keys

The remaining settings in the Other Options section, which are the same settings as those located in the Standard mode PIF Editor, pertain to shortcut keys. Other shortcut keys are possible in 386 Enhanced mode, and keystrokes can be reserved in one mode and not in another. All other uses of the shortcut key settings are the same as in Standard mode.

The Application Shortcut Key field assigns a shortcut key to a program, enabling you to switch over to the program to make it the foreground task simply by pressing its shortcut key combination. You can use the shortcut key in Windows, in a Windows program, or in another DOS program. If you press the shortcut key combination, Windows immediately switches you to the DOS program to which it is assigned.

The key sequence must consist of a combination of the Ctrl, Alt, and Shift keys, and a single character. The character can be any keyboard character—a letter, number, symbol, or function key. You can, for example, press Ctrl+Q, Alt+Q, Ctrl+Shift+F1, or a similar

III

Putting Windows to Work

combination. You assign a shortcut keystroke by selecting the box in the PIF Editor and then pressing the key sequence you want as the shortcut key.

Naming a PIF

After you have created a PIF with the PIF Editor, save it using any name you like (you must use the PIF extension). Even so, the name you choose can affect the way the PIF is used.

The following items explain the options for naming a PIF:

- ✔ **Name matches program name.** When you start a DOS program without directly specifying a PIF (use the program's executable name in the File, Run dialog box, for example), Windows searches for a PIF with a name that matches the program. If it does not find one, it uses the default PIF settings. If it finds a PIF with a name that matches the program's executable file name, it uses the settings in the PIF to run the program. If you want to use a PIF by indirect association in this way, specify the program's executable file name for the Command Line property. Then, create a PIF with a matching name and place it in the Windows directory.

- ✔ **PIF name is unique.** If the PIF name does not match the DOS program's executable file name, you must reference the PIF directly. Create the PIF, give it whatever name you want, then specify the PIF's file name as the Command Line property for the program item.

Giving a PIF a name that matches, at least to some degree, the name of its associated program file makes it easier to keep track of which program is associated with a particular program.

Using Multiple Configurations for a DOS Program

You might have a DOS program that you would like to run in different configurations. Perhaps you have a word processor that you want to be able to start with different working directories, according to the type of file on which you want to work at any given time.

There are a few options for running DOS programs with multiple configurations. The first option is to use multiple PIFs and program items.

Multiple PIFs and Program Items

You can create a PIF for each program configuration you want to use, changing the Optional Parameters and Start-up Directory PIF entries accordingly. Save each PIF with a unique name. Then, create a program item for each PIF in one of your Program Manager groups. Double-clicking on a program item will start the DOS program with whatever settings you specified in the associated PIF.

Single PIF, a Batch File, and the /? Setting

The other option is to create a PIF-and-batch-file combination that will enable you to specify options at program start-up. This technique takes advantage of replaceable parameters in a batch program. This is how replaceable parameters work: Each batch program can be passed up to 10 command-line parameters. These parameters are entered on the command line following the batch file's name, as in the following example:

```
STARTIT \DOCS TEST.DOC /W
```

In the previous example, STARTIT is the name of the batch file (STARTIT.BAT), \docs is the first parameter, test.doc is the second parameter, and /w is the third parameter.

Next, the batch program must include placeholders for the replaceable parameters. Each placeholder is preceded by a percent sign (%) and includes a number from 0 through 9. The following is a sample batch file that uses replaceable parameters:

```
rem   This is startit.bat
@ECHO Using %0 with %1 %2 %3
CD %1
WORD.EXE %2 %3
```

Using the previous STARTIT command-line example, the result from running the batch program would be as follows:

```
Using STARTIT with \docs test.doc /w
CD \docs
WORD.EXE test.doc /w
```

To use a batch program with replaceable parameters, create a PIF for the batch file. As the Optional Parameters setting, use /?. This causes Windows to prompt you for parameters each time the PIF is executed. Supply the same parameters you would provide if typing the batch command at the DOS command line.

III

Putting Windows to Work

Using PIFs with Document Files

You can associate a DOS program's document files with a PIF and start the application by double-clicking on the document icon. To do so, you first must associate the program's document file type with the DOS program. To associate a file with a program, perform the following steps:

1. Open File Manager and select one of the DOS program's document files.

2. Choose File, Associate. File Manager displays the Associate dialog box, shown in figure 15.10.

Figure 15.10
The Associate dialog box associates documents with programs.

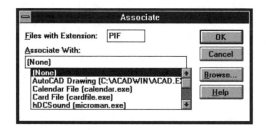

3. If the program is not listed in the Associate With combo box, choose the Browse button to locate the DOS program's executable file.

4. After you have located and selected the executable file, click on OK in the Associate dialog box to form the association between the document file and the program.

After you have associated a document type with its program, create a general PIF for the document's program. Give the PIF a name that matches the program's executable file name. For WORD.EXE, for example, create a PIF named WORD.PIF. Give the PIF whatever settings are required for the program.

Next, create a program item for the document in one of your Program Manager groups. At the Command Line entry, specify the path to the document file, such as c:\docs\test.doc. When you double-click on this document item, Windows checks for an association between the document file and a program. It finds the association, starts the program, and, because the PIF name matches the program's file name, Windows uses the PIF to run the program.

Adjusting the Default PIF

Now that you know what a PIF is, how to create one, and what the settings in a PIF do, you are ready to learn about the default PIF.

As mentioned earlier in the chapter, Windows uses default PIF settings if it does not find a PIF when it starts a program. These default settings come from a default PIF called _DEFAULT.PIF, as shown in figure 15.11. This file normally is located in the Windows directory. To view the settings in _DEFAULT.PIF, simply load it into the PIF Editor as you would any other PIF.

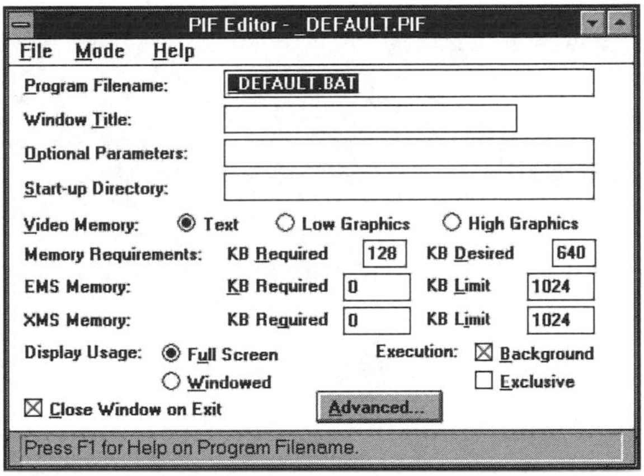

Figure 15.11
The PIF Editor-
_DEFAULT.PIF
dialog box.

If _DEFAULT.PIF does not exist, Windows uses a set of built-in default values. (Windows also uses the same set of built-in defaults when you start a new PIF.) If _DEFAULT.PIF does exist, Windows uses its settings whenever it starts a program for which it can find no PIF. Review the settings in it to make sure they fit your situation (remember that each PIF has two modes and you should check both sets of settings).

Simply load _DEFAULT.PIF to review the settings for yourself. If you make changes to it and resave it, the changes affect any DOS program for which Windows cannot find a PIF. They do not, however, change the settings used to create a new PIF. If you want to return to Windows' original set of defaults and include them in the _DEFAULT.PIF, follow these steps:

1. Activate the PIF Editor.

2. Choose the New command in the PIF Editor's File menu.

3. Choose the File menu's Save As command to save it as _DEFAULT.PIF.

Adjusting the PIF for the DOS Prompt

When you choose the MS-DOS Prompt icon from the Main program group, Windows starts a new copy of COMMAND.COM. A full-screen DOS session appears on the display, and you can issue any DOS command or execute programs (except another copy of

Windows) that you can run from the DOS command line outside of Windows. The MS-DOS Prompt icon gives you access to the DOS environment without having to leave Windows.

The DOS session you see when you choose the MS-DOS Prompt icon is not the same COMMAND.COM session you used to start Windows. It does, however, have the same characteristics as the original COMMAND.COM session.

If you run Windows in 386 Enhanced mode, you might want to set up the DOS prompt to run in a window rather than full-screen. To do so, simply change the DOS prompt's PIF by following these steps:

1. Open the PIF Editor and load the file DOSPRMPT.PIF from the Windows directory.

2. Click on the Windowed radio button in Display Usage.

3. Choose File, Save.

4. Exit the PIF Editor and choose the MS-DOS Prompt icon to start it in a window.

You also might want to change the DOS prompt item's properties or other PIF settings to use a different start-up directory or window title.

Customizing DOS Programs

In Windows 3.1 a DOS application's Control menu includes a selection labeled Fonts. If you choose the Fonts command, the Font Selection dialog box shown in figure 15.12 appears on-screen.

Changing the size of the DOS application's window is simple—just choose the desired character size, and the sample window shows the resulting change in window size. When you are satisfied with the window size, click on OK.

Keeping Changes to DOS Programs

The Font Selection dialog box includes a Save Settings on Exit check box. Windows keeps track of DOS application settings in the file DOSAPP.INI. If the Save Settings on Exit box is checked when you exit the application, Windows stores various information about the application in DOSAPP.INI. If a setting already exists, Windows replaces the values for the application with the current settings. If an entry does not exist in DOSAPP.INI for an application, Windows creates one. The entry is created and maintained even if the application never runs in windowed mode (that is, if you always run the program in full-screen mode).

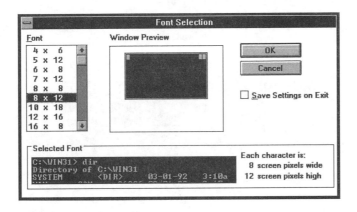

Figure 15.12
The Font Selection dialog box for a DOS application.

Among the settings stored in DOSAPP.INI are the location of the DOS application's window on the Windows desktop, the size of the window, and the DOS window's font size. These settings configure the application window to open at exactly the same location each time it is run and to use the same window and character size as in the previous session.

To cause a DOS program to open at its previous location and size, check the Save Settings on Exit check box. To cause Windows not to save a program's position and size, clear this check box.

Using the Mouse with DOS Programs

One feature of Windows 3.1 and later versions is the capability to use the mouse in windowed DOS programs (DOS programs that run in a window, instead of full-screen). When the pointer is inside the DOS program's window, it is mapped to the DOS program. When it is outside of the DOS program's window, it is mapped to Windows.

When you run a DOS text-based program in full-screen mode and a mouse driver has been installed, you generally have a block pointer for a mouse pointer. The block pointer follows the mouse, moving from one character position to another as the mouse moves. The mouse pointer is somewhat jerky because it must follow text columns and rows. If you are accustomed to the smooth mouse pointer movement in Windows, you might be disappointed by mouse movement in full-screen DOS programs.

However, when you run the program in a window, the Windows graphical mouse pointer is retained, as is the smooth movement it provides. You therefore might want to run DOS programs in a window to get smoother mouse response.

Figure 15.13 shows Microsoft Word for DOS running in a window. The mouse has been used to highlight a selection of text. Note that even though Word is running in text mode, the Windows graphical mouse pointer is still used.

Figure 15.13
Using the mouse in a DOS-program window.

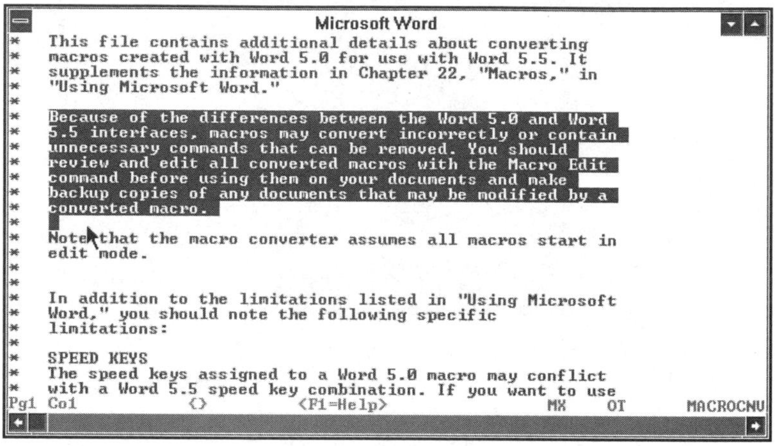

If you want to use the mouse in your DOS programs under Windows, make sure you use the driver supplied with Windows for your mouse. Setup copies the device driver to the Windows directory for you, but does not install it. Edit the current entry in AUTOEXEC.BAT (or add a new entry) to point to the correct file. The mouse driver supplied with Windows enables you to use the mouse in a windowed DOS program, just as you would use it in full-screen mode.

Locating the Mouse Driver

The mouse driver that Windows uses for the Windows environment has a DRV extension and is located in the \WINDOWS\SYSTEM directory. The DOS-supported mouse driver has an extension of COM or SYS, depending on the mouse type. The driver is located in the \WINDOWS directory. Make sure you install the COM driver in AUTOEXEC.BAT, or the SYS driver in CONFIG.SYS. You must reboot the system to use the new mouse driver.

Running a DOS Graphics Program

Windows 3.1 adds the capability to run DOS graphics programs in a window in addition to DOS text-based programs. Figure 15.14 shows the MS-DOS Shell program (DOSSHELL.EXE) configured for graphics mode and running in a window. Figure 15.15 shows the same program running in low-resolution text mode.

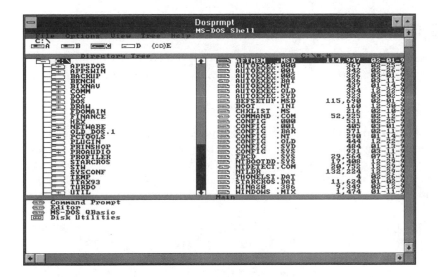

Figure 15.14
The MS-DOS Shell program in graphics mode running in a window.

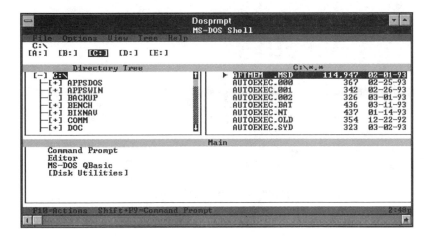

Figure 15.15
The MS-DOS Shell program in text mode running in a window.

Support for DOS graphics programs is well integrated with Windows 3.1 and later. When you create a PIF for the program, make sure you specify High Graphics for the Video Memory option. This option allocates enough memory to the program for Windows to properly maintain its display. You also might need to set High Graphics and Retain Video Memory in the PIF's Display Options, depending on the program.

Your system's display driver first must be capable of running DOS graphics programs in a window. Make sure you are using one of the compatible display drivers supplied with Windows 3.1 or later, or a third-party display driver that provides support for windowed DOS graphics programs.

Exiting a DOS Program

You usually have to exit a windowed DOS program from within the program, not from Windows. In other words, you cannot choose Close from a DOS program's Control menu and exit the program. By default, when you exit a DOS program, the window closes automatically. This process occasionally presents problems.

Some DOS programs display information about the program or about your data after you exit the program. Usually, this information appears on the display after you return to the DOS prompt. After you exit these programs under Windows, however, you return to the Windows display without seeing the DOS screen or its messages. When you execute a DIR command, for example, the output disappears before you can read the results. Windows enables you to terminate a DOS program to an inactive window (see fig. 15.16), instead of returning directly to the Windows desktop. The information generated by the program shows up on the inactive window, which you can read before you close the window.

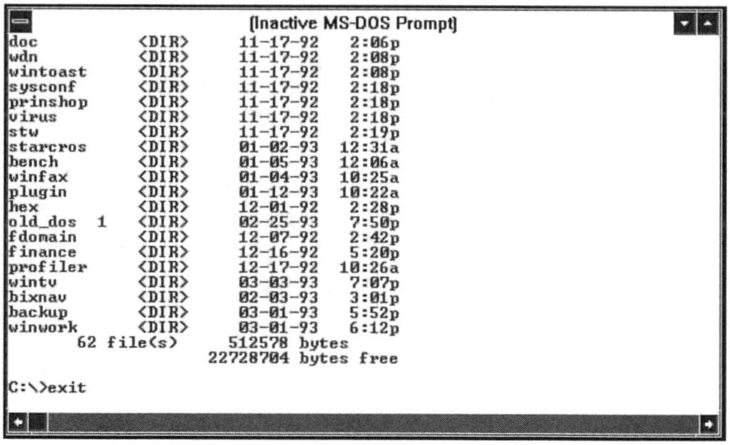

Figure 15.16
A terminated DOS program.

```
[Inactive MS-DOS Prompt]
doc           <DIR>       11-17-92    2:06p
wdn           <DIR>       11-17-92    2:08p
wintoast      <DIR>       11-17-92    2:08p
sysconf       <DIR>       11-17-92    2:18p
prinshop      <DIR>       11-17-92    2:18p
virus         <DIR>       11-17-92    2:18p
stw           <DIR>       11-17-92    2:19p
starcros      <DIR>       01-02-93   12:31a
bench         <DIR>       01-05-93   12:06a
winfax        <DIR>       01-04-93   10:25a
plugin        <DIR>       01-12-93   10:22a
hex           <DIR>       12-01-92    2:28p
old_dos    1  <DIR>       02-25-93    7:50p
fdomain       <DIR>       12-07-92    2:42p
finance       <DIR>       12-16-92    5:20p
profiler      <DIR>       12-17-92   10:26a
wintv         <DIR>       03-03-93    7:07p
bixnav        <DIR>       02-03-93    3:01p
backup        <DIR>       03-01-93    5:52p
winwork       <DIR>       03-01-93    6:12p
         62 file(s)       512578 bytes
                        22728704 bytes free

C:\>exit
```

To make a DOS program terminate to an inactive window, use the Windows PIF Editor to change the program's PIF file. The Close Window on Exit option controls the method Windows uses to close the program. If the box for that option is not checked, Windows terminates the program to an inactive window. To close an inactive DOS program window, choose Close from the window's Control menu.

Exiting a Locked DOS Program

Occasionally, a DOS program running under Windows improperly terminates or locks up, preventing you from closing the DOS program. Although you can continue to use Windows and run programs without addressing the problem, the memory that is allocated to the DOS program is not free for use by the system. A "dead" program can cause instability within the system, resulting in problems with other programs.

When a DOS program "dies" and you cannot exit the program, you can use a special command in the DOS program's Control menu. Press Alt+Esc to return to Windows from the DOS program, or press Ctrl+Esc to access the Task List so that you can return to the Program Manager. Select the Settings option from the program's Control menu, and then choose Terminate to close the program. The dialog box is shown in figure 15.17.

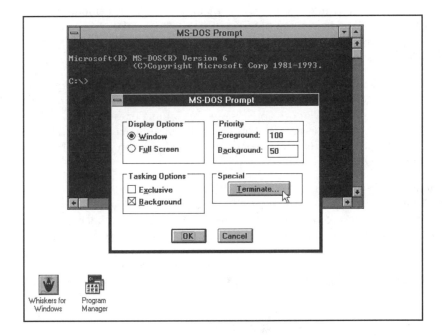

Figure 15.17
The Terminate option in the Control menu.

The Terminate option is a last resort that should be used only in the event of a program crash. Exit a DOS program the normal way whenever possible because Terminate can leave the system in an unstable condition. On the other hand, this procedure enables you to save data in other active programs before restarting Windows. Terminate the dead program, save the other data, and restart Windows.

Balancing Windows and DOS Programs

Because Windows 386 Enhanced mode enables you to multitask Windows and DOS applications, Windows gives you a way to control how Windows allocates CPU priority to applications. This enables you to reduce the amount of CPU time that DOS applications have, which makes your Windows programs run better whenever a DOS application is running. Or, you might want to give DOS programs a larger share of the CPU time.

III

Putting Windows to Work

To control multitasking priority, double-click on the 386 Enhanced icon in the Control Panel. Three options in the Scheduling group control the amount of CPU time Windows applications receive relative to any DOS applications that might be running:

✔ **Windows in Foreground.** This setting specifies the amount of CPU time (in timeslices) that Windows applications share when a DOS program is running in the background. The Windows applications will have the specified amount of CPU time before the CPU switches away to service the DOS application. Increase this number if you want Windows applications to have more CPU time. Decrease the number if you want the DOS applications to have more CPU time.

✔ **Windows in Background.** This setting specifies the amount of CPU time (in timeslices) that Windows applications share when a DOS program is running in the foreground (and the Windows applications are running in the background). Increase this number if you want the Windows applications to have more CPU time when a DOS program is active. Decrease the number if you want the DOS program to have more CPU time.

✔ **Exclusive in Foreground.** This check box, if checked, causes Windows applications to have exclusive use of the CPU whenever a Windows application is active. This prevents DOS programs from running in the background, regardless of the Execution setting in their PIFs. Check this box if you want Windows to use the CPU exclusively and do not want DOS programs to run in the background. Clear the check box if you want to be able to run DOS programs in the background.

Controlling Individual Programs

In the Advanced Options window of the PIF Editor are two settings that control the amount of CPU time that the DOS program associated with the PIF has:

✔ **Background Priority.** This setting specifies the relative amount of CPU time that the DOS program receives when it is running in the background. Increase this number if you want the program to have a larger share of the CPU's time when running in the background.

✔ **Foreground Priority.** This setting specifies the relative amount of CPU time that the DOS program receives when it is running in the foreground. Increase this number if you want the program to have more CPU time when it is active.

Chapter Snapshot

Technological and price breakthroughs in Windows hardware and software have revolutionized the way you can work with graphics in Windows. No longer is graphics design a domain closed to all but graphics illustrators and desktop publishers. Instead, hardware advances such as local bus video, grayscale scanners, and 600-dpi laser printers empower ordinary Windows users to produce professional-looking graphics in business documents, newsletters, annual reports, and presentations on their own. Windows desktop publishing and graphics software now are more affordable and easier to use by the typical business user.

This chapter introduces you to the world of Windows 3.1 graphics by focusing on the following topics:

Whether you are interested in graphics from a professional or personal viewpoint, this chapter offers tips that help you make the most of your PC's graphics hardware and Windows.

16

CHAPTER

Inside Windows
Graphics

Many factors determine the speed and power of a PC's graphics hardware and
software. An understanding of the different ways the PC can represent graphics
is important to using graphics effectively. The first section of this chapter
examines the differences between bitmapped and vector graphics.

Working with Bitmapped and Vector Graphics

You can work with two primary types of graphics in Windows: bitmapped and vector graphics. Both kinds of graphics are designed specifically for some uses but not for others, making the decision of which graphics to use a highly individualized choice.

Bitmapped Graphics

A bitmapped graphic is the most widely used graphics type in the Windows environment. A *bitmap* is a pattern of dots that, when combined, form an image on-screen or on the printer. Each dot is known as a *pixel*. You can use a paint program, such as Windows Paintbrush, to create bitmapped graphics (see fig. 16.1), or you can use a scanner to scan a real-world image (see fig. 16.2).

Figure 16.1

A bitmapped image created in a paint program.

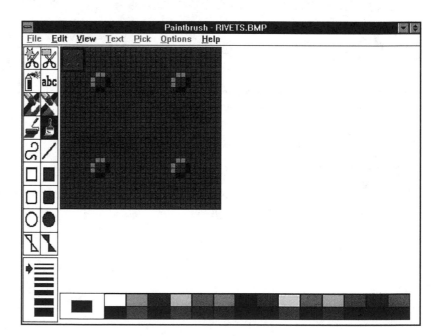

The quality of bitmapped images can be remarkable, because you can work with more than 16.8 million colors. The downfall of bitmapped images is the loss of quality that you get when you try to resize or scale them. Many refer to this loss of quality as the "jaggies" (for the jagged edges). For example, figure 16.3 shows an image at a 100 percent level of magnification; figure 16.4 shows the same image at a 500 percent level of magnification. If you want to get detailed, figure 16.5 shows the same image at a 1,400 percent level of magnification. Notice that at this extreme level of magnification, the image looks mosaic.

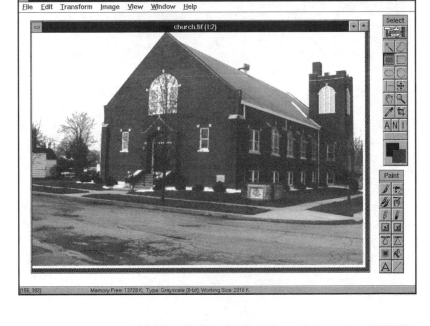

Figure 16.2
A bitmapped image created by scanning a photograph.

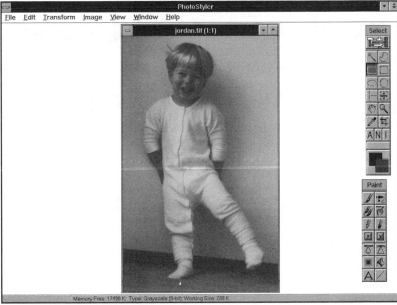

Figure 16.3
JORDAN.TIF at a 100 percent level of magnification.

III

Putting Windows to Work

Figure 16.4
JORDAN.TIF at a
500 percent level
of magnification.

Figure 16.5
JORDAN.TIF at a
1,400 percent
level of
magnification.

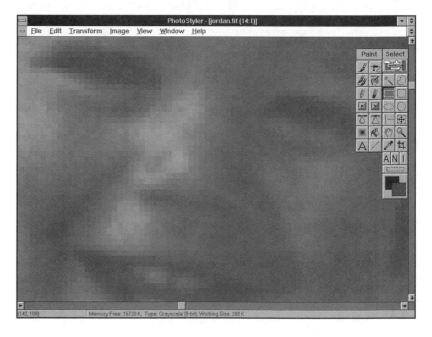

Bitmaps Defined

A bitmapped image contains data that is represented in terms of its gray or color values. You can use several different types of bitmaps, as shown in table 16.1.

Table 16.1
Types of Bitmaps

Bitmap Type	Bits Per Pixel	Number of Colors
Black-and-white	1	2
Grayscale	8	256 shades of gray
4-bit	4	16
8-bit	8	256
24-bit	24	16.8 million

Tip

If you plan to use 24-bit images, you need to have plenty of RAM (at least 16 MB) and disk space. Although 24-bit bitmaps look incredibly lifelike on-screen, this realism comes at a considerable cost. A large 24-bit image can take up at least 16 MB of disk space.

A bitmap is defined by the number of bits that store data about each pixel and the number of color components that make up the image. These images can be grouped into the following categories:

✔ **Black-and-white.** Each pixel in a black-and-white bitmap is either white (value of 1) or black (0).

✔ **Grayscale.** Each pixel in a grayscale bitmap is defined by 8 bits with values ranging from 0 (black) to 255 (white). Each value is a different shade of gray.

✔ **Indexed color.** Each pixel in an indexed color bitmap is represented by 4 or 8 bits whose values represent a color in a color table.

✔ **RGB true color.** Each pixel in an RGB true color bitmap is defined by three 8-bit numbers, which correspond to red, blue, and green intensities.

Paint Programs and Bitmaps

To create and work with bitmapped images, you need a paint program. You can use three kinds of paint programs, depending on your needs:

✔ **8-bit paint.** The basic paint tool is an 8-bit paint program. This type of program is designed to work with black-and-white, indexed 4-bit, and indexed 8-bit graphics. Windows Paintbrush is an example of a basic paint program (see fig. 16.6).

✔ **24-bit paint.** Far superior to a basic paint program, a 24-bit paint program can work with 24-bit images and includes a wider assortment of painting tools. Examples of 24-bit paint programs include CA-CricketPaint and Fractal Design Painter.

✔ **Image processing.** Image-processing programs are similar to 24-bit paint programs, but also include gamma correction, resampling, and four-color separation capabilities to work with true color photographs. Image-processing software is sometimes referred to as an "electronic darkroom." Aldus PhotoStyler is an example of an image-processing application (see fig. 16.7).

Figure 16.6
Windows
Paintbrush.

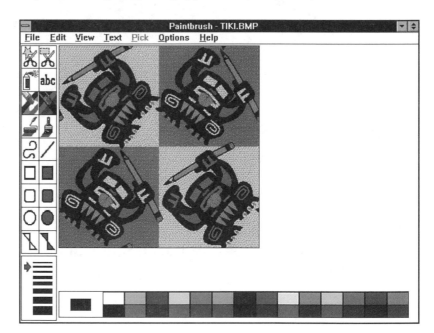

The difference between high-end paint and image-processing programs is subtle. Think of a paint program as a tool for creating images, and an image-processing program as a tool for manipulating images.

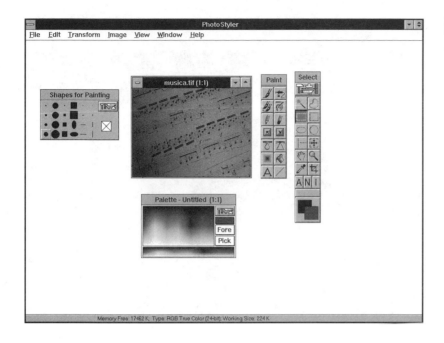

Figure 16.7
Aldus PhotoStyler.

Vector Graphics

Unlike bitmaps, *vector graphics* (also called *object-oriented graphics*) are not made up of series of pixels, but of shapes, such as circles, lines, arcs, and squares (see fig. 16.8). These objects can be scaled to any size because they are generated from mathematical definitions. For example, the two objects shown beside each other in figure 16.9 are identical, but the large object is scaled to look many times the size of the small image. There are no "jaggies" present on the large object. Vector graphics are ideal for technical drawings and line art because you can pay attention to detail in drawing programs far more easily than in paint programs.

Vector graphics are always created within a drawing or illustration program, such as CorelDRAW!, Arts & Letters, Micrografx Draw, and Aldus Freehand. Drawing programs usually have a distinct set of tools; paint programs do not have such tools because they are designed to create and manipulate pixels, not objects. Many users find that drawing programs are not as intuitive as paint programs. Thus, if you have experience only with paint programs, it might take a while to get adjusted to a drawing program. Instead of drawing free-form as you might expect, you actually layer objects to create a desired effect.

III

Putting Windows 'o Work

Figure 16.8
Vector graphics
consist of a
number of
different shapes.

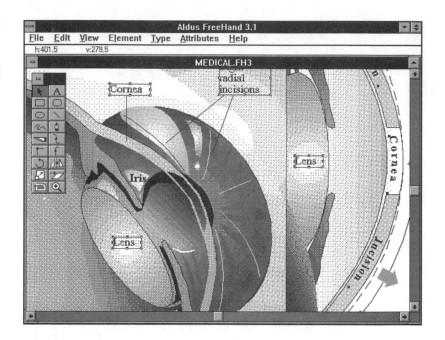

Figure 16.9
Vector graphics do
not become
distorted as their
sizes increase.

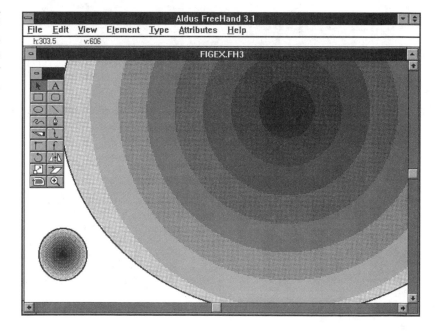

Drawing Programs and Vector Graphics

If you decide that you want to use a vector-based drawing program, you should make your selection according to your drawing needs. If you plan to make detailed technical drawings, you will need a drawing program; if you work with scanned grayscale photographs, you will need a paint or image-processing program. Other choices may be more subtle, however. Table 16.2 provides a brief summary of some of the capabilities of paint and drawing programs.

Table 16.2
Choosing the Right Graphics Program

Category	Paint Application	Drawing Application
Supports bitmapped graphics	X	X
Supports vector graphics		X
Painting tools	X	
Drawing tools		X
24-bit images	X	
Scanned photographs or image manipulation	X	
Custom blending	X	
Pixel-level editing	X	
Manipulation of shapes		X
Technical drawing		X
Text manipulation and special effects		X
Clip art included		X

Examining Graphics File Formats

Although there are two major types of graphics file formats, there are at least two dozen common graphics file formats you can work with under Windows. Fortunately, most

Windows-based graphics, desktop publishing, and business applications support at least a few standard file formats. Table 16.3 lists the 16 most popular formats supported under Windows.

Table 16.3
Major Windows Graphics Formats

Format	Description	Type
BMP	Windows Bitmap	Bitmap
CDR	CorelDRAW!	Vector
CGM	Computer Graphics Metafile	Vector
DIB	Device-Independent Bitmap	Bitmap
DRW	Micrografx Draw/Designer	Vector
EPS	Encapsulated PostScript	Vector/bitmap
GIF	Graphics Interchange Format	Bitmap
JPEG	Joint Photographic Experts Group	Bitmap
MSP	Microsoft Paintbrush	Bitmap
PCX	PC Paintbrush	Bitmap
PIC	Picture	Vector
PICT	Mac Picture File Format	Vector
TGA	Targa	Bitmap
TIF	Tag Image File Format	Bitmap
WMF	Windows Metafile	Vector
WPG	WordPerfect/DrawPerfect Graphic	Bitmap/vector

Although many Windows applications provide better support for TIF files and other graphics formats, BMP is considered the standard Windows bitmap format, and WMF is the standard vector graphics file format.

Types of Bitmapped Graphics

Nine major bitmapped graphic formats are used in the Windows environment today. These are discussed in the following sections.

BMP

BMP (Bitmap) is the de facto standard graphics file format for Windows. It is supported by nearly all Windows applications, but is rarely supported outside of Windows. Windows Paintbrush saves bitmaps in BMP format by default, and graphics displayed as wallpaper on the Windows desktop must be in BMP format. BMP files are device-independent and support black-and-white, 4-bit, 8-bit, and 24-bit image types.

DIB

DIB (Device-Independent Bitmap) is the standard bitmapped graphic format for OS/2. Only a few Windows applications provide support for DIB files. Paintbrush, for instance, can open a DIB file, but cannot save the file in its native format.

GIF

GIF (Graphics Interchange Format) is a standard format used to store graphics on CompuServe and other bulletin board systems. The format was designed to create the smallest file size to minimize the time required to transfer files to and from CompuServe. GIF is basically a utility format, although more and more applications support it. You can use a number of commercial and shareware paint programs, however, to convert GIF files into other bitmap formats. Both PC and Macintosh platforms support GIF. There are two GIF file versions: 87a and 89a (applications that were originally written to work with the 87a format might not be able to read the 89a format). GIF format supports black-and-white, 4-bit, and 8-bit image types.

 GIF supports an encoding method known as interlacing. *Interlacing* involves a process of saving an image in four passes rather than the standard single pass. Interlacing is helpful if you are downloading a GIF image from CompuServe and your communications program enables you to view the file while it is being downloaded. (WinCIM is such a program.) The result is that you can see an outline of an image while it is being downloaded. This facility enables you to abort the file transfer if the image is not what you expected it to be.

IMG

IMG (Image) was the standard graphics format for the GEM environment and Ventura Publisher. Most Windows applications do not support IMG; probably the only application you will find that supports IMG files is Ventura Publisher for Windows.

JPEG

JPEG (Joint Photographic Experts Group) is a new format designed to provide extremely high compression ratios (up to 100:1). The JPEG compression scheme achieves these remarkable ratios by leaving some of the data out during the compression process. You usually can use JPEG format for images, however, without any noticeable loss of quality of the image. JPEG is especially useful for storing 24-bit color photographic images, which can take up a great deal of disk space. Most applications do not currently support JPEG images.

MSP

MSP (Microsoft Paint) was the standard graphics format used by Microsoft Paint in earlier versions of Windows (prior to version 3.0). Paintbrush enables you to import MSP files and save them in BMP or PCX format.

 If you need to use MSP graphics, you should convert them to BMP or PCX for greater acceptability in Windows 3.1.

PCX

PCX (PC Paintbrush) is probably the standard graphics format for the entire PC platform (Windows and DOS). PCX was one of the first graphics formats available for the PC and was the native format for Zsoft Paintbrush. PCX probably is supported by more Windows and DOS applications than any other format. The PCX format supports black-and-white, 4-bit, and 8-bit image types.

 PCX files usually require less disk space than the equivalent BMP or TIF files.

TGA

TGA (Targa) is used primarily for 16-bit (64 KB color) graphics. Because of the popularity of 24-bit video cards, however, 16-bit images are much less popular, making TGA format of less value than it once was. Only a few high-end image processing applications, such as Aldus PhotoStyler, support TGA.

TIF

TIF (Tag Image File) format is one of the most popular and widely used file formats in the PC and Macintosh environments. Most Windows applications with graphics import capabilities support TIF. Almost all scanning software works with TIF files, as does fax software. TIF is an extremely flexible format and provides a wide variety of compression routines, including the following:

✔ Noncompressed

✔ LZW Compressed

✔ Huffman

✔ Pack Bits

✔ Fax Group 3

✔ Fax Group 4

Not all Windows applications provide support for each of these encoding routines, so an uncompressed TIF file is your safest choice to ensure compatibility. TIF format supports black-and-white, grayscale, 4-bit, 8-bit, and 24-bit image types.

 Earlier versions of the Windows Clipboard did not support TIF format, but Windows 3.1 does for easy graphics transfer between applications.

Types of Vector Graphics

Although there are exceptions, vector graphics formats tend to be specific to an application, which is much different from the more generic bitmapped graphics. Windows supports the following seven major vector formats.

CDR

CDR (CorelDRAW!) is the native file format of CorelDRAW!. Because its file format was proprietary and not available to other software vendors until recently, no other current Windows application currently provides support for CDR files.

CGM

CGM (Computer Graphics Metafile) is the vector-graphics equivalent to PCX because of its widespread use on both DOS and Windows platforms. Most drawing programs provide support for CGM format.

DRW

DRW (Micrografx Draw) is the native file format of Micrografx Draw and Designer and is supported by several Windows desktop publishing (such as Aldus PageMaker), graphics (Aldus FreeHand), and business applications (Word for Windows).

EPS

EPS (Encapsulated PostScript) format uses the PostScript page-description language to generate an image. EPS files are extremely complex and can contain wide varieties of information (including PostScript text and bitmapped graphics). EPS provides high-quality output at a steep storage price. A 1 MB Windows metafile, for example, takes at least five times that amount of space if saved as an EPS file. You can manipulate the entire EPS image by resizing or moving it, but you cannot edit or make any changes to elements within the image. EPS supports black-and-white, grayscale, and 24-bit image types. If you import an EPS file into an application, the program might not be able to display it on-screen, but should be able to print the file on a PostScript printer.

If you have text in an EPS image, the fonts used by the text must be available on your system or printer for the graphic to print correctly.

PIC

PIC (Picture) is used to store Lotus 1-2-3 charts and graphs. Many Windows applications support PIC files.

WMF

WMF (Windows Metafile) is targeted as the standard vector-graphics format for Windows. Many applications now provide support for WMF format. WMF files can include both bitmapped and vector images.

WPG

WPG (WordPerfect Graphic) is the graphic format used by WordPerfect for Windows and DrawPerfect. Not many non–word processing applications support WPG files, and no drawing programs (except DrawPerfect) provide editing capabilities.

Converting between Different Graphics File Formats

Because such a vast number of possible graphics formats can be used in Windows, you might find that your application does not provide direct support for a graphic you want to use. When this occurs, the first step is to copy the graphic to the Clipboard and attempt to paste it into the receiving application. However, in situations when this is not successful (such as pasting a vector drawing into a paint program), you need to convert the graphic into an alternative format. You can use one of the following four file-conversion paths:

✔ **Converting between bitmap formats.** A bitmap-to-bitmap conversion probably is the easiest file conversion and can be accomplished by using Paintbrush (see table 16.4) or a popular utility such as PaintShop Pro. Additionally, most paint programs enable you to import and export bitmaps in a variety of formats.

Table 16.4
Paintbrush File-Conversion Capabilities

Format	Opens	Saves
BMP	Yes	Yes
DIB	Yes	No
MSP	Yes	No
PCX	Yes	Yes

✔ **Converting between vector formats.** Because most vector graphics are application-specific, drawing programs are the best tools to convert between vector formats. Most of the major drawing programs let you simply import most other vector formats.

✔ **Converting bitmap to vector format.** You can convert bitmaps to vector graphics by tracing the edges of a bitmap and transforming the dot patterns into a line-art vector image. Micrografx Draw and Adobe Illustrator have autotrace capabilities, and other drawing programs provide manual tracing tools. Additionally, Adobe Streamline and CorelTRACE! are two stand-alone autotracing programs that you can use to transfer a bitmap to vector format easily.

✔ **Converting vector to bitmap format.** Many drawing programs can save a vector graphic in a bitmapped format. If your drawing program cannot do this, you can display the vector graphic on-screen and capture the image with screen capture software or by pressing Print Screen to copy the screen image to the Clipboard. After you import the screen shot into a paint program, you can crop the image as needed.

If you plan to do much graphics conversion or are trying to convert between lesser-used formats, you should consider getting HiJaak for Windows, a powerful commercial conversion utility.

One shareware utility you might want to consider getting is PaintShop Pro. It might be one of the most economical ways to convert between bitmap formats, providing import and export capabilities for BMP, DIB, GIF, IMG, JAS, MAC, MSP, PCX, PIC, RAS, RLE, TGA, TIF, and WPG formats.

As you have seen in this chapter, a wide variety of graphics options are available on the Windows platform. Not only can you choose between bitmap and vector types, you also can specify one of several graphics formats. Fortunately, with such data exchange mediums as Clipboard and object linking and embedding, Windows enables you to worry less about the format of the graphic so that you can concentrate on the actual content of the graphic. This trend toward interoperability will undoubtedly continue in future versions of Windows, making the task of using graphics easier and easier.

Chapter Snapshot

Do you spend too much time entering information rather than creating information? If so, you should consider optical character recognition (OCR) technology. Although scanning technology has been available for some time, lower hardware costs, breakthroughs in scanning software, and the success of Windows have made OCR a technology useful for every business and computing requirement. A few years ago dedicated-scanning systems cost at least $50,000. Today, an investment of less than $1,000 can increase your productivity remarkably, even if you require only occasional use of the scanner. This chapter looks at the new world of OCR by focusing on:

This chapter will help you understand how to apply OCR and scanning effectively with Windows.

Scanning, OCR, and Windows

Computers automate much of the work we do today. Unfortunately, paper documents are still very much a part of the business world. The use of fax machines to transmit documents has risen considerably, and many users find it necessary to modify received faxes. The first section of this chapter examines one technology that makes it possible to modify these types of documents: OCR.

Understanding OCR

Optical character recognition (OCR) is a process by which real-world documents are digitized by a scanning device; the resulting bitmapped image then is analyzed by OCR software to determine the known characters and formatting that can be extracted from the image. In one way, OCR technology is no different from desktop publishing (DTP) and computer-aided design (CAD): just like DTP and CAD, OCR technology uses its own special hardware—scanners—and software. Real-world documents (letters, reports, newspapers, magazines, and so on) can be scanned by a scanner, turned into a bitmapped file, and then decoded into usable text and graphics by optical character recognition software. Figure 17.1 shows the important parts of a successful (time-saving) OCR system.

Figure 17.1
An OCR system.

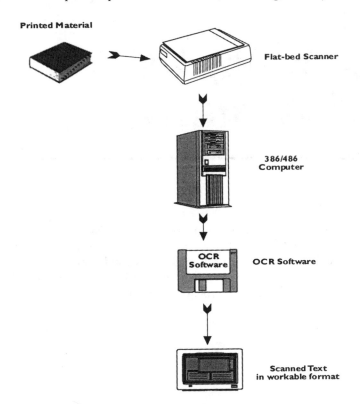

Printed Material

Flat-bed Scanner

386/486 Computer

OCR Software

Scanned Text in workable format

OCR is a wonderful technology, but in many ways it is a double-edged sword. High-quality software, hardware, and readable documents make it possible for you to scan text that the OCR software can read at an accuracy rate of over 99 percent. Inferior equipment or poor-quality documents, however, might produce such poor quality that you spend more time correcting errors than you would have spent typing the material.

Although OCR technology is light-years ahead of what was available a few years ago, keep in mind that it is not a miracle worker. If you have a hard time reading the document, your OCR software will, too.

If you are serious about OCR, you need a PC with at least an 80386 CPU and 4 MB of RAM. Some OCR software can run on a 286, but more recent advanced versions do not. As with virtually any application, a higher-performance CPU will make the software perform better. Although an 80386 is the minimum CPU required in many situations, a 486 or Pentium system will provide the best performance.

PC Scanners

Aside from a capable PC, you need a scanner to begin the process of optical character recognition. A *scanner* digitizes a physical document or image into a bitmapped image. The physical dimensions and quality of available scanners differ, depending on whether they are hand-held, flatbed, or drum scanners.

Flatbed Scanners

Scanning a document on a flatbed scanner closely resembles photocopying a document. After you place the document on a glass plate and cover it with a lid, the scanner passes over the page with a light. Flatbed scanners can be used to scan all types of documents, even bound materials such as books. Many flatbed scanners also have an optional document feeder to automate the document entry process.

Hand-Held Scanners

Easy to use and inexpensive, hand-held scanners are a much smaller investment than flatbed scanners. Hand-held scanners are perfect if you are interested primarily in scanning graphics.

As with all scanned material, the quality of the character-recognition process (the amount of text the OCR software can translate into workable text) is directly related to the quality of the scanned bitmap. To scan material accurately with a hand scanner, a little more accuracy is required. You must move a hand scanner across the page slowly and steadily; jerky movement makes it more difficult for the software to recognize characters. Another concern is the width of the hand-held scanner. Unlike flatbed scanners, which scan the entire document in one pass, the narrow widths of hand-held scanners require two to three passes for a typical document. Because you are doing this by hand, you need to maintain a consistent speed as you pass the scanner over the material.

These drawbacks to hand-held scanning can be minimized with OCR software that corrects skewing and irregular scanning speed.

If you plan on scanning more than a page daily, you need a flatbed scanner.

Regardless of the type of scanner, resolution and color support are two important parts of every scanner's capabilities (see table 17.1). Most scanners have a minimum scanning resolution of 300 dpi, which is acceptable for most material. A scanner also can support anywhere from 1 to 24 bits per pixel. The current affordable grayscale scanners (most are 8-bit scanners) are ideal OCR candidates. If you plan to use the scanner for true color graphics, you need a 24-bit color scanner.

Table 17.1
Resolution and Color Support

Bitmap type	Bits per pixel	Number of colors
Black-and-white	1	2
Grayscale	8	256 shades of gray
4-bit	4	16
8-bit	8	256
24-bit	24	16.8 million

Some older scanners are full-page and feed the document through themselves. This produces a good scan but does not allow books or odd-sized documents to be used.

Examining the OCR Process

As mentioned earlier, the successful scan and recognition of text and graphics requires a scanner that can work seamlessly with OCR software. OCR software processes the character bitmaps of the image and converts the bitmaps into ASCII characters (some packages also preserve the formatting of the original text). OCR software uses a four-step process to read and translate bitmapped images into workable text:

1. Input

2. Decomposition

3. Character recognition

4. Proofing

Step One: Input

The first step in OCR is scanning the image. Most OCR software enables you to scan a document directly or from a TIFF file that previously has been scanned. If your plans are to scan magazine articles or other documents with shaded backgrounds, make sure the OCR software is capable of recognizing text with shaded backgrounds. Without any special technology to handle this characteristic, a complete page of text on a shaded background might not be readable for the OCR software.

Hewlett-Packard and Caere solved the problem of scanning text on shaded backgrounds by developing proprietary technologies known as Hewlett-Packard AccuPage and Caere AnyPage. Each technology uses a process called dynamic thresholding to analyze a document and look for contrasts between light and dark portions of the page. When AccuPage or AnyPage locates a shaded region, it adjusts the threshold at which the OCR software turns on or off a pixel (that is, determines if it is part of the text). AccuPage and AnyPage perform this process at a microscopic level, recognizing backgrounds at dimensions smaller than a millimeter.

Step Two: Decomposition

The next step, known as *decomposition,* involves breaking up the different regions of a page into textual and nontextual areas. After the nontextual material is tossed aside, textual regions are analyzed to determine the flow of the text. With sophisticated OCR software, you can specify text regions for decomposition or have the software do it automatically (see fig. 17.2). In addition, you can manually set template regions of text to scan in multiple-page documents. Templates enable you to eliminate page headers and numbers between pages.

More advanced OCR packages go one step further during decomposition. OmniPage, for example, determines the white space between each line of text, enabling it to recognize drop caps.

 The capability to recognize drop caps improves the accuracy during translation of the TIFF to text. (A TIFF file is a bitmapped image, which is not necessarily the same as a BMP file.)

Step Three: Character Recognition

The third step of scanning text is the heart of OCR—recognizing the characters from a page. OCR software uses one of two different methods to recognize text:

- ✔ **Pattern matching.** Character recognition is performed through a pixel-by-pixel evaluation of a character's bitmap. This bitmap is compared to a database of possible choices; the exact letter chosen is determined by a probability analysis. A *c*, for example, has a 72 percent chance of being an *e*, but an 80 percent chance of being a *c*.

Pattern matching has two major flaws. First, it isn't always reliable because of substitution errors. Second, pattern matching is more time-intensive because the software must be trained for each new font you want it to support—an exhausting, tedious process.

Figure 17.2
Manually setting the text regions on a page.

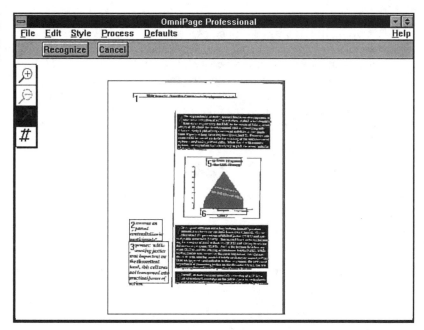

✔ **Omnifont recognition.** Omnifont software does not need to be trained when you use new fonts because it recognizes characters through a different process. OmniPage, for example, sends each character through to a series of filters called "experts," each of which is responsible for identifying the character.

Each "expert" is a separate part of the program that receives the data, analyzes it from a database of fonts, and then spits out the answer to another part of the program. When an expert is not capable of identifying the character, it passes the character to the next expert. This process continues until a character is recognized—no guessing occurs. Omnifont software can recognize most fonts unless the characters are small, large, or unusual. Most of the Windows OCR software available today, such as OmniPage and WordScan Plus, uses omnifont technology.

The capability of OCR software to recognize characters is in large part based on the quality of the original document. You will receive poor results if the page has small type (six points or smaller), unusual fonts, or unreadable text. When the document is of high quality, the results are nearly perfect. Figure 17.3 shows a page taken from *Inside Paradox for Windows* (New Riders Publishing). With an HP ScanJet IIP and OmniPage Professional, the page was scanned and inserted into Word for Windows (see fig. 17.4). The accuracy rate: no misspelled words and only two errors (a missing space between two sets of words).

Creating Design Documents **257**

most probable common fields, Paradox looks first at the indexed fields in the detail table and tries to find a field from the master table that matches in name and type. If a match is found, fields from both tables are shown in the dialog box's link diagram section.

If Paradox cannot determine which fields match, the boxes are left blank. Select the matching fields from the field list of the master and detail tables by double-clicking on the field (or by clicking on the field and then clicking on the Add Field arrow). If you decide to clear the fields inside the link diagram, click on the Unlink button.

NOTE *If you previously defined a referential integrity relationship between two tables, you can bypass the Define Link dialog box. Paradox automatically links the matching fields from the referential integrity relationship as you drag the mouse from the master table to the detail table.*

If you have a composite key in your detail table, the link diagram shows each field of the composite key. Select the field from the master table field list that matches one of the composite key fields.

When you are satisfied with the link, click on the OK button to return to the Data Model dialog box. Notice that the data model picture now includes an arrow that shows the relationship between the tables (see fig. 9.8). This double arrow represents the one-to-many relationship between the INVOICE and ITEMS tables.

To complete the data model, you need to establish a link between the CLIENT and INVOICE tables and a link between the ITEMS and DOCUMENT tables. Figure 9.9 shows the finished data model after these links are created. Notice the single arrow that represents the one-to-one relationship between the ITEMS and DOCUMENT tables. (A single arrow also can signify a many-to-one relationship.)

Figure 17.3
A page taken from a book.

III

Putting Windows to Work

Figure 17.4
Virtually a 100
percent accuracy
rate after
scanning.

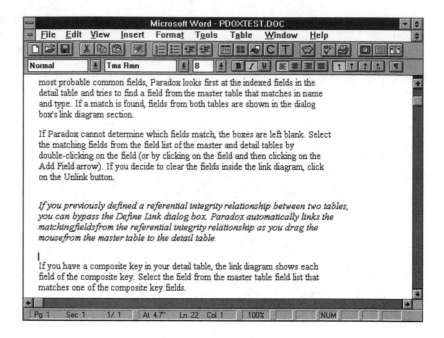

Don't think you can scan and print copies of *Inside Windows, Platinum Edition,* or any other book. Copyright laws protect the scanning and photocopying of copyrighted material. Make sure you know whether you need permission to scan material protected by copyright.

Is omnifont software really "omnifont"? As an ad hoc test, the sentence "Omnifont software does not need to be trained when you use new fonts" was listed 17 times in a Word document, with each line using a different font.

The fonts selected in the test are fairly common serif, sans serif, and monospaced fonts. A few decorative fonts were thrown in to enhance the test. The document, as shown in figure 17.5, was scanned by an HP ScanJet IIP. OmniPage Professional was used to convert the page into text format. The results are shown in figure 17.6. If you take out the decorative fonts, the only common error was mistaking a letter O with the number 0. The usual serif and sans serif fonts, which are used on most normal documents, produced no errors.

Even at 99 percent accuracy, 20 mistakes could be on a typical 2,000-character page. For this reason, allow time for spelling checking and proofreading.

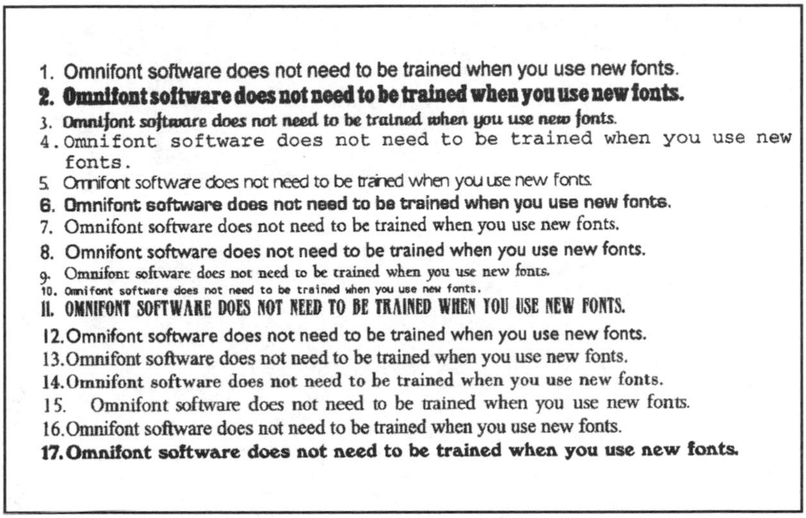

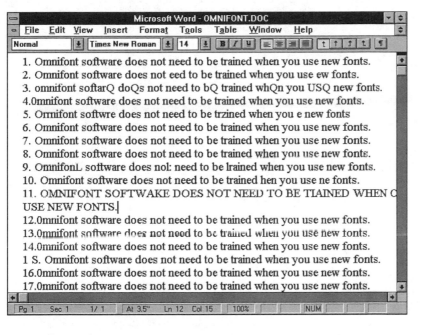

Figure 17.5
The omnifont test document.

Figure 17.6
The scanned text in a Word document.

III

Putting Windows to Work

Step Four: Proofing

The final step in the OCR process involves recognizing characters the software could not identify. Whenever the software encounters an unrecognizable character, it substitutes a tilde (~) or asterisk (*) for the character. Many OCR packages enable you to jump through each place to correct the text. Some software, such as OmniPage, enables you to double-click on a word to enlarge and correct it (see fig. 17.7). OmniPage also includes an Auto Spell feature that tries to correct any misspelled words for you.

Figure 17.7

Proofing a document in OmniPage.

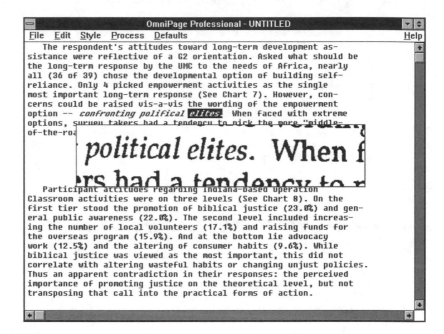

The auto spell feature of OCR packages is a mixed blessing. Although it helps figure out words without your help, you still need to scroll through the document. Auto spelling sometimes makes matters worse—understandable words with one missing or misspelled letter can suddenly become crazy words.

Training

Many OCR packages can be trained to improve their chances of recognizing unusual characters. If you choose the Process, Train Recognition command in OmniPage, for example, a dialog box appears showing characters that were out of context by the software—that is, were unrecognized. You can specify the unrecognized character by double-clicking on the desired box in the dialog box (see fig. 17.8).

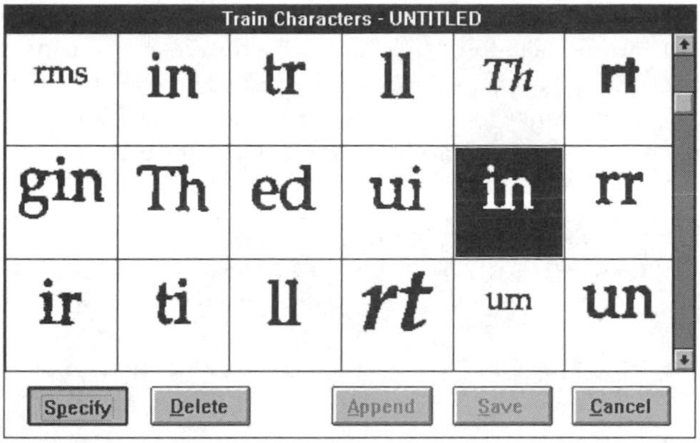

Figure 17.8
Double-clicking on *in* to train the OCR software.

Using OCR

OCR technology can be used in a variety of ways to simplify the work you do in Windows. A prime candidate for OCR technology is an office that receives large amounts of paper documents that must be modified electronically. Even if you are not buried in paper, however, you can benefit from OCR technology in word processing, desktop publishing, databases, and spreadsheets.

OCR in Word Processing

Suppose you are a research associate for a small nonprofit organization and you are in charge of synthesizing several research papers for a special report to the organization's supporters. Because of a hard disk crash several months earlier, however, none of the research documents are available electronically. You might have to face the difficult task of reassembling these research papers in a short amount of time. Instead of staying up all night retyping the text, use OCR. In a couple hours, you might be able to scan all the research papers (see fig. 17.9) and import them into Word for Windows to begin preparing the new report (see fig. 17.10).

OCR in Desktop Publishing

Scanning also is very useful for digitizing graphical images, such as photos, logos, clip art, and other material for use in desktop publishing.

Imagine you are a desktop publisher for a big company. Each week you put together a newsletter for your clients to update them on current business news. You often receive press releases from Fortune 500 companies, but you have a difficult time retyping them for use in the newsletter. In addition, you receive so many press releases that photocopying them for everyone would take forever. With OCR software and a scanner, you easily can scan the press release (a sample is shown in figure 17.11), copy the text to the Clipboard, and paste it into your PageMaker publication (see fig. 17.12). Because of the print quality of the press release, you rarely have to correct any errors.

Figure 17.9
A page from a research report.

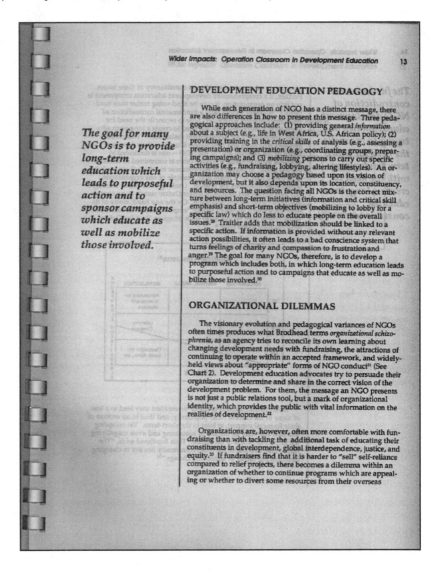

Wider Impacts: Operation Classroom in Development Education 13

DEVELOPMENT EDUCATION PEDAGOGY

The goal for many NGOs is to provide long-term education which leads to purposeful action and to sponsor campaigns which educate as well as mobilize those involved.

While each generation of NGO has a distinct message, there are also differences in how to present this message. Three pedagogical approaches include: (1) providing general *information* about a subject (e.g., life in West Africa, U.S. African policy); (2) providing training in the *critical skills* of analysis (e.g., assessing a presentation) or organization (e.g., coordinating groups, preparing campaigns); and (3) *mobilizing* persons to carry out specific activities (e.g., fundraising, lobbying, altering lifestyles). An organization may choose a pedagogy based upon its vision of development, but it also depends upon its location, constituency, and resources. The question facing all NGOs is the correct mixture between long-term initiatives (information and critical skill emphasis) and short-term objectives (mobilizing to lobby for a specific law) which do less to educate people on the overall issues.[28] Traitler adds that mobilization should be linked to a specific action. If information is provided without any relevant action possibilities, it often leads to a bad conscience system that turns feelings of charity and compassion to frustration and anger.[29] The goal for many NGOs, therefore, is to develop a program which includes both, in which long-term education leads to purposeful action and to campaigns that educate as well as mobilize those involved.[30]

ORGANIZATIONAL DILEMMAS

The visionary evolution and pedagogical variances of NGOs often times produces what Brodhead terms *organizational schizophrenia*, as an agency tries to reconcile its own learning about changing development needs with fundraising, the attractions of continuing to operate within an accepted framework, and widely-held views about "appropriate" forms of NGO conduct[31] (See Chart 2). Development education advocates try to persuade their organization to determine and share in the correct vision of the development problem. For them, the message an NGO presents is not just a public relations tool, but a mark of organizational identity, which provides the public with vital information on the realities of development.[32]

Organizations are, however, often more comfortable with fundraising than with tackling the additional task of educating their constituents in development, global interdependence, justice, and equity.[33] If fundraisers find that it is harder to "sell" self-reliance compared to relief projects, there becomes a dilemma within an organization of whether to continue programs which are appealing or whether to divert some resources from their overseas

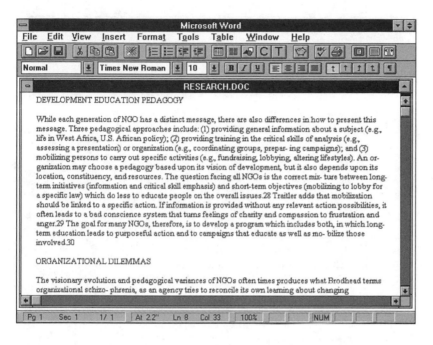

Figure 17.10
Scanned text can
now be edited in
Word for
Windows.

You might ask, Why not keep it as a bitmap if quality is good? As a bitmap, the press release (or any other document) is just an image—you cannot do anything with it or to it. By converting the document using OCR, you make it possible to edit the text, change its formatting, and integrate it with other text. In addition, editable text takes only a fraction of the storage space of a TIFF file.

OCR in Databases

Are you an insurance salesman? OCR is perfect for this business too. Suppose you often solicit potential customers by looking through the phone book. You typically open a page out of the book and try to call each number. You then take notes on each call and enter the information into a Quattro Pro for Windows spreadsheet. In doing so, you still have to type in the name, address, and phone number of each customer.

By using OCR software, you can scan a page out of the phone book (see fig. 17.13), save it as a spreadsheet file, and import it to Quattro Pro. When the page is in the spreadsheet, you can perform minor formatting changes and then use it as a weekly log by adding columns to take notes about each call you make. Figure 17.14 shows the phone book entries in the spreadsheet. When completed, you can import this data into a database for long-term use.

N E W S

FOR IMMEDIATE RELEASE

Contact:
James Strohecker
Borland International
(408)439-4765

Terry Kalil
Great Plains Software
(701)281-3130

Borland and Great Plains Software Form Strategic Alliance

SCOTTS VALLEY, Calif. — October 1, 1991 — Borland International, Inc. (NASDAQ:BORL) and Great Plains Software jointly announced today a strategic alliance that will include a Great Plains Edition of Borland's ObjectVision for Windows, version 2.0.

The Great Plains Edition of ObjectVision is expected to ship in November simultaneous with the release of ObjectVision 2.0, which Borland announced today.

"ObjectVision is creating entirely new markets and opportunities for vertical software developers, such as Great Plains," said Philippe Kahn, Borland chairman, president and CEO. "We're eager to bring ObjectVision and other Borland products to Great Plains' installed base of customers and developers. Our leadership in Visual Application Creation and object-oriented technology enables Great Plains to deliver unsurpassed computing power to users in the accounting profession."

"ObjectVision's Visual Application Creation capabilities and its Btrieve data connectivity are an entirely new approach to addressing the flexibility needs of our customers," said Douglas J. Burgum, Great Plains president and CEO. "This joint development with Borland demonstrates Great Plains' continued commitment to providing VARs and customers with leading-edge technology. We believe the power and ease of ObjectVision 2.0 will increase the functionality of Great Plains Accounting for our customers."

The Great Plains Edition of ObjectVision will be marketed and supported by Great Plains Software. Additional information on the Great Plains Edition of ObjectVision will be announced separately by Great Plains.

(more)

1800 GREEN HILLS ROAD
P.O. BOX 660001
SCOTTS VALLEY, CA
95067-0001

B O R L A N D

Figure 17.12
The text of the press release is easily integrated into PageMaker.

Spreadsheets

Suppose you make a number of business calls each month on your home phone. When the time comes to sort through and itemize personal and business phone calls, you hole up in the home office for a day and develop a headache figuring out what calls were which. You usually type the amount for each call into a Quattro Pro for Windows spreadsheet and separate the calls into two categories. Afterward, you track the amounts and integrate the data into a monthly expense report.

With OCR, you can speed up by many times the amount of work it takes to enter mounds of expenses into a spreadsheet. You simply scan the phone bill, save it as a spreadsheet, and then import the file into Quattro Pro (see fig. 17.15). You then are able to separate the calls easily into two different categories and total them. A process that used to take 2 hours can now be done in 10 minutes.

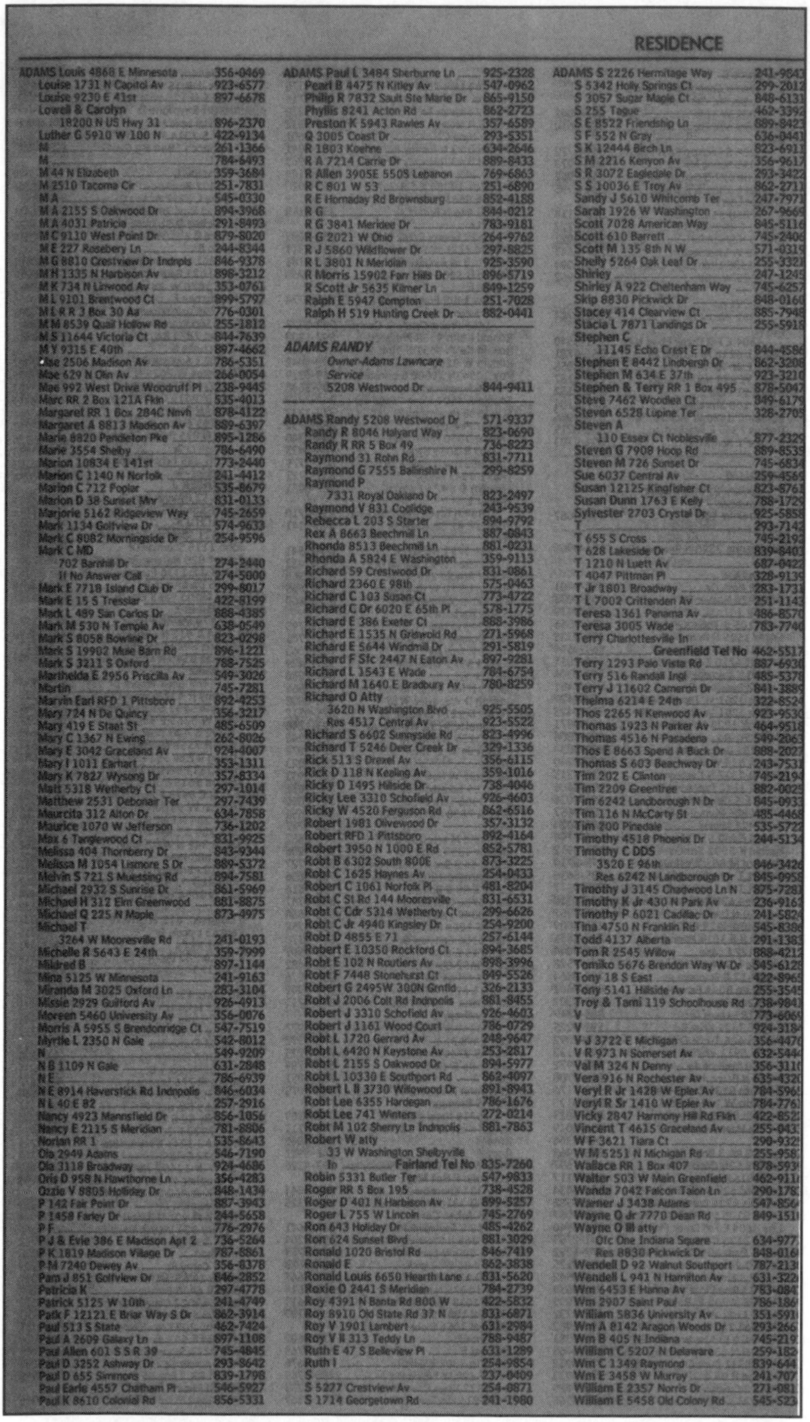

RESIDENCE

ADAMS Louis 4868 E Minnesota	356-0469
Louise 1731 N Capitol Av	923-6577
Louise 9230 E 41st	897-6678
Lowell & Carolyn 18200 N US Hwy 31	896-2370
Luther G 5910 W 100 N	422-9134
M	261-1366
M	784-6493
M 44 N Elizabeth	359-3684
M 2510 Tacoma Cir	251-7831
M A	545-0330
M A 2155 S Oakwood Dr	894-3968
M A 4031 Patricia	291-8493
M C 9110 West Point Dr	879-8020
M E 227 Rosebery Ln	244-8344
M G 8810 Crestview Dr Indnpls	846-9378
M H 1335 N Harbison Av	898-3212
M K 734 N Linwood Av	353-0761
M L 9101 Brentwood Ct	899-5797
M L R R 3 Box 30 Aa	776-0301
M M 8539 Quail Hollow Rd	255-1812
M S 11644 Victoria Ct	844-7639
M Y 9315 E 40th	897-4662
Mae 2506 Madison Av	786-5351
Mae 629 N Olin Av	266-0054
Mae 992 West Drive Woodruff Pl	238-9445
Marc RR 2 Box 121A Fkln	535-4013
Margaret RR 1 Box 284C Nmvh	878-4122
Margaret A 8813 Madison Av	889-6397
Marie 8820 Pendleton Pke	895-1286
Marie 3554 Shelby	786-6490
Marion 10834 E 141st	773-2440
Marion C 1140 N Norfolk	241-4412
Marion C 712 Poplar	535-8679
Marion D 38 Sunset Mnr	831-0133
Marjorie 5162 Ridgeview Way	745-2659
Mark 1134 Golfview Dr	574-9633
Mark C 8082 Morningside Dr	254-9596
Mark C MD 702 Barnhill Dr	274-2440
If No Answer Call	274-5000
Mark E 7718 Island Club Dr	299-8017
Mark E 15 S Tresslar	422-8199
Mark L 489 San Carlos Dr	888-4385
Mark M 530 N Temple Av	638-0549
Mark S 8058 Bowline Dr	823-0298
Mark S 19902 Mule Barn Rd	896-1221
Mark S 3211 S Oxford	788-7525
Marthelda E 2956 Priscilla Av	549-3026
Martin	745-7281
Marvin Earl RFD 1 Pittsboro	892-4253
Mary 724 N De Quincy	356-3217
Mary 419 E Staat St	485-6509
Mary C 1367 N Ewing	262-8026
Mary E 3042 Graceland Av	924-4007
Mary I 1011 Earhart	353-1311
Mary K 7827 Wysong Dr	357-8334
Matt 5318 Wetherby Ct	297-1014
Matthew 2531 Debonair Ter	297-7439
Maurcita 312 Alton Dr	634-7858
Maurice 1070 W Jefferson	736-1202
Max 6 Tanglewood Ct	831-9925
Melissa 404 Thornberry Dr	843-9344
Melissa M 1054 Lismore S Dr	889-5372
Melvin S 721 S Muessing Rd	894-7581
Michael 2932 S Sunrise Dr	861-5969
Michael H 312 Elm Greenwood	881-8875
Michael Q 225 N Maple	873-4975
Michael T 3264 W Mooresville Rd	241-0193
Michelle R 5643 E 24th	359-7999
Mildred B	897-1144
Mina 5125 W Minnesota	241-9163
Miranda M 3025 Oxford Ln	283-3104
Missie 2929 Guilford Av	926-4913
Moreen 5460 University Av	356-0076
Morris A 5955 S Brendonridge Ct	547-7519
Myrtle L 2350 N Gale	542-8012
N	549-9209
N B 1109 N Gale	631-2848
N E	786-6939
N E 8914 Haverstick Rd Indnpolis	846-6034
N L 40 E 82	257-2916
Nancy 4923 Mannsfield Dr	856-1056
Nancy E 2115 S Meridian	781-8806
Norlan RR 1	535-8643
Ola 2949 Adams	546-7190
Ola 3118 Broadway	924-4686
Oris D 958 N Hawthorne Ln	356-4283
Ozzie V 8805 Holliday Dr	848-1434
P 142 Fair Point Dr	887-3943
P 1458 Farley Dr	244-5658
P F	776-2976
P J & Evie 386 E Madison Apt 2	736-5264
P K 1819 Madison Village Dr	787-8861
P M 7240 Dewey Av	356-8378
Pam J 851 Golfview Dr	846-2852
Patricia K	297-4778
Patrick 5125 W 10th	241-4749
Patk F 12121 E Briar Way S Dr	862-3914
Paul 513 S State	462-7424
Paul A 2609 Galaxy Ln	897-1108
Paul Allen 601 S S R 39	745-4845
Paul D 3252 Ashway Dr	293-8642
Paul D 655 Simmons	839-1798
Paul Earle 4557 Chatham Pl	546-5927
Paul K 8610 Colonial Rd	856-5331
ADAMS Paul L 3484 Sherburne Ln	925-2328
Pearl B 4475 N Kitley Av	547-0962
Philip R 7832 Sault Ste Marie Dr	865-9150
Phyllis 8241 Acton Rd	862-2723
Preston K 5943 Rawles Av	357-6589
Q 3085 Coast Dr	293-5351
R 1803 Koehne	634-2646
R A 7214 Carrie Dr	889-8433
R Allen 3905E 550S Lebanon	769-6863
R C 801 W 53	251-6890
R E Hornaday Rd Brownsburg	852-4188
R G	844-0212
R G 3841 Meridee Dr	783-9181
R G 2021 W Ohio	264-9762
R J 5860 Wildflower Dr	297-8825
R L 3801 N Meridian	925-3590
R Morris 15902 Farr Hills Dr	896-5719
R Scott Jr 5635 Kilmer Ln	849-1259
Ralph E 5947 Compton	251-7028
Ralph H 519 Hunting Creek Dr	882-0441
ADAMS RANDY *Owner-Adams Lawncare Service* 5208 Westwood Dr	844-9411
ADAMS Randy 5208 Westwood Dr	571-9337
Randy R 8046 Halyard Way	823-0690
Randy R RR 5 Box 49	736-8223
Raymond 31 Rohn Rd	831-7711
Raymond G 7555 Balinshire N	299-8259
Raymond P 7331 Royal Oakland Dr	823-2497
Raymond V 831 Coolidge	243-9539
Rebecca L 203 S Starter	894-9792
Rex A 8663 Beechmill Ln	887-0843
Rhonda 8513 Beechmill Ln	881-0231
Rhonda A 5824 E Washington	359-9113
Richard 59 Crestwood Dr	831-0861
Richard 2360 E 98th	575-0463
Richard C 103 Susan Ct	773-4722
Richard C Dr 6020 E 65th Pl	578-1775
Richard E 386 Exeter Ct	888-3986
Richard E 1535 N Griswold Rd	271-5968
Richard E 5644 Windmill Dr	291-5819
Richard F Sfc 2447 N Eaton Av	897-9281
Richard L 1543 E Wade	784-6754
Richard M 1640 E Bradbury Av	780-8259
Richard O Atty 3620 N Washington Blvd	925-5505
Res 4517 Central Av	923-5522
Richard S 6602 Sunnyside Rd	823-4996
Richard T 5246 Deer Creek Dr	329-1336
Rick 513 S Drexel Av	356-6115
Rick D 118 N Keeling Av	359-1016
Ricky D 1495 Hillside Dr	738-4046
Ricky Lee 3310 Schofield Av	926-4603
Ricky W 4520 Ferguson Rd	862-6516
Robert 1981 Olivewood Dr	357-3132
Robert RFD 1 Pittsboro	892-4164
Robert 3950 N 1000 E Rd	852-5781
Robt B 6302 South 800E	873-3225
Robt C 1625 Haynes Av	254-0433
Robert C 1061 Norfolk Pl	481-8204
Robt C St Rd 144 Mooresville	831-6531
Robt C Cdr 5314 Wetherby Ct	299-6626
Robt C Jr 4940 Kingsley Dr	254-9200
Robt D 4855 E 71	257-6144
Robert E 10350 Rockford Ct	894-3685
Robt E 102 N Routiers Av	898-3996
Robt F 7448 Stonehurst Ct	849-5526
Robert G 2495W 300N Grnfld	326-2133
Robt J 2006 Colt Rd Indnpolis	881-8455
Robert J 3310 Schofield Av	926-4603
Robert J 1161 Wood Court	786-0729
Robt L 1720 Gerrard Av	248-9647
Robt L 6420 N Keystone Av	253-2817
Robt L 2155 S Oakwood Dr	894-5977
Robt L 10330 E Southport Rd	862-4097
Robert L II 3730 Willowood Dr	891-8943
Robt Lee 6355 Hardegan	786-1676
Robt Lee 741 Winters	272-0214
Robt M 102 Sherry Ln Indnpolis	881-7863
Robert W atty 33 W Washington Shelbyville In Fairland Tel No	835-7260
Robin 5331 Butler Ter	547-9833
Roger RR 5 Box 195	738-4528
Roger D 401 N Harbison Av	899-5257
Roger L 755 W Lincoln	745-2769
Ron 643 Holiday Dr	485-4262
Ron 624 Sunset Blvd	881-3029
Ronald 1020 Bristol Rd	846-7419
Ronald E	862-3838
Ronald Louis 6650 Hearth Lane	831-5620
Roxie O 2441 S Meridian	784-2739
Roy 4391 N Banta Rd 800 W	422-5832
Roy 8910 Old State Rd 37 N	831-6871
Roy V 1901 Lambert	631-2984
Roy V II 313 Teddy Ln	788-9487
Ruth E 47 S Belleview Pl	631-1289
Ruth I	254-9854
S	237-0409
S 5277 Crestview Av	254-0871
S 1714 Georgetown Rd	241-1980
ADAMS S 2226 Hermitage Way	241-9843
S 5342 Holly Springs Ct	299-2012
S 3057 Sugar Maple Ct	848-6131
S 255 Tague	462-3392
S E 8522 Friendship Ln	889-8423
S F 552 N Gray	636-0441
S K 12444 Birch Ln	823-6911
S M 2216 Kenyon Av	356-9617
S R 3072 Eagledale Dr	293-3422
S S 10036 E Troy Av	862-2711
Sandy J 5610 Whitcomb Ter	247-7971
Sarah 1926 W Washington	267-9669
Scott 7028 American Way	845-5116
Scott 610 Barrett	745-2406
Scott M 135 8th N W	571-0319
Shelly 5264 Oak Leaf Dr	255-3321
Shirley	247-1249
Shirley A 922 Cheltenham Way	745-6257
Skip 8830 Pickwick Dr	848-0160
Stacey 414 Clearview Ct	885-7948
Stacia L 7871 Landings Dr	255-5918
Stephen C 11145 Echo Crest E Dr	844-4586
Stephen E 8442 Lindbergh Dr	862-3208
Stephen M 634 E 37th	923-3210
Stephen & Terry RR 1 Box 495	878-5047
Steve 7462 Woodlea Ct	849-6179
Steven 6528 Lupine Ter	328-2705
Steven A 110 Essex Ct Noblesville	877-2329
Steven G 7908 Hoop Rd	889-8539
Steven M 726 Sunset Dr	745-6834
Sue 6037 Central Av	259-4569
Susan 12125 Kingfisher Ct	823-8761
Susan Dunn 1763 E Kelly	788-1729
Sylvester 2703 Crystal Dr	925-5858
T	293-7142
T 655 S Cross	745-2193
T 628 Lakeside Dr	839-8403
T 1210 N Luett Av	687-0422
T 4047 Pittman Pl	328-9139
T Jr 1801 Broadway	283-1731
T L 7002 Crittenden Av	251-1143
Teresa 1361 Panama Av	486-8570
Teresa 3005 Wade	783-7740
Terry Charlottesville In Greenfield Tel No	462-5517
Terry 1293 Palo Vista Rd	887-6930
Terry 516 Randall Ingl	485-5378
Terry J 11602 Cameron Dr	841-3889
Thelma 6214 E 24th	322-8524
Thos 2265 N Kenwood Av	923-9530
Thomas 1923 N Parker Av	464-9518
Thomas 4516 N Pasadena	549-2063
Thos E 8663 Spend A Buck Dr	888-2027
Thomas S 603 Beachway Dr	243-7531
Tim 202 E Clinton	745-2194
Tim 2209 Greentree	882-0025
Tim 6242 Landborough N Dr	845-0933
Tim 116 N McCarty St	485-4468
Tim 200 Pinedale	535-5722
Timothy 4518 Phoenix Dr	244-5134
Timothy C DDS 3520 E 96th	846-3426
Res 6242 N Landborough Dr	845-0959
Timothy J 3145 Chadwood Ln N	875-7281
Timothy K Jr 430 N Park Av	236-9163
Timothy P 6021 Cadillac Dr	241-5824
Tina 4750 N Franklin Rd	545-8386
Todd 4137 Alberta	291-1383
Tom R 2545 Willow	888-4212
Tomiko 5676 Brendon Way W Dr	545-6129
Tony 18 S East	422-8965
Tony 5141 Hillside Av	255-3545
Troy & Tami 119 Schoolhouse Rd	738-9841
V	773-6069
V	924-3184
V J 3722 E Michigan	356-4470
V R 973 N Somerset Av	632-5444
Val M 324 N Denny	356-3110
Vera 916 N Rochester Av	635-4320
Veryl R Jr 1428 W Epler Av	784-5965
Veryl R Sr 1410 W Epler Av	784-7761
Vicky 2847 Harmony Hill Rd Fkln	422-8522
Vincent T 4615 Graceland Av	255-0431
W F 3621 Tiara Ct	290-9325
W M 5251 N Michigan Rd	255-9587
Wallace RR 1 Box 407	878-5939
Walter 503 W Main Greenfield	462-9114
Wanda 7042 Falcon Talon Ln	290-1783
Warner J 3438 Adams	547-8564
Wayne O Jr 7770 Dean Rd	849-1510
Wayne O III atty Ofc One Indiana Square	634-9777
Res 8830 Pickwick Dr	848-0160
Wendell D 92 Walnut Southport	787-2130
Wendell L 941 N Hamilton Av	631-3220
Wm 6453 E Hanna Av	783-0843
Wm 2987 Saint Paul	786-1866
William 5836 University Av	351-5910
Wm A 8142 Aragon Woods Dr	293-2664
Wm B 405 N Indiana	745-2197
William C 5207 N Delaware	259-1825
Wm C 1349 Raymond	839-6444
Wm E 3458 W Murray	241-7077
William E 2357 Norris Dr	271-0813
William E 5458 Old Colony Rd	545-5234

Figure 17.13
A page from the phone book.

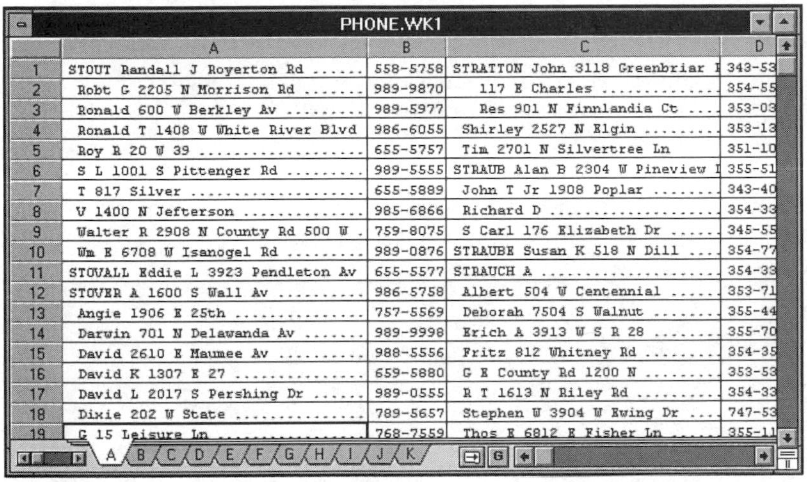

PHONE.WK1

	A	B	C	D
1	STOUT Randall J Royerton Rd	558-5758	STRATTON John 3118 Greenbriar I	343-53
2	Robt G 2205 N Morrison Rd	989-9870	117 E Charles	354-55
3	Ronald 600 W Berkley Av	989-5977	Res 901 N Finnlandia Ct	353-03
4	Ronald T 1408 W White River Blvd	986-6055	Shirley 2527 N Elgin	353-13
5	Roy R 20 W 39	655-5757	Tim 2701 N Silvertree Ln	351-10
6	S L 1001 S Pittenger Rd	989-5555	STRAUB Alan B 2304 W Pineview I	355-51
7	T 817 Silver	655-5889	John T Jr 1908 Poplar	343-40
8	V 1400 N Jefterson	985-6866	Richard D	354-33
9	Walter R 2908 N County Rd 500 W .	759-8075	S Carl 176 Elizabeth Dr	345-55
10	Wm E 6708 W Isanogel Rd	989-0876	STRAUBE Susan K 518 N Dill	354-77
11	STOVALL Eddie L 3923 Pendleton Av	655-5577	STRAUCH A	354-33
12	STOVER A 1600 S Wall Av	986-5758	Albert 504 W Centennial	353-71
13	Angie 1906 E 25th	757-5569	Deborah 7504 S Walnut	355-44
14	Darwin 701 N Delawanda Av	989-9998	Erich A 3913 W S R 28	355-70
15	David 2610 E Maumee Av	988-5556	Fritz 812 Whitney Rd	354-35
16	David K 1307 E 27	659-5880	G E County Rd 1200 N	353-53
17	David L 2017 S Pershing Dr	989-0555	R T 1613 N Riley Rd	354-33
18	Dixie 202 W State	789-5657	Stephen W 3904 W Ewing Dr ..	747-53
19	G 15 Leisure Ln	768-7559	Thos E 6812 E Fisher Ln	355-11

A / B / C / D / E / F / G / H / I / J / K

Figure 17.14
Phone book lists now in spreadsheet format.

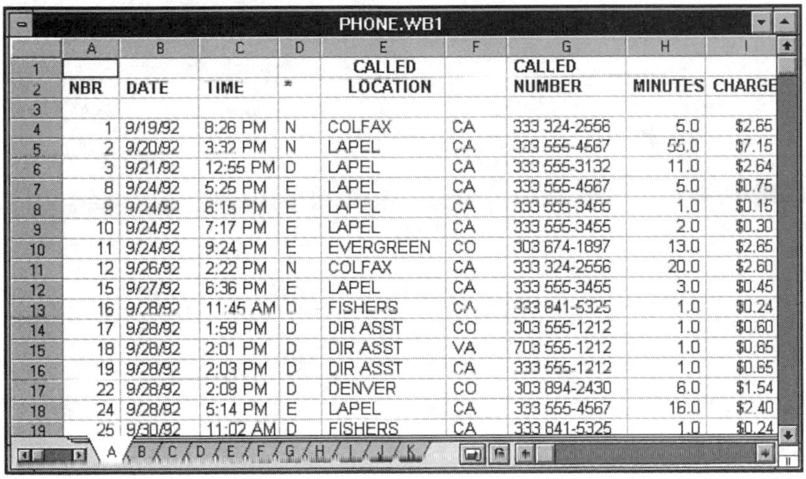

PHONE.WB1

	A	B	C	D	E	F	G	H	I
1					CALLED		CALLED		
2	NBR	DATE	TIME	*	LOCATION		NUMBER	MINUTES	CHARGE
3									
4	1	9/19/92	8:26 PM	N	COLFAX	CA	333 324-2556	5.0	$2.65
5	2	9/20/92	3:32 PM	N	LAPEL	CA	333 555-4567	55.0	$7.15
6	3	9/21/92	12:55 PM	D	LAPEL	CA	333 555-3132	11.0	$2.64
7	8	9/24/92	5:25 PM	E	LAPEL	CA	333 555-4567	5.0	$0.75
8	9	9/24/92	6:15 PM	E	LAPEL	CA	333 555-3455	1.0	$0.15
9	10	9/24/92	7:17 PM	E	LAPEL	CA	333 555-3455	2.0	$0.30
10	11	9/24/92	9:24 PM	E	EVERGREEN	CO	303 674-1897	13.0	$2.65
11	12	9/26/92	2:22 PM	N	COLFAX	CA	333 324-2556	20.0	$2.60
12	15	9/27/92	6:36 PM	E	LAPEL	CA	333 555-3455	3.0	$0.45
13	16	9/28/92	11:45 AM	D	FISHERS	CA	333 841-5325	1.0	$0.24
14	17	9/28/92	1:59 PM	D	DIR ASST	CO	303 555-1212	1.0	$0.60
15	18	9/28/92	2:01 PM	D	DIR ASST	VA	703 555-1212	1.0	$0.65
16	19	9/28/92	2:03 PM	D	DIR ASST	CA	333 555-1212	1.0	$0.65
17	22	9/28/92	2:09 PM	D	DENVER	CO	303 894-2430	6.0	$1.54
18	24	9/28/92	5:14 PM	E	LAPEL	CA	333 555-4567	16.0	$2.40
19	25	9/30/92	11:02 AM	D	FISHERS	CA	333 841-5325	1.0	$0.24

A / B / C / D / E / F / G / H / I / J / K

Figure 17.15
Scanned phone bills as a spreadsheet.

III

Putting Windows to Work

Integrating OCR Software with Other Windows Applications

One of the advantages of OCR in the Windows environment is that you can integrate OCR with other programs that take advantage of Windows' integration technology. Suppose you scan a number of documents daily and then import the text into your word processor. It would be easy to scan the text, save it as a text file, open your word processor, and import the file. An even easier solution is available, however.

Suppose you have Word for Windows and OmniPage Professional. OmniPage comes with a WordBasic macro you can install (OmniPage even installs the macro automatically) that enables you to scan a document while working in Word for Windows and then have the text inserted into the current document. What could be easier? Figures 17.16 through 17.19 illustrate a step-by-step example.

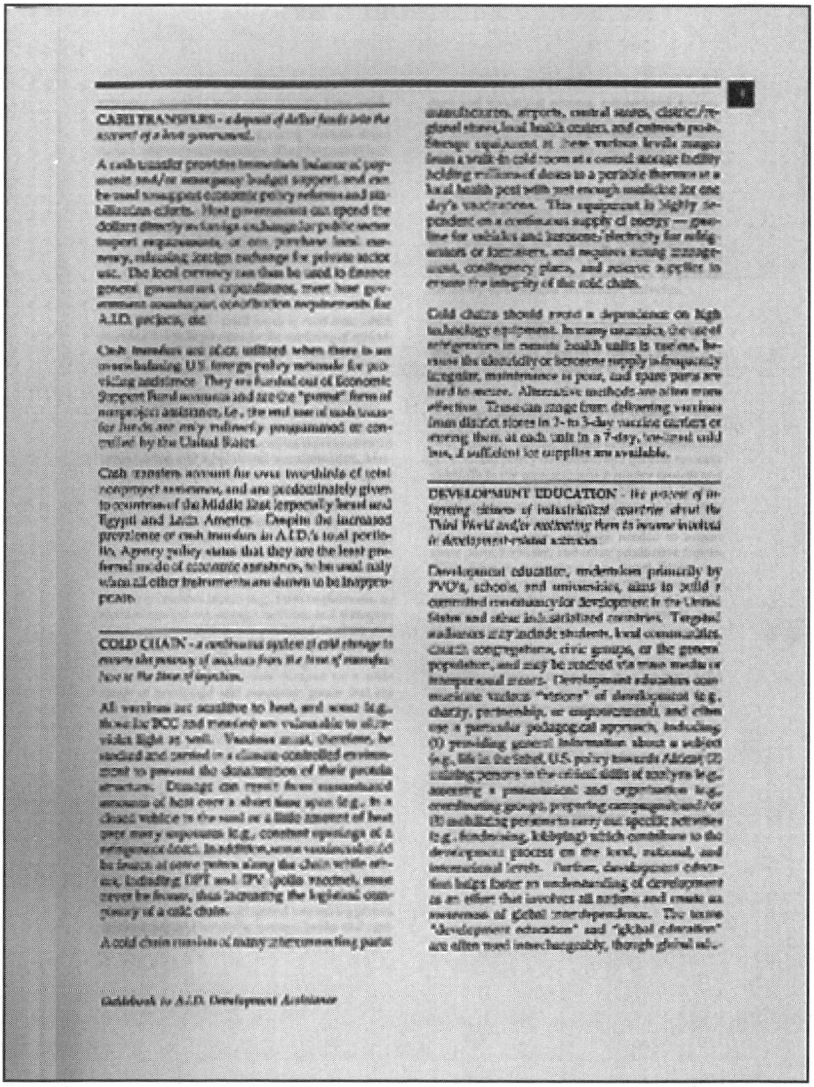
CASH TRANSFERS
COLD CHAIN
DEVELOPMENT EDUCATION
Guidebook to A.I.D. Development Assistance

Figure 17.16
Step 1: Find the document and place it into the scanner.

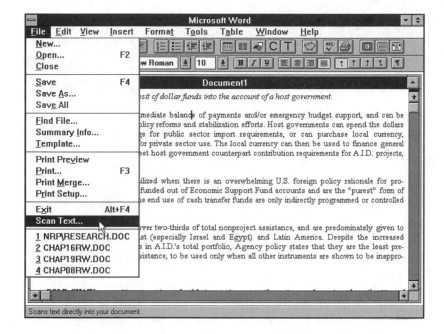

Figure 17.17
Step 2: Choose File, Scan Text from the Word menu.

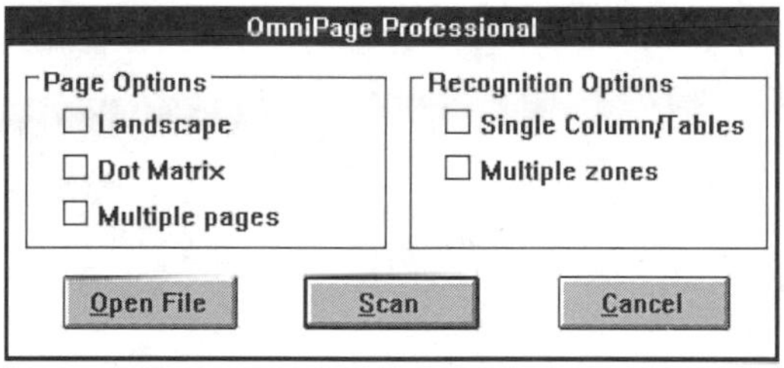

Figure 17.18
Step 3: Set the scanning options.

OCR opens up a world of possibilities for businesses today. As prices for quality scanning hardware and OCR software continue to drop, character recognition technology continues to improve and reach higher accuracy rates. As more companies see the value of maintaining and working with information in electronic form, OCR will continue to be more mainstream. Look for a true "paperless office" coming to your neighborhood soon.

III

Putting Windows to Work

Figure 17.19
Figure 17.19
Step 4: OmniPage
quickly and
seamlessly inserts
the text into a
Word document.

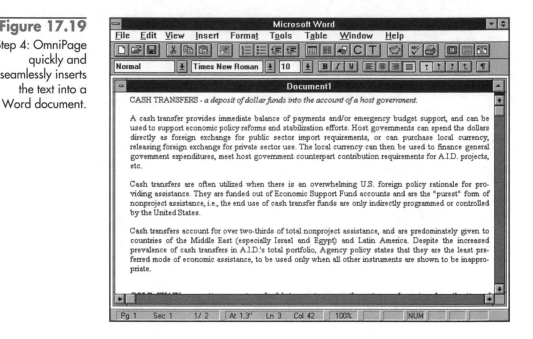

Chapter Snapshot

There are many aspects to communicating under Windows. If you are using Windows for Workgroups 3.11, you have additional capabilities for communicating with other users, including built-in e-mail and fax capability. Chapters 29 and 30 cover communicating from Windows for Workgroups. This chapter examines general Windows communications issues.

Windows, by virtue of its multitasking capabilities, is a natural platform for communications. In this chapter, you take a look at the following issues and how they relate to the Windows PC:

In this chapter you will learn about a number of data communications topics and how they relate to the Windows operating environment. For further reference, you might want to consult the Windows Resource Kit, as well as the SYSINI.WRI file that is placed in your Windows subdirectory during installation.

CHAPTER

Communicating through Windows

A personal computer that cannot communicate is like an island in the middle of a vast ocean of data. You can perform many complex tasks on such a computer, but you are limited to working with the data on your hard disk (or floppy disk). Without a communications mechanism, you are cut off from the outside world—and the almost limitless data that is out there.

Fortunately, a phone line can help your computer access that data. When you equip your system with a modem and communications software (and connect the modem to your phone line), you open the door to literally hundreds of computer data networks, and thousands of computer bulletin board systems, all of which bring the world to your PC.

First, take a look at fax technology and how it is integrated with the Windows operating environment.

Faxing under Windows

Fax technology has come a long way in the past decade. Once an obscure technology that was affordable only to the largest of corporations, faxing has grown to be one of the most integral parts of the business community. Few businesses could function without the services of in-house fax machines, and the phrase "fax it to me" has become almost as common as "it's in the mail."

Coinciding with the rising popularity and lowered costs of faxing is the proliferation of personal computers within the corporate enterprise. The idea of a PC on every desk, once only a fantasy, is now very much a reality as today's hardware prices fall more into the reach of small- to medium-sized businesses.

For many users, the natural reaction has been to try to integrate these two technologies, creating a single, combined computing and communications device that is as seamless as your local desktop printer. And no better platform is available to aid in this integration than Windows. Windows, with its what-you-see-is-what-you-get (WYSIWYG) interface, built-in support for graphical images, and inherent device-independence, has proven to be an excellent platform for fax applications.

Comparing Windows Faxing with Other Fax Technologies

Faxing under Windows is quite possibly one of the simplest endeavors you'll ever undertake. Because Windows is a graphical environment, it is easy to preview your faxes to see exactly how they will look when sent. In addition, by utilizing the device-independence of Windows, a fax software package can fully integrate itself into the Windows environment. This usually is accomplished by a special-purpose device driver that is bundled with the fax software application. Posing as a printer driver, this driver intercepts the print jobs sent to its phantom printer and redirects them to the fax application for processing. The result is seamless WYSIWYG faxing from Windows, as demonstrated by figure 18.1.

Windows for Workgroups 3.11 includes a product called At Work Fax that integrates shared fax capability with Microsoft Mail (which also is included with Windows for Workgroups). Windows 3.11 does not include At Work Fax, but there are numerous third-party fax applications that you can use in Windows. For information on At Work Fax, refer to Chapter 28, "Sharing Resources in Windows."

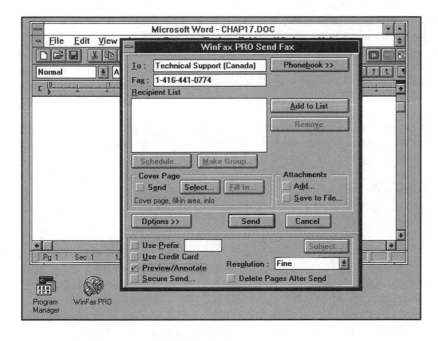

Figure 18.1
WinFax Pro 3.0 is an excellent example of the seamlessness of Windows-based faxing.

Stand-Alone Fax Machines

Faxing under Windows differs greatly from traditional, stand-alone faxing. With Windows, you can utilize the power of the personal computer not only to send and receive faxes, but to manage them as well. Faxes can be indexed and stored in a fax database, and then retrieved by using keywords and other data. Most fax applications also can compress fax images, which saves disk space.

In addition, because Windows is a multitasking environment, you can process faxes in the background while you continue to work productively in the foreground. Windows fax applications can be configured to remain minimized on the Windows desktop, monitoring the fax modem and waiting for a call. Then, when a fax arrives, these applications spring into action, processing the incoming fax, then saving it for later viewing or editing.

DOS-Based Faxing

Faxing under Windows also differs from DOS-based faxing, but not as significantly as it does from the traditional, stand-alone approach. With DOS-based faxing, you often are limited by the available video hardware and CPU processing power. Fax applications must be written to support a variety of video boards so that they can function in a sufficient number of environments.

In contrast, Windows fax applications need not concern themselves with video or other hardware issues. Windows is, by nature, a device-independent environment. Each application communicates with the system (and its hardware) through established application programming interfaces (APIs). As a result, a fax application need only make the proper API calls; Windows takes care of the rest and draws the windows, dialog boxes, and bitmapped images as the application requires them.

DOS-based fax applications do not have the multitasking advantages that Windows applications possess. Instead, they must rely on terminate-and-stay-resident programs (TSRs) and complex DOS device drivers to achieve true background operation. This makes installation and configuration that much more difficult, and introduces the possibility of a TSR conflicting with an important piece of application software.

Sending Faxes

Sending faxes under Windows is a relatively straightforward process. As noted earlier, most Windows fax applications provide a custom device driver, one that emulates a Windows printer driver. If you want to fax a word processing document to a colleague in another city, you simply select the fax driver as the current printer and then print the document to the fax. A sample fax driver dialog box is shown in figure 18.2.

Figure 18.2
The WinFax
printer driver
dialog box.

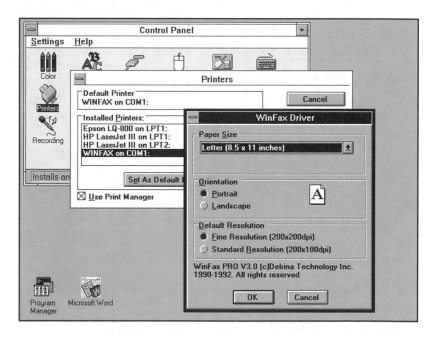

After you have sent your print job to the fax printer driver, it gathers the application's output and converts it to the appropriate resolution and format for transmission by the fax modem. It then launches the fax application, enabling you to select a recipient for the fax. Most fax applications provide a phone book–like mechanism for storing frequently used numbers, and in many cases you also can specify whether you would like to preview and possibly annotate the fax before sending. Figure 18.3 shows the dialog box in WinFax Pro that provides access to the WinFax phone book, which you use to store recipients' names and fax phone numbers.

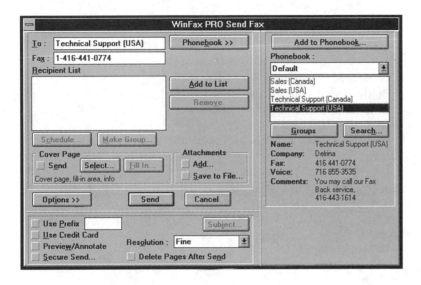

Figure 18.3
With the WinFax Pro Send Fax dialog box you can choose a recipient from a phone book and set other options.

After you have selected an appropriate target user, the fax application then minimizes itself on the Windows desktop and begins the process of dialing the target system and transmitting the fax in the background. Depending on the complexity of the images and the number of pages involved, you might see little or no degradation in foreground system performance as your fax application operates behind the scenes.

Receiving Faxes

Receiving a fax in Windows is even simpler than sending one. With most fax applications, all you have to do is have the application running and configured to receive; you then minimize the application and continue working in the foreground. If a fax call occurs while you are working, the fax application will answer the call, receive the fax in the background, and then hang up and reset the modem.

Managing Faxes

What you can do with faxes after they have been received is highly dependent on the fax management capabilities of your fax application. Full-featured products, such as WinFax Pro, offer a number of options for searching, sorting, and storing your faxes. Faxes typically are saved into send or receive logs upon transmission/reception, and you perform your various manipulation operations on the entries in these logs.

One of the most useful features of any management-capable fax application is the capability to search the fax logs. Most applications enable you to do a search based on a number of criteria, including the date/time of the fax event, the number of pages, the identity of the sending station, and in some cases on keywords that you assign to a fax after it has been processed.

Fax annotation is a feature in many high-end fax applications. By incorporating a set of basic drawing tools into an application's viewing module, many vendors make it possible for you to edit directly a sent or received fax image. The tools range from freehand paintbrushes to geometric shapes and even text. In many cases, you can direct the fax application to provide a preview of a fax as it processes that fax for transmission. This enables you to see how the fax will look and to annotate directly the image before it is sent. A good example of this can be seen in the viewing module of WinFax Pro 3.0, as shown in figure 18.4.

Figure 18.4
The WinFax Pro 3.0 viewer module features a basic set of fax annotation tools, enabling you to edit directly your sent or received faxes.

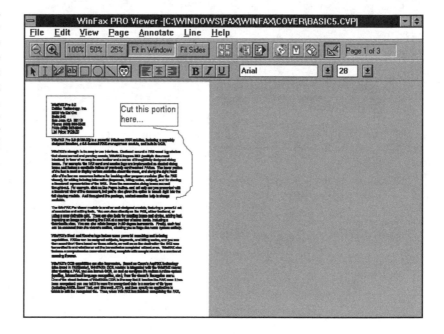

Another useful feature is the capability to compress faxes. Faxes are usually bitmapped images, so they often are easily compressed to as little as 20–30 percent of their uncompressed size. This in turn frees up disk space and enables you to store more faxes than would be possible without compression.

Probably the most important feature of any complete fax solution is the integration of optical character recognition (OCR) into the application. With the addition of OCR capabilities, fax applications enable you to recognize the received faxes and turn a bitmap image into editable text.

Users of fax software, be warned! The quality of OCR implementations varies greatly from application to application, and many software vendors incorporate existing technology from leading OCR developers—as opposed to creating their own systems.

To be safe, stick with the packages that are based on established OCR systems, which are technically mature and offer a high degree of speed and accuracy.

Understanding Modem Communications

Traditional data communications (modem to modem, modem to host, and so on) also has become an important application for the Windows environment. As with faxing, communicating with a modem has benefited from the user-friendly interface and multitasking capabilities of Windows.

Even though modern Windows communications applications take much of the sting out of communicating with other computers, there still are many issues that no amount of interface creativity can overcome. Modem-based communication is, by nature, a complicated endeavor.

First, consider the modem itself. This device looks deceptively simple, but it actually is one of the more complex peripherals around. The modem's job is to convert the digital data from your computer into a series of analog signals, which can be carried over traditional, voice-grade telephone lines.

The modem communicates with other modems by *modulating* (encoding) the frequency of the analog signal, and in turn *demodulates* (interprets) the incoming analog signal that is being transmitted by the other modem. Thus you have the term *modem*, which is an acronym for MOdulator/DEModulator.

Second, consider the issue of compatibility. Modems must adhere to a common set of modulated analog signals to form a basis for communication. These modem communication standards are overseen by the Committee Consultative International for Telephony and Telegraphy (CCITT).

The CCITT sets down international guidelines on the interaction of modems at various speeds, defining the link negotiation (*handshaking*, wherein the modems establish an initial connection), *signaling* (the modulation itself), error correction procedures, and data compression algorithms to be used during a modem conversation. The CCITT guidelines are well established and widely accepted, so you should always look for modems that feature these standards.

III

Putting Windows to Work

Finally, consider the issue of a modem's software interface. Most modems feature a subset (or superset) of the de facto industry standard Hayes AT command set. The Hayes AT command set is the interface used by one of the more popular modem vendors, Hayes Microcomputer Products, Inc., and is almost universally accepted as the standard way that a communications application should interact with a modem.

Most communications applications, including those that run under Windows, assume that you will be communicating with a Hayes-compatible modem. If your modem has additional features, such as a proprietary error correction or data compression system for communicating with a modem from that same vendor, it normally is enabled through a command that is part of a superset of the normal Hayes AT command set.

Other issues that pertain to modems include *terminal emulation* (how your computer's console interacts with the system on the other end), file transfer protocols, and how your Windows communications application handles multitasking. You will learn more about all these issues as the following section delves into the world of Windows-based communications software.

Using Windows Communications Software

Communications software has benefited greatly from the user interface and multitasking capabilities of the Windows environment. By using the inherent graphical nature of Windows, communications applications are now able to provide an unparalleled level of visual feedback. Archaic configuration options are now made clearer by the use of pull-down list boxes, integrated dialog boxes, and colorful, interactive configuration controls.

User-Friendly Communications Software

Communications software often is complex. Parameters for modem configuration, terminal emulation, and serial port control can overwhelm even the most experienced PC user. Much of the problem lies in the interface of the communications software itself; the sheer number of options make integrating the software into a cohesive whole nearly impossible. The result is a product that is difficult to master and that forces you to navigate through countless menus and submenus as you search for the appropriate option.

Environmental Advantages

Windows eliminates feature confusion by enabling a software vendor to organize logically various options, incorporating them into compound dialog boxes that interact with each other. In addition, by using multiple windows, an application can display more information on-screen, making the process of trial-and-error less time-consuming. A good example of an integrated configuration interface is shown in figure 18.5.

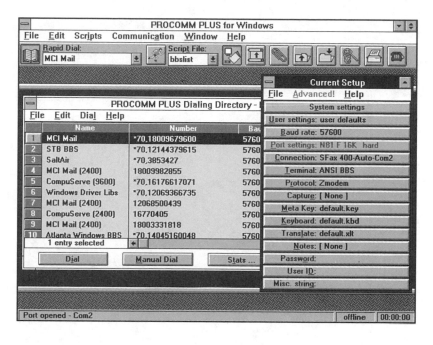

Figure 18.5
The ProComm Plus for Windows interface.

Another advantage of using multiple windows and dialog boxes is seamlessly managing multiple communications sessions. By utilizing the Windows Multiple Document Interface (MDI), an application can maintain multiple client windows within its own window. MDI often is utilized by communications applications to provide numerous virtual consoles, enabling you to view multiple online sessions simultaneously. In many cases you can even copy and paste data from one window to the next. Figure 18.6 shows an application that makes good use of MDI to facilitate multisession operation.

Background Operation

Because Windows is a multitasking environment, one of the major advantages enjoyed by any Windows-based communications application is the capability to operate in the background. By operating in the background, a communications application frees you to continue working in the foreground. This is especially useful during time-consuming operations, such as large file transfers and long screen-capture sessions. Instead of waiting for your PC to complete the operation, you can continue to be productive and better utilize your Intel-based PC's capabilities.

Configuring Communications Software

The most difficult issue you face when working with a communications application is the configuration phase. Although Windows has enabled vendors to eliminate the headaches from this process (through the use of dialog boxes, custom controls, and so on), it still is a complex process that requires some understanding of what each option represents.

Figure 18.6
HyperACCESS for
Windows utilizes
MDI to facilitate
multisession
operation.

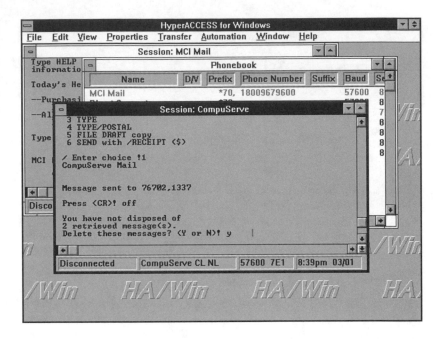

Figure 18.6
HyperACCESS for
Windows utilizes
MDI to facilitate
multisession
operation.

Terminal Emulation

A critical part of configuration is that of setting the appropriate terminal emulation. Most communications applications emulate a number of different terminal types to facilitate interaction with a wide variety of host systems. Because each host system (IBM mainframes, DEC minicomputers, and so on) expects to be interacting with a certain type of terminal (3270 or 5250 for IBM, VT series for DEC), your communications application must be configured to emulate the appropriate type of host system.

This type of configuration is true for all aspects of interaction, from keyboard mapping (what key sends which escape sequence) to display attributes (does the host system require 25 lines on screen? 40 lines?). Your communications application must take all these factors into consideration when sending and receiving data to and from the host system.

Terminal emulation is one area in which Windows-based communications applications really shine. Windows is a graphical environment, so communications applications are not limited to the hardware-based text mode that restricts many DOS communications applications. As a result, they can display any number of lines on-screen, as well as emulate graphics terminals (normally a difficult feat for DOS-based applications).

Another advantage of being Windows-based is the way in which an application enables you to configure terminal emulation. Beyond traditional dialog boxes (for setting terminal type, character translation, and so on), Windows communications applications often put the graphical nature of the Windows interface to good use in areas such as keyboard remapping. By creating a complete, virtual keyboard on-screen, a Windows-based communications application enables you to reconfigure keyboard settings through a simple point-and-click operation. ProComm Plus for Windows features just such a virtual keyboard, as illustrated in figure 18.7.

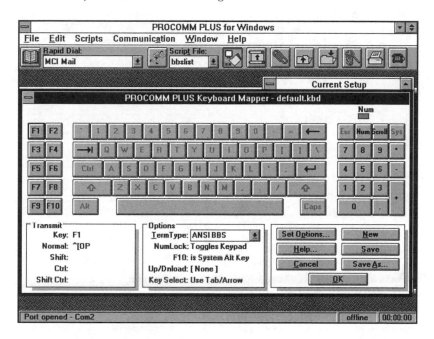

Figure 18.7
The ProComm Plus for Windows keyboard remapping module.

Modem Settings

Another configuration area that benefits greatly from the Windows interface is modem configuration. By grouping most of the major configuration options into a logical series of nested dialog boxes, a Windows-based communications application enables you to access the most important functions, such as interface flow control and pulse or tone dialing. An excellent example of integrated, nested configuration dialog boxes is found in HyperACCESS for Windows, shown in figure 18.8.

Possibly the most important piece of configuration data is the modem initialization string. This complex series of AT commands is used to configure a variety of your modem's operational parameters. Everything from flow control, to the type of error correction and data compression to use, is controlled by your modem's initialization string. Most Windows-based communications applications provide a list of supported modems, and then use a custom initialization string database to look up a string for, and then configure, your modem.

III

Putting Windows to Work

Figure 18.8
HyperACCESS for
Windows uses
logically grouped
dialog boxes to
facilitate modem
configuration.

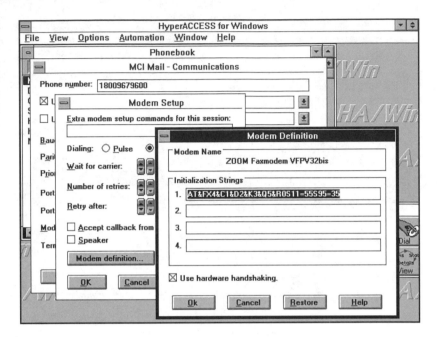

After you have settled on an optimal initialization string, it often is useful to write that string into your modem's nonvolatile RAM (NVRAM). Most modems provide onboard EEPROMs for storing these configuration parameters, and can be instructed to load them when the modem is turned on or receives a certain command (usually ATZ). You then can use the initialization string options in your communications software to make any run-time changes that might be required.

File Transfer Protocols

When two computers want to transfer files between one another, they normally must settle on a common transfer protocol to facilitate the operation. *Transfer protocols* define how the data is to be encapsulated or encoded during the transfer, and often also include a number of error-correction mechanisms such as checksums, cyclical redundancy checks (CRCs), and acknowledgment blocks.

The encapsulation and encoding enables the data to be transferred without being interpreted as an actual terminal command (many files contain byte streams that might trigger a terminal or terminal emulator's functions). The error-correction mechanisms work to maintain the integrity of the transferred data in case of such problems as line noise and overruns.

The most popular general-purpose file transfer protocol is Zmodem. Developed by Chuck Foresberg, Zmodem has a number of powerful features that make it the protocol of choice among experienced users. First, it enables a type of transfer known as a *streaming transfer,* wherein the entire file is sent in a series of blocks without any acknowledgment from the receiving end. Error correction is facilitated by the use of 16- or 32-bit CRCs, and the fact that the receiver need not answer back for each block received makes it a very fast and efficient protocol.

Zmodem also is highly configurable. Most aspects of the protocol's behavior, from transmission type to error correction used, can be adjusted. Finally, it has the capability to resume a file transfer, restarting the procedure where the previously interrupted transfer left off. This latter feature is especially useful when a long transfer is interrupted after much of the data has been transmitted. Instead of having to resend the entire file, Zmodem enables you to use what you've already received while simply transmitting the remaining bytes.

Other popular protocols include Ymodem, Xmodem, Kermit, and CompuServe B/B+. Xmodem, Ymodem, and Kermit all are *block-oriented protocols;* that is, they send data in a predefined block size, and the receiver always acknowledges each block. The acknowledgment aspect of these protocols reduces their overall throughput, because the sending system must pause after each block as it waits for the receiver to verify the data (through checksums or CRCs) and acknowledge its uncorrupted reception.

CompuServe B/B+ is a special-purpose protocol designed for performing file transfers through the CompuServe Information Service. It too is a block-oriented protocol, and features an autoresume feature similar to Zmodem's. Kermit also is a special-purpose protocol, primarily used for performing file transfers with minicomputers. These protocols are compared in table 18.1.

III

Putting Windows to Work

Table 18.1
Common File Transfer Protocols

Protocol	Transfer Type	Error Correction	Auto-resume	Application
Xmodem	Block-Oriented	CRC or Checksum	No	General Purpose
Ymodem	Block-Oriented	CRC or Checksum	No	General Purpose
Ymodem-G	Streaming	None	No	General Purpose
Zmodem	Streaming	CRC	Yes	General Purpose
CompuServeB/B+	Block-Oriented	CRC	Yes	CompuServe
Kermit	Block-Oriented	CRC or Checksum	No	PC-Host

Windows provides little in the way of enhancement to file transfer protocols. Other than an improved interface—for instance, in the form of integrated dialog boxes for configuration—file transfer protocols are handled in the same way as in DOS-based communications applications. As long as you tell the host system to transmit using a protocol that your application supports, you should be in good shape.

Host Mode

Most communications applications provide some sort of *host mode,* whereby the application configures your PC to act as host to a calling PC. Host modes vary among applications, in both the number and types of options provided. Some applications provide only the most basic file transfer capabilities, whereas others are more extravagant and offer limited e-mail and conferencing features.

As with file transfer protocols, little has changed in the transition from DOS to Windows-based communications applications. Most of the functions remain the same, and the only major benefit from Windows is the capability for a host mode communications application to operate in the background.

Special-Purpose Windows Communications Software

Until now, you have been learning mostly about general-purpose Windows communications software and the unique features these applications provide due to their graphical environment. A number of special-purpose applications also have arrived on the scene, however, and you might find that the integrated, more focused set of capabilities they provide makes interacting with their supported services considerably less painful.

General- vs. Special-Purpose Communications Software

The primary differences between general-purpose and special-purpose communications applications center around the number and type of features available. A general-purpose application might support dozens of terminals in an effort to be as flexible as possible, but a special-purpose application needs only to support the terminal type required for its supported service.

Similarly, the general-purpose application usually provides a number of file transfer protocol options, but a special-purpose application is more selective, offering only those required for transferring files to and from a particular online system.

These differences also are reflected in the applications' interfaces. Whereas a general-purpose application might provide a toolbar with options for uploading, downloading, and initiating a call, a special-purpose application might use that same toolbar concept, yet stock it with options unique to its supported online service.

CompuServe Information Manager for Windows

One of the more widely used special-purpose applications is the CompuServe Information Manager for Windows (WinCIM). WinCIM builds on the success of the DOS-based CompuServe Information Manager, utilizing Windows' MDI features to create an environment of overlapping windows and nested dialog boxes that correspond to the various menu layers of the CompuServe Information Service itself (see fig. 18.9).

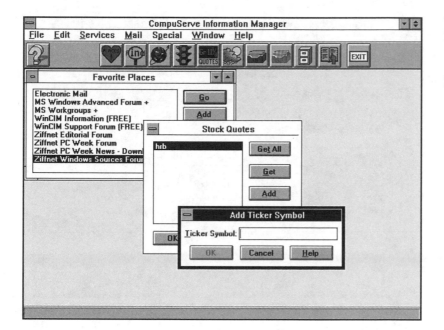

Figure 18.9
The CompuServe Information Manager for Windows.

WinCIM makes good use of color and custom controls, providing a toolbar of colorful icons that represent various services offered by CompuServe. Clicking on the icon with a cloud and sun, for example, brings you to the service's weather section. Other options include the capability to download forum messages in the background and to create and reply to messages offline.

A Note from the Author

CompuServe also offers an application called CompuServe Navigator that automates access to virtually all of CompuServe's services. With CompuServe Navigator you can automate the process of reading and responding to e-mail and forum messages, saving a considerable amount of money on connect-time charges. CompuServe Navigator also automates access to other CompuServe services and enables you to mark and automatically upload and download files. CompuServe Navigator is available for $30 (with a $10 usage credit) in the CSNAV forum on CompuServe.

MCI Mail: The Wire

The Wire from Swfte International is another special-purpose communications application. Its features are geared toward interaction with the MCI Mail e-mail network. Options for organizing and indexing messages, as well as the capability to download messages in the background and automatically poll your MCI Mail account at configurable intervals, make The Wire a popular choice among Windows-based MCI Mail users (see fig. 18.10).

Figure 18.10
The Wire from Swfte International.

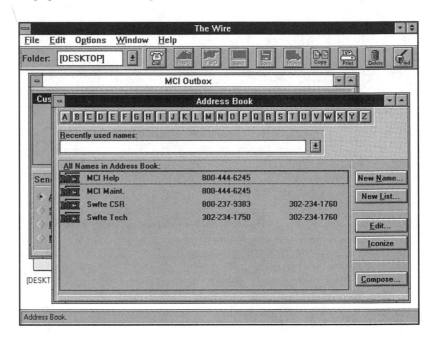

One nice feature of The Wire is the way it uses the Windows graphical environment to implement a series of organizational folders. This hierarchical folder system makes it easy to categorize messages and keep your MCI Mail account under control.

Using Windows by Remote Control

Remotely controlling the Windows environment is a difficult process. A tremendous amount of data, including GDI (Graphical Device Interface) coordinates and mouse position, all must be transmitted to the remote site for processing and replication. This requires considerable data communications bandwidth; the link between the host and remote PCs must be very fast to create a responsive environment.

Differences between Dial-In and LAN-Based Remote Control

To compensate for the high volume of data, most remote control applications require that you use high-speed modems when dealing with a dial-in system, and a high-bandwidth network architecture when dealing with LAN-based systems. A minimum of a V.32 modem (which has a theoretical throughput of 38,400 bits per second) usually is required for dial-in support, and 10 megabits per second Ethernet for LAN-based remote control. Even with such high-speed links, the responsiveness of the environment rests heavily on the efficiency of your particular remote control software.

Modem-based communications, for example, require the remote control application to make the data as compressible as possible so that your error correcting/data compressing modem can approach its theoretical maximum throughput. In contrast, LAN-based systems have no hardware-based data compression to rely on, and instead must implement compression in their own remote control code. Applications that support both environments (dial-in and LAN-based) must feature dual personalities and adapt appropriately to the transmission media in use.

LAN-Based Remote Control

Most LAN-based remote control applications are designed for use as corporate help-desk tools. These applications feature extensive network transport protocol support so that they can run across a number of different network operating system environments. They also provide extended features, such as the capability to remain connected to the PC as it exits Windows. This enables you to perform DOS-level tasks, such as editing a target user's AUTOEXEC.BAT and CONFIG.SYS file. In many cases you can even force the remote system to reboot and then automatically reestablish a connection when the system is booted.

An excellent example of a sophisticated LAN-based remote control application is Proxy from Funk Software. Proxy enables you to connect simultaneously to multiple workstations, and then provides you with total control over their operation. You can force them to exit Windows, cause them to reboot, and have them automatically reestablish their remote control sessions, all from across the network. Proxy also enables you to view multiple remote control sessions simultaneously; it implements its viewer modules as independent Windows applications, which can be arranged side-by-side on your Windows desktop (see fig. 18.11).

Dial-In Remote Control

Dial-in remote control is more difficult to implement than LAN-based remote control, primarily because of the relatively low bandwidth provided by today's modems. Even the fastest V.32bis connection (the current top of the line, as designated by the CCITT) represents only a fraction of the bandwidth available on a LAN. As a result, remote control vendors go to great lengths to optimize the performance of their dial-in products, and the interfaces often feature few frills.

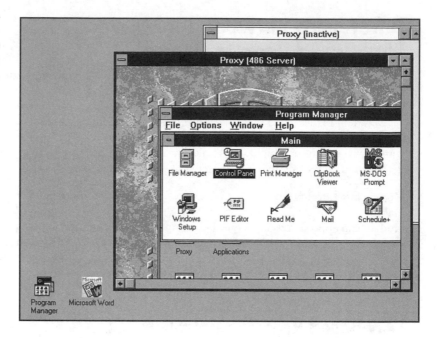

Figure 18.11
Two Proxy remote
control sessions on
the desktop.

The first thing you notice about dial-in remote control applications is their lack of multisession support. Unlike LAN-based products such as Proxy, dial-in applications normally are geared toward a single remote/host connection. In addition, the overhead from trying to provide multiple remote control sessions would make the performance of such a product unbearably slow.

Another distinct feature of most dial-in applications is the file transfer module. Unlike LAN-based remote control, with which you can simply copy a file to a network server to gain access to it at the remote site, dial-in applications must compensate because they are providing the only link between remote and the host. No other common ground exists between the two locations, and the remote control application must provide some sort of file transfer capabilities to be truly useful. Figure 18.12 illustrates the simple interface of a typical dial-in remote control package.

Using Communications Ports under Windows

Working with serial communications under a multitasking environment such as Windows requires some knowledge of how the environment interacts with your PC's hardware. Unlike the DOS world, in which only a single application is executing at any given time (and that application is granted exclusive access to the PC's hardware), a multitasking environment must keep track of the interactions between multiple applications, each executing simultaneously within the PC. At any given time, one or more of those applications might require access to a particular hardware component within the PC. The operating environment (in this case, Windows) must arbitrate access to each PC hardware component so that multiple applications can effectively share a limited set of resources—namely, the hardware and peripherals of the PC.

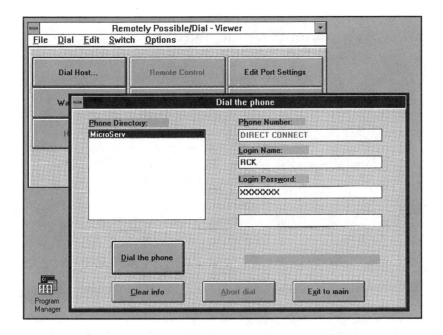

Figure 18.12
Remotely Possible/Dial's user-friendly interface.

One way that an operating environment achieves this sort of arbitration is through a technique known as *device virtualization.* By creating a virtualized interface to a device (usually in the form of a device driver), and then requiring that each application go through appropriate operating system channels to gain access to this virtual device interface, you easily can create an environment in which no two applications step on each other's toes. Because the operating environment arbitrates access to the virtual device interfaces, it can control which application gets control and for how long. As a result, the process of device virtualization provides the basis upon which any multitasking operating environment is built.

How the Serial Ports Function under Windows

Windows is no exception to the device virtualization rule. Like any true multitasking environment, it virtualizes each hardware device and requires that applications make explicit API calls to access them. This is clearly evident in the design of the Windows communications subsystem. Windows features a number of device drivers and virtual device drivers, all of which work in unison to provide a virtualized interface to both Windows and DOS applications running under Windows. What your application sees is

III

Putting Windows to Work

(what appears to be) a traditional PC serial port; in reality, it is interacting with a software representation of that port, which in turn interacts with the rest of the Windows communications subsystem to perform the requested I/O operation. The various drivers and the functions they perform are outlined in table 18.2.

Table 18.2
Components of the Windows Communications Subsystem

Driver Name	Function
COMM.DRV	Provides the low-level interface functions, including the interrupt handling routine that directly services the serial port's registers and buffers
VCD	Arbitrates access to the serial port and provides the virtualized interface to DOS communications applications
COMMBUFF	Works in conjunction with VCD to provide buffering between a DOS communications application and the serial port

All these drivers are installed at run time and defined in the Windows SYSTEM.INI file. COMM.DRV is by far the most critical component in the subsystem; it provides the low-level interface between the serial port and the rest of the communications subsystem, and the other drivers build upon it. COMM.DRV also provides the all-important interrupt handling routine, which is a special program that the operating system installs at run time and uses to handle interrupt requests as they are made by various hardware devices.

When the serial port needs to be serviced (for example, a byte has arrived at the port), it generates an interrupt request to the CPU. The CPU examines which interrupt line the request came in on, then looks up the memory location of the corresponding interrupt handling routine in a special internal table called the interrupt descriptor table. It then turns control of the operating system over to the interrupt handler (in this case, COMM.DRV) and waits while the handler services the request. Control then is returned to the CPU, and execution continues. The preceding interrupt-driven scenario is the basis upon which Windows multitasks its communications sessions.

Data communications are, by nature, very timing-sensitive. If data arrives in a particular place and at a particular time (the serial port), and the operating environment isn't ready for it, that data might be lost.

Timing becomes even more of an issue in a cooperatively multitasked environment such as Windows. Under Windows, each application must yield to the system for multitasking to occur; the Windows scheduler has no way of preempting a running Windows application. As a result, the system always is at risk of a misbehaving application hogging the CPU and consequently bringing all other applications to a halt.

This sort of situation would prove unacceptable to a communications application. If the application is unable to process incoming data, that data might very well get lost at the serial port (data not retrieved from the serial port will be overwritten with subsequent incoming data).

Because the cooperative multitasking architecture of Windows makes guaranteeing CPU time for any one application nearly impossible, Windows itself controls the processing of data from the serial port. By relying on the COMM.DRV and its role as an interrupt handling routine, Windows is able to guarantee that the data will have a place to go once it arrives at the PC. This is true even if the communications application itself is unable to respond (for example, when another application is in control of the CPU).

COMM.DRV can do this because it is defined as an interrupt handling routine by Windows. The CPU cannot ignore an interrupt request (see the following section for situations when Windows appears to ignore an interrupt request); it is forced to respond by the architecture of the Intel-based PC itself. After it has switched control to COMM.DRV, COMM.DRV then retrieves the data from the port and places it into a temporary holding buffer, usually 8–16 KB in size and defined by the communications application when it opens the port. The data waits there until the communications application regains the CPU.

Overall, the current system works well. Data is consistently retrieved from the port, regardless of the state of the communications application, and thus data loss is avoided.

Using the 16550 UART in Windows

Unfortunately, the Windows communications subsystem does break down, usually at the hardware level. COMM.DRV, like any other interrupt handler, is at the mercy of the CPU's interrupt flag. This flag can be set by any operating system–level component (another device driver, for example) so that the CPU will refuse to respond to interrupt requests until the flag is reset. The interrupt request will not be lost—just delayed until the flag is reset. Device drivers often set this flag as they enter critical sections of execution, when interrupting them would be dangerous to the system. If written properly, they reenable interrupt processing after they have finished executing.

During these interrupt-disabled situations, the CPU is rendered temporarily blind to interrupt requests. If the CPU refuses to answer a request from a peripheral (in this case, the serial port), it also fails to execute the interrupt handling routine. As a result, timing-sensitive operations, such as communications sessions, can run into trouble.

Earlier, you learned that if the serial port is not serviced regularly to retrieve the incoming data, that data is overwritten at the serial port by the next piece of incoming data. COMM.DRV, the Windows interrupt handling routine assigned to service the serial ports, is responsible for keeping the data flowing into the system, and if it does not get executed, the data is lost at the port.

Data overrun is a problem that plagues any true multitasking environment. Fortunately, you can do something about it: you can upgrade your serial ports so that they include some sort of buffering mechanism to compensate for the often-delayed interrupt response of Windows. The simplest way to perform this type of upgrade is to replace your serial port's Universal Asynchronous Receiver/Transmitter (UART).

The UART is the critical component of most PC-based serial ports. Its job is to translate the incoming serial data into the parallel format used internally by your PC. In most configurations, it features a set of buffers capable of holding a single byte of incoming or outgoing data, where it stores the data as it processes it. The UART is the linchpin of any serial port design, and also is the major stumbling point for Windows.

Because most UARTs are capable of holding only a single byte of data at any given time, you can see how such a device could get overrun, especially at high speeds. When a byte of data arrives at the UART, the serial port normally issues an interrupt request to let the CPU know that data is available for retrieval. If for some reason the CPU is slow in responding (if interrupts are disabled by another driver, for example), there is a good chance that another byte will arrive at the UART before COMM.DRV can retrieve the existing data. The incoming byte then overwrites the previous byte, causing a phenomenon known as a *UART overrun*. The previous byte is then lost and must be retransmitted.

So the real source of the problem lies in the UART itself. Fortunately, upgrading it is often as simple as switching your existing UART (probably an 8250A or 16450 model) with one based on the National Semiconductor 16550 series. The 16550 features a set of dual, 16-byte FIFO (First In, First Out) buffers, as well as a level-sensitive interrupt trigger that can be configured to issue an interrupt request when one of the buffers fills to a certain point.

If you configure the trigger to go off at eight bytes, for example, the 16550 receives eight bytes worth of data and then prompts the serial port to issue an interrupt request. As the UART waits for the interrupt handler to service it, a full eight bytes of additional data can arrive at the port. The 16550 simply stores them within the receive FIFO buffer, and as a result, overruns are all but eliminated. The Windows COMM.DRV directly supports the 16550's operation and automatically enables it if it detects a 16550.

Windows features a SYSTEM.INI switch that controls the enabling/disabling of 16550 support. The entry COMxFIFO=<Boolean> is listed in the SYSINI.WRI file that accompanies Windows. The interpretation of this entry includes a bug, however. Though the .WRI file indicates it is a Boolean expression and, as such, accepts any Boolean value (such as true/false and yes/no), in reality it responds to only one type of entry: 1/0. All other entries are interpreted as false, prompting Windows to turn off your 16550's buffering.

A statement of COM1FIFO=TRUE would in reality be interpreted as false, for example. The only valid true entry is COM1FIFO=1. And because Windows turns on 16550 support by default, there's really no reason to even include this entry in SYSTEM.INI. Its only real use is for disabling 16550 support, something you probably do not want to do anyway.

Replacing your UART is a relatively simple process. If your serial port is part of an expansion board, look for a large, 40-pin chip with the number 8250 or 16450 on it. These are older UARTs, the kind that feature single-byte buffers. The 16550 is pin-compatible with them, so you should be able to simply pop out (or desolder, if your UART is soldered on) the older UART and replace it with a 16550.

If your UART is integrated with other components into a VLSI (Very Large Scale Integration) device, you have to purchase a completely new I/O card. This also is true if your UART is integrated with your motherboard; few motherboards feature full-sized UARTs. Your best bet is to look for a card with one or more 16550-equipped serial ports already on it. These usually cost only a few dollars more than a 16450-equipped model and are well worth the additional cost.

Moving Beyond the 16550

Although the 16550 solves the problem of data overruns on most systems, its 16-byte buffers simply are not enough at times. This is true, for example, when you need to run numerous DOS applications while performing background communications. DOS virtual machines are notorious for causing sporadic UART overruns, even with a 16550 installed. In addition, although the Windows COMM.DRV does indeed support the 16550, it does not necessarily make the best use of its features (for example, it sets the receive interrupt trigger at 14 bytes, leaving only 2 bytes of space for incoming data to accumulate). Fortunately, there are alternatives to the basic Windows solutions.

The first, and arguably simplest, upgrade is TurboCom from Bio-Engineering Research Labs. TurboCom is a set of device drivers and virtual device drivers that effectively replaces the entire Windows communications subsystem. Designed to work exclusively with the 16550 UART, TurboCom makes better use of the chip's features and generally is more efficient than COMM.DRV. It also provides you with direct control over all aspects of 16550 operation, including the position of the interrupt trigger (by far the most critical item in the 16550).

If you are losing characters at high speeds, you can adjust the 16550 interrupt trigger downward through a SYSTEM.INI switch, increasing the amount of buffer space reserved for incoming data.

Finally, TurboCom supports both of the 16550's FIFO buffers. Windows only supports the receive buffer, which can limit the throughput of outgoing data.

If TurboCom proves to be inadequate—it does, after all, rely on the same 16550 UART as Windows does, and as a result is not completely immune to overruns—you can try one of the coprocessed serial adapters from Hayes or Telcor. The Hayes ESP adapter features an onboard CPU and 1 KB of buffer memory; the ESP's CPU handles the flow of data into the port, eliminating any possibility of an overrun. Similarly, the Telcor T/Port adapter features a CPU and a set of dual 16 KB buffers, giving it a maximum throughput of 115,200 bps (the ESP is rated at 57,600 bps). Either one of these adapters will eliminate data overruns once and for all.

An attractive alternative to TurboCom is KingCOM, from OTC Corporation (Tustin, CA). In addition to managing the system's COM ports and eliminating COM port conflicts, KingCOM integrates your e-mail, communications, and fax programs. KingCom can manage up to nine communications programs at one time under a single modem or fax modem, and even enables you to define which program will answer calls to the modem if more than one communications program is running at one time.

How To Configure the Serial Ports

Windows provides a number of mechanisms for configuring your PC's serial ports. These include several SYSTEM.INI settings, as well as a dialog box that you access from within the Windows Control Panel.

The Ports Dialog Box

To access the Windows serial port configuration dialog box, first launch Control Panel from the Program Manager's Main group, then double-click on the Ports icon to display the Ports dialog box (see fig. 18.13).

Figure 18.13
The Ports dialog box.

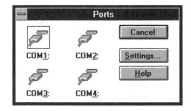

To access configuration information about a particular port, click on that port's icon, then click on the Settings button. You will be presented with a dialog box such as the one shown in figure 18.14.

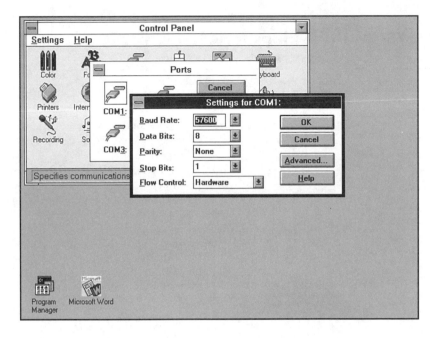

Figure 18.14
The Settings
dialog box.

Within the Settings dialog box are the following configuration options:

- ✔ **Baud Rate.** The speed at which data is to be sent through the port, normally measured in bits per second (bps).

- ✔ **Data Bits.** The number of bits to use when transmitting characters serially.

- ✔ **Parity.** The type of error correction to use during transmission.

- ✔ **Stop Bits.** The number of spaces to place between characters.

- ✔ **Flow Control.** The technique to use for managing the flow of data.

All these settings will be overridden by your communications software when the port is opened; altering these settings is normally necessary only when you are establishing a manual connection, perhaps to a printer or printer-sharing device.

SYSTEM.INI Settings

In addition to the Ports dialog box in Control Panel, Windows enables you to configure a number of communications parameters through the SYSTEM.INI configuration file. Table 18.3 lists a number of these parameters, their default values, and what they do.

III

Putting Windows to Work

Table 18.3
SYSTEM.INI Settings for Communications under Windows

Setting	Default Value	Purpose
COMBoostTime= (example: COMBoostTime=5)	2 milliseconds	Specifies the amount of time, in milliseconds, that a DOS virtual machine is allotted for processing interrupts. Increasing this value might keep your DOS communications applications from dropping characters at high speeds.
COMxFIFO= (example: COM1FIFO=1)	1 (true)	Specifies whether the Windows COMM.DRV will recognize and utilize the FIFO buffers of a 16550 UART when one is installed in the system.
COMxBuffer= (example: COM1Buffer=768)	512 bytes	Specifies the size of the COMM.DRV buffer that will be allocated when a DOS virtual machine opens the serial port.
COMMDrv30= (example: COMDrv30=True)	False	Specifies whether the communications driver provides its own interrupt handler; Windows 3.0's COMM.DRV does not.
COMIrqSharing= (example: COMIrqSharing=True)	False	Specifies whether to enable the sharing of interrupts between one or more serial ports. The ISA bus does not support this feature, but EISA and MCA machines do. Adjust it accordingly.

Managing Multiple Ports

Managing multiple communications ports is relatively straightforward. Windows can be very forgiving in this regard. If, for example, you accidentally try to open the same port using two different applications, Windows warns you and asks you which application should be given control of the port. This port access arbitration is part of the Windows VCD, and you can configure the VCD's arbitration behavior in the 386 Enhanced dialog box (see fig. 18.15), launched through the Control Panel.

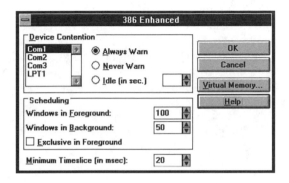

Figure 18.15
The Device Contention portion of the 386 Enhanced dialog box.

Another area of concern centers around the allocation of interrupt request lines within the system. Most ISA-based PCs do not support the sharing of an interrupt request line between two different devices (both EISA and MCA systems support this, so if you use one of these systems, you can basically ignore this section). Yet in many systems, the serial ports are configured in just such a manner. This is especially true in systems that have more than two serial ports.

The common practice is to assign IRQ4 to the first and third serial ports (COM1: and COM3:) and IRQ3 to the second and fourth serial ports (COM2: and COM4:). This scenario works fine if you avoid simultaneously using the two ports that share an interrupt line. If you try to use them at the same time, one port wins the fight for the interrupt line, and the other port becomes disabled.

Unfortunately, there are only 16 interrupt lines available in an AT-type PC, and that places them at a premium. Often there simply aren't enough available interrupts to spend 4 of them just to satisfy the serial ports (other devices that use interrupts include the hard disk controller, floppy controller, parallel port, keyboard, system timer, and network adapters). In these cases, you can get away with sharing an interrupt line as long as you use the two ports separately.

If you need to communicate through COM1:, do not try to open another session through COM3:. One common mistake made by many users is to place a serial mouse on COM1: and a modem on COM2:. Although this configuration itself works fine, many users become bewildered when they add a third serial port (COM3: on IRQ4) and their mouse suddenly goes dead. If a similar situation occurs on your system (a port goes dead for no apparent reason after installing a new adapter), check for an interrupt conflict first.

Chapter Snapshot

Windows provides a help system common to all applications. Microsoft's intention in providing help was to make a consistent and user-friendly interface for getting online help. Windows applications provide hypertext help that takes advantage of a rich set of features. In addition (and perhaps more importantly), you can create custom help files to provide users with help for using custom applications.

This chapter explains both using the Windows Help system and creating custom help files. The following topics are covered:

A later section in this chapter—"Understanding Windows Help Technology"—describes the tools Microsoft provides for creating help. The "Examining Why To Create Help Files" section describes issues you must consider in designing useful help files. The "Creating Help Files" section describes—step-by-step—the creation of a custom help file.

Using and Building Windows Help

sing the Windows Help system is in fact quite easy. The Help application has a standard interface that is the same for any Windows application. The consistent interface makes navigating Help and extracting information simple.

Running Help

To ask for help with a Windows application, click on the Help menu (see fig. 19.1) or press the F1 key. Windows starts the Help application (WINHELP.EXE) and loads the Help file specific to your application. If your application supports context-sensitive help, Windows automatically jumps to the screen that applies to the information you need.

Figure 19.1
Starting Help
using the Help
menu for an
application.

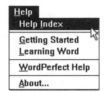

When Help is running, you can jump from one screen of information to another by clicking on any block of colored text. The blocks of colored text indicate that more information is available on that topic. If the colored text has a solid underline, you will jump to another Help screen (also called a Help topic). If it has a dotted underline, a pop-up window appears containing additional information. This window remains on-screen until you click the mouse button again. (You also can use the Tab and Enter keys to move the focus among the colored blocks.) Whenever a jump is possible the pointer changes to an index finger, as shown in figure 19.2.

Figure 19.2
The index finger
mouse pointer,
which signifies a
jump is possible.

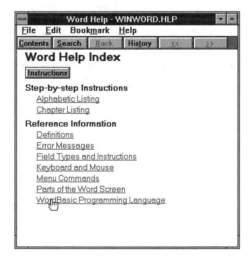

You can start WINHELP.EXE from File Manager by double-clicking on its file name. You also can create a program item icon for it in any program group in Program Manager.

One benefit of each of these methods is they enable you to view two Help files simultaneously. (Most applications enable you to start only one instance of the Help application from their menus.) To view two Help files, start the instances from File Manager or set up a program item icon for the Help application.

You can automatically associate a Help file with the Help application by specifying the Help file name as an argument on the command line in the Program Manager's Properties dialog box.

Opening a Help File

When Help is running, you can open any Help file you want to view. Select File, Open and choose the desired Help file name in the Open dialog box, as shown in figure 19.3. When you click on the OK button, Help will load and display the Help file you have selected.

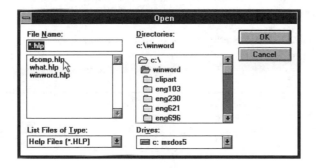

Figure 19.3
Using the Open dialog box to open a Help file.

Searching a Help File

Windows Help provides a powerful search facility for navigating Help files when you are not certain which topic to select. Keywords and key phrases are associated with each topic (or screen) in the Help file, and you can use these keywords to search information in the Help file. To access this facility, click on the Search button on Help's button bar to display the Search dialog box (see fig. 19.4).

When you type a word in the text box, Help automatically scrolls the list of keywords and key phrases in the list box to the section beginning with the characters you typed. After you find the keyword you need, highlight it and click on the Show Topics button. The lower list box displays the topics associated with that keyword. Select one of these topics and click on the Go To button. Help will jump to that Help screen and display it.

Figure 19.4

The Help
application's
Search dialog
box.

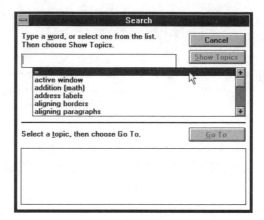

Placing and Sizing the Help Windows

The size of the Help window and where it appears on-screen are determined randomly the first time you use Help. Afterward, the size and position of the Help window are stored in the [Windows Help] section of WIN.INI. You can alter this position by running Help and positioning the window where you would like it to appear. You also can set it to the size you desire. When you exit Help, the new size and position are stored.

You might want to edit WIN.INI directly to set the position and size of the Help window. You can use the following four settings to control the size and location of the Help window:

Setting	Purpose
M_WindowPosition=	Determines the position and size of the main Help window. Enter the coordinates *x1,y1,x2,y2,maximized*.
H_WindowPosition=	Determines the position and size of the History dialog box. Enter the coordinates *x1,y1,x2,y2,maximized*.
A_WindowPosition=	Determines the position of the Annotations dialog box. Enter the coordinates *x1,y1,x2,y2,maximized*.
C_WindowPosition=	Determines the size and position of the Copy dialog box. Enter the coordinates *x1,y1,x2,y2,maximized*.

In all cases, the *x1* and *y1* coordinates indicate the position of the upper left corner of the window in pixel coordinates. The *x2* and *y2* coordinates give the width and height of the window. The final value indicates whether the window is maximized to full screen (1) or opened using the coordinates in the WIN.INI entry (0). The coordinates for each entry must be enclosed in brackets, as shown in figure 19.5.

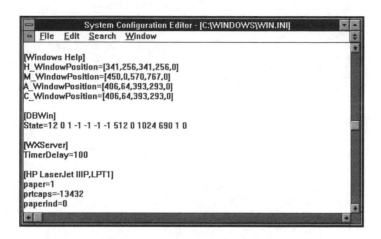

Figure 19.5
The WIN.INI
settings for the
Help window size
and location.

Controlling Jump and Pop-Up Colors

You can use WIN.INI settings to control the color of the blocks of text that signify jumps
to Help topics or to pop-up windows. You might want to set custom colors if the default
green does not show up well against your selected color scheme. To change the colors,
edit (or add) the following lines in the [Windows Help] section of WIN.INI:

Setting	Purpose
JumpColor=	Determines the color of text that signifies a jump to a Help topic. Enter values for red, green, and blue.
PopupColor=	Determines the color of text that signifies a jump to a pop-up window. Enter values for red, green, and blue.

The entries for these settings should be three values ranging from 0 to 255, each separated by a blank space (see fig. 19.6). These numbers represent the red, green, and blue
components of the color you desire. Windows combines these values to produce the color
for presentation on the screen.

To determine the values to use for your color settings, click on the **D**efine
Custom Colors button in the Color dialog box (which is opened by double-
clicking on the Color icon in the Control Panel). The dialog box that appears
enables you to create custom colors by dragging a cursor over a color palette.
The dialog box shows you both the color you have selected and the red, green,
and blue values of the color. After you have selected the color you want, write
down the red, green, and blue values for it. Enter these values in the correct
line, either JumpColor or PopupColor, in WIN.INI.

III

Putting Windows to Work

Figure 19.6
The color settings
in the [Windows
Help] section of
WIN.INI.

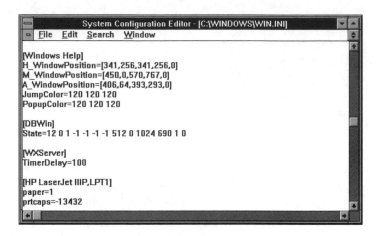

Advanced users of Windows Help also might want to set the colors for the more rarely used hypertext features. The IFJumpColor= setting determines the color of text that signifies a jump to a Help topic in another Help file. The IFPopUp= setting controls the color of text signifying a jump to a pop-up window residing in another Help file. The MacroColor= setting controls the color of text signifying that it runs a Help macro.

Each of these settings takes the same values as the other color settings.

Placing Bookmarks

You can place electronic bookmarks in a Help file to return to an often used topic quickly. To place a bookmark, go to the desired topic in the Help file and choose Bookmark, Define. When the dialog box appears, either allow the Help topic to remain in the text box or enter your own text for the bookmark, as shown in figure 19.7. Click on the OK button. The text in the text box appears as an option appended to the bookmark menu. When you select that option, you jump directly to the Help topic associated with the bookmark.

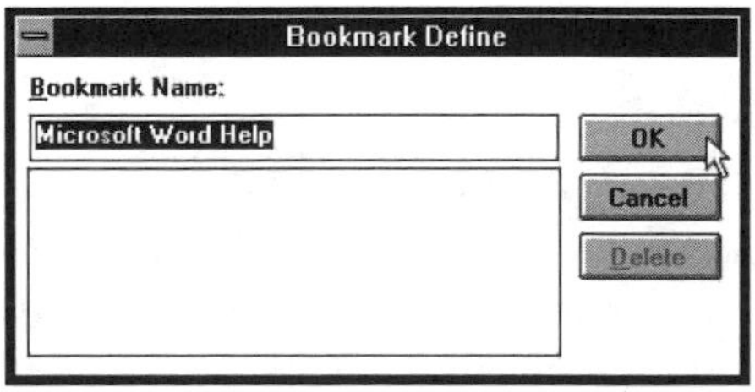

Figure 19.7
Creating a
bookmark in a
Help file.

Editing and Deleting Bookmarks

To change the text of a bookmark or to delete a bookmark, choose Bookmark, Define. When the Bookmark Define dialog box appears, select the bookmark you want to alter in the list box (see fig. 19.8). Either enter new text for the bookmark or click on the Delete button. The changes you make appear on the Bookmark menu.

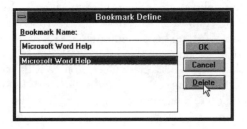

Figure 19.8
Using the Bookmark Define dialog box to edit or delete a bookmark.

Adding Notes to Help Pages

You can add annotations to Help files to supplement the information provided on any topic screen. To add an annotation, select Edit, Annotate. In the Annotate dialog box, shown in figure 19.9, enter the text of your annotation and click on the Save button. A paper clip icon appears next to the section heading to indicate that the topic has been annotated. You can view the annotation at any time by clicking on the paper clip icon.

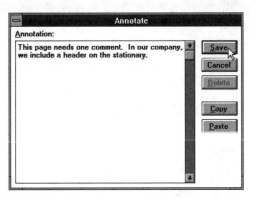

Figure 19.9
Annotating a Help file.

III

Putting Windows tc Work

Editing or Deleting an Existing Note

After you have added annotations to a Help file, you can edit or remove your notes at will. Click on the paper clip icon to open the Annotation dialog box. To edit a note, make the necessary changes in the text and click on the Save button. To delete a note, click on the Delete button (refer to figure 19.9).

Using Help Bookmark and Note Files

Windows uses separate files to store Help bookmarks and notes. You can use these files to your advantage under certain circumstances.

When you create bookmarks, Windows stores all Help bookmarks, regardless of the Help file involved, in a file called WINHELP.BMK. You can use this file for two special purposes. If you want to create multiple sets of bookmarks so that your Help files are custom indexed for particular projects, set up each set of bookmarks as described in previous sections. When you have completed a set, rename the WINHELP.BMK file. Set up your next set of bookmarks, and again rename the WINHELP.BMK file. When you are working on the project associated with a custom bookmark file, simply copy the custom-named bookmark file to WINHELP.BMK. Be careful not to overwrite a set of bookmarks you have not yet renamed. In addition to maintaining custom sets of bookmarks, you can eliminate all bookmarks efficiently using this file. Simply delete the file; all your Help files will be cleared of bookmarks.

Annotations are stored in special annotation files with the name of the Help file and an ANN extension. Annotations for CONTROL.HLP, for example, are stored in CONTROL.ANN. You can use this file for one special purpose: if you want to delete every annotation from a Help file, delete the annotation file. The related Help file will be cleared of all paper clip icons.

To print an annotation, open it by clicking on the paper clip icon. Click on the **C**opy button in the Annotation dialog box. Open Notepad and use the **E**dit, **P**aste menu option to copy the contents of the clipboard into the workspace. Then choose **F**ile, **P**rint to print the annotation.

Understanding Windows Help Technology

Windows Help technology is a set of tools for creating Windows hypertext Help files and for accessing these files from Windows applications. The core of this technology is the Windows Help application WINHELP.EXE. This file, which is discussed in preceding sections of this chapter, displays Windows Help files.

As a companion to WINHELP.EXE, the Windows Software Development Kit includes the Windows Help Compiler, a DOS program that combines text and graphics files to create a Windows Help file. These two programs enable you to create and display online documentation with the following characteristics:

✔ Text in various fonts, sizes, and colors

✔ Keywords for searching a Help file

✔ Cross-reference jumps that link two similar explanations

✔ Graphics in up to 16 colors

✔ Bitmaps containing hot spots that initiate jumps when clicked

✔ Pop-up windows containing text and graphics

✔ Secondary windows that display information without the buttons and menu found in the Windows Help window

Windows Help technology enables you to create feature-rich online documentation. Figure 19.10 shows the Windows Help application and a sampling of its features. You can use different fonts (including different colors) for different types of information. You can include keywords to guide searches of Help topics. You can include lists of cross-referenced topics that, when an item on the list is clicked, jump straight to the cross-referenced information.

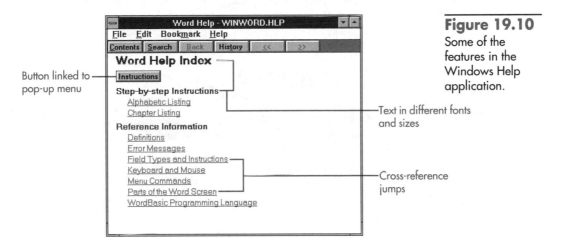

Button linked to pop-up menu

Text in different fonts and sizes

Cross-reference jumps

Figure 19.10
Some of the features in the Windows Help application.

If you need to use pictures, you can include them. If you want the user to click on a part of a picture to get more information, you simply embed a hot spot in the picture. If you would like definitions of key terms to appear in pop-up windows when the user clicks on them, you can link a pop-up window containing the definition to each instance of the key term. If you want to display Help information without providing access to the button and menu features of the full Help window, you can use a secondary window. Windows Help technology enables you to create sophisticated hypertext Help documents easily.

The Common Help System

The key to the success of Windows Help technology is the Windows Help application, which provides a common user interface for all Help documents. The user can click on four standard menus to gain access to File, Edit, Bookmark, and Help functions. The user also can use four buttons, Contents, Search, Back, and History, to navigate the Help file. Two browsing buttons enable you to move in a predefined sequence topic by topic. Whenever the mouse cursor changes to a pointing hand, the user can click to jump to new information or to pop up a window containing additional information.

The Windows Help button bar can be customized to include up to 22 buttons for navigation. You create a button with the CreateButton macro, explained in a later section, which you insert in the [CONFIG] section of the Help project file. (Some Help authoring tools automate the addition of buttons to the button bar.)

Help's common interface is a blessing for the bewildered Windows user. When the Help window appears, the user knows a list of cross-linked topics in a table of contents will appear. To move from topic to topic, you click either on the desired topic or on a button. You can always get back to the table of contents, and you can always retrace your steps through the Help file. If you cannot find what you need, you can use the Search dialog box (shown in figure 19.11) to hunt through the key concepts covered in the file. When you need to use Windows Help, the last thing you want to worry about is learning how to use it. Fortunately, the Help interface and the way you find information are always the same.

Figure 19.11
The Help Search
dialog box.

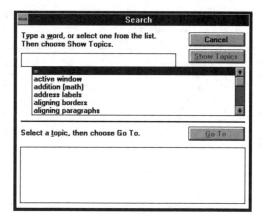

The Help Compiler

The Windows Help Compiler (HC.EXE, HC31.EXE or HC30.EXE, depending on the version of Windows) is a program that combines the raw materials of Help files into the finished Help file. The program uses three kinds of raw materials. The first are the topic files—the actual text of the Help file—which is stored in rich text format (.RTF). The second are the graphics files used in the Help file, which are stored in bitmap (.BMP), device-independent bitmap (.DIB), metafile (.WMF), multiple-resolution bitmap (.MRB), or segmented-graphics bitmap (.SHG) format. The third raw material is the Help project file, a text file that contains the instructions for the Help Compiler to use as it makes the Help file. This file can be created using any ASCII editor, but it must have an HPJ extension.

Rich text format (RTF) is a process for encoding text and graphics information in a file. The name *rich text format* means all the information is stored as text. Plain text is "enriched" by commands that describe how to format the text on the printer and on-screen. Italic, for example, is indicated by the command \i. RTF format enables users of different computers and operating systems, such as Windows, OS/2, and Macintosh, to exchange files easily.

To create a Help file, you obviously need a text editor that can create rich text format files and ASCII text files. Many word processors, including Word for Windows, enable you to create rich text format and ASCII text files. If you do not have access to a word processor that supports rich text format, you can write your text file in an ASCII editor such as Windows Notepad and insert the rich text format commands by hand. (These commands are described in Chapter 3 of the Programming Tools manual for the Windows Software Development Kit.)

If you are using Word for Windows 6.0 to create RTF files for the Windows Help Compiler, you will experience problems when attempting to compile the Help file because of changes to the RTF file format in Word 6.0. You must acquire an updated copy of the Help Compiler to use Word for Windows 6.0 RTF files. The updated Help Compiler is available as the file VBHC505.EXE from the MSL forum on CompuServe, from the Microsoft Download Service (206-936-6735), and through the Internet at anonymous FTP at ftp.microsoft.com. The file VBHC505.EXE is a self-extracting archive containing all the files you need to update the Help Compiler.

If you want to add pictures to your online documentation, you also need graphics editing software. Fortunately, Windows Paintbrush supports an appropriate graphics file format (BMP file format).

When the Help Compiler creates a Help file, it reads the Help project file to determine what it should do. The Help Compiler then compiles the topic files and the graphics files into a form that WINHELP.EXE can display, and then writes the finished Help file, which has the HLP extension. You view this Help file by loading it into WINHELP.EXE.

Examining Why To Create Help Files

Windows Help technology removes the creation of online documentation from the realm of the programmer and places it within the realm of the user. This capability might seem useless considering that Windows applications already include help. Nevertheless, when you examine the needs of users in a company setting, there are a number of advantages to Windows Help technology.

No single Help file can meet the needs of every situation. Although clear, understandable help might be only a keystroke away, the Help file might not present information in a helpful manner—the user might need a different type of organization. Special Help files fill these needs.

One example of special help is the Cue Cards that appear in Microsoft applications. These special Help files instruct a user to perform a single operation step by step. Strictly speaking, Cue Cards are not necessary—the information also is included in the application's main Help system. This Help file is more complicated, however. When you start it, you first must locate the procedure for which you need assistance, and then locate the directions. These directions might not fit on-screen at the same time you perform the procedure, even if you select the Always on <u>T</u>op menu item from the Windows Help application's <u>H</u>elp menu.

You can start a custom Help file from within an existing application if the application includes a macro for launching other programs. For example, Word for Windows includes the SHELL macro to start other applications. To launch a custom Help file from somewhere in Word, use the macro statement SHELL "WINHELP.EXE MYFILE.HLP" at the point in your macro where custom help is necessary.

Cue Cards are perfect for stressed moments when you need timely information on-screen. Cue Cards are always on top. The window in which they appear can be kept small because it needs to present only one instruction at a time. The cards can be invoked on a context-sensitive basis. When you ask for help during a procedure, you can be taken directly to the Cue Cards for the procedure you are undertaking. Although special Help files at first appeared redundant, these new special Help files clearly have time-saving applications.

Although any Help files you create will be independent of a particular application, their design is influenced by the following:

✔ Meeting the needs of users

✔ Documenting special needs

✔ Creating hypertext documents for use in your company

Meeting the Needs of Users

In general, users consult Help files for the following reasons:

✔ To learn ways to perform procedures or to jog their memories

✔ To learn basic operations in the application

✔ To find information about a specific operation they need to perform

✔ To explore the capabilities of the application

Any Help file you create meets one or more of these specific needs. People in your organization might think of a list of spreadsheet features they use rarely, for example. Employees might benefit from a spreadsheet Help file that jogs their memories easily without the need for searching through the main Help file. New employees might need a help file that covers only the essential features they need to get started.

Regardless of the audience, special help files solve problems encountered with the main Help file, including the following:

✔ The main file does not provide the necessary answers

✔ Using the main file interrupts work

✔ Using the main file is disorienting

Help files either fill certain niches in a user's working style or they remain as unused as the main Help file.

Documenting Your Special Needs

Most companies create their own word processor and spreadsheet templates to facilitate the efficient flow of work. The designers of applications cannot anticipate such templates, however, and therefore cannot design help files to accommodate them. As a result, you might need to create help for templates, macros, DDE conversations, and OLE objects just for your company. A help file is easier to update than paper documentation. You can easily maintain one shared copy over a network; when the file is updated, everyone has the latest documentation.

Creating Hypertext Documents for Your Company

In addition, you might want to create online documents that have nothing to do with the software you use. You might want to keep an employee manual online, or explanations of ordering and invoicing procedures. Help files created using Windows Help technology do not have to be used in conjunction with software applications. They might serve as stand-alone documents. These documents can be updated centrally and distributed easily over a network.

III

Putting Windows to Work

Creating Help Files

The process of creating a help file has five stages:

1. Creating the topic files

2. Creating the graphics files

3. Creating the help project file

4. Running the Help Compiler

5. Testing the help file

Several methods and tools are available for creating help files. Your choices obviously depend on the tools you have available already and the budget you have for acquiring new tools. Still, some methods clearly are preferable over others.

The best information about how to create help files is on the Microsoft Developer Network CD. The compact disc includes the Windows SDK documentation on help files, the Windows Help Compilers, the Windows Help Project Editor (WHPE), and the Windows Help Authoring Template (WHAT). *The Windows Help Authoring Guide,* the manual for WHPE and WHAT, contains a wealth of information about creating help files. The CD is currently available by subscription from Microsoft ($195.00). You can purchase the Microsoft Developer Network CD by calling (800) 759-5474.

Creating Help Files by Hand

You can, of course, create help files by hand using any text editor. This method, however, is the most tedious and difficult. To build help files by hand, you must master the 89 RTF statements and accurately place them in the text file. You also must master the 57 help macro statements, and create the help project file in all of its details. Creating a help file by hand requires virtually becoming a help programmer. This takes too much effort.

Regardless of the hassle of coding help files by hand, a brief look at some coding features explains the help tools. Topic files are straightforward text. As a result, to write each topic, you simply enter text into the file. Each page in the topic file, as represented by a hard page break, defines a separate topic within the file. Each topic file can therefore contain several different help topics. The use of page breaks to define topics simplifies the process of creating help files by reducing the number of topic files you must manage. For the average help file, you probably need only one topic file.

A *help topic* is a single page of information displayed by the Windows Help application. A help file consists of several interlinked topics. When you execute a jump, you jump from one topic to another.

Footnotes to each page define such things as end points of jumps, the title of the topic displayed in the Search dialog box, and keywords used in association with the title in the Search dialog box. Jumps, for example, are created by providing each topic in the topic file with a footnote called a *context string*. The context string is attached to each topic page as a footnote using the pound sign (#) as the footnote symbol. The text of this footnote uniquely identifies the topic as a destination of a jump.

To initiate the jump, you create a jump hot spot somewhere as a part of another topic. A *jump hot spot* is a block of text formatted using double underlines. The double underlines signal the compiler to create a jump from this text to some other location in the Help file. The line after this double-underlined text is the context string, which identifies the destination formatted as hidden text. The hidden text is exactly the same text that appears in the pound-sign footnote of the destination topic. The compiler matches the two, creating a jump from the hot spot, with the context string attached, to the topic page, bearing the context string as a footnote.

The Windows Help Compiler uses various character formats to determine which kind of jump to create between topics.

All other types of jumps in a Help file are created in a similar fashion, involving specified context strings as the beginning point and ending point of jumps. If you use a graphic as a hot spot, by using the Hot Spot Editor, the hot spot has a context string attached to it that specifies the destination topic to display when the user clicks on the graphic.

Pop-up windows use a context string attached to a word in a topic file. The word specifies which topic will appear in the pop-up window. A Help file is basically a complex web of footnotes. (Figure 19.12 shows the set of footnotes used for the Ultimate Windows On-Line Advisor table of contents.)

The Ultimate Windows On-Line Advisor, which is freeware, is available on CompuServe in the Macmillan Computer Publishing Forum (GO MACMILLAN), in the "Windows and Utilities" library section. Many of the following sections in this chapter use the Ultimate Windows On-Line Advisor as an example of a custom help file.

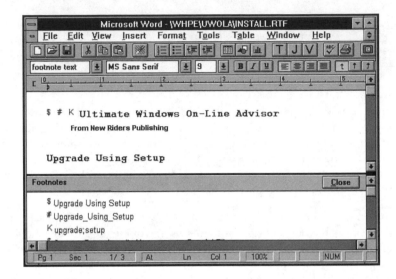

Figure 19.12

The web of
footnotes for the
Ultimate Windows
On-Line Advisor.

Other features of the Help screens are set using RTF statements embedded in the topic files. Bitmaps are inserted in topic files using an RTF statement. Attributes of the text you want to appear on-screen, such as an italic font or a color, are set using the appropriate RTF command. You set tab stops, line breaks, and all other aspects of text formatting using RTF commands.

If you are using a word processor that supports the RTF file format, such as Word for Windows, the task of creating the topic file is easier. You can embed graphics and set text-formatting attributes using your word processor's graphics-embedding and text-formatting features. Your word processor writes the correct RTF commands to the topic file for you as it saves the topic file in RTF format.

The Help project file contains sections that look like the sections in the Windows initialization files (see fig. 19.13). One section lists all the topic files; another lists all the graphics files. Other sections contain specific directions for the Help Compiler. The Help Compiler examines the Help project file to determine what topic and graphics files to compile and how to handle them.

You invoke the Help Compiler from the DOS command line much as you would any compiler. The command line has its fair share of arguments and switches. Fortunately, no one needs to be concerned about how to master this command—several Windows-based tools manage this command for you. The only thing you need to know is that help files are webs of interconnected footnotes. Your word processor can write files in RTF format correctly so that you can use these tools. The remaining mysteries of help files, however, can be safely hidden behind the tools you use to create them. Thanks to these tools, you need not become a programmer to write custom help.

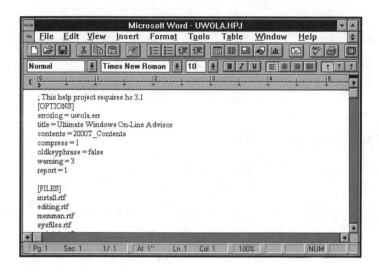

Figure 19.13
The Help project
file for the
Ultimate Windows
On-Line Advisor.

Using Tools

The original release of the Windows Help Compiler required that you build help files by hand. The manual section describing how to create the files suggested using a spreadsheet such as Excel to keep track of all the files that would be included in the final compile. A sample spreadsheet, called a help tracker, was shown in a figure in the documentation. No other tools were provided by Microsoft to simplify the help construction process.

Software developers eventually created tools to simplify the help writing process. Document templates for Microsoft Word for Windows appeared in the Microsoft forums on CompuServe, and management tools that kept track of files also appeared. Shortly after the introduction of the Help Compiler, writing Help files was a far simpler task than the Windows Software Development Kit described.

Tip

The number of tools for authoring help increases almost daily. Periodically check the Windows SDK forum on CompuServe to see what new tools are available. The WinHelp library is devoted to help authoring tools. As of this writing, updated versions of the Windows 3.0 and 3.1 Help compilers are available for downloading in the WinHelp library.

Taking Advantage of Windows Help Tools

The following sections describe the tools currently available for managing the help construction process. The first section describes tools that were used to create the Ultimate Windows On-Line Advisor: WHPE and WHAT. This section steps you through the creation of a topic for the Ultimate Windows On-Line Advisor. This example explains how these tools work and what process is used to create a Help file. WHPE and WHAT have their advantages, but they unfortunately are not supported by other software companies. As a result, the sections that follow provide capsule summaries of six other tools available for creating Help systems for Windows. These products range in price and functionality, and they each include some form of support. The capsules are intended to help you identify a tool, or type of tool, that meets your needs.

Using WHPE and WHAT

The Windows Help Project Editor (WHPE) is a tool that automates the creation of your Help project file. The Windows Help Authoring Template (WHAT) is a Word for Windows document template that automates formatting topic files. These two tools work together to simplify the creation of help files. Both are available on the Microsoft Developer Network CD.

This section uses the Ultimate Windows On-Line Advisor to demonstrate how a help file is created. Although this example clearly illustrates creating help files, it should not be used as a substitute for the Windows SDK documentation on help or the Windows Help Authoring Guide, which both are available on the Developer Network CD. You might want to explore many features of help files on your own, just as you might want to use other tools (discussed later in this chapter) to construct your files. This section starts you on your way by showing you how to create a basic, fully functional help system.

Creating a Help Project

To start a new Help project using WHPE and WHAT, you must install these two packages from the CD. These software tools need to be installed in a new directory using File Manager. You should create this directory off the directory containing WHPE (named by default WHPE).

Next, start WHPE. Select the File, New Project command, as shown in figure 19.14. WHPE is now ready to work on a new project.

Figure 19.14
Starting a new project in WHPE.

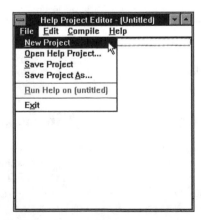

Creating the RTF Files

To work on your project, you need to create at least one topic file. To create a topic file, select the Add New or Existing File option from the Edit menu. Change the active directory to your project directory in the dialog box. Type the name of a file in the text box, and then click on OK (see fig. 19.15). WHPE creates a topic file that is based on WHAT.

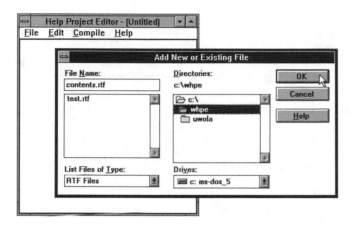

Figure 19.15
Creating a topic file.

If you try to save your project before you create a topic file, WHPE presents a warning message that the project contains no valid files. If you save the project anyway and reopen it, WHPE presents an error message that warns that the Help project file contains no valid files. These errors in no way damage your project. Simply close the error message dialog box and continue. To avoid the error message in the future, create at least one topic file before you save your project.

Creating Topics

To create topics in your topic file, open the RTF topic file by double-clicking on its name in the WHPE workspace. (You also can highlight it and use the Edit File option on the Edit menu.) If Word for Windows is not running, WHPE starts it and then loads the RTF file for editing. To create your first topic, choose the Topic option from the Insert menu. The dialog box shown in figure 19.16 appears.

Word for Windows is the default RTF editor installed by WHPE because WHAT is a Word for Windows document template. If you want, however, you can use any other RTF editor instead. Start help for WHPE and click on the Changing Your Default RTF Editor topic. This help topic includes a macro that will change your editor for you. Simply click on the button that appears in the help topic.

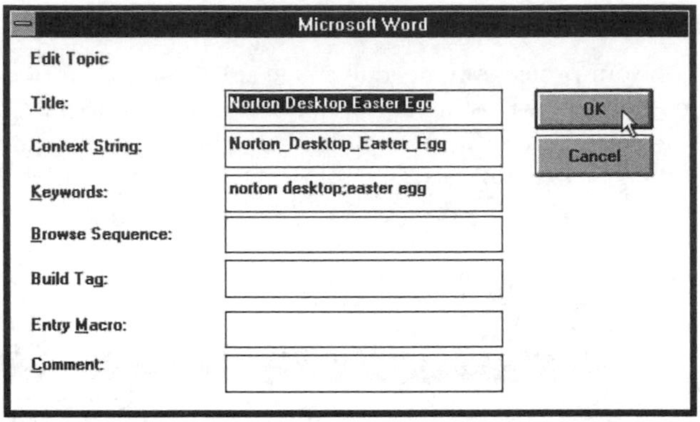

Figure 19.16
The Edit Topic
dialog box
provided by
WHAT.

The Edit Topic dialog box gives you the opportunity to enter the following items into text boxes:

✔ **Title.** Type the title of the topic. Windows Help uses this string to present the title of the topic in dialog boxes.

✔ **Context String.** Enter the context string. Windows Help uses this string internally like a label to indicate both the target and destination points of any jump.

✔ **Keywords.** Enter the keywords for searching. Separate each keyword with a semicolon. These keywords appear in the Search dialog box.

✔ **Browse Sequence.** Enter a number that represents the browsing order for this topic. This number indicates the order in which the topic will appear when the user clicks on the browse buttons. Each topic can be assigned a sequential number, but it is best to number them by tens or twenties. If you later need to insert a topic in the browse sequence, you avoid having to renumber every topic.

The last three boxes in the Edit Topic dialog box are used for special purposes.

✔ **Build Tag.** If you want to include some topics in one build of a Help file but not in others, you can use build tags in the Build Tag box to control the compilation conditionally.

Suppose, for example, you are supporting both a Windows 3.0 and a Windows 3.1 version of Help. You enter the build tag **windows_31** for all the Windows 3.1 topics, and then include windows_31 in the [BUILDTAGS] section of the Help project file to compile for Windows 3.1. You then exclude it to compile for Windows 3.0.

You can see from this example that the Help Compiler includes topics with build tag footnotes in the Compilation when tags are included in the Help project file. The Help Compiler excludes them otherwise.

✔ **Entry Macro.** You can enter the name of a Help macro that runs when the Help topic is displayed. You can add a special button to the button bar, for example, for use by only the Help screen being displayed. To do so, enter the following macro in the Entry Macro box:

```
CreateButton("Related_Topics","&Related Topics",
"JumpID("thisfile.hlp" ,"related_topics")")
```

This macro creates a button the Help application identifies with the string `Related_Topics` (as identified by the first parameter). The text on the button is Related Topics, as shown by the second parameter. (The & identifies where the hot key is.) This button executes a jump macro (the third parameter) that jumps to a help topic in THISFILE.HLP. The topic in THISFILE.HLP has the context string `related_topics`. The screen for this help topic contains the list of related topics.

The Microsoft Developer Network CD contains complete documentation for all the Help macros.

✔ **Comment.** This box is for any comment you want to include as the help file designer. These comments do not appear in the compiled help file; they are simply for your reference.

As you enter topics, check the Place new topic at end of file check box. Check this setting to prevent new topics from being inserted accidentally in the middle of an existing topic page.

After you finish entering this information in the Edit Topic dialog box, click on OK. WHAT macros insert a topic page with the appropriate footnotes.

Topic Text

To continue constructing the Help file, add the topic text to the topic page. When you finish, set the styles for your topic appropriately. The Ultimate Windows On-Line Advisor uses a nonscrolling region at the top of each topic to identify the user's current location. The nonscrolling region is defined as the first paragraph in the file that has the Keep With Next style. To define the nonscrolling region, highlight the first two paragraphs as shown in figure 19.17 and select the Keep With Next style in the Format, Paragraph dialog box.

Nonscrolling regions enable you to keep the name of your Help file on-screen at all times.

III

Putting Windows tc Work

WHAT provides special styles, Lb1 and Lb2, to format numbered and bulleted lists. Lb1 applies to the first item in a list; Lb2 applies to the remaining items. Set these styles by highlighting the appropriate items and choosing the correct style from the drop-down list box on the ribbon bar (see fig. 19.18).

Figure 19.17
Creating the nonscrolling region.

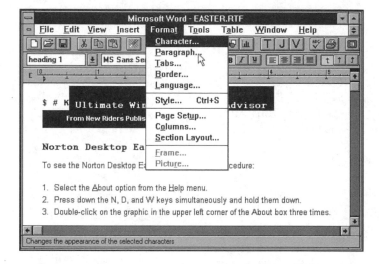

Figure 19.18
Setting WHAT styles from the ribbon.

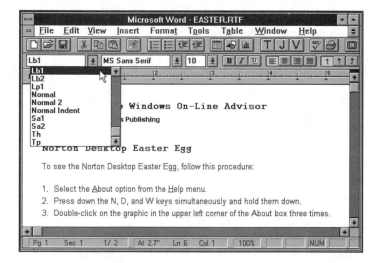

Creating a Contents Page

Continue creating topics as necessary. At some point, however, you will need to insert jumps between topics. Most of the jumps in the Ultimate Windows On-Line Advisor originate from a set of tables of contents. Each table of contents is a topic in a topic file. For convenience, these pages were gathered into a file named CONTENTS.RTF, and are known as contents pages.

Creating a Jump

To insert jumps, open CONTENTS.RTF and fill in the nonscrolling region as shown earlier in this section. To insert a jump, select the Jump or Popup Hotspot option from the Insert menu to display the Jump dialog box (see fig. 19.19). Fill in the Context String of the desired destination topic and the Text for the jump itself. Select the Hotspot Type using the option buttons, then click on OK. WHAT inserts an appropriately formatted jump into the topic file at the cursor.

Microsoft Word
Insert Jump or Popup Hotspot
Text: `Norton Desktop Easter Egg`
Context String: `Norton_Desktop_Easter_Egg`
Hotspot Type
● Jump
○ Popup
☐ Unformatted
File Name:
Window Name:

Figure 19.19

Inserting jumps onto the table of contents topic pages.

Creating a Pop-Up Window

Three features of the Windows Help system that WHAT and WHPE can automate are not used in the Ultimate Windows On-Line Advisor. These features are demonstrated in the next three sections, however. The first of these is the use of a pop-up window, which often is used to display definitions or explanations of key terms and phrases.

Tip

You can take advantage of several of the Help Compiler's more advanced features that are not automated by WHPE and WHAT, including secondary windows, macros, and links among Help files. For complete documentation of these features, see the Microsoft Developer Network CD.

To create a pop-up hot spot, place the cursor in the text of your help file. Choose Insert, Jump or Popup Hotspot, or click on the J button on the button bar. In the Jump dialog box (see fig. 19.20), enter the text for the hot spot in the Text text box and the context string that will be the destination for the jump in the Context String text box. Click on the Popup option button. Add a topic to the file that has the same context string and contains the information to be displayed in the pop-up window. When the Help Compiler creates the help file, it creates a pop-up window to display the information in the topic rather than the usual topic page.

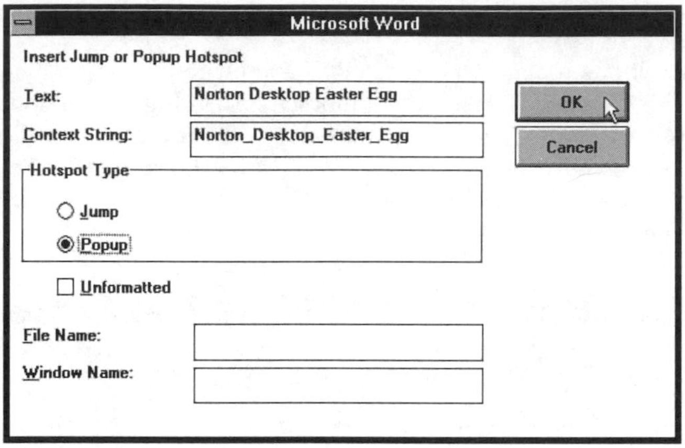

Figure 19.20
Creating a pop-up
hot spot.

```
┌─────────────────────────────────────────────────────────────┐
│ ─                     Microsoft Word                          │
├─────────────────────────────────────────────────────────────┤
│  Insert Jump or Popup Hotspot                                 │
│                                                               │
│  Text:            │Norton Desktop Easter Egg │   ┌─────────┐  │
│                                                 │   OK    │  │
│  Context String:  │Norton_Desktop_Easter_Egg │   └─────────┘  │
│  ┌─Hotspot Type──────────────────────────┐     ┌─────────┐   │
│  │                                        │     │ Cancel  │   │
│  │     ○ Jump                             │     └─────────┘   │
│  │     ⦿ Popup                            │                   │
│  │                                        │                   │
│  └────────────────────────────────────────┘                  │
│       ☐ Unformatted                                           │
│                                                               │
│  File Name:      │                      │                     │
│                                                               │
│  Window Name:    │                      │                     │
│                                                               │
└─────────────────────────────────────────────────────────────┘
```

Adding a Graphic

Adding a graphic to a custom Help file using WHAT and WHPE is quite easy:

1. Place the cursor in the file where you want the graphic to appear.

2. Choose Insert, Graphic.

3. When the Graphic dialog box appears, type the path and file name for the graphic and use the Position group to choose which way you want to align the image (see fig. 19.21).

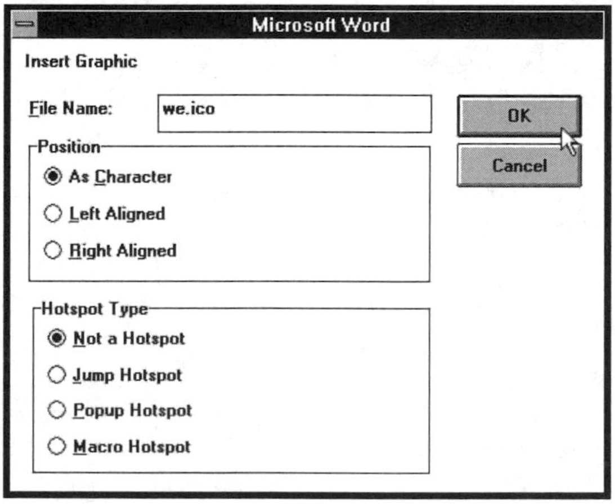

Figure 19.21
Inserting a
graphic in WHAT.

```
┌─────────────────────────────────────────────────────────────┐
│ ─                     Microsoft Word                          │
├─────────────────────────────────────────────────────────────┤
│  Insert Graphic                                               │
│                                                               │
│  File Name:    │we.ico              │      ┌─────────┐        │
│  ┌─Position─────────────────────┐          │   OK    │        │
│  │  ⦿ As Character              │          └─────────┘        │
│  │  ○ Left Aligned              │          ┌─────────┐        │
│  │  ○ Right Aligned             │          │ Cancel  │        │
│  └──────────────────────────────┘          └─────────┘        │
│                                                               │
│  ┌─Hotspot Type──────────────────┐                            │
│  │  ⦿ Not a Hotspot              │                            │
│  │  ○ Jump Hotspot               │                            │
│  │  ○ Popup Hotspot              │                            │
│  │  ○ Macro Hotspot              │                            │
│  └───────────────────────────────┘                           │
│                                                               │
└─────────────────────────────────────────────────────────────┘
```

4. Type the name of the graphics file directory in the Graphics dialog box in WHPE.

5. Choose Edit, Graphics and enter the name of the graphic file's directory in the Directory text box.

By default, the directory that appears in Directory is your project directory. The easiest method for inserting graphics is to place the graphics files in the project directory, where WHPE will find them automatically.

When the Help Compiler compiles the file, it locates the graphics file in this directory and inserts it in the appropriate place in the help file.

Creating a Hypergraphic

To convert the graphic to a *hypergraphic*—the user can click on it to jump somewhere else—select the appropriate jump type in the Hotspot group in the Graphics dialog box. When you click on the OK button to insert the graphic, the appropriate Jump dialog box will appear. (Figure 19.22 shows an example of a standard jump to another Help topic.) Enter the context string that represents the destination of the jump in the Context String text box, adjust the option buttons for the appropriate type of jump, and click on OK. When the Help Compiler builds the Help file, it creates a jump from the graphic to the appropriate Help topic. Creating a hypergraphic is just like creating a hypertext jump. The only difference is that the origination point of the jump is a graphic rather than a line of text.

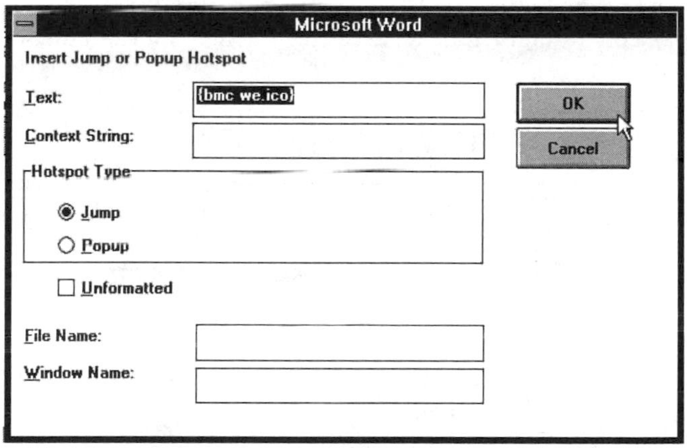

Figure 19.22
Creating a hypergraphic using WHAT.

III

Putting Windows to Work

Setting the Project Parameters

After you have entered all your topics and created the necessary jumps, you need to set the parameters necessary for compilation using the WHPE Edit menu. The dialog boxes provided by this menu enable you to set most of the parameters you otherwise would have to insert into the Help project file by hand. WHPE creates the project file and updates it for you.

First, you must identify your project using the Project dialog box, which appears in figure 19.23. Enter the title of the help file in the Title text box. Windows Help uses this title internally. You also need to enter the context string for the table of contents page that appears as soon as the help file is started. This context string is entered in the Contents box. Select your target Help platform in the Help Version box and then click on OK.

Figure 19.23
Defining the project parameters.

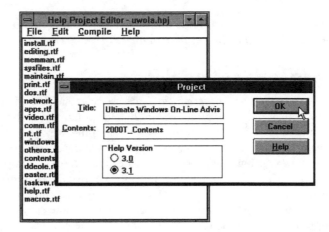

Next, select the Compression option from the Edit menu. Select the level of file compression you prefer using the radio buttons in the dialog box (see fig. 19.24). The higher the compression, the slower the response time for accessing the help file, and the smaller the file for distribution.

Figure 19.24
Selecting the compression for the help file.

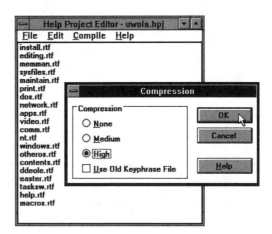

Tip

If you select High compression, you should not check the Use Old Keyphrase file check box. Although checking this box saves compile time, the old file may not reflect changes made to the topic files since the last compile. It is better to wait a little longer on the compiler rather than wonder why a new topic does not appear where it is supposed to in the Help file.

Finally, select the Window Definitions option from the Edit menu. In the dialog box shown in figure 19.25, select the desired options for color and window position. Click on the Define button to accept the settings, then click on OK.

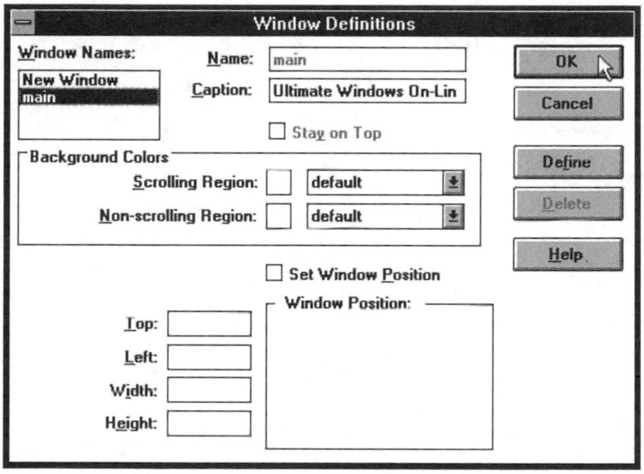

Figure 19.25
Selecting the window definitions.

Although you have completed editing the parameters necessary for compiling the On-Line Advisor, for other projects you might need to select other options from the Edit menu. If you include graphics in your help file, you need to select the Graphics option and enter the names of the bitmap files you want to include. If you want to embed comments into the Help project file, select the Comments option and enter the necessary text. If your help file will be accessed from a Windows application, you need to build a header file of context strings. To do so, select the Application Contexts option. For directions on using WHPE and WHAT features, consult the help files that accompany these applications or the documentation on the Microsoft Developer Network CD.

Compiling the Help File

After you have set all the necessary parameters, you are ready to compile your help file. Select the Start option from the Compile menu (see fig. 19.26). WHPE opens a DOS session in which the appropriate Help Compiler runs. If you encounter errors, you can view them using the Compile, View Errors menu option. You do not need to keep the compiler DOS session open to view the errors.

III

Putting Windows to Work

Figure 19.26
Starting the Help
Compiler.

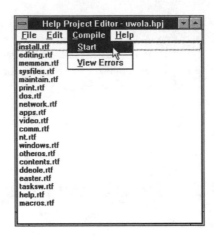

Testing the Help File

The final stage in preparing your help file is viewing the finished product and reviewing it for accuracy. You can start your help file using the Run Help on option on the File menu (see fig. 19.27). This option launches Windows Help and loads your new help file. As you view the file, take special care to ensure that all jumps target the correct topic. An error in data entry can create an erroneous jump. The Help Compiler cannot verify whether the context string you entered as the destination for a jump matches the topic file you intended as the destination.

Figure 19.27
Starting the new
help file.

Using Other Tools

Other tools besides WHAT and WHPE are available to assist you in creating help files that are supported. These tools range from high-end commercial products to simple shareware programs. Each product has defined a particular niche in the custom help market. As always, base any purchase decision on your needs and preferred working style. The following sections provide brief sketches of six tools other than WHAT and WHPE for creating help files.

RoboHelp

RoboHelp provides a Word for Windows document template that automates the construction of Help topics. The template provides a specialized menu and a floating toolbar that enable easy access to each of the operations necessary to creating a help topic. Creating a topic page and adding the footnotes are simple matters. Saving, compiling, and viewing your help file require only three button clicks. With RoboHelp, Word for Windows becomes your help authoring environment. It is perhaps the most functional environment for authoring help files from scratch. You have to provide the Help Compiler, however—it is not included with RoboHelp.

RoboHelp is available from Blue Sky Software, (800) 677-4946 or (619) 459-4365. List price is $495.

Blue Sky Software is currently developing a product called WinHelp Power Add-Ons that will enable you to integrate multimedia video and sound in a Windows Help file. WinHelp Power Add-Ons should be available in August of 1994. The suggested list price of the product is $199, or $99 for registered users of RoboHelp.

Doc-to-Help

Doc-to-Help is a set of Word for Windows document templates that help you convert product documentation to help files. If you have existing documents that you want to convert, or if you want to produce a written document and a help file, this package probably is your best choice. The document templates provided automate most of the conversion process. You might find yourself inserting some cross-reference jumps by hand, but this step is unnecessary. All of your work takes place within Word for Windows. Doc-to-Help provides macros that launch the Help Compiler from within Word; the Windows Help Compilers are also included. (Doc-to-Help is the only package that includes the Help Compilers.)

Doc-to-Help is available from WexTech Systems, (212) 949-9595. List price is $295.

WexTech Systems also offers a utility called Quicture that speeds help file development by replacing all bitmapped graphics in a Help project with placeholders, increasing scrolling and printing speed while you are authoring the help file. When the finished help file is compiled, the images are incorporated into the help file. The suggested list price for Quicture is $59.

Help Magician

Unlike most help authoring tools, Help Magician provides its own RTF-file editor. It works much the same way as Word for Windows templates offered by other tools. Help Magician provides menus and buttons that facilitate the creation of topics and jumps.

Other features of Help Magician include the capability to import RTF files created by other Help tools and the capability to display and print a list of links between topics. The Help Magician editor does impose some limits on the size of your help file. You can now exceed 512 topics, 512 graphics, 20 fonts, and 30 browse groups, and the file can be larger than 1 MB. If you are writing large help files, the extra features provided may make Help Magician the best tool to use.

Help Magician is available from Software Interphase, (800) 54-BASIC or (401) 397-2340. List price is $199.

Universal Help

Universal Help also provides a Word for Windows document template that facilitates creating help files. Universal Help can create Windows and OS/2 help files. If you have to support both platforms, Universal Help is the clear choice. This authoring environment does have some limitations, however. Universal Help provides no access to the Help Compiler from within the word processor. Another concern is that this tool uses a dBASE file to store information about your help file. As a result, your help file is limited to 5,000 topics, 999 links for each topic, 999 pop-up links for each topic, and 254 characters for the length of the keyword list for a topic. These limitations are minimal, however, when compared to Universal Help's compatibility with Windows and OS/2.

Universal Help is available from Softronics, (800) 225-8590, (900) 884-7638, or (719) 593-9550. List price is $645.

QD Help

Unlike the other help authoring tools available, QD Help (Quick and Dirty Help) takes a minimalist approach. This program requires you to choose your own ASCII editor for writing help files. You write the file with your editor and insert a set of special commands that QD Help uses to convert your text file to RTF format. Although QD Help is only slightly removed from embedding RTF statements yourself, it does provide a set of utilities that anyone writing help might find useful. One of them, QDMenu, examines a Windows executable file, extracts its menu structure, and writes a text file based on the menu structure that can serve as the starting point for creating your help file. This feature alone might be worth the small shareware investment.

QD Help is shareware and can be downloaded from the Windows SDK forum on CompuServe. You can contact author Phil Allen directly at CompuServe ID 72047,2134. Registration is $35.

Xantippe

Xantippe takes a different approach to creating help files. It uses electronic index cards to store information that goes into the help file. You can sort the cards into file boxes, create links between topics, and assign keywords to a card. Because of its flexible sorting capabilities, you can use Xantippe to outline your help file. After your outline suits your needs, Xantippe can create the RTF file, header file, and project file that you feed to the Help Compiler.

Xantippe is shareware and can be downloaded from the Windows SDK forum on CompuServe. Registration is $15. A commercial version of the program is available from IRIS Media Systems, (510) 256-4673, or CompuServe ID 76547,706.

Chapter Snapshot

Macro and scripting utilities are playing an increasing role for many users in automating tasks and integrating applications. This chapter examines the macro capabilities of the Windows Recorder and a selection of third-party macro and scripting utilities you can use to automate tasks and integrate applications in Windows. The chapter covers the following topics:

Although the Windows Recorder is somewhat limited in what it can do, it nevertheless offers a good way for you to become familiar with simple recorded macro techniques.

Automating Tasks with Macros and Scripts

Macros are an increasingly important part of the Windows environment. More and more users are learning how macros can make their work easier and less tedious. The Recorder applet that comes with Windows offers limited capabilities, but it will not be long before Microsoft's Visual Basic for Applications revolutionizes the way many users perform simple and complex actions in and between Windows applications. Although Visual Basic for Applications is available only for Excel and a select few other Microsoft applications, you still can take advantage of the Recorder and many third-party macro and script utilities.

If you have never used macros before, the Recorder may be a good place for you to start. You do not have to learn a language or study a thick manual about "If Then" or "Goto" statements. Instead, you can use the Recorder to record tasks you perform every day. In addition, many Windows applications have a macro language.

Although most of these macro languages enable you to record a macro, what sets them apart from the Recorder is their capability to edit the macro after you create it. When you become more experienced with macros, you also can write actual code instead of recording a macro.

Exploring the Windows Recorder

The Recorder, one of the least known of all the Windows applets, is an easy-to-use tool for recording and playing back a sequence of keystrokes or mouse actions. Although the Recorder is limited in scope, you can use it to automate tasks you currently are doing manually. For novice macro users, the Recorder is worth your time because it incorporates many of the standard techniques of most macro tools at a reduced level of complexity. For limited purposes, the Recorder can be a no-frills time-saver. This section looks at how to use the Recorder and suggests which purposes the Recorder can serve.

The Recorder can be used for more than just "Windows-wide" activities. If a Windows application does not have a macro language, you can create custom Recorder macros for it.

Recording a Macro

Because the Recorder has no "macro language" to learn, creating a Recorder macro is easy. In fact, you already know how to perform the action you want to automate; the only thing you have to learn is how to use the Recorder. To create a macro by using the Recorder, simply follow this five-step process:

1. Start the Recorder (click on its icon).

2. Assign a name, shortcut key, and other options for the macro.

3. Perform a series of actions you want to automate (keystrokes and mouse actions).

4. Stop the Recorder.

5. Save the macro into an REC file.

To start the Recorder, double-click on its icon in the Accessories group of Program Manager. You see the screen shown in figure 20.1.

Select Macro, Record from the menu. The Recorder displays the Record Macro dialog box (see fig. 20.2).

In this box, you set a number of macro record and playback options:

✔ **Record Macro Name.** Enter the macro's name in the text edit box.

✔ **Shortcut Key.** Specify a shortcut key to activate the macro. Type a letter or select a letter from the combo box list; check one or more of the Ctrl, Shift, and Alt check boxes.

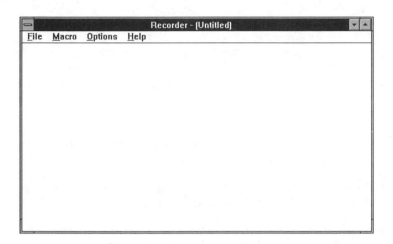

Figure 20.1
The Recorder window.

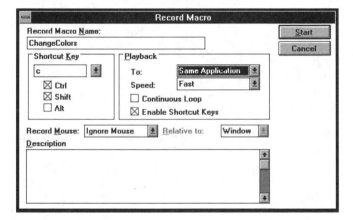

Figure 20.2
The Record Macro dialog box.

✔ **Playback.** Specify how the macro is to be replayed.

✔ **To.** Specifies whether you want the macro to execute in only the application in which it was recorded or in any application. The list box has the following two choices:

    ✔ **Same Application.** Plays a macro only in the application in which it was recorded.

    ✔ **Any Application.** Plays back the macro in any application.

✔ **Speed.** Specify the speed at which you want the macro to execute. This box has the following two options:

    ✔ **Fast.** Plays back in fast speed.

✔ **Recorder Speed.** Plays back at the speed in which it was recorded. This option is helpful when you need to delay a command for a specified period of time before the macro continues.

✔ **Continuous Loop.** Check this box to make the recorder continue in an infinite loop until you terminate the macro with Ctrl+Break. This option is useful for showing demos or automating tasks.

✔ **Enable Shortcut Keys.** Check this box to enable the use of shortcut keys of other Recorder macros during playback.

✔ **Record Mouse.** Records and plays back keystrokes and mouse movements based on the options in the Record Mouse list box. Options include:

> ✔ **Clicks + Drags.** Records keystrokes and mouse actions that occur when a mouse button is depressed, and excludes movements or actions when the buttons are not pushed. This is the default setting and is the safest way to record mouse movements while still enabling most actions to occur.

> ✔ **Ignore Mouse.** Records all keystrokes while ignoring all mouse moves. This option is the best and safest way to record macros and ensures that macros are portable from one environment to another. In addition, with this option you can perform mouse actions that you do not want recorded as part of the macro.

> ✔ **Everything.** Records all mouse actions, regardless of button status. Use this option as little as possible. To stop recording under the Everything option, use Ctrl+Break because the motion of the mouse selecting the Recorder icon also is captured, and the click action is registered by another application.

✔ **Relative To.** Choose one of two options:

> ✔ **Window.** Records mouse actions relative to a window.

> ✔ **Screen.** Records mouse actions relative to the whole screen.

✔ **Description.** Enter a description of the macro in the box. This is optional.

Most of the settings (Record Macro **N**ame, Shortcut **K**ey, **P**layback, and **D**escription) can be modified after you record the macro. After you finish defining the macro settings, click on **S**tart to begin recording the macro. When the recording process begins, the Recorder is displayed as a blinking icon. Perform the activity you want to automate. Make sure that you enter the actions accurately, because the Recorder captures your input exactly as it is entered. When you are finished, click on the blinking Recorder icon to stop recording or press Ctrl+Break (if enabled). The Recorder dialog box appears, as shown in figure 20.3.

Figure 20.3
The Recorder
dialog box.

You cannot create a Recorder macro that completely exits Windows. If you try, the Recorder stops recording at the "This will end your Windows session" dialog box message. You must click on OK to exit Windows.

Choose $\underline{S}$ave Macro to save the macro (you also can resume or cancel the recording of the macro). After clicking on OK, the Recorder icon still appears, but it is not flashing. Do not close the Recorder yet. The macro has been temporarily saved, but it has not yet been saved to a file. When you create a macro and save it, the Recorder stores it in an REC file, which can contain multiple macros. If you close the Recorder without saving an REC file, you lose the macro you just recorded. Restore the Recorder window and save the macro into an REC file by choosing $\underline{F}$ile, $\underline{S}$ave. Finally, check the macro to make sure it works.

The Recorder cannot record a Ctrl+key combination as the first keystroke in a macro recording session. To work around this problem, perform some action before recording the Ctrl+key combination.

Running a Recorder Macro

You can run a Recorder macro in three different ways: from the Recorder window, through a shortcut key, or by clicking on an icon in Program Manager.

Recorder Window

If the Recorder window is displayed, you can select a macro from the Recorder list and choose $\underline{M}$acro, $\underline{R}$un from the menu, or double-click on the macro title.

If you have the Playroom Software Makeover package and use its CapsKey utility (forces the Caps Lock key to remain active until you press the Shift key), always run CapsKey first before using Recorder. If not, macros might not execute properly.

III

Putting Windows to Work

Shortcut Key

If you define a shortcut key for the macro, you can run a macro any time its REC file is open. The Recorder window can be in any state and can be opened in the background. When a macro's shortcut key is pressed, the macro executes no matter which Windows application is active. A Recorder cannot run a macro, however, if a shortcut key is pressed while a DOS application is active.

Program Manager Icon

The easiest way to run a macro is to run it from an icon in Program Manager. To enable a macro to run from Program Manager, you need to take advantage of a little-known command-line argument for the Recorder:

```
RECORDER -H ShortcutKey RecorderFileName
```

To represent the *ShortcutKey* parameter, use the alphanumeric key, special key name (such as Insert, Page Down), or the following to represent the Ctrl, Shift, and Alt keys:

Special Character	Key It Represents
^	Ctrl
+	Shift
%	Alt

To create a macro icon, activate a program group in Program Manager and choose File, Properties. In the Properties dialog box, enter the information, paying particular attention to the Command Line box. Your entry should look similar to the one shown in figure 20.4. When you want to run the macro, double-click on the icon you just created.

Figure 20.4
The Program Item
Properties dialog
box.

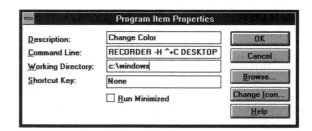

If you are executing a macro from the macro icon you defined earlier in Program Manager, make sure the Run Minimized box is not checked. If it is, an error message displays and your macro stops.

Viewing a Macro

A little-known feature contained in the Recorder is a window that lists a macro's events. To access this hidden window, hold down Shift and choose <u>M</u>acro, <u>P</u>roperties. The Macro Events dialog box, as shown in figure 20.5, displays a numbered list of events. You cannot edit this list, but it does give you an idea of each event recorded in a macro.

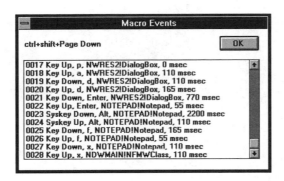

Figure 20.5
The Macro Events dialog box.

To determine the meaning of each line, look at the following example:

```
0124 Key Down, d, WINWORD!OpusApp, 55 msec
```

You can break this example into several elements, as shown in table 20.1.

Table 20.1
Breaking Down a Recorder Event

Line Item	Identifies
0124	Number of event in the macro
Key Down	Name of event
d	Specific key pressed
WINWORD!OpusApp	Program in which the action is carried out
55 msec	Duration of event

III

Putting Windows to Work

Ten Tips for Using the Windows Recorder

You now have a basic understanding of how the Recorder works. Next, you need to know what the Recorder can and cannot do and when you should use it. This section lists the ten most important things you should know about the Recorder. With an understanding of the Recorder's capabilities and limitations, you can use it to simplify your work on the desktop.

If you choose to use some of the options that are not recommended in this chapter, do so with care.

Do Not Entrust the Recorder To Modify Critical Files

First and foremost, use the Recorder to simplify your work, not to damage it. Use the Recorder to automate safe tasks, not those that can result in lost data or work. You could, for example, create a macro that opens SysEdit and modifies your CONFIG.SYS and AUTOEXEC.BAT. But don't! As you learn in the following tips, macros have potential pitfalls. Keep it simple. Keep it safe.

Never create a macro that automatically edits system files, such as AUTOEXEC.BAT, CONFIG.SYS, WIN.INI, or SYSTEM.INI.

Do Not Record Mouse Actions

The Recorder gives you the option of recording a macro based on keyboard and mouse actions. Whenever possible, use the keyboard exclusively when you are recording a macro. Mouse actions are relative to the screen resolution and position of the controls that invoke mouse events, such as push-button position, the sequence of files in a list box, the selections within groups of option buttons, and so on.

Macros recorded using mouse actions simply are not reliable because these macros depend on reference points, such as locations and sizes of windows and other objects on-screen. Windows can change shapes and sizes from session to session. This means that an object in the wrong place could cause the macro to perform an action entirely different from what you originally intended. Any inadvertent reconfiguration of the application interface causes errors in macros that rely heavily on mouse actions. In contrast, this cannot happen during the execution of a keyboard macro because you are using menu commands that do not change.

Crucial to your understanding of how the Recorder works is the information it stores when you record a macro. Suppose you record a macro to open Quattro Pro for Windows and perform an action. To open the application, you could record the click of a mouse on the Quattro Pro icon in Program Manager. What if, however, the Program Manager window is arranged differently when you try to play back the macro? Your macro will run incorrectly, and you might run a different program.

Macros with mouse actions do not run correctly because when you click on an icon in Program Manager, you view the action as opening Quattro Pro, but the Recorder interprets your action as a mouse double-click at the 125×95 screen coordinate. The Recorder does not look at the actual result of the mouse action and then perform that action; the Recorder simply performs the action.

If you are used to recording macros in other applications, this might seem a bit strange. When you record a macro in Word, for example, and perform a command, such as File, Open, Word does not record the keystrokes (Alt+F, O), but converts the action to a specific WordBasic command: FileOpen.

Use Only Ctrl+Shift Key Combinations for Shortcut Keys

The Recorder enables you to set a shortcut key for a macro of virtually any key or combination of keys on your keyboard. Do not get excited over this flexibility. If this shortcut key conflicts with another shortcut key already in use by an application in which you are working, the Recorder beats your application to the punch and executes the macro. The results can be surprising.

Suppose, for example, that you have the Recorder open with a Ctrl+B macro designed to format a page in Works for Windows. While you are working in Word for Windows, however, you try to bold text by pressing Ctrl+B. The Recorder begins to execute the macro. If the macro was set to play back into any application, the keystrokes that were supposed to execute in Works are sent to Word instead.

If the macro was set to play back into the same application, the Recorder attempts to switch control to Works and then play back the macro into Works. If Works is not running, Recorder terminates the macro with an error message. To avoid this type of problem, use a Ctrl+Shift key combination, such as Ctrl+Shift+Q or Ctrl+Shift+0. Windows applications usually avoid using Ctrl+Shift key combinations for built-in commands.

III

Putting Windows to Work

Break Long Macros into Smaller Macros

If you are going to record a macro with a large number of keystrokes (or mouse actions), break it into two or more shorter macros. This saves you time because Recorder macros cannot be edited. If you make a mistake during the recording process, you are forced to start over and re-record the macro. If, however, you break up the entire process, you can have one macro call another by pressing the shortcut key while the macro is being recorded. (The Options, Shortcut Keys command must be checked, as shown in figure 20.6.) You can nest up to five macros within a single macro or link together an indefinite number of macros.

Figure 20.6
Shortcut Keys enables you to call a macro within a macro.

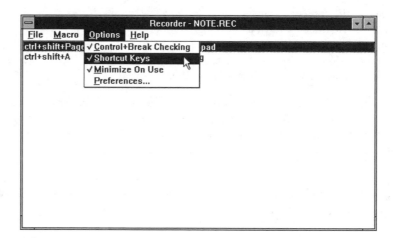

Enable Ctrl+Break Checking

When you run a macro, always make sure the Control+Break Checking item in the Options menu is enabled (checked), as shown in figure 20.6. This option enables you to terminate a running macro by pressing Ctrl+Break. If this option is not enabled, the only way to stop a running macro is by rebooting your system. If you press Ctrl+Alt+Del to terminate the Recorder, your system will freeze.

The only time you might want to disable Control+Break Checking is during a looping procedure (such as a continuous demo) in which you do not want someone to stop the macro.

Avoid Using a Macro in Dynamic Situations

As was stressed earlier, you should avoid using mouse actions because you never can be sure of the relative position of the windows and other interface objects. You also should avoid using keystrokes in dynamic situations. You could, for example, record a macro that calls the Task List and finds Program Manager by typing **P** because an application beginning with that letter will be selected. Suppose, however, that you also have Paradox for Windows, PageMaker, PhotoStyler, ProComm Plus for Windows, PackRat, and Paintbrush also running. Chances are Program Manager will not be the first "P" application selected. You cannot control which P application runs at any one time.

Do Not Simulate Keystrokes in DOS Applications

The Recorder does not record keystrokes you make in DOS applications. This is because the Recorder records the commands you perform as Windows messages. These messages, generated by the Recorder upon playback, are sent to the applications while they are running. DOS applications, however, have no way of understanding these types of messages and cannot participate in this form of communication.

You can automate keystrokes to a DOS application indirectly if the DOS program is running in a window or as an icon. Open Notepad, enter the keystrokes, then copy them to the Clipboard. Open the DOS application's control menu and paste the text from the Clipboard into the DOS application.

Run on Windows Start-Up, but Not from WIN.INI

You can set a Recorder macro to execute upon Windows start-up, but you cannot execute a macro by typing a command line in the Run= or Load= line of WIN.INI. To run a macro when Windows starts, create a Program Manager icon as shown earlier in this chapter, and then move that icon to the StartUp group of Program Manager (see fig. 20.7). Each item in the StartUp group runs at the start of Windows.

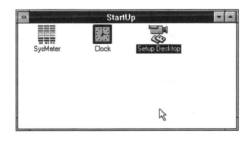

Figure 20.7
A macro icon placed in StartUp group runs at the start of a Windows session.

Be Watchful of Shortcut Key Conflicts When Merging REC Files

You can merge macros from multiple REC files into a single REC file by choosing File, Merge. The Merge option enables you to create a single master REC file for access to all your macros. When you merge REC files, however, the Recorder flags any duplicate shortcut key assignments and removes the key assignment from the incoming macro. This default action has one important implication. Suppose that a macro calls another macro by using a shortcut key, but the called macro has its shortcut key assignment stripped during a merge process. The calling macro mistakenly calls another macro, producing unintended results.

Have Just One Instance of Recorder Open at Any One Time

Windows prevents more than one instance of the Recorder being open at any one time. If you try to run Recorder a second time, only the current Recorder window is activated. This means that you cannot perform a command within the Recorder; if you click on the Recorder icon to activate it, the macro stops. If you try to start Recorder a second time, nothing happens.

Using Macros in Windows Applications

Most high-end Windows applications have a macro or script language you can use to automate repetitive tasks and develop advanced solutions (as discussed later in this chapter). In contrast to the Windows Recorder, you typically can use two methods to create a macro. First, you can turn on a macro recording command in an application and record a series of keystrokes through the Windows Recorder. These keystrokes are later played back to the application as if you were typing the keystrokes at playback time.

Second, you can write a set of instructions and store these instructions in a file. You can play back these instructions when desired. The language you use for describing what the application should do is called a *macro* or *script language*.

Macro languages often look like true programming languages, such as BASIC, Pascal, or C. The macro language explored in this section—WordBasic, the Word for Windows macro language—is based on the BASIC programming language. Even if you feel uncomfortable with "programming," make sure your unease does not prevent you from using macros. The macro recording facility in Word for Windows enables you to accomplish many of the things you can accomplish by writing a macro in WordBasic.

Word for Windows 2.0 is used in the examples in this section. The menu structure is somewhat different in Word for Windows 6.0, although the general process used to record a macro is very similar.

Word for Windows supports both methods of creating a macro. Recording a macro is by far the easiest method to use. The basic process is similar to that of the Recorder:

1. Choose Tools, Record Macro.

2. Assign a name and shortcut key (optional) for the macro.

3. Perform a series of actions you want to automate (keystrokes and mouse moves).

4. Choose Tools, Stop Recorder to end the recording process.

5. Save the template in which the macro was created.

To demonstrate, suppose you must follow office convention and distribute a memo in a plain Courier font, but want to create the memo in Times New Roman. A macro that changes the text of a document to Courier on the fly would be helpful. This is a simple process, but one that can be made even simpler by using a macro.

To record this Times-to-Courier process, choose Tools, Record Macro (see fig. 20.8). Enter a name for the macro, and define a shortcut key. Figure 20.9 shows that the macro name is **NiceFontToBlandFont** and the key assignment is Ctrl+Shift+V.

III

Putting Windows to Work

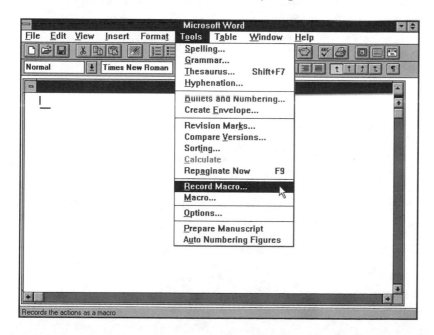

Figure 20.8
The Record Macro option.

Figure 20.9
The Record Macro
dialog box.

Avoid assigning more than one macro to the same shortcut key. Although you do not erase any of the macros by doing so, you might lose track of a macro you need if you reassign its keystroke to another macro. The last macro assigned to a keystroke is the only macro assigned to the keystroke. The previously assigned macro becomes a macro that has no keystroke assignment.

Click on OK and the Macro dialog box appears. Use this box to define the context of the macro. Global is available to all documents; Template is available only to documents created with the current document template.

The Macro dialog box pops up to give you the choice of Global or Local context only when you are working with a document template other than NORMAL.DOT, in which all global macros are stored. Use the global macro context for macros that you want to use in any Word document you create. Use the template macro context for macros specific to the document type defined by the document template you are using.

The recording process now begins. Perform the events you want to record. For this example, perform the following steps:

1. Choose Edit, Select All.

2. Choose Format, Character.

3. Select Courier from the Font list.

4. Click on OK.

When you are finished, choose Tools, Stop Recorder to end the recording process. The macro is saved to the template; make sure you save the template by choosing File, Save All from the menu. This ensures that your macro has been saved. In the future, whenever you need to change all the text in a document to Courier, simply press Ctrl+Shift+V.

The Word macro recorder provides limited mouse support during the recording of a macro. You can use the mouse to choose menu items or settings in dialog boxes, but you cannot perform any mouse action on a document's text, such as selecting text.

After you finish recording a macro, you can view and edit the WordBasic macro generated from the recording session. Choose Tools, Macro and choose the name of the macro from the list box. Click on the Edit button. Word opens the WordBasic macro. Figure 20.10 shows the statements for the NiceFontToBlandFont macro in the macro window.

Figure 20.10

A macro shown in the macro editing window.

Using WordBasic To Write Macros

Word for Windows also enables you to create a macro by writing statements in its macro language, WordBasic. To create a WordBasic macro, choose Tools, Macro. Enter a macro name and click on Edit. Word opens a document window with a special toolbar that enables you to test and debug your WordBasic statements (see fig. 20.10). Enter the WordBasic statement that accomplishes the task you have in mind. Close the document window just as you close any other document window in Word. Your macro then is ready to use.

III

Putting Windows to Work

Tip

Word for Windows enables you to include dialog boxes in your macros. Several predefined dialog boxes are available, or you can create your own by using a dialog editor called MACRODE.EXE, located in the Word directory.

You start the MACRODE.EXE dialog editor by using Program Manager's File, Run. To use dialog boxes effectively to collect information from a user, you must master the rudiments of the WordBasic language. You must write WordBasic statements to display the dialog box, collect the information, and place the collected information into your document.

Macro languages enable you to automate time-intensive tasks and be more productive.

You have seen the obvious shortcomings of the Windows Recorder, and you also have seen the potential for macros as demonstrated in many Windows applications, such as Word for Windows. In the future, look for macro languages to become more tightly integrated. Microsoft is working on a Windows-wide macro language called Visual Basic for Applications, which has language similarities to Visual Basic and WordBasic. As of this writing, Visual Basic for Applications is available only in Excel 5.0, but will soon be available for many other Microsoft applications. In addition, Lotus offers its own general macro language, Lotus Script, for automating tasks and integrating Lotus applications.

Using Third-Party Macro Utilities

There are a number of third-party utilities that are useful for automating tasks in applications that do not provide their own macro languages. These third-party utilities are also very useful for integrating applications.

Third-party automation utilities generally fall into two categories: macro recorders and script languages. Macro recorders are similar to the Windows Recorder, but these third-party recorders generally offer much better control over macro actions. Script languages are much more like programming languages. In fact, many Windows-based scripting tools use a command structure very similar to the BASIC programming language.

Whichever type of utility you choose, there are many different ways you can automate tasks and improve your productivity in Windows. The following list offers just a few suggestions for using macro recorders and scripting utilities in Windows:

✔ **Automate actions in programs that do not have native macro languages.** Many applications do not include their own macro languages. Although you can automate tasks in these applications with the Windows Recorder, the Recorder does not offer the same level of capability and flexibility as other macro utilities.

✔ **Launch applications.** Virtually all macro and scripting utilities provide commands or features that enable you to automate the launching of applications.

If you have a set of applications that you work with, you can create a macro that not only opens all of the applications for you, but also positions them on the desktop to your preferences.

✔ **Perform system backup.** System backup is an extremely important task that many users forgo. By automating system backup, you relieve yourself of the burden of performing the backup manually. PC Tools and Norton Utilities both provide the capability to schedule unattended backups. If your backup utility does not support scheduling, you can use a third-party macro or scripting language to automate the backup process.

✔ **Automate system configuration changes.** Although Windows 4.0 will support on-the-fly configuration changes, most changes in Windows 3.1 and 3.11 require that you restart Windows for the change to take effect. If you often change hardware configuration, you can automate the process using a macro or script.

✔ **Coordinate e-mail and communications applications.** Many Windows communications programs do not work together. If WinFax is monitoring the communications port for incoming faxes, for example, other communications applications cannot access the port to retrieve e-mail or perform other communications tasks. You can create a script that integrates all your communications programs, enabling them to acquire control of the communications port when necessary.

✔ **Program the mouse.** A number of utilities—including Whiskers (Numbers & Co.), Logitech MouseWare, and Power Mouse (hDC Computer Corporation)— enable you to assign shortcut keys and macros to your mouse buttons. These utilities, which can be very effective means of automating tasks in Windows, are described in Chapter 10, "Input Devices: Keyboards and Mice."

✔ **Create custom toolbars.** Some utilities, such as hDC Computer Corporation's Power Launcher, enable you to create your own custom toolbars for automating system and application tasks.

✔ **Integrate applications.** You can use scripts and macros to integrate applications and provide your own custom software solutions. You could, for example, create a script that uses a communications program to retrieve sales information and pass the information to a spreadsheet. The spreadsheet could then organize the information and pass it to a word processor to generate an automatic report. The report could then be e-mailed or faxed to coworkers. All of this process could execute unattended.

These are just a few examples of the things you can do to automate tasks and make yourself more productive with your applications. The key point to understand is that virtually any task, whether simple or complex, probably can be automated using a macro recorder or script language.

III

Putting Windows to Work

Now that you are familiar with some of the things you can do with these types of utilities, you are ready to learn about some specific third-party applications and utilities that can help you automate tasks in Windows.

Script Utilities

There are many good script languages for the Windows environment. *Scripts* are much like DOS batch files, except that script utilities and scripts generally provide much more powerful automation than do batch files. Many script languages are just a small step behind full-blown programming environments in terms of capability. They enable you to automate tasks, communicate with applications with DDE, access native Windows API functions, display dynamic dialog boxes, and much more.

You might already have a scripting language available to you. PC Tools for Windows includes a scripting utility called ScriptTools. Norton Desktop for Windows includes a scripting utility called ScriptMaker. Both script languages are similar and enable you to create complex and powerful scripts to automate tasks and integrate applications. Another notable script utility is WinBatch, from Wilson WindowWare. WinBatch offers the same level of functionality as ScriptTools and ScriptMaker, and was included in earlier versions of Norton Desktop. Each of these three utilities provides an editor for writing and testing scripts. Figure 20.11 shows the editor for Norton's ScriptMaker.

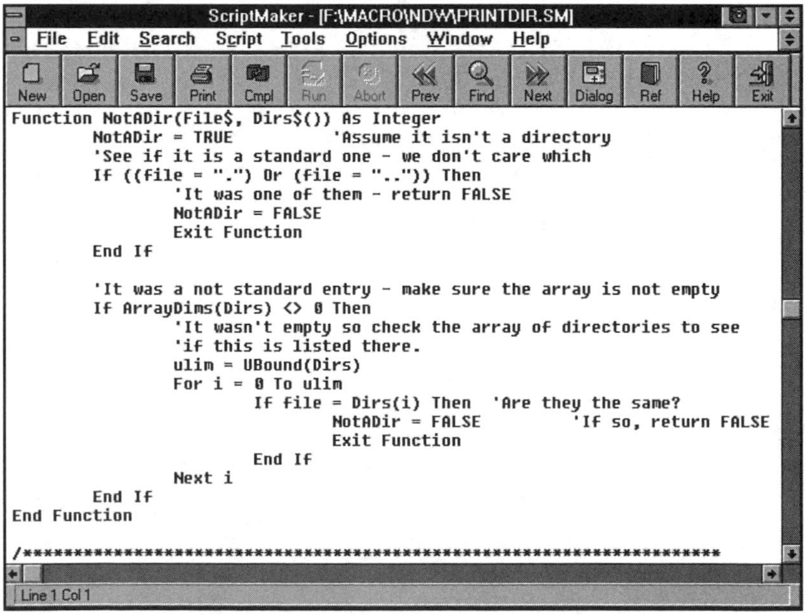

Figure 20.11
ScriptMaker includes its own editor for creating and compiling scripts.

```
ScriptMaker - [F:\MACRO\NDW\PRINTDIR.SM]
File  Edit  Search  Script  Tools  Options  Window  Help
New  Open  Save  Print  Cmpl  Run  Abort  Prev  Find  Next  Dialog  Ref  Help  Exit
Function NotADir(File$, Dirs$()) As Integer
        NotADir = TRUE              'Assume it isn't a directory
        'See if it is a standard one - we don't care which
        If ((file = ".") Or (file = "..")) Then
                'It was one of them - return FALSE
                NotADir = FALSE
                Exit Function
        End If

        'It was a not standard entry - make sure the array is not empty
        If ArrayDims(Dirs) <> 0 Then
                'It wasn't empty so check the array of directories to see
                'if this is listed there.
                ulim = UBound(Dirs)
                For i = 0 To ulim
                        If file = Dirs(i) Then  'Are they the same?
                                NotADir = FALSE            'If so, return FALSE
                                Exit Function
                        End If
                Next i
        End If
End Function

/****************************************************************
Line 1 Col 1
```

If you have some experience in programming with BASIC, Visual Basic, or any other language, you should have no trouble learning to use any of the Windows-based scripting languages. Whether you have any experience, the selection of sample scripts included with most script utilities will help you learn to use the language with little trouble. Information services such as CompuServe, Prodigy, and America Online also have areas dedicated to many of these utilities, which contain additional sample scripts and scripts developed by users.

All of the three scripting utilities mentioned in this chapter (ScriptMaker, ScriptTools, and WinBatch) have advantages over one another. ScriptMaker (Norton Desktop for Windows) and ScriptTools (PC Tools) are bundled with popular utility packages. WinBatch is available as a stand-alone product, which is an advantage if you do not need the other features provided in the integrated utility products such as PC Tools or Norton Desktop for Windows.

Another issue to consider when deciding which script utility to use is the utility's capability to compile the script into a stand-alone executable program that can run without the direct support of the script utility. If you use the scripts only on your system, or you are distributing the scripts to other users who have the same utility, the capability to compile the script is not a major concern. If you need to distribute the scripts to other users who will not have the script utility, the capability to compile the script into a stand-alone application is important.

Central Point's ScriptTools does not include a compiler, and there is no optional compiler available. ScriptTools scripts must be run using the script player that comes with PC Tools. Symantec's ScriptMaker does include the capability to compile the script into an EXE file that can be executed on any PC, including those that do not have ScriptMaker or Norton Desktop installed on them. Wilson WindowWare's WinBatch does not include a compiler, but an optional compiler is available from the company at an additional cost.

Macro Utilities

The Windows Recorder is useful in many situations, but it does not offer the same level of capability found in many third-party macro utilities. These macro utilities offer the capability to easily edit a macro, work with data, and integrate applications. They are a step down in capability from scripting utilities, but they offer an excellent means for automating tasks in applications and in the general Windows environment, and for integrating applications.

A number of macro utilities are available for the Windows environment. Some of the more popular ones include ProKey for Windows (CE Software), Power Launcher (hDC Computer Corporation), and Whiskers (Numbers & Co.). Most scripting utilities also include the capability to record and play back macros and to record actions for inclusion in scripts. Figure 20.12 shows Power Launcher's Launch Command Line dialog box, which you can use to record macros, create program launchers, and build complex macros from predefined actions as well as user-defined actions.

Figure 20.12
Power Launcher's
Launch Command
Line dialog box.

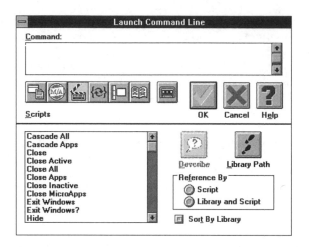

Each of the macro utilities for Windows uses a somewhat different approach to recording and editing, but they all share similar capabilities and methods. Rather than recording literal keystrokes (actions), these macro utilities generally record the results of keystrokes. Instead of recording the key sequence Alt+F+O to open the file menu, for example, these utilities record the fact that the File menu is opened. This *intelligent recording* is an important feature because it ensures a higher level of reliability for your macros. Rather than blindly issuing keystrokes, the macro can intelligently cause actions to occur.

Many of the macro recorders also support the creation of macros using objects. ProKey for Windows is a good example of this type of utility. Figure 20.13 shows ProKey being used to record a macro. To insert a delay into the macro, you simply can double-click on the Delay icon in the Record dialog box. ProKey prompts you with a dialog box to specify the length of the delay. To insert a message dialog box into a macro (which would be displayed when the macro executes), you simply double-click on the Message icon in the Record dialog box. ProKey then prompts you to specify the content of the message and set options for its display, including whether the message will include an alert beep.

Figure 20.13
ProKey for
Windows supports
recording using
objects.

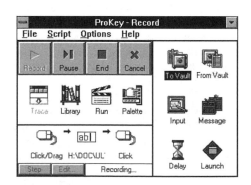

The capability to create macros using objects simplifies the macro recording process and makes it possible for you to include features in your macros that otherwise would require a scripting language to support. The capability to insert delays, messages, and other events in a macro make the macro more professional and useful. Many macro utilities include predefined objects that perform fairly complex actions, eliminating the need for you to create your own "submacros" to perform these functions.

If you have used the Windows Recorder and have experienced its limitations, acquiring a third-party macro utility would probably be a good investment. If you want to automate tasks using dynamic dialog boxes, DDE, or other high-level features, a script language is a better choice.

Part Four

Integrating Applications

Chapter Snapshot

Windows users work with many more applications on their desktops than do DOS users because of the ease of data exchange in the Windows environment. Windows uses a storage area known as the Clipboard to enable you to send data from one application and to insert a copy of that data into a second application. This chapter explores the following issues about the Windows Clipboard:

If you have used Windows for any length of time, using the Clipboard probably has become second nature to you. Cut, copy, and paste are some of the most-used terms in the Windows vernacular. By learning how the Clipboard works with the source application and the receiving application, and seeing how it manages several data formats, you can better understand its strengths and weaknesses as a data-exchange medium.

CHAPTER

Exchanging Data Using the Clipboard

I t is not difficult to use the Clipboard, but if you have never used it before, the Clipboard bears some explaining. The following section provides some general tips on using the Clipboard. Later sections in this chapter examine more specific issues.

Understanding Clipboard 101: The Basics

Nearly all Windows applications use the Clipboard. To use it, choose one of the following three commands that are found under the **E**dit menu:

✔ Cu**t** removes the selection from the active window and places it in the Clipboard.

✔ **C**opy duplicates the selection from the active window and places it in the Clipboard.

✔ **P**aste inserts the contents of the Clipboard into the active window at the position of the cursor.

Suppose you want to move text between two applications: from Write to PageMaker. After selecting the text in your source application (see fig. 21.1), choose **E**dit, Cu**t** from the menu. Next, activate the application in which you want to insert the text. Place the cursor at the position in which you want the text to be inserted, and choose **E**dit, **P**aste. The text has been moved from one application to the other (see fig. 21.2).

Figure 21.1
Selecting text in Write to be cut.

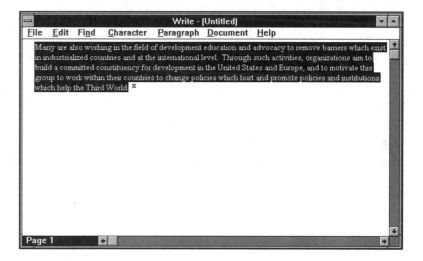

Graphics are transferred between applications in the same way as text. Suppose you want to transfer an image from Aldus Freehand to Quattro Pro for Windows. Select the portion of the graphic you want to copy in Freehand, using the selection arrow tool (see fig. 21.3), and copy it to the Clipboard by choosing **E**dit, **C**opy. Activate Quattro Pro, and select the cell in which you want to insert the image. Choose **E**dit, **P**aste; the graphic is inserted into the spreadsheet, as shown in figure 21.4. After you paste the data, the data remains in the Clipboard until something else replaces it. Thus, you can paste multiple copies of the same graphic if desired.

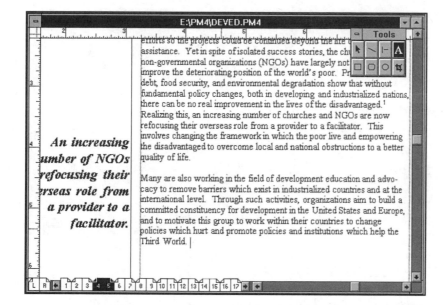

Figure 21.2
The pasted text in a PageMaker story.

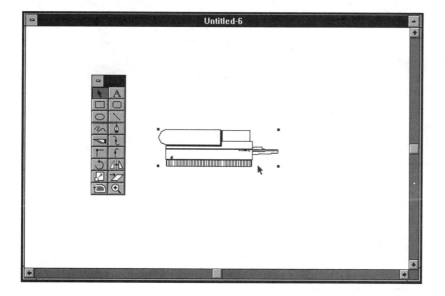

Figure 21.3
Selecting a Freehand graphic to be copied to the Clipboard.

Figure 21.4

Pasting the Freehand graphic into a Quattro Pro spreadsheet.

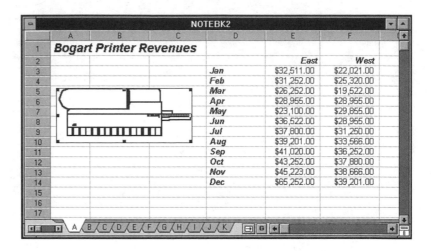

The Clipboard is also very useful for copying text from (or pasting text into) a text field in a dialog box. Because you cannot access the menu commands directly from a dialog box, use their shortcut keys (discussed in this section) instead.

The Cut, Copy, and Paste commands from the Edit menu have keyboard shortcuts. By learning these, you can speed up the process of data exchange within and between applications. There currently are two different sets of shortcut keys you can choose from, as shown in table 21.1.

Table 21.1
Cut, Copy, and Paste Keyboard Equivalents

Function	Windows 3.0 Shortcut Keys	Windows 3.1 Shortcut Keys
Cut	Shift+Del	Ctrl+X
Copy	Ctrl+Ins	Ctrl+C
Paste	Shift+Ins	Ctrl+V

The Windows 3.0 keys formerly were the Windows standard, but Microsoft introduced a new set of shortcut keys for Windows 3.1. All Microsoft Windows Solution Series applications, as well as many new products from other software vendors, use the new shortcut keys. If you are used to using the old shortcut keys, however, you can continue to do so (although this is undocumented).

If the Windows 3.1 shortcut keys look familiar to you, perhaps it is because you have used a Macintosh. These are the same Cu**t**, **C**opy, and **P**aste keyboard equivalents that are found on the Apple platform.

Using Clipboard Formats

The capability to exchange data between Windows applications is not as simple as it might appear. To understand this complexity, think about the unique data types of the applications you might use, as described in table 21.2.

Table 21.2
Variety of Available Data Types

Application	Works Primarily With
Word for Windows or Ami Pro	Formatted text
Notepad	Unformatted text
WordPerfect for DOS	OEM text
Excel or Quattro Pro for Windows	Spreadsheet data (including numbers and formulas)
Paintbrush	Bitmap graphics
Micrografx Draw or Aldus Freehand	Vector graphics
MS Sound System	Sound

The variety of data types that exists between applications can lead to some potential problems. For instance, how can you transfer formatted text from WordPerfect for Windows to Notepad (which accepts only unformatted text)? If you ever have tried to open a WordPerfect or other word processing file with Notebook or another text editor, you know that the result is garbled: text is sandwiched between formatting specifications.

Does this same logic carry over to Clipboard data exchange between WordPerfect and Notebook? No: WordPerfect data is not pasted as unintelligible text into Notebook, because of the way the source application (the Clipboard) and the receiving application work together.

IV

Integrating Applications

The contents of the Clipboard are always treated as a single unit. You can never paste part of the Clipboard contents into a document.

When you copy data to the Clipboard, the source application sends data in as many formats as it is able to send; for example, among the formats that WordPerfect transfers to the Clipboard is Text (consisting of unformatted characters). Notepad is able to accept the WordPerfect data because it also supports Text format; it is thus able to paste the data correctly into a document.

The source application is ultimately in control of the way the data is formatted. The source application determines the type of formats to support; the receiving application determines which format to accept when it pastes the data. As a result, some of the formatting or information on the data may be lost if the same data formats are not supported in the receiving application.

The amount of data you can store in the Clipboard is limited only by the amount of memory in your computer. Imagine the drain on system resources if the source application had to supply the Clipboard with multiple formats of the same data. To avoid this problem, most applications simply tell Clipboard the types of formats that they support, and furnish data in that format when a receiving application requests it from the Clipboard.

The actual storage area for your data is not the Clipboard Viewer (CLIPBRD.EXE), which you can use to view the contents of the Clipboard. The Clipboard is much more of an ethereal entity: a class of application programming interface functions located in the USER library that manages the exchange of data between applications.

You have no control over which formats are copied and pasted. The source application determines which formats to send to the Clipboard; the receiving application looks at the available formats, and accepts the highest available format. In other words, you cannot force Notepad to accept RTF—Notepad makes that determination.

The lone exception to this rule is when a receiving application has a Paste Special command on the Edit menu. This command enables you to have some say in the way data is pasted into your document. If you copy a range of cells from Quattro Pro to the Clipboard, for example, and then choose Edit, Paste Special in Word, the Paste Special dialog box appears, as shown in figure 21.5.

Figure 21.5
Word's Paste
Special dialog
box.

You can paste or paste link the data as unformatted text, a bitmap, or a device-independent bitmap. If you choose Unformatted Text from the Data Type list and click on the Paste button, the inserted data looks like that shown in figure 21.6. If you choose Bitmap, the data looks much different, as shown in figure 21.7.

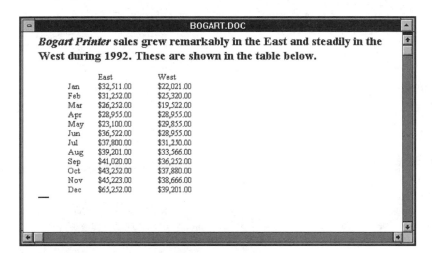

Figure 21.6
A Quattro Pro
spreadsheet block
pasted as text.

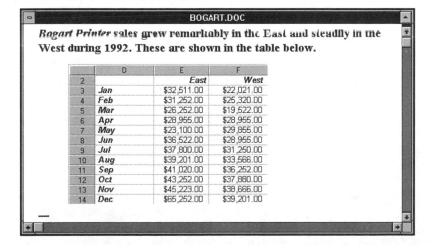

Figure 21.7
The same Quattro
Pro spreadsheet
block pasted as a
bitmap.

IV

Integrating Applications

See Chapter 24, "Inside Dynamic Data Exchange," for information on Paste Link.

As seen in this example, there are many possible formats of Clipboard data. The order in which these formats are sent by the source application to the Clipboard also is important because the order represents the data-format rankings. In other words, the application sends the format with the greatest amount of information about that data first, the next most preferred format is second, and so on. For example, Word for Windows 2.0b places data in the Clipboard in the following format order:

Rich Text Format (RTF)

Text

Native

OwnerLink

Picture

Link

ObjectLink

OEM Text

When you paste the data into another application, RTF is the first format chosen if the receiving application accepts RTF text. If not, Text is the second alternative. Or, if you want to paste Word data as a picture or OLE object (OwnerLink or ObjectLink), you can use the Paste §pecial command in the receiving application to bypass the normal Clipboard procedures. The only time that OEM Text is used is when you are pasting to a DOS-based application.

Word 2.0 and 2.0a send data to the Clipboard in a different format order:

Rich Text Format (RTF)

Native

OwnerLink

Picture

Text

Link

ObjectLink

OEM Text

Thus, if you try to paste Word 2.0 or 2.0a text into Write or another word processor that does not support Rich Text Format, the Word icon (representing an OLE object) is pasted into the document instead of the actual text. This happens because the OwnerLink format is higher on the list than is text. You can get around this in Write by choosing **E**dit, **P**aste **S**pecial rather than **E**dit, **P**aste from the menu, and selecting Text from the **D**ata Type list in the Paste Special dialog box.

Table 21.3 lists the standard data formats that are stored by the Clipboard.

Table 21.3
Clipboard Data Formats

Data Type	Format	Description
	Owner	Identifies data stored in a format that requires the source application to be running. If the source application is closed, you cannot display the data in Owner format.
	Native	Identifies data stored in a source application's internal data format.
Text	Text	Identifies unformatted text using the ANSI character set.
	OEM Text	Identifies unformatted text using the Original Equipment Manufacturer (OEM) character set.
	RTF Text	Identifies formatted text (including typeface and font style specifications) in Microsoft's Rich Text Format (RTF).
Spreadsheet/ Database	SYLK	Identifies tabular data in Microsoft's Symbolic Link (SYLK) format (used by older Microsoft applications, such as Multiplan and early versions of Excel).
	DIF	Identifies data in Software Art's Data Interchange Format (DIF). Originally used to transfer VisiCalc data, DIF now is used for transferring Lotus 1-2-3 data.

continues

IV

Integrating Applications

Table 21.3, Continued
Table 21.3, Continued
Clipboard Data Formats

Data Type	Format	Description
	BIFF	Identifies data in Microsoft's Binary File Format (BIFF). BIFF is used for transferring Excel data.
	WK1	Identifies spreadsheet data stored in Lotus 1-2-3 version 2 format.
	CSV	Identifies data stored in Comma-Separated Variable (CSV) format. Each line consists of comma-delimited spreadsheet cells or database fields, and is terminated with a carriage return and line feed.
Graphics	Bitmap	Identifies graphical data stored as a bitmap image. A *bitmap* consists of a series of small dots, or pixels.
	DIB	Identifies a Device-Independent Bitmap (DIB). Unlike a normal bitmap, a DIB image is independent of the device on which it is displayed.
	Picture	Identifies graphical data stored as a metafile. In contrast with a bitmap, a *picture* consists of a series of drawing commands from the Windows Graphical Device Interface (GDI). These commands are stored and generate an image each time you view or use the graphic.
	Palette	Identifies a Windows color palette. A palette can be stored in the Clipboard with a graphic.
	TIFF	Identifies graphical data stored in Tag Image File Format (TIFF).
Sound	WAVE	Identifies waveform data, the standard Windows sound format.
Link	Link	Identifies data that can be linked (DDE/OLE) through DDE into a receiving document.
	OwnerLink	Identifies a data object that can be embedded through OLE into a compound document. OwnerLink contains an object's class, document name, and name, although the document name is not used because the data object is embedded, not linked.

Data Type	Format	Description
	ObjectLink	Identifies a data object that can be linked through OLE into a compound document. ObjectLink format contains an object's class, document name, and name; the document name is used to link the file to the compound document.

The Owner, text, and graphics formats are used most frequently by the average Windows user. These formats are described in the following sections.

Owner Format

The Owner format is available for textual and graphical data. A source application that copies Owner format data to the Clipboard is responsible for displaying that data in the Clipboard Viewer if the Owner display command is selected from the Display menu. Because the Clipboard is dependent on the source application to display the data, the Owner format is lost if you close the source application while the data is in the Clipboard.

Text Formats

Although a word processing application typically sends data to the Clipboard in Owner format, it probably also sends data in one, two, or all three of the following textual formats:

✔ *Text format* is the simplest data format in Windows, consisting of unformatted ANSI characters. Each line of text ends with a carriage return and line feed. If you look at Text data in the Clipboard Viewer, it is displayed in the System font. The System font is determined by the FONTS.FON= entry in the SYSTEM.INI file. Figure 21.8 shows the Clipboard Viewer with data in Text format.

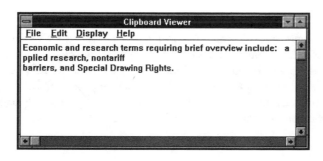

Figure 21.8
Text displayed in Text format.

IV

Integrating Applications

✔ *OEM Text format* consists of unformatted characters from the OEM character set. Coming from DOS-based applications, the OEM character set is based on the code page used on the system (U.S. standard is code page 437). As with Text format, each line ends with a carriage return and line feed. OEM Text data is displayed in the Clipboard Viewer using the OEM font (determined by the `OEMFONTS.FON=` entry in the SYSTEM.INI file). Figure 21.9 shows the Clipboard Viewer with data in OEM Text format.

Figure 21.9
Text displayed in
OEM Text format.

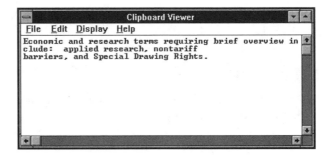

 You cannot display all the characters from the OEM character set in Windows by using an ANSI font. Although ANSI and OEM character sets use identical characters in positions 32–127 for most of the code pages, OEM characters 0–31 and 128–255 do not have an ANSI equivalent, or are in a different position than the corresponding ANSI character. As a result, if you want to display nonmatching characters, you must use OEM Text format to display such characters.

✔ *Rich Text Format* (RTF) retains the formatting characteristics of text, including typeface, point size, and font style (bold, italic, underline). If both the source and receiving application support RTF, you can cut and paste between those applications without losing the text's formatting attributes.

 Aldus PageMaker 4.0 does not properly paste RTF text copied from Word for Windows 2.x. If you try to paste Word text into PageMaker, only a single line of unintelligible text is displayed. You must either import a saved DOC file into PageMaker by using **F**ile, **P**lace in PageMaker, or paste the Word text into Notepad, copy the Notepad text, and paste it into PageMaker. Note that the latter workaround causes you to lose text formatting.

Graphics Formats

Although a graphics application can hold data in the Clipboard in Owner format, it also usually sends the image as a bitmap or a metafile, as well as an accompanying color palette. These images are described as follows:

✔ A *bitmap image* consists of a series of small dots or pixels (the smallest picture element recognized by the computer) that form a rectangular object (see fig. 21.10). A bitmap is stored as a table of numeric values and other data that helps define the image. This table is sometimes referred to as a *map;* each value in the map is represented by one or more bits. The term *bitmap* has become the term used to define this table.

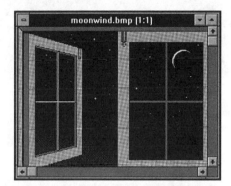

Figure 21.10
A bitmap graphic.

The file size of a bitmap depends on the number of colors it contains (16, 256, 24-bit) and its actual size dimensions. It is also dependent on the resolution of the display driver and monitor, and the number of dots-per-inch that the monitor is capable of displaying. A bitmap cannot be scaled or resized without losing some of its original quality.

For example, figure 21.11 shows the image from figure 21.10 enlarged four times. As you can see, it becomes grainy. A bitmap also loses some quality when you shrink it in size—the more dense the pixels, the more you lose the original colors.

✔ A *picture metafile* consists of a series of GDI drawing commands that produce a variety of graphical objects such as points, lines, and curves. When you view a picture metafile in the Clipboard Viewer or paste it into an application, Windows renders the image (see fig. 21.12) by running through these drawing commands. A picture metafile can be scaled or resized without losing its original sharpness or quality because the objects generated by the GDI commands are scaled according to the resolution (see fig. 21.13). Because the drawing commands come from the Windows GDI, a picture metafile is not dependent on the source application to generate an image.

Integrating Applications

Figure 21.11
The resized enlargement of a bitmap becomes grainy and loses its original quality.

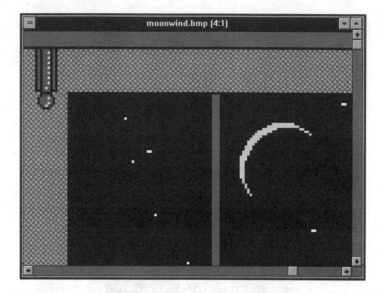

Figure 21.12
A picture metafile.

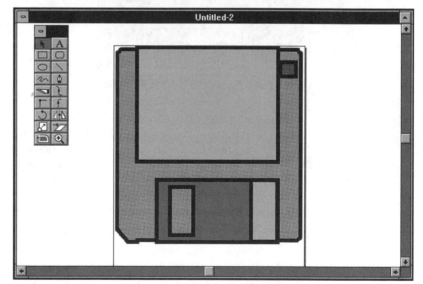

Data in picture format can include a variety of data structures, including bitmaps. Scaling or resizing pictures distorts the bitmap element of the image, however.

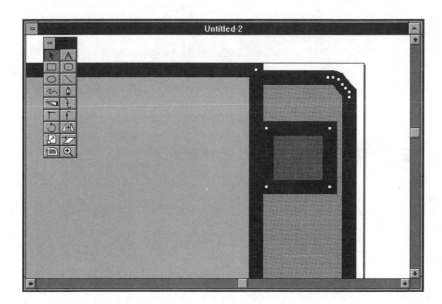

Figure 21.13
Even as a picture metafile is resized, it maintains its original quality.

✔ When you copy a graphic to the Clipboard, you copy a palette to accompany the image. The palette is used by the Clipboard to render the graphical image. A palette is based on a 256-color spectrum, even if you do not have a 256-color driver on your system. If you are running a 16-color display driver, for example, the first 16 colors of the palette are the standard 16 Windows colors; all the remaining colors are shown as black (their color values are zero).

If you try to paste a 256-color bitmap into a Word 2.x document, the image appears in 16 colors. To get around this limitation, double-click on the bitmap after it has been inserted in your Word document to activate Microsoft Draw. (Draw supports the required palette management to display 256-color bitmaps.) After the image is displayed in Draw, update the embedded object in your document by choosing **U**pdate or E**x**it and Return to Document from the **F**ile menu.

If you have several 16-color graphics, each of the palettes will be identical because the same 16 standard colors are always used to generate the graphic. Palettes for 256-color images are not always the same, however. The exact colors that make up a palette vary with each graphic, making a palette specific to a particular graphical object. A graphic and palette can separate under some instances. If, for example, you paste a 256-color graphic into Paintbrush while another 256-color graphic is already there, the pasted image takes on the existing palette in Paintbrush.

A palette in the Clipboard does not overwrite an existing palette in a receiving application.

Using the Clipboard Viewer

Windows 3.1 includes a handy utility called the Clipboard Viewer (CLIPBRD.EXE), which you can use to view, save, and delete the contents of the Clipboard. Remember that the Clipboard Viewer is not the Clipboard—it is only a window showing the contents of the Clipboard. Thus, the Clipboard Viewer does not need to be running to be able to use the Clipboard.

Starting the Clipboard Viewer

To run the Clipboard Viewer, activate the Main program group in Program Manager and double-click on the Clipboard Viewer icon. The Clipboard Viewer window opens, and you can view the contents of the Clipboard or take further action with the File, Edit, and Display menus.

Clearing the Contents of the Clipboard

To delete the contents of the Clipboard, activate the Clipboard Viewer window, and choose Edit, Delete from the menu or press Del. You are asked to confirm this deletion by clicking on the Yes button in a message box.

A second way to clear the contents of the Clipboard does not require the Clipboard Viewer at all. Instead, it can be done within the application in which you are working. If you are in a word processing application, for example, select a space and then choose Edit, Copy. The space is inserted into the Clipboard, overwriting its previous contents.

Viewing Data in Different Formats

The Display menu in the Clipboard Viewer lists the data formats sent by the source application to the Clipboard. If you cut a paragraph of Word text to the Clipboard, for example, the Clipboard Viewer's Display menu displays several formats, as shown in figure 21.14.

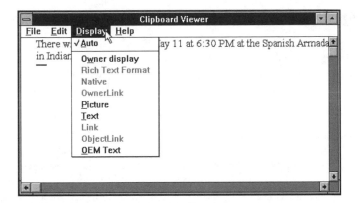

Figure 21.14
The Clipboard
Viewer's Display
menu, shown with
Word for
Windows data in
the Clipboard.

Notice that Auto initially is checked. Auto is not a format—it is a setting that signifies that the Clipboard has selected the format being displayed from the list of available formats. If the source application is running, Auto displays the contents of the Clipboard in the format preferred by the source application. If the source application is not running, the Clipboard selects the best format left available.

Note also that several formats are shown as dimmed text in the list. These formats still are available in the Clipboard for pasting into receiving applications (or else they would not be listed), but the Clipboard Viewer itself cannot display them in these formats.

When the source application is closed, the Display list of available formats often changes, as shown in fig. 21.15. The formats that are removed (such as Owner display, Link, ObjectLink, and OwnerLink) are dependent on the source application, and cannot be used without it running.

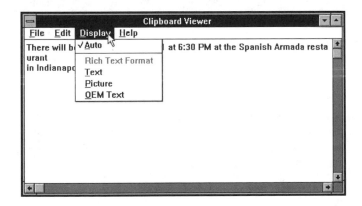

Figure 21.15
The list of
available formats
often changes
when the source
application is
closed.

IV

Integrating Applications

Saving the Contents of the Clipboard

You might need to save data in the Clipboard for a later time. A Clipboard file can be useful when you want to save data temporarily in a location apart from a specific document or file. To save the contents of the Clipboard, choose File, Save As. Type a file name in the Save As dialog box, and click on OK. Clipboard files have a default extension of CLP.

A CLP file has some limitations, which makes it a less-than-ideal means of data storage. A CLP file is device-dependent, meaning that when you save it, you must open that file using a display driver that supports the same number of colors as it did when you saved the file. Thus, if you saved a CLP file when you were running in 256 colors, be sure to use that file only when you are using a 256-color display driver. If you try to use it when you have a 16-color display driver, it cannot be pasted properly in an application. Note that the resolution (640×480, 800×600, or $1,024 \times 768$) of the display driver is inconsequential; only the colors used in the driver matters.

Moreover, you cannot save formatted text in a CLP file. When you try to save a CLP file with formatted text, it immediately is converted to Text format (even if the source application is still running).

Capturing Screens with the Clipboard

There are many screen-capture utilities available for Windows, but you can use the Clipboard to capture the contents of the screen as well. The image is held in the Clipboard in bitmap format. To capture the complete screen display, press the Print Screen key. You then can paste the image into any application that supports bitmap format, such as Paintbrush, by using Edit, Paste.

You also can capture the contents of the active window by pressing Alt+Print Screen or Shift+Print Screen (depending on your keyboard). To capture a dialog box, press Alt+Print Screen or Shift+Print Screen while the dialog box is displayed.

If you want to capture the contents of the active window by using Alt+Print Screen or Shift+Print Screen, keep in mind that this command copies the parent window—not a child window—in a multiple document interface application.

Chapter Snapshot

The phrase "Information At Your Fingertips" is now well known in the PC community. It was introduced by Bill Gates, chairman of Microsoft, at the 1990 COMDEX, and is Microsoft's strategy in personal computing. The idea behind Information At Your Fingertips is that personal computers will become more "personal" and easier to use in the 1990s.

Perhaps no technology demonstrates this new ease of use more than OLE (object linking and embedding). As you discover in this chapter, OLE can transform how you work by providing capabilities that the Clipboard and Dynamic Data Exchange (DDE) cannot. This chapter also shows you how OLE makes it easier to focus on the task at hand rather than on the tool used to perform the task. You also read about the following topics:

This chapter provides a primer on OLE and prepares you for Chapter 23 "Using OLE 2," which explains the latest version, OLE 2.

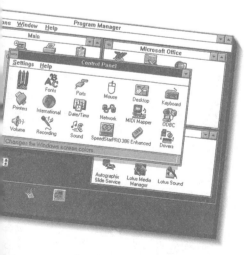

CHAPTER

Introducing Object Linking and Embedding

OLE (pronounced O-LAY) provides a unique method of document integration that makes it possible for you to combine data from many different source applications. To use OLE effectively, you need to have an understanding of basic terms and concepts that apply to OLE. The first section of this chapter provides an overview of OLE.

Exploring OLE

OLE combines some of the features of the Clipboard and DDE, and adds a host of new capabilities to form the highest level of integration in the Windows environment. *Object linking and embedding (OLE)* is a Windows communications protocol that enables one application to use the services of other applications by placing information from the source application into the receiving application's document. As with DDE, the application receiving the data is called the *client application,* and the source of the data is known as the *server application.*

A *communications protocol* is a set of rules that Windows applications must follow to talk with each other. DDE and OLE are examples of two Windows communications protocols.

OLE is much more powerful than the Clipboard method of data exchange. In the traditional cut, copy, and paste method, no linkage exists between the application that creates the data and the application that receives it. OLE, however, enables the information being inserted into the receiving application to maintain a link to the original application, making it possible to update the information automatically. While you read about OLE, consider its advantages:

- ✔ **OLE is task-oriented.** OLE enables users to focus on the task rather than on the application required to perform the task.

- ✔ **OLE is document-centered.** OLE is designed to change the traditional application-centered view of computing that most people have today. When you create a compound document, you can integrate data from a variety of applications. The focus, however, remains on the document, not the source application.

A *compound document* is a document that consists of elements created in more than one application.

- ✔ **OLE is a dynamic form of data exchange.** Like DDE warm and hot links (refer to Chapter 24 "Inside Dynamic Data Exchange (DDE)"), a linked OLE object can be updated dynamically. A change to the source data automatically changes the representation of that data in the linked object.

- ✔ **OLE decentralizes your desktop.** With OLE, each application can specialize in the things it does best. An application is not required to be a "mega-app"—a word processor, spreadsheet, drawing program, and presentation package all rolled up into one. Rather, OLE enables the drawing tool to concentrate on what it does best (drawing), the spreadsheet to concentrate on what it does best (crunch numbers), and so on.

✔ **OLE is flexible.** An OLE client does not care which objects are embedded or linked in a document, or what an object's native format is or will be. As a result, a compound document is assured compatibility with a future version of a server application.

Understanding a World of Objects

As you work with OLE, you first must understand the term *object*, which is really the center of attention in OLE. An *OLE object* is a data element that can be displayed or manipulated by the user. An object can be a spreadsheet file, a word processing document, an audio or video clip, or a bitmapped image. Figure 22.1 shows a Word document with a number of OLE objects.

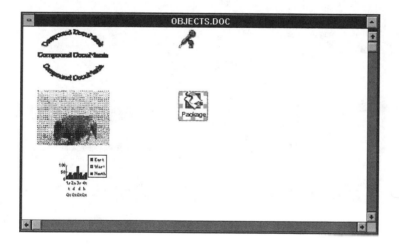

Figure 22.1
Word document containing OLE objects.

OLE objects are placed in a document known as a compound document (or container document). A *compound document* is maintained by the client application and can receive objects from one or more server applications. The server provides data in the form of an object to the client and enables these objects to be played or edited or both in the server application when the server is requested. A server application must be installed on a user's system, although a source document (where the OLE object originated) can be located on a local area network.

IV

Integrating Applications

Tip

When using OLE in a networked environment, a server application must be on your local drive. A source document, however, can be on a networked drive.

Objects are the elements embedded or linked in a compound document, but they are not all of the same type or have the same function. When you double-click on an object, the type of object it is determines what it can do. You can "play" or "edit" a video clip, but you can only "edit" an embedded spreadsheet. The actions an object can perform are called *verbs*. In the video clip example, double-clicking on the object causes it to play; this is its *primary verb*. A server also can perform other actions, called *secondary verbs*. These usually are accessed using a menu item (see fig. 22.2). Some objects have a single verb; others have more than one.

Figure 22.2
A Paradox menu showing the verbs of an object.

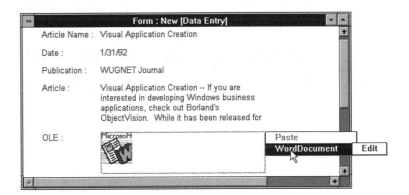

Linking and Embedding Objects

As stated earlier in this chapter, a compound document contains OLE objects, which are data elements from other applications. An OLE object can be attached to the compound document in one of two ways, as described in this section.

Embedding an Object

When you embed an object into a document, the object becomes part of the document. You physically store the object's data in the receiving application. The data contained in the object includes the following:

- ✔ Data the client uses to display the object

- ✔ Data to associate the object with the application that created it

- ✔ Native data passed to the server application to edit the object

Because an embedded object contains the native data of an object instead of simply a pointer to a file that contains the data, it will always be larger than a linked object. Keep this in mind as you decide whether to embed or link an object.

An embedded object can be placed through a Clipboard copy-and-paste process or through the Insert, Object command from the client application's menu (if the client provides this command). Suppose that you want to embed a video clip into a Word document. Figure 22.3 shows the AVI file being copied to the Clipboard as an object. This object is then pasted into the document by using the Edit, Paste Special command (see fig. 22.4). The clip now can be played by double-clicking on the object.

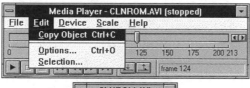

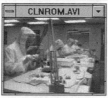

Figure 22.3

Copying a video clip to the Clipboard.

Figure 22.4

Inserting the video clip into Word by using the Paste Special dialog box

IV

Integrating Applications

Linking an Object

When you link an object, the actual data remains separate from the client document. A pointer to that data is stored in the compound document, and a representation of that object is displayed. The actual object data remains in its original location.

You can continue to work with a linked object in the server application (the application that created the object), apart from the client application. A linked object is independent of the compound document; an embedded object exists only within the confines of the compound document. A linked object must be copied and pasted through the Clipboard, just as a DDE link is created. If the client application supports OLE, it treats the data as an OLE object.

The key difference between an embedded and a linked object is the way the object is stored. An embedded object does not exist outside of the compound document, but a linked object does. As a result, a linked object requires much less storage space because the data is contained in an external file.

The difference between linked and embedded objects, however, should be transparent for the user because double-clicking on a linked or an embedded object invokes the source application to play or edit the object.

Object linking excels in a networked environment because it enables a single source document to be represented in many compound documents throughout the network. The use of embedded objects would be a nightmare.

To illustrate the benefits of linking objects, suppose that you embed a video clip in an e-mail message to 10 people in your workgroup. The video clip is rather lengthy and takes up 5 MB of space. Because the object is embedded (the video clip is stored within the mail message), the mail message's size becomes 5 MB. When you send the message to 10 e-mail addresses, the network devotes 50 MB of space to a single 5 MB message.

If you store the video clip file on a networked drive and link it to the mail message, each member of your workgroup can access the same linked object, and the linked object requires just over 5 MB of space.

When sending a compound document to others in a multiuser environment, object embedding frees you from worrying about whether everyone has access to a networked directory in which the source document resides.

Packaging Objects

OLE is more flexible than DDE. For a DDE conversation to take place, you must have two applications that support DDE. OLE, however, enables you to wrap (or encapsulate) data in an OLE object so that virtually any application's document can be attached to a compound document. This object is called an *object package,* and it is represented in a compound document as an icon. An object package can wrap itself around non-OLE Windows applications and even around DOS applications, batch files, and DOS commands.

Windows understands what to do with the object package because the package provides information about the source application to Windows that the source application itself cannot provide. When the user double-clicks on an object package, the package is "unwrapped." An object package can be created by using some hidden capabilities of File Manager or by using the Object Packager.

Object Packaging in File Manager

The easiest way to create an object package is by dragging and dropping a file from File Manager into a client document. A package is created instantly. For example, figure 22.5 shows a file selected in File Manager that is dragged and dropped into a Word document. It becomes an object package instantly, as shown in figure 22.6.

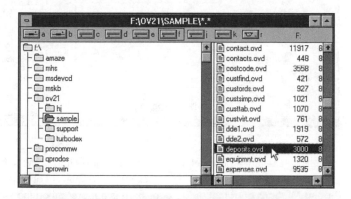

Figure 22.5
Selecting a file from File Manager.

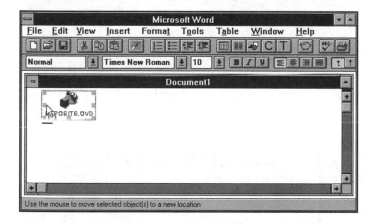

Figure 22.6
The new object displayed in Word.

By double-clicking on the icon, you invoke, or unwrap, the package (see fig. 22.7). To create a linked package, hold down Ctrl+Shift while performing the drag-and-drop process. The client must support all OLE conventions for this technique to work. You can perform this technique in Word, for example, but not in Quattro Pro for Windows.

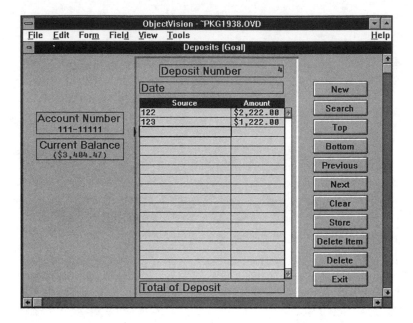

The `IconTitleFaceName=` parameter in the `[desktop]` section of WIN.INI does not apply to the icon used by the Object Packager. The Object Packager uses only 8-point MS Sans Serif font. If MS Sans Serif is not present on the system, it uses the closest match (such as Arial).

Object Packaging with the Clipboard

You can also copy a file to the Clipboard by using the File, Copy command from the File Manager menu (see fig. 22.8), and then choosing Paste, Paste Link, or Paste Special from the client menu (client applications differ in how they handle these objects). You can use the Clipboard only with client applications that are fully supportive of OLE.

Figure 22.8
The Copy dialog box in File Manager.

Using Object Packager

As shown in the previous two sections, you can use the Clipboard and File Manager to create object packages quickly. You can also create an object package by using the Object Packager directly. The Object Packager can be started from Program Manager (in the Accessories group) or by choosing Insert, Object from the client application menu. Either way, the Object Packager window appears, as shown in figure 22.9.

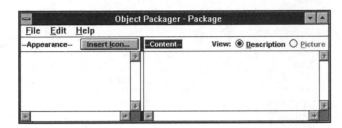

Figure 22.9
Object Packager.

If the data you want to wrap has been copied to the Clipboard, select the Content side of the Object Packager with your mouse, and choose Edit, Paste. If you want to embed a command-line statement, choose Edit, Command Line from the menu to display the Command Line dialog box (see fig. 22.10).

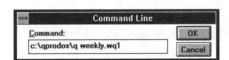

Figure 22.10
The Command Line dialog box.

An OLE object is represented graphically. Object Packager enables you to define a graphical icon or use the default icon. If no icon is present in the Appearance side, or if you want to change the existing icon, click on the Insert Icon button. Select an icon from an ICO, EXE, DLL, or other resource file, and click on OK to insert the image into the Appearance side of the Object Packager. The package is complete.

Choose Edit, Copy Package from the Edit menu to copy the package to the Clipboard. Activate the Windows application in which you want to embed the object, and choose Edit, Paste Special. (If you are using Word or another Microsoft application, you can select the object's Clipboard data type. In the Paste Special dialog box, select Package Object from the Data Type list, and click on the Paste button.) The package is now an embedded object in the compound document (see fig. 22.11).

Figure 22.11

An object package embedded in a document.

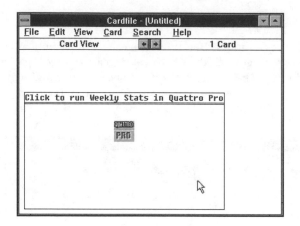

You normally can use the drag-and-drop technique only if the client application provides full OLE support. Otherwise, you must create an object package by using the Object Packager.

To save time, you can use the following technique:

1. Drag and drop the desired file into a full-support client, such as Word.

2. Edit the package by choosing **E**dit, O**b**ject Package.

   If you have an object package selected in Word, the menu changes dynamically from Object to Object Package.

3. Copy the object package by using the Object Packager's **E**dit, Copy Pac**k**age command.

4. Activate the desired OLE client, and choose **E**dit, **P**aste or **E**dit, Paste **S**pecial.

Looking Inside the Registration Database

The *registration database* is the source OLE client applications use to retrieve information about OLE server applications. When the **I**nsert, **O**bject command is selected by the user, the client application looks at the registration database and compiles a list of the type of objects available at that time. When a user double-clicks on an OLE object, Windows looks to the registration database to locate the server application. Server applications register the types of objects they serve (support) and the verbs they can perform on objects, as well as their program DOS file names and location of those files on your hard disk.

Although the registration database is used primarily for OLE activities, additional information is stored there that is used by File Manager and other shell applications. Applications can register (enter in the database) command lines and switches to execute, or DDE messages to send when an associated file extension is dragged and dropped, opened, or printed from File Manager.

The actual registration database is a file called REG.DAT, located in your Windows directory. If you want to view or edit the registration database, you must run a utility called RegEdit (REGEDIT.EXE). RegEdit also is located in your Windows directory. An icon for it is not created automatically when you install Windows because of its advanced nature. To run RegEdit, create a program item for it in Program Manager, or run it from File Manager. The window looks like that shown in figure 22.12.

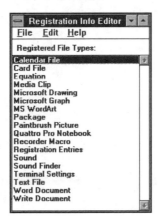

Figure 22.12
The default RegEdit window.

Another view of the registration database can be seen by running REGEDIT.EXE /v. The /v switch brings up the advanced version of RegEdit. As you can see in figure 22.13, the registration database looks like a hierarchical tree. Each branch of the tree has a key name. A key name can be associated with a text string that provides more details about the key.

Tip

If you back up your WIN.INI and SYSTEM.INI files regularly, add REG.DAT to the backup list. If your REG.DAT file is corrupted or lost, you can rebuild your registration database.

First, get rid of the old REG.DAT file by deleting or renaming it, and restart Windows. Next, in File Manager, double-click on SETUP.REG in the WINDOWS\SYSTEM subdirectory to rebuild your original registration database (Windows applets, and so on). Use File, Search to locate all REG files (*.REG), and then double-click on each of these in the Search Results window to rebuild each application record in the registration database.

IV

Integrating Applications

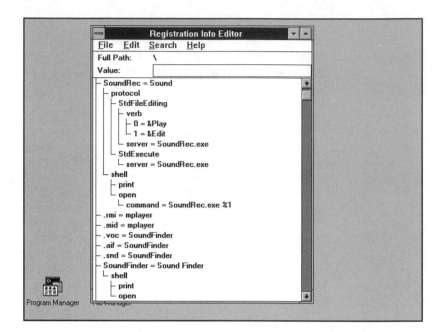

Figure 22.13
The advanced
RegEdit window.

The shift from "application-based" to "document-based" computing will be a gradual one, but the shift is beginning to build momentum. The latest version of OLE, version 2.0, is being supported by an increasing number of applications. It provides a much more powerful integrating environment, such as enabling you to edit OLE objects within the compound document. Chapter 23, "Using OLE 2," explains OLE 2 in detail.

Chapter Snapshot

Object linking and embedding (OLE) is an evolving
standard. Although OLE 1 provided the capability to create
compound documents, these compound documents weren't
"seamless." You always knew each object belonged to its
parent application and had to think about which application
created each object. The newest version of OLE is OLE 2.0,
which adds to OLE's capabilities (and seamlessness) with
the following capabilities:

This chapter discusses these topics and offers demonstrations of how these new capabilities of OLE add to your
ability to create seamless compound documents or to easily
develop custom business applications.

CHAPTER

Using OLE 2

C hances are you have already used the capabilities of OLE 1. When you copy an Excel chart to the Clipboard and then paste it into a Word document using Paste Special, you create an embedded object in the Word document. This object knows which application created it and is required to edit it. When you double-click on this embedded object, the system knows it needs to start Excel (if it's not already running) and that Excel should then automatically have the object open and ready for editing. Close Excel and you return to your Word document with the changed Excel object automatically updated in Word.

At the point in which you embedded the object, your Word document became a *compound document,* made up of pieces from two different applications. Even when using some of Word's features, such as Picture Editor or Equation Editor, you actually are creating a compound document. This is because those two programs are not actually part of Word itself—they are OLE servers that come packaged with Word. Other programs, such as WordPerfect for Windows 6, offer similar add-in capabilities through the mechanism of OLE.

The eventual goal of OLE technology is to enable you to work with documents and not worry about which application you are using. All your applications would offer system objects that all other applications can use through the mechanism of OLE. Although OLE 2 brings us closer to that vision, it still is not perfect. It is, however, where the technology is leading. The vision starts to become much clearer when you work with applications that use OLE 2, such as Microsoft Excel 5, Microsoft Word 6, Microsoft Project 4, and a number of other applications.

This chapter shows you the benefits of OLE 2, which adds to OLE 1's capabilities by making the integration of applications more seamless.

Understanding OLE Terms

Before you can become an OLE whiz, you need to familiarize yourself with the necessary terms (see table 23.1).

Table 23.1
OLE Terms

Term	Meaning
Server application	An application that is providing OLE services to a client application. With an Excel chart embedded in a Word document, for example, Excel is the OLE server and Word is the OLE client.
Client application	An application that is using the services of another application through OLE.
DDE	Dynamic data exchange. OLE is partly built upon DDE's interapplication communications capabilities.
In-place editing	The capability to edit an embedded object within the main document without leaving the main application.
Drag and drop	The capability to grab an object, drag it across the screen, and drop it into a client document.
Compound document	A document composed of objects generated by a number of different applications, all linked through OLE.
Container object	An object (such as a document) that contains other objects.

Term	Meaning
OLE automation	The capability of a server application to expose, or make available, its own objects for use in another application's macro language. Microsoft applications that use Visual Basic for Applications support OLE automation. Many other applications that support OLE 2 also support OLE automation.

Examining In-Place Editing

With OLE 1, when you double-clicked on an embedded object, the source application automatically started (if it wasn't already running), took over the foreground, and automatically loaded the object, ready for editing. But if the source application was set to take up the whole screen, you could not see your main document behind it. Even if it did not take up the whole screen, you still could not easily see the actual document you were working on—only the individual object you were editing with its originating application.

OLE 2 adds a new capability called in-place editing. Now, when you double-click on an embedded object, you are not taken away from your document. Instead, after a brief period, the menus and toolbar change to reflect the capabilities of the source application while you are still looking at your entire document. This in-place editing capability adds to the seamlessness of OLE.

Two examples demonstrate how this works. The first example uses WordPerfect 6 for Windows and its included application, WordPerfect Chart. This example shows how an OLE 1 link works. The second example uses Microsoft Word 6 and Excel 5, showcasing the in-place editing features of OLE 2.

Examining OLE 1

To see the differences between object editing with OLE 1 and OLE 2, here are a couple of brief demonstrations. This first demonstration uses WordPerfect for Windows 6 and WordPerfect Chart, and uses OLE 1.

First, from the main WordPerfect screen, select the Insert menu and then choose Object, as shown in figure 23.1.

You then see the Insert Object dialog box, shown in figure 23.2. From the dialog box, choose WordPerfect WP Chart 2.1 and click on OK.

Figure 23.1
Inserting an object
in WordPerfect.

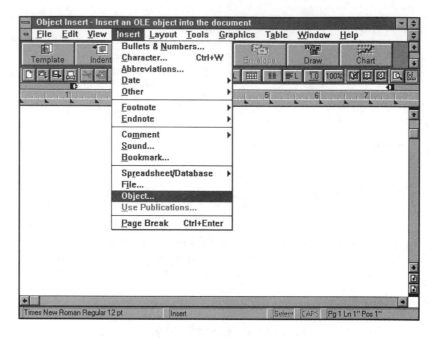

Figure 23.2
Choosing WP
Chart from the
Insert Object
dialog box.

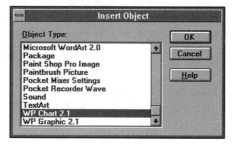

Tip

In WordPerfect for Windows 6, you also can perform the same task by choosing **G**raphics, Cha**r**t.

Finally, WP Chart opens, as shown in figure 23.3.

Because WP Chart automatically comes up with a complete sample chart that is fine for this example, you can consider the chart complete and click on the Return button at the bottom of the screen to close WP Chart and embed the object into the document. When you click on the Return button, you are asked if you want to save changes to your document. Click on Yes to update the document with the new chart. The result is shown in figure 23.4.

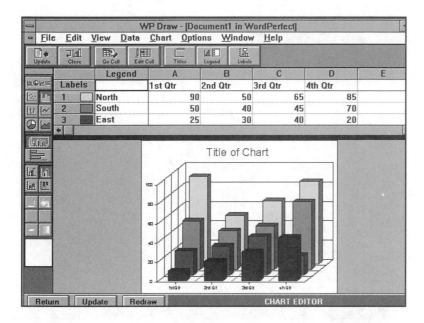

Figure 23.3
The WP Chart
main screen.

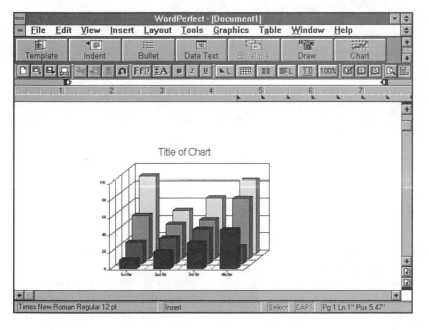

Figure 23.4
An embedded
chart in
WordPerfect.

As you would expect, to edit the chart you double-click on it. When you do this, WP Chart
is automatically reopened with the chart ready for editing, as shown in figure 23.5.

Figure 23.5
Editing a chart
with OLE 1.

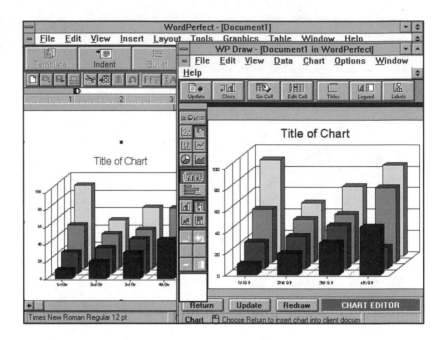

This is certainly better than not being able to edit the chart at all, as if you had performed a simple copy-and-paste operation. Still, in OLE 1 you must leave your main document, which might interrupt your thought process. In addition, you have to mentally change gears as you change to the charting application.

OLE 2 addresses this potential problem by offering, among other features, in-place editing. Here is how it works:

First, start with your document in Word, as shown in figure 23.6.

Then, choose Insert, Object to display the Object dialog box, shown in figure 23.7. From the Create New tab, choose Microsoft Excel Chart and click on the OK button.

When you are finished, you see a sample inserted chart from Excel in your Word document, as shown in figure 23.8.

Several things in figure 23.8 should be noted. First, although you are seeing the Word document and the Excel chart together, you see the Excel toolbar and menus. If you access those menus, they are Excel menus rather than Word menus. Yet you can still see the ruler from Word. This is the core of in-place editing. To return to Word's menus and toolbar, click outside the chart. To return to Excel's menus, double-click on the chart.

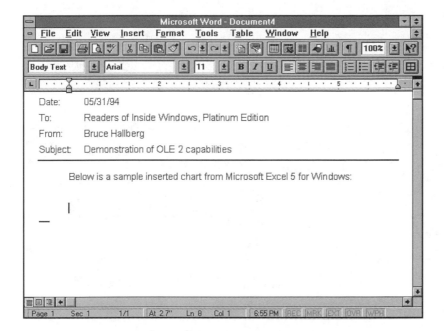

Figure 23.6
Starting with the document in Word.

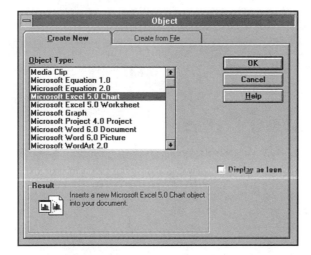

Figure 23.7
The Create New tab in the Insert Object dialog box.

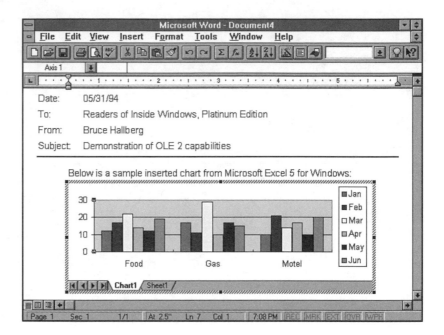

Word's add-in programs work in a similar fashion. When you use WordArt, it behaves the same way as Excel. Similarly, you can perform the same trick from within Excel.

In-place editing is something you do not have to be concerned with, but you might want to be aware of this powerful feature and take advantage of it when appropriate.

Using Drag and Drop

One new feature in OLE 2 is support for drag-and-drop operations. This enables you to grab an object in one application and simply drag and drop it into a destination application. Consider figure 23.9, for example.

You already know how to Copy the graph and then do a Paste Special into the destination document. You also can grab the chart in Excel and drag your mouse pointer to the Word screen. The Word pointer changes to the insertion pointer as you do this. Release the mouse button and the chart is automatically moved to the Word document, as shown in figure 23.10.

Tip

Like many things in Windows, a drag operation moves an object. To duplicate the chart from Excel into Word, hold down the Ctrl key as you make the drag. A small plus symbol next to the Word insertion pointer indicates you are creating a copy of the object rather than moving it.

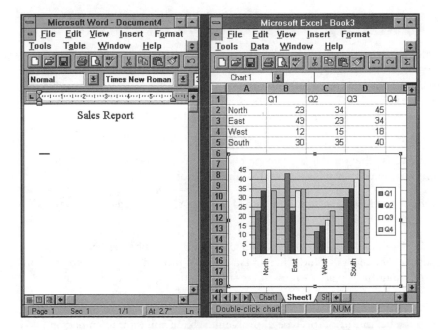

Figure 23.9
Word and Excel,
before drag and
drop.

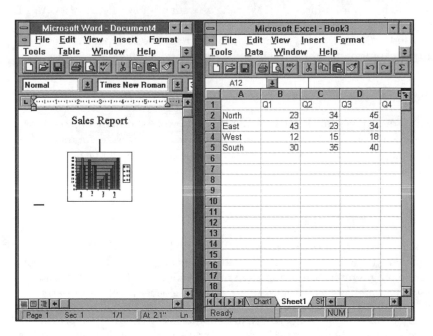

Figure 23.10
The chart dragged
into the Word
document.

IV

Integrating Applications

Understanding Component Architecture

In the good old days of software development (actually, last week), most programs were written using monolithic design. *Monolithic design* refers to the fact that all applications did only what their programmers designed into them, no more and no less. If you needed the occasional spreadsheet table in your word processing document, you had to rely on that capability being a part of your word processor. In fact, you had only one of several choices:

✔ Hope like crazy that the current version of your word processor could use the current version of your spreadsheet files directly (not very likely, really)

✔ Upgrade to the newest version of the word processor, in which a crummy spread-sheet capability had just been added

✔ Work copier miracles, and make your document *look* as if it had an embedded spreadsheet-like analysis table, when in fact you just printed from each application separately and then created a mess doing manual cutting and pasting in the conference room

And this is only the beginning of this type of problem. What if you want to embed an organization chart into your business plan? What if you want to show a figure of a GANTT chart in a project status report? What if you want to use the results of a database query in an analysis spreadsheet? The list goes on and on, and no matter what capabilities are designed into your applications, there will be some types of things that they *just won't do.*

Understanding Objects

The way in which these problems are starting to be solved involves software objects. A *software object* contains both programming code and data that are necessary for the operation of the object. For example, a word processing document might be designed as an object, wherein the words are the data, and the programming code in the object contains instructions for formatting the object, printing the object, and so forth.

Programming Objects

To a programmer, however, software objects are quite a bit more complex. In an object-oriented system, everything in the system is an object of one sort or another. Each object contains data and programming code (the programming code is called a *method* in an object-based system, whereas data usually is referred to as the *properties* of the object).

It bears mentioning that objects are, in reality, just another way to think about programming. Computers, at their core, function by executing one instruction right after another. Sometimes they branch to other locations in a program, but basically they all operate in a procedural manner. For a long time, programs operated in exactly the same way. Programs and programmers mimicked the operation of the computer hardware, albeit at a somewhat higher logical level.

Object-oriented systems work in exactly the same way at the machine level: instruction after instruction. However, they are organized differently from a programmer's perspective, and operate differently at that level. Even though they still are just programs executing sequentially, they are programmed and thought of in different ways, and these differences offer many benefits. Here is a brief overview of how object-oriented programming is different from procedural programming:

✔ Objects can borrow programming code from other, similar objects, and then modify that code for their own specific results. This is called *polymorphism*; when you do it, you are said to be *subclassing* an object. When objects are created in the system, they automatically receive all the properties (data and methods) of their parent object; this is called *inheritance.*

✔ Objects work by communicating with other objects in the system. You might, for instance, have a button in a dialog box that you designed that, when clicked, draws a circle. When you click on the button, the button object sends a message to the circle object that says, in effect, "Hey, you! Draw a circle!" This communication is carried out through an object interface. All the objects in a given system will use the same object interface so that all objects can communicate with all other objects.

✔ Because objects communicate through a rigid communication protocol and do not actually share data or programming code, a bug in one object will not mess up the internal programming of another object. Thus, objects are said to be *encapsulated;* each one is independent of the other objects.

✔ The programmer has to know how the objects in the system are arranged. This is called the *object hierarchy.*

Now, that's a lot of concepts to absorb all at once. However, for the purposes of this discussion, the key concepts to remember are the following:

✔ Objects communicate with one another in order to accomplish tasks.

✔ Objects are individual entities in the system.

✔ Objects contain, within themselves, everything that they need to function.

Learning To Think about Objects

Objects offer many benefits to both programmers and users. However, changing your thinking about computers from the procedural model (wherein everything is merely a

IV

Integrating Applications

series of instructions) to the object model (wherein your system is composed of many individual objects, all working in concert) can be difficult. Certainly it would not be worth thinking about if there were no benefits, but there are many:

✔ Objects increase programmer productivity. Because you can reuse old objects that you know already work, you can more easily write new applications using slight modifications of those objects, instead of starting from scratch every time.

✔ Objects can make a system more bug-free. Because you can use existing, debugged objects in your programs rather than writing the whole thing from scratch, you are less likely to have a buggy application when you are done. Also, because each object is separated from the others, you avoid the problem of a bug in one part of a program causing problems in another part of the program.

✔ If your system were composed entirely of objects, you could more easily integrate existing objects with new objects. You could, for instance, buy an object that performed spelling checking; in theory, every application that you own could then use that spelling checking object.

✔ You could create compound documents. If you think about it, many documents that you create often need capabilities of many different types of programs. For instance, it is very common to include drawings or spreadsheets into a word processing document. If everything in your system were composed of objects, you could more easily integrate the capabilities of your different applications. The exciting thing here is that this support would be automatic. Instead of relying on each software vendor to provide support for the different applications you use, each application would automatically be able to work with all the others. If a brand-new application comes onto the market, you can buy it knowing that it will work seamlessly with your existing software investment.

✔ Developing custom business applications would be a breeze. Instead of writing monolithic programming code for every project, you can just integrate existing application objects in order to achieve whatever goal you wish.

As you can begin to see, objects offer many advantages. Fortunately, these capabilities are here today in the form of Windows' object linking and embedding, or OLE.

Understanding OLE's Component Architecture Model

Object-oriented programming languages are really not new; they have been around for a while. What was lacking was a practical way for each one to operate in a framework that enabled them to operate together. This requires, among other things, a common protocol, which all the objects in a system can use to communicate with one another.

Microsoft has created such a tool with OLE and its Component Object Model. Using a standard like OLE is important for a variety of reasons:

✔ **Standards.** By having a common standard available for the creation and communication of objects, you are assured that applications written to that standard will be able to work together.

✔ **Stability.** One can easily imagine a system made up of millions of objects, all communicating with one another. In such a system, you must be sure that all objects will work and communicate properly, without risk of incorrect connections between objects. OLE provides such a solution.

✔ **Networking.** You probably also can imagine a system wherein different objects exist in different places in a network of computers. OLE provides a programming model that is the same, from the programmer's perspective, whether an object is in the local program or is on a computer located at the other end of the country. And, although OLE does not have security for such a network built in presently, it has been designed with security in mind, and those capabilities can be added at a future time.

Exploring OLE Automation

OLE automation refers to OLE 2's advanced capability to enable objects to be used by programmers across applications. Applications built on OLE 2 have the capability to expose, or provide, object libraries that other applications can see and use. A program in Excel, for instance, can create and edit Microsoft Project objects. Or, a Visual Basic program can create and use Excel objects as if those objects were being used in the original application.

At this time, OLE automation relies heavily on Visual Basic and Visual Basic for Applications, languages that were designed to take advantage of objects and of OLE automation.

The benefits of OLE automation are found mainly in higher productivity for programmers. Because you can reference objects from many applications without worrying about the more cumbersome details of interapplication communication, you can develop business solutions that use capabilities of multiple applications much more easily.

At this time, it is mainly Microsoft applications that support OLE automation, but even within Microsoft applications that support is not complete. As OLE 2 gains popularity, however, more and more applications emerge that can use this capability, both from Microsoft and from other vendors. Table 23.2 contains an overview of Microsoft applications and their respective OLE automation capabilities.

IV

Integrating Applications

Table 23.2
Microsoft Applications and OLE Automation

Application	Level of Support
Access 2	Access can control other OLE automation programs through AccessBasic, but cannot be used by other OLE automation programs. Access can be accessed through ODBC drivers, however, which most Windows programs support.
Excel 5	Excel was the first Microsoft application to support Visual Basic for Applications (a key component of OLE automation) and therefore can control other OLE automation applications. Excel fully supports OLE automation, including exposing a library of Excel objects for use in other applications.
PowerPoint 4	PowerPoint 4 does not support OLE automation.
Project 4	Microsoft Project 4 fully supports OLE automation, both as a server and client.
Word 6	Word 6 can be controlled through OLE automation, but cannot control other OLE automation applications because it lacks Visual Basic for Applications. Microsoft has said that a future version of Word will gain Visual Basic for Applications.

Understanding OLE Automation Functions

Three functions are key to using OLE automation: Set, CreateObject, and GetObject. These three functions are all you need to master in order to start using OLE automation in your Visual Basic programs.

Set

The Set function enables you to set a local variable to "point" to an object in a different application. For example, `Set MySheet = MSExcel.ActiveSheet` causes the variable `MySheet` to point to the active sheet in the open Excel workbook. From then on, you can reference the properties and methods of the `MySheet` object locally, but they actually impact the workbook in Excel.

CreateObject

CreateObject does two things: it creates the specified object, and it returns an object that is linked to the new object. You then use Set to take the returned object and link it to an object variable.

The syntax for CreateObject is `CreateObject("className")`. The class name must be specified in quotation marks, and follows this order: *ApplicationName.ObjectType*.

Therefore, you can use a construction like this:

```
Set ANewObject = CreateObject("Excel.Sheet")
```

When you use CreateObject like this, it automatically starts the application that provides the object, if it has not already been started. In this case, Excel would be started. Then, when the application is started, the object you specify is created, and the object variable is created that can reference that object. You then can use that object variable, for instance with the following two examples:

```
ANewObject.Insert "Some Text to Insert"
ANewObject.FileSaveAs("C:\EXCEL\MYSHEET.XLS")
```

GetObject

GetObject functions somewhat similarly to CreateObject, except it accesses its source object from a file. So, you would use GetObject like this:

```
Set SomeObject = GetObject("C:\OBJECTS\TEST.OJB")
```

Using the Object Browser

Microsoft Excel for Windows 5 and Microsoft Project for Windows 4 each contain a program known as an object browser. An *object browser* is a tool that enables you to see all available object libraries and then, within each library, the available objects and their methods.

To view objects available for use in Excel or Project VBA-based programs, access the **O**bject Browser command in the **V**iew menu while you are editing a VBA macro. The browser appears as shown in figure 23.11.

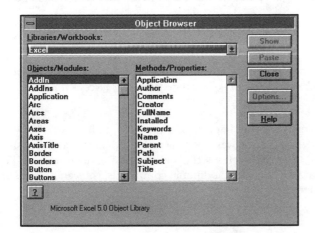

Figure 23.11
Excel's Object
Browser.

Integrating Applications

Access the Libraries/Workbooks section to see the available object libraries. You then can select an object in the Objects/Modules list box. When you click on an object, the available methods and properties for that object appear in the Methods/Properties list box.

Controlling Available Object Libraries

Excel and Project contain a dialog box that enables you to select which object libraries are available to your VBA program. This dialog box is found by choosing Tools, References, which brings up the References dialog box shown in figure 23.12. To use this dialog box, select or deselect from the available object libraries.

Figure 23.12
The References
dialog box.

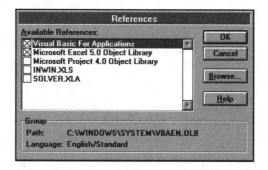

Creating and Using an Object

Figure 23.13 shows a brief subroutine that creates and manipulates a Word for Windows object within an Excel workbook. When this subroutine is run, it embeds a Word document object into the Excel worksheet. When run, you see the results as in figure 23.14.

Notice a couple of characteristics shown in figure 23.14. First, the embedded object is surrounded by a crosshatched border commonly seen around embedded objects when they are active. Second, although you can clearly see the Excel worksheet, you also can see Word's ruler bar at the top of the object. The screen also shows Word's toolbar and menus. When you click outside the object and deactivate it, Excel's normal controls return.

Also, consider the power of the simple piece of code shown in figure 23.13. With only eight VBA commands, the program was able to activate a specific Excel worksheet, insert a Word document into the worksheet, select a font size for the document, and then insert text into the document. With very few additional commands, you can easily control any aspect of that embedded object.

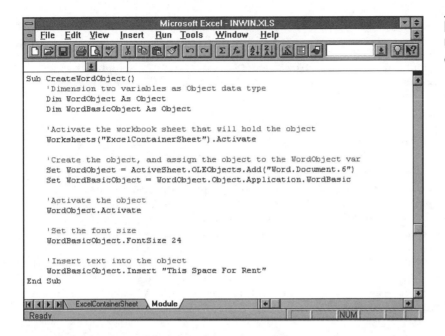

Figure 23.13
Using a Word object in Excel.

```
Sub CreateWordObject()
    'Dimension two variables as Object data type
    Dim WordObject As Object
    Dim WordBasicObject As Object

    'Activate the workbook sheet that will hold the object
    Worksheets("ExcelContainerSheet").Activate

    'Create the object, and assign the object to the WordObject var
    Set WordObject = ActiveSheet.OLEObjects.Add("Word.Document.6")
    Set WordBasicObject = WordObject.Object.Application.WordBasic

    'Activate the object
    WordObject.Activate

    'Set the font size
    WordBasicObject.FontSize 24

    'Insert text into the object
    WordBasicObject.Insert "This Space For Rent"
End Sub
```

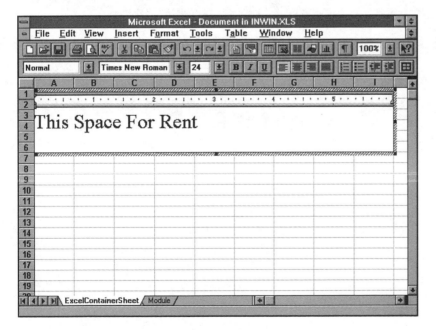

Figure 23.14
An embedded Word document in an Excel worksheet.

This Space For Rent

IV

Integrating Applications

Using Visual Basic for Development

As you can see, Microsoft applications that support OLE automation can be linked in powerful and simple ways, making development of custom business solutions far easier than otherwise possible. Many times, however, it does not make sense for an application you are developing to be based in any one particular application—you want the capabilities of many applications.

Visual Basic 3 is a worthy tool for application development in these cases. You can use Visual Basic to develop your own custom application which is built by piecing together parts from whichever shrink-wrapped application makes sense. Need a small word processing function in part of your custom Visual Basic program? Just include a Word object. Need some spreadsheet capabilities in another place in your custom application? Just include an Excel worksheet object. These objects can be fully controlled by your code, without you having to code all the details necessary to accomplishing word processing or spreadsheet tasks.

Provided your end users have the applications already installed that offer these object services, you can make your development efforts much easier with Visual Basic and with the capabilities of OLE automation.

Learning More about OLE Automation

Many sources give detailed information about using OLE automation in a number of ways. You can start by reading the documentation that comes with Excel and Visual Basic. You also can contact Microsoft and order the Office Development Kit or the Word for Windows Developers Kit. Finally, a number of good books on the market teach Visual Basic development; look for those that also cover OLE automation, which is relatively new technology.

Chapter Snapshot

Welcome to the undocumented world of dynamic data exchange (DDE)! Although much has been written about DDE for the programmer, what about the rest of us? It is difficult finding much useful information about the DDE capabilities of Windows applications. This chapter unveils the dark, mystical world of DDE and shows how you can use it to revolutionize your work. In doing so, this chapter discusses the following:

For more information about DDE, see *Integrating Windows Applications,* from New Riders Publishing.

Inside Dynamic Data Exchange

Dynamic data exchange (DDE) enables you to transfer data or instructions between Windows applications with little user interaction. It has many uses, including the following:

✔ Automatic updating of Excel spreadsheet data inside a Word for Windows annual report

✔ Electronic mailing of an Ami Pro document without leaving the word processor

✔ Querying a remote mainframe database without leaving Excel

✔ Directly linking a Quattro Pro for Windows spreadsheet to real-time data, such as stock market quotes or scientific measurements

To use DDE, you have to establish a conversation between a *client* (an application that sends or receives data to or from another application) and a *server* (an application that responds to the client application's requests by providing the necessary information). Think of a DDE conversation as a phone call: someone initiates the conversation, and if the intended receiver is available, you can begin a conversation and exchange ideas. When you finish talking, you end the conversation by hanging up the receiver. Obviously, many possible options can occur during the phone call, but basically DDE is no more complicated than a phone call.

Using DDE

Windows provides two ways to use DDE: interactively or through a macro language. Interactive DDE is based on the Clipboard copy-and-paste metaphor; macro DDE is based on establishing conversations in user-written macros from an application's macro language.

Interactive DDE Links

Many applications provide DDE capabilities through their menus. This feature enables you to copy data interactively from one application and "paste-link" it into a second application. A good example is copying a cell from a Quattro Pro for Windows spreadsheet using the Edit, Copy command (see fig. 24.1) and paste-linking it into Word for Windows using Edit, Paste Special (see fig. 24.2). In the Paste Special dialog box shown in figure 24.3, you choose the Unformatted Text data type and click on the Paste Link button.

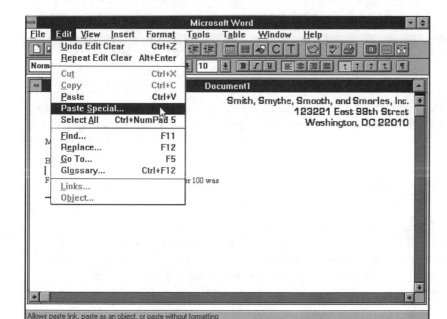

Figure 24.1
Copying data from the source document.

Figure 24.2
Linking the data into the receiving document using the Paste Special command.

Figure 24.3
Paste-linking the
data into Word.

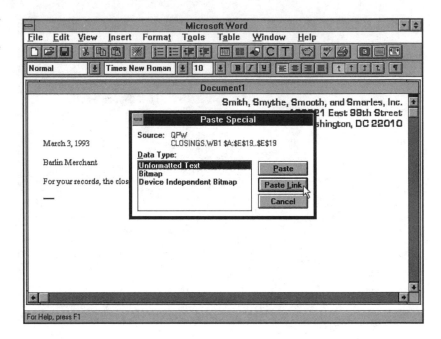

You cannot globally insert a paste-link into a document. Some applications use an Edit, Paste Special command; others use an Edit, Paste Link command.

Looking at the Word document (see fig. 24.4), the value inserted in the document looks no different from the other text around it. If, however, you choose View, Field Codes, you can easily see that the text you pasted in is now what Word calls a DDEAUTO field (see fig. 24.5). Other Windows applications might implement the paste-link differently, but the effect is the same: the data item pasted in the Word document is inexorably linked to the Quattro Pro spreadsheet cell. When the value in the Quattro Pro cell changes in the original document, so does the value in the Word document.

When you create a DDE link between two applications, you set up a permanent link between the two applications. The data link is a channel the server uses to inform the client whenever the data in the source document changes. It is permanent because the server will continue to inform the client until the link is deleted.

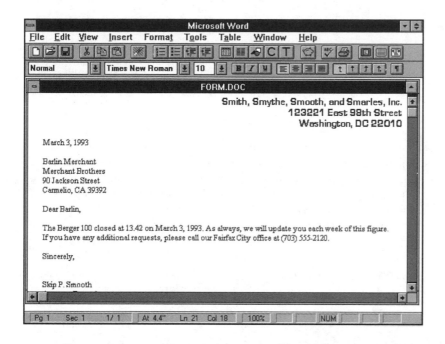

Figure 24.4
Quattro Pro data is now part of the Word document.

Figure 24.5
Word uses the DDEAUTO field for automatic links.

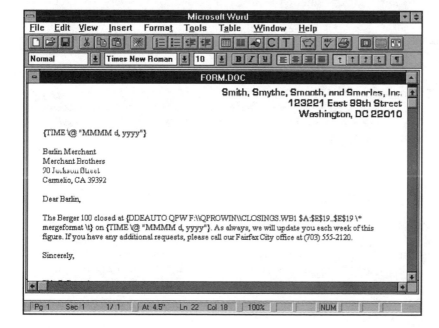

IV

Integrating Applications

A permanent link can be either hot or warm. A *hot* (or persistent) *link* automatically updates the receiving document when the data in the source changes. A *warm link* notifies the client that a change has been made, but the client must specifically make a request to the server for the data to be updated. Even if the linked data in the source document has changed, a warm link does not update the receiving document until the user asks for it. A permanent link is usually implemented by a user through a Paste Link or Paste Special menu command.

Given that a hot link is easier to use (because all updates are performed instantly), why not use a hot link all the time? The reason is that hot links take up system resources. Thus, if you have a sizable number of hot links open at the same time, your system performance can be adversely affected. Warm links, on the other hand, are not persistent and therefore do not put a continuous strain on Windows. Because DDE links require system memory, the actual number of possible links for a document is limited.

Some Windows applications, such as Ami Pro and Word for Windows, enable you to edit hot and warm links through an **E**dit, **L**inks command.

When you open the receiving document, you are prompted as to whether you want to update the data links to that document. If you respond affirmatively, the client looks for the application and source document. If it cannot find one of these, it then asks you whether you want to open the application. This can happen even if the server is opened but the source document is not opened.

If you have to load the server application to update a data link, it must be in your PC's path (from the PATH line in the AUTOEXEC.BAT file). Otherwise, the client will not be able to load the server and update the DDE link.

Macro DDE Conversations

Although many people think of DDE solely in terms of the Clipboard metaphor, a far more powerful way to use DDE also exists. Many Windows applications have a macro or script language that enables you to establish DDE conversations between two applications. DDE conversations managed by the macro language of the DDE client (or possibly the server) can be called *macro DDE*.

Although this section uses application-specific examples in illustrating DDE macros, these principles generally apply to all Windows applications supporting a DDE-capable macro language. Moreover, the macro code examples are simple enough to understand even if you have never used those applications before.

In a macro or script, a DDE conversation is created by writing code that initiates a conversation with a server, pokes data to or receives data from the server application, and terminates the DDE conversation. Suppose that you want to receive address information from the current record in a Paradox for Windows database without ever having to leave Word for Windows. You can create a WordBasic (Word's macro language) macro to provide seamless access to Paradox data. The following WordBasic code retrieves data from Paradox, stores the returning values in variables, and inserts values in the current document at the text cursor.

```
Sub MAIN

' Initiate DDE Conversation
ChanNum = DDEInitiate("PDOXWIN", ":BUSADD:BUSINESS.DB")

' Request data from current record
Business$ = DDERequest$(ChanNum, "Name")
Address$ = DDERequest$(ChanNum, "Address")
City$ = DDERequest$(ChanNum, "City")
State$ = DDERequest$(ChanNum, "State")
ZipCode$ = DDERequest$(ChanNum, "Zip")

' Insert Into Word Document
Insert Business$
*** BeginPara
Insert Address
Insert City$ + " " + State$ + ", " + ZipCode$
InsertPara
InsertPara

' Terminate DDE Conversation
DDETerminate ChanNum

End Sub
```

In a second example, suppose that you work with two applications on your desktop—Word for Windows and ObjectVision. ObjectVision is used as a database front end; Word is used for basic word processing tasks. Without ever leaving an ObjectVision form, you want to generate a form letter in Word using data from an ObjectVision form. To perform this action, you need to prepare both Word and ObjectVision.

IV

Integrating Applications

In Word, you need to set up a preformatted letter. To do this, insert a letterhead and the body of the letter in the document, leaving blanks where the address information will be placed. The document looks like figure 24.6.

Figure 24.6
Leave blanks where ObjectVision data will be poked.

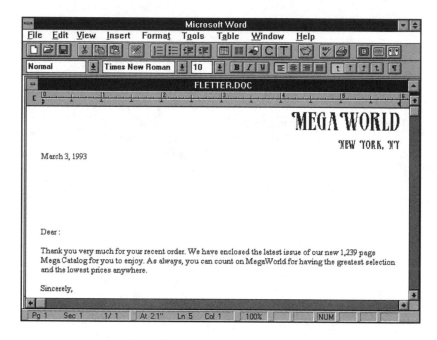

Before ObjectVision can send the data to the document, you first need to define place-holders for that data. In Word, a bookmark serves this function by marking a specific location in a document. To define a bookmark in Word, go to the line in which the name of the company will be inserted and choose Insert, Bookmark. In the Bookmark dialog box shown in figure 24.7, type **Company** to name the bookmark, then click on OK. Move the cursor down to the next line and create a bookmark named **Dept** at that location. On the next line, place an **Address** bookmark. Continue this process for the remaining address fields—**City**, **State**, and **ZipCode**, except place them all on the same line, separating City and State bookmarks with a comma and a space and State and ZipCode with a single space. Add a final bookmark called **Contact** and insert it just after the "Dear" greeting. Save the document as **FLETTER.DOC** and close the document.

Now that Word is up as a DDE server, a series of ObjectVision functions can be written that send address data into Word and ask Word to print a copy of the document to the default printer. The ObjectVision functions would look like the following:

```
' Initiate DDE Conversation
@DDEOPEN("WordLink","WINWORD","C:\WINWORD\FLETTER.DOC",
"Company, Dept, Address, City, State, ZipCode, Contact",
"Company, Dept, Street, City, State, Zip Code, Contact")
```

```
' Poke data from current record
@DDEPOKE("WordLink","Company",Company)
@DDEPOKE("WordLink","Dept",Dept)
@DDEPOKE("WordLink","Address",Street)
@DDEPOKE("WordLink","City",City)
@DDEPOKE("WordLink","State",State)
@DDEPOKE("WordLink","ZipCode",Zip Code)
@DDEPOKE("WordLink","Contact",Contact)

'Print and close form letter
@DDEEXECUTE("WordLink","[FilePrint]")
@DDEEXECUTE("WordLink","[FileClose 2]")

' Terminate DDE Conversation
@CLOSE("WordLink")
```

These functions can be attached to a push button on a form (see fig. 24.8).

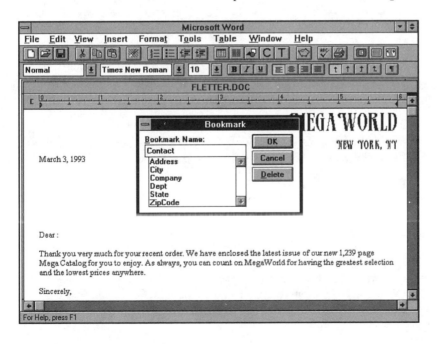

Figure 24.7
Entering
bookmarks in a
Word document.

Figure 24.8
Adding a new
push button to a
corporate address
form.

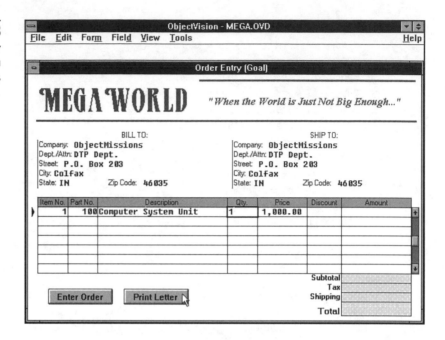

Figure 24.8
Adding a new
push button to a
corporate address
form.

When the user clicks on the Print Letter button, data is sent to Word and inserted in the form letter using the @DDEPOKE statement. Print and close FLETTER.DOC using the @DDEEXECUTE statement. The @DDEEXECUTE statement sends the DDE server instructions to perform a specific command(s), the syntax of which typically is based on a server's script or macro language.

Because of the nature of this type of conversation, a macro DDE conversion is considered a *cold link*, or a one-time exchange of data. In addition, because a macro DDE conversation can be coded in a macro, no user interaction is required.

Macro DDE is a very underrated capability of Windows 3.1. Macro DDE can be used to create seamless solutions to the labor-intensive tasks you find yourself doing routinely. Some tasks that require working with several different applications can be controlled with DDE by the client application. The result is that the user might never have to leave the client application to perform those processes in other applications. This lowers the learning curve with new applications and increases efficiency. Each of the following four examples demonstrates a seamless solution. Each can be implemented using nothing more powerful than a macro language. Study them closely to determine how these principles can be applied to your needs.

✔ **Rolodex-style database.** Suppose you want to create a simple address database you can query within Word for Windows. You can use DDE to integrate Word with PackRat (see fig. 24.9).

Figure 24.9
A Rolodex
database example.

The following are the steps for querying an address database from within Word for Windows:

1. Word sends your address query to PackRat.

2. PackRat queries its database and returns the result.

3. The address is placed in your document.

✔ **Real-time stock quotes.** Suppose you want to generate an Excel graph that logs the real-time performance of your company's stock. You can use DDE to integrate Excel with ProComm Plus for Windows (scc fig. 24.10).

Figure 24.10
A real-time stock
quotes example.

The process of this link is straightforward:

1. Excel periodically asks ProComm Plus to log in to CompuServe and retrieve the current stock quote.

2. ProComm Plus returns the quote in the appropriate Excel cell.

3. Excel uses the new figure to update a graph based on these figures.

✔ **Order fulfillment.** Suppose you want to automate some of the work of your company's order fulfillment operators, who are using an ObjectVision application as they take phone orders. After an order, they have to provide a copy to the shipping department to begin processing. The operators also have to send a letter to the customer to confirm the order. Figure 24.11 diagrams the process.

You can use DDE to perform these actions with a click of a button:

1. ObjectVision sends a copy of the order to the shipping department through Microsoft Mail.

IV

Integrating Applications

2. At the same time, ObjectVision sends a letter confirming the order to the customer by poking the address information to Ami Pro.

3. Ami Pro generates a form letter and determines from the information provided by ObjectVision whether to fax the confirmation letter using WinFax or to print the letter on the network printer.

Figure 24.11
An order fulfillment example.

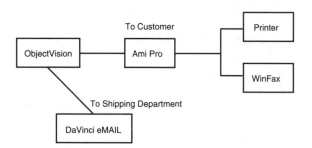

✔ **Information dissemination.** Suppose you want to receive data from multiple sources (a Quattro Pro spreadsheet, Access database, and statistical information from Project), combine it in Word, and send it through multiple channels (fax, e-mail, or CompuServe e-mail) to your company's sales representatives.

You can use DDE to solve this problem by having Word retrieve the information from all sources, combine that information into a Word template, and enable users to distribute the information as they want. This process is shown in figure 24.12.

Figure 24.12
An information dissemination example.

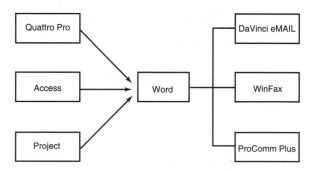

Following the Rules: DDE Protocol

For applications to converse using DDE, there has to be a strict protocol defining how the conversation can be conducted. DDE protocol ensures that two applications are in sync to carry out the conversation. Otherwise, some part of the conversation can fail, losing the link between the two applications and possibly the data. Fortunately, adhering to DDE protocol is the responsibility of the application programmer, not the end user.

If you are using macro DDE, make sure you pay attention to DDE protocol. If you find your DDE conversation cannot be established or you are having problems with it, chances are you are not adhering to protocol correctly. Before looking further at the protocol, take a close look at the actors taking part in the following conversation:

✔ A client application initiates a DDE conversation with another application and asks the server application to send data to or receive data from it, or asks the server to perform a command. The client typically is in charge of a conversation and terminates the conversation when it is finished.

✔ A server application responds to the request of the client application. Upon a poke, a server will accept data from the client and place it in the appropriate location. Upon a request for data, a server finds the data the client desires and sends it back to the client. (If the server cannot find the data, it also informs the client of that as well.) Upon request to perform an action, the server carries out the command if possible.

Because most of the major Windows applications can function as both a client and a server, how you use them depends on your needs. The ideal DDE client application is simply the one in which you spend the most amount of time, such as a word processor, spreadsheet, or database application. The ideal DDE server is one that stores or works with data or can access remote data. Examples include e-mail, fax, and communications software; spreadsheet or database applications; and database front ends to connect you to remote (that is, SQL server) data.

You also can use a DDE server to perform a function for you automatically behind the scenes, such as using a word processor to create a form letter.

Although each conversation involves a single client and single server, you can have multiple DDE conversations taking place simultaneously. A client can have concurrent conversations with two or more servers. If an application can function both as a client and server, it can be utilized as both in two different conversations. To hold multiple conversations with the same application, however, you must have multiple instances of the application opened at once. A conversation always occurs between two application windows.

Establishing DDE Conversations

In a DDE conversation, a client establishes communication with the server using one of three levels of identification:

✔ At the top level is the *application name* of the server. Each DDE server has an assigned application name to which it responds. A server's application name usually is the name of the file (minus the extension). If not, a client cannot start a DDE server if the server is not running when the client attempts to begin a conversation.

✔ At the second level is the *topic,* which identifies the range of information with which the conversation is going to interact. A common example of a topic most DDE servers use is an open document.

DDE protocol requires that a conversation be confined to a single topic; thus, a conversation cannot work with more than one document in the DDE server. Although you can access data from multiple documents, you need to define a new conversation for each new document. Within a particular topic, several data elements can be exchanged during the conversation.

✔ At the bottom level is the *item,* which identifies the exact data element the client wants to use. The client then either requests that data element or pokes data to that data element. An item typically is a reference to a value, such as a cell address (A1B2) or block coordinates (A1B1... ...A10B1) in a spreadsheet, a field or bookmark in a word processor document, a field in a database application, or a defined variable in a communications program. Data usually is exchanged through a standard Clipboard format (that is, Text) or through a special registered Clipboard format.

Keep in mind the application name, topic, and items are always defined by the server. Although a client is in control of a DDE conversation, it is always doing so within the boundaries set forth by the server.

Figure 24.13 illustrates the DDE protocol hierarchy for Word for Windows with a single opened document called FORMS.DOC, which contains four bookmarks (the data items).

Although topics are specific to an application, most servers support a standard topic called System. The System topic can be used by the client to query the server and to retrieve information that might be relevant to a conversation. You might be able to receive a list of the available topics and items available under those topics, depending on the server. Table 24.1 lists the items typically available under the System topic.

Table 24.1
Items Typically Available under the System Topic

Item Name	Purpose
SysItems	A tab-delimited list of names of the items available under the System topic

Item Name	Purpose
Formats	A tab-delimited list of Clipboard formats the server supports
Topics	A tab-delimited list of topics currently available to the client
Status	Current status of the DDE server (usually "Ready" or "Busy")

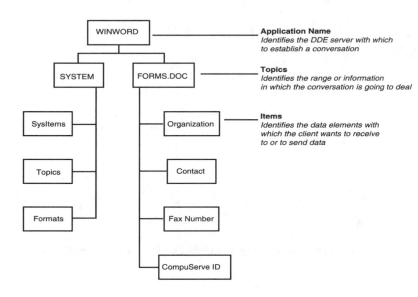

Figure 24.13
FCDDE protocol hierarchy.

You can use the System topic to make decisions in your macro code. The following WordBasic macro, for example, is designed to retrieve a value from an Excel spreadsheet called MTLFUNDS.XLS. The macro uses the Topics item of the System topic to interrogate Excel to see if MTLFUNDS.XLS is returned as a topic. If so, the macro moves on to establish a new conversation with that particular spreadsheet. If it is not opened, the macro sends a DDEExecute statement that opens MTLFUNDS.XLS.

```
Sub MAIN

'Initiate DDE Conversation with Excel
ChanNum = DDEInitiate("Excel", "System")

' Retrieve a list of available topics. If MTLFUNDS.XLS is not opened,
' open it.
Topics$ = DDERequest$(ChanNum, "Topics")
If InStr(Topics$, "MTLFUNDS.XLS") = 0 Then
```

IV

Integrating Applications

```
                      DDEExecute ChanNum, "[OPEN(" + Chr$(34) + "MTLFUNDS.XLS" +
                      ➡Chr$(34) + ")]"
            End If


            ' Initiate a new conversation; this time using MTLFUNDS.XLS as the
            ' topic. Retrieve cell value.
            ChanNum2 = DDEInitiate("Excel", "MTLFUNDS.XLS")
            SalesFig$ = DDERequest$(ChanNum2, "D3G4")


            ' Place the value in a Word document.
            EditGoTo .Destination = "PlaceNumber"
            Insert SalesFig$


            Bye:
            ' Terminate DDE conversations.
            DDETerminateAll


            End Sub
```

A Note from the Author

Most developers of Windows applications with both client and server capabilities stress the software's capabilities as a DDE client but virtually ignore how they can be used as a DDE server. As a result you might find that the single most frustrating factor in working with Macro DDE is trying to determine a software program's application name, set of topics, and set of items.

Software documentation often fails to provide DDE server information in a clear and concise manner or even neglects to mention it. For example, try to find documentation from Microsoft on how you can use Word for Windows as a DDE server. Table 24.3, shown later in this chapter, helps eliminate some of these headaches by providing an extensive list of DDE server protocols.

Understanding DDE Messages

Windows provides several application programming interface messages for implementing DDE. Although the low-level programming specifics of these DDE messages is of no concern to even an advanced Windows user, understanding what these messages do is important. No matter how you work with DDE, either interactively or through a macro language, your DDE conversations will in some way be through these messages. The nine DDE messages can be divided into three groups:

✔ System group, which includes Initiate, Terminate, Acknowledge, Advise, and Unadvise. These commands focus on parts of communication between the client and server.

✔ Data group, which contains Poke, Request, and Data. These commands are primarily concerned with the actual exchange of data between the client and server application.

✔ Task group, which contains a single command, Execute. This message enables you to perform native commands of the server application from within a client application.

Table 24.2 lists each of the DDE messages and their categories.

Table 24.2
Categorizing DDE Messages

DDE Message	Category
Acknowledge	System
Advise	System
Data	Data
Execute	Task
Initiate	System
Poke	Data
Request	Data
Terminate (and Terminate All, which is implemented in some macro languages)	System
Unadvise	Data

The DDE commands most often found in macro languages include Execute, Initiate, Poke, Request, and Terminate.

IV

Integrating Applications

The uses of the DDE commands are discussed in the following list.

✔ **Acknowledge.** The Acknowledge message is sent from one application to the other informing that a message has been received. If you are writing DDE macros, familiarize yourself with Acknowledge. The Acknowledge message is used almost exclusively at the programming level and is rarely implemented in a macro language.

✔ **Advise.** The Advise message is used by a client to ask a server to inform it whenever the value of a data item changes. A parameter in the Advise message tells the server whether to send the data back to the client automatically (in a hot link) or simply to inform the client the value has changed (in a warm link). Because most macro languages do not have a DDEAdvise command, this message is used primarily behind the scenes in a hot or warm link.

✔ **Data.** The Data message is used by a server to notify a client that an item's value has changed and to send the data back to the client application, such as by a hot link. The Data command also is used by the server in response to a Request command.

✔ **Execute.** The Execute message is used by the client to post a command the server is to execute, making it an ideal way to access another application's script or macro language. The command must follow a strict syntax defined by the server and usually is delimited by brackets. In many respects, Execute is the most powerful of all DDE messages because you can actually take full control over the server application. Execute is not concerned with data; in fact, a data item is not utilized in an Execute command.

✔ **Initiate.** The Initiate message is sent by a client application to a server application to establish a DDE conversation.

✔ **Poke.** The Poke message is used by the client application to send a value to a data item in the server application. Poke overwrites any existing value held by the item.

✔ **Request.** The Request message is used by a client to retrieve the value of a data item in the server application.

✔ **Terminate.** The Terminate message is sent by the client to the server application to end the conversation immediately.

✔ **Unadvise.** An Unadvise message is sent by a client application to the server when it no longer needs a data item updated.

Figure 24.14 diagrams the flow of a DDE conversation using these messages.

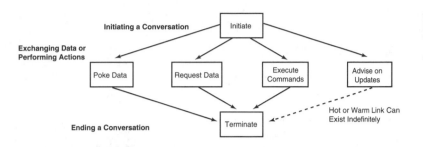

Figure 24.14
The flow of a DDE conversation.

Expert DDE Tips

As has been stressed throughout this chapter, DDE is one of the most neglected subjects in Windows software documentation. To compensate for this, this section pieces together undocumented or poorly documented DDE tips and tricks.

When working with DDE, keep in mind that DDE is not an exact science. Working with DDE applications is more like working with temperamental artists: each is unique, and to work with them successfully, you need to know the subtleties of communications. With that in mind, this section also uncovers the anomalies that you might run into as you work with these applications.

DDE Obfuscation? The benefits of DDE outweigh the headaches that result from inconsistencies and differences between product implementations of DDE. Software DDE inconsistencies are really due to the lack of well-defined standards for user interaction with DDE. The best advice is to experiment and learn the unique traits of the applications you use.

DDE Server Protocol for Major Applications

Table 24.3 provides one of the most extensive compilations of DDE protocol information to date. Use it as a reference instead of thumbing through the back pages of your software documentation. In some cases, this information is not even mentioned in your product documentation.

Many applications enable Execute commands when the conversation has been established with the System topic.

DDE Server Protocol for Major Windows Applications

Application	DDE Server Application Name	Topics Supported	Items Supported
Access	ACCESS	System Name of .MDB file Name of Table [Database Name]:TABLE Table Name Name of Query [Database Name]:QUERY Query Name SQL Statement [Database Name]:SQL Expression	System: SysItems, Formats, Status, Topics Database: TableList, QueryList, MacroList, ReportList, FormList, ModuleList, MacroName TableName, QueryName, SQL Statement: All Data, FieldNames, NextRow, PrevRow, FirstRow, LastRow, FieldCount, MacroName
Ami Pro	AMIPRO	System Name of .SAM file	System: SysItems, Formats, Status, Topics
Crosstalk for Windows	XTALK	System	System: Status Script variables
DaVinci eMAIL	EMAILW30	Name of a phone book entry System SendMail Mail	Numerous (see product documentation)
DynaComm	DYNACOMM	System (for DDE Initiate and DDE Terminate commands only) Server	Items typically defined in scripts
Excel	EXCEL	System Name of .XLS file	System: SysItems, Topics, Formats, Status Cell address (R1C1 format) or block coordinate
Lotus 1-2-3	123W	Name of .WK? file	Cell address (R1C1 format) or block coordinate
ObjectVision	VISION	System Name of .OVD file	Name of Field
PackRat	PACKRAT	System Numerous topics (see product documentation)	Numerous items (see product documentation)
Paradox for Windows	PDOXWIN	Name of a .DB or .DBF file	Name of field
Procomm Plus for Windows	PW	System	Predefined script variable
Program Manager	PROGMAN	Name of .WAX or .WAS file PROGMAN	PROGMAN
Project 3.0	WINPROJ	System Name of .MPP file	
Q+E Database Editor	QE	System Query window name Query file name SQL SELECT statement	Cell Address
Quattro Pro for Windows	QPW	System Name of .WB? file	System: SysItems, Topics, Formats, Status Cell address (R1C1 format) or block coordinate
SuperBase	SB4W or SUPERBASE	System	System: SysItems, Topics, Formats, Status, ReturnMessage, Fields, (expression)
Toolbook Visual basic Design Time Visual Basic Run Time WinFax	TOOLBOOK Name of .MAK File Name of .EXE File FAXMNG	Name of .SBF file Name of .TBK file Program specific Transmit Control	Name of Field Program specific Program specific Fax Number, Receiver, Sendfax DoneReceivingFax, NumberFaxesReceived, TimeUntilNextgoing, Status
Word for Windows	WINWORD	System Name of .DOC file	System: SysItems, Topics, Formats Document: Name of bookmark
WordPerfect for Windows	WORDPERFECT	System Commands	System: SysItems, Topics, Formats

Ami Pro

Excel link anomaly. Before attempting to update a link to Excel in an Ami Pro document, have Excel and the source document open first. If Excel is open but the source document is not, Ami Pro does not recognize that Excel is open and asks you if you want to start Excel. If you click on the No button, your links are not updated. If you click on the Yes button and a GLOBAL.XLM or other file was loaded on start-up, Ami Pro prompts you to open these documents read-only, only after you click on the second Excel icon (which should be flashing). If Ami Pro is maximized, though, you will be unable to see the flashing icon; instead, it will appear as if the system has hung.

Word link anomaly I. Suppose you want to create a hot link from Ami Pro to Word by paste-linking Ami Pro text in a Word document. Word shows the link as being automatic, but in reality it is not. To update the Ami Pro text, you must update the link manually. Moreover, if you open the receiving document and click on the Yes button to link to external documents, Word tries to launch Ami Pro without asking first. An hourglass appears on screen as Word tries to establish a link to Ami Pro. Word eventually displays the message "Word is waiting for the server to release object." Press the Retry button and wait? Sorry, but Word won't respond or allow you to exit the operation. The solution: reboot your system.

Word link anomaly II. Suppose you avoid Word link anomaly I by having Ami Pro open when you try to update the link. If you do not have the source document open, Word receives the updated information, but closes Ami Pro after it is finished.

Microsoft Access

Anomaly. If you try to access data from an open DDE server in which the data does not exist, you receive the message "Remote data not accessible. Start *[application]* application name?" The Yes button loads a second instance of the DDE server application with the name of the nonexistent topic (document) in the title bar.

Note You cannot use DDE to query the SYSTEM.MDB.

Pass-through SQL tip. Although Access does not support direct pass-through SQL, you can perform pass-through SQL indirectly by using a DDE link with the Q+E Database Editor.

Microsoft Excel

Data format tip. When a client application requests data from Excel, it sends data to the client in comma-delimited format.

Link tip. If you cannot establish a conversation with Excel, be sure the Ignore Remote Requests box in the Workspace dialog box is not checked.

DDE initiate anomaly. When you initiate a conversation with Excel, use the System topic. If you use a spreadsheet (XLS) file as the initial topic, Excel might open a second instance of Excel even if the XLS file you are using as a topic is already opened.

Microsoft Word

Excel link anomaly. An Excel spreadsheet cannot be used as a data file linked to Word by a DDE or DDEAUTO field for use in a print merge. Any field that displays a table places a paragraph mark before the table. This paragraph mark cannot be deleted.

International version workaround. Each language version of Word for Windows has the macro language in its native language. To send a WordBasic command to an international version of Word using DDE, you first must know its language version. DDEExecute statements to Word depend on the language of the particular version of the Word server. If you need to send a DDEExecute statement to several international versions of Word or to an unknown version, you need to use the SendKeys command. SendKeys is the only language-independent WordBasic command.

Bookmark anomaly. Word's built-in bookmarks (such as \Line, \Char, and \Para) are not recognized as DDE items and cannot be used in a DDEPoke or DDERequest command.

DDETerminateAll tip. The WordBasic command DDETerminateAll ends all conversations in which Word is the client application. It has no effect on any other ongoing DDE conversations (including those in which Word is a DDE server).

Hidden-text tip. Word never sends hidden text via a DDEPoke command as a client or returns hidden text to a client application upon a DDERequest command.

ObjectVision

@DDEOPEN alert. Even if you use the Link Tool to create a DDE link, it is best to "back up" that link with a @DDEOPEN event tree somewhere in your application. If you created a link using the Link Tool and the server application is not open when you open the OVD file, you receive a "Remote Data Not Accessible. Start Application?" message. If you click on No, the DDE link is lost to that application. If you save the OVD file in that state, your link is irretrievable.

> If you cannot establish a conversation with an ObjectVision application, be sure that the Ignore Remote DDE Requests check box is not checked in the Data Links dialog box.

DDE request workaround. ObjectVision has no @DDEREQUEST function. If, however, the server application to which you are trying to link has a macro language, you might be able to perform a workaround. Before establishing a link, write a macro in your server application that pokes the data you need back to ObjectVision. After setting this up, send an @DDEEXECUTE statement from ObjectVision to the server to run that macro. The macro then gets the data you want, establishes a new conversation with ObjectVision, and pokes the data back to your application.

PackRat

System topic anomaly. A file must be opened before attempting to establish a conversation with PackRat using the System topic.

Paradox for Windows

DDE client limitations. As a DDE client, Paradox for Windows can be used to obtain data from or poke data to other Windows applications. Paradox, however, is limited in how it can perform as a DDE client. Specifically:

- ✔ Warm links to DDE servers are not supported by Paradox.

- ✔ You can establish a hot link only with alphanumeric fields. For the link information to properly fit inside the field, it must be over 35 characters in length.

- ✔ You cannot directly view the value of a hot link within a Paradox table. Instead, you view the DDE reference information about that link. To view the actual values, you must activate the server application.

- ✔ You can use the DDE paste link command only from within table view.

DDE server limitations. As a DDE server, Paradox for Windows can receive data from other Windows applications, and other Windows applications can access data from Paradox tables. When using Paradox as a server, however, keep in mind the following limitations:

- ✔ When performing a paste-link, you can copy values only from a table in table view. Paradox provides no DDE support in forms or reports.

- ✔ You can paste-link a single value only in a table, a single record, or an entire table. You cannot paste-link a single record or multiple values within a field or column.

✔ Paradox does not accept DDEPoke and DDEExecute statements from a client application. As a result, you can receive values from a Paradox database from a client application, but you cannot execute ObjectPAL methods or perform any other action remotely. The only alternative is to use SendKeys.

Paste link note. DDE paste links in Paradox tables are not very useful because they only display a reference to the data, not the actual data itself. Consider using a cold link or OLE as an alternative to a hot link.

System topic note. Paradox does not provide support for the System topic.

ProComm Plus for Windows

DDEExecute note. You can send ProComm Plus a DDEExecute statement to perform any WAX script file or a limited number of script commands. These include Capture, ClosePW, Dial, Dialload, Dialname, Execute, Getfile, Halt, Hangup, Sendfile, and Transmit. ProComm Plus does not enable a client application to execute every Windows Aspect script command—only those listed here.

Program Manager

Controlling Program Manager. Unless you have the Windows SDK, you probably did not even realize that you can perform a variety of functions in Program Manager using DDE. These include the following:

✔ Adding, removing, and restoring program groups

✔ Changing the state of the program group window (maximize, minimize, or restore)

✔ Adding, removing, and replacing program items (or icons)

✔ Setting the icon, shortcut key, or position of an item

✔ Closing the Program Manager

 Program Manager is the only Windows applet that supports DDE.

To perform one of these commands, you must establish a conversation with Program Manager and send one or more of the following commands to it through a DDEExecute statement. Table 24.4 shows the complete list of commands available.

Program Manager DDE Commands

Command	Command Syntax	Parameters
CreateGroup creates a new program group or activates an existing group's window.	CreateGroup(*GroupName*,[*GroupPath*])	*GroupName* identifies the group to be created or, if the group already exists, activated.
		GroupPath identifies the path and name of the group (.GRP) file. (optional) *GroupName* identifies the group to be activated.
ShowGroup changes the state of a group's window to maximized, minimized, or restored.	ShowGroup(*GroupName*, *ShowCommand*)	*ShowCommand* is an integer that specifies an intended action:
		Activates the group window; if it is minimized or maximized, the group window is restored. 2 Activates and minimizes the group window. 3 Activates and maximizes the group window. 4 Activates the group window and restores it in its most recent size and position. 5 Activates the group window and maintains its current size and position. 6 Minimizes the group window. 7 Minimizes the group window while keeping the active group window in an active state. 8 Displays the group window in its current state while keeping the active group window in an active state
DeleteGroup deletes a program group.	DeleteGroup(*GroupName*)	*GroupName* identifies the group to be deleted.
Reload removes and reloads a program group.	Reload(*GroupName*)	*GroupName* identifies the group to be reloaded
AddItem creates a new program icon in the active group.	AddItem(*CommandLine*,[*Name*],[*IconPath*],[*IconIndex*], [*xPos,yPos*],[*DefDir*],[*HotKey*],[*StartMinimized*])	*Note: If no group name is specified, Program Manager removed and reloads all groups CommandLine contains the complete command line information needed to execute the application. (same as the Command Line box in the Program Item Properties dialog box)*
		Name identifies the title of the icon. (optional)
		IconPath identifies path and name of the file containing the icon (e.g., EXE, DLL, ICO file). (optional)
		IconIndex is an integer which acts as an index to identify the exact icon contained in the *IconPath* file. The default is 1. (optional)
		xPos is an integer specifying the horizontal position of the icon in the group window. (optional)
		yPos is an integer specifying the vertical position of the icon in the group window. (optional)
		DefDir identifies the default or working directory as you run the application. (optional)
		HotKey is an integer which specifies the value of the desired short cut key. (optional) If you want to use a key combination using the Alt, Ctrl, or Shift keys, add the following values to the key's ASCII value:
		Alt - 1024 Ctrl - 512 Shift - 256 Extended - 2048
		StartMinimized is an integer that specifies whether to start the application in a minimized state: 0 application in a normal or maximized state. 1 starts the application in a minimized state.
ReplaceItem deletes the desired program icon from the active window and records the location of the deleted item. The next AddItem()command places the icon at that position.	ReplaceItem(*ItemName*)	*ItemName* specifies the name of the program icon to be replaced.
DeleteItem deletes the desired program icon from the active window.	DeleteItem(*ItemName*)	*ItemName* specifies the name of the program icon to be deleted.
ExitProgman closes Program Manager.	ExitProgman(*SaveState*)	*SaveState* is a boolean value identifying whether to save the current settings on exit: RUE saves the current Program Manager state. FALSE does not save the current Program Manager state.
Note: You can only use the ExitProgman() command when Program Manager is not the active Windows shell.		

DDE request tip. Using the PROGMAN item, you can send a DDE Request command to Program Manager to retrieve a list of groups. The list of group names is returned in Text format and separated by carriage returns. For example, note the following WordBasic macro:

```
Sub MAIN
ChanNum = DDEInitiate("PROGMAN", "PROGMAN")
Groups$ = DDERequest$(ChanNum, "ProgMan")
Insert Groups$
DDETerminate ChanNum
End Sub
```

This macro returns the following list of groups in this format:

Main

App Utilities

Norton Desktop Applications

Accessories

Borland Applications

Non-Borland Applications

Windows Sound System

Microsoft Knowledge Base

Multimedia Tools

StartUp

Microsoft Tools

Games

Communications

Quattro Pro for Windows

DDEExecute note. When you send Quattro Pro for Windows a DDEExecute command, use curly brackets {} rather than square brackets [] to surround the macro command or function. Note that this is different from most other Windows applications.

Topics item anomaly. If you use the System topic to interrogate Quattro Pro to retrieve a list of available topics, the Topics item fails to return the last opened notebook (for instance, if a single notebook called SALES.WB1 is opened). The following WordBasic macro code returns just the System topic:

```
ChanNum = DDEInitiate("QPW", "System")
Topics$ = DDERequest$(ChanNum, "Topics")
MsgBox Topics$
DDETerminateAll
```

If you want to determine if a notebook is opened, use the following workaround. Before retrieving the list of available topics, send a DDEExecute command to create a new notebook:

```
ChanNum = DDEInitiate("QPW", "System")
DDEExecute ChanNum, "{FileNew}"
Topics$ = DDERequest$(ChanNum, "Topics")
MsgBox Topics$
DDETerminateAll
```

In this way, you can be assured that the notebook you are searching for is not the last opened notebook.

WordPerfect for Windows

DDE server limitations. As a DDE server, WordPerfect for Windows will accept only DDEExecute commands. You cannot poke data to or request data from WordPerfect using the Poke and Request commands.

The original release of WordPerfect for Windows 5.1 did not provide DDE server capabilities. You need the interim release of Version 5.1 (dated 4/30/92), Version 5.2, or later versions.

DDEExecute note. You can execute any macro command from a client application using a DDEExecute statement except for DocSummaryGetData, GetWPData, MergeVariableGet, and MergeVariableSet.

You can send the following three commands to WordPerfect in a DDEExecute statement. These are not commands supported in the macro language and are available only with DDE.

✔ AppActivate( ), which activates the WordPerfect window.

✔ AppClose( ), which closes WordPerfect.

✔ MacroPlay(MacroName:"MacroName"), which executes a predefined WordPerfect macro.

Chapter Snapshot

Windows is an ideal environment for making applications work together. Although DOS applications are less cooperative than Windows applications, you still can mesh information from DOS files with Windows documents. This chapter shows you a few techniques for integrating DOS-based information, such as:

Chapters 20 to 24 demonstrate how you can use macros, the Clipboard, dynamic data exchange, and object linking and embedding to integrate multiple Windows applications seamlessly. Regardless of the new features and ease of use of Windows applications, you probably still use a few DOS-based applications. If so, you can apply some of the same principles you learned in previous chapters to incorporate your DOS applications into your Windows desktop.

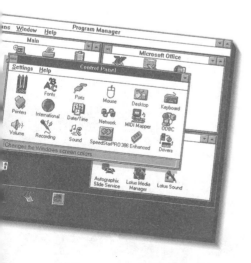

Data Exchange with DOS Applications

For years, working in the DOS environment required that you work within "self-encapsulated" programs; you not only had to learn how to use 1,001 user interfaces and command structures, but also had to figure out some way to break down the walls that existed between isolated programs to transfer data from one program to another.

There was (and is) no way to exchange data on-the-fly, making any data transfer limited to importing and exporting a common file format (usually the lowest common denominator—ASCII text). Because of the programs' incompatibility, a single DOS application typically was used to create a document with little access to outside text or graphics.

One step above ASCII format is Rich Text Format (RTF). *RTF* is a format that enables you to transfer formatted text and graphics between some DOS (and Windows) applications. RTF is a more sophisticated standard, but you still have to perform an import/export process to use those files.

Windows is much more advanced in its capabilities to transfer data between different programs and to integrate applications for a common task. Even DOS applications can use Windows' integration capabilities. Although DOS applications are not designed to take advantage of some of the most powerful data exchange capabilities of the Windows environment, you can still tap into the power of Windows to make your work easier and more efficient when you use your trusty DOS applications.

Although Windows applications are growing increasingly popular, DOS applications are not dead. In fact, many loyal DOS users continue to work primarily in the character-based environment they grew accustomed to over many years. Although the future of personal computing will be a graphical environment, it will be years before everyone migrates to Windows exclusively.

DOS Applications: Revealing Expert Integrator's Tricks

Before diving into the nuts and bolts of integrating DOS applications, keep in mind four general rules:

1. Text can be transferred from DOS to Windows, from Windows to DOS applications, and between DOS applications using the Clipboard (see fig. 25.1).

Figure 25.1
Text transfer between DOS and Windows applications.

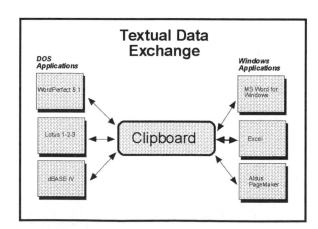

2. Graphics can be transferred from DOS to Windows applications using the Clipboard. Capturing the entire screen or part of a DOS screen allows you to use that image in Windows as a bitmap graphic. This is a one-way process from DOS to Windows—you cannot paste a Windows graphic into a DOS application or move a graphic between DOS applications (see fig. 25.2).

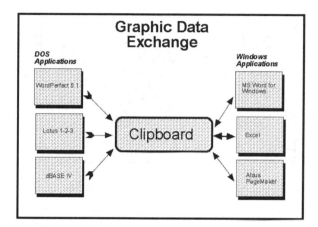

Figure 25.2
Graphics transfer between DOS and Windows applications.

Windows looks at the type of data held in the Clipboard. If it is graphical data, you get a message box stating that there is no text in the Clipboard.

3. DOS applications and documents can be embedded as an OLE object within a Windows document by using the Object Packager. DOS applications are linked using OLE the same way non-OLE-compliant Windows applications are (see fig. 25.3).

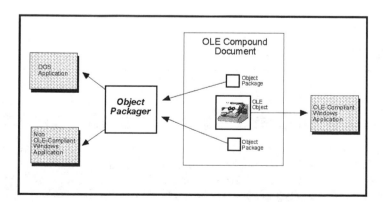

Figure 25.3
Using DOS applications with OLE.

IV

Integrating Applications

4. Dynamic data exchange provides no support for DOS applications. All forms of DDE work only between DDE-supported Windows applications (see fig. 25.4).

Figure 25.4
DOS Applications cannot utilize DDE.

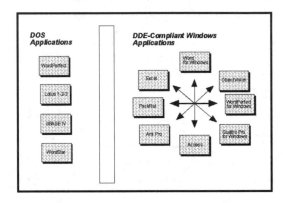

Table 25.1 shows the data-exchange capabilities that exist between DOS applications and Windows.

Table 25.1
Data Exchange Capabilities with DOS Applications

	Clipboard	DDE	OLE
Text: DOS → Windows	X		X
Text: Windows → DOS	X		
Text: DOS → DOS	X		
Graphics: DOS → Windows	X		X
Graphics: Windows → DOS			
Graphics: DOS → DOS			

Using the Clipboard To Exchange Data

As discussed in Chapter 21, Windows uses an internal storage area known as the Clipboard to enable you to send data from one application and insert a copy of that data into a second application. The Clipboard itself is a storage area located in the Windows USER library that manages the exchange of data between applications. You can view the contents of the Clipboard by running the Clipboard Viewer (CLIPBRD.EXE).

Experienced Windows users appreciate the simplicity of the Clipboard's cut, copy, and paste actions. Some DOS applications have their own "clipboard," but no DOS clipboard exists for transferring text and graphics between applications. The transfer of text between applications usually means using a file conversion utility or saving the document as an ASCII text file and importing it into the other application.

Running Windows in 386 Enhanced Mode is strongly recommended when integrating DOS applications. 386 Enhanced Mode provides many additional capabilities essential to DOS-Windows data exchange.

The capability to exchange graphics between DOS programs is even more limited. There have been a few standard graphic formats for DOS, such as PCX and CGM, but many DOS-based programs either do not accept imported graphics at all or have their own proprietary formats.

When you run DOS applications under Windows, however, a whole new world of opportunities appears that makes even some die-hard DOS fans think twice about Windows. You can use the Clipboard to exchange static text from DOS to Windows applications, Windows to DOS applications, and even between DOS applications. You can also exchange graphics in a more limited fashion from DOS programs to Windows.

Keep in mind that you will lose all formatting of text exchanged between DOS and Windows applications and between two DOS applications. Clipboard only exchanges text between DOS and Windows in Text and OEM Text formats.

Text format is a fixed-pitch ANSI font used to display the text in the Clipboard. OEM Text, which is sometimes listed as Terminal, is a fixed-pitch font using the OEM character set (instead of ANSI), which is supported by some Windows applications.

Such enhancements as bold, italic, underline, etc. are lost during a Clipboard transfer. You also lose tabs (which are converted to five spaces) and soft returns, but not hard returns.

Moving DOS Text to Windows

When you transfer DOS text in Windows, you perform a one-time exchange of data using a "mark, copy, and paste" process. Mar**k**, Cop**y**, and **P**aste all are commands found by accessing the Control menu of a DOS window (under the **E**dit menu).

To illustrate this process, suppose you want to copy a group of cells from a Quattro Pro 4.0 spreadsheet and paste it into a Word for Windows document.

1. You start by running Quattro Pro in a window (not full-screen).

2. You then choose **E**dit, Mar**k** from Quattro Pro's Control menu, as shown in figure 25.5.

Figure 25.5

Choose the Mark command from the Edit menu.

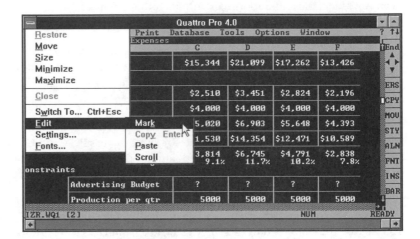

3. Mark the text you want to copy by dragging the mouse over it (see fig. 25.6) and choose **E**dit, Cop**y** from Quattro Pro's Control menu to copy the text to the Clipboard.

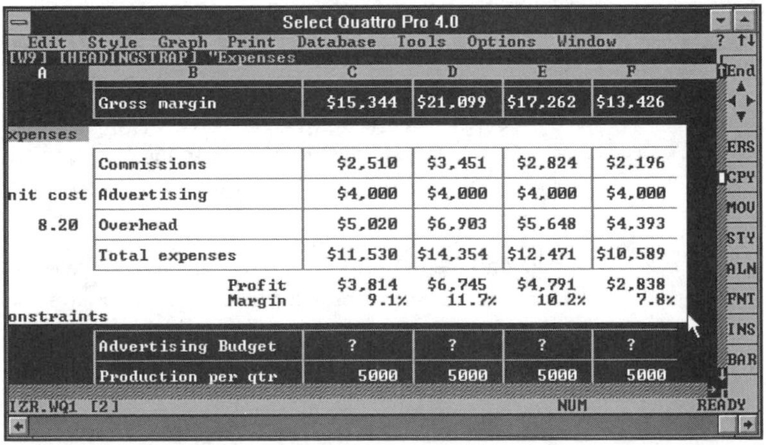

Figure 25.6

Drag the mouse to select text to be copied.

4. Activate the Word window and choose the **E**dit, **P**aste command to paste the text into the Word document (see fig. 25.7).

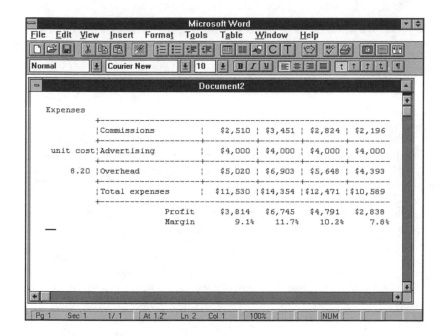

Figure 25.7
Quattro Pro text is pasted into Word for Windows.

If you want to copy the contents of the entire Quattro Pro screen, or if you are running Windows in Standard mode, press the Print Screen key while you are running the DOS application full screen. (If Print Screen does not work, try using Alt+Print Screen or Shift+Print Screen.) This action copies the Quattro Pro screen to the Clipboard as text. You can then paste it into your document as desired.

Tip

If you are running Windows in Standard mode, you can still exchange data with DOS applications, although there are a few restrictions. Windows operates in Standard mode on computers which have a 286 processor or less than 2 MB of RAM. In Standard mode, DOS applications fill the entire screen instead of being able to run in a window. You cannot mark a portion of text for copying to the Clipboard; you must copy the entire contents of the screen.

Note

The Print Screen key can be very useful when you want to copy the entire contents of a DOS screen to the Clipboard.

IV

Integrating Applications

Transferring Windows Text to DOS Applications

Windows also enables you to move text from a Windows program to a DOS application. To illustrate the steps, suppose you want to move text from Word for Windows to Quattro Pro 4.0.

1. Select the text you want to copy in Word for Windows and choose Edit, Copy command from Word's menu.

2. Switch to the Quattro Pro window (make sure it is in a window and not full-screen) and place the text or mouse cursor on the location where you want to paste the text.

3. Choose Edit, Paste from the Control menu of the Quattro Pro window. The text now appears in the Quattro Pro spreadsheet.

If you are running your DOS application full screen or are in Standard mode, you need to copy the text from the Windows program in the same manner. To make a DOS window full-screen, choose Settings from the Control menu and Full Screen in the Display Options group. You can also set up the PIF file to go to full screen or window by default.

To shrink a full-screen DOS application to an icon, press Alt+Esc. If this does not work, check to ensure that the shortcut key has not already been reserved by the application in your PIF file.

Activate the DOS program so that it comes up full-screen and immediately press Alt+Spacebar to switch back to Windows. The DOS program will now be shown as an icon. Choose Edit, Paste (or Paste if you are running in Standard mode) from the Control menu of the icon (see fig. 25.8). The text is inserted in Quattro Pro.

If you have difficulty pasting text into your DOS application, it might be because your DOS application is not able to accept the text as quickly as Clipboard is sending it. To solve this problem, if you are running the application from a PIF file, try unchecking the Allow Fast Paste option. The Allow Fast Paste option is found in the Advanced Options dialog box (Enhanced mode) of the PIF Editor.

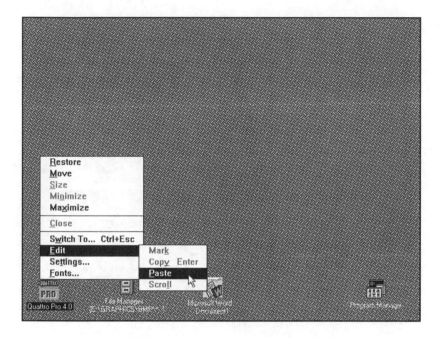

Figure 25.8
Control menu of
the Quattro Pro
icon.

Transferring from DOS to DOS

Not only does Windows provide static data exchange between DOS and Windows
applications, it also enables you to move data between DOS applications. Even if you use
only DOS applications, you can still take advantage of the data-exchange power of the
Windows environment.

When you paste text into a DOS application, the Clipboard simulates the "typing" of the
text into the DOS program. This is because DOS applications do not understand Windows messages.

To illustrate this process, suppose you want to copy text from a Quattro Pro 4.0 spreadsheet and insert it into a WordPerfect document.

1. Open both applications in DOS windows.

2. Switch to Quattro Pro and choose Edit, Mark from its Control menu. Mark the
text you want to copy by dragging the mouse over it (see fig. 25.9).

Integrating Applications

Figure 25.9
Selecting text in
Quattro Pro.

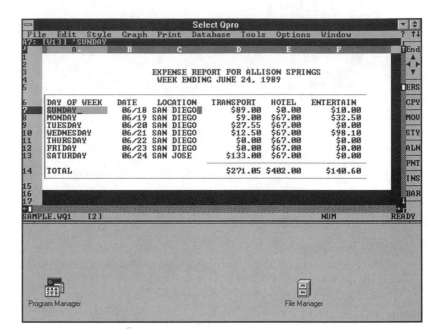

3. Choose **E**dit, Cop**y** from Quattro Pro's Control menu to copy the text to the Clipboard.

4. Switch to the WordPerfect window (make sure it is a window and not full-screen) and place the text or mouse cursor where you want to insert the text.

5. Choose **E**dit, **P**aste from WordPerfect's Control menu. The spreadsheet data is now inserted in the WordPerfect document, as shown in figure 25.10.

If you are running both applications full-screen or are in Standard mode, you need to activate Quattro Pro and press the Print Screen key. (If this does not work, try using Alt+Print Screen or Shift+Print Screen.) Use Alt+Spacebar to switch back to Windows. If WordPerfect is not running, start it and press Alt+Spacebar to switch back to the Windows desktop. WordPerfect will now be shown as an icon. Choose **E**dit, **P**aste (or **P**aste if you are running in Standard mode) from WordPerfect's Control menu. The text will be inserted into the WordPerfect document.

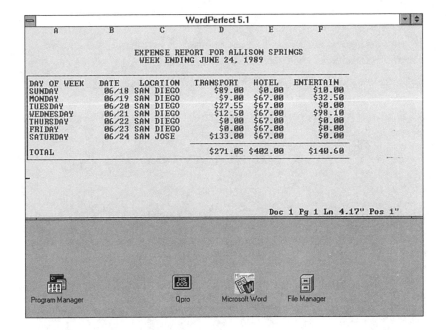

Figure 25.10
Inserting a
Quattro Pro
spreadsheet into
WordPerfect.

Transferring Graphics

Besides exchanging text with DOS applications, you can also copy graphics or graphical screens to the Clipboard and use them in Windows applications. This capability is important to many users who have created graphics in a DOS application and would like to convert them to a Windows bitmap or other graphic format file. In addition, others may want to capture the contents of the entire screen in graphic form for use in a presentation or documentation.

You can only transfer graphics from DOS applications if you are running Windows in 386-Enhanced mode. Windows does not provide graphic data exchange in Standard mode.

The Windows Clipboard is limited by the data types the source application sends to the Clipboard and the capability of the receiving application to handle at least one of those data types. For example, the Clipboard can handle 256-color bitmaps. Just be sure the receiving application can accept them.

Integrating Applications

Tip

Word for Windows has a bug in its use of graphics with the Clipboard. See Chapter 21 for details on its workaround.

Suppose you want to import a graph created in Quattro Pro into Word for Windows. To do this, you would follow these steps:

1. Begin by displaying the Quattro Pro graph in a DOS window, as shown in figure 25.11.

Figure 25.11
Displaying a graphic in Quattro Pro.

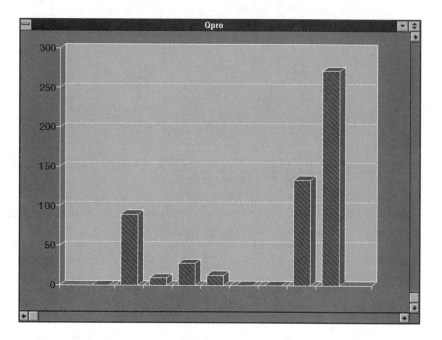

2. Press Alt+Print Screen to copy the contents of the window to the Clipboard. (If you are running Quattro Pro full-screen, press the Print Screen key.)

3. Activate Word and use Edit, Paste to paste in the chart (see fig. 25.12).

You can also copy a portion of a DOS screen as a graphic. For instance, if you have a WordPerfect graphic (WPG) and would like to import it into your Word document, open WordPerfect 5.1 in a window (not full-screen) and display the graphic. Choose Edit, Mark from WordPerfect's Control menu and mark the portion of the graphic you want to copy by dragging the mouse over it (see fig. 25.13). Choose Edit, Copy from the Control menu to copy text to the Clipboard. When the graphic is copied to the Clipboard, the graphic is in bitmap format. Switch to Word and use Edit, Paste from Word's menu (see fig. 25.14).

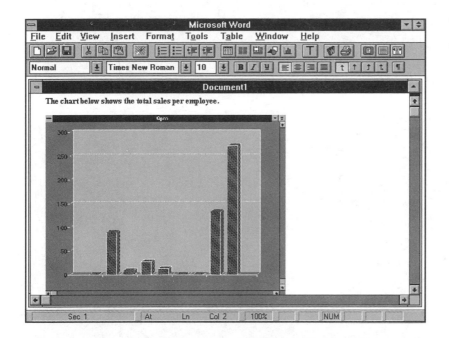

Figure 25.12
Quattro Pro chart pasted into Word.

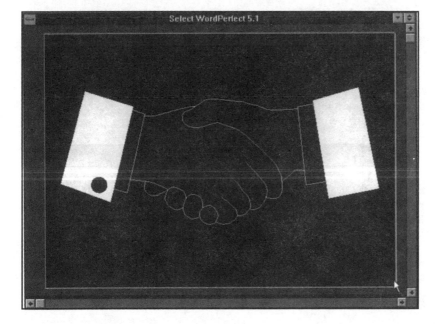

Figure 25.13
Drag the mouse over the portion of the graphic you want to copy.

IV

Integrating Applications

Figure 25.14
WordPerfect graphic pasted into Word.

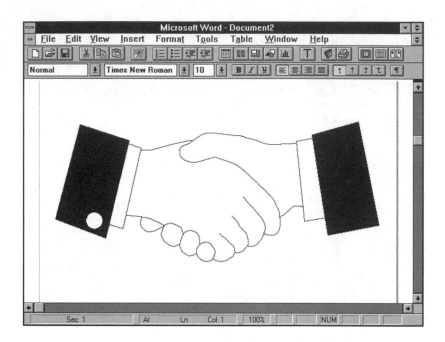

You also can exchange graphics between Windows and DOS applications by saving the graphic in a format accepted by both environments. The BMP (bitmap) format is currently the standard graphic file format in Windows, but virtually no DOS applications support it. Some DOS applications support PCX format, however, enabling you to use Windows Paintbrush as a conversion tool. If you cannot save a graphic in an interchangeable format, you may need to invest in a graphic conversion utility that can transfer graphics between many DOS and Windows file formats.

Using OLE To Embed DOS Applications in Windows Documents

Even though DOS applications do not support OLE, you can link DOS applications and documents to Windows compound documents using the Object Packager. The Object Packager is a Windows 3.1 utility that enables you to encapsulate non-OLE data in an object package and embed that data package into a compound document. This data is presented as an icon in the client application. When you want to access the data contents of the package, you simply double-click on the icon. The DOS application starts loading the data file. When you exit the program, you return to the client application.

Tip

Not only can you use the Object Packager to wrap itself around DOS and non-OLE Windows applications, but also DOS commands and batch files.

To create an object package with a DOS application, follow these simple steps:

1. Start the Object Packager by double-clicking on its icon in Program Manager.

2. Choose Edit, Command Line from the menu to display the Command Line dialog box. In the dialog box, type the name of the DOS or PIF file followed by the data file you want to embed as its command-line parameter. To run a batch command, type:

   ```
   C:\UTILITY\CLEANUP.BAT
   ```

3. Click on the Insert Icon button to select an icon to represent the package in the compound document. Select an icon from an ICO, EXE, DLL, or other resource file (type its file name in the File Name field) and click on OK to insert the icon image into the Appearance side of the Object Packager, as shown in figure 25.15.

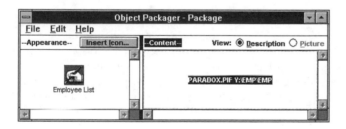

Figure 25.15
Completed object package.

Note

Windows includes a file named MORICONS.DLL, located in your Windows directory. MORICONS.DLL contains more than 100 icons you can use to represent object packages.

4. The package is complete. Choose Edit, Copy Package from the menu to copy the package to the Clipboard.

5. Activate the Windows application you want to embed the object into and choose Edit, Paste Special from its menu. (If you are using Word or another Microsoft application, you will be able to select the object's data type. Select Package Object from the Data Type list and click on the Paste button.) The package is now an embedded object in the compound document.

IV

Integrating Applications

Tip

You can use any graphic to represent an OLE package. Copy a graphic to the Clipboard and choose **E**dit, **P**aste to insert it into the Appearance side of the Object Packager.

When you use the compound document, you can view the packaged data by double-clicking on the embedded icon. The DOS application runs with the appropriate file open.

Using Macros To Integrate DOS and Windows Applications

Windows enables you to run many Windows and DOS applications at the same time, limited only by the memory you have on your system. You can switch between these applications by using the Task List, Alt+Tab, or the Alt+Esc keys. To start each of these programs, however, you need to minimize your application, restore the Program Manager, click on the appropriate icon, and then perform the necessary tasks. Fortunately, you can use the macro language of several Windows applications to link more closely two or more applications, eliminating the need to use the Program Manager to start programs.

Most Windows applications have macro languages that provide a command to launch another program. You can use this command to make your Windows desktop easier to work with. To illustrate this special macro command, this section uses the built-in capabilities of a Windows macro language to integrate Windows and DOS applications. The macros themselves are nothing complicated—just single-line commands. The end result, however, greatly simplifies your work.

Many people use a word processor and spreadsheet for daily tasks. Suppose your office is using a Windows word processor and a DOS spreadsheet. Is there any easy way to move between applications quickly? You can use Program Manager, but the most speedy way is to customize the Word menu by adding a command that starts Quattro Pro.

In Word for Windows, create a macro in your global template (NORMAL.DOT) by choosing T**o**ols, **M**acro from the menu. Name the macro **StartQP** and click on the Edit button. Type the following command in the macro edit window (assuming you have a PIF file for Quattro Pro):

```
Sub MAIN
Shell QUATTRO.PIF, 1
End Sub
```

Close the macro edit window after saving the StartQP macro and choose Tools, Options from Word for Windows' menu bar. Then select the Menus icon from the Category list. Select the T&ools option from the Menu pull-down menu. Add a separator to the menu by selecting - - - - - - - from the Macros list and clicking on the Add button.

Select StartQP from the Macros list and type **Start &Quattro Pro** in the Menu Text combo box and click on the Add button. Click on the Close button and save changes to the global template by choosing File, Save All from the menu.

When you are finished setting up the macro and menu, select Start Quattro Pro from the Tools menu to run Quattro Pro from within Word. Quattro Pro now opens in a window.

Windows moves far beyond the DOS environment in its capabilities for transferring data between different programs and integrating applications for a common task. Even with this sophistication, Windows continues to include DOS applications in the process.

IV

Integrating Applications

Part Five

Networking and Windows

Chapter Snapshot

The PC originally was intended to be used by one person; thus, the phrase *Personal Computer*. As the PC evolved, the expectations of what it could be used for also evolved; today, PCs are rapidly replacing minicomputers and mainframes for many applications. *Networks* enable PCs to be connected together to share information and resources such as printers in much the same way that multiple users accessed older minicomputers and mainframes.

This chapter explains how networks operate, and covers a few other points:

Using network resources is not difficult. Using network resources effectively, however, requires that you understand some underlying concepts about networks. The first section of this chapter provides an overview of general network topics.

CHAPTER

Understanding Networks and Workgroups

Types of networks vary, depending on the way the computers in those networks are connected. A *local area network* (LAN), for example, is a group of computers connected together within a particular geographic area. Multiple LANs in different geographic locations are sometimes connected together to form a *wide area network* (WAN).

A network uses a combination of network hardware—usually consisting of a network interface card (NIC) with cabling—and software to connect multiple computers together physically and to enable them to "talk" to each other.

Understanding the Purpose of a LAN

A LAN enables previously separate computers to share disk drives, printers, and other external devices. LANs enable you to do the following:

✔ Store programs and data in a common location available to other users

✔ Provide access to a particular program (and associated data) for more than one person at a time

✔ Access and use printers connected to other computers

✔ Use e-mail to communicate with others

✔ Transfer data between different types of disk drives

With a LAN, one computer can be designated as a central location to store program and data files that are used by many computers. In addition, users have access to a printer that might be connected to a different computer; this option provides flexibility as to the number and types of printers available, and also saves money because a printer is not needed for each computer.

CD-ROM drives are gaining in popularity as a way to access large amounts of data. With a LAN, one CD-ROM drive can be accessed from any other computer in the network.

The capability to store programs and data in one location can help many business users with accounting. With the network version of an accounting software package, two people can enter invoices into the system while a third person enters accounts receivable information. When invoices need to be printed, the users who entered them can print to the same printer.

Another popular use of a LAN is for database management. Many companies maintain lists of clients (or prospective clients) in a database. A telemarketing team, for example, can use its database when it calls clients and notify them of a new product offering or a special the company is running. By keeping all the client information in a common database as a record is added or changed, it is available for everyone to access and use.

Suppose that each prospective client record contains a field that is checked if the client asks for additional information, and a field that is checked after the information has been sent. The telemarketers would check the request for additional information field, and another person could be scanning the database searching for those prospective clients who want information.

After the information is sent, the person who sent the information would update the record indicating that information had been sent and then the telemarketers could follow up. This universal access among the telemarketing team is made possible by a network connecting everyone's PCs.

Electronic mail, or e-mail, is another important aspect of networking and workgroup computing. E-mail enables messages and files to be sent to users connected to the network. LANs make it easy to schedule meetings and appointments with others who are connected to your network. With the appropriate software, you can access the schedules of others and determine the best time to schedule a meeting or appointment.

LANs also can solve hardware problems. If you need to read data from a 3½-inch disk, but you have only a 5¼-inch disk drive on your computer, a LAN can enable you to access the 3½-inch drive on another computer.

One of the most common uses of a LAN is information exchange. Suppose you are preparing a report that needs to include information being prepared by a co-worker. Instead of transferring the information from one computer to another with a disk (a process often referred to as *sneakernet*), you can access the file by way of the network— without even getting up from your desk.

Understanding LAN Hardware

Most LANs require a network interface card (NIC) in each computer on the network. The NIC provides the hardware interface between the network and the computer in which it is installed. It performs the task of transmitting data from the computer onto the network and receiving data from the network to the computer.

Each NIC has some type of connector on the back of the card that enables a cable to be connected to it. Each computer is connected to the others in the network with a network cable.

As network technology advances, many new methods and techniques are being used to increase network speed and flexibility. Wireless NICs use radio transmission techniques to connect computers on the network. Infrared technology is being used to transmit network signals between buildings and other straight line-of-sight applications in much the same way that your remote control operates your television. Microwave technology also is being used to provide LAN connections between buildings. Fiber-optic cabling offers the transmission of data over longer distances and has higher network speed than conventional copper cabling. Fiber-optic cabling also is not affected by electromagnetic interference that degrades the signals of conventional network cabling.

Understanding LAN Software

The *network operating system* (NOS) provides your computer with the functions and commands necessary for it to operate in a network. The NOS processes network requests, communicates with the network, and provides a smooth integration with the computer's operating system.

Network software must be installed on your computer before you can access the network. Each network operating system (NetWare, LANtastic, Windows for Workgroups, and so on) uses a slightly different procedure to boot the network software. Usually, a *NIC device driver*, which is the software interface between the network adapter and the network operating system, is loaded first. The NOS is loaded next; it usually consists of one to five programs, depending on the type of network and the specific function that your computer will have in the network.

In the case of LANtastic, the NOS program called REDIR.EXE gives the computer the capability to access disk drives and printers on other computers. Running the NOS program SERVER.EXE after REDIR.EXE also enables the computer to share its disk drives and printers with others.

Depending on the type of network, the network software is usually loaded in the CONFIG.SYS file, the AUTOEXEC.BAT file, a separate batch file, or a combination of these before Windows starts. Windows for Workgroups 3.11 improves network performance by using virtual network device drivers that are loaded after Windows starts, rather than by CONFIG.SYS or AUTOEXEC.BAT. This conserves memory and enables the network to perform better. Some NICs, however, do not provide support for these virtual network device drivers, although manufacturers are developing new drivers. NICs that are not supported by virtual network device drivers are supported by real-mode drivers, which are installed by CONFIG.SYS and AUTOEXEC.BAT, just as with previous versions of Windows.

When you first power up your computer, it automatically looks for the CONFIG.SYS and the AUTOEXEC.BAT files, and executes the instructions within them. The CONFIG.SYS file usually contains loading instructions for device drivers; the AUTOEXEC.BAT file is a DOS batch file that can contain almost any command typed at a DOS prompt.

Understanding the Physical LAN

Although wireless LANs now are available, a typical LAN consists of a given number of workstations that are connected to one another by cables. On the network, each workstation is called a *node*. You can consider nodes to be just access points to data, or doorways that you use to access the network. The distinction between nodes is important only to the network operating system so that it can distinguish one request from another and provide services when a specific user requests them from a given node. In other words, the network operating system must be able to identify the doorway from which you make your request.

Network Interface Cards

Each workstation requires special hardware to connect to the network and access the network's resources. This hardware consists of a network interface card (NIC) that performs the task of sending and receiving messages across the network. Each NIC uses a unique network address to enable messages to be directed specifically to it, in much the same way you send mail to a specific house address. The network card monitors all the packets of data (a *packet* is data that has been encapsulated in some way) that travel across the network, checks the address to which the data packet is addressed, and acts on the packet accordingly. If the packet is meant for another node, the network card passes it on. Otherwise, the network card intercepts the packet and passes the data on to the workstation's CPU.

To a large extent, the network card determines the network's performance. It serves as a communications link in one direction between the computer and the network when sending data, and in the other direction as a link between the network and computer when receiving data. The data is transferred one bit at a time at speeds that vary according to the type of network and card being used.

Generally, the network card processes data more slowly than the network can carry it, and more slowly than the computer can send it. The card, therefore, must *buffer* the data, or hold it in temporary storage until the card can process it. For this reason, a slow network card can become a bottleneck to performance, and a fast network card can improve network performance considerably.

Media

The network requires a means to enable data packets to move between nodes. These connections between nodes often are called the network media. Common network media include twisted-pair cable, coaxial cable (also called coax), fiber-optic cable, and free space. Twisted-pair, coaxial, and fiber-optic cables are physical connections and often are referred to as *bounded media*. The term *free space* refers to wireless network connections, which are achieved by using radio waves or light (as in infrared networks). These kinds of media often are referred to as *unbounded media*.

Twisted-Pair Cable

Twisted-pair cable is the most commonly used form of network medium, similar to the cabling used for standard telephone lines. Token Ring networks (see the section

"Network Topology" later in this chapter for an explanation of Token Ring) use a form of twisted-pair wiring that is considerably sturdier than standard phone wire. This special type of twisted-pair cable contains pairs of wires enclosed by metallic-foil shielding, with the entire bundle shielded by a metallic braid. Other types of Token Ring cabling are used, consisting of additional twisted pairs, fiber-optic cables, and voice/data lines contained in the same bundle. In addition, less expensive unshielded twisted-pair wiring also can be used.

In some cases, existing phone lines can be used for twisted-pair network media, but the quality of the lines limits the distance between nodes and the number of nodes that can be connected to the network. If you are installing new cabling, install Category 5 cable for maximum performance.

Coaxial Cable

Coaxial cable is another commonly used network medium. Ethernet and ARCnet networks both use coaxial cable. Some coaxial cable used in networks is similar to that used in cable television. Coaxial cable generally offers higher data-transfer rates over longer distances than does twisted pair, due to lower signal loss and interference. Coaxial cable uses standard BNC connectors to connect cables together and to connect the network cable to the network card (see fig. 26.1).

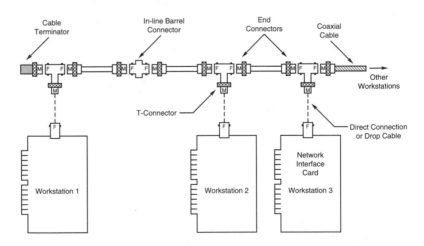

Figure 26.1

Typical coaxial cable components.

Some types of networks that use coaxial cabling require that the cable be directly connected to the network card by a T-connector. Other networks allow a drop cable (a short, single length of cable) between the main network cable and the computer, which enables you to run the main cable through the wall or ceiling and run a drop cable from the main cable to the computer.

Fiber-Optic Cable

Fiber-optic cables are more expensive than other types of cabling, but provide the highest transmission rates and best signal security. Fiber-optic networks are now available from many vendors and will become less expensive as vendors begin competing for market share. Fiber-optic cabling is used extensively in building-to-building and site-to-site connections, enabling users in different buildings or at different sites to communicate and share data and other resources.

Unbounded Media

Radio networks have been used to connect systems for which a physical connection was not possible. The latest twist on unbounded media is the wireless infrared network. These networks use infrared transmitter/receivers to send data through the office without a cable connection. The primary benefit of this type of network is the elimination of planning for cable installation or special construction to accommodate the cables.

Network Topology

The term *network topology* sounds more imposing than it really is. This term refers to the way in which a network's nodes are physically connected to one another. Common topologies in use today are star, ring, and bus topologies.

A simple *star topology* network consists of a hub to which workstations are connected, much like the points of a star (the nodes) connect to its center (the hub). Figure 26.2 illustrates both simple star topology and distributed star topology. A *distributed star topology* network essentially is a number of stars with hubs connected together. Star topology offers easy fault detection (detecting faulty cables and other components) and an easy means to expand the network in multifloor installations. The network shown in figure 26.2 consists of two simple stars connected together to form a distributed star network.

The hubs in a star topology network control network communication, serving to control transmission errors, boost the signal, and route data packets. Although star topology networks appear similar in configuration, the hub's function varies not only across different networks, but also within the same network. ARCnet networks, for example, use both passive and active hubs. *Passive hubs* route data packets without performing any other processing, such as signal boosting, on the packet. *Active hubs* also amplify and retime the signals.

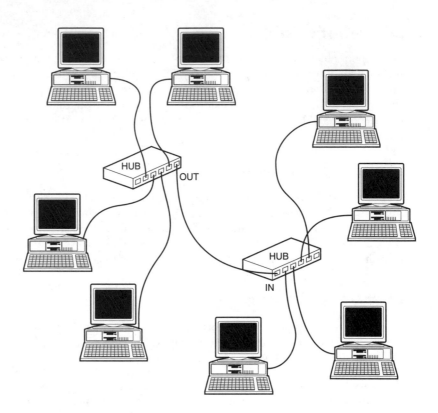

Figure 26.2
A distributed star
topology network.

A *bus topology* network uses one or more linear bus segments to which networks are connected (see fig. 26.3). The nodes are connected in a series along the main cable, or *backbone.* Nodes often are connected to the backbone with drop cables. Bus topology simplifies adding nodes linearly, such as in the same office or on the same floor of a building, but complicates the addition of nodes on different floors. The primary drawback to bus topology is that if a cable fails, the entire network is affected. With star topology, on the other hand, only the node to which the cable is connected is affected.

In *ring topology* networks, nodes are connected to the server in a continuous ring, forming a closed circle. Ring topology works well for small workgroups and departments in which all the nodes on the network can easily be connected to the ring. Ring topology, however, is more difficult to implement if nodes are separated by longer distances or by different floors of a building.

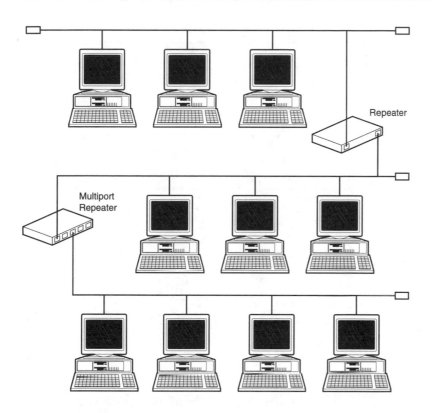

Figure 26.3
A bus topology
network.

Repeater

Multiport
Repeater

Network Layers

Most networks follow a standard network-layering scheme that separates the various parts of the network into logical layers. The standard, defined as the OSI Reference Model, is illustrated in figure 26.4.

The first two layers define the way data is physically transferred across the network. Layers 3, 4, and 5 define the way the data is processed before being passed on to the workstation's operating system (such as MS-DOS). Layer 6 defines the workstation's operating system, and layer 7 defines the workstation's network software. Above layer 7 are the applications that require access to the network, such as Windows and your other applications.

This layering of the network enables different types of hardware and software to be used on a single LAN. Your network can, for example, mix workstations that use different operating systems. Some workstations might run UNIX while others use MS-DOS. The network also can employ different network transport systems, with some workstations running IPX, others running NetBIOS, and still others using TCP/IP (transport systems are discussed a little later in this chapter).

Figure 26.4
The OSI Reference
Model.

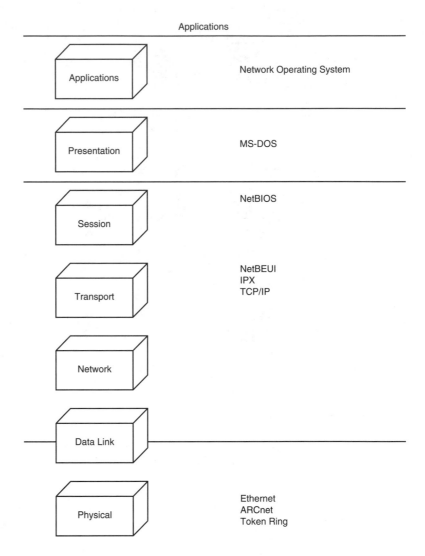

Figure 26.4
The OSI Reference
Model.

Without network layering, connecting different types of workstations to a common LAN would be expensive or impossible. You also would have to purchase different versions of the same network operating system to support different network adapters. With layering, for example, the network operating system at layer 7 sends a request to the operating system at layer 6. The operating system communicates the request to the network transport layers, translating it into whatever form is needed by the transport layers. These transport layers convert the request into a form the hardware layers (layers 1 and 2) can interpret. These lowest two layers then perform the physical transfer of data.

It does not matter to the network operating system which type of network interface card is being used, because the NOS does not interact with the network at that low a level. Instead, the transport layers take care of communicating with the network adapter. When the data comes back, it filters through the layers in reverse order, eliminating the need for the network operating system to interpret the information at the hardware level.

Network Architectures

Various networks use different methods and rules to transfer data along the network. These different data-transfer methods are called the network's *architecture.* Common network architectures include Ethernet, ARCnet, and Token Ring. These architectures control the method by which data passes physically between workstations.

Ethernet started as a de facto standard, but has become an officially recognized international standard. Ethernet is a contention architecture because it handles contention between two or more nodes that try to access the network at the same time (in this context, *network* refers to the cabling connecting the nodes). When two nodes have data on the network at the same time, a data collision occurs.

With the Ethernet architecture, the physical network layer senses the presence of a carrier signal, which indicates that data is moving on the network. If data is traveling on the network, the physical layer signals the data link layer not to transmit data. If the physical layer does not detect a carrier, it signals the link layer that it may transmit data.

If the physical layer detects a data collision, it signals the network that a collision has occurred. All other nodes then fall back to receive mode. The transmitting node then waits a random amount of time before it attempts to retransmit the data packet. This random wait time helps ensure that the two nodes that caused the collision do not attempt to retransmit at the same time, causing another collision.

The Token Ring and ARCnet architectures operate differently from the Ethernet architecture. Token Ring and ARCnet both represent noncontention architectures. These types of networks are called *token-passing networks.* They function by passing a special data frame, called a token, around the network. If a node has data to send, it captures the token and appends its data to the token. The packet then is retransmitted across the network. The receiving node strips its intended data from the token and passes the token around the network again. Because only a single token is being passed around the network, no possibility exists for data collisions.

Although Token Ring and ARCnet architecture both employ token passing, they differ in the way the token is passed from node to node. With Token Ring, the token is passed from node to node in sequence around the ring. With ARCnet, the token passes node-to-node from the lowest to the highest network address.

Transport Layers and Stacks

The layers that translate the data coming from the media-access layers (the physical LAN connection) are called the *link control layers.* These layers implement different transport methods to convert the data into a form that the higher layers of the network (the node's operating system) can understand. In reverse, the transport layers convert data coming from the node's operating system into a form that can be passed on to the physical network. The different transport protocols used are also referred to as *transport stacks.*

The NetBIOS (Network Basic Input/Output System) serves as a link between the computer's operating system and the network protocol stacks. NetBIOS is a set of software routines that provide basic network access services, just as a computer's BIOS (Basic Input/Output System) provides basic hardware services to applications running on the computer (see fig. 26.5).

Figure 26.5
Functions of the
BIOS and
NetBIOS.

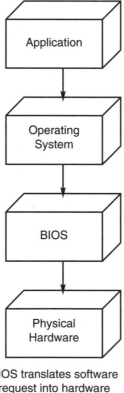

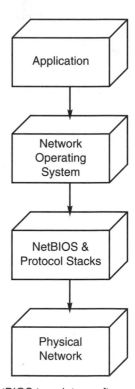

When the operating system requests network resources, the request goes to the NetBIOS. The NetBIOS then translates the request to the appropriate transport stack, which then translates the request to the LAN's physical layers.

Common network transport protocols include NetBEUI, TCP/IP, and IPX. NetBEUI stands for NetBIOS Extended User Interface. NetBEUI was developed by IBM for use on Token Ring networks. The NetBEUI stack for Windows for Workgroups installs as a terminate-and-stay-resident (TSR) program when your computer boots.

TCP/IP stands for Transmission Control Protocol/Internet Protocol and was developed by the Department of Defense. TCP/IP is commonly used to connect different types of computer systems. You can implement TCP/IP with Windows for Workgroups to connect to UNIX-based systems, for example.

If you are running Windows for Workgroups on top of Novell NetWare, you probably are familiar with the Internetwork Packet Exchange (IPX) protocol. IPX is the transport protocol that NetWare uses to translate data across the network.

The important point to remember about transport protocol stacks is that you can use more than one protocol at a time. This enables you to connect to different systems from a single Windows for Workgroups session. You can read a file from disk resources down the hall using IPX or NetBEUI, for example, and send it to a UNIX host using TCP/IP.

Looking At Client/Server Relationships

The relationship that computers in a network have with each other is a client/server relationship. For each task that is performed in that relationship, one computer uses, or accesses, the resources of another computer.

A *server* is a computer that shares its resources with others. The resources shared can include disk drives, printers, and other peripherals such as fax modems. If, for example, you make the hard drive on your computer (or a portion of it) available for other users to access from their computers, your computer is acting as a server.

A *client* is a computer that accesses or uses the resources shared by another computer. When you print to a printer that is connected to another computer or modify a file located on another computer, your computer is the client.

Understanding How a LAN Operates

By connecting multiple computers as a LAN, you add a great deal of functionality to each computer. Once connected, you instantly have access to and the use of resources on other computers. The client/server concept is common to most LANs, and is implemented by first specifying the shared resources on a server, and then using the shared resources from the client.

Each computer that acts as a server is configured to specify which resources on that computer will be shared with other users on the network. Once the server(s) has been configured, you can use the shared resources on the server(s) from your workstation.

Understanding Resource Sharing

The computer or computers configured as servers can share their resources with others. *Configuration* is accomplished when you specify the resources that will be shared and give a name to each resource. Resources usually consist of disk drives, individual directories on those disk drives, and printers.

When configuring the shared resources on a server, you specify a name for the resource that will be seen by other computers on the network, and then specify the device that the resource name is actually pointing to. You can, for example, create a shared resource with the name of C-DRIVE that actually points to drive C. Or, you can create a shared resource named WINDOWS that actually points to C:\WINDOWS.

When a shared directory resource is used by a client, the shared directory (and any directories below it) is available to the client; any directories above the shared resource are not used.

If a resource named WINDOWS, which points to C:\WINDOWS, is created on the server, the client (when connected to the WINDOWS resource) can access C:\WINDOWS and C:\WINDOWS\SYSTEM on the server, but not the server's root directory C:\.

Printers are handled in a similar way. You can, for instance, create a resource named HPLASER, which actually points to the LPT1: printer port (which has a Hewlett-Packard laser printer connected to it).

Using Shared Resources

A client accesses the resources on a server by creating a network drive or network printer.

A network drive is created on your computer by using a command or utility program provided with your network operating system. Usually, you specify a network drive letter that you use from your workstation to access a server. When you specify the network drive letter, you also specify the name of the server and the resource name of the drive you want to use. Once specified, any action you perform using the chosen network drive letter actually uses the drive/directory you specified on the server.

For example, a network drive is created on the client, which is given a drive letter such as K, and is connected to a resource name (such as WINDOWS) on the server. When K is accessed from the client, the WINDOWS resource on the server actually is being used. Because the WINDOWS resource actually was defined as being the C:\WINDOWS directory on the server, you know that when you access K from the client, you actually are accessing C:\WINDOWS on the server.

Printers are accessed in a similar way. A network printer port such as LPT3: is created on your computer, which actually is connected to a printer resource (such as HPLASER) on the server. When something is sent to LPT3:, it actually is being sent to the resource HPLASER on the server (HPLASER points to LPT1: on the server, which is what the HP laser printer is connected to).

Understanding LAN Processing Operation

When you run a program, all processing is done on the computer you are using. This means that if you run a program located on the hard drive of another computer, the program is not being run on that computer; it is being run on yours. The program files are actually being transferred from the other computer (over the network) to your computer, where the program is executed using your CPU.

The best way to understand this is to think that the resources you are using actually are part of, or connected to, your computer. If, for example, you have created a network drive K, which points to drive C of another computer, think of K as being a physical drive on your computer. When you change to drive K and run a program, think of the program as being loaded into the memory of your computer from a disk drive located on your computer.

Examining Types of LANs

LANs are categorized by one of two types: dedicated server or peer-to-peer. The difference between the two types is substantial, and these differences are discussed in the following sections.

Dedicated Server Networks

A *dedicated server network* has one or more servers that contain the resources shared with other clients. Usually the server is dedicated for use as a server only, and cannot be used as a workstation; its only purpose is to share disk drives, printers, modems, and other peripherals with other computers on the network.

More than one server can be in a dedicated server network, and, in some cases, the server also can be used as a workstation. Novell NetWare v3.11 is a dedicated server network, in which the server cannot be used as a workstation. Novell NetWare v2.2 is a dedicated server-type network, in which the server can be used as a workstation, however.

In a dedicated server network, the clients can use the shared resources available on a server, but those clients usually cannot use resources that exist on the other client workstations. This is an important distinction between a server-based network and a peer-to-peer network.

In a server-based network, if computer A is the server, and computers B and C are client workstations, computers B and C can access resources on computer A, but B and C usually cannot access each other's resources.

In some situations in a server-based network, clients can share some resources with other clients. Third-party products are available, such as LANtastic for NetWare which gives LANtastic peer-to-peer capabilities to a Novell NetWare network. Windows for Workgroups also gives clients the capability to act as servers when used in conjunction with NetWare and other network operating environments.

Peer-to-Peer Networks

A *peer-to-peer network* enables any computer to be a client workstation and a server at the same time. This means that you can work on your computer, access the resources on another server, and share the resources on your computer with others at the same time.

In addition, most peer-to-peer networks have the option of being configured as a dedicated server-type network, or being configured somewhere between a true dedicated and peer-to-peer network. You can, for example, choose to configure five of your computers as server/client workstations and five as client workstations only. In this scenario, the five server/client workstations share their resources; the client workstations can only access the shared resources of others.

LANtastic, Windows for Workgroups, and NetWare Lite are examples of peer-to-peer networks.

Administering Windows Networks

After you set up a LAN, you need to manage or administer the network. Not only is it important for you to establish standard locations for certain programs and data, but you also must determine which users will have access to this information.

A dedicated server network usually is much easier to administer than a peer-to-peer network because the client workstations in a dedicated server network can access only one common server for shared directories and printers. In this case, the administrator has to worry only about how to organize and manage the shared information on the dedicated server. Usually, with a dedicated server network, users store their own programs and data on their hard drive; programs and data available for access are stored on the server.

In a peer-to-peer network, specific computers can be designated to contain certain types of programs and data in their shared directories. If the network is managed properly, administration becomes much easier.

Contrary to popular belief, a peer-to-peer network that is properly administered can, in some situations, provide better performance than a dedicated server network. An example of this is having both database and accounting programs that are used by many users.

If the database and accounting programs are located on a single dedicated server, that server is accessed by all users of those two programs. If you use a peer-to-peer network and you put the accounting program on one computer and the database on another computer, the workload required of the server is cut in half.

A peer-to-peer network can be much more difficult to administer than a dedicated server network, however, because every hard drive in the network potentially can be accessed and used by others. While this results in a great deal of flexibility for the users, administration of such a network can cause headaches. The administrator might have to worry about every computer in the network (instead of just a single dedicated server), for instance.

Suppose that the high-speed laser printer that everyone in the network uses is connected to John's computer, and everyone stores their word processing documents on the hard drive on Sally's computer. If, at the end of the day, Sally or John turn off their computer, printing jobs that are sent to John's computer can be interrupted or, worse yet, someone working on a document at the time Sally turns off her computer can lose his information.

Managing Resources

Any LAN needs an organization plan to eliminate confusion and the possibility of misplaced or lost data. As a system administrator, your first task is to decide which programs and information will be shared, where they will be located, and the kind of access that will be allowed. With this information in mind, you then can create the shared resources and directories.

Managing Users

After you have decided which resources and directories will be shared with others, you need to create accounts for the various users on the computers that they will be allowed to access. When creating and managing user accounts, you can specify the privileges of each user. User privileges can include the following:

✔ **No access at all.** For certain users.

✔ **Read access only.** Allows users to read and copy data, but does not allow the addition or modification of existing data; the original remains unchanged.

✔ **Full read-write access.** A full access similar to the access you have to files located on your own hard drive; the user can add, delete, and modify files as needed.

Some privileges can be controlled in the user account, while others can be specified when managing the shared resources.

Implementing a Backup Strategy

Maintaining a current backup is extremely important. When data has been lost or damaged, a backup can save you a tremendous amount of time and effort.

The extent and frequency of backups vary with each network installation, depending on the type of data used and its importance. In most situations, the network administrator is responsible for making sure that the shared directories in the network are backed up regularly. It often is the user's responsibility to make sure that the individual hard drive is backed up.

In any kind of network environment, it is essential to have a backup strategy or plan that is written down and reviewed with anyone who will be using the network. The plan should include the following information:

✔ When the backups occur

✔ What information is backed up

✔ Who performs the backups

✔ Whether the backups are full backups or backups of the modified files only

Included in the backup strategy should also be a plan for users to back up their own computers.

After the plan has been reviewed by each network user, some adjustment might be needed to ensure that the proper data is being backed up as often as necessary. Some users might need to implement their own temporary backup strategy to ensure that critical data is temporarily backed up until the next regular network backup is performed.

The medium that is used for backups in a LAN environment usually is a tape backup. Some LAN administrators even maintain a separate hard drive on the system that is used for backups. Some network operating systems support backup strategies that include disk mirroring and duplexing. These are techniques that write data to two different hard disks at the same time.

Exploring Network Features Available with Windows

Microsoft Windows 3.0, 3.1, and 3.11 are network-aware, and include features that enable you to access and use shared network resources from within Windows. Shared network drives and directories are accessed from File Manager, and shared printers can be configured from the Printers section in the Control Panel.

Network-aware applications know when they are operating in a network environment. Often when programs are network-aware, additional features are incorporated into the programs, enabling you to take advantage of the features provided to you by the network.

Programs don't have to be network-aware to be used in a network environment. Prior to Windows 3.0, Windows/286 usually operated well in a network environment. When Windows 3.0 came along, some of the network features that worked well under Windows/286 no longer operated.

Accessing Shared Directories

File Manager provides the capability to establish a connection to a shared directory on another computer. After the connection is established, any other program can use the network drive.

To establish a network connection to a shared directory on another computer, start File Manager by double-clicking on the File Manager icon in the Main program group. From the menu, choose Disk, Network Connections to access the Network Connections dialog box (see fig. 26.6).

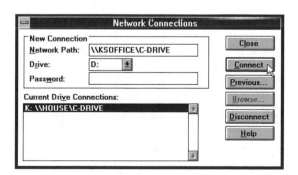

Figure 26.6

File Manager's Network Connections dialog box.

The Network Connections dialog box displays the current network connections and enables you to establish new connections. The example in figure 26.6 shows a connection using the network drive letter K, which is redirected to the C-DRIVE resource on the server named HOUSE.

In the New Connection box, the Network Path is the name of the resource to which you will be connecting. The information you specify here consists of the name of the server, followed by the resource name. The example in figure 26.6 is the format used for LANtastic. Other networks might have a slightly different format.

The Drive selection connects a network drive letter to the resource specified in the Network Path box. If a password is required, you can specify it in the Password box. Choosing the Connect button connects you to the resource, which appears in the Current Drive Connections box.

To disconnect from a shared resource, select the resource you want to disconnect from in the Current Drive Connections box, and click on the Disconnect button.

Clicking on the Previous button shows you a list of shared network resources to which you previously have been connected. If you are connecting to one of these, you can select the resource from here instead of typing it in the Network Path box.

After you have established a new network drive, the drive is available for use. The drive letter icons located just under the window title bar (see fig. 26.7) show physical disk drive A, physical hard drive C, and network drives D and K. When displaying a window for a network drive, the network drive and path also are displayed on the same bar as the drive letter icons. In figure 26.7, the network path is shown as D: \\KSOFFICE\C-DRIVE.

Figure 26.7
File Manager, showing drive icons and the network drive and path.

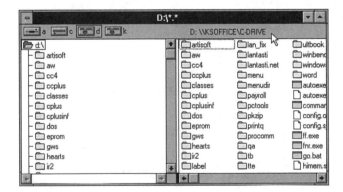

Accessing Shared Printers

The Printers section of the Control Panel provides the capability to establish a connection to a shared printer on another computer. After the connection is established, any other program can use the network printer.

To establish a network connection to a shared printer located on another computer, start the Control Panel by double-clicking on the Control Panel icon in the Main program group. Double-click on the Printers icon to display the Printers dialog box, as shown in figure 26.8.

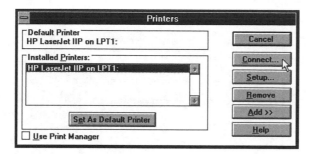

Figure 26.8
The Printers dialog box.

The Printers dialog box displays a list of currently installed printers. This list shows the port that the printer is connected to and the name of the printer, but it does not show whether it is a network printer. Because most networks have a print spooler built in, do not select the Use Print Manager box.

Choosing the Connect button from the Printers dialog box displays the Connect dialog box (see fig. 26.9), in which the Ports box shows the ports and what they are connected to. Choosing the Network button in the Connect dialog box displays the Printers - Network Connections dialog box (see fig. 26.10).

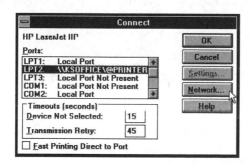

Figure 26.9
The Connect dialog box.

The Current Printer Connections box displays the current network printer connections and enables you to establish new connections. Figure 26.10 shows a network printer connection using port LPT2:, which is redirected to the @PRINTER resource on the server named KSOFFICE. In the New Connection box, the Network Path is the name of the network printer resource to which you will be connecting. The information you specify here consists of the name of the server, followed by the printer resource name. The example shown is the format used for LANtastic; other networks might have a slightly different format.

Networking and Windows

The Port selection is the port used to access the shared network printer resource, pointed to by the information in the Network Path box. If a password is required, you can specify it in the Password box. Choosing the Connect button connects you to the network printer resource, which appears in the Current Printer Connections box.

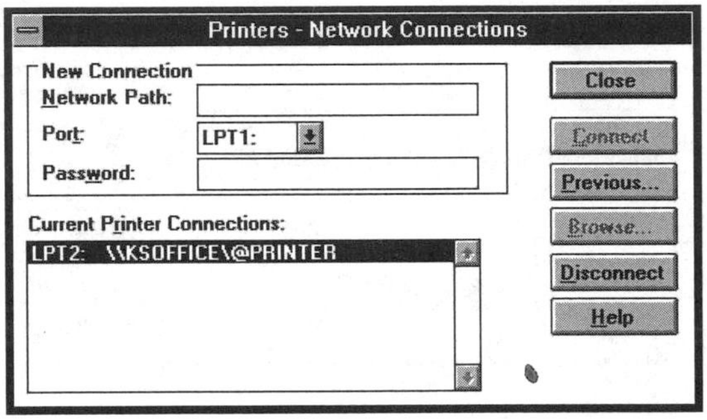

Figure 26.10
The Printers - Network Connections dialog box.

To disconnect from a shared network printer resource, you can select the resource from which you want to disconnect in the Current Printer Connections box, and then click on the Disconnect button.

The Previous button shows you a list of shared network printer resources to which you previously have been connected. If you are connecting to one of these resources, you can select the resource from here instead of typing it in the Network Path box.

After you have established a network printer connection, the network printer is available for use.

Operating Particular Networks within Windows

Each network has certain requirements and limitations when operating in a Windows environment. The following sections have additional information that is specific to the most popular networks used with Windows.

Artisoft LANtastic

LANtastic is a popular and feature-rich peer-to-peer local area network. Although not required to use network functions in Windows, LANtastic for Windows includes network utility programs that incorporate the features of LANtastic in a Windows-style interface.

To run LANtastic with Windows, you must have LANtastic v3.0 or higher. To run Windows in 386 Enhanced mode on a LANtastic server, you must have LANtastic v4.0 or higher.

If you are using Artisoft's 2 Mbps adapter cards, you must include the `EMMExclude=` statement in your SYSTEM.INI file. If your RAMBASE address is D800-DFFF, the statement appears as follows:

```
EMMExclude=D800-DFFF
```

A floppy disk cannot be formatted in File Manager. To format a floppy, execute the FORMAT command from a DOS prompt.

The Fast Printing Direct to Port option in the Printers section of the Control Panel must be turned off for proper printing. LPT1: always shows Local Port, even if it is connected to a network printer.

Novell NetWare

Novell NetWare is the leading dedicated server-based network in the world. To run Windows under NetWare, you might need to replace your NetWare shell with NETX.COM, which is provided with Windows.

If you are running Novell's IPXODO.COM and LSL.COM, you must be using v1.20 or higher. The current versions of these files are included with Windows and are located in the System subdirectory of Windows.

If you are going to run Windows in Standard mode, load the TBMI2.COM TSR first.

If you are running IPX.COM, the system administrator needs to build a new version using the IPX.OBJ provided with Windows.

Do not perform network functions from an MS-DOS prompt while in Windows. Use File Manager or the Control Panel for these activities.

Make sure the MS-DOS SHARE program is not loaded. This can cause problems when trying to run programs from the file server.

Running Windows for Workgroups in a NetWare environment is different from running Windows 3.1 or 3.11 under NetWare. The following section of the chapter explains many of the issues involved with Windows for Workgroups. For specific tips on integrating Windows for Workgroups and Novell NetWare, consult Chapter 32, "Integrating Windows and Novell NetWare."

V

Networking and Windows

Using Windows for Workgroups

You must understand a number of concepts to effectively implement Windows for Workgroups in an existing or new network environment. Even after you have installed Windows for Workgroups (see Chapter 1, "Configuring Windows"), a number of issues still remain relating to network structure and implementation. This section of the chapter examines the following issues:

✔ Understanding workgroups

✔ Defining workgroups

✔ Allocating resources

✔ Defining a common file structure

✔ Structuring the network

In this section you learn what workgroups are and how the concept of workgroups can apply to your organization's use of Windows for Workgroups. You also learn how to define new groups and address workgroup-planning issues, such as who should be in each group, which users should share resources, and how to divide responsibilities among users.

You also examine other global network issues, such as defining a common directory structure to facilitate resource sharing, allocating printer resources, and controlling your applications. The discussions of these topics can help you determine your network's logical structure.

Even if you are not responsible for setting up, configuring, or maintaining the network, the material in this section of the chapter will be useful to you. Specifically, the following section provides an overview that shows you how to relate to the other members of your workgroup, as well as to other workgroups.

Whatever your responsibilities might be within the workgroup, the first step is to understand what workgroups are all about.

Understanding Workgroups

Workgroups do not represent a new concept; if you work with other people toward a common goal, you are part of a workgroup. Your softball team, the PTA, your department at work, and your family all represent different kinds of workgroups. In essence, a workgroup simply is a group (large or small) that is made up of people who share common responsibilities, tasks, and goals.

In a networked computer environment such as Windows for Workgroups, a workgroup usually comprises a group of people who share job responsibilities. In the average organization, people often belong to more than one workgroup (see fig. 26.11). You might be part of a department, for example, that represents a workgroup. In addition, you also might share tasks and responsibilities with a few other individuals in the department. Perhaps you are a group supervisor, part of a design team, or one of the department's secretaries. In any case, you might share a job title or a specific set of duties with other members of your department. These people who share your job title or duties often form a workgroup, of which you are a part. As a result, you belong to two workgroups—this smaller group of individuals and the entire department.

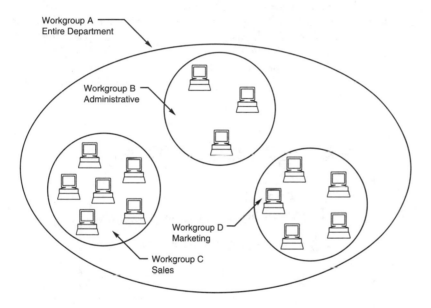

Figure 26.11
Examples of workgroups within a department.

But how do workgroups relate to the network? A network's primary function is to connect users together and enable them to share resources, access common data and applications, and communicate with one another. Because they generally work on the same project or goal, the workgroup's members need to communicate with one another and share information. The network serves as a link between these users by enabling them to share data that relates to a common project and to communicate through e-mail.

Windows for Workgroups not only enables the network's users to share resources across the network and to send and receive mail, it also enables users to interact with one another in other ways. An example is the Schedule+ program (covered in detail in Chapter 30, "Using Schedule+"), which enables users to schedule meetings, view each others' schedules, and even enter an appointment in another user's schedule. Although this type of user interaction does not require workgroups per se, workgroups add a logical structure to the ability to communicate and share resources.

Putting Workgroups in Windows for Workgroups

In Windows for Workgroups, a *workgroup* is really nothing more than a logical grouping of users. Workgroups, instead of offering any real physical separation or organization of users, primarily offer a means of organizing the way resources are displayed to users. In essence, workgroups enable you to view the overall network as a collection of smaller logical entities, which are the workgroups themselves.

Picture it this way: Assume that your traditional network comprises 200 workstations. To access a resource (such as a directory or a printer) on another workstation, you must specify its machine name, which is assigned to the workstation when it boots. Next, you must specify the resource share name, which is assigned by the user of the workstation that contains the shared resource. If you know the name of the workstation that you want to access as well as the resource share name, you simply can type the name in the appropriate dialog box in File Manager or Print Manager and connect to the other workstation. Figure 26.12 shows an example of this process, using the Connect Network Printer dialog box.

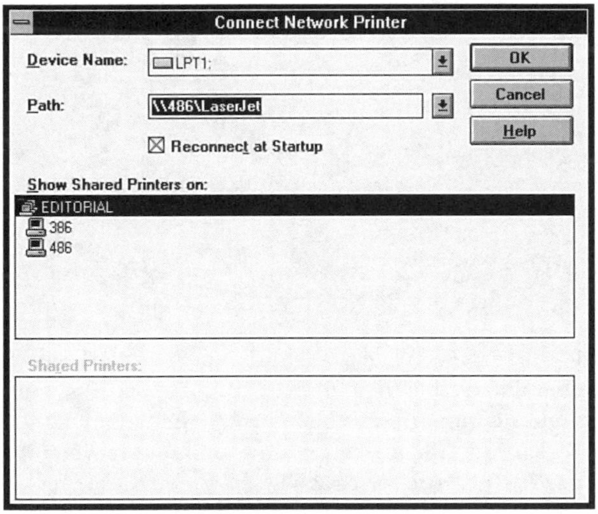

Figure 26.12

Connecting to a shared printer.

But what if you forget the machine name or the share name? Or, what if you need to connect to a directory that you have never accessed before? In both cases, you probably do not know the machine name or the name of the resource to which you want to connect. You must browse through File Manager's list of connected systems to find the one you want. If the network has 200 workstations and each one offers three or four different directory shares, you must browse through 600 to 800 different items to find the resource you want.

This type of environment is far from useful or efficient. Computers and operating environments such as Windows are designed to make it easier to communicate and work with other users, not more difficult. Workgroups help serve that purpose by providing a means to group resources into different categories.

Organizing Users

As mentioned previously, workgroups do not offer any real physical organization or separation of users. A member of any workgroup potentially can share resources and communicate through Microsoft Mail and Schedule+ with members of any other workgroup. You do not need to belong to the same workgroup as another user if you want to access her disk or printer; nor does the user have to belong to your workgroup to use the resources connected to your node.

You do not have to belong to a particular workgroup to send mail or schedule meetings (or perform any of the other tasks that Mail and Schedule+ provide) with other members of that workgroup. If the other workgroup shares a common electronic post office with your workgroup (as shown in fig. 26.13), you can communicate freely with that workgroup's members. You also can communicate directly with members of other workgroups by using the Chat program; again, they do not have to belong to your workgroup.

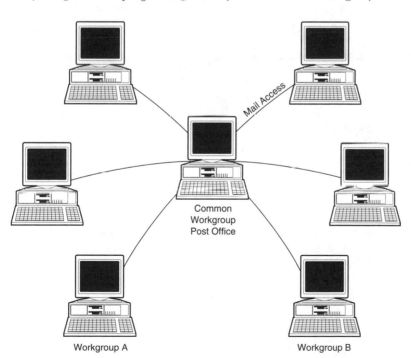

Figure 26.13
Workgroups sharing a common post office can communicate through Mail.

Mail Access

Common
Workgroup
Post Office

Workgroup A

Workgroup B

If workgroups do not provide any separation of users, what purpose do they serve? Workgroups in Windows for Workgroups offer a means of displaying resource information in an organized and easily digestible way. Instead of showing you 200 workstations and 600–800 resources, for example, Windows for Workgroups enables you to break the network into logical units—workgroups. The primary purpose of workgroups from a physical standpoint, therefore, is to organize the browse dialog boxes that display network resources. The workgroup name is just a category tag you can use to organize the list of available resources across the network.

Before you decide how to structure your company into workgroups, you must understand how resources are displayed in Windows for Workgroups. This understanding will help you decide whether to organize and create workgroups based solely on resource access, or to base your workgroups on other criteria. The next section explains the way workgroups appear in Windows.

Viewing Workgroups

The way workgroups appear in Windows depends primarily on whether any workstations are running Windows under a particular workgroup. If at least one node is running under a workgroup, that workgroup's name appears in the network browse dialog boxes when other users are browsing for resources. If no nodes are running under a workgroup name, that workgroup name does not appear in the browse dialog boxes. If the last workgroup member has just exited from Windows, the workgroup's name still appears. Over a period of a few minutes, however, the workgroup's name disappears from the resource lists.

In the same manner, when a user changes to a new workgroup and reboots his node, the new workgroup might not appear right away in other users' browse dialog boxes. Further, a machine might actually be duplicated in two different workgroups. If the user's node is booted under a particular workgroup and he switches to a new workgroup, his machine might appear for a short period of time in two places—once in the old workgroup and again in the new one. Over a period of time, however, the duplicate entry disappears from the old workgroup.

Workgroups and the resources they contain appear in a collapsible tree format. In figure 26.14, for example, the EDITORIAL group is shown expanded, and the MARKETING group is collapsed. The workgroup names appear next to a multiple-workstation icon, as shown in figure 26.14. The multiple-workstation icon illustrates the concept of workgroups—a group of users (and their workstations) that collectively form a workgroup.

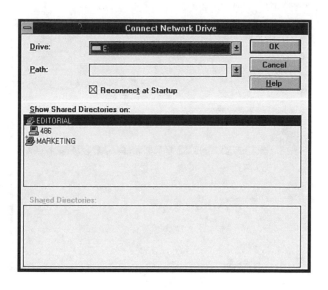

Figure 26.14
Workgroups
displayed in a
browse dialog
box.

If the workgroup tree is collapsed, you see only the workgroup name, and not the resources in it. A plus sign (+) beside the workgroup name indicates that the workgroup tree is collapsed and that you can view more information about that workgroup. Double-click on a workstation name to expand the tree and display the machine names that are assigned within the workgroup. The plus sign then is replaced by a minus sign. Double-click on the workstation name again, and the workgroup tree collapses; the names of the machines that are online again disappear.

Users of Windows for Workgroups 3.11 often experience a Not Enough Memory error when attempting to browse connections on the network. This is a known bug, and Microsoft is examining the issue. Currently, there is no direct workaround for this bug. You can, however, simply specify the name of the resource, including the machine name and share name, such as \\SERVER\SHARE.

By default, only the resources that belong to the nodes in your current workgroup appear in expanded format. All other groups appear in collapsed format when you first display the dialog box. This simplifies the search for resources. Usually, you will want to attach to resources within your workgroup, and attach to resources in other workgroups less often.

Each machine's available resources appear in a separate list box in each network browse dialog box. After double-clicking on a workgroup name to view its tree of available machines, you can double-click on a machine name to view the resources that are available on that machine. These resources appear in the Shared Printers or Shared Directories list box, depending on which type of resource list you are viewing (see fig. 26.15).

Figure 26.15
Available
directories in the
Shared Directories
list box.

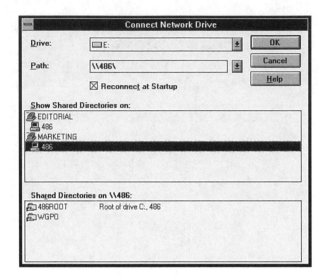

Now that you know how workgroups appear in Windows, you can understand their affect on your network's structure. If your primary goal is to provide access to resources, you can structure your workgroups according to the way you want the resources to appear in Windows rather than according to which users you want to bring together. If the structure of your e-mail system (comprising Mail and Schedule+) is more important than resource sharing, you probably will orient your workgroups around users rather than resources.

Windows for Workgroups uses the concept of workgroups primarily as a tool for organizing the display of network resources, but you put the concept of workgroups to work organizing your department or business. The manner in which you implement workgroups—whether by resource allocation or by user grouping—is completely up to you, so you need to do some planning.

Defining Workgroups

Now that you know what workgroups are and the way they appear in Windows for Workgroups, you are ready to create some physical workgroups from your list of network users. The way you define these workgroups depends on the type of interaction the users require, their common tasks and goals, and how you want to organize the display of resources in Windows.

Gathering Users into Workgroups

If your network is small, you probably need only one or two workgroups. If you purchased the Windows for Workgroups Starter Kit and your network consists of only two workstations, for example, you only need one workgroup. Resource sharing is no doubt your primary objective.

The more workstations you add to the network, however, the more necessary it is to create additional workgroups. E-mail and user interaction also become important considerations as the network grows in size. As your need to organize resources into workgroups becomes more important, therefore, so does your need to organize users into workgroups. Defining your network's structure then becomes a matter of balancing these two sets of needs.

Before you actually define your workgroups, answer the following questions:

✔ Will you use workgroups primarily to organize the display of shared directories and printers?

✔ Will you use workgroups primarily to provide structure and segregation of users for e-mail and other communication services?

✔ Do you need to balance resources against communication services?

If you are creating workgroups primarily to impose a structure on the resources that will be shared across the network, those resources (not the users) are the key factor in setting up the workgroups. If you are creating workgroups to facilitate communication and interaction among groups of users, then your users are the key factor and their resources are secondary. If both factors are important, you will have to balance the two when creating the workgroups.

You might find that a happy medium is to organize the workgroups according to resource access and create a single workgroup post office to enable all workgroups to share mail. Or, if you are using primary servers to provide access to applications and data, you can place these servers in their own workgroups to give them an "identity" on the network. Figure 26.16 illustrates this concept.

When defining which users should belong to a particular workgroup, bear in mind that with very few exceptions (those exceptions being Mail and Schedule+), it really does not matter from a functional standpoint to which workgroup a user belongs. You do not have to log in as a member of a specific workgroup to use resources that are allocated under that workgroup. The only real consideration in defining workgroups, therefore, is which structure will make the most sense to everyone who uses the network. This depends primarily on how you use the network in your organization; there are no tried-and-true guidelines for you to follow.

In most cases, if you mimic your company's structure when setting up workgroups, your network environment should make sense to the users. They are familiar with the company's logical structure, and they should view that structure as a logical organization for the network.

Figure 26.16
Giving servers an identity on the network.

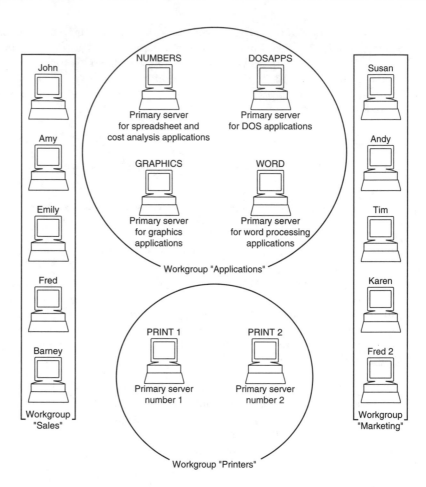

Creating Workgroups

When you have decided the way to organize your workgroups and which users will belong to each workgroup, you can begin setting them up. When you install Windows for Workgroups on a Windows workstation (or Workgroup Connection on DOS workstations), the Setup process prompts you for a workgroup name. This name becomes the default workgroup name when the user starts Windows on the workstation and logs in to Windows for Workgroups.

Choose the Control Panel's Network icon to open the Microsoft Windows Network dialog box. This dialog box includes a Workgroup combo box, which enables you to join an active group or create a new group. Figure 26.17 shows the Microsoft Windows Network dialog box.

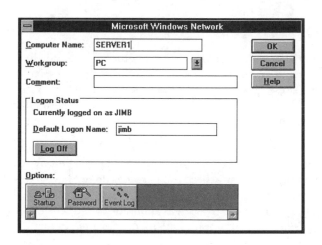

Figure 26.17
Creating a workgroup in the Microsoft Windows Network dialog box.

You can enter the name of a workgroup in the box or choose an existing group from the **W**orkgroup drop-down list. The list shows only currently active groups—in other words, the groups in which at least one member is running Windows. If no users are running Windows under a particular workgroup, that workgroup name does not appear in the list, even if your workstation has been used to run Windows under that workgroup before.

To create a new workgroup in Windows, just type the new workgroup name in the **W**orkgroup combo box. When you click on OK, the Control Panel prompts you to reboot the system or continue. If you choose to continue, the new workgroup appears in your browse dialog box, but other users cannot see the change until you reboot your system. If you choose the **R**eboot option, the system reboots to change your workgroup. The change then appears to other users across the network (although it happens gradually, as explained earlier).

For the most part, you probably will not change workgroups very often. The primary reason to change workgroups is to change the way your local resources appear to other users. Note that you do not have to be in a particular workgroup to send mail to members of that workgroup. You do, however, need a mail account in the workgroup's post office.

You can use several different methods to send mail to users in a different workgroup. These methods are explained in Chapter 29, "Using Microsoft Mail and Fax."

You need to consider some other issues in addition to defining workgroups when you plan your network. Among these are how you will make resources available to users and where those resources will be located physically.

Sharing Resources

As you plan your network, you also should consider whether it should include primary servers. *Primary servers* are much like nondedicated servers on networks that do not offer peer-to-peer capability. These servers house the majority of shared resources, such as printers and file systems, but they also can be used as workstations. Nodes that function primarily as workstations and not servers, but which also share some of their local resources, are called *secondary servers*.

Windows for Workgroups does not require primary servers per se. Resources can be scattered across the network nearly anywhere you like; they do not have to reside on just a handful of primary servers. The word *scattered,* however, is a good indication that this is not the best option. By locating resources such as applications and sensitive data on a single node, you simplify network administration and provide greater network security.

If Windows for Workgroups is your only network operating system, consider allocating as few workstations as necessary as primary servers. These workstations will house the majority of common applications to which the users need access. Applications that only one workgroup uses (or which only a few members of a particular workgroup use) can reside on one of that workgroup's nodes rather than a primary server. This arrangement enables the workgroup or person who is most familiar with the application to be responsible for maintaining it. Figure 26.18 illustrates this concept.

The primary servers also house sensitive data that requires more security than data that is stored on the secondary servers. Increased security includes access security as well as file maintenance. If you want to control which users have physical access to sensitive data (other than across the network), place it on a primary server. If your network includes data that you want to back up regularly, place the data on a primary server where the system administrator can easily include it in the backup process. (Data on a secondary server can be backed up across the network. By placing the data on a primary server, however, you can simplify the backup process.)

The capability to back up remote nodes requires the nodes to run the shared directories. Backups across the network generally degrade network performance. As a result, you should consider backing up during off-hours.

If you are running Windows for Workgroups on top of another network operating system, you probably already have at least one dedicated server that contains your users' applications. This dedicated server might also contain much of your users' data. The applications should remain on the server for a number of reasons, including ease of program management and customization.

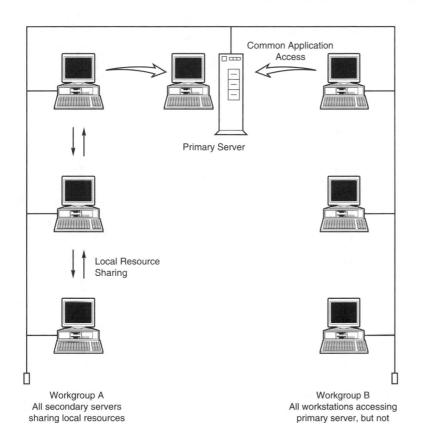

Figure 26.18
Primary and
secondary servers
in Windows for
Workgroups.

Common Application
Access

Primary Server

Local Resource
Sharing

Workgroup A
All secondary servers
sharing local resources

Workgroup B
All workstations accessing
primary server, but not
sharing local resources

Tip

You probably will want to move users' data to their workstations so that they can more easily share data with one another. This arrangement also decreases the server's load and ultimately improves overall network performance. If the data is sensitive, however, you might want to leave it on the server for security.

Another point to consider regarding resource sharing is which stations are running DOS and which ones are running Windows for Workgroups. DOS users still can access the network through Workgroup Connection and attach to resources on other nodes, but they cannot share their local resources with other users. Only a node running Windows for Workgroups in 386-Enhanced mode can function as a server, sharing its resources with other nodes on the network. Figure 26.19 shows an example of a simple network and the capabilities that each of its nodes has for accessing resources.

Figure 26.19
All nodes can access the mail system.

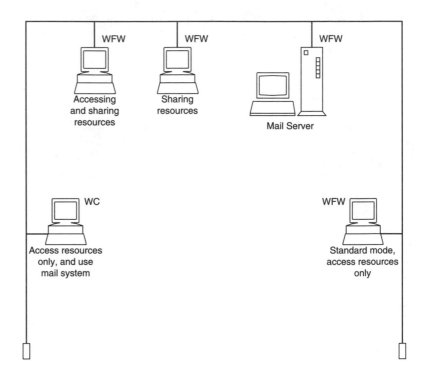

WFW = Windows for Workgroups
WC = Workgroup Connection

WFW — Accessing and sharing resources

WFW — Sharing resources

WFW — Mail Server

WC — Access resources only, and use mail system

WFW — Standard mode, access resources only

Tip

Windows for Workgroups 3.11 runs only in 386-Enhanced mode. It does not support Real or Standard modes.

Users who run DOS without Windows for Workgroups cannot share their resources, although third-party utilities exist that enable DOS users to share their resources with other users on a Windows for Workgroups, LAN Manager, and Novel network environment. Plan the layout of the network resources accordingly.

Setting Up Resource Sharing

When you have decided how the resources on the network will be allocated, you can set up those resources to be shared. You can set up resource sharing of a workstation's resources only at that workstation; you cannot set it up across the network. After the sharing is established, however, the resources can be shared *persistently,* or each time Windows for Workgroups is started on the workstation. This ensures that resources are consistently available to all users.

Use File Manager to configure disk and directory sharing, and use Print Manager to configure printer sharing. Chapter 28, "Sharing Resources in Windows," shows you how to set up resource sharing under Windows.

Keeping Resources Available

After resources are shared, you want to ensure that they will always be available so that users can count on data and applications being available. This is particularly important with a primary server, which is being accessed by a number of users. It is less important that secondary servers always be accessible, but still important nonetheless.

 To ensure that resources are always available, consider leaving the workstations running all the time. When users leave for the day, have them log out from the network, but leave Windows running on their workstations. Instead of shutting off the computer, tell them just to turn off the monitor.

In general, leaving a computer turned on is less damaging than turning it on and off every day. Hard disk head damage, when it occurs, often happens when the disk is powered down (the heads fly over the surface of the disk, and "land" on the disk when the disk is powered down). By always leaving the system on, you can actually increase disk life.

You should provide surge protection for your workstations whether they are left on all the time or are turned off periodically. In addition, you might want to add uninterruptible power supplies (UPS) to the most critical workstations.

To ensure that Windows starts on each workstation when it is turned on, include an appropriate WIN command in each workstation's AUTOEXEC.BAT file. If you then want to prevent users from leaving Windows, you can customize Program Manager to prevent them from doing so. (Chapter 6, "Customizing Windows," shows you how to customize Program Manager.) When users need to access the DOS prompt, they can open a DOS box in Windows. For tips on running and optimizing DOS applications under Windows, refer to Chapter 15, "Integrating Windows and DOS," and to *Maximizing Windows 3.1,* from New Riders Publishing.

Defining a Common File Structure

If you share only selected directories at each workstation, then the workstations do not need to share a common directory structure. Users can set up their hard disks as best suits them. The few shared directories can appear under whatever name the user configures them for. If it simplifies network browsing for your users, you can develop a standard share-naming convention that all users can implement on their workstations. This convention can be as simple as naming directory shares containing applications with the share name APPS, and directory shares containing data with the share name DATA. If a user is searching for some data on the network and knows that it is located on the machine named \\FRED, the user knows that the shared data resides in \\FRED\DATA. Figure 26.20 illustrates such a share-naming convention.

Figure 26.20
A typical example
of share-naming.

```
        Barney              Fred               Alice
       [computer]        [computer]         [computer]

         Root             ┌─APPS             ┌─APPS
    (entire drive shared) ├─ EXCEL           ├─ EXCEL
                          └─ WORD            └─ WORD

                          ┌─DATA             ┌─DATA
                          ├─ DOCS            ├─ DOCS
                          ├─ GRAPHICS        ├─ GRAPHICS
                          └─ SPREADSH        └─ SPREADSH
```

If you choose to share the entire hard disk on each workstation, or a large portion of it, consider developing a common directory structure on each workstation. This helps users locate disk resources more easily, because when they become familiar with the directory structure on their own machines, they are familiar with the directory structure of all the machines on the network.

It naturally is much easier to develop a common directory structure across the network if you are installing new workstations and assembling the network from scratch. Because you are setting up the hard disks at the same time you are setting up the network, you can plan ahead and create the same structure on each workstation. Using File Manager, however, it is easy to rename or move existing directories to conform to the workgroup's conventions if a few changes are needed.

The development of a common directory structure on existing machines is much more difficult, particularly if the machines have been used for any length of time. Users create their own directories using whatever scheme they like. The benefits of standardizing are real, however, so you should consider redefining the directory structure on your existing workstations. In general, this requires backing up each hard drive, creating the proper directory structure, then moving the appropriate files into each directory.

The larger the network, the more trouble this becomes, but the less likely it will be that you need a common directory structure on all workstations. As the network grows in size, so does the need (usually) for a greater number of workgroups. It also becomes less likely that you will be sharing the entire disk on each workstation. If your network is relatively small, consider creating a common directory structure on each workstation. If the network is large, standardize the way shared directories are named.

Chapter Snapshot

The trade press has expressed so many opinions about Windows NT that it is difficult to tell whether Windows NT is the serious high-performance operating system for the future or the slow hog operating system of the future. Actually, both arguments have their merits. Windows NT requires a lot of computer hardware and runs some applications slower than Windows 3.11 and DOS. However, Windows NT offers acceptable performance under a wide range of conditions, security, compatibility with a varied installed base of software, and crash protection of a variety of types. Whether you should adopt Windows NT depends on your specific needs. This chapter acquaints you with the advantages and disadvantages Windows NT offers by discussing the following topics:

The information presented in this chapter will help you decide whether to upgrade to Windows NT. For many installations, Windows NT is a superior choice to Windows 3.11, especially when you need solid security for your computer system. It also offers a very robust operating environment for users who are involved in networking and mission critical computing.

CHAPTER

Understanding Windows NT

I n 1993, Microsoft released the much-hyped Windows NT (for *new technology*), which promised to be the next-generation Windows operating system. This version of Windows was touted as bringing a whole new computing technology to the desktop. Microsoft promised a 32-bit operating environment, security, true multitasking, multithreading, and compatibility with applications built for a variety of operating systems. It promised solutions to some common problems with managing Windows in a business environment, as well as a clear migration path from a diversity of operating systems to a single, enterprise-wide operating system that could run your installed base of software.

Whether Microsoft delivered on the promises made in the prerelease publicity depends on your point of view. Initial sales were disappointing. Initial reviews complained of the hardware requirements being too massive and the speed of operation being too slow. In the months since those initial complaints and disappointing sales figures, however, different sorts of stories have appeared in the computer trade press: stories of Windows NT being adopted by a variety of businesses for large-scale computer operations.

Note For a more complete discussion of Windows NT, see *Inside Windows NT* and *7 Keys to Learning Windows NT,* both from New Riders Publishing.

Looking Over Windows NT

When you first see Windows NT running, you will be hard-pressed to notice the difference between Windows NT and Windows for Workgroups 3.11. You see the same Program Manager. If you open the program groups, you see the same applets as are included with Windows for Workgroups. In fact, after Windows NT is first installed and enabled to search your hard disk for applications, its interface seems very familiar.

A few differences between Windows NT and Windows for Workgroups are noticeable at first glance, however (see fig. 27.1). First, the title bar of the Program Manager window is different. In Windows NT, the title bar shows two names: the first is the name of the computer (ALFRED); the second is the name of the user who is currently logged in (Forrest).

Figure 27.1

The Program Manager in Windows NT.

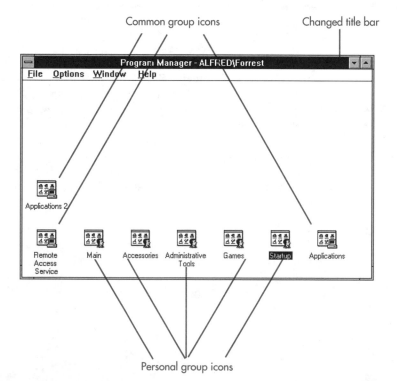

In addition to this difference, you also notice two types of program group icons. One type, with a small computer on its right side, is called a *common program group*. Common program groups appear for every user on the Windows NT system and contain program items available to all users. The other type, with a picture of a person on its right side, is called a *personal program group*. Personal program groups contain program items available only to the user logged in to the computer.

Finally, you notice a new program group, the Administrative Tools group. Windows NT is an operating system that requires administration. That is, someone must supervise the system. A supervisor is necessary to govern the advanced functions that Windows NT provides, such as logins and user profiles. Windows NT, as a result, requires more planning and organization than Windows 3.11.

Tip

The Windows NT Program Manager also has three additional menu items. See "Working with Program Manager" later in this chapter for an explanation of using these menu options.

These visible differences between Windows NT and Windows for Workgroups point to some of the new features in Windows NT. First, each computer running NT is a secure system. It is identified by a name in order to provide unique identification of each node on a network. The computer displays the user name to show who is working on the system and to be able to provide this information to other users across a network, if one is installed. The system enforces security by using a system of user accounts, passwords, and security privileges. If you do not have the rights to access a file or program, the system denies you access permission.

Second, Windows NT is a multiuser system; one computer can be used by any number of individuals. Each individual user can have his own custom setup for Windows NT, and this custom setup includes more than the wallpaper, screen colors, and screen saver the user favors. The system also can make different software programs available to different users. As a result, a company president can have access to all the financial data and financial analysis packages that chart the company's progress, while the president's administrative assistant can have access only to the programs he routinely uses to support the president's work. The Windows NT operating system prevents users from getting access to each other's programs and data using the security features mentioned previously.

Third, Windows NT is optimized for networking. Secure networking is built in, and even at its lowest level this networking is more advanced than peer-to-peer schemes. Windows NT can serve as both a server and a workstation operating system. The Advanced Server version provides all the features you would expect of any server operating system. The new technology Microsoft brought to Windows NT extends Windows into the realm formerly dominated by mainframe operating systems. This new technology means that you can have mainframe features on your desktop and downsized network. As a result, it is important that you understand what this new technology really is.

Understanding the New Technology

Prior to Windows NT's release, the new technology dimension was the subject of much discussion. Microsoft Press even released a book on Windows NT months before the operating system was available for purchase. The main purpose behind this book was to acquaint potential users with the new technology built into Windows NT.

In retrospect, much of the new technology seems fairly commonplace today. Part of the reason is that the battle between Windows and OS/2 has made the buzz words of the new technology household words for power users. Anyone who reads computer magazines has to know the terms, because knowing them is the passport for entering the community of power computer users. But the new technology is not for technogeeks only; it has important implications for the average user as well. Regardless of your level of experience, you need to know what *new technology* means and what it can bring to you.

Understanding 32-Bit Operating Systems

The number of bits in your operating system has very real implications for you as a user. This number of bits refers to the size of the microprocessor's *address space,* or the largest block of memory the computer's central processing unit can access. An *address* is a number that uniquely identifies the location of a byte in memory, the smallest location that can store a character. The address space is filled with a list of such bytes, each uniquely identifiable by a number. The length of the address space is important. The more bits in the address space, the larger a memory address it can store, and therefore, the more memory your computer can use.

Practical examples from the history of personal computers illustrate the importance of address space. The Apple II computer used an 8-bit address space, and could access up to 64 KB of RAM. The early IBM PC had a 16-bit address space; it could accommodate up to 1 MB of RAM. The PC-compatibles you are familiar with today must perform extraordinary efforts to access memory above the 1 MB barrier. They must install a special memory manager, such as HIMEM.SYS, that routes and translates calls to higher memory locations. With a 32-bit address space (available with 80386, 80486, and Pentium processors), no such extraordinary effort is necessary. The microprocessor can directly address up to 4 GB of RAM.

Although 4 GB seems like an immeasurable amount of memory, keep in mind that in 1982, 64 KB seemed to be an immeasurable amount, more than any program would ever need. Memory is a resource that programs can easily consume. Features planned for the next generation of software, such as voice recognition and voice command, will take more and more memory. Although you may not imagine 4 GB to be a restrictive limit, someday users might see it as one.

When you choose Windows NT as your operating system, you can take full advantage of this large amount of memory that your 80386 or newer microprocessor can access. The advantages of having this large address space are as follows:

✔ The amount of memory available for running applications is huge, hundreds of times greater than any single application needs.

✔ Program designers can write applications that run faster and work with the resources of your computer more efficiently because they do not have to work through a memory manager.

✔ When you work with a suite of applications, you work more efficiently because you have the memory and the speed that enables you to run all the applications in your suite simultaneously.

The size of the address space is not the only advantage of a 32-bit microprocessor. These processors can manipulate data 4 bytes at a time (as opposed to 2 bytes at a time for a 16-bit processor, or 1 byte at a time for an 8-bit processor). What this means to you might not seem obvious. All data must pass through the microprocessor in order for any operation, such as addition in your spreadsheet, to take place. The old 8-bit microprocessor can take in the equivalent of 1 number at a time to process the addition problem. A 16-bit microprocessor can take in 2 numbers at a time. A 32-bit microprocessor can take in 4 numbers at a time. As a result, the actual work of computing happens much more rapidly on a 32-bit microprocessor. Windows NT can take advantage of the microprocessor's capability to process data 32 bits at a time.

As a 32-bit operating system, therefore, Windows NT offers you lots of memory and lots of processing speed. The following provisions need to be added to this statement, however:

✔ You have to have the memory installed before Windows NT can take advantage of it. Like Windows 3.11, Windows NT makes use of virtual memory by establishing a swap file on your disk. But swap files are slower than actual memory. You are able to take advantage of 32-bit power, insofar as you have the actual memory available to access.

✔ You need to have applications written for a 32-bit operating system to take advantage of the 32-bit features. Most existing Windows applications are written for Windows 3.11 and DOS, the combination of which provides a 16-bit operating system. These applications run in a 16-bit emulation mode under Windows NT, which is slightly slower than they run under DOS/Windows.

✔ The software marketplace has been slow to create 32-bit Windows applications. You can invest in Windows NT and a Pentium-based computer with 4 GB of memory, but you might wait a considerable amount of time before you have the applications that you need to take advantage of the operating system.

As a result, if you are evaluating Windows NT for possible purchase, you must realize that Windows NT brings you incredible processing power with its 32-bit architecture. This feature alone might not be enough to attract you to Windows NT, however.

Understanding Multitasking

You probably are familiar with multitasking from Windows 3.11. *Multitasking* is the phenomenon of the operating system enabling more than one program to run simultaneously. Multitasking in Windows NT is different, however, than multitasking in Windows 3.11. The difference is most easily demonstrated by the new cursor that appears in Windows NT. You can notice the new cursor, for instance, when the operating system loads. The cursor is a combination of the hourglass and the arrow (see fig. 27.2), and it means that you can go ahead and work with another application while one or more applications is busy enough to display the hourglass cursor.

Figure 27.2
The combined hourglass and arrow cursor.

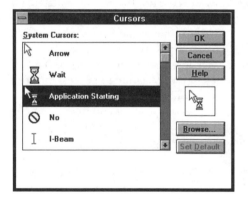

The difference represented by this cursor is often called *true* or *preemptive multitasking*. True multitasking means that the microprocessor is providing services in small timeslices to each application running. Each application is accorded its timeslice in turn, and the microprocessor enforces each application's time limit. After an application's timeslice expires, the next application takes its timeslice, and so on in turn until all running applications have had a chance to use a bit of the microprocessor's time. Then the sequence starts over again. The cycle repeats so rapidly that all programs appear to execute as though they were the only program running.

The type of multitasking used by Windows 3.11, depends on the good behavior of each individual program to function. Each program must yield the microprocessor to others at appropriate intervals. If one program fails to yield appropriately, the multitasking scheme immediately becomes a single-tasking scheme until the program finishes its task.

True multitasking means that no application can take over and control the microprocessor, as can happen in Windows 3.11. Long computations—such as when a complicated spreadsheet recalculates, a database compacts records, or a statistics program does an analysis of variance—cannot cause the hourglass cursor to appear for the entire system. Such computations cannot prevent you from performing other work. The microprocessor is in control, and it makes sure that each application keeps running.

Formally, a task consists of a program's machine-executable instructions, the associated data, and the memory necessary to hold the task. Under Windows NT, each task is kept separated in memory. If one task attempts to infringe on another task, Windows NT creates an error known as an *exception* or a *trap*. When such an error occurs, Windows NT stops the offending process in order to protect the infringed process. Only the offending task is interrupted; all other tasks continue running normally.

As a result, Windows NT provides a significant amount of crash protection. One program, no matter how badly behaved, cannot damage another program. Therefore, a Windows NT system is much more robust than a Windows 3.11 system. The dreaded general-protection fault, one program trying to write into another program's area of memory, is much less likely to occur, and if such a catastrophic error does occur, it should not lock up the system. Windows NT's true multitasking feature provides, as a result, improved system performance and improved system productivity. These are significant advantages over other operating systems.

Understanding Multithreading

Multithreading is a system capability that is less well known than multitasking—the average user cannot see multiple threads in action as well as he can see multiple tasks in action. Multithreading is like multitasking, but it occurs only within one program. *Threads* are separate tasks within a single program, such as opening a file or creating a table. *Multithreading* means that different threads in the same program can execute simultaneously.

What advantages does multithreading offer to you? The main advantage is that your programs run faster and more efficiently. When a program executes within its timeslice, it can perform a calculation and enable you to access the menu at the same time. As a result, you work more rapidly, with fewer delays while you wait for a single program to finish one task before you can start another task.

A second advantage of multithreading is that your system is more productive. In the overall management of your work, you want each system activity—calculating a spreadsheet, accessing data from a database, and printing, for example—to finish in an orderly and timely fashion. You need your spreadsheet calculated, data delivered, and report printed at roughly the same time. With both multithreading and multitasking, your system is more likely to fulfill such complex demands. As a result, both your system and you are more productive.

Understanding Multiprocessing

Multiprocessing refers to an operating system's capability to use more than one microprocessor to execute programs on a computer. Windows NT enables you to take advantage of *symmetric multiprocessing,* in which the computer has more than one microprocessor installed and each processor accepts the next available task for processing. For instance, the computer might be designed with two or more 80486 chips in place. Under this circumstance, Windows NT schedules any task or thread to any of the 80486 chips available, making the best use of the available central processing resources.

 Another version of multiprocessing, asymmetric multiprocessing, is possible. In *asymmetric multiprocessing,* each microprocessor installed on the computer has a dedicated task; one microprocessor might be dedicated to running the operating system, and the other to running user programs, for example. In this design, bottlenecks can occur if one processor is relatively free and the other is overworked. Such bottlenecks do not occur in symmetric multiprocessing, because the operating system schedules tasks on the first available microprocessor.

In general, multiprocessing means that your computer has to have more than one microprocessor installed to take advantage of this capability. Most users do not own such systems, and not many systems of this type are available. Why should this capability be important to you? As a user of a single workstation, it is minimally important. Given the speeds of current single processor designs, multiprocessing architectures are not likely to appear on the desktop soon.

If you are considering Windows NT as a server operating system, however, multitasking might be of considerable importance. Most multiprocessor computers are intended for server applications. A busy server easily can become a data processing bottleneck. Multiprocessor designs improve the capability of a single server to handle transactions. If you are considering installing a server that must quickly handle a steady stream of client requests, a multiprocessor design and Windows NT might be your best solution.

Understanding Subsystems

Windows NT is organized into separately running *subsystems,* independently running tasks that perform dedicated operating system functions. These tasks communicate with one another by passing messages that represent requests for services. The subsystem receiving the request schedules the service, executes it, and returns information about the completed service to the subsystem that requested the service. In general, this provides for an efficient operating system, because each subsystem runs as a separate, multithreaded task.

Why should you care how your operating system is organized? Mainly because you need to be concerned with evaluating the efficiency and maintainability of the operating system. Windows NT offers subsystems that, from the bottom up, help to prevent operating system problems.

The lowest level in Windows NT is known as the hardware abstraction layer (HAL). The HAL translates each request for an operating system service into machine-executable statements coded correctly for the microprocessor and other hardware installed on the computer. The HAL enables Windows NT to be ported easily from one computer architecture to another. To move from the Intel family of microprocessors to the DEC Alpha chip, the porting team needs to rewrite only the HAL. This fact is important to you in an enterprise-wide implementation of Windows NT, because it means that Windows NT running on different hardware platforms functions substantially the same from computer architecture to computer architecture. The only differences lie in the HAL.

The next layer in Windows NT is the *kernel,* which receives requests from other subsystems, schedules them, coordinates multitasking and multithreading, and responds to exceptions or interrupts. The kernel is the mediator between the other subsystems and the HAL. Windows NT contains the following other subsystems:

✔ **Virtual memory manager.** Handles all swapping to disk through the swap file.

✔ **Object manager.** Creates and manages the abstract data types, or objects, that represent system resources.

✔ **Security reference monitor.** Handles all security functions.

✔ **Local procedure call facility.** Manages communications between subsystems and user applications.

✔ **I/O system.** Manages all input/output requests to disks, networks, disk caches, and similar devices that can receive input or generate output.

What this means to you is that each of these subsystems receives all the protection that Windows NT provides to any other task. Each subsystem is isolated from the other so that errors in one subsystem do not crash all the others. Windows NT is therefore a more robust operating system than DOS, which does not provide such protection.

The use of subsystems also enables Windows NT to exploit multiple modes of operation. The operating system subsystems run in kernel mode, in which all system services and commands are accessible. User programs, however, run in user mode, in which access to many system commands and services is limited. As a result, Windows NT can prevent an errant program from damaging the operating system because the program simply does not have access to the kernel level. Windows NT also can prevent programs such as viruses from causing damage because programs that are not known subsystems of the operating system do not have access to kernel mode.

Windows NT also implements the notion of *security privileges,* a set of permissions that a program must possess in order to perform a task. Security privileges are set at the time a program is started, and they match the user's security profile. If a program does not have permission to perform an operating system task, such as accessing a particular file, the program is not permitted to perform the task. As a result, you can be certain that the subsystem organization of Windows NT provides you with the most robust PC operating environment available. Not only do you have crash protection of the sort provided by OS/2, but you also gain the security aspects of mainframe operating systems, such as virtual memory system (VMS).

A privilege is like a DOS file attribute, only more powerful. Using the ATTRIB command, for example, you can set a DOS file to read-only, preventing the operating system from writing to the file. Using privileges in Windows NT, you can determine which users should have read-only access to a file, which users should have read-write access, which users should have delete access, and which users should have the authority to execute programs. You can set these privileges on an individual basis, if you want.

Understanding NT Networking

Windows NT includes networking in both Workstation and Advanced Server versions. The form of networking included in the Workstation service is a very high-end peer-to-peer network. Each workstation can contain a network adapter card and can be linked by a network cable to every other workstation. Other users can be granted access to each computer on the network. Users must be granted accounts on each computer they might want to log in to on the network. Windows NT automatically configures each workstation with a guest account that grants minimal privileges, however. On your peer-to-peer network, you can configure the guest account to enable appropriate access to resources on any given system, and you even can set a password for it to prevent unauthorized use.

Although a workstation can be run as a central server for the network, Windows NT offers the Advanced Server version that enables you to provide the kinds of fault tolerance mechanisms you might prefer for your network server. You can implement disk striping, disk mirroring, and other data protection features favored on network servers. You also can implement connectivity features for Macintosh computers so that you can run a mixed-platform network with ease. The Advanced Server also provides a remote access service, which enables someone to dial up your server using a modem and connect to your network. The remote user sees the network drives and resources exactly as if she were using her home workstation.

Disk striping is a method of writing data to multiple disks or disk areas at once in regions called stripes. Disk striping improves read-write access times, but can increase the chance that data might accidentally be lost from the system. *Disk mirroring* is a method of writing data to two disks simultaneously so that you have a duplicate of the primary disk on the secondary disk. If one disk fails, you have an immediate backup available.

Windows NT offers built-in networking of both peer-to-peer and client/server types. These networks offer advanced security and fault tolerance, and feature easy operation across differing hardware platforms. As a result, they give Windows NT a serious advantage over competing operating systems.

Understanding Security

Windows NT offers what the U.S. government refers to as Class C2 security. Class C2 security requires the following:

✔ A login system that requires users to identify themselves with a unique name and password combination

✔ Discretionary access control, in which one user who owns a resource, such as a file or program, can decide which other users can have access to it

✔ Auditing, which enables the system to detect and record security events, such as unauthorized attempts to access a file

✔ Memory protection, which enables files to be read- and write-protected from others on a network

When you start your computer, Windows NT asks you to log in by entering your name and password. Windows NT includes boot protection as a part of this process. You must press Ctrl+Alt+Del before you see the Login dialog box. As a result, it is virtually impossible for someone to substitute a program that mimics Windows NT, tricking you into typing your name and password so that he can steal the name/password combination. To get into Windows NT, you must be known to the system.

In addition to login names and passwords, Windows NT creates an access token for each process you initiate. This token is a repository of the security information about a user. It records such information as the following:

✔ Your security ID

✔ Your group ID

✔ Your privileges

✔ The default owner of any objects (like files) that you create

✔ Your primary group

✔ The default access control list for any objects involved in the process

Windows NT checks the access token for any process before it enables a process to access a system service, such as opening a file. If your access token does not show the privileges necessary for the task, you are denied the right to perform the task. Information from the access token is then copied into the security event log as Windows NT logs the security violation.

Groups literally are groups of users. Members of groups are granted certain security privileges, and the fastest way to assign security privileges is to make a user a member of a group. Administrators, for instance, have all security privileges, whereas Guests have hardly any privileges at all. Backup Administrators have enough privileges to copy all files on the system to a backup storage device, but they do not have the full control of the system that Administrators have. The *primary group* in a security token is the collection of security IDs that can have access to the process.

Windows NT also enables you to use access control lists (ACLs). An ACL is a list of which system users can access an object, such as a file. Using an ACL, which you can set using the **P**ermissions option on the File Manager's **S**ecurity menu, you can list groups of users or individual users who have access to a file. As a result, you can limit access to any system resource to a restricted list of users. This powerful device enables you to create as secure an environment as you want on your Windows NT system or network.

Understanding Compatibility

Windows NT aims to provide you with a migration path from a diverse range of other operating systems. As a result, Windows NT includes compatibility subsystems that emulate other operating systems. You can run DOS programs using the DOS subsystem, OS/2 1.*x* programs using the OS/2 subsystem, and POSIX-compliant UNIX programs using the POSIX subsystem. To run such applications, you need only to install their executable files as program items in Program Manager or use the **R**un option on the Program Manager's **F**ile menu. Windows NT automatically invokes the correct compatibility subsystem and runs the program.

Compatibility with Windows NT is not perfect. For instance, DOS programmers often circumvent the operating system and address hardware directly to improve the speed of the application program. Windows NT attempts to trap all such programming methods and route them appropriately, but Microsoft has been unable to guarantee that Windows NT can trap all such methods.

Examining the New Features

In addition to a new operating system technology, Windows NT brings you a set of new features that implement the new technology. These features provide you the means of interacting with the new technology in order to use the key elements of the operating system. If you are considering using Windows NT, you should examine each of these features carefully. You might have to make some trade-off decisions to make the best use of Windows NT in your installation. Which features you trade for a successful Windows NT installation depends on your needs as a computer user.

Installable File Systems

Windows NT allows installable file systems. This feature enables you to select the file system you wish to use from the following list:

- ✔ DOS File Allocation Table (FAT) system

- ✔ High Performance File System (HPFS) used with OS/2

- ✔ NT File System (NTFS)

Each file system has its advantages and disadvantages. The DOS FAT system offers the greatest compatibility with your existing Windows/DOS installation. You work with files in exactly the same way as you did before installing Windows NT. If you elect to use the FAT system, however, the security you can implement on your system is limited to login level security. You cannot use access control lists, for example, with the FAT file system.

The High Performance File System (HPFS) offers the greatest compatibility if you are upgrading from an OS/2 installation that used HPFS. It also offers speed advantages over the FAT system, as well as the capability to use long file names. If you choose HPFS, however, you do not get the full implementation of Windows NT security features, just as with the FAT system.

The Windows NT File System (NTFS) enables you to take full advantage of Windows NT's features. You get full security, protection from data corruption, long file names, and improved speed over the FAT system. You cannot migrate easily back to an earlier file system, however. After you have converted to NTFS, you cannot convert the file system back to FAT or HPFS. You can copy files to FAT or HPFS disks without trouble, but there is no conversion program. You have to back up the drive, repartition your hard drive, format the partition, and restore your files from your backup.

On the other hand, you can convert FAT or HPFS disks to NTFS anytime you want by running a conversion program. The conversion is simple and painless. In the command prompt window, simply type **convert /fs:ntfs**. The conversion program runs, and your system reboots to take advantage of the new file system. As a result, you can leave old hard disk volumes in their current format and convert them only after you are certain of your file system choice.

Windows NT uses the FAT file system for floppy disks exclusively. As a result, Windows NT maintains both 8.3 and long file names for any file on the system. The NTFS and HPFS file systems are used only on hard disk drives. Windows NT translates between long and 8.3 file names transparently.

Disk Administrator

Windows NT offers a command-line language similar to DOS. Virtually all system tasks can be handled from a Windows program, however. Disk Administrator (see fig. 27.3) is the program that enables you to manage disks. You still format disks from the File Manager. Disk Administrator offers you additional, advanced functionality, however.

Figure 27.3
The Disk
Administrator
window.

Using Disk Administrator, you can create or delete partitions on a hard disk drive, set the active partition, and change drive letters. You also can create volume sets and stripe sets (assuming you are using NTFS), or implement disk mirroring. In addition, you get a graphical display of disk information, such as partition type, drive letter, and disk size.

A *volume set* is disksa set of disks organized so that the NTFS treats them as a single partition. *Stripe sets* are regions of a disk organized to duplicate data storage and to improve data access speed.

User Manager

User Manager, shown in figure 27.4, is a program that enables you to handle the tasks associated with creating and managing user accounts. Because you must set up at least two accounts, one for the system administrator and one for yourself, you must use User Manager on at least an occasional basis.

The user information that you can set is grouped into three policy areas: account, user rights, and audit. You access the dialog boxes that enable you to set these policies from the Policies menu. In the account category, you can determine policies relating to passwords, such as when the user must change the password. Under the user rights category, you can determine what access a user has to what privileges on the system, such as changing the system time or whether the user can log in from a network. In the audit category, you can determine whether system events, such as file access, will be logged for each user.

You also can create, copy, and delete user accounts from the <u>U</u>ser menu. These procedures work much like creating program groups and program items in Program Manager.

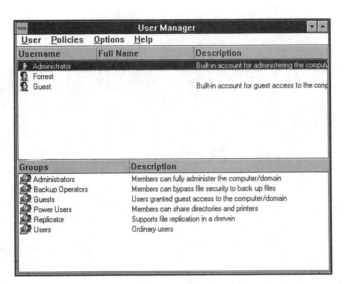

Figure 27.4

The User Manager window.

Performance Monitor

Windows NT includes a Performance Monitor program that enables you to monitor the performance of your system. You can monitor processor time, privileged time, user time, and the number of interrupts per second. Each of these events can be displayed on a chart (see fig. 27.5), which enables you to visualize how efficiently your system—or any system on the network—is working.

In Performance Monitor, the key menus are the <u>V</u>iew menu and the <u>E</u>dit menu. The <u>V</u>iew menu enables you to select from <u>C</u>hart, <u>A</u>lert, <u>L</u>og, and <u>R</u>eport views. The <u>E</u>dit menu enables you to display an Add dialog box, which is invoked by the first item on the menu, to determine what to display in each view.

In chart view, you see a line chart that represents system performance. With a little experience, you soon recognize when the system is slowing down. In alert view, you can set critical values for the counters associated with processor time, privileged time, user time, and interrupts per second. When the counter exceeds or falls below the critical value, you can run a program that either alerts you to the situation or corrects the problem. (If you need an explanation for any of the counters, click on the <u>E</u>xplain button in any dialog box that has one.) In log view, you can create a log that is updated at a time interval you set. You can choose to create a log of the activity associated with any of the system services. The log can show current activity, or it can save activity to a file for later display. In report view, you can create a report that shows the counters for the items you chose to log in log view or for current system activity.

Figure 27.5

The Performance Monitor window showing the performance chart.

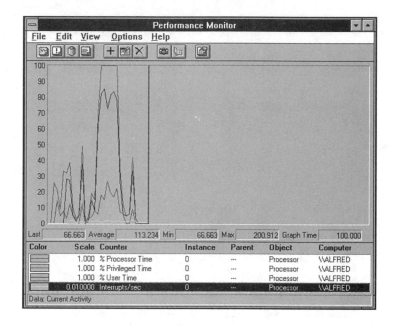

Using Performance Monitor, you can check on system activity. If a system slows down, you can check to see which counters are showing unusually high or low activity. When you clarify a problem, you can create macros or run programs that automatically deal with the problem. If monitoring your physical disk shows that a file system check is in order, for example, you can automatically run CHKDSK to diagnose and repair the problem.

Event Viewer

Windows NT also provides an Event Viewer program to monitor events on your system. Event Viewer does not present information about system performance related to events like Performance Monitor. Instead, Event Viewer presents a list of all significant events that take place on your system (see fig. 27.6). You can examine these events to determine if your system is both operating correctly and secure.

From Event Viewer's Log menu, you can select whether you are viewing System events, Security events, or Application events. An *event* is literally anything that happens on the system. System events reveal anything of interest about any of the system services, drivers, or servers. You can reveal the details of any event, including an explanation of why it was logged, by double-clicking on the event in the list. This action reveals a dialog box like that shown in figure 27.7.

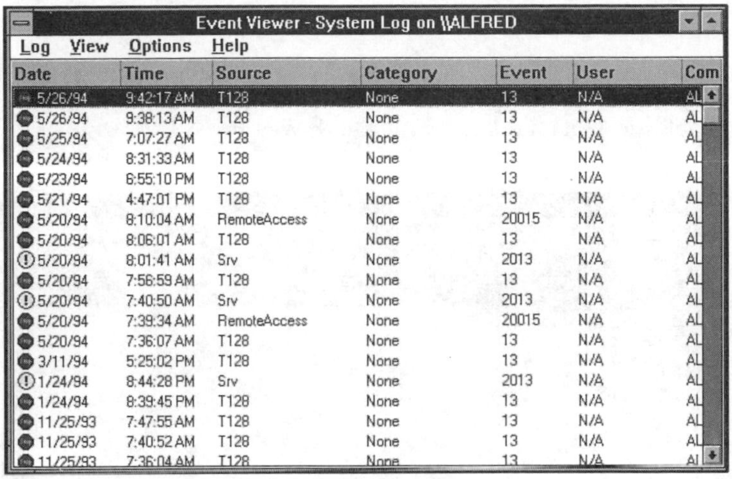

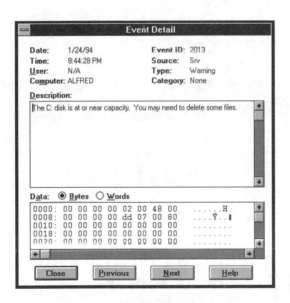

V

Networking and Windows

Figure 27.6
The Event Viewer window showing a log of system events.

Figure 27.7
An Event Detail dialog box for a system event.

You can review the Event Detail dialog boxes to diagnose problems with your system, applications, and security. (The event shown in figure 27.7 shows that the server detected the C drive was nearly full. The solution is to migrate some files to another location.) You should regularly review this log, especially the security log, to make certain that your system is in top form.

Backup

Windows NT provides a Backup program to assist you with maintaining your system (see fig. 27.8). This program is much like others on the market for DOS; however, you should know that it is probably the weakest utility provided with Windows NT.

Figure 27.8
The Backup program's window.

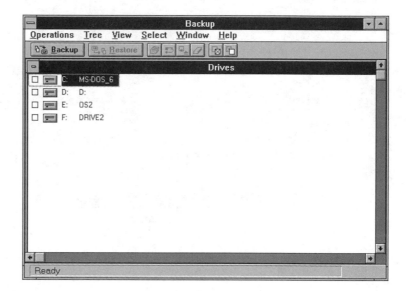

Although the Backup program is fully functional and enables you to back up files effectively, it does not have the full range of features you might want. It does not work with a wide range of tape drives, for example, nor does it support file compression. You should contact Microsoft or visit the Windows NT forum on CompuServe (**GO WINNT**) to get the latest hardware compatibility list before selecting a tape drive. You also might want to consider a third-party backup program as a substitute.

Understanding Windows NT Workstation and Windows NT Advanced Server

You can buy two different versions of Windows NT: Windows NT Workstation and Windows NT Advanced Server. Which edition you choose depends on your planned installation and how much you want to invest in Windows NT. The Workstation edition supports an individual workstation and provides the advanced peer-to-peer networking (or low-level server networking) supported by Windows NT. It is priced on a per workstation basis. The Advanced Server edition, on the other hand, supports a single network server and is priced on a server licensing basis, depending on the number of workstations to be attached to the server.

The choice between the two editions is easy to make. If you are setting up a single workstation or a small network (15 or fewer workstations), you should use the Workstation edition. If you are going to base a larger network with a file server on Windows NT, you should select the Advanced Server edition. Configuring a workstation as a server with the Workstation edition is theoretically possible, just as it is with Windows for Workgroups 3.11. This option is hardly an ideal solution, however, if your network approaches 15 or more workstations.

Deciding To Use Windows NT

Deciding to use Windows NT instead of a competing operating system can be a difficult decision. Recent press articles offering month-long tests of Windows for Workgroups 3.11, OS/2, Windows NT, and Chicago have concluded that Windows for Workgroups 3.11 is the best business operating system available. OS/2 has its devotees among developers who need an operating system that does not allow a poorly behaved program, such as one that is under development and therefore contains bugs, to crash the entire system. If you are considering high-end workstations, UNIX is a definite competitor. Despite what some elements in the computer trade press say, Chicago (also known as Windows 4) is still too far from release to be a serious contender. But you should review its purported characteristics carefully as you weigh your choice. You might decide to wait for Chicago rather than upgrade to Windows NT.

Every major operating system on the market has its audience. The real question in choosing to use Windows NT is whether you are a part of its audience. The next section is designed to help you discover whether you are.

Who Should Use Windows NT?

If you choose an operating system on the basis of all the features that it offers, you might as well resign yourself to buying a high-end mainframe system. Such systems are the only ones that can offer all the features you could ever want with all the performance you could ever want. In selecting an operating system for a personal workstation, you need to get all the features you must have to do your work and none of the features that you would never use. Buying extra features means buying files that take up valuable space on your hard drive.

So who is Windows NT really for? The next few sections offer profiles that help you to see what kind of user needs Windows NT. If you see yourself in one of the profiles, you are a very good Windows NT candidate.

The High-End User

Window NT offers the following features that a high-end or power user of a personal workstation might need or prefer:

✔ Crash protection

✔ 32-bit architecture

✔ True multitasking

✔ Multithreading

✔ Built-in networking

✔ Built-in remote access

✔ Protection against viruses

✔ Built-in recovery of a damaged operating system

✔ Compatibility with a variety of operating systems

What kinds of activities does a high-end user engage in that require all of these features? The following list helps to explain:

✔ **Running multiple applications simultaneously.** You always have a word processor, spreadsheet, database, presentation graphics, and communications program loaded at the same time. These programs are doing work in the background (for example, downloading files) while you are working in the foreground. Window NT's multitasking and multithreading features improve your working environment.

✔ **Linking to multiple machines simultaneously.** You are logged in to a peer-to-peer network or server-based network most of the time. Windows NT provides superior networking over DOS/Windows.

✔ **Dialing into the home system.** You are frequently traveling or working at home and, as a result, dial in to the desktop system to retrieve files and use programs often. Windows NT has a built-in remote access server and client.

✔ **Working on mission-critical data.** You work with data and programs critical to the success of your business, and you need bullet-proof protection of files from both corruption and viruses. You also need to make sure your system does not crash and corrupt files during the crash. The file protection and crash protection of Windows NT fit these needs.

✔ **Several users sharing a single workstation.** You work in an office where several users must work on a single workstation, or you work in an office where users frequently work on different workstations. Each user wants to set up his own working environment. Windows NT provides superior multiple user environments.

✔ **Working in an environment of mixed operating systems.** You work in an office that uses DOS for desktop systems and has UNIX or OS/2 1.*x* programs running on various other platforms. Windows NT has more operating system compatibility modules than other options.

✔ **Stressing the DOS/Windows environment heavily.** You repeatedly find your DOS/Windows environment slowing down, or you constantly have to wait to continue work in one application while another application displays the hourglass for a long operation. Windows NT can relieve such stress by managing your applications' tasks more efficiently.

If any or all of these descriptions fit you, you might benefit from moving to Windows NT as an individual user. You should keep in mind that you might experience some performance penalties in 16-bit Windows applications, and you might trade a small amount of speed for the added security of Windows NT.

Windows NT 3.5, the next version of Windows NT, will be out by fourth quarter 1994. Reviews of the beta test version so far indicate that version 3.5 requires less memory than version 3.1 and performs faster with 16-bit Windows applications.

The Secure User

Windows for Workgroups 3.11 provides password security for its network. But if someone wants to break into your workstation, pressing Ctrl+Alt+Del enables them to reboot the system to DOS. Windows NT provides better login security, because pressing Ctrl+Alt+Del only causes the Login dialog box to reappear. Therefore, if you need security on a workstation or a network, Windows NT is superior to DOS and Windows.

In addition, the NT File System enables you to implement advanced security features available heretofore only on mainframe operating systems. You can use access control lists to limit file access to designated individuals; you can audit who has accessed a file and when; you can monitor system events; and you can monitor specific security events to see if your data and programs are in danger. Users who must be security conscious ought to consider Windows NT seriously.

The Advanced Network

Among the various network operating systems, Banyan VINES is reputed to be the best for technical excellence. Novell NetWare has captured most of the corporate networking market. Microsoft LAN Manager and Artisoft LANtastic hold their own in niche markets. Who should choose Windows NT instead of one of these players?

If you are planning to build a network or change your network operating system, Windows NT offers the following advantages:

✔ A graphical user interface is supplied for all network management programs.

✔ Management utilities come as a part of the package rather than as add-ons.

✔ Network services are easy to set up and manage.

✔ Peer-to-peer or server architectures are easy to implement.

✔ Workstations integrate well with servers.

✔ Workstations can run DOS/Windows, Windows NT, or Macintosh System 7.

✔ Windows NT offers advanced network and file security.

✔ Workgroup utilities (Mail, Schedule+, Chat, and so on) are included.

✔ Remote access is a part of the network, not a complicated add-on.

If you find yourself gravitating to any set of these features, Windows NT might well be the network operating system of choice. You should especially consider price versus performance as you make your decision, as well as the availability of a manufacturer-sponsored consulting service, such as Microsoft Consulting Services, that can help you make the transition to your new network environment.

What Are the Hardware Requirements?

If you are considering Windows NT, you need to be aware of the hardware requirements. You might indeed have to upgrade hardware in order to run this operating system. In making your decision, you need to factor in these costs as well. Table 27.1 lists the hardware requirements for Windows NT 3.1.

Table 27.1
Minimal Hardware Requirements for Windows NT 3.1

Hardware	Intel x86-Based System	RISC-Based System
Processor	80386/25 or better	MIPS R4000 or DEC Alpha
Video	VGA or better	VGA or better
Hard drive	At least one with 75 MB free	At least one with 92 MB free
Floppy/CD drives	High-density floppy drive	SCSI CD-ROM drive
Minimum memory	12 MB RAM	16 MB RAM

Hardware	Intel x86-Based System	RISC-Based System
Pointing device	Optional	Optional
CD-ROM drive	Optional	Required
Network adapters	Optional	Optional

Keep in mind that these are minimal hardware requirements. Windows NT will load and run with this minimum hardware. You might be much happier as a user, however, if you add at least 4 MB of RAM to the minimum requirements, get the fastest processor you can afford, and a large hard drive with a fast access time.

How Much Security Do You Need?

The question of how much security to implement is in part a question about which file system you want to use. If you want maximum security, you must use the NT File System. If you want minimal security, you can use any of the file systems that NT supports and, if you select NTFS, implement only the security features you need. But the real question is what you need.

For the average single user of a computer, wherein no one else uses the computer workstation but the user and the workstation is not networked, Windows NT offers login security that is quite good. The only way to violate this security is to reinstall Windows NT and create a new administrative password. You can guard against this possibility by disabling the boot from floppy option in the ROM setup and setting a hardware-level password in your system's setup. As a result, you can be reasonably certain that no one can invade your system and compromise data. Under these circumstances, any file system will do.

After you network the workstation, however, or after multiple users use the same workstation, the advanced security features offered by NTFS make sense. Not only can you set security on individual program and data files, but you can audit who has used them. If a security breach somehow occurs, you can track down how it occurred and close out the account that has been compromised. Or, if a serious security breach has occurred, you can lock out all users and reestablish different accounts for those who use the networked workstations. NTFS is the file system of choice under these circumstances.

A number of different security needs fall in between these two extremes. Windows NT can accommodate each of them with some combination of the correct file system and security features. A central issue in deciding how much security to implement is how much administrative time you want to put into monitoring security. Security features that are never monitored can easily be compromised. You should implement the security that keeps your data and programs as safe as you think they should be, and then you should monitor your secure environment regularly by checking the security log for abnormal activity.

What Are the Differences from Windows 3.11?

As you think about whether to upgrade to Windows NT, you might want to note the main differences from Windows 3.11 in working with key programs. These differences give you a sense of how all the new features will impact on your working style. In general, working with Windows NT is only slightly different from working with Windows 3.11. There are a couple of habits you have to develop, and a few new menus here and there to deal with.

Starting Windows NT

A key difference between Windows 3.11 and Windows NT is the start-up sequence. With Windows 3.11, you boot into DOS and then start windows using the WIN command. If you are using Windows for Workgroups, you must enter a password in a dialog box (if you have enabled networking features) for your system to be ready for use.

Windows NT has a different start-up sequence. When you boot the computer, Windows NT loads. It has no DOS layer. As a result, there is no command line that you type at a prompt of any sort to start Windows. When the boot sequence ends, you must press Ctrl+Alt+Del to log in to the system. After you press this key combination, you enter your login name and password in a dialog box. If you have typed everything correctly, clicking on the OK button admits you to the system. Then the familiar Windows screen appears.

Working with Program Manager

Windows NT's Program Manager contains a few key differences from that of Windows 3.11 in operation. When you create program groups using the New item on the File menu, for example, you must specify whether the group is common or personal. In addition, on the Options menu, there is a Save Settings Now item. You can select this item at any time to save the settings for the Program Manager's organization of the desktop.

These added menu options, one of which has been long desired by Windows 3.11 users, are the most minor of the changes, however. The File menu sports two new items: Logoff and Shutdown (see fig. 27.9). These two new items are central to the way you interact with Windows NT.

In Windows NT, you do not just exit Windows; you must decide which of the two ways to exit you wish to use. Logoff is the appropriate procedure if you wish to end your Windows NT session without shutting off the computer. When you use Logoff, Windows NT returns to the login screen and displays the dialog box that asks the next user to press Ctrl+Alt+Del to login.

When you use Shutdown, you inform Windows NT that you want to log off and shut the computer off. After Windows NT logs you off, it initiates its shutdown sequence. You must wait until you see a dialog box that says it is safe to shut off the power before powering off your system. If you power the system off before you see this dialog box, you might corrupt operating system files or prevent your system settings from being saved.

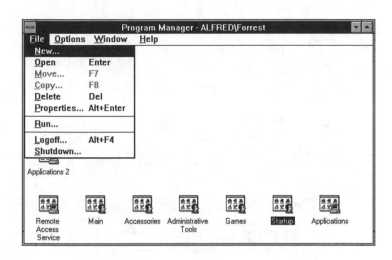

Figure 27.9
The File menu in
Program
Manager.

Networking and Windows

Other than these changes, you work with Program Manager in Windows NT the same way you do in Windows 3.11. You should notice no difference in the way you launch and use programs.

Working with Control Panel

The Windows NT Control Panel contains many of the same icons as the Windows 3.11 Control Panel. You work with these icons, for the most part, in the same way you do in Windows 3.11. The Windows NT Control Panel contains the following icons that do not appear in Windows 3.11, however, as shown in figure 27.10:

- ✔ Cursors

- ✔ Devices

- ✔ Server

- ✔ Services

- ✔ System

- ✔ UPS

Each of these new icons opens a dialog box that enables you to set Windows NT–specific settings. The Cursors icon, which presents the dialog box shown in figure 27.11, enables you to customize the cursors used for each system event. If you do not like the hourglass cursor, for instance, you can change it. You can even install animated cursors, so your wait cursor could be a dashing race horse instead of an hourglass.

Figure 27.10
The Windows NT
Control Panel.

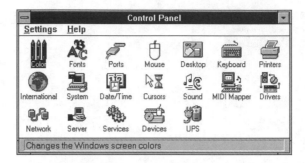

Figure 27.11
The Cursors
dialog box.

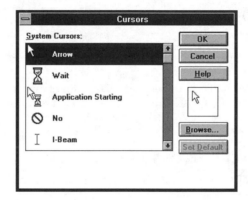

The Devices icon, which presents the dialog box shown in figure 27.12, enables you to configure, start, and stop device drivers. You will not need to use this dialog box often unless you notice that some needed device such as a mouse port is not activating when the computer starts. Windows NT enables this sort of control over each device on your system. As a result, you have detailed control over how the operating system interacts with your hardware.

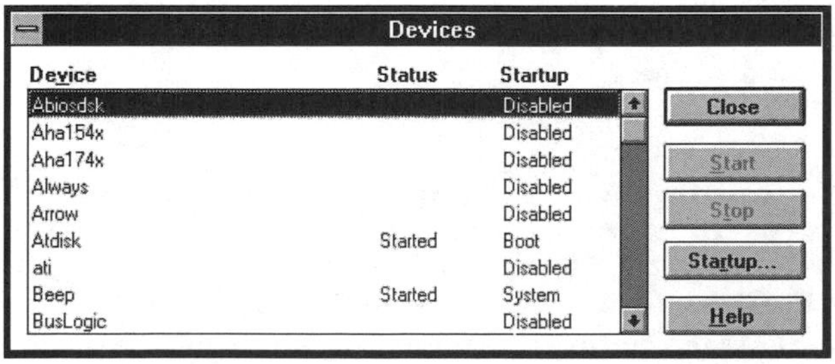

Figure 27.12
The Devices dialog
box.

The Server icon, which presents the dialog box shown in figure 27.13, enables your control over the server characteristics of your computer. The Server dialog box manages the print, file, and communications services on your computer. This dialog box controls how your computer acts as a network host.

Figure 27.13
The Server dialog box.

The Services icon enables you to control each operating system service. The Services dialog box (see fig. 27.14) enables you to start, stop, and pause system services such as Event Log, Alerter, or Net Logon. Most of the time you will not need to interact with this dialog box. There may be times, however, when you wish to prevent network logins or prevent the Alerter from sending alert messages to selected users.

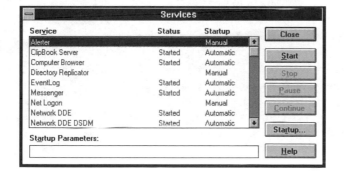

Figure 27.14
The Services dialog box.

The System icon displays the System dialog box shown in figure 27.15. In the System dialog box, you set the default operating system, if you are using the dual boot feature that enables you to retain a copy of your previous operating system; use controls to manage virtual memory; and set your personal path and other environment variables. You can expect to use the System dialog box at least occasionally.

Windows NT enables you to retain a copy of your old operating system during the installation process. This feature, known as *dual boot,* then presents a menu each time your system starts asking you which operating system to boot. You

continues

should select the dual boot feature on installation if you own programs that might not run in one of the compatibility modes. Some DOS games, for example, may circumvent DOS in ways that Windows NT does not allow. You might need to keep a copy of DOS to run such programs.

Figure 27.15
The System dialog box.

```
┌─────────────────────── System ───────────────────────┐
│                                                       │
│  Computer Name:  ALFRED                    ┌─────OK────┐│
│  ┌─Operating System──────────────────┐     ├──Cancel──┤│
│  │  Startup: [MS-DOS            ▼]    │     ├Virtual Memory...┤│
│  │                                   │     ├─Tasking...─┤│
│  │  Show list for [30 ▲] seconds     │     ├──Help─────┤│
│  └───────────────────────────────────┘                 │
│  System Environment Variables:                         │
│  ┌───────────────────────────────────────────────────┐│
│  │ ComSpec = D:\winnt\system32\cmd.exe               ││
│  │ Os2LibPath = D:\winnt\system32\os2\dll;           ││
│  │ Path = D:\winnt\system32;D:\winnt                 ││
│  │ windir = D:\winnt                                 ││
│  └───────────────────────────────────────────────────┘│
│                                                       │
│  User Environment Variables for Forrest                │
│  ┌───────────────────────────────────────────────────┐│
│  │ path = c:\windows;c:\windows\system;c:\winword    ││
│  │ temp = D:\temp                                    ││
│  │ tmp = D:\temp                                     ││
│  └───────────────────────────────────────────────────┘│
│                                                       │
│  Variable: [                              ]  [ Set  ]  │
│  Value:    [                              ]  [Delete]  │
└───────────────────────────────────────────────────────┘
```

The UPS icon, which presents the dialog box shown in figure 27.16, enables you to control an uninterruptible power supply (UPS). Whether you use the UPS icon depends on whether you have a UPS attached to your system. If you use your system as a server, or if you are engaged in mission-critical work, you should strongly consider getting a UPS. Power outages are somewhat rougher on Windows NT than they are on Windows 3.11. There are more system files open and more system data to lose than in the earlier Windows environment. (Fortunately, repairing a Windows NT system is much easier as well.) A UPS might be a wise investment as a result.

Windows NT can occasionally be damaged. Power outages and similar events can corrupt even the best operating systems. You can invoke the Last Known Good menu on start-up, however, to start the last version of the operating system that was known to boot. If this version fails, you can use the same menu to conduct repairs using your Emergency Repair Disk. Windows NT is very capable of protecting you against operating system failures.

A major difference between working with the Control Panel in Windows NT and the Control Panel in Windows 3.11, especially when you start working with Windows NT, is that Windows NT might deny you permission to use a Control Panel icon. The reason is that some Control Panel functions can be made only by someone logged in as the system administrator. If you are not the system administrator, you cannot change many settings yourself, perhaps not even the date and time. Permission to make such changes is limited for security reasons. As a result, by switching to Windows NT, you might be handing some control of your system over to a system administrator.

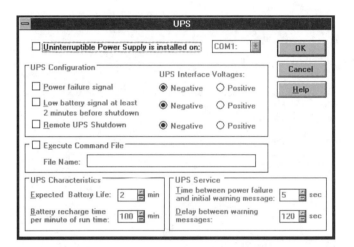

Figure 27.16
The UPS dialog box.

Working with File Manager

The central difference between the Windows 3.11 File Manager and the Windows NT File Manager is the presence of a Security menu (see fig. 27.17). Using the Security menu, if you have appropriate privileges, you can set permissions, auditing, and ownership for files and directories. If you do not have the system privileges to perform a particular operation, the menu item for that operation is dimmed or the system presents a dialog box informing you that you cannot take the action you indicated in a dialog box.

Figure 27.17
The File Manager's Security menu.

If you are used to working in a command-line mainframe environment, you might be pleased to see how easy security operations are in Windows NT. To set permissions, choose Security, Permissions to invoke the Directory Permissions dialog box (see fig. 27.18). You use drop-down list boxes and list boxes to determine which users have what privileges. You easily can review the permissions granted; there is little guesswork involved. Security under Windows NT is easy to administer.

Figure 27.18

The Directory
Permissions dialog
box.

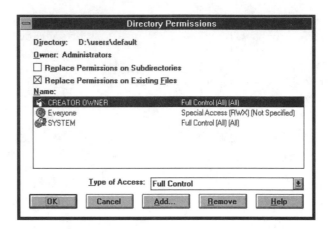

To take advantage of the security features shown in this section, you must be
using the NT File System.

Working with Print Manager

The Print Manager in Windows NT is radically different from the Print Manager in
Windows 3.11. The Printer, Document, and Security menus appear on the menu bar, as
shown in figure 27.19. All printing management is controlled from the Windows NT Print
Manager. The functions of the Printers icon in the Windows 3.11 Control Panel have
been merged into the Windows NT Print Manager.

Figure 27.19

The Print Manager
in Windows NT.

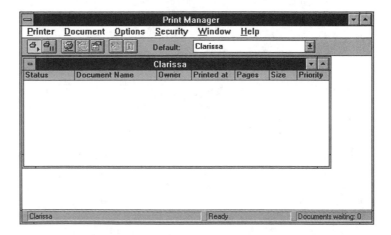

You use the <u>P</u>rinter menu to connect to a printer (either on a local machine or a network), create a printer, remove a printer, set the properties of a printer using its Printer Driver dialog box, set paper types and print margins, pause a printer, resume a paused printer, and purge a printer's queue. You use the <u>D</u>ocument menu to remove a document from a queue, examine details of a print job, pause a print job, resume a paused print job, and start a document's printing over. You use the <u>S</u>ecurity menu—like the <u>S</u>ecurity menu in the File Manager—to set permissions, auditing, and ownership for printers.

Managing printers in Windows NT is different mainly in that functions that are included in the Control Panel in other versions of Windows are now included in the Print Manager. After you become accustomed to this change, you manage printers in basically the same way as you do in Windows 3.11.

Working with the Registry

You will either be pleased or saddened to learn that Windows NT has done away with the WIN.INI and SYSTEM.INI files. In their place is a database called the System Registry. If you liked tinkering with settings in the INI files for Windows 3.11, the developers of Windows NT have some advice for you about tinkering with the System Registry: Don't!

Although this sounds like rude advice, there is a simple reason for it. Data is not stored in the System Registry the same way it is stored in the INI files. Some values are binary values, some are 32-bit integers, and some are stored as special-purpose strings of characters. The typical computer user will find mastering these special data formats difficult. Making a mistake with one of these data formats has a simple side effect: Windows NT probably will refuse to boot. As a result, the advice to leave the System Registry alone is very good advice.

Not tinkering with the system configuration is a central change in the way you work with Windows NT. It is radically different from the way you work with Windows 3.11. Very often with Windows 3.11, the advice for troubleshooting is to change a setting in one of the INI files and see what happens.

If you must explore the System Registry, however, you can do so by running a program called REGEDT32.EXE using the <u>R</u>un option on the <u>F</u>ile menu in either Program Manager or File Manager. This program presents the Registry Editor, which enables you to make changes in the System Registry (see fig. 27.20).

The Registry is organized as a database with keys representing locations in the database where values that represent system settings can be attached. There are four predefined or first-level keys. HKEY_LOCAL_MACHINE is a predefined key containing subkeys that hold values that represent the configuration data for your computer's hardware and software. HKEY_USERS contains subkeys that hold values representing information about the active users on the system. HKEY_CURRENT_USER contains subkeys that hold values representing information about the current user of the system who started the Registry Editor. HKEY_CLASSES_ROOT contains subkeys that hold values defining Windows 3.11 compatibility and OLE support.

Figure 27.20
The Registry Editor.

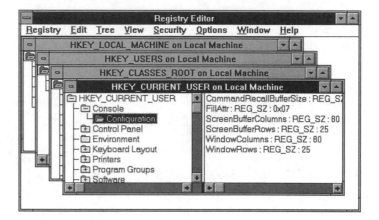

Each predefined key is represented as a document window in the Registry Editor's workspace. A tree view of the subkeys for the predefined key appears in the left pane of this document window. You navigate this tree like you navigate the tree in File Manager. The right pane contains the values of the subkeys. You can edit one of the values by double-clicking on it. This action starts an editor that enables you to enter only the appropriate value type for that key.

Before you modify a value, make certain that you know what the value should be. If you are not certain, check with Microsoft Technical Support. The Registry Editor is not a place to play out hunches or to test hypotheses. As programmers like to say, you can really hose your system.

Chapter Snapshot

A major advantage of Windows for Workgroups is its peer-to-peer networking. With Windows for Workgroups you can share resources such as disks, printers, and fax-modems across the network. This chapter focuses on sharing resources across the network. The topics covered in this chapter include the following:

If you are unfamiliar with networks and you have not read Chapter 26, "Understanding Networks and Workgroups," read it first before you proceed with this chapter. Chapter 26 provides an overview of networks and the benefits they offer, and also explains what peer-to-peer networks provide that other networks cannot. These topics, particularly peer-to-peer networking, are important to using Windows for Workgroups.

28

CHAPTER

Sharing Resources
in Windows

This chapter provides the information you need to begin sharing resources such as free disk space, applications, data, and printers with other users. Your first step is to understand how Windows for Workgroups makes resources available across the network.

Starting Windows and Logging In

Windows for Workgroups is a peer-to-peer network operating system. Unlike more traditional dedicated networks, which do not enable workstations to share resources with one another, Windows for Workgroups enables resources on one workstation to be used by another workstation. This means that another user can access files on your workstation just as if your local hard disk were connected to the other user's workstation. You can access disks and printers on other workstations in the same way.

Windows for Workgroups 3.1 runs in Standard and 386-Enhanced modes. Windows for Workgroups 3.11, however, runs only in 386-Enhanced mode. This edition of *Inside Windows, Platinum Edition* assumes you are running Windows for Workgroups 3.11, which offers additional features that are not available in Windows for Workgroups 3.1.

Logging In at Start-Up

To understand the login process for Windows for Workgroups, you must understand the password list file and the way security is implemented in this environment. Windows for Workgroups implements security differently from many other network operating systems. Many network environments require you to have an existing user account to which a system administrator has granted specific access privileges. Windows for Workgroups, however, allows anyone, including DOS clients, to log in with a new user name and password. This enables new users to, in essence, create their own user accounts for Windows for Workgroups.

When you log in to the network in Windows (see fig. 28.1), Windows checks the user name you provide to see if it matches an existing password list file on your workstation (or in your home network directory if you are booting from a diskless workstation). If it does match an existing password list file and the login password you provide is valid, the password list file is unlocked, giving you access to its contents. If the login password does not match the password required by the user name, the file remains locked and you are denied access.

Figure 28.1
The Welcome to Windows for Workgroups dialog box.

Welcome to Windows for Workgroups

Type a logon name and password to log on to the Microsoft Windows Network.

Logon Name: JIMB

Password: ********

OK

Cancel

Help

This chapter covers the login process and resource sharing under Windows. For information on logging in and using network resources from a DOS client running Workgroup Connection, refer to *Inside Windows for Workgroups*, from New Riders Publishing.

The password list file is used to store the passwords required by remote resources. These passwords represent the complete security system implemented in the Windows for Workgroups network, both in DOS (including Workgroup Connection) and in Windows.

When you access new resources from Windows, the name of the resource and its password are stored in the password list file. The next time Windows connects to that resource, it checks the password list file for an appropriate password. If the password matches the one required by the resource to which Windows is attempting to connect, the connection is reestablished. If the stored password does not match the requested password, Windows prompts you for a password for the resource (discussed later).

When you provide a new user name and password during login (and therefore, no password list file exists), Windows asks if you want to create a password list for the user name. If you choose the Yes button, Windows for Workgroups creates a password list file for your user name. Even though you have never logged in to the workstation with this user name, Windows attempts to reestablish connections to the resources that were in place during the previous session. If the resources require passwords, Windows prompts you for them. If no password is required, the reconnection takes place without any additional input from you. As you access additional network resources, those resources and their required passwords are added to the new password list file.

If you choose No when prompted to create a new password list file, Windows does not create a password list file for your user name. You still are logged in to Windows, however.

The final option you have when prompted to create a new password list file is Cancel. This cancels the current dialog box and returns you to the Welcome to Windows dialog box. If you choose Cancel at this point, the login dialog box closes without logging you in. You still have access to the features in Windows, but you do not have access to remote resources until you log in. To log in after Windows is started, use the Control Panel.

Using Control Panel To Log In and Out

The Windows for Workgroups Control Panel includes a Network icon that provides options for logging in to the network and controlling network operation. If you choose the Network icon, the Microsoft Windows Network dialog box appears, as shown in figure 28.2.

Figure 28.2
The Microsoft
Windows Network
dialog box controls
network access
and performance.

Microsoft Windows Network

Computer Name: OFFICE1

Workgroup: PC

Comment:

OK
Cancel
Help

Logon Status
Currently logged on as JIMB
Default Logon Name: JIMB
[Log Off]

Options:
Startup   Password   Event Log

The Microsoft Windows Network dialog box controls a number of different network features and operating parameters. The **W**orkgroup item, which enables you to change to another workgroup or create a new workgroup, is discussed in Chapter 26, "Understanding Networks and Workgroups." The rest of the options and controls are discussed in various areas of this chapter.

The Logon Status group box enables you to log in and out of the network. If you are not currently logged on, the button at the lower left corner of the Logon Status group box displays the label **L**og On. Clear the **D**efault Logon Name edit box and choose the **L**og On button to display the Welcome to Windows for Workgroups dialog box (refer to figure 28.1), which is the same dialog box Windows displays by default at start-up if the system is not configured for automatic login. The most recent user name is displayed in the **L**ogon Name edit box.

To log in with the displayed login name, type your password in the **P**assword edit box of the Welcome to Windows for Workgroups dialog box and press Enter, or click on OK. If you want to use a different login name, type the name in the **L**ogon Name edit box, then type the password associated with that user name. When you press Enter or click on OK, Windows for Workgroups then logs you in to the network and reestablishes network connections.

If you plan to leave your workstation and are concerned that someone will access the remote resources to which your workstation is connected, you should log out. You also should log out when you leave work. To log out without exiting Windows (and leave your local resources available to other nodes), use the Network item in Control Panel.

To log out, open the Control Panel and double-click on the Network icon to display the Microsoft Windows Network dialog box. In the Logon Status group, the button in the

Logon Status group box displays <u>L</u>og Off, indicating that you currently are logged in. To log out, choose the <u>L</u>og Off button. If you currently are connected to remote resources, Windows warns you that logging out will disconnect you from those resources (see fig. 28.3). To log out, choose <u>Y</u>es. To cancel the logout process and remain connected to remote resources, choose <u>N</u>o.

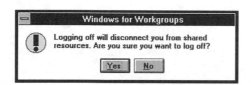

Figure 28.3

Logging out disconnects you from remote resources.

If you want to log in and out of the network quickly, open the Network group in Program Manager and choose the Log On/Off icon. Windows will log you out of the network quickly without displaying any prompts or dialog boxes. To log back in, choose the Log On/Off icon again.

You do not have to log out to exit Windows for Workgroups. When you exit Windows, you are automatically logged out, and no other users on the network can access your local resources. If disks, printers, or other resources are shared from your workstation, and other users need them, you should leave Windows running on your system but log out of the network.

The process of logging out prevents someone else from using your workstation to access sensitive remote resources, but it does not prevent them from accessing your local resources. To protect local resources, Windows includes utilities called screen savers that enable you to password-protect your workstation and prevent anyone else from using it even when Windows is running. Screen savers also prevent burn-in from occurring on your display. *Burn-in* occurs when a single image remains on a computer display for extended periods of time and results in a ghost image on the monitor.

The use of screen savers as a security tool is discussed later in this chapter in the section on resource and workstation security.

Controlling Login

By default, Windows for Workgroups attempts to log in automatically at start-up. If you rely on remote connections extensively, this enables you to log in immediately and reconnect to those resources without having to go through the steps involved in logging in using the Control Panel. If you use remote resources only rarely, however, you might want to log in only when you need to access network resources, instead of immediately when Windows for Workgroups starts.

The Microsoft Windows Network dialog box includes a button labeled Startup that displays a dialog box you can use to control Windows for Workgroups' start-up (see fig. 28.4). The Startup Settings dialog box includes a check box labeled Log On At Startup. If this box is checked, Windows for Workgroups logs in using the default user name as soon as Windows starts. If you clear the box, you will not be prompted to log in until you open the Control Panel, select Network, then use the Logon button to log in.

If your program groups include items such as documents and programs that are located on other nodes, leave your system configured to log in at start-up. This ensures that these items are available immediately after you start Windows for Workgroups.

In addition to controlling login at start-up, the Startup Settings dialog box contains other controls that define the way Windows for Workgroups functions at start-up. The check box labeled Enable Network DDE determines whether you will be able to use network DDE on your workstation. If this item is disabled, you will not be able to use applications such as the Clipbook Viewer or Chat. If you do not use network DDE, consider disabling this option to improve Windows' performance on your workstation.

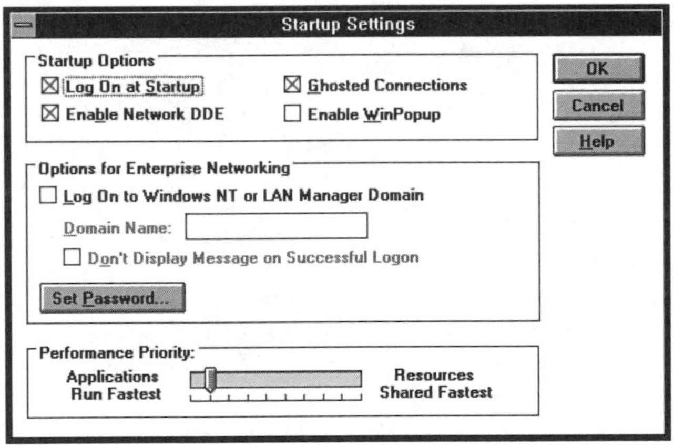

Figure 28.4

The Startup Settings dialog box.

The check box labeled Ghosted Connections determines whether Windows attempts to reestablish network resource connections automatically at start-up. If this option is checked, Windows attempts to connect to resources as soon as Windows starts. If this option is disabled, Windows does not attempt to establish a connection to previously defined remote resources until you actually attempt to access those resources. Windows does, however, reserve a drive ID at start-up to accommodate each disk resource.

The Enable WinPopup check box controls whether or not WINPOPUP.EXE executes automatically when you start Windows for Workgroups. WinPopup enables you to send messages to other users or to every user in a workgroup. In many ways, WinPopup is similar to a simplified e-mail system. If you disable WinPopup, you will not receive notification of messages when other users attempt to send messages to you. Place a check in the Enable <u>W</u>inPopup check box if you want to send and receive messages on the network.

The check box labeled <u>L</u>og On to Windows NT or LAN Manager Domain enables you to have Windows for Workgroups automatically log in to a Windows NT or LAN Manager domain as soon as Windows starts. You must specify a domain name in the <u>D</u>omain Name edit box. If you do not need to connect to a Windows NT or LAN Manager domain at start-up, leave the check box cleared.

Now that you are familiar with the options you can use to start Windows and the way Windows for Workgroups uses passwords to protect resources, you are ready to begin connecting to some of those resources.

Sharing Disks, Directories, and CDs

You can use Windows for Workgroups to share an entire disk (either hard disk or floppy disk), one or more directories, or a CD-ROM. The process of sharing these resources is relatively simple—you only need to use the File Manager to set it up. This chapter covers the commands in File Manager that enable you to connect to shared resources across the network and to share your local resources with other users. The other features and commands in File Manager are covered in Chapter 3, "Managing Files."

Sharing Your Directories and Disks

When you open File Manager, it displays a directory window of the currently selected disk. The split window shows a directory tree at the left and a file list at the right. As you select directories in the directory tree, the file list window changes to display the currently selected directory. Figure 28.5 shows File Manager with some of its components labeled.

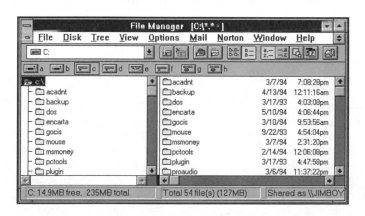

Figure 28.5
Parts of the File Manager.

To choose a different disk, click on its drive icon. These icons are located below File Manager's menu and toolbar (if the toolbar is being displayed). Figure 28.5 shows the four types of drive icons displayed by File Manager: local floppy disk (drives A and B), local hard disk (C, D, and F), local CD-ROM drive (E), and remote network drive (G and H).

To make your local resources available to other users, open the File Manager and share the disk or directory. Choose the drive icon of the drive you want to share, or of the drive that contains the directory you want to share. In the directory tree, choose the directory you want to share with other users. If you want to share the entire disk, choose the root directory (the uppermost directory in the tree).

With the proper directory selected, choose Disk, Share As to display the Share Directory dialog box (see fig 28.6). By default, File Manager fills in some of the items in the Share Directory dialog box for you. The Share Name edit box, which is the name other users see for the resource when they are browsing for it, contains the name of the directory being shared. If you are sharing the root directory, the Share Name edit box contains the drive ID (such as C).

Figure 28.6
The Share Directory dialog box.

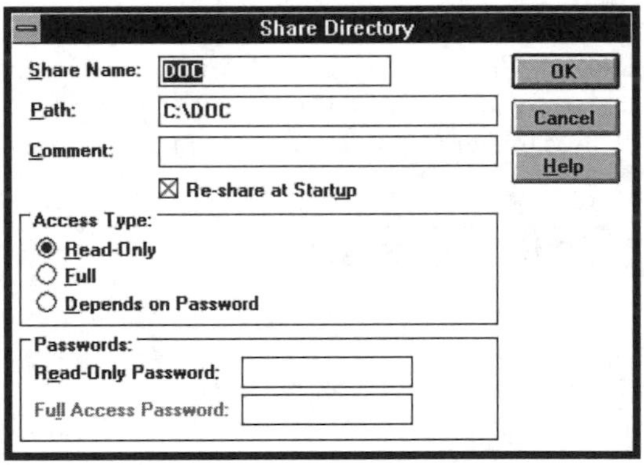

To change the name by which other users see your resource, double-click in the Share Name edit box to highlight the existing entry and type the name you want to use. The share name can be up to 12 characters long and can contain letters, numbers, and the following special characters:

! # $ % & ( ) - . @ ^ _ ' { } ~

Normally, the share name you specify appears in other users' browse dialog boxes when they are browsing for resources on the network. If you end the share name with a dollar sign ($), however, the share name does not appear in their browse dialog boxes. Users still can connect to the resource if they know its name. This enables you to share these resources with selected users without the entire network knowing that these resources are available. This adds an extra layer of security to these resources in addition to the security provided by passwords.

Give each local resource a share name that makes sense to other users when they see it in their browse boxes. A directory name QRX2Z may make sense to you, but it probably means nothing to anyone else. Choose a descriptive name, such as REPORTS, PRO-GRAMS, or DOCUMENTS.

The **P**ath edit box specifies the local path of the resource being shared. By default, the path of the currently selected directory appears in this edit box. If the path is correct, leave it as is. If you selected the wrong path in the File Manager directory tree, you can simply specify the correct path in the **P**ath edit box—you do not have to return to the directory tree to reselect the correct directory.

The **C**omment edit box enables you to enter a comment that appears next to the resource when other users see the resource in their browse boxes. The comment can consist of up to 48 characters. Figure 28.7 shows a few resources with comments in a browse dialog box.

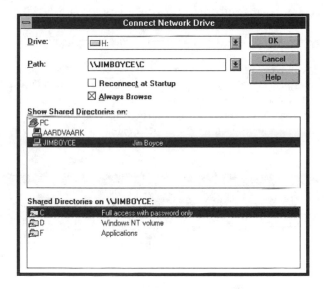

Figure 28.7

Comments can appear next to resources in the browse dialog box.

The Re-share at Start**u**p check box in the Share Directory dialog box controls whether the resource is shared automatically each time you start Windows for Workgroups on your system. If the box is checked, the resource is automatically reshared and is available to other users each time you start Windows for Workgroups. You do not have to log in to the network for these resources to be shared. If the box is cleared, the resource will not be reshared again automatically. If other users rely on your resources being available consistently, check the Re-share at Start**u**p check box. If you want to make the resource available only during your current Windows session or for a short time, clear the check box.

The Access Type group box contains three radio buttons that define the level of access other users will have to the resource you are sharing. The **R**ead-Only option gives other users the ability to read files in the shared directory, but they cannot change or erase files, or add new files to the directory. The Full option gives other users the ability to read, change, erase, and add new files to the shared directory. The Depends on Password option grants either read-only or full access to the user, depending on which password the user provides when connecting to the resource.

When Read-Only is selected, the Read-Only Password edit box is available (not dimmed) in the Passwords group box (just below the Access Type group box). If you leave the Read-Only Password edit box empty, no password is required to read files in your shared directory. If you want to require other users to provide a password so that they can view the files in your shared directory, enter it here.

When the Full radio button is selected, the Full Access Password edit box is available. As with read-only access, you can require users to provide a password for access to the shared directory. Protecting the shared directory with a password is more important if the user has full access than if he has read-only access.

To give some users read-only access and other users full access to your shared directory, choose the Depends on Password radio button. This option makes both the Read-Only Password and Full Access Password items available in the Passwords group box. Enter a different password for each one.

When you have all the items in the Share Directory dialog box the way you want them, click on OK. The shared directory then becomes available to other nodes. In File Manager, its icon changes from a standard folder to a shared folder icon (an outstretched hand holding the folder). Figure 28.8 shows a number of shared folder icons in File Manager.

Figure 28.8
Shared directories in File Manager.

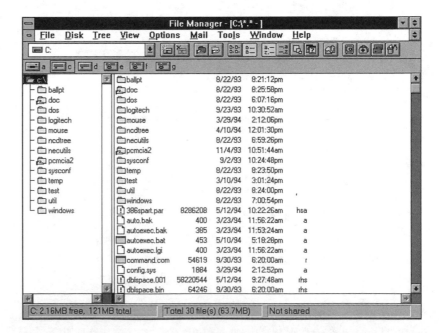

If you have the standard toolbar displayed in File Manager (choose Options, Toolbar to turn it on and off), you can open the Share Directory dialog box by selecting the directory to be shared and then pressing the Share As button. This has the same effect as choosing Share As from File Manager's Disk menu. Figure 28.9 shows the toolbar buttons for directory sharing.

Figure 28.9
Connection and sharing buttons in the toolbar.

Removing a Directory from Sharing

The Stop Sharing command in File Manager's Disk menu and the Stop Sharing button in the toolbar enable you to stop a directory from being shared. If you no longer want a shared directory to be available to other users, choose the Stop Sharing command or button. If you choose the command or the button, the Stop Sharing Directory dialog box appears (see fig. 28.10).

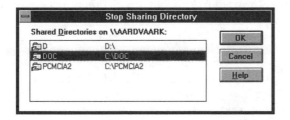

Figure 28.10
The Stop Sharing Directory dialog box.

The Stop Sharing Directory dialog box displays all the directories on your workstation currently being shared. Select the directory you no longer want to share, then choose OK. If you want to select a block of directories to stop sharing, choose the first directory in the block, then press and hold down the Shift key while you click on the last directory in the block. All the directories in between are selected. If you want to select multiple directories but skip some, press and hold down the Ctrl key and click on the directories you no longer want to share.

If you use File Manager to stop sharing a directory, and users still are connected to that directory, File Manager displays the warning dialog box shown in figure 28.11. If you choose Yes to disconnect the resource, File Manager determines whether users who are connected have files open in the shared directory. If they do, a second warning dialog box shown in figure 28.12 appears, warning you that disconnecting the resource might cause these users to lose data. You should not disconnect these users unless absolutely necessary. If possible, use Chat or the phone to contact these users and ask them to close their files so that you can disconnect the resource.

Figure 28.11

The first disconnect resource warning message box.

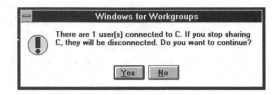

Figure 28.12

The second disconnect resource warning message box.

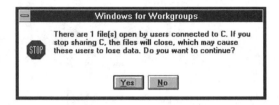

If the File Manager toolbar is displayed, you can access the Stop Sharing Directory dialog box by clicking on the Stop Sharing button (refer to figure 28.9).

Connecting to a Shared Directory

Now that your local resources are set up to be shared with other nodes, you might want to access resources on other nodes. You connect to remote disk resources as easily as you share a directory—with a few quick commands in File Manager.

To connect to a remote disk being shared by another node, open File Manager, then choose the Disk menu. Choose the Connect Network Drive menu item to display the Connect Network Drive dialog box, as shown in figure 28.13. This dialog box enables you to browse the network for resources and to connect to those resources.

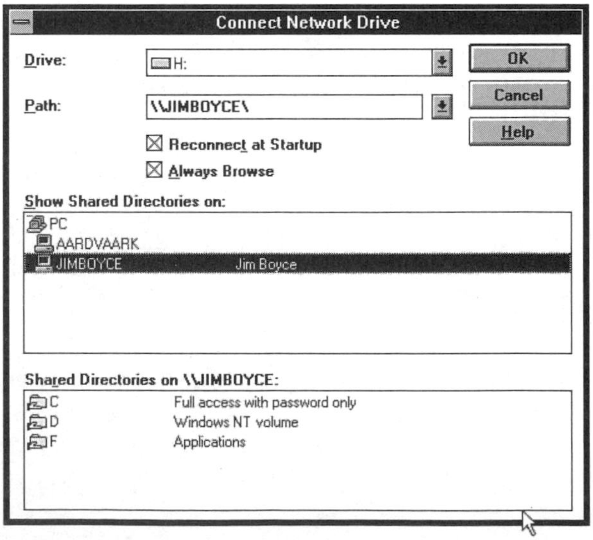

Figure 28.13

The Connect Network Drive dialog box.

Use the <u>D</u>rive drop-down list box to select a logical drive ID to associate with the remote resource. Windows displays the next available drive ID in the list, but you can select any available drive ID. When you complete the connection process, the remote resource appears to be connected to your system as a physical drive with that ID.

The <u>P</u>ath combo box is used to specify the path to the remote resource. The path name consists of the machine name and the remote share name, separated by a backslash, as in *machine**sharename*. If you know the name of the machine and remote share name, you can enter it directly in the <u>P</u>ath combo box.

If the share name of a resource you want to connect to has a dollar sign ($) as the last character in the name, you must enter the path to the resource manually. The dollar sign character ($) hides the resource from the browse list.

If you do not know the machine name or share name to which you want to connect, you can browse the network for the machine and share name. The list box labeled <u>S</u>how Shared Directories on displays the logged-in machines in each workgroup. By default, your current workgroup appears in expanded form; all other workgroups appear in collapsed tree form. Expanded groups show a minus sign (-) beside the workgroup icon, and collapsed workgroups show a plus sign (+) beside the icon.

Attempting to browse for network connections in Windows for Workgroups 3.11 sometimes causes a "Not Enough Memory" error. This is a known bug, but you might be able to overcome it by changing the setting `MaintainServerList` in the `[Network]` section of SYSTEM.INI on the system to read `MaintainServerList=Yes`. If this does not overcome the problem, you can connect to resources by entering their share names directly, instead of browsing for the available shares.

To display the available resources on a particular machine, click on its machine name in the list box. The available resources on the selected remote machine appear in the list box at the bottom of the Connect Network Drive dialog box. This list box is labeled Sha<u>r</u>ed Directories on *machine,* in which *machine* is the name of the remote node.

To connect to a resource, select it in the Sha<u>r</u>ed Directories list box. The path of the selected resource then appears in the <u>P</u>ath combo box. Click on OK to connect to the resource. If the resource requires a password, File Manager prompts you for one. If no password is required, the resource is connected immediately.

If you want the resource to be reconnected each time you log in to the network, make sure the Reconnec<u>t</u> at Startup check box is checked. This places the resource name in your system's CONNECT.DAT file, which Windows scans at login to determine which resources to reconnect automatically. If you want to use the resource only for a little while, or only during the current network session, clear the Reconnect at Startup check box.

If File Manager's toolbar is displayed, you can access the Connect Network Drive dialog box by clicking on the appropriate button in the toolbar. Figure 28.14 shows the Connect and Disconnect buttons in the File Manager toolbar.

Figure 28.14
The Connect and
Disconnect buttons
in File Manager.

Disconnecting a Remote Directory

To disconnect a remote directory, open File Manager and choose <u>D</u>isk, <u>D</u>isconnect Network Drive. The Disconnect Network Drive dialog box appears, as shown in figure 28.15.

Figure 28.15
The Disconnect
Network Drive
dialog box.

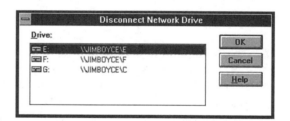

From the <u>D</u>rive list box, choose the remote resource you want to disconnect from your session, then click on OK. If you are not using any files on the selected drive, File Manager disconnects the resource without any further action from you. If you have files open on the remote disk, however, File Manager displays a dialog box warning you of open files and a loss of data if you disconnect the drive (see fig. 28.16). At this point, you should choose <u>N</u>o to cancel the disconnection process and close the files before attempting to disconnect the resource again.

Figure 28.16
You should close
files on a disk
before
disconnecting it.

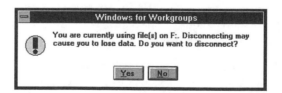

Sharing CD-ROMs

CD-ROM drives generally are recognized as logical drive IDs by the system. For this reason, you easily can share a CD-ROM across the network. On the workstation that is sharing the CD, load the MSCDEX device driver using the /S switch before starting Windows. The drive appears in Windows on that workstation as a logical drive ID, such as D.

Next, open File Manager and select the root directory of the CD. Choose the Share As command from File Manager's Disk menu and assign the CD a share name and password as you would a directory on a hard disk.

Connecting to a Remote CD

If the CD does not require a special loader program, other users can access the CD as if it were a shared directory on a local hard disk. To share a CD, follow the same steps you would for connecting to a remote directory on a shared hard disk.

If the CD requires a loader program, you must configure the loader program to access the remote drive. First, use File Manager's Connect Network Drive command to assign a drive ID to the remote CD. Browse for the CD as you would any other shared remote resource. After the drive is connected, make sure the loader program is configured to read from the drive ID you assigned to the remote CD.

Disconnecting a Remote CD

To disconnect a remote CD from your system, first exit the CD's viewer program (if any). Then use File Manager's Disconnect Network Drive command to disconnect the CD the same way you disconnect a directory on a hard disk.

Sharing Floppy Disks

The processes for sharing, connecting to, and disconnecting from a floppy disk are identical to those for a directory on a hard disk. The primary difference is the floppy disk might not be available consistently. Usually, you connect to a floppy disk only when you need to copy files from a drive that is not the correct size or capacity of your system's floppy drive.

When you connect to a shared floppy disk, clear the Reconnect at Startup check box. This prevents Windows from attempting to reconnect to the floppy each time you log in to the network.

Setting Up Printers

Another resource you can share across the network in Windows for Workgroups is printers. You can make your local printer available to other users by sharing it in much the same way you share your local disks. You also can print to printers that are connected to other nodes, just as you access disks on other nodes. Shared printers in Windows for Workgroups, such as expensive laser printers, can be used more efficiently and effectively than printers that are not shared. Shared printers also pay for themselves in a shorter period of time and assist in scheduling a large number of print jobs by enabling you to distribute the printing load across the network. If your printer is busy and you need to print a document, you can send it to a printer connected to someone else's workstation.

Although the process for sharing printers is somewhat different from sharing disk resources, it is just as easy. Rather than use the File Manager to share printers, you use the Print Manager. The Print Manager services your local print jobs and print jobs that other users send to your workstation from across the network.

An important part of setting up and sharing printers is understanding the purpose of parallel printer ports (LPT) and how they are used in Windows for Workgroups.

Understanding LPT Ports

Printers usually are connected to a computer's parallel ports. These ports also are called *LPT* ports, which is an acronym taken from *line printer*. Your workstation might include a single LPT port, or as many as three. Standard DOS systems without special hardware provide a maximum of three installed LPT ports. Each LPT port is referenced by a number, such as LPT1, LPT2, and LPT3.

These ports are called *parallel ports* because data travels through them in parallel. Unlike a serial port, which uses only one wire to transmit data in each direction, data travels through the parallel ports one byte at a time. A byte consists of eight bits, and the cable connecting your printer to your workstation uses eight wires—one for each bit—to send the data. The parallel ports also include other lines that control the transfer of data through the port.

Windows uses one of two methods to print to an LPT port. When you print to a local printer, Windows normally accesses the port directly, bypassing even the system's BIOS. This results in faster printing, but is not always possible due to hardware incompatibility. The other method Windows uses to print is the same as the one DOS applications use: Windows opens the port as a standard DOS device and uses standard DOS file services (interrupt 21) to print to the port. Print jobs that use DOS services eliminate any compatibility problems, but also are slower than printing directly to the port.

When you configure a printer in Windows, one of the steps is to connect the driver to a particular port. This associates the printer driver with a logical port. When you print to a local printer, the logical port corresponds to the physical port that the printer is attached to—logical port LPT1 corresponds to physical port LPT1.

When you print to a remote printer, the logical port designation you set up in your local Windows environment does not necessarily correspond to the physical port to which the printer is connected on the remote node. You might specify LPT1 on your system, for example, but the printer might actually be attached to LPT2 or LPT3 on the remote node. As far as Windows is concerned on your workstation, however, it is printing to LPT1. The network then redirects the print job from LPT1 across the network to the other node. The other node's Print Manager then directs the print job to the proper physical port.

When you configure a printer, an important point to remember about LPT port entries is that you do not have to configure your printer driver to print to the same port as the one to which the printer is physically connected on the other node.

The Printers icon in Control Panel provides access to the Printers dialog box (see fig. 28.17). The Connect button in the Printers dialog box opens the Connect dialog box, also shown in figure 28.17, which enables you to specify the port to which your printer is connected. The method Windows uses to print depends on the port entry you use to connect the printer in the Control Panel, and whether the printer port is local or redirected across the network.

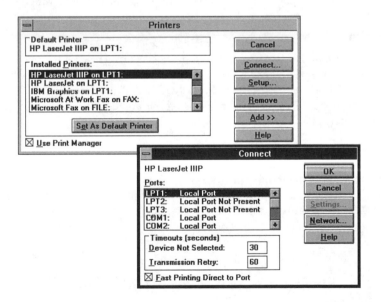

Figure 28.17

The Printers and Connect dialog boxes.

The Ports list box in the Connect dialog box displays 10 different port selections by default. The system's COM ports represent 4 of those 10 selections (sharing a serial printer is discussed in a later section). The majority of the other default entries relate to LPT ports.

If LPT1:, LPT2:, and LPT3: are physical ports on your workstation, Windows recognizes these entries as hardware port entries and controls the ports directly. If the ports are not physically present, but are redirected to a network device, Windows uses DOS services to print to them.

Most entries other than LPT1:, LPT2:, and LPT3: are considered by Windows to be nonhardware accessible. Windows therefore uses DOS services to access them, instead of controlling them directly. These nonhardware ports include the EPT: and FILE: entries. The FILE: port entry is used when directing a print job to a file. The EPT: port entry is used with special hardware that only a few printers, such as the IBM Pageprinter, use.

The FAX: entry is used in conjunction with At-Work Fax (explained in Chapter 29, "Using Microsoft Mail and Fax").

Configuring Printer Drivers

Windows uses a device driver to send data to the printer when you print from a Windows application. A *device driver* is a miniprogram that enables Windows to communicate with the printer and take advantage of any special features the printer offers. Printer drivers enable a programmer to create a standard print function without having to worry about how the application communicates with the printer. The application directs Windows to print some data, and Windows passes the information off to the print driver, which then takes care of sending the information to the printer. The application does not interact directly with the printer.

Although many printers can emulate more common printers by sacrificing features, most printers provide optimum performance when used with a driver written specifically for them. When you install a printer in Windows, you actually install a printer driver. The printer configuration process involves setting operating parameters for the driver, which then controls the printer.

Whether you print to a local printer or to a printer located elsewhere on the network, you must install a printer driver for the destination printer. If your local printer is a Panasonic KXP-1124, for example, and you want to print to an HP LaserJet IIIsi across the network, you must have the HP IIIsi driver installed on your system—you cannot use the Panasonic driver you use for your local printer to print to the LaserJet.

To configure a printer in Windows, you first must install the driver. To do so, follow these steps:

1. Open the Control Panel and choose the Printers icon to display the Printers dialog box.

2. If the printer driver you need is not yet installed, choose the Add button. The Printers dialog box expands to display the List of Printers box, as shown in figure 28.18.

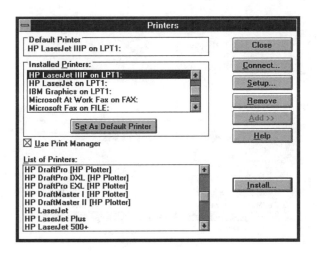

Figure 28.18

Installing a new printer driver through the Printers dialog box.

3. Locate the printer driver you need and choose the Install button. The Control Panel then prompts you to insert one or more of your Windows for Workgroups distribution disks.

4. Insert the requested floppy disks when prompted, and click on OK.

Next, you need to choose a port to associate with the printer driver. Follow these steps:

1. Select the installed printer driver and then choose the Connect button in the Printers dialog box. The Connect dialog box appears and displays the Ports list.

2a. If you are associating the driver with a local printer, choose the appropriate port from the Ports list.

2b. If you are associating the driver with a printer across the network, choose the Network button to display the Connect Network Printer dialog box, shown in figure 28.19.

3. In the Connect Network Printer dialog box, click on the Device Name drop-down list and choose the logical port ID you want to associate with the printer driver. If you have a local LPT port, choose a different logical port for your network connection.

4. Choose the machine in the Show Shared Printers on list box that controls the printer you want to access. In the Shared Printers on list box, choose the printer you want to use. If you want the printer to be reconnected each time you start Windows for Workgroups, make sure the Reconnect at Startup check box is checked.

5. After you make the selections you want, click on OK.

Figure 28.19

The Connect
Network Printer
dialog box.

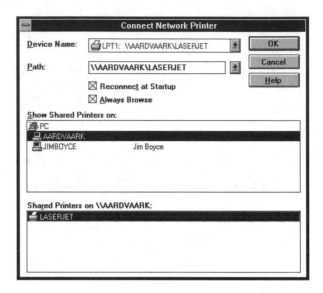

6. If you know the name of the machine and shared printer to which you want to connect, you do not have to select it from the list in the dialog box. Instead, you can enter the machine name and shared printer name in the Path combo box, as in *machine**printer*.

7. When the Control Panel returns to the Connect dialog box, verify that the port you selected for the network printer appears in the Ports list box with the machine and printer share name beside it. In addition, verify that this port is selected.

8. When the port selection is correct, click on OK to return to the Printers dialog box.

9. Set up the printer driver for the options installed on the destination printer. Choose the Setup button and change settings for the printer as necessary. The dialog box you use to do this varies with the printer type.

   Figure 28.20 shows an example of the HP LaserJet IIIP options.

10. When your printer finally is configured properly, click on OK to return to the Printers dialog box. Click on OK again to complete the printer setup process.

You also might need to adjust the Device Not Selected and Transmission Retry settings in the Connect dialog box. The Device Not Selected setting specifies the number of seconds Print Manager (on your local workstation) waits for the printer to reach online status and become ready to print. The Transmission Retry setting specifies the length of time Print Manager attempts to send data to the printer after its buffer has filled before informing you that the printer cannot accept any more data. You generally need to change these settings only for local printers.

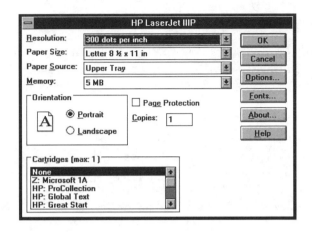

Figure 28.20
The HP LaserJet
IIIP options.

Your printer driver is now configured and ready to use to print. If you do not need to print to a serial printer (one connected to a COM port), skip the following section and begin reading the section "Understanding Print Manager." If you want to share a serial printer or connect to a serial printer, the next section helps you do so.

Sharing Serial Printers (COM Ports)

The current version of Windows for Workgroups does not enable you to share COM (serial) ports directly with another node, although At-Work Fax does enable indirect sharing of a fax modem. You cannot, for example, share your local modem with other users.

Although you cannot share a COM port, you can share a local printer that is connected to a COM port. If another user has shared a serial printer, you can print to it across the network.

The key to sharing serial printers is that Print Manager controls the printing process across the network. When you send a document from your node to a remote printer, your print request is received on the remote node by Print Manager. Your print request is directed to a shared printer by name, not to a specific COM port. The remote node Print Manager simply receives your print request, adds it to its queue, and sends it to the appropriate printer when the printer is available.

To print to a remote serial printer, first install and configure the appropriate printer driver as described in the previous section. Choose the Connect button in the Printers dialog box, choose an available logical LPT port, then choose the Network button. When the Connect Network Printer dialog box appears, choose the remote server machine and shared printer from the list, or type its name in the Path combo box, just as you would for a parallel printer. Click on OK to exit the Connect Network Printer dialog box, and perform any other printer driver configuration steps required by the printer (such as setting print options). When the configuration is complete, you are ready to print to the remote printer.

Understanding Print Manager

Print Manager performs printer sharing in Windows for Workgroups. Print Manager is a print spooler. A *spooler* schedules multiple print jobs in a queue and manages the transmission of these jobs to the printer. The Print Manager performs this task in the background, enabling you to continue working while you print. Figure 28.21 shows the Print Manager program window.

Figure 28.21
Print Manager displays installed printer drivers and pending print jobs.

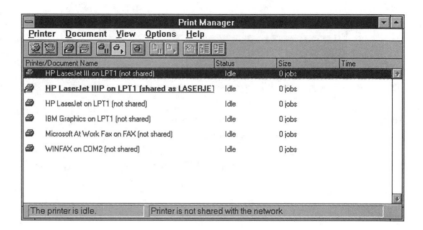

By default, Windows channels all Windows printing through Print Manager. To determine whether Print Manager is controlling printing on your system, choose the Printers icon in Control Panel. When the Printers dialog box appears, verify that the Use Print Manager check box is checked. This indicates that all Windows printing will be handled by Print Manager. When this check box is cleared, Windows printing is directed to the current printer port, bypassing the Print Manager.

When you print from a Windows application to a local printer, the print request goes to Print Manager, which generates a temporary print file for each page in the print job. When the print files have been created, the application regains control so that you can continue to work. Print Manager then begins sending these print files to the printer.

When you print to a network printer, a similar process takes place. Print Manager creates local temporary files for each page of the document, then returns control to the application when the files are created. Instead of sending the files to the printer, however, Print Manager sends the files to the remote node that functions as a print server. The copy of Print Manager running on the remote node receives the files and begins sending them to the printer, just as if the files had been created on the remote node and not copied across the network.

If you disable Print Manager, these temporary files still are created on your local workstation, then transferred to the remote node. Therefore, no real benefits are gained from disabling Print Manager for network printing.

Print Manager starts automatically when you print a document. It also starts automatically if you have a shared printer connected to your system and that printer is configured to share automatically at start-up. You can start Print Manager yourself and must do so when you want to connect or disconnect a network printer, specify background printing options, view your print queue, and perform other print management tasks.

The Print Manager program icon is located in the Main program group. To start Print Manager, double-click on the icon, or select it and press Enter. The Print Manager then appears on your display.

Sharing a Local Printer

To share a local printer with other users on the network, Print Manager must be running to process print requests from other nodes. To share a printer, open Print Manager as described previously. The printer drivers configured for your system then appear in Print Manager's window. Choose the printer you want to share, then choose Printer, Share Printer As. If Print Manager is displaying its toolbar, you can choose the Share button instead. Figure 28.22 shows the Print Manager toolbar with its buttons labeled.

Figure 28.22
Buttons in the Print Manager toolbar.

After you choose the Share Printer As command or click on the Share button, the Share Printer dialog box appears (see fig. 28.23). The currently selected printer appears in the Printer drop-down list box. If you want to share a different printer, click on the list box and choose the desired printer.

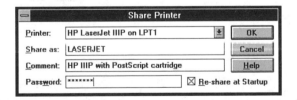

Figure 28.23
The Share Printer dialog box.

Next, click in the Share as edit box and type a description for the printer. This is the description network users will see when they browse for your printer in Print Manager. The description can be up to 12 characters long and can contain the following special characters:

> ! # $ % & ( ) - . @ ^ _ ` { } ~

If you want to hide the printer from other users' browse dialog boxes, end the share name with a dollar sign ($). This adds an additional level of security to your printer.

Other users still can connect to your printer by directly specifying your node's machine name and the share name of the printer in the Browse dialog box in each user's Print Manager.

Use the Comment field to enter a descriptive comment about the printer. This comment appears beside the printer's share name when other users browse for printers on the network. The Comment field can contain up to 48 characters.

The Password field enables you to password-protect your printer. If you want only selected users on the network to be able to send documents to your printer, include a password for it in the Password field. Then, give these users the password.

If you want the printer to be available consistently, check the Re-share at Startup check box. With this box checked, Print Manager starts automatically when you start Windows and makes the printer available to other users.

When you have the options set the way you want them, click on the OK button to begin sharing the printer.

Removing a Printer from Sharing

To remove a printer from sharing and to prevent other users from accessing it across the network, choose the Stop Sharing Printer command from Print Manager's Printer menu, or choose the Stop Sharing button from the toolbar. When you do, the Stop Sharing Printer dialog box appears, as shown in figure 28.24.

Figure 28.24
The Stop Sharing
Printer dialog box.

Select the printer(s) you want to stop sharing, then click on OK. If print jobs currently are waiting in the queue for the selected printer(s), Print Manager warns you with a dialog box and asks if you want to continue. Choose Yes to remove pending print jobs from the printer's queue and remove the printer from sharing. The current print job in progress is not removed, however. Choose No to cancel the command.

When you remove a printer from sharing, Print Manager also prompts you if other users are connected to your printer, even if they are not printing. In general, you should avoid removing your printer from sharing unless all network users have disconnected from it.

Using a Remote Printer

When you want to print to a remote printer, you first must connect to it in Print Manager. To connect to a remote printer, choose the Connect Network Printer command in Print Manager's Printer menu or choose the Connect button from the toolbar to display the Connect Network Printer dialog box. This is the same dialog box you use to configure a printer driver for a network printer. This process is described in the section on configuring printer drivers earlier in this chapter.

To print to a remote printer, choose the Print Setup command from your application's menu. Choose the connected remote printer from the printer selection list, then print as you normally would to a local printer.

Disconnecting a Remote Printer

To disconnect a remote printer from your Windows for Workgroups session, open Print Manager and choose the Disconnect Network Printer command from the Printer menu or choose the Disconnect button. Select the printer(s) you want to disconnect and click on OK.

Using Print Manager's Other Features

Print Manager offers a number of other features for managing your print jobs and controlling the way Print Manager functions. The Set Default Printer command, also found in the Printer menu, enables you to specify the default printer for your Windows applications without having to access the Control Panel. The default printer is used when you print unless you specifically select a different printer in your application.

To set the default printer, select a printer from the list of printers in the Print Manager window, then choose the Set Default Printer command or click on the Default Printer button in the toolbar.

Managing Print Jobs

The Pause Printer and Resume Printer commands in Print Manager's Printer menu enable you to start and stop a printer's queue. If you have a problem with a printer that you need to correct, you can pause it by selecting the Pause Printer command or by clicking on the Pause Printer button in the toolbar. After the problem is solved, choose the Resume Printer command or the Resume Printer button to restart the printer.

The Document menu provides commands for managing documents in the print queue. The first command in the menu, Pause Print Document, enables you to pause a print job. If you are printing on your own workstation, you can pause anyone else's print job as long as it is not currently printing. You cannot, however, pause your own print jobs. When you are printing on a remote workstation, you can pause your own print jobs if they are not currently printing, but you cannot pause anyone else's print jobs.

When you pause a print job, other pending jobs after it in the queue begin to cycle ahead of the paused print job. Print Manager continues to print other jobs. This is similar to standing still in a moving line of people—those who were behind you begin to move ahead. If you leave a print job paused long enough, it eventually becomes the last job in the queue.

The Resume Printing Document command changes the status of a paused print job back to active. When you resume a paused print job, it "steps back into line" in the queue, advancing in the queue as documents are printed. You can resume only those print jobs that you have paused.

The Delete Document, Move Document Up, and Move Document Down commands in Print Manager's Document menu control a print job's position in the queue. The Delete Document command removes the print job from the queue. To delete a document from the queue, choose the document, then choose the Delete Document command or the Delete Document button, or press the Del key on the keyboard. Print Manager prompts you to confirm the print job's deletion.

You can delete any job on your local workstation, including your own jobs or jobs scheduled by someone else on the network. On remote nodes, you can delete only the jobs you scheduled. If you want to delete all the pending jobs in the print queue, you can exit Program Manager.

The Move Document Up and Move Document Down commands do just what their command names imply—move a print job up or down one slot in the queue. To move a job, first select it, then choose either the Move Document Up or Move Document Down command. You also can choose the Move Up or Move Down buttons from the toolbar.

If you want to move a print job more than one position in the queue, select it, then drag it into the desired position using the mouse.

You can drag a print job only within its own printer queue—you cannot drag a print job to a different printer.

Controlling Print Manager's Appearance

By default, Print Manager displays the status of a job, its size (in kilobytes), and the time and date the job was placed in the queue. You can use Print Manager's View menu to control the way the job status appears in the Print Manager window.

The first three commands in the View menu—Time/Date Sent, Print File Size, and Status Text—are toggle commands that turn these display items on and off. When an item is displayed, a check mark appears next to its menu item. When the item is not being displayed, the check mark does not appear next to it.

To update the print queue status, press the F5 key or choose the Refresh command from the View menu.

You also can change the font and column width Print Manager uses to display its information. To change fonts, choose the Font menu item from the Options menu. A standard Font selection dialog box appears (see fig. 28.25) in which you can choose a new font or change the size of the existing font.

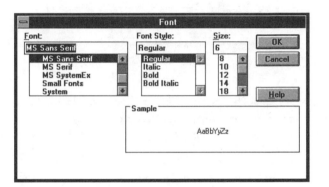

Figure 28.25
The Font dialog box enables you to change Print Manager's font.

To change column width, you can either choose the Set Column Widths command from the Options menu, or move the pointer to the column edge in the status line and drag it to a new position. If you use the Set Column command to change column widths, use the Tab key (or Shift+Tab) to move between the different columns. As you move the mouse or cursor keys, the column resizes accordingly. To resize columns with the mouse, click on the column you want to change and drag it to its new position.

You also can turn on and off the toolbar and status bar. Both of these items are controlled through the Options menu. Use the Toolbar and Status Bar menu items in the Options menu to turn on and off the toolbar and status bar.

Viewing Other Network Queues

By default, Print Manager displays the queue on your local workstation. You also can view the queues on other nodes across the network. This enables you to control the print jobs you schedule on remote printers.

To view the queue of a remote printer, choose View, Other Network Printer to display the Other Network Printer dialog box, as shown in figure 28.26. In the Network Printer edit box, enter the machine name for the node that is controlling the queue you want to view, then choose the View button.

Figure 28.26
The Other
Network Printer
dialog box.

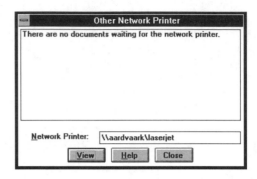

Unfortunately, the Other Network Printer dialog box does not include a Browse button to locate network printers quickly. As a result, you must know the machine and printer share name of the remote printer you want to view.

When you choose <u>V</u>iew, the documents scheduled to print in the printer's queue, if any, appear in the dialog box. When you are finished viewing the files, click on the Close button. You also can view the print queue of another network printer just by connecting to it using the <u>C</u>onnect Network Printer command in Print Manager's <u>P</u>rinter menu.

Controlling the Way Print Manager Performs

A few commands in Print Manager enable you to control Print Manager's priority relative to other applications, define the way it handles warning messages, and generate separator or banner pages at the beginning of each print job to help you find your print jobs.

Controlling Priority and Messages

To control printing priority and message handling, choose the <u>B</u>ackground Printing command from the <u>O</u>ptions menu. This displays the Background Printing dialog box shown in figure 28.27.

The three radio buttons in the Printing Priority group box control the relative amount of CPU time Print Manager receives. The <u>N</u>ormal option is the default setting. If printing is slowing down your other applications, you might want to choose the <u>L</u>ow radio button instead. The <u>L</u>ow button allocates a smaller share of the CPU's attention to Print Manager, which makes your other Windows applications run faster.

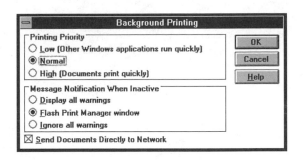

Figure 28.27
The Background
Printing dialog
box.

The High radio button allocates more CPU time to Print Manager. This can improve printing speed, but at the expense of your other Windows applications. If you are going to start a few print jobs and then leave your workstation for a while, you can set Printing Priority to High to speed printing while you are away.

These print priority settings affect local printers only. They have no effect on how fast your remote print jobs are executed.

The group box labeled Message Notification When Inactive contains three options that control the way Print Manager handles warning messages when it runs in the background (when it is not the active application).

By default, when Print Manager experiences a printer problem that requires your attention, it flashes its icon if it is running as an icon or flashes its title bar if it is running in a window. This informs you of a problem with a print job. When you make Print Manager active or restore it to a window, it displays a message regarding the printing problem. The Flash Print Manager window radio button sets this behavior for Print Manager.

To have Print Manager display warnings and error messages immediately, even when it is running in the background, choose the radio button labeled Display all warnings. If you select Ignore all warnings, Print Manager does not take any action to indicate an error if it is running as an icon. It does, however, display the message(s) when you restore it to a window.

Using Separator Pages (Banners)

When you are the only one printing to your local printer, it is easy to keep track of printed documents—all of them are yours. If other users are printing to your printer from their workstations, however, you need some way to discern whose documents are whose so that you can send the completed documents to the right people. When you print to a remote printer, the person responsible for the remote workstation needs to know if the document is yours so that you can receive it when it is done.

Print Manager enables you to include a separator page (also called a banner page) at the beginning of each print job. You can choose from two Windows-generated separators, or you can create your own separator page. By default, Print Manager does not include a separator page with each print job.

The selection you make for a separator page affects only the documents printed on your workstation—either documents you create or print jobs sent from other users across the network. You cannot create your own separator page and print it on someone else's workstation, but you can create a custom separator page for your workstation. When you print to a remote printer, the separator page configured at the remote node, if any, is used to print your document.

Use the Separator Pages command in Print Manager's Options menu to specify the type of separator page to be printed with each document on your workstation. The Separator Pages dialog box shown in figure 28.28 appears when you select this command.

Figure 28.28
The Separator
Pages dialog box.

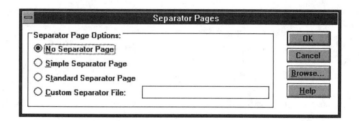

By default, the No Separator Page radio button is selected. This option does not print a separator page between each document.

The Simple Separator Page option causes Print Manager to print a separator using a small Courier font and no graphics. The separator page output looks similar to the following:

```
Microsoft(R) Windows(TM) for Workgroups
-------------------
Document:          Notepad - SHORTS.TXT
Printed By:  BARTS
Date and Time:     10:32 AM 12/05/92
```

Use the Simple Separator Page option when printing to a dot-matrix or daisy-wheel printer, or for the fastest possible printing time to all printers.

The Standard Separator Page radio button is used primarily with laser printers. This option creates a separator page with a graphical Microsoft Windows logo and the heading Microsoft Windows for Workgroups at the top of the page. The document name, user name, and time and date are printed below the heading in large type.

The Custom Separator Page option enables you to create your own custom header. The separator page header file you specify must be a Windows Metafile Format file (WMF) or a Clipboard file (CLP). To create your custom separator header, use a program that can create WMF files, or copy your header from any program to the Clipboard, then save it as a Clipboard file. Specify the name of your custom file in the file name edit box in the Separator Pages dialog box, or use the Browse button to locate the file you want to use. When a document is printed on your workstation, your custom separator header appears on the separator page, followed by the user and document information described previously.

You now are familiar with the Windows login process, directory sharing, and printer sharing. You now need to consider how you can make your resources consistently available—even when you are away from your workstation—without compromising your workstation's security.

Maintaining and Securing Resources

When you are the only one using your workstation's resources, it does not matter if you turn off your printer, exit Windows, or turn off your system completely. When your resources are shared across the network, however, these resources should be available at all times to other users, even when you are away from your computer.

If security is not a problem, you can leave Windows for Workgroups running on your system so that requests by other nodes for access to your shared resources can be serviced. If security is a concern, however, you simply cannot walk away from your workstation. If you are logged in, anyone can sit down at your computer and access any remote resources you are connected to. Even if you are not logged in to the network, someone can access your local resources, including private documents.

Fortunately, Windows for Workgroups provides a number of screen savers you can use to password protect your workstation when you are away from it. You do not even have to log out of the network to make your system secure. Before you learn how to password-protect your workstation, however, you should make sure your shared resources are always available to other users.

Keeping Resources Available

To provide network user access to your workstation's resources at all times, your computer must be turned on and running Windows for Workgroups in 386-Enhanced mode. The following tips ensure that other users always can access the shared resources on your workstation:

✓ **Leave your computer running.** Consider leaving your computer on all the time, even when you are not in your office. The solid-state components in the computer are not damaged by continuous use. In fact, the heating and cooling caused by turning the system on and off can, over a long period of time, cause socketed chips in the system to work loose. If you turn on and off the system frequently, you also can shorten the hard disk's life. When you leave for an extended period, turn off only your monitor to prevent burn-in (a permanent image on the display).

✔ **Start Windows for Workgroups at boot.** If possible, include the necessary login and WIN commands in your AUTOEXEC.BAT file to start Windows for Workgroups automatically as soon as you turn on your computer and it boots. This way, if you turn off your system at the end of the day, you will not have to remember to start Windows the next morning when you turn on your system.

✔ **Use the Re-Share at Startup option.** Check the Re-Share at Startup check box when you configure shared resources that you want to be available to other users automatically when you start Windows for Workgroups. This avoids the possibility of forgetting to share a particular resource manually, or accidentally sharing it using a new share name.

✔ **Use Windows for DOS tasks.** If you usually exit Windows to perform DOS command-line tasks at the DOS prompt, do these tasks from within Windows instead. Choose the MS-DOS Prompt icon in the Main program group to execute DOS commands. In addition, run DOS applications from within Windows.

If your system is always on and Windows for Workgroups is always running, you probably want to ensure a level of security for your local resources and for remote resources connected to your Windows for Workgroups session.

Securing Your Workstation

The Desktop icon in the Control Panel provides an option that enables you to set up a screen saver for Windows. Although screen savers generally are not required with VGA systems, a screen saver prevents monitor burn-in. *Burn-in* occurs when a single, static image is displayed on a monitor for an extended period of time. Over time, the static image becomes permanent—it "burns" itself into the phosphor on the back side of the monitor's screen. In Windows, screen savers perform an additional task: they enable you to secure your workstation from unwanted access or snooping.

A *screen saver* is a program that creates a moving pattern of one kind or another on the display. The image constantly changes, eliminating the possibility of an image burning in the screen's phosphor coating. The constantly changing image also helps security—the image takes over the whole display, preventing anyone else from seeing what you were working on when you left your workstation.

Screen savers in Windows can include password-protection. When the system has been idle for a user-specified length of time, the screen saver blanks the display and begins to display its moving image. If the screen saver is configured with a password, you cannot return to your normal Windows display or access any Windows features, applications, or data until you provide the correct password. In effect, you are locked out of your computer until you provide the correct password.

To set up a screen saver and password security for your workstation, choose the Desktop icon in Control Panel to display the Desktop dialog box, shown in figure 28.29.

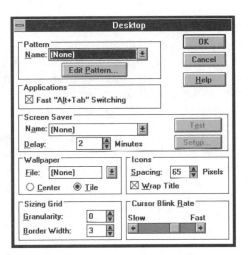

Figure 28.29
The Desktop dialog box.

To select a screen saver, choose the N**a**me drop-down list box in the Screen Saver group box. Windows for Workgroups includes five different moving images you can use on your workstation. If you want to see how the screen saver looks after you select it, choose the T**e**st button. The screen saver's test image appears until you move the mouse or press a key on the keyboard.

To change options for the selected screen saver, choose the Set**u**p button. This displays a dialog box of options that vary according to the screen saver you have selected. Figure 28.30 shows the Setup dialog box for the Mystify screen saver.

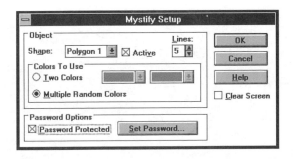

Figure 28.30
The Setup options for the Mystify screen saver.

To password-protect your workstation, choose any screen saver except Blank Screen. The Blank Screen screen saver does not offer any setup options, and therefore cannot include a password.

After you select the screen saver you want to use, choose the Setup button and set whatever options you want to customize for the screen saver. Remember to set an appropriate Delay time. This is the length of time the system can be idle before the screen saver activates.

Next, check the Password Protected check box and choose the Set Password button. Enter your new password in the New Password edit box, then type it again in the Retype New Password edit box to confirm it. If the screen saver is active and you move the mouse or press a key, the password entry dialog box for the screen saver appears. Enter your password and press Enter or choose OK to unlock your system and return to Windows.

If you forget your password, reboot your system to return to the DOS prompt. Then, edit your SYSTEM.INI file and delete the screen saver entry from it. For example, change the entry `SCRNSAVE.EXE=screen.saver.name` in the `[boot]` section to read `SCRNSAVE.EXE=`, then restart Windows. If you do this, you then have to reconfigure your screen saver.

Chapter Snapshot

Communicating with other users is becoming an increasingly important aspect of networking and workgroup computing. This chapter shows you how to use all the features of the Mail program in Windows for Workgroups to send and receive e-mail. This chapter teaches you how to perform the following tasks:

In addition to examining e-mail, this chapter also explains the use of a feature that is new to Windows for Workgroups 3.11—Microsoft At Work Fax, which enables you to send and receive faxes using a shared fax modem.

29

CHAPTER

Using Microsoft Mail and Fax

To use Microsoft Mail effectively, you should have a basic understanding of your network's mail system. The first section of this chapter provides a brief overview of how Mail works.

Understanding the Mail System

Electronic mail, also called e-mail, has become an important part of network computer use in the last few years. E-mail's origins as a local message service that sent messages within a LAN has evolved into a full-fledged communication service capable of sending and receiving messages around the world. In the past, the process of sending messages across the continent or around the world was tedious for the average user. Today, the entire process can be transparent—simply choose an address from an electronic address book, and the message is routed on its way.

The Mail application included with Windows for Workgroups does not offer such wide-ranging communications as gateways to external mail systems, but it can serve as an excellent mail system for your LAN. Windows for Workgroups Mail is a scaled-down version of Microsoft Mail 3.2 that provides all the local area mail features included with the full package. Mail 3.2 also is capable of communicating between different workgroup post offices and through gateways to other mail systems.

The Workgroup Post Office

When you start Mail, it connects to a workgroup post office, or WGPO. The WGPO is nothing more than a shared directory structure located on one of the workstations on the network. The WGPO's post office manager creates the WGPO, which contains your mail account and the mail accounts of other users. The WGPO post office manager can be a network administrator or a member of the workgroup that uses the WGPO. Figure 29.1 shows the shared WGPO directory structure displayed in File Manager.

Figure 29.1
The WGPO directory structure displayed in File Manager.

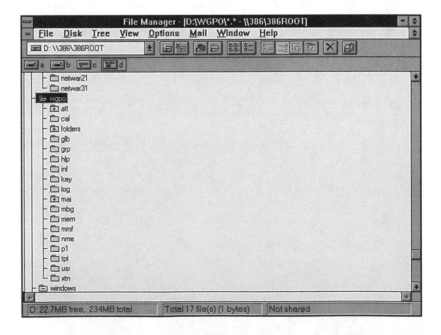

To communicate with another user, both you and the user must have mail accounts in the same WGPO. If you do not have a mail account in the same WGPO as the person to whom you want to send a message, you will not be able to send the message. (Mail 3.2 enables you to send mail to other workgroup post offices.) Any user, however, can have a mail account in a WGPO, regardless of the workgroup that user is logged in to on the network.

If your network is relatively small, your Mail system administrator can create a single WGPO for all network users, enabling everyone to communicate with each other. If your network is large and divided into many workgroups, multiple WGPOs probably exist. If you are not sure if you have a Mail account yet or where it is located, contact your Mail system administrator.

Sending and Receiving Messages

When you send a message to someone, Mail places the message in the WGPO as a temporary file. When the recipient starts Mail and connects to the WGPO, Mail copies the file to the recipient's message file. The message file, which can reside on either the WGPO or the user's own workstation, contains all the user's mail messages, as well as other Mail-related items.

As a mail server, Mail is really nothing more than an automatic file-transfer utility. You create a file, place it in the WGPO, and Mail transfers it to the recipient when the recipient signs in to the mail system. This process is the same when you need to send a message to more than one user. The only difference is that Mail transfers the file to more than one recipient.

Using Mail

If you are running Windows for Workgroups, your Mail application is a Windows-based program that enables you to send and receive messages, reply to messages, forward messages to other users, and organize your messages. If you are connecting to the network from DOS using Workgroup Connection, your Mail application is a DOS-based program that offers the same capabilities as the Windows version.

The important point to remember about Mail is that you must have a mail account in a WGPO, and that to communicate with other users, they also must have an account in the same WGPO.

Understanding Windows Mail

The Mail program item icon usually is located in your Main program group. To start Mail, double-click on its icon, or select the icon and press Enter. If you have never run Mail on your workstation before, Mail displays the Welcome to Mail dialog box shown in figure 29.2.

Figure 29.2
The Welcome to
Mail dialog box.

The Welcome to Mail dialog box enables you to connect to an existing WGPO or to create a new WGPO. If a WGPO for your workgroup already exists, you should choose the **C**onnect to an existing postoffice radio button.

When you select the option to connect to an existing WGPO and then click on OK, Mail displays a Network Disk Resources dialog box you can use to locate the desired WGPO (see fig. 29.3). To connect to the WGPO, choose from the **S**how Shared Directories list the machine name on which the WGPO is located. The shared directories, of which the WGPO is one, then appear in the Sha**r**ed Directories list.

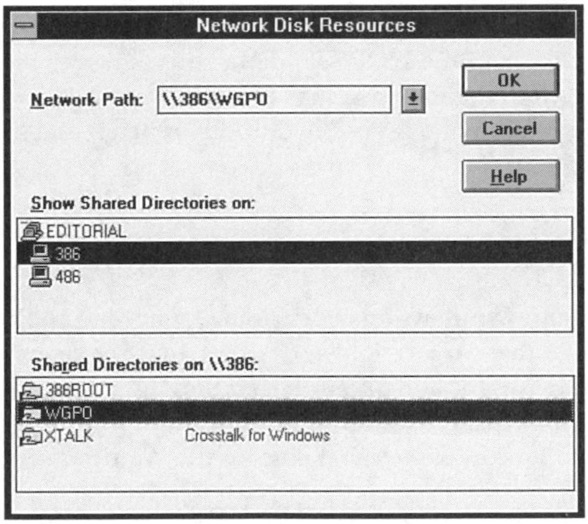

Figure 29.3
The Network Disk
Resources dialog
box.

From the Sha**r**ed Directories list, select the WGPO share name. If you are not sure which directory is the correct one, contact the WGPO's post office manager. Generally, however, the WGPO will be shared with the name WGPO, unless the post office manager opted to use a different name when sharing the directory. After you locate and select the correct shared directory, click on OK.

Mail then asks if you have an existing account in the WGPO. If the post office manager has already created an account for you, choose <u>Y</u>es. If you do not yet have an account, choose <u>N</u>o.

If you choose <u>Y</u>es, the Mail main program window appears (discussed a little later). If you do not have an account and choose <u>N</u>o, a dialog box labeled Enter Your Account Details appears, as shown in figure 29.4.

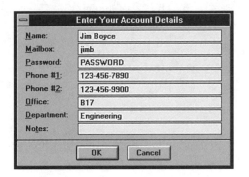

Figure 29.4
The Enter Your Account Details dialog box.

The first two items in the dialog box, <u>N</u>ame and <u>M</u>ailbox, are mandatory; the other entries are optional. The following list describes the fields you can use to define your Mail account:

✔ **Name.** List your user name as you want it to appear to other workgroup members when they browse the list of mail accounts in the WGPO. Include your first and last name, up to a maximum of 30 characters. Mail defaults to the name you used when installing Windows for Workgroups on the system (which might not be your own). This entry is associated by Mail with your <u>M</u>ailbox account name.

✔ **Mailbox.** List the name you want to use for your mail account. The name can be anything up to 10 characters, but enter a unique name that will be easy for you to remember. For example, use your last name plus your first initial, as in JBOYCE.

✔ **Password.** Enter the password you want to use to access your mail account. It does not have to match your login password. The Mail password is limited to eight characters, and the default is PASSWORD. If you do not want to have a password for your mail account, highlight the word PASSWORD in the <u>P</u>assword field, then press the Del key. This blanks the password entry. Bear in mind that any user will be able to read your mail if you do not include a password.

✔ **Phone #1.** Enter the phone number at which you can normally be reached. Usually, this is your main office phone number. This field can include letters and numbers, so that you can include optional remarks. Example: (123) 456-7890 (Voice).

✔ **Phone #2.** Enter an optional extension number or a fax number. As with the Phone #1 entry, this field can include text. If you place your fax number here, you might want to add a note beside it indicating that it is your fax number. Example: (123) 999-1234 (fax).

✔ **Office.** You usually will use this field to indicate your physical office location. This might be a room number, such as B-102, or a mail stop. The entry can be a maximum of 32 characters.

✔ **Department.** Enter the name of your department. This entry does not have to coincide with your workgroup name in any way.

✔ **Notes.** Add any additional comments about your mail account here. The maximum length for this field is 128 characters.

After you have filled in the information in the dialog box, click on OK. The main Mail program window then appears on your display.

If you answered Yes when asked by Mail if you have an existing account on the system, the Mail Sign In dialog box appears. This dialog box also appears each time you start Mail. If you prefer, you can have Mail start and sign you in automatically. This is discussed later in this chapter.

You must sign into the mail system before you can use Mail. In the Name edit box, type the name of your mailbox. Ask your post office manager for your mailbox name if you did not create your Mail account. Otherwise, enter the name you provided in the Mailbox entry in the Enter Your Account Details dialog box.

Next, type your Mail Password, if any, in the Password edit box. For security, asterisks appear in place of your password as you type.

Using the Mail Program Window

Mail is a standard Windows application. It includes a resizable window, child windows, a menu bar, a toolbar, and other common Windows interface components. Figure 29.5 illustrates the different parts of the Mail window.

You can turn on and off the toolbar and status bar. The toolbar provides quick access to the most common Mail commands, duplicating commands found in Mail's menu.

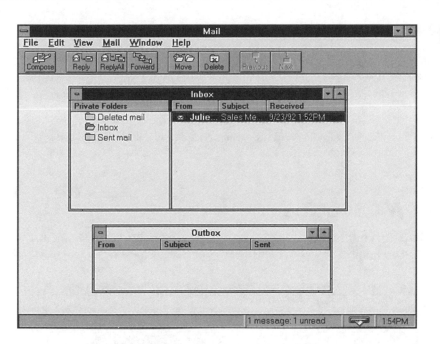

Figure 29.5
Components of the
Mail window.

Networking and Windows

Understanding Folders and Child Windows

The Outbox and Inbox are two standard child windows that Mail provides. Both can be minimized to icons and resized to unclutter the Mail window. The Outbox is used to hold messages temporarily until Mail is able to place them in the WGPO. If you are working offline, such as on a notebook computer that is not connected to the system, the Outbox enables you to store messages until you connect the notebook to the network and deliver the messages.

The Inbox is used to hold messages that you receive, copies of mail you send to others, and messages that you have deleted. As figure 29.5 indicates, the Inbox window has three standard message folders, which are used to store these three types of items.

Folders are logical storage areas you can use to organize your messages. You can use the standard set of folders or create your own. Folders can include other folders, which are called *subfolders*. You might create a folder called Project, for example, and use it to store messages related to a specific project. In the Project folder, you can create subfolders called Engineering, Marketing, and Sales. These subfolders help you organize messages according to the source of the message or to whom it was directed. (Creating and managing folders is discussed later in this chapter.)

If you want to view the contents of more than one folder at a time, you can open additional Inbox windows by choosing the <u>N</u>ew Window command from Mail's <u>W</u>indow menu.

When you receive a new message, it is placed in your Inbox folder (not to be confused with the Inbox *window*). You then can open the Inbox folder and view the messages in it. When you delete a message, it is placed in your Deleted messages folder. You can configure Mail to erase messages from the Deleted messages folder when you exit Mail, or leave them in the folder. You also can configure Mail to place in the Sent mail folder a copy of all the messages you send to other users.

Now that you are familiar with folders and the basic parts of Mail's window, you are ready to begin sending and receiving mail.

Sending Messages

Mail provides a special window for creating messages. The send note window shown in figure 29.6 includes a number of features that make composing a message an easy task.

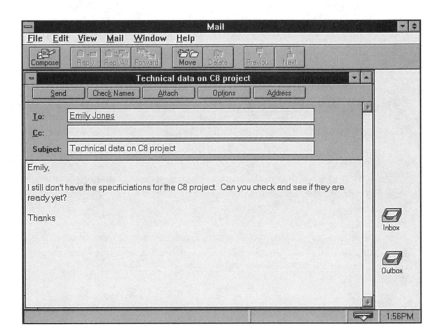

Figure 29.6
The send note window enables you to compose messages quickly.

To create a message, click on the Compose button from the toolbar or choose Compose Note from the Mail menu. This displays the send note window.

When the send note window appears, the cursor is located in the To edit box. If you know the mail account name of the person to whom you want to send the message, you can type it in the To edit box. Another way to address the message is to enter a few letters of the name, then choose Check Names or press Alt+K. Mail then displays the Check name dialog box (see fig. 29.7), which offers a list of mail users whose first or last names match the characters you entered. Select the recipient's name from the list and click on OK.

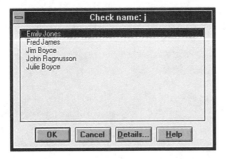

Figure 29.7
The Check name
dialog box.

If you want to view additional information about one of the accounts in the Check name dialog box, select the name and choose the Details button. A dialog box appears that gives you additional details about the account's owner. When you are finished viewing the information, choose the Close button to close the dialog box. You also can copy the information to your personal address book by choosing the personal address book button. The personal address book is discussed later in this chapter.

When you have selected the recipient's name from the Check name dialog box, click on OK to return to the send note window and to place the name in the To edit box.

Although the entry of the first few characters of the recipient's name can speed up your search for the right mail account, you do not have to use this option. You can choose the Address button to display the Address dialog box (see fig. 29.8), which displays a list of all the mail accounts in the WGPO.

Figure 29.8
The Address
dialog box

To choose an addressee, click on the recipient's name in the Postoffice List, then choose the **T**o button. This places the user's name in the To list box. If you want to send copies to other users, select their names and choose the **C**c button. This places these users' names in the Cc list and directs a copy of the message to them. You can select additional names one at a time, or use the Shift and Ctrl keys to select a group of names.

As with the Check name dialog box, you can select a user's name and choose the **D**etails button to view additional information about the user.

If your WGPO contains many names, you can choose the magnifying glass button (the Search button) to search for a user by name. This button displays a Name Finder dialog box (see fig. 29.9) in which you enter a text string to use as a search pattern. When you choose the **F**ind button, Mail checks all the users' names to find those that contain the specified string.

Figure 29.9
The Name Finder
dialog box.

If you want to list all the users whose names contain the string "John", for example, enter the string in the Name Finder dialog box. This string locates the user names John Doe and Albert Johnson because both contain the same string. When you perform the name search, Mail returns to the Address dialog box to display the results of the search. Only those names that match the search string are displayed. You then can select the names you want from the displayed list. To display all the names again, choose the Search button again and clear the edit box in the Name Finder dialog box. Then, press Enter to return to the Address dialog box.

When your address information is correct, click on OK to return to the send note window.

Creating the Message Contents

The messages you create in Mail can include text, graphics, and attached objects (files). You can enter text directly in the message window by typing it on the keyboard, or you can copy it to the message window from the Clipboard. Formatted text loses its formatting, however, when copied to the message window. (Graphics and other valid Clipboard data types also can be copied from the Clipboard to the message window.)

To add text to your message, enter it directly from the keyboard or place it in the Clipboard with another application, then choose the **P**aste command from Mail's **E**dit menu.

You also can insert the contents of a file by choosing the Insert from File command from Mail's Edit menu. This is useful for inserting text files into your message. If you want to send someone a copy of your system's CONFIG.SYS file, for example, you simply insert it using the Insert from File command. Then, you can add additional text as desired.

If you want to paste nontext data from the Clipboard to the message in a particular format, place the data in the Clipboard, then choose Paste Special instead of the Paste command. This displays the Paste Special dialog box, which you can use to select from the Clipboard's multiple data formats (see fig. 29.10). Note that the application that places the data in the Clipboard must place it there in multiple formats for these different formats to be available for pasting. The Clipboard does not provide support for multiple data formats on its own.

Figure 29.10
The Paste Special dialog box.

Select an appropriate format from the Data Type list, then choose the Paste button to place the data in your message.

Inserting Objects

The Insert Object command enables you to embed objects from other applications into your message. These objects can be portions of spreadsheets, selected text from documents, graphics, recorded sounds, and other types of data. Inserting objects relies on Mail's object linking and embedding (OLE) capability. Because OLE is such a large topic in itself, embedding objects in Mail messages is discussed in Chapter 22, "Introducing Object Linking and Embedding."

For now, keep in mind that you can embed an object in a message. When you embed an object, the object's source application opens so that you can create the necessary data. If you have a sound adapter and microphone in your system, you can create voice messages and mail them to other users. To listen to the message, however, the recipients also must have sound capabilities in their system.

Attaching Documents to a Message

In addition to copying parts of a document to the message from the Clipboard and embedding objects through OLE, you also can attach documents and other files to your message. As with objects, these documents are embedded in the message. The difference is that the attached files can be saved on the recipient's system as separate files. You can, for example, send someone a copy of a spreadsheet you have created or a report you have written. You also can attach program files. If someone accidentally deletes a vital program file, you can mail another copy.

To attach a file to your message, choose the <u>A</u>ttach button from the toolbar. This displays the Attach dialog box shown in figure 29.11. The Attach dialog box is identical to the standard file browse dialog box included with Windows.

Figure 29.11

Use the Attach dialog box to attach a file to a message.

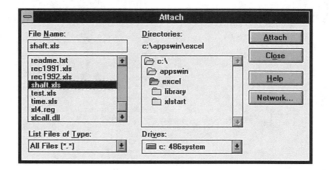

If the file you want to attach is not displayed in the current directory, use the controls in the dialog box to locate the file. If the file you need is located on a remote network disk to which you are not yet connected, click on the Network button to connect to the machine and to display its contents.

When you have located the file, select it in the file list and choose <u>A</u>ttach. Mail inserts an icon in the message to represent the file. You can attach multiple files to the same message. When you are finished attaching files, choose the Cl<u>o</u>se button.

Attached files appear in a message as an icon. If the file contains an icon, the icon is used to represent the file in the message. If the file does not contain an icon, Mail uses a standard blank-sheet document icon to represent the attached file. Figure 29.12 shows an assortment of files attached to a message.

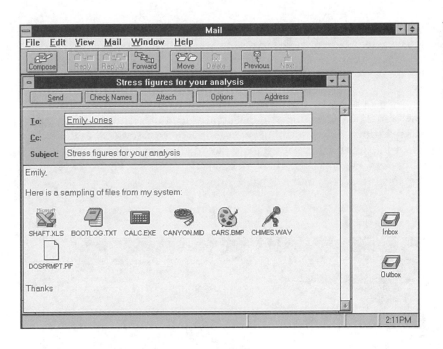

Figure 29.12
Files attached to a
message are
represented by
icons.

Setting Message Options

The **O**ptions button in the send note window enables you to specify a handful of options for the message. The **O**ptions button displays the Options dialog box, shown in figure 29.13.

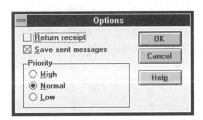

Figure 29.13
The Options
dialog box.

If the **R**eturn receipt check box is checked, you will be sent a confirmation message that the recipient has received the file when the recipient opens the message. This is a useful feature when you need to ensure that an important message is read.

The Save sent messages check box, which is checked by default, controls whether a copy of your message is saved in the Sent mail folder when you send it to its recipient. This is similar to keeping a photocopy of paper messages you send to people through a regular mail system.

The Priority group box contains three radio buttons that you can use to specify the priority of the message. This defines the icon that appears next to the message's description in the recipient's Inbox. Low-priority messages show a down arrow next to the envelope, a normal-priority message displays the standard envelope icon, and a high-priority message displays a red exclamation mark beside the envelope. Figure 29.14 shows three messages in the Inbox, each with a different priority.

When your message options are set, click on OK to return to the message window.

Figure 29.14
Icons indicate
message priority
in the Inbox.

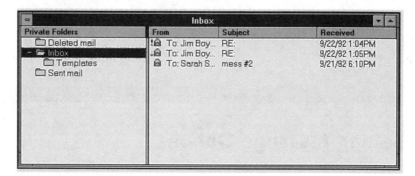

Sending the Message

When your message is complete and you are ready to send it, choose the Send button from the toolbar. Mail moves the message to your Outbox. If you are working online (connected to the WGPO), the message remains in the Outbox for a short period of time and then is moved to a temporary file in the WGPO. When the recipient signs in to the WGPO, Mail downloads the message to her message file.

If you are working offline (your computer is not connected to the network), the messages remain in your Outbox until you connect to the WGPO. The messages then are moved to the WGPO.

Tip

Many applications, including Excel, Word, File Manager, and others, provide a Mail menu by which you can directly mail documents from the application. These applications communicate with Mail to compose and send the message.

Receiving and Working with Messages

When you start Mail and sign in, Mail checks to see if you have any new messages. If you do, it places them in your Inbox. Depending on how many other programs are running and whether you are entering commands with the mouse or keyboard, Mail might not check for new messages right away. You can direct it to check for new messages by choosing View, New Messages. Mail then checks for new messages and places any new ones it finds in your Inbox.

Mail also checks for new mail periodically as you are running the program. You learn later in this chapter how to specify the time Mail waits before checking for new messages.

Descriptions for messages in the Inbox that you have not yet read appear in bold; descriptions for messages you have read appear in normal text. To read a message, select it in the Inbox by highlighting it with the cursor keys and press Enter, or double-click on it with the mouse. The Read Note dialog box then appears, as shown in figure 29.15.

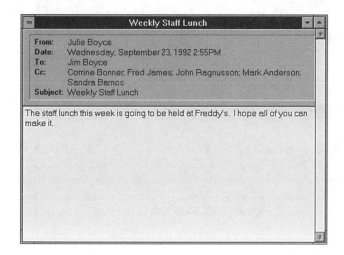

Figure 29.15
The Read Note dialog box containing a message.

If the message does not fit in the window, use the scroll bar to view it or resize the window to make the message fit.

Viewing and Saving Attachments

When you receive a message that contains attachments, the message identifier in your Inbox displays a document paper-clipped to the message envelope icon. You can view the attached files (or play them in the case of sounds and other files) by displaying the message, then double-clicking on the attached files with the mouse. The associated application starts and displays the attached file.

Note that this only works if the file type is associated with an application on your system. The application that is used to display or play the document might actually be located elsewhere on the network, but the association for the attached file must exist in your copy of WIN.INI or your registration database.

Unlike embedded objects and information you place in a message by pasting, an attached file can be copied from the message to a file. In a way, this resembles detaching the file from the message and placing it on your disk, except that the file remains attached to the message and a copy of it is created instead.

To copy one or more attached files from a received message to individual files on your disk, display the message, then choose File, Save Attachment. This displays the Save Attachment dialog box shown in figure 29.16.

Figure 29.16

The Save Attachment dialog box.

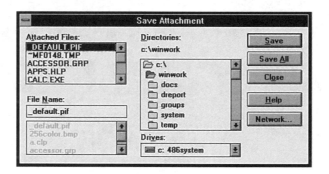

Begin by selecting an item from the Attached Files list. To save it with a different name, click in the File Name edit box and type a new file name. If you want to replace an existing file in the current directory, choose the file from the file list located below the File Name edit box. If you want to place the file in a different directory, local drive, or unconnected remote drive, use the Directories, Drives, and Network items in the dialog box to choose the file's destination.

When you have set the options the way you want them, choose the Save button. The file then is copied from the message to the file name you have selected.

If you want to save a selection of files, choose them from the Attached Files list, then choose the Save button. To save all the attached files, simply choose the Save All button. When you are finished saving attached files, choose the Close button to close the dialog box and return to the message window.

Sorting Messages

Mail provides four options for sorting your messages. The View menu includes the commands Sort by Sender, Sort by Subject, Sort by Date, and Sort by Priority. Each command sorts the list of messages in the Inbox window according to its sort criteria. Select one of these commands to sort and display your messages.

You also can sort the display according to sender, subject, or date by clicking on one of the three buttons at the top of the message list in the Inbox window. You must use the View menu, however, to sort by priority.

Replying to a Message

To reply to a message you have received, display or select the message, then choose either the toolbar's Reply button or Mail, Reply. Either action opens a new window ready for you to enter a reply (see fig. 29.17).

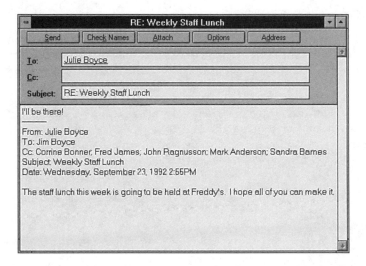

Figure 29.17
Replying to a message.

The contents of the message appear at the bottom of the window and the cursor at the top of the window. The sender's name automatically appears in the To field, and the subject of the original message appears in the Subject field. Attachments that were in the original message are replaced by references in double brackets, as in <<OLE Object: Microsoft Excel Macrosheet>>. The attached files are not included in the reply message unless you manually attach them.

Compose your reply as you would any other message—by adding text, embedding objects, and attaching other files. To reattach a file from the original message, open the original message and select the attached file. Choose Edit, Copy to copy the file to the Clipboard. Then, return to the reply message window and choose Paste or Paste Special to attach the file.

The Options button in the reply message window enables you to specify a few options for the return message.

When the message is ready, choose the Send button to send the reply. If you want to send a copy to someone else, use the Address button to display the Address list and then add the recipient's name to the Cc list.

Using Reply All

If you want to reply to everyone in the original message's From and Cc lists, choose either the toolbar's Reply All button or M̲ail, Reply to A̲ll. This enables you to send the message quickly to everyone involved without the need to add their names manually to the To and Cc lists.

Compose the reply message as you would for a single recipient, then use the S̲end button to send it to all the users in the To and Cc fields.

Forwarding a Message

Occasionally, you will receive messages that need to be passed on to other users. You might be waiting for a bit of crucial information that you promised to someone else, for example, or want to share a message with someone else to keep them up-to-date on a project.

To forward a message that you have received, select the message in the Inbox or display it, then choose the Forward button from the toolbar or M̲ail, F̲orward. This displays a message editing window containing the original message and a Subject header of FW to indicate that the message is being forwarded (see fig. 29.18).

Figure 29.18
A message being prepared for forwarding.

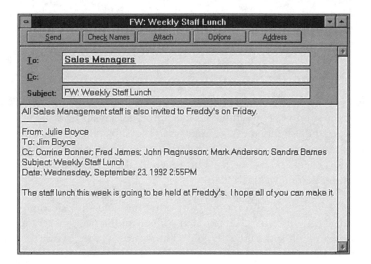

If you want, add your own comments at the top of the message or make notations in the original message. Use the A̲ddress, Chec̲k Name, and Opt̲ions buttons to choose recipients and set options for the message. When it is ready to be forwarded, choose the S̲end button.

Using Additional Mail Features

The functions examined in the previous section are fairly straightforward. Additional features in Mail make composing, sending, and maintaining messages much easier. The first of these, message templates, is really more a method than it is a feature.

Using Message Templates

If you find yourself creating the same messages over and over again, you can create a common message and save it as a template for use any time you want it. The template message can contain the names of the people to whom you normally send the message, as well as any stock text you normally include in the message. A *message template* is simply a message that you compose but never send. When the time comes to create a message from the template and send it, you use the Forward command instead of the Send command. This keeps the original template message and sends a copy to the message's recipients.

To create a message template, choose the Compose button or Mail, Compose Note. When the send note window appears, fill in as much of the note as you want, including the To and Cc fields, the Subject field, and the body of the message. When the template is completed, close the send note window by double-clicking on its control button or by pressing Ctrl+F4. Mail then asks you if you want to save a copy of the message in your Inbox (see fig. 29.19). Choose the Yes button to save the template.

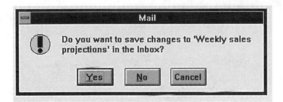

Figure 29.19
Mail prompts you to save the message (message template) that was not sent.

To use a template you have created, select it in the Inbox, then choose the toolbar's Forward button or Mail, Forward. When the message appears in the FW (Forward) window, add any additional information to the message and use the Options button to set the message's options. When the message is ready, choose Send to send it to the list of recipients.

It is a good idea to keep your message templates separate from your other messages to avoid the chance of accidentally deleting them. Folders enable you to separate not only your template messages, but all your other messages as well.

Working with Folders

As you learned earlier in this chapter, Mail creates three standard folders in your Inbox: Inbox, Sent mail, and Deleted mail. You also can create your own folders.

Folders are nothing more than logical storage areas for messages. Folders can contain other folders, which are called *subfolders*. Subfolders enable you to organize your messages even more thoroughly. You can create a top-level folder for each project on which you are currently working, for example, and create subfolders in each folder for the different message categories you need for each project.

Folders can be either private or shared. Private folders are stored in your own message file. Only you have access to your private folders and can read the messages in them. Shared folders are stored in the WGPO. Other Mail users can read, write, and delete messages in shared folders, depending on how the shared folder is created.

To create a private folder, choose File, New Folder. This displays the New Folder dialog box shown in figure 29.20.

Figure 29.20
The New Folder dialog box.

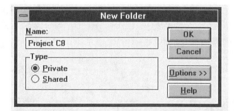

The Name field specifies the name of the folder. (You can include spaces in the folder name.) This is the name that appears beside the folder's icon in your Inbox. The Type group box contains two radio buttons labeled Private and Shared for specifying the folder as either private or shared. Choose the appropriate radio button for the folder you are creating.

Next, choose the Options button to expand the dialog box to include some additional options as shown in figure 29.21. The Level group box enables you to specify whether the folder is a Top Level Folder or a Subfolder of another folder. To create a top-level folder, choose the Top Level Folder radio button. To create a subfolder, choose the folder that is to contain the new folder.

Another group box, labeled Other Users Can, defines the access rights other users have for the folder. These options are valid only for shared folders. To enable other users to read messages in a shared folder you are creating, check the Read check box. If you want other users to be able to place messages in the shared folder, check the Write check box. To enable other users to delete messages from the shared folder, check the Delete check box. If you want all three to apply, check all three check boxes.

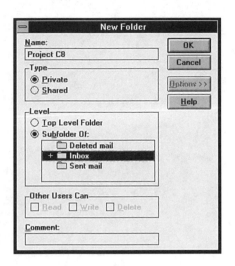

Figure 29.21
Additional options in the New folder dialog box.

The Comment field enables you to include a comment in the folder's properties. This comment does not appear in the Inbox window, but does appear if you select a folder and change its properties in Mail (discussed next).

When you have the folder's properties set the way you want them, click on OK to create the folder.

Changing Folder Properties

Like program item icons in Program Manager, folders have properties. These properties are the parameters that are used to create the folder, including its name, subfolder location, and comments.

To view or change a folder's properties, select the folder in Mail, then press Alt+Enter or choose File, Folder Properties to display the Folder Properties dialog box (see fig. 29.22).

To change any of the properties, simply change the new setting as you did when you created the folder. Note that you can change the properties of folders you created, but you can change only the Comment property of the Deleted mail, Sent mail, and Inbox folders. You cannot change the other properties of these three folders.

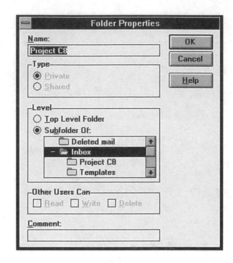

Using Folders

To work in a different folder from your current one, select it from the Inbox window using the cursor keys and pressing Enter, or double-click on it with the mouse. If it is a subfolder, open its parent folder, then select the subfolder. When you select a folder, its contents appear in the message portion of the Inbox window.

Mail displays a plus (+) or minus (-) sign beside a folder's icon if it contains subfolders. The plus sign indicates that the folder is collapsed and contains subfolders. You can expand the folder by pressing the plus sign on your keyboard. A folder that is already expanded to display its subfolders includes a minus sign beside its icon.

You can copy and move messages between folders using either the mouse or Mail's menu. To move or copy a message to a different folder using the menu, choose either the Copy or Move command from the File menu. The Move Message or Copy Message dialog box appears, according to which menu item you select. Both dialog boxes are identical. The Move Message dialog box is shown in figure 29.23.

Figure 29.23
The Move
Message dialog
box.

To specify the location for the move or copy, choose the destination from the Move to or Copy to list. If you want to switch between private and shared folders, choose the appropriate radio button from the Type group box. If you want to create a new folder in which to place the message, choose the New button. When your options are correct, click on OK to move or copy the message. If you have more than one message selected in the source folder, all the selected messages are copied or moved to the new destination folder.

You also can use the mouse to move and copy messages to other folders. If both the source and destination folders are displayed in the Inbox window, open the source folder to display its contents. To move a message, select the message in its source folder, then drag it on top of the destination folder and release the mouse button. To copy the message rather than move it, hold down the Ctrl key while you drag the message.

If both the source and destination folders are not visible, as may be the case when moving or copying files between private folders and shared folders, open another Inbox window to display both folders. Choose Window, New Window to open another window. Use the Shared Folders or Private Folders command in the View menu to switch the view in the window as necessary (you also can click on the Shared Folders or Private Folders button inside the Inbox window). Then, simply copy or move the messages between the two Inbox windows. Figure 29.24 shows a message being copied from a private folder in one window to a shared folder displayed in another window.

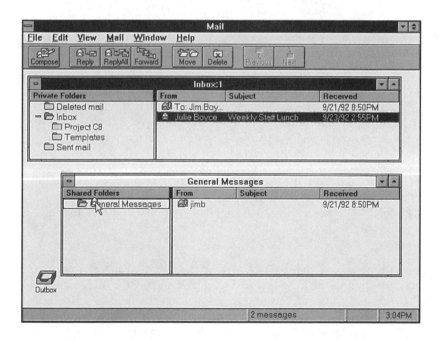

Figure 29.24
Copying a message from a private folder to a shared folder.

V

Networking and Windows

Importing and Exporting Folders

In addition to working with folders within your own message file, you can export some or all of your folders to a new message file that can be shared with other users. You also can import folders from other message files. The import and export features of Mail enable you to share a large number of messages and folders with other users easily without having to place them in a shared folder. You also might want to export folders to create a smaller message file to use on another system, such as your notebook or laptop system.

To export folders and the messages they contain to a new message file, choose File, Export Folders. Mail prompts you for the name and location of the export message file. If the file you specify exists, Mail opens it and displays the Export Folders dialog box shown in figure 29.25. If the export message file does not exist, Mail asks if you want to create the file. If you answer Yes, Mail creates the file.

Figure 29.25
The Export Folders dialog box.

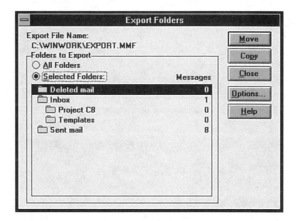

You can export all the folders in your message file or select a group of folders to export. To export all the folders, choose the All Folders radio button. To export only selected folders, choose the Selected Folders radio button.

If you are exporting selected folders, use the Shift and Ctrl keys in combination with the mouse to select the folders you want to export. If you select a folder that contains subfolders, all the subfolders also are selected. If you then deselect a subfolder that contains other folders, the deselected folder is exported as a placeholder, but the messages in it are not exported.

The Options button displays the Options dialog box (see fig. 29.26), which enables you to determine the messages that you want to export. As its name implies, the All Messages radio button, when selected, causes all messages to be exported. The Messages Received or Modified button enables you to set a date range. Any messages that were received or modified within that range of time are exported—other messages are not exported.

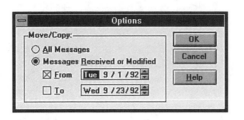

V

Networking and Windows

Figure 29.26
The Options
dialog box.

When your selection of folders and message options is complete, choose the **M**ove button to move the folders and messages from your current message file to the new message file. Note that the folders themselves are not moved—only the messages in them are removed from your local message file and placed in copies of the folders in the export message file.

To retain the messages in your message file and make a copy in the export file, choose the **Cop**y button instead. When you are finished exporting folders and messages, choose the **C**lose button.

Using Address Books

Another useful feature in Mail is the capability to create your own personal address book. You can copy mail addresses quickly from the Postoffice List or create custom entries in your personal address book.

To view the personal address book, choose **M**ail, A**d**dress Book. The Address Book dialog box appears and displays the Postoffice List, as shown in figure 29.27.

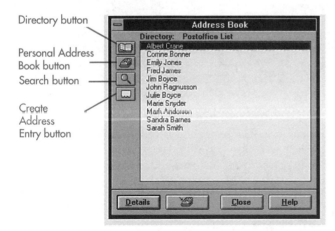

Directory button

Personal Address
Book button

Search button

Create
Address
Entry button

Figure 29.27
The Address Book
dialog box.

The Postoffice List includes the names of all user accounts in the WGPO. If your organization is small, you probably have no need to create a personal address book. If your WGPO includes a large number of users, however, a personal address book can make locating addresses much easier. A personal address book displays only the addresses you have added to the address book yourself.

To view the Personal Address book, click on the Personal Address Book button (refer to figure 29.27). By default, the Personal Address Book is empty. To copy addresses from the Postoffice List, click on the Directory button, then choose the Postoffice List from the Open Directory dialog box and click on OK.

When the Postoffice List reappears, select every user name you want to add to your personal address book. You can use Shift and Ctrl when selecting with the mouse to select more than one address. To select multiple addresses with the keyboard, press Shift+F8, then highlight addresses using the spacebar. To copy the selected user addresses to your personal address book, click on the Copy button. To switch back to the personal address book, click on the Personal Address Book button.

To view the details of a user's account, either in the Postoffice List or the Personal Address Book, choose the user's name, then choose the **D**etails button. A dialog box appears that contains complete information about the user's account (see fig. 29.28).

Figure 29.28
A mail account details dialog box.

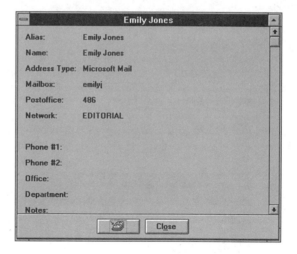

If you want your address book to be used by default instead of the Postoffice List, choose the Personal Address Book button and select Personal Address Book from the list. Then, choose the Set **D**efault button. When you select the A**d**dress button in a Mail window, such as the send note window, Mail displays your personal address book instead of the Postoffice List.

Using Personal Groups

Another useful Mail feature is the capability to create personal groups. Personal groups appear in your personal address book under a single descriptive name but actually represent a group of people. You can create a personal group called Sales Managers, for example, that contains the names of all the managers in the Sales department. When you want to send a message to all your sales managers, you select Sales Managers in the personal address book. This description then appears in the To field of your message, as shown in figure 29.29.

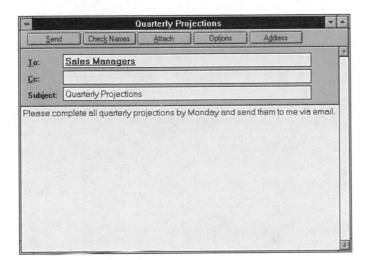

Figure 29.29
A Sales Managers group used to send multiple messages.

When you send the message, it goes out to everyone on the Sales Managers list automatically. This saves you the trouble of building an address list one name at a time each time you want to send a message to a group of people.

To create a personal group, choose **M**ail, Personal **G**roups to display the Personal Groups dialog box shown in figure 29.30. Your new personal groups list will be empty, so to create a new group, choose the **N**ew button.

Mail then prompts you for the name of the new group. Type a name and click on OK. A dialog box similar to the Address List dialog box appears (see fig. 29.31), which you use to add mail accounts to the group.

Select the names of the people you want to place in the group, then choose **A**dd. You can add one name at a time, or select a group of names and add them at the same time. As you add names to the group, the names appear in the Group Members list at the bottom of the dialog box. When the list is complete, choose **O**K to return to the Personal Groups dialog box.

To edit a personal group, choose the **E**dit button. The Personal Groups creation dialog box appears again, enabling you to add new names to the group in the same manner as when you first created the group. To delete a name from the group, click on the name in the Group Members list and press Del. When the list is correct, choose **O**K to return to the Personal Groups list again.

Figure 29.30
The Personal
Groups dialog
box.

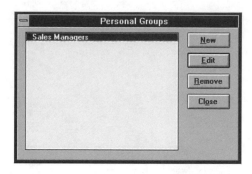

Figure 29.31
The Personal
Groups creation
dialog box.

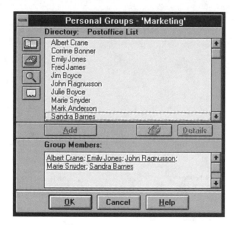

To delete a group from your Personal Groups list, select the group, then choose **R**emove. Mail prompts you to verify the deletion. To delete the group, choose **Y**es. To cancel the deletion, choose **N**o.

When you finish with the Personal Groups list, choose Cl**o**se to close the dialog box and return to the main Mail window.

Personal groups appear in your personal address book with individual names. The group names are in bold, and individual names appear in normal type (see fig. 29.32). To send a message to a personal group, begin the message using either the compose or forward options. Choose the A**d**dress button to display your personal address book. If the Postoffice List appears, your personal address book is not set as the default. Choose the Personal Address Book button to display it.

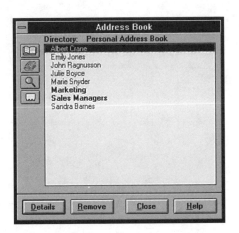

Figure 29.32
Group names in
the personal
address book.

Next, choose the group name to which you want to send the message (you can choose
more than one group). If you want to send it to individual users, add their names to
either the To or Cc lists. When your address list is finished, choose OK. Complete the
message as you normally would, then choose the Send button. Note that the individual
names in a group never appear in the message's header; the group name appears instead.

Searching for Messages

If you receive a large number of messages, it can become difficult to retrieve specific
messages. You might recall that you received a message concerning a certain topic, for
example, but you just cannot remember who sent it to you or in which folder you placed
the message. Fortunately, Mail includes a function that enables you to search for just such
messages.

The Message Finder command in the File menu displays a Message Finder dialog box
similar to the one shown in figure 29.33. With Message Finder, you can search for a
message according to its sender, its subject, its recipients, or text within the message. You
also can direct Message Finder to look in all your folders, or just in a specific folder. You
even can open multiple Message Finder windows to perform a number of different
searches.

To search for a message, choose File, Message Finder. In the Message Finder dialog box,
enter the necessary search criteria to locate the message. If you know that you received
the message from a specific user, type the user's name in the From field. If you know the
subject of the message, type it in the Subject field. To search for a message according to
the users that are in its recipient's list, enter the recipients in the Recipients field. If you
recall a keyword that appeared in the message or a string of text from it, enter this in the
Message Text field.

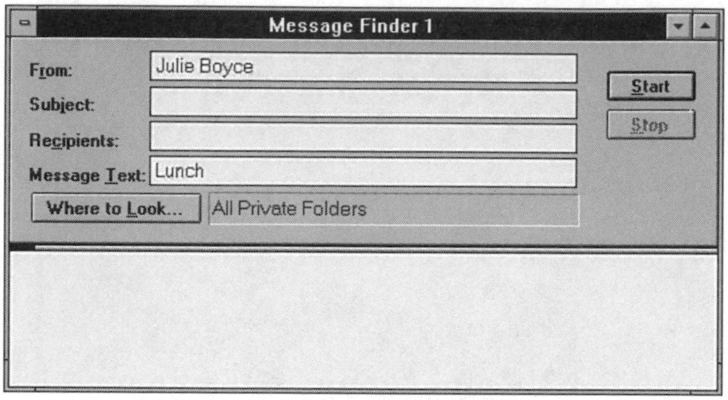

Figure 29.33
The Message
Finder window.

Message Finder 1

From: Julie Boyce
Subject:
Recipients:
Message Text: Lunch
Where to Look... All Private Folders

Start
Stop

To specify in what area Message Finder should search for the message, choose the Where to Look button. This displays the Where to Look dialog box shown in figure 29.34. To have Message Finder search through all your folders, choose the radio button labeled Look in all folders. To search a specific folder, choose the radio button labeled Look in, and choose the folder from the displayed list. When you have the options set, click on OK.

Figure 29.34
The Where to
Look dialog box.

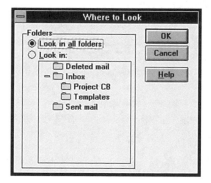

When you are ready to start the search, choose the Start button. Message Finder begins searching for the message. To cancel a search after it has started, choose Stop. When Message Finder completes its search, it displays in the bottom part of the window a list of messages that fit the search criteria. Note that a search can result in any number of messages matching your search criteria.

To view a message the Message Finder locates in its search, select it with the keyboard or double-click on it with the mouse. Mail then opens a window to display the message. You can include additional information in the message, then choose Reply, Reply All, or Forward to send the message to another user.

When you no longer need the results of the search, choose Close from the Message Finder control menu to close the window. If you think you might need Message Finder later, minimize it to an icon.

Setting Mail Options

The Mail menu includes the Options command, which enables you to set various options to control the way Mail operates. When you choose the Options command, the Options dialog box appears, as shown in figure 29.35.

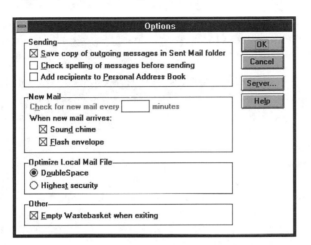

Figure 29.35
The Options dialog box.

The Sending group box features two check boxes that enable you to control the options that are available to you when you send a message. The first check box is labeled Save copy of outgoing messages in Sent Mail folder; this option determines whether Mail keeps a copy of the messages you send. If you check this box, Mail saves a copy of each sent message in your Sent mail folder. If you clear the box, Mail does not keep a copy. This is a global control, but you can override it for a specific message. To do so, select the Options button when you compose a message, then clear the Save sent messages box in the individual message's Options dialog box.

The third check box in the Sending group is labeled Add Recipients to Personal Address Book. When you check this option, Mail automatically adds the names of message recipients to your personal address book if they are not already included in the book. To prevent Mail from adding recipients to your personal address book when you send a message, clear this check box.

The New Mail group box controls the way Mail handles incoming messages. At the top of the group, an edit box enables you to specify how often Mail checks for new messages while it is running. The default setting is 10 minutes. If you prefer to have Mail check more frequently for new messages, decrease the number in the edit box accordingly. To make Mail check for messages less often, increase the number.

The Sound chime check box, when checked, causes Mail to sound a chime whenever new messages arrive. If you clear this check box, Mail does not provide an audible alert.

The Flash envelope check box, when checked, causes Mail to change the mouse pointer to an envelope whenever new messages arrive. If you are working in another application and Mail is running as an icon, for example, you still see the cursor change briefly to display an envelope, providing a visual alert that mail has arrived.

The final check box is labeled Empty Wastebasket when exiting. When you check this box, any messages in your Deleted mail folder are deleted when you exit from Mail. This option provides an automatic means of removing deleted messages. If you do not want messages to be deleted automatically from the Deleted mail folder, clear this check box.

The Server button in the Options dialog box generally is dimmed, making it unavailable. You can make it available by editing your MSMAIL.INI file and changing the NoServerOptions= setting to read as follows:

```
[Microsoft Mail]
NoServerOptions=0
```

When you restart Mail, the Server button will be available. Choose Server to display the Server dialog box, as shown in figure 29.36. You can use the options in the Storage group box to determine where your message file is stored. By default, the Local radio button is selected and your messages are stored in the file MSMAIL.MMF in your Windows for Workgroups directory. If you prefer to use a different message file (useful if you are sharing the workstation with another user), change the file name in the File edit box. You also can use the edit box to move your message file to a different directory.

Figure 29.36
The Server dialog box.

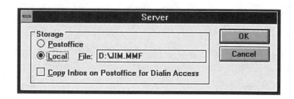

To locate your message file in your Mail server's WGPO, choose the Postoffice radio button. If you choose this option, Mail creates a message file name on its own; you cannot specify a message file name.

The check box labeled Copy Inbox on Postoffice for Dialin Access causes a duplicate copy of your Inbox to be maintained in the WGPO. This feature enables you to dial in to the network and check your mail. This feature requires the full Mail 3.2 package, however, and might also require third-party software to operate on your network.

Managing Your Mail

Your message file is the heart of your local Mail system. All your messages and private folders are stored in your message file. Therefore, if your message file becomes corrupted or is accidentally deleted, you lose all your messages and folders. You should back up your message file regularly to avoid these problems.

To back up your message file, choose <u>M</u>ail, <u>B</u>ackup; the Backup dialog box appears, as shown in figure 29.37. If you have backed up your message file before, Mail displays the existing backup file's location and name. To back up to the same file, click on OK. To specify a different file name or directory, use the controls in the dialog box to specify the path and file name for your new backup. When you click on OK, Mail makes a complete copy of your message file according to your selections.

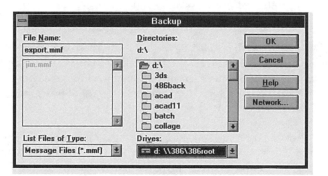

Figure 29.37
The Backup dialog box.

The Dri<u>v</u>es list box lists the network drives to which you already are connected. You can locate your message file on one of these drives simply by selecting it, just as you select a local disk. To connect to a new remote disk, click on the Network button.

If Mail cannot locate or read your message file when Mail starts, it displays the Open Message File dialog box, shown in figure 29.38. Locate your backup message file, select it, and click on OK. If you want to create a new message file, choose the N<u>e</u>w button.

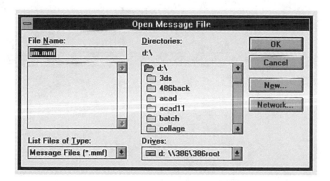

Figure 29.38
The Open Message File dialog box.

If you have a backup file, or if you think that your old message file still exists, you should try to locate it before creating a new one. Remember that if you create a new message file, it will not retain your old folder structure or old messages.

Using At Work Fax

Windows for Workgroups 3.11 includes a new feature called At Work Fax that enables users to send and receive faxes through either a fax modem connected to the user's node or a shared fax modem located elsewhere on the network. At Work Fax can be used as a stand-alone application or in conjunction with Microsoft Mail. In both cases, outgoing faxes are routed to the appropriate device (local fax modem or shared remote fax modem).

At Work Fax enables you to attach files to fax messages. If the receiving system supports the feature, the attached files are transferred as e-mail rather than as faxes. This makes it possible for you to fax a file to another user. If the recipient's system does not support the feature (it is a standard Class 3 fax machine, for example), the file is transmitted as a standard fax.

Incoming faxes from other At Work Fax systems (and compatible systems) are routed to intended recipients automatically as e-mail. Incoming faxes from Class 3 fax machines are stored in a designated fax attendant's inbox. The attendant is responsible for forwarding the faxes to the proper destination on the network.

Setting Up a Fax Modem

Before you can begin using At Work Fax, you must configure a fax modem. The fax modem can be located on your workstation or on a remote workstation elsewhere on the network. To configure a local fax modem, use the following procedure:

1. Open the Control Panel and choose the Fax icon. This displays the Fax Modems dialog box shown in figure 29.39.

Figure 29.39
The Fax Modems
dialog box.

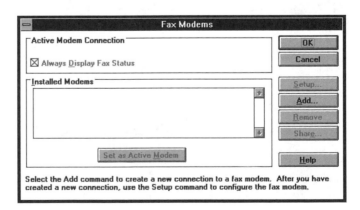

2. Choose the **A**dd button to open the Add Fax Modems dialog box (see fig. 29.40).

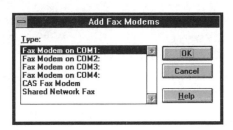

Figure 29.40
The Add Fax
Modems dialog
box.

3. If you are configuring a local fax modem, choose the appropriate device from the Type group box. Choose Fax Modem on COM*n:* (substituting the appropriate COM port number for *n*) if you are configuring a Class 1 or Class 2 modem, or choose CAS Fax Modem if you are configuring a CAS modem. Verify that your modem is connected to the system and turned on, then click on OK.

4. At Work Fax will attempt to locate and test the fax modem. When the fax modem has been recognized, At Work Fax displays a dialog box prompting you to enter the phone number of your fax modem. Type the number, then click on OK.

The modem is now configured.

Sharing the Fax Modem

If you want other users to be able to use the modem, you must create a shared directory to contain outgoing faxes and share the modem. To share a fax modem with other users on the network, use the following procedure:

1. If the Fax Modems dialog box is not currently open, open the Control Panel and choose the Fax icon.

2. From the Installed Modems group, select the fax modem you want to share with the network, then choose the Share button. The Share Local Fax Modem dialog box (fig. 29.41) appears.

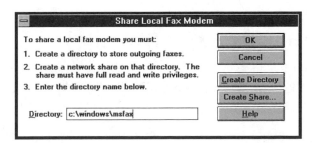

Figure 29.41
The Share Local Fax
Modem dialog box.

3. In the **D**irectory edit box, enter the name of the directory in which you want outgoing faxes to be stored. If the directory does not exist, choose the **C**reate Directory button to create it.

4. After specifying and creating the directory, choose the Create **S**hare button. The Control Panel displays the Share Directory dialog box shown in figure 29.42.

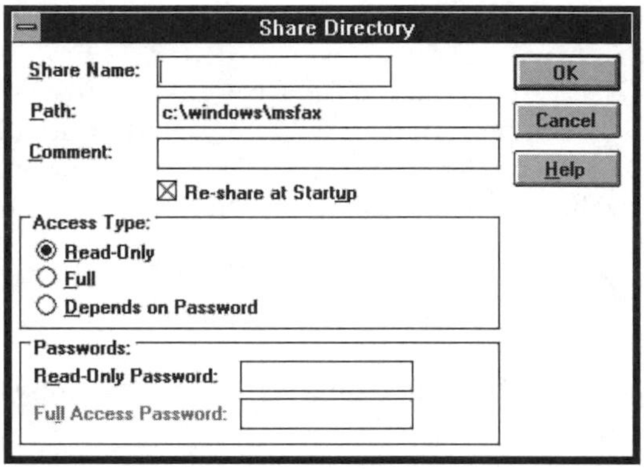

Figure 29.42

The Share Directory dialog box.

5. In the **S**hare Name edit box, enter the name for the shared fax modem. The name can be a maximum of 12 characters. Ending the name with a dollar sign ($) will hide the shared resource, preventing it from appearing when other users browse for resources on the network.

6. Set the Access Type and Password according to your preferences.

7. To share the directory each time Windows starts, place a check in the Re-share at Start**u**p check box.

8. Add a comment in the **C**omment edit box (optional).

9. Click on OK, then click on OK again, then close the Control Panel.

The modem can now be accessed by other users.

Connecting to a Shared Fax Modem

To use a shared fax modem that is connected to a remote note, you must connect to the fax modem. Use the following procedure to connect to the shared fax modem's directory:

1. Open the Control Panel and choose the Fax icon.

2. Choose the **A**dd button to display the Add Fax Modems dialog box (refer to figure 29.40).

3. Choose Shared Network Fax from the **T**ype list box, then click on OK.

4. In the Connect Network Fax dialog box, choose the shared directory assigned to the fax modem. If the shared directory does not appear in the list, choose the Network button and browse for the fax modem's shared directory. Choose the shared directory, then click on OK. Click on OK again to close the Fax Modems dialog box, then close the Control Panel. You now are ready to access the fax modem.

Setting Fax Options

At Work Fax provides many options you can use to control the quality of faxes, default message format, transmission times, and other settings. To set these options, open Microsoft Mail and choose Fax, Options. This displays the Default Fax Options dialog box shown in figure 29.43.

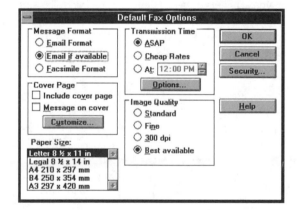

Figure 29.43

The Default Fax Options dialog box.

The option buttons in the Message Type group control the format for outgoing fax messages. Choosing the Email Format causes At Work Fax to attempt to send the message in e-mail format, instead of as a fax. The option button labeled Email if available also causes At Work Fax to attempt to send the message in e-mail format, but if e-mail format is not supported by the recipient system, At Work Fax transmits the message as a fax.

The options in the Cover Page group control whether outgoing faxes include a cover page and whether your fax message will be included on the cover page. If you place a check in the check box labeled Include cover page, At Work Fax will include a cover page with the following items:

✔ Recipient's name, address, and phone number

✔ The names of other recipients of the same fax

✔ Sender's name and fax phone number

✔ Current date, subject of the fax, and number of pages (including the cover page)

If you want to include a bit map on the cover page, choose the Customize button. At Work Fax displays a dialog box that you can use to select a bit map file from disk.

The Paper Size and Image Quality options control the size of paper format and resolution of the outgoing fax. Set these options according to your preferences and to the capabilities of the receiving system.

The Transmission Time options control how outgoing faxes are scheduled. If you select the ASAP option, faxes are sent as soon as the system is free to do so. The Cheap Rates option causes At Work Fax to send the fax during off-peak hours, which you define by choosing the Options button in the Transmission Time group. By using the At option, you can specify an exact time at which to send the fax.

In addition to setting default options for a fax, you also can set options for a specific fax when you schedule it. When you send the fax, Microsoft Mail will appear on the display with the fax message in the Compose window. Choose the Options button, then choose Fax. This causes the Fax Message Options dialog box to open, which you can use to set fax options.

Sending a Fax

Sending a fax using At Work Fax is simple, and is very similar to most other Windows-based fax programs. From the source application (such as your word processor), choose the Print command from the File menu. Select the Microsoft At Work Fax on FAX: printer. Set options for the print (such as page range), then click on OK. The At Work Fax driver intercepts the print job and opens Mail, displaying the fax in the compose window (see fig. 29.44).

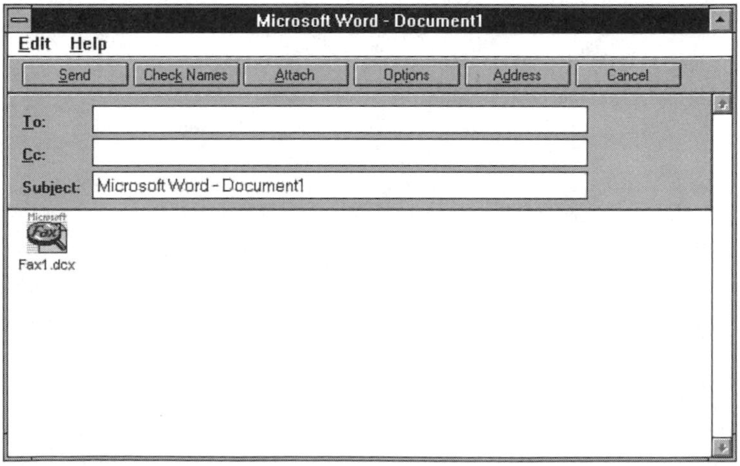

Figure 29.44
A fax message in the compose window.

Microsoft Word - Document1
Edit Help

Send | Check Names | Attach | Options | Address | Cancel

To:
Cc:
Subject: Microsoft Word - Document1

Fax1.dcx

Place the cursor in the **T**o field, then choose the A**d**dress button to open the address book. If you have a fax address for the recipient in the address book, select it as you would a regular e-mail address, then click on OK. If you do not yet have a fax address entry for the recipient, choose the blank address book entry button to create a new address. In the New dialog box (see fig. 29.45), choose Microsoft At Work Fax, then click on OK.

Figure 29.45
Use the New dialog box to add a fax address.

Enter an alias name (such as the person's real name) in the Alias field of the New User dialog box (see fig. 29.46). Enter the fax number in the Fax Number field. If you are sending to another At Work Fax user, specify the fax number using the format *username@+country-area-prefix-number*, where *username* is the user's local e-mail address, *country* is the country phone code, *area* is the area code, *prefix* is the local phone prefix, and *number* is the local phone number. The following is an example for a user named jboyce:

jboyce@+1-123-555-9999

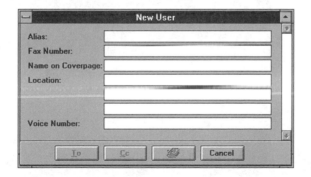

Figure 29.46
The New User dialog box.

Place the user's name in the Name on Coverpage edit box to have the user's name included on the fax cover page. Fill in any additional information for the user (optional), then choose **T**o or **C**c (whichever is applicable). Repeat this process for any other To or Cc recipients. When you are ready to send the fax, choose the **S**end button. The fax then will be sent according to your Send Time settings for the fax.

Using Chat

When you need to communicate with someone right away, you pick up the phone and call them. Windows for Workgroups includes a program called Chat, which serves much the same function. Chat enables you to communicate directly with other users across the network by using Windows for Workgroups' Network DDE (NetDDE) capability.

Why should you use Chat? Some users think of the program as a novelty more than anything else. In some situations, however, Chat is a very useful program. When it is essential that you contact someone immediately and that person's phone is busy, you can use Chat instead. The other user's computer beeps; if a sound card is installed in the system, it rings like a telephone. In a way, Chat serves as a second phone line to the other user's office.

Another situation in which Chat is useful is when you are running a program that is communicating with another user's workstation. This communication might be something relatively unimportant, such as a game of Hearts, or it may be a crucial data transfer. Either way, Chat enables you to communicate with the other user.

Making and Answering Calls

Chat usually is located in your Accessories group. Figure 29.47 shows the main Chat program window.

Figure 29.47
The Chat program
window.

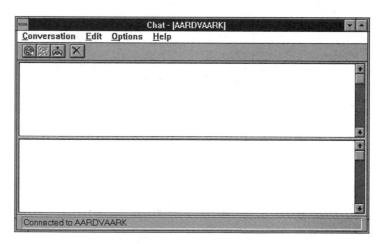

To initiate a call, click on the Call button from Chat's toolbar. (This icon depicts a hand operating a rotary telephone dial.) Alternatively, you can choose the Dial command from the Conversation menu. When you select either item, Chat displays the Select Computer dialog box, as shown in figure 29.48. This dialog box lists the workgroups on the network, along with the computers in each workgroup. To dial another node, enter its computer name in the Computer Name edit box or select it from the Computers list, then click on OK.

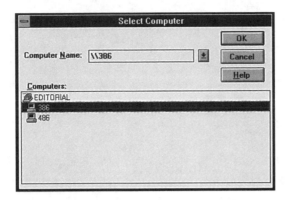

Figure 29.48
The Select
Computer dialog
box.

When you click on OK, Chat attempts to connect to the selected computer. If the other node is not currently running Chat, Chat starts on the other system as an icon. The remote system beeps and Chat's phone icon changes to show the receiver moving as if it were ringing off the hook. If Chat is already running in a window on the remote node, its title bar flashes instead.

To answer a call, choose the Answer button from the toolbar. This icon depicts a telephone receiver being lifted from its cradle. Otherwise, you can choose the <u>A</u>nswer command from the <u>C</u>onversation menu.

The text you type on your local workstation appears in the top window. Text that the remote user types appears in the bottom window. The text appears on both screens in real time—that is, as you type it. You do not have to wait for the other user to finish typing a line before you can type. Both of you can type at the same time. If you make mistakes and use the Backspace key, the mistakes and the backspacing appear on the other system's display as you press the keys, just as it does on yours.

When you are finished with the conversation, indicate in some way to the other user that you are signing off, then click on the Hang Up button in the toolbar. This button depicts a telephone receiver being returned to its cradle. Alternatively, you can choose the <u>H</u>ang Up command from the <u>C</u>onversation menu.

Using Expressions

In a face-to-face conversation, you can easily convey your true meaning. You can smile, scowl, grin, wink, and use other facial expressions to add meaning to your words. When you are communicating electronically through typed words, however, it is easy to type one thing and mean another, just because of the way the other person interprets what you have typed. Sometimes, the other person might even become offended because there is no way for you to convey that you are joking or being facetious.

Because of these communication problems, a system of symbols has come into common use on many electronic bulletin board services and online communication services such as CompuServe and GENie. These symbols enable users to inject facial expressions, emotions, and tone into their written messages. These symbols are often called *emoticons,* for Emotional Icons, or *smilies.*

Table 29.1 lists some of the more common expressions and techniques you might want to include in your messages when you are using Chat.

Table 29.1
Chat Emoticons

Symbol	Meaning
:-)	A smile
;-)	A wink
P-)	A wink
:-O	Uh, oh!
I-O	Bored
:-I	No comment
(-:	Left-hand smile
I-D	Ho, ho
I-)	Hee, hee
:-o	Shock or surprise
:-\	Undecided
#-)	Hung over
:-#	My lips are sealed

In addition to common emotional expressions, many common phrases have been shortened to acronyms. Use these phrase-acronyms to speed your written conversation by eliminating the need to type long strings of text when a few letters will serve the purpose. Table 29.2 lists some common online expressions and their shortcuts.

Table 29.2
Common Online Phrases and Their Shortcuts

Shortcut	Phrase
B4	Before
CUL8R	See you later
BTW	By the way
FWIW	For what it's worth
FYI	For your information
G	Grin
GD&R	Grinning, ducking, and running
GMTA	Great minds think alike
IAE	In any event
IMO	In my opinion
IMHO	In my humble opinion
IOW	In other words
MOF	Matter of fact
NBD	No big deal
OIC	Oh, I see
OTOH	On the other hand
ROFL	Rolling on the floor laughing
RTM	Read the manual
RTFM	Read the * manual
TIA	Thanks in advance
TTYL	Talk to you later

When you use Chat, symbols can get your message across in the right way, and phrase shortcuts can save quite a bit of typing.

Using the Clipboard

You can cut and paste text from the Clipboard as you use Chat. If you want to keep a section of text that the other user has sent or text that you have entered, just highlight it and choose Edit, Copy. This places a copy of the text in the Clipboard. From the Clipboard, you can insert the text into Chat or into documents you create in other applications.

To remove text, select the text, then choose Edit, Cut. This removes the text from the window and places it in the Clipboard. To paste text into a Chat window from the Clipboard, make sure the text is in the Clipboard, then choose the Paste command.

Setting Preferences

Chat's Options menu provides a number of commands that change Chat's appearance and function. The Preferences command enables you to switch from top-and-bottom windows to side-by-side windows. You also can change the way your Chat partner's font appears. You can set Chat to display your partner's messages in your own font, or in the font your partner is using on the other system.

The Font command enables you to change the font used in your conversation window. If your partner has configured Chat to display your message using your font, the font you select with the Font command shows up for your text in your partner's Chat window.

The Background Color command sets the background color of your conversation window on your workstation, as well as the color of your conversation window on the remote system. You can change only your own window's color. Your partner's color selection determines the background color of his conversation window both locally and remotely.

Status Bar commands turn on the toolbar and status bar on your display. The Sound command determines whether you hear an audible alarm when you call another user or when another user calls you. If your system has a built-in sound adapter, and you want to change the sound that is assigned to incoming and outgoing Chat calls, use the Sound icon in the Control Panel to assign the new sound.

Chapter Snaphot

In Chapter 29 you read about one of Windows for Workgroups' bundled network applications—Mail. You can use Mail to send and receive messages across the network, and possibly replace your current paper interoffice memo system completely.

Windows for Workgroups includes a second bundled application called Schedule+. Schedule+ is a personal scheduling program that enables you to maintain a schedule of pending tasks, meetings, and appointments. You can view your schedule on-screen or print it for your appointment book. Schedule+ also can be used as a workgroup scheduling tool, enabling you to schedule appointments electronically with other members of your workgroup. You can set up appointments from your computer without picking up a phone or leaving your office.

This chapter covers all the features of Schedule+, including the following topics:

Schedule+ uses Mail as its message transport system. If you have not yet configured Mail on your network, you should do so now. You then will be ready to start using Schedule+.

Using Schedule+

S chedule+ is a Windows application that provides a range of tools for managing your
work schedule. With Schedule+, you can maintain a daily schedule of appointments, schedule recurring appointments, maintain a list of tasks you need to
perform, set reminders to yourself, and schedule the use of resources, such as conference
rooms. You can delegate another user as your assistant to help manage your schedule.
You also can set up Schedule+ so that other users who share your workgroup post office
can view your schedule. Access to your schedule enables users to locate times when you
are free to attend meetings, as well as optionally make changes to your schedule. Figure
30.1 shows the Schedule+ program window.

Figure 30.1
The Schedule+
program window.

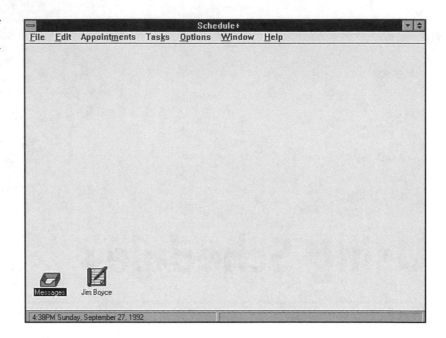

Figure 30.1
The Schedule+
program window.

Not only does Schedule+ enable you to keep track of your own schedule and view the schedules of others, but it also enables you to schedule meetings electronically with other users. This feature can automate much of your meeting scheduling process, eliminating the need to send paper memos and make phone calls.

Schedule+ Overview

Schedule+ includes many features, but the program is simple enough to use that you can soon become comfortable using it. The first facet of Schedule+ to understand is the Appointment Book.

The Appointment Book

The Schedule+ Appointment Book is, in many ways, the heart of the program. With it you maintain your own daily schedule and keep reminders about appointments. In addition to maintaining your schedule, the Appointment Book also serves as a daily calendar. Figure 30.2 shows the Appointment Book.

Different icons are used to identify different types of appointments. Beside the description for meetings is a handshake icon. Appointments for which you have set an alarm include an alarm-bell icon. Recurring appointments, which are appointments that happen on a regular basis, include a looping arrow to indicate that they are recurring appointments rather than single-occurrence appointments.

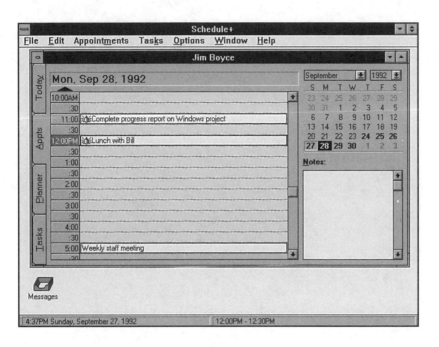

Figure 30.2
The Schedule+
Appointment
Book.

The Planner

The Planner provides a visual interface for scheduling meetings and other appointments over a longer span of time than does the Appointment Book. Rather than display a single day's worth of appointments, the Planner displays as many days as it can within its time allocation window. Like the Appointment Book, it displays a calendar you can use to switch your Planner view quickly to a different day, month, or even year. Figure 30.3 shows the Planner window.

When you want to schedule a meeting, you do so using the Planner. As you select attendants for the meeting using the same address book as you use in Mail, the attendants' busy times appear as colored bars overlaid in your Planner window. This enables you to select a time for the meeting when all attendants will be free. Those who are invited to the meeting appear in a list at the lower-right corner of the Planner window.

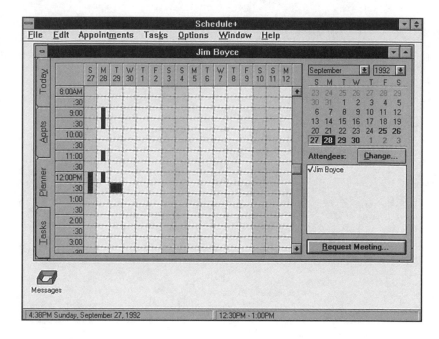

Figure 30.3
The Planner
window displays
a longer time
range.

The Task List

Schedule+ also can help you manage tasks. The Schedule+ Task List enables you to keep track of tasks, assign to them priorities and due dates, and add tasks to your schedule. Figure 30.4 shows the Task window in Schedule+.

In the Task List, you can add and delete tasks, change their priorities, assign due dates, assign descriptions, mark tasks as completed, edit task properties, and add tasks to your schedule. The Task List offers an excellent means of organizing your projects and integrating them with your daily schedule.

Working with Messages

Schedule+ also enables you to send and receive messages, although you are limited to requesting meetings and responding to such requests. If you need to send any other type of message, you can use Mail to do so. Schedule+ provides a Messages window for displaying messages of meetings you have requested and responses from other users to your request. Figure 30.5 shows the Messages window.

As in Mail, you can select messages and display them in separate windows, as figure 30.5 illustrates.

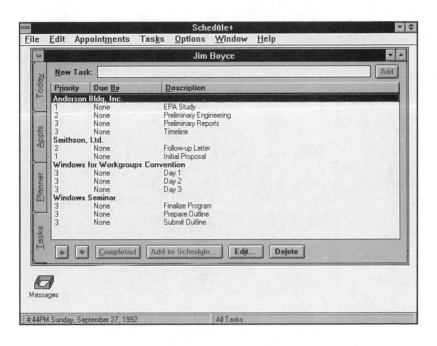

V

Networking and Windows

Figure 30.4
The Task List is
used to prioritize
and manage tasks.

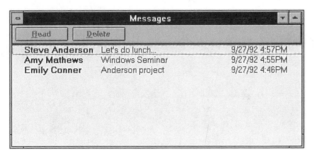

Figure 30.5
The Messages
window displays
meeting requests.

If you are not familiar with scheduling programs, Schedule+ may seem complex. It is simple to use, however, and is an excellent alternative to manual methods for managing your schedule. When combined with the Windows for Workgroups Mail program, Schedule+ can go a long way toward eliminating paper shuffling and help you more closely coordinate with other users on your network.

The first step in putting Schedule+ to work for you is to start the program. The next section discusses some of the options you have for starting Schedule+.

Starting Schedule+

Setup adds the Schedule+ program item to your Main Program Manager group when you install Windows for Workgroups. You can double-click on the Schedule+ program icon to start the program, or you can use Program Manager's or File Manager's Run command (in the File menu) to run the executable file SCHDPLUS.EXE, which is the Schedule+ application file.

When you start Schedule+, it prompts you to sign in to the mail system, unless you currently are running Mail and are already signed in to the mail system. Schedule+ displays the Mail Sign In dialog box shown in figure 30.6.

Figure 30.6
Schedule+
requires signing in
to the mail system.

If you already are running Mail and are signed in to the mail system, Schedule+ starts immediately and does not prompt you to sign in to the mail system.

The Name field in the Mail Sign In dialog box is the name of your mail account in the WGPO (Workgroup Postoffice). The Password entry is your mail account password. Schedule+ uses the same password as your mail account, although it maintains a separate copy of your password.

If you change your password in Mail, Schedule+ still tries to start with whatever password you specified in your last Schedule+ session. When the passwords do not match, Schedule+ displays a Confirm Password dialog box (see fig. 30.7) prompting you to enter your previous password. Enter your old Mail password, which was used in the previous Schedule+ session.

Figure 30.7
Schedule+
prompts you to
confirm your
password.

When the password you enter matches the old password, Schedule+ then prompts you to confirm your new Mail password. Enter your new Mail password in the dialog box and choose OK. Schedule+ then updates its copy of your new password and gives you access to the program.

When Schedule+ is up and running, you are ready to begin making appointments.

Scheduling Appointments

You can use your Appointment Book in Schedule+ to display appointments you have outside of the office, meetings to which you have been invited, meetings you have scheduled, and simple reminders. All these types of appointments can include an alarm that reminds you of the appointment ahead of time. You control the lead time between the alarm and the appointment, giving you plenty of time to make an important engagement or meeting.

To schedule a general appointment, start Schedule+ and display the Appointment Book. You can display the Appointment Book by clicking on <u>A</u>ppts or Toda<u>y</u> in your appointment planner window, or by entering their shortcut keys from the keyboard (Alt+A or Alt+Y). Figure 30.8 shows the Appointment Book displaying the current day.

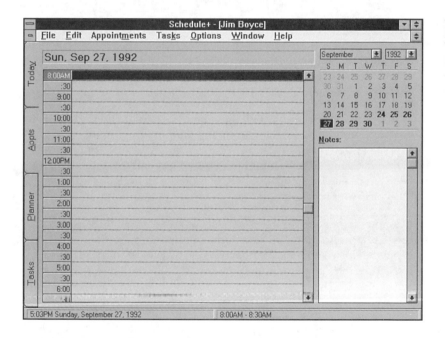

Figure 30.8
The Appointment Book displaying the current day.

As you can see in figure 30.8, the Appointment Book displays a calendar in the upper right corner of the window, a daily schedule broken up into half-hour segments in the left half of the window, and a <u>N</u>otes window in the lower right portion of the window for keeping daily notes.

To schedule an appointment for a specific time, highlight the time slot that applies to the appointment. If it requires 30 minutes or less, click on the appropriate time. If it requires more than 30 minutes, highlight the range with the mouse (click on the first 30-minute slot and drag the mouse to the last slot in the appointment). To specify a time range with the keyboard, locate the cursor in the first time slot, then press and hold down the Shift key and use the cursor key to highlight the desired block of time.

With the time block allocated, choose the **N**ew Appointment command from the Appointments menu or press Ctrl+N. Either action displays the Appointment dialog box shown in figure 30.9.

Figure 30.9
The Appointment dialog box.

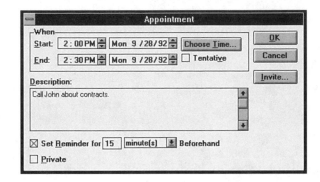

The Appointment dialog box provides controls for setting the date and beginning and end times for an appointment. This dialog box also is used to create a description for the appointment.

If you want to change the time block for the appointment, use the **S**tart and **E**nd controls to specify the starting time and date, as well as the ending time and date. In most cases, appointments do not span more than one day. If you are going on vacation, attending a convention, or will be unavailable for a long period of time, block out the entire time you will be gone. With the entire time range blocked off, other users know that you are unavailable when they view your schedule.

The Choose **T**ime button displays the Choose Time dialog box (see fig. 30.10), which offers a visual means of selecting a time. The time format displayed in the Choose Time dialog box is similar to the one used in the Planner window, which you will read about later in this chapter. Unlike the Planner window, however, the Choose Time dialog box displays a maximum of only 11 days.

To select a time range in the Choose Time dialog box, use the mouse or cursor keys to highlight the block of time. If the time range you need exceeds the Choose Time dialog box display, choose Cancel to return to the New Appointment dialog box and use the list controls to set the time and date.

If you are having trouble locating a block of time of the necessary length to allocate to the appointment, choose the **A**uto-Pick button. Schedule+ then searches your schedule for the next available block of time that fits the amount of time you need for the appointment. To view a different day, choose the day from the calendar. To view a month or year, use the month and year drop-down lists to select the desired month and year. The rest of the Choose Time dialog box changes to reflect the month and year you select. After you select the desired time, choose OK to return to the Appointment dialog box.

In the Appointment dialog box, click in the **D**escription text box or press Alt+D to switch to it. Enter a description for the appointment. This description appears in your Appointment Book for the appointment. Figure 30.11 shows a half-hour appointment in the Appointment Book with a description added to it.

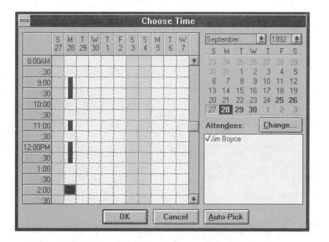

Figure 30.10
The Choose Time dialog box.

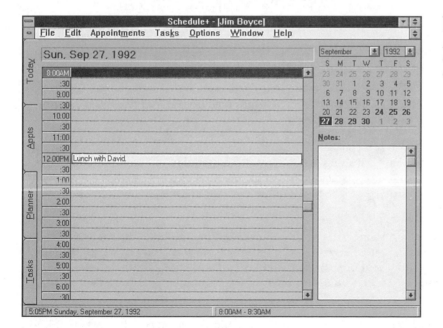

Figure 30.11
A half-hour appointment with a description.

A schedule is no good if you forget to look at it or get involved in your work and forget about an upcoming appointment. Fortunately, Schedule+ provides audible reminders for appointments.

Setting a Reminder

To set a reminder for an appointment, display the Appointment dialog box. If you are setting or changing a reminder for an existing appointment, double-click on the appointment in your Appointment Book to display the Appointment dialog box.

The check box labeled Set Reminder controls whether Schedule+ displays a reminder message and plays an audible alarm to remind you of the upcoming appointment. The edit box and drop-down list box beside the Set Reminder check box enable you to specify the length of time before the appointment for which Schedule+ issues the reminder. The default is 15 minutes, but you can set a reminder to be issued months before the appointment if you need to. Figure 30.12 shows a typical reminder message generated by Schedule+.

Figure 30.12
Schedule+ can issue reminders about your appointments.

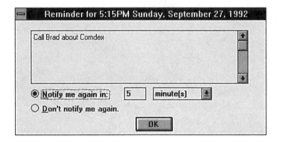

Setting Other Appointment Options

The Private and Tentative check boxes in the Appointment dialog box enable you to specify whether the appointment should be considered private, and whether it is a firm appointment or a tentative appointment.

If the Private check box is checked, Schedule+ does not let other users view the appointment, even if they have full access privileges to your schedule file. Even your assistant cannot view your private appointments. In your Appointment Book, private appointments appear with a key icon beside them to indicate that they are "locked out" from sight of other users.

Although other users cannot view your private appointments, these engagements still show as busy times when others try to book meetings with you. Your private appointments are no different from your other appointments to users who view your schedule. The other user simply sees that the time for the private appointment is already filled in your schedule.

If you want to prevent other users from viewing an appointment, even if they have full access privileges to your schedule file, check the Private check box to make it private.

Working with Tentative Appointments

The Tentative check box in the Appointment dialog box specifies whether the appointment is tentative. Normally, when you set aside time for an appointment and add it to your appointment book, other users see that this time is unavailable to meet with you. You can, however, mark an appointment as tentative. Tentative appointments resemble other appointments, but the time slots set aside for them do not appear to other users as busy. You can schedule a tentative appointment and continue to keep its time available for other users.

Tentative appointments are useful for setting reminders to yourself for specific hours of the day. If you want to remember to place a phone call overseas at a certain hour, for example, you can enter a tentative appointment for it, and even set a reminder. If other users try to schedule a meeting with you during that time, they can see that the time slot is open.

When you have set all the options for your appointment in the Appointment dialog box, choose OK. The appointment description then appears in a blocked out area of time in your Appointment Book (see fig. 30.13).

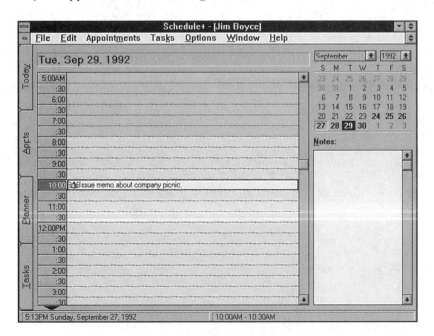

Figure 30.13

A scheduled appointment in the Appointment Book.

V

Networking and Windows

Editing Appointments

Appointments often change after they are made. To edit an appointment, select it and then choose the Edit Appt command from the Edit menu, or double-click on the appointment. Either action displays the Appointment dialog box, which is the same dialog box you use to create a new appointment.

Use the controls in the dialog box to edit the appointment information, just as you did when you originally created the appointment.

Copying, Moving, and Deleting Appointments

You can copy, move, and delete appointments easily in Schedule+. To delete an appointment, select the appointment and choose Delete Appt from the Edit menu or press Ctrl+D. Schedule+ does not prompt you to verify the deletion. Instead, it immediately deletes the appointment. To restore a deleted appointment, choose the Undo Delete command from the Edit menu immediately after deleting the appointment.

Moving an appointment is equally easy. To move an appointment with the mouse, select it to make it active. Then, locate the cursor on the top line of the appointment's time block. This changes the cursor to an up-down arrow. Click on the top line of the time slot and drag the appointment into its new position.

To move an appointment with the menu, select the appointment, and then choose Move Appt from the Edit menu. Schedule+ displays a simple dialog box that you use to specify a new starting time and date. Set the new time using the provided spin controls, then choose OK.

To copy an appointment, first select it, and then choose Copy Appt from the Edit menu. This copies the appointment to the Clipboard. Next, select the starting time slot for your new appointment. Then, choose the Paste command from the Edit menu to paste the new appointment into position.

If you simply want to change the length of time allocated to an appointment, you do not need to use the Edit Appt command to do so. Instead, select the appointment, then place the cursor on the bottom line of its time slot. The cursor changes to an up-down arrow. Click on the bottom line and drag the ending time for the appointment to specify its new block of time.

Working with Recurring Appointments

Another type of appointment is the *recurring appointment*. These are appointments that happen on a regular basis. You may have a weekly staff meeting every Monday morning, lunch with the same group of people one day a week, or some other appointment that happens regularly. You can enter these appointments manually in Schedule+, but doing so over and over not only wastes time, but increases the chance you will forget to schedule it.

Schedule+ simplifies setting up recurring appointments by enabling you to specify them only once. Then, Schedule+ takes care of placing the appointment in your Appointment Book and optionally reminding you about the appointment.

To create a recurring appointment, choose the New **R**ecurring Appointment command from the Appoin**tm**ents menu, or press Ctrl+R. Either action displays the Recurring Appointment dialog box, which resembles the one you use to create single-event appointments.

The group box labeled This Appointment Occurs contains the appointment's frequency. By default, Schedule+ sets up recurring appointments weekly on the day and current time the appointment is created, but you can change this by choosing the **C**hange button. When you choose the **C**hange button, the Change Recurrence dialog box, which is shown in figure 30.14, appears.

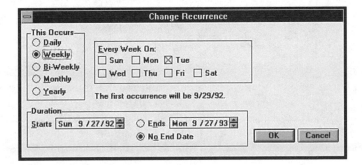

Figure 30.14
The Change Recurrence dialog box.

Use the radio button in the This Occurs group box to specify the frequency of the appointment. You can select from **D**aily, **W**eekly, **B**i-Weekly, **M**onthly, and **Y**early. When you select one of the radio buttons in the This Occurs group box, the group box to the right of your selection also changes to reflect the frequency you have selected. Figure 30.15 shows a composite of the different options available in the Change Recurrence dialog box according to your selected frequency.

If the **D**aily radio button is selected, your choices are simple. You can have the appointment occur every day, which includes Saturday and Sunday, or you can have it occur only on weekdays.

The **W**eekly or **B**i-Weekly radio buttons enable you to specify the day of the week on which the appointment is to recur. Check the check box beside the appropriate day.

Figure 30.15
Composite of
frequency settings
in the Change
Recurrence dialog
box.

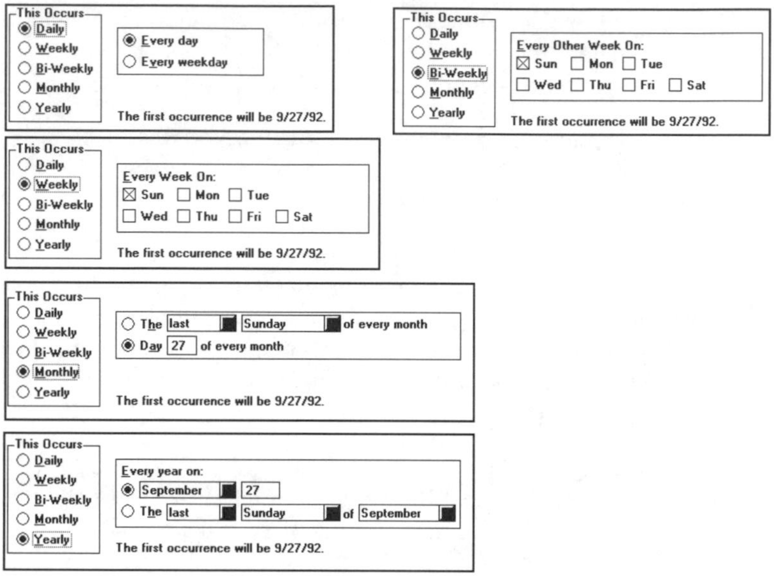

Select the Monthly radio button to mark the appointment so that it occurs on the first, second, third, fourth, or last occurrence of a given day in the month. If you have a meeting that regularly takes place on the second Tuesday of each month, use the drop-down lists in the Change Recurrence dialog box to set the option. You also can specify a date. You can set up an appointment, for example, to be scheduled on the 20th of each month.

The Yearly radio button enables you to specify the month and date on which the appointment will recur, such as September 23. As with regular monthly appointments, you also can associate the appointment with a weekday in the month, such as the third Friday in each September.

The Duration group box is used to set the time and duration of the recurring appointment. You can specify that the appointment continue to recur by choosing the No End Date radio button. You also can cause the recurring appointment to terminate by specifying a stop date with the Ends radio button and scroll list.

When your recurring appointment is configured properly, choose OK.

Editing Recurring Appointments

You can edit a single instance of a recurring appointment in the same way that you edit nonrecurring appointments. Select the appointment and choose Edit Appt from the Edit menu, or double-click on the appointment in the Appointment Book. Schedule+ then displays the Appointment dialog box, which you can use to change any of the properties of the appointment.

You also can copy, delete, move, and resize recurring appointments in exactly the same ways as described previously for non-recurring appointments.

Note that when you copy a recurring appointment to another time slot, it does not copy recurringly. In other words, only one copy of the appointment is added to the new time slot, not multiple copies.

To change the starting and ending times for a recurring appointment, or to change other global parameters, such as the appointment's description or reminder, choose Edit Recurring Appts from the Appointments menu. The Edit Recurring Appointments dialog box is shown in figure 30.16.

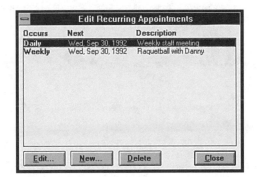

Figure 30.16
The Edit Recurring Appointments dialog box.

The Edit Recurring Appointments dialog box lists every recurring appointment. Select the appointment you want to edit, and then choose the Edit button. This displays the same Recurring Appointment dialog box that you use to create the appointment. Edit its properties as desired, and then choose OK to make the change. You return to the Edit Recurring Appointments dialog box, from which you can select other appointments and use the same procedure to edit them.

To delete a recurring appointment using the Edit Recurring Appointments dialog box, select the appointment and choose the Delete button. To create a new recurring appointment, choose the New button. When you are finished editing your recurring appointments, choose the Close button.

Creating Short or Overlapping Appointments

Although Schedule+ allocates a full 30-minute slot to an appointment by default, you can create shorter appointments of any duration. You also can create a number of appointments that share the same time slot.

To create a 15-minute appointment, choose the 30-minute block of time that contains the 15-minute appointment. Choose the <u>N</u>ew Appointment command from the Appointments menu or press Ctrl+N. In the Appointment dialog box, use the <u>S</u>tart and <u>E</u>nd spin control to change the ending or starting times to 15-minute increments. Click on the minutes portion of the time, then use the up and down scroll buttons to change the time.

If you create two 15-minute appointments that share the same 30-minute block, they both appear in the Appointment Book, side-by-side in the appropriate slot. The second 15-minute appointment displays its start time at the beginning of its description, as shown in figure 30.17.

Figure 30.17

Two 15-minute appointments sharing a time slot.

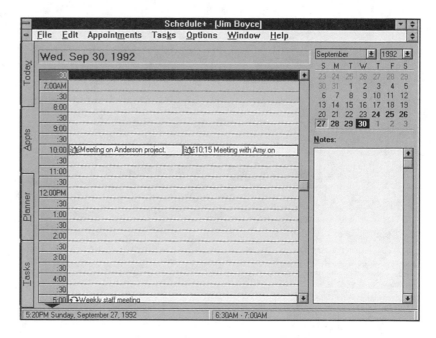

To create appointments of less than 15 minutes, just edit the start and end time manually to specify the duration of the appointment. Select the 30-minute block in which you want to place the appointment, then press Ctrl+N or choose <u>N</u>ew Appointment from the Appointments menu. In the Appointment dialog box, click on the minutes portion of the <u>S</u>tart spin control and enter (with the keyboard) the exact time for the start of the appointment, such as 8:<u>42</u>. Then, click on the minutes portion of the <u>E</u>nd spin control and enter the exact ending time.

You can add as many as 30 one-minute appointments in each half-hour time block, if necessary. Schedule+ automatically includes the start time in each appointment's description, as shown in figure 30.18.

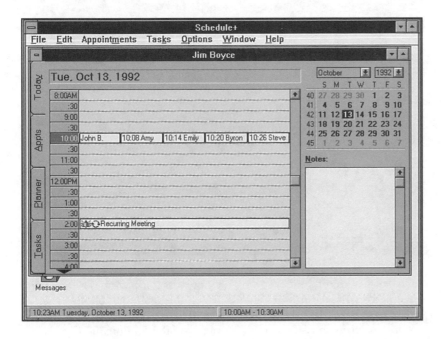

Figure 30.18

Five appointments in the Appointment Book.

Note that these three appointments only appear to be 10 minutes long. Schedule+ still considers them to be 30 minutes in length. You can change the reminder lead time for each appointment to notify you at a different time for each of the appointments.

In addition to maintaining appointments with Schedule+, you also can maintain a list of daily notes.

Using Daily Notes

You often will have items to add to your Appointment Book that are not associated with a specific time slot. These items are simply things you want to accomplish at some time during the day, or reminder notes for certain appointments. These notes appear in the Notes window of your Appointment Book.

To add a note, simply click in the Notes list and type the note. You can add as many notes as you want. Keep in mind, however, that these notes are not associated with any particular time slot on your schedule. As you switch the Appointment Book view to a different day, the Notes for the new display appear in the Notes list. If there are no notes for the day, the Notes list is empty.

Figure 30.19

A complex
appointment
group in the
Appointment
Book.

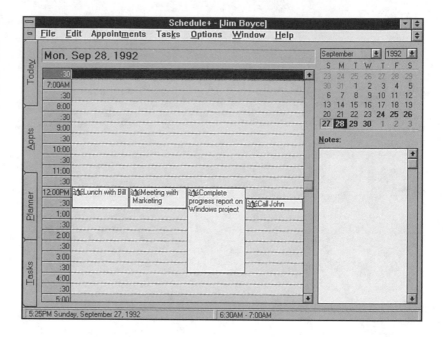

By default, Schedule+ displays a reminder showing the notes for the current day the first
time you start Schedule+ on that day. If you want to turn off this reminder, choose
Options, then General Options. Clear the Set Reminders for Notes check box in the
resulting General Options dialog box (this dialog box and its other options are discussed
in detail later in this chapter).

Scheduling appointments and maintaining notes are only two ways to use Schedule+. You
also might want to use Schedule+ to schedule meetings with other users.

Scheduling Meetings

The process of scheduling meetings with other users using Schedule+ is fairly simple. The
steps are as follows:

1. Choose the desired time slot for the meeting.

2. Select the prospective attendees from the list of Mail accounts in your WGPO.

3. Determine if the attendees are free to come at the selected time.

4. Choose a new time slot if a scheduling conflict exists with the other users.

5. Invite the prospective attendees to the meeting.

You can schedule a meeting through your Appointment Book or through the Planner. When you schedule a meeting through the Appointment Book, you cannot view the other users' free and busy times.

To request a meeting through the Appointment Book, select the time slot for the meeting. If you have already created an appointment for the meeting, use one of the methods described previously to edit the appointment. If you have not yet created the appointment, choose the New Appointment command from the Appointments menu or press Ctrl+N. This displays the Appointment dialog box.

Choose the Invite button to invite other users to attend the meeting. The Invite button displays the Select Attendees dialog box shown in figure 30.20.

Figure 30.20
The Select Attendees dialog box.

The Select Attendees dialog box resembles closely the Address dialog box that you use to select user addresses in Mail. By default, Schedule+ displays the entire Postoffice List of users. You can click on the Address Book button to choose your personal address book. You also can set your personal address book to be displayed as the default, just as you can in Mail.

Select from the list the users you want to invite to the meeting. Choose the Add button to add their names to the Attendees list at the bottom of the dialog box, or select the names and drag them into the Attendees list with the mouse. After you select the prospective attendees, choose OK to return to the Appointment dialog box. To request the meeting, choose OK.

When you choose OK, Schedule+ displays a dialog box you can use to create an invitation message for the meeting. The names of the prospective attendees appear in the To list. The description of the appointment appears in the Subject edit box. The date and time of the meeting appear below the subject.

Place the cursor in the message box and enter whatever message you want to send to each prospective attendant. If you want these users to respond to your invitation, check the Ask for **R**esponses check box. If you do not want them to reply, clear the check box.

To send the message to each user in the **T**o list, choose **S**end. If you do not want to send a message, choose Cancel. When you view the **A**ttendees list in the Appointment dialog box, a letter icon appears next to the names of any attendees to which you sent a message about the meeting. If you did not send a message to a particular attendant, no icon appears next to the name.

Scheduling Meetings with the Planner

An easier way to schedule meetings is to use the Planner, because it provides a visual picture of other users' free and busy times. Planner's visual calendar ensures that you can select a meeting time that fits into everyone else's schedules.

To schedule a meeting with the Planner, first make the Planner window active by clicking on **P**lanner in the Schedule+ window or by pressing Alt+P (see fig. 30.21).

Figure 30.21

The Planner window in Schedule+.

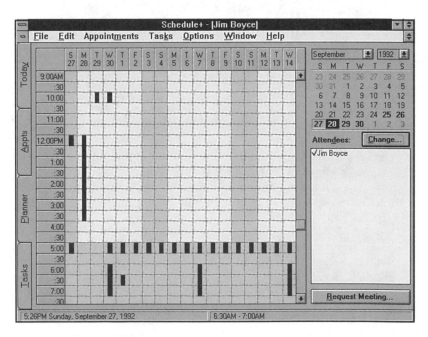

Your busy times appear in your Planner as colored bars. Select a time slot that offers enough time for the meeting. Then, choose the **C**hange button to select attendees for the meeting. The **C**hange button displays the same Select Attendees dialog box as described previously (see fig. 30.20). Choose from the list prospective attendees for the meeting, then choose **A**dd to add them to the list at the bottom of the dialog box. When all prospective attendees are selected, choose OK.

After you choose OK in the Select Attendees dialog box, Schedule+ overlays the schedules of the selected attendees onto your own schedule. Busy times are displayed in a different color from your own busy times. If you and another users' busy times coincide, the overlapping time slot shows as a combination of the two colors. By default, your busy times display in blue; other users' busy times display in gray. As you learn later in this chapter, you can change either color. Figure 30.22 shows other users' schedules overlaid to schedule a meeting.

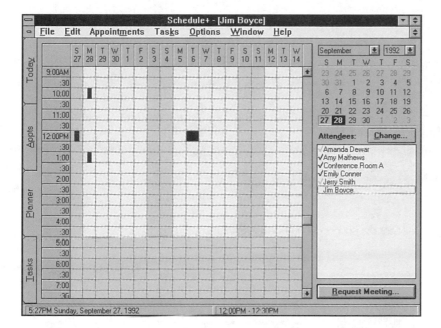

Figure 30.22
Other users' schedules overlaid in the Planner.

To turn off the display of a specific users' busy times, click on the user's name in the Attendees list. The check beside the user's name disappears. To turn it back on, click on the name again. A red X appears beside the name of any users whose schedules conflict with the time you have selected for the meeting. To view one attendant's schedule, double-click on the attendant's name.

To choose a different meeting time, simply choose the appropriate time slot with the mouse or cursor. If you want to have Schedule+ automatically select a time when all other users are available, choose Auto-Pick from the Appointments menu. Schedule+ then searches the schedule for the next possible time slot that is free for all selected attendees.

When you have identified a time for the meeting, choose the Request Meeting button. The Send Request dialog box appears, as shown in figure 30.23, with the list of addressees in the To field. Enter the subject for the meeting and a message. If you want the attendees to respond to your meeting request message, leave the Ask for Responses check box checked.

Figure 30.23
The Send Request
dialog box.

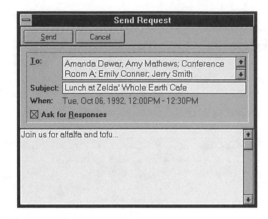

When your message is ready, choose the <u>S</u>end button to send it to every user in the <u>T</u>o list.

Responding to Meeting Requests

When someone else schedules a meeting with you, they generally send you a message requesting that you attend, as described in the previous section. These messages appear in your Schedule+ Messages window. They also appear in your Inbox in Mail, as shown in figure 30.24.

Figure 30.24
Meeting requests
appear in
Schedule+ and
Mail.

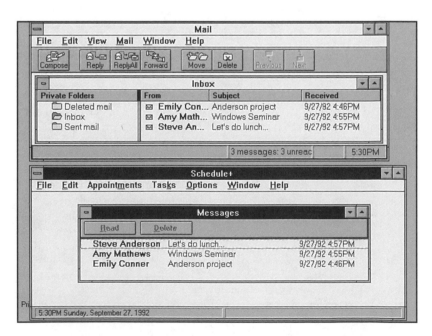

To view your messages in Schedule+, double-click on the Messages icon in the Schedule+ window or choose the **M**essages command in the **W**indow menu. To view a meeting request in Mail, open it as you would any other Mail message. Both Mail and Schedule+ recognize the meeting request as a special type of message and display the Meeting Request dialog box shown in figure 30.25.

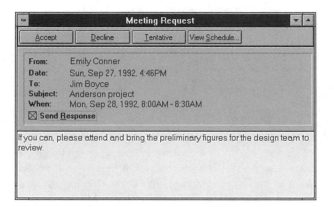

Figure 30.25
The Meeting Request dialog box in Mail and Schedule+.

To determine if the meeting conflicts with your schedule, choose the View **S**chedule button. If you select View **S**chedule in Schedule+, your Appointment Book appears. If you choose the View **S**chedule button in Mail and Schedule+ is running, focus switches to Schedule+ and the Appointment Book appears. If Schedule+ is not running, Mail starts Schedule+ and the Appointment Book appears in it.

When the Appointment Book appears, the requested meeting time is highlighted, giving you a visual indicator of whether the meeting time conflicts with your schedule. Return to the Meeting Request dialog box to accept or decline the invitation, or to schedule it as a tentative appointment. Choose either the **A**ccept, **D**ecline, or **T**entative buttons.

If you choose the **A**ccept button, Schedule+ books the meeting in your Appointment Book. If a response was requested by the person booking the meeting, Schedule+ (or Mail) then displays a Send Response dialog box like the one shown in figure 30.26, which you can use to respond to the invitation. When your message is ready, choose the **S**end button to send it. Note that Schedule+ does not remove the meeting request message from your Messages window.

If you choose the **D**ecline button, the parameters in the Send Response dialog box are a little different, indicating that you will not be attending the meeting. Similar to a meeting request, you can add a short note to your response before sending it.

When you decline a meeting, Schedule+ does not alter your schedule in any way, nor does it remove the request message from your Messages window. You can select a meeting request message that you have previously declined and change your response. If you decline the meeting and then decide you can attend, you can send a new reply accepting the meeting. Schedule+ then books the meeting in your Appointment Book.

Figure 30.26
The Send
Response dialog
box.

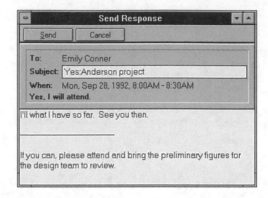

If you choose the <u>T</u>entative button rather than <u>A</u>ccept or <u>D</u>ecline, Schedule+ books the appointment in your Appointment Book as being tentative. If a response was requested, you are prompted to create a reply, as you are when accepting or declining. When you book a tentative appointment, other users who view your schedule still see that time as being available. If you want to make the appointment firm so that its time slot appears as busy, edit the appointment as described earlier in this chapter (double-click on it in the Appointment Book) and clear the Tentati<u>v</u>e check box.

Keeping Track of Meeting Requests

Note that when a meeting request comes in while you are running Schedule+, you do not receive an audible indicator that the request has arrived. If the Messages window is open, the message appears in its list. If the Messages window is minimized, however, a red arrow appears in the icon as a visual indicator that a new message has arrived.

If Mail has been configured to provide an audible alarm when new messages arrive and you receive a meeting request from another user, an audible indicator sounds. To learn how to set up this Mail feature, see Chapter 29.

To ensure that you know of each meeting request, either check the Messages icon in Schedule+, leave the Messages window open so that you can see new messages as they are added, or leave Mail running all the time on your workstation.

Working with an Assistant or Other Users

If you have a secretary, it is likely that he or she has the responsibility of maintaining at least a part of your schedule. In Schedule+, you can assign another user as your assistant.

The assistant can modify and maintain your schedule, respond to meeting requests, and schedule meetings on your behalf. Appointments that you set up as private, however, cannot be viewed by your assistant.

Working with (or as) an Assistant

To identify another person as your Schedule+ assistant, choose Options, then Set Access Privileges. The Set Access Privileges dialog box appears as shown in figure 30.27. The Users list displays the names of any users who have access privileges to your schedule other than the default setting. When you first start using Schedule+, only the Default setting appears in the Users list, and the Default privilege is set to View. This means that other users can overlay your schedule on their own to view your free times and busy times.

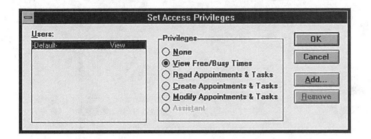

Figure 30.27

The Set Access Privileges dialog box.

To change the default access privileges for users who are not specifically listed in the Users list, make sure Default is selected in the list, then choose one of the radio buttons in the Privileges group box. The following list summarizes the access privileges that these radio buttons control:

- ✔ **None.** Other users cannot access your schedule at all. They cannot overlay your schedule on their own to view your free times and busy times.

- ✔ **View Free/Busy Times.** Other users can overlay your schedule on their own to view your free times and busy times.

- ✔ **Read Appointments and Tasks.** Other users can open your schedule and view any nonprivate appointments and tasks in it. They cannot create new appointments or tasks, or modify existing ones.

- ✔ **Create Appointments and Tasks.** Other users can view your schedule and create new appointments for you. They also can modify and delete any appointments that they have created.

- ✔ **Modify Appointments and Tasks.** Other users can view, create, and modify any appointments and tasks in your schedule, except those you mark as private.

✔ **Assistant.** A user designated as your assistant has the same privileges as in
Modify Appointments and Tasks. In addition, your assistant receives meeting
requests on your behalf, can respond to meeting requests, and books meetings for
you.

To designate a user as your assistant, or provide other users with different access privileges
for your account, you first must add the user's name to the Users list. If the user's name is
not already listed in the Users list, choose the Add button. This displays the Add Users
dialog box, which resembles the other dialog boxes you use in Schedule+ and Mail to
select users from the Postoffice Directory or your Personal Address Book. The Add Users
dialog box is shown in figure 30.28.

Figure 30.28
The Add Users
dialog box.

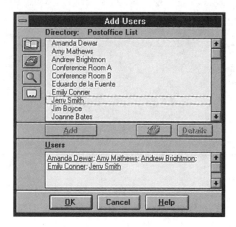

Select from the directory list the user whom you want to assign as your Assistant, then
choose the Add button or drag the name into the Users list. Next, choose OK. The name
of the user you select then appears in the Users list in the Set Access Privileges dialog box.
Select the user to whom you want to assign Assistant privileges, then choose the Assistant
radio button. The description beside the user's name in the Users list changes to read
Assistant.

When someone attempts to schedule a meeting with you, the meeting request is sent to
both you and your assistant. Either you or your assistant can reply to the message. If your
assistant accepts the meeting time, your schedule is updated automatically to include the
new appointment. When you later view the Meeting Request, it indicates that the meeting
has already been added to your schedule.

If you are someone else's assistant (assume the person is your supervisor) and you want to
book a meeting for him or her, you use the same process you normally use for a meeting.
Select the desired time, then choose the prospective attendees, including your supervisor.
Choose the Request Meeting button to book the meeting. Schedule+ then asks
if you want to schedule the appointment for your supervisor. If you choose Yes, the

appointment is added to this person's appointment book. If you choose <u>N</u>o, the meeting request is sent to both you and your supervisor for later response. The appointment is not scheduled in your supervisor's Appointment Book.

Modifying Your Supervisor's Schedule

When you are given Assistant status for someone else's schedule, you can load, view, and modify that schedule. To load another user's schedule, choose <u>F</u>ile, then choose <u>O</u>pen Other's Appt Book. Schedule+ displays the directory list. Choose the users whose schedules you want to display, then choose <u>A</u>dd or drag them to the <u>U</u>sers list. Choose <u>O</u>K to open the schedules.

The additional schedules appear in their own windows, as shown in figure 30.29. To view a schedule, create new appointments, or modify existing appointments, choose the appropriate schedule window, then manipulate the schedule as you would your own. When you close another person's schedule window, it is removed from your Schedule+ window (closing your own schedule just minimizes it).

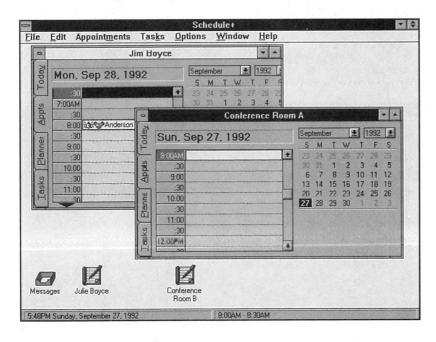

Figure 30.29
Additional schedules displayed in Schedule+.

Working with Other Users

You can allow other users to load, view, and modify your schedule on their workstations by granting them privileges. You also can load, view, and modify another user's schedule if you have the necessary access privileges.

To allow users other than your assistant to view or modify your schedule, use the same procedure described previously for adding an assistant. Instead of giving these other users Assistant privileges, choose the appropriate privilege from the Privileges group box. These other users then will be able to access your schedule to the degree provided by their privilege level.

Note that if you give a specific user the same access privilege as the Default privilege, the user's name disappears from the Users list because the user will have the same level of access anyway.

When you have access to another user's schedule as an Assistant or with specific privileges, you also have access to that user's Task List. The Task List stores a list of dated, prioritized tasks.

Using the Task List

In Schedule+, you can use your Task List to keep track of tasks you need to work on over a period of time. Common tasks include completing reports, making important phone calls, beginning new projects, and writing memos and letters. Figure 30.30 shows the Task List in Schedule+.

Figure 30.30
The Task List window in Schedule+.

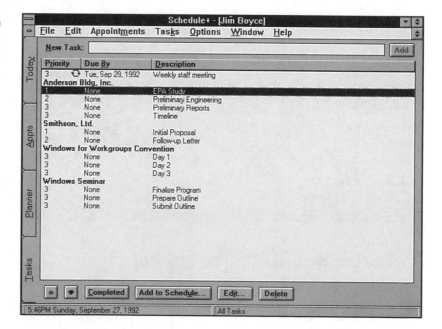

V

To display the Task List, click on the Tasks tab or press Alt+T. Uncompleted tasks appear as a list in the Task List. The information that appears includes the task's priority, its due date, and a description. You can sort the Task List by simply clicking on one of three key buttons at the top of the Task List. These buttons are labeled Priority, Due By, and Description.

Although you do not need to assign a task to a specific project, doing so adds an additional layer of organization to your Task List. To create a new project name, choose Tasks, then New Project. The Project dialog box, shown in figure 30.31, appears. Enter the description of the project in the Name edit box. If you want to make the project and all tasks in it private, check the Private check box. Tasks and projects that are private cannot be viewed by other users, even if they have Modify or Assistant access privileges to your schedule. A key icon appears beside private project descriptions to indicate that it is locked from view by other users.

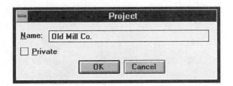

Figure 30.31
The Project dialog box is used to create new projects.

Use the New Project command to create as many projects as you need. These project names then appear in the Task List. Any tasks that you assign to a specific project appear under that project's description.

To create new tasks, choose Tasks, then New Task, or press Ctrl+T. Either action displays the Task dialog box shown in figure 30.32.

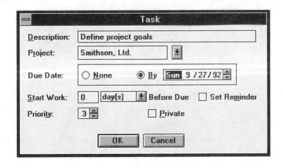

Figure 30.32
The Task dialog box is used to create and modify tasks.

Enter a description for the task in the Description field. This is the description that appears in the Task List for the task. To assign the task to an existing project, choose the Project combo box and choose the desired project name. If the project does not yet exist, highlight any existing entry in the Project combo box, then enter the description for the new project. When you finish creating the task, Schedule+ creates the new project. To assign the task to no specific project, choose <None> from the Project list.

Next, set the due date for the task. To assign no due date to the task, choose the <u>N</u>one radio button in the Due Date group box. To assign a specific due date to the task, choose the <u>B</u>y radio button, then use the date spin control to select the task's due date.

When you choose the <u>B</u>y radio button, the <u>S</u>tart Work control becomes available. This enables you to specify a date when the task will become active and enables you to set a reminder for when to begin working on the project.

The Priority spin button enables you to assign a priority level to the task. You can use the numbers one through nine and letters A through Z as priority indicators. In the Task List you can then sort your pending tasks by priority.

The <u>P</u>rivate check box controls whether a task is private. Private tasks cannot be viewed by other users.

When your new task is configured the way you want it, choose OK. The task then appears under its project name (if any) in the Task List.

Note that you can create tasks when viewing the Appointment Book or Planner. Select the New <u>T</u>ask command or press Ctrl+T when either view is displayed to open the Task dialog box.

Modifying Tasks

To modify a task, select it in the Task List, then choose the Edit button to display the Task dialog box for the task. Optionally, you can double-click on a task or press Enter when it is selected to display the Task dialog box.

Adding Tasks to Your Schedule

To add a task to your schedule, select the task, then choose the Add to Schedule button. Schedule+ then displays the Choose Time dialog box shown in figure 30.33 Select the date and time you want to assign to the task, then choose OK. For short tasks, such as writing a memo or making a phone call, the appointment date and time generally is when you execute the task. For longer tasks, the date and time is generally when you start working on the task.

Tasks that you add to your schedule appear in your Appointment Book the same as other scheduled appointments. The task name appears in the appointment description, followed by the name of the project. If you have set a reminder, the reminder icon also appears beside the appointment description.

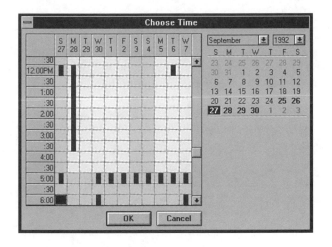

Figure 30.33
The Choose Time
dialog box.

Networking and Windows

Changing Task Priority

You can click on the up or down arrow buttons at the bottom of the Task List to change the priority of a task. The priority of the selected task moves up one priority level when you click on the up arrow, and down a priority level when you click on the down arrow.

Completing Tasks

To mark a task as completed, select the task, then click on the Completed button or press Alt+C. Schedule+ removes the task from your task list and places a note in your appointment book indicating that the task was completed on the current date (the date when you mark the task as completed).

Deleting a Task

To delete a task, select it from the Task List, then choose the Delete button. Schedule+ removes the task from your Task List. To delete a project, select the project name from the Task List, then choose Delete. If the project has any uncompleted tasks still listed in the Task List, Schedule+ asks you if you want to delete all the remaining tasks associated with the project. Choose Yes to delete the tasks, or No to cancel the command.

Sorting the Task List

You can display the Task List in one of four ways. Each of these display options is controlled from the Tasks menu. If the View by Project menu item is selected from the Tasks menu, Schedule+ displays your pending task the way tasks are organized in the list. You also can set these sort display options by clicking on the Priority, Due By, and Description buttons at the top of the Task List.

Setting Schedule+ Options

In addition to setting access privileges to your schedule for other users, you can set other options that control the way Schedule+ appears and functions. To change your password, for example, choose Options, then Change Password. Schedule+ prompts you to enter your current password, then enter and confirm your new password.

Choose Display from the Options menu to set colors for your Schedule+ display. This opens the Display dialog box shown in figure 30.34.

Figure 30.34
The Display dialog box controls the display options in Schedule+.

The following list explains the options you can set in the Display dialog box:

✔ **Appointment Book Background.** Sets the background color of your Appointment Book.

✔ **Planner Background.** Sets the background color of the Planner window.

✔ **Planner User.** Sets the color used to display your appointments in the Planner window.

✔ **Planner Others.** Sets the color used to display other users' appointments when you overlay their schedules in your Planner window.

✔ **Page Background.** Sets the background color of the Schedule+ window.

✔ **Font Size.** Specifies the size of font used for the time and day/date column and row headers in the Planner and Appointment Book.

The Options menu also includes a number of general options. To set general Schedule+ options, choose Options, then General Options. This displays the General Options dialog box shown in figure 30.35.

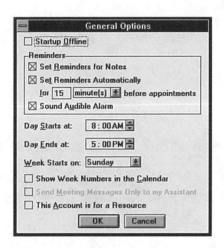

Figure 30.35
The General
Options dialog
box.

The Startup Offline check box controls whether Schedule+ starts up online or offline by default. Check this check box if you want Schedule+ to start offline automatically. Note that you can switch between online and offline status using the Work Offline and Work Online commands in the File menu.

The Reminders group box in the General Options dialog box controls the way reminders are generated by Schedule+. The Set Reminders for Notes check box, when checked, causes Schedule+ to generate a reminder showing the current day's notes the first time you start Schedule+ during the current day.

The check box labeled Set Reminders Automatically controls whether Schedule+ automatically includes a reminder for each appointment you create. You can override this setting individually for each appointment by clearing the Set Reminder check box in the Appointment dialog box when you create the appointment. The Set Reminders Automatically check box in the General Options dialog box also controls the global default time for reminders.

The check box labeled Sound Audible Alarm controls whether Schedule+ plays an audible alarm when it displays a reminder message. If you do not want Schedule+ to issue an audible alarm, clear this check box.

Two spin controls in the General Options dialog box—Day Starts at and Day Ends at—set the starting and ending time for your average work day. These settings change the colors of time slots displayed in the Planner. 30-minute blocks of time that fall within the two times specified by these two spin controls appear in a different color from time blocks outside your regular work day. By default, the day starts at 8:00 a.m. and ends at 5:00 p.m.

The list box labeled Week Starts On enables you to specify which day of the week represents the start of your work week. The default value is Sunday. Select a different day to control which day is displayed first (at the left-most column) in the Planner. It does not change the five-day period identified as your work week, which runs from Monday through Friday.

The check box labeled Show Week Numbers in the Calendar determines whether Schedule+ includes the week number (relative to the year) at the left of the calendar in the display. Figure 30.36 shows week numbers displayed beside the calendar.

Figure 30.36
Week numbers
displayed in the
calendar.

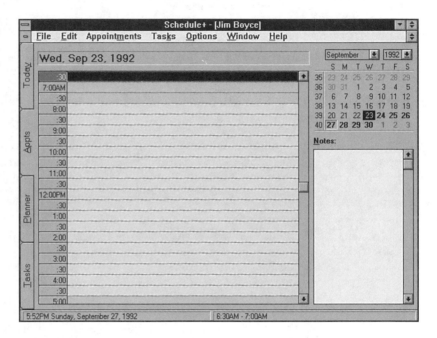

The check box labeled This Account is for a Resource, when checked, specifies that the Schedule+ account you are currently working with is for a resource such as a conference room or item of equipment. Scheduling resources is examined in the next section of this chapter.

The check box labeled Send Meeting Messages Only to My Assistant is dimmed by default unless you have assigned another user as your Schedule+ assistant. If you have an assistant, you can check this check box to have Schedule+ send meeting request messages only to your assistant. If this option is checked, you do not receive meeting request messages. You instead rely on your assistant to reply to the meeting requests for you.

Scheduling Facilities

In Schedule+, *resources* are support items like conference rooms and special equipment you might need for a meeting, such as VCRs, projection systems, and even computers. You can use Schedule+ to create schedules for these resources.

Creating a Resource Schedule

To create a schedule for a resource, first create a Mail account for the resource. If you are not the post office manager for your WGPO, you must have the WGPO post office manager create the account for you. Choose a name for the resource that matches its physical use, such as Conference Room A, VCR #1, or Demo Computer. Afterward, choose a Mail account name that you can easily associate with the resource, such as confa, for Conference Room A. This helps you remember the name of a resource you must manage.

Next, start Schedule+ on any workstation and sign in to the Mail system using the resource's mail account and password. If this is the first time you have worked with the resource's schedule, Schedule+ prompts you to verify that this is the first time you have used Schedule+ for the resource on the current workstation. Choose <u>Y</u>es to create a schedule file for the resource on your workstation.

If you choose <u>N</u>o, Schedule+ displays the Find Local File dialog box shown in figure 30.37, which you can use to locate the resource's calendar file. The resource's calendar file name matches its Mail account name, and has the file extension CAL. Locate the resource's schedule file and choose OK. If no local schedule file for the resource exists, choose N<u>e</u>w to create a new one.

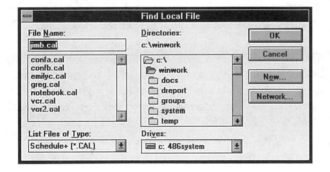

Figure 30.37
The Find Local File dialog box.

To associate the schedule with a resource, choose <u>O</u>ptions, then <u>G</u>eneral Options to display the General Options dialog box (refer to figure 30.35). Check the check box labeled This <u>A</u>ccount is for a Resource.

Next, determine if another user is to serve as an assistant for this resource. Generally, you will want to assign someone as a resource assistant to respond to scheduling requests for the resource. Close the General Options dialog box by choosing OK, then choose <u>O</u>ptions and Set <u>A</u>ccess Privileges. Use the <u>A</u>dd button to add the new assistant's name to the <u>U</u>sers list. Then, in the Set Access Privileges dialog box, select the assistant's name and choose the Assi<u>s</u>tant radio button.

Note that by default, a resource's access privileges are set to <u>C</u>reate Appointments and Tasks. This enables other users to load the resource's schedule into Schedule+ and to book meetings. If you prefer to have the resource's assistant be the only person who can schedule the resource, change the Default privilege to View Free/Busy Times. This enables other users to overlay the resource's schedule on their own to locate a time when the resource is free, but they cannot actually schedule the appointment for the resource.

You might want to set up a user as an assistant for the resource's schedule, but still enable other users to schedule appointments directly. The assistant in such cases may be responsible for providing or maintaining the resource, but not actually scheduling appointments for it. For example, if you are scheduling a piece of equipment for a meeting and need an operator for the equipment, set up the operator as the resource's assistant. This ensures that the assistant receives meeting request messages for the resource.

The last step in setting up a resource is to turn off meeting requests to the resource's account because the resource has an assistant who manages its schedule. Meeting requests to the resource's account also are of little use because other users can create and modify appointments for the resource.

To turn off messages to the resource's account, choose Options, then General Options to display the General Options dialog box. Check the check box labeled Send Meeting Messages Only to My Assistant. Then choose OK.

Scheduling a Resource Appointment

Although it may seem strange at first, you schedule a resource the same way you schedule a meeting with another user—you invite the resource to attend the meeting, even if the meeting is *in* the resource. Because the resource's schedule is the same as any user's schedule, you can overlay the resource's schedule over your own to locate a time slot when the resource is available. If you need to use more than one resource for a meeting, such as the VCR #1 and Demo Notebook Computer in Conference Room A, invite all these resources to the meeting.

Scheduling a Resource Indirectly

To schedule an appointment for a resource when you are not its assistant, or when you do not have the privileges necessary to schedule appointments directly for the resource, start Schedule+ and sign in under your own Mail account. Display the Planner window and locate the time and date on which you want to schedule the meeting. Choose the Change button to include the needed resources in the Attendees list. When you return to the Planner window, these resources' schedules are overlaid on your own, enabling you to locate a time when all the resources are available.

Identify a time slot when all the resources and other attendees are available. If necessary, use the Auto-Pick command to locate the next available time slot. After you identify the time for the meeting, choose the Request Meeting button and issue the meeting request as you would for any other meeting. The resource's assistant receives a copy of your meeting request automatically.

Scheduling a Resource Directly

If you have the necessary access privileges for a resource, you can schedule it yourself without going through the resource's assistant. To do so, choose File and Open Other's Appt Book. Select the resource from the directory, choose Add to place the resource name in the Users list, then choose OK. If you want to schedule more than one resource, add them all to the Users list before choosing OK.

When you choose OK, the schedules for the resources in the Users list appear on your display. If you have the necessary privileges, you can schedule appointments for the resources just as you do for your own schedule.

Printing Your Task List and Schedule

If you have a notebook computer that you carry with you on trips, you probably keep a copy of your schedule on it. You can use Schedule+ to view and manipulate your notebook's existing schedule. If you use a paper schedule book and planner, you may find it useful to print your schedule and task list from Schedule+ to be used with your schedule book.

To print your schedule or task list, choose File, then Print. The Print dialog box appears as shown in figure 30.38.

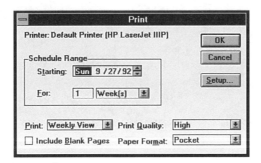

Figure 30.38
The Print dialog box in Schedule+.

Use the controls in the Schedule Range group box to define the starting date for your printed output and the For controls to define the range of time to include in the print-out.

The Print list box offers five options for the type of view to print. These options are illustrated in figures 30.39 through 30.43

Select the desired output option from the Print drop-down list. Note that you still must use the Schedule Range controls to define how much information will be included in the printout.

The check box labeled Include <u>B</u>lank Pages controls whether Schedule+ prints pages in the Daily, Weekly, and Monthly Views that have no appointments scheduled in them. To include these blank pages in the printout, check this box.

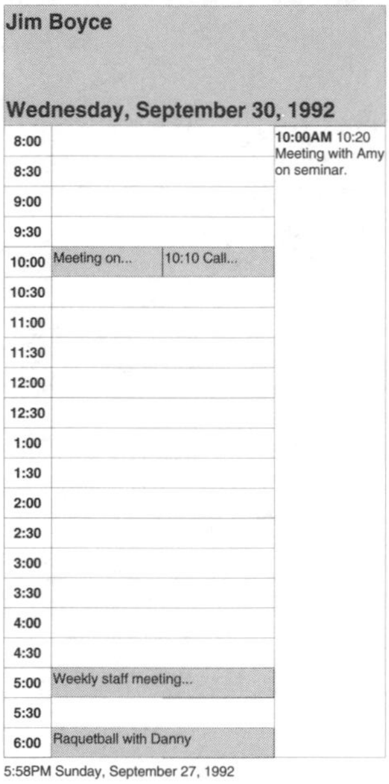

Figure 30.39
A Daily View.

Jim Boyce	
Wednesday, September 30, 1992	

			10:00AM 10:20 Meeting with Amy on seminar.
8:00			
8:30			
9:00			
9:30			
10:00	Meeting on...	10:10 Call...	
10:30			
11:00			
11:30			
12:00			
12:30			
1:00			
1:30			
2:00			
2:30			
3:00			
3:30			
4:00			
4:30			
5:00	Weekly staff meeting...		
5:30			
6:00	Raquetball with Danny		

5:58PM Sunday, September 27, 1992

Figure 30.40
A Weekly View.

9/27/92						Jim Boyce	
	Sun	Mon	Tue	Wed	Thu	Fri	Sat
8:00		And...					
8:30							
9:00							
9:30							
10:00			Issu...	Me...			
10:30							
11:00							
11:30							
12:00	Lun...	Lunch with...					
12:30							
1:00							
1:30							
2:00							
2:30							
3:00							
3:30							
4:00							
4:30							
5:00	5:1...			We...	We...	We...	Wee...
5:30							
6:00				Raq...			
More		12:00P M M... 12:00 Com... 12:30		10:00A M 10:1 0. 10:00 1 0:20 Meet...	6:30P M s... 6:30 S etup meet...		9:00PM hubba
Notes:							

5:59PM Sunday, September 27, 1992

6:00PM Sunday, September 27, 1992

Figure 30.41
A Monthly View.

Sep 28 - Oct 4, 1992   **Jim Boyce**

Monday, September 28, 1992
8:00AM-8:30AM	Anderson project
12:00PM-1:00PM	Lunch with Bill
12:00-1:00	Meeting with Marketing
12:00-4:00	Complete progress report on Windows project
12:30-1:00	Call John about contracts.

Tuesday, September 29, 1992
10:00AM-10:30AM	Issue memo about company picnic.

Wednesday, September 30, 1992
10:00AM-10:30AM	Meeting on Anderson project.
10:00-10:30	10:10 Call Danny to cancel
10:00-10:30	10:20 Meeting with Amy on seminar.
5:00PM-5:30PM	Weekly staff meeting
6:00-7:30	Raquetball with Danny

Thursday, October 01, 1992
5:00PM-5:30PM	Weekly staff meeting
6:30-7:00	setup meeting
6:30-7:00	Setup meeting 2

Friday, October 02, 1992
5:00PM-5:30PM	Weekly staff meeting

Saturday, October 03, 1992
5:00PM-5:30PM	Weekly staff meeting
9:00-9:30	hubba

Sunday, October 04, 1992
5:00PM-5:30PM	Weekly staff meeting

6:00PM Sunday, September 27, 1992

Figure 30.42
A Text View.

Task List   **Jim Boyce**

3	Tue, Sep 29, 1992	Weekly staff meeting

Anderson Bldg, Inc.

1	None	EPA Study
2	None	Preliminary Engineering
3	None	Preliminary Reports
3	None	Timeline

Smithson, Ltd.

1	None	Initial Proposal
2	None	Follow-up Letter
3	Sun, Sep 27, 1992	Define project goals

Windows for Workgroups Convention

3	None	Day 1
3	None	Day 2
3	None	Day 3

Windows Seminar

3	None	Finalize Program
3	None	Prepare Outline
3	None	Submit Outline

6:01PM Sunday, September 27, 1992

The Print Quality drop-down list enables you to choose the quality of the printed output. Selections include High, Medium, Low, and Draft.

The Paper Format drop-down list provides three choices for determining the size of the printed output. The choices include Standard, Junior, and Pocket. The only difference among these options is the size at which the reports print. Choose the size that fits your schedule book.

When your print options are set correctly, choose OK to start the print job.

Chapter Snapshot

Although Windows NT has been adopted somewhat slowly, NT and NT Advanced Server are gaining momentum in distributed network environments. Windows for Workgroups integrates very well with Windows NT. This chapter examines some of the issues involved in integrating Windows for Workgroups with Windows NT and Windows NT Advanced Server, including the following issues:

If you are not very familiar with Windows NT, refer to Chapter 27, "Understanding Windows NT," which provides an overview of the NT and NT Advanced Server operating systems. If you are interested in an overview of remote access services from a Windows for Workgroups perspective, refer to Chapter 34, "Using Remote Access Services."

31

CHAPTER

Integrating Windows and Windows NT

The Windows NT operating system offers many advantages over other operating environments. These advantages include distributed processing, advanced security, support for remote access, and central administration. Because of NT's disk and memory requirements, NT often is not a good choice as a user environment except in vertical applications requiring the processing power that NT provides (such as CAD and application development).

Windows for Workgroups, however, is an excellent general user operating environment for many reasons. Windows for Workgroups 3.11 offers improvements in disk and network performance not available in Windows 3.11. Its peer-to-peer and workgroup components make it a good environment for many businesses. Even so, many companies require more extensive server capabilities than Windows for Workgroups can provide. Security also is a concern with many users. Although it offers good security, the nature of peer-to-peer networking makes Windows for Workgroups a poor choice in situations where security is critical.

For this reason, many companies have opted to install Windows NT and NT Advanced Server on their primary servers to provide data and applications security. Windows for Workgroups is a good choice as a user environment to integrate with NT because of its tight integration with the Windows interface, its support for the same protocols supported by NT, and its built-in features for integrating in NT server environments.

Understanding Protocol Support Under NT

The primary issue making Windows for Workgroups 3.11 a good choice for a user environment in an NT server environment is the fact that Windows for Workgroups, NT, NT Advanced Server, and the Workgroup Add-on for MS-DOS (the MS-DOS networking client) all use the same set of network protocols. For this reason, integrating these systems in a distributed network requires very little effort and virtually no configuration.

In addition, these four systems all share the same logical structure for sharing resources— shared file and printer resources appear the same under Windows for Workgroups as they do under NT (see figs. 31.1 and 31.2).

Figure 31.1
A remote shared resource viewed in NT.

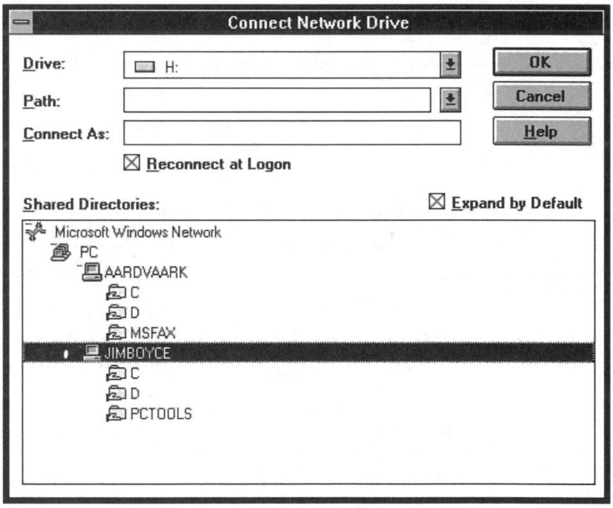

Even though Windows for Workgroups and NT share the same default protocols, other options exist for choosing a protocol. By default, the NetBEUI protocol is installed during setup for Windows for Workgroups, NT, and NT Advanced Server. This means that no additional configuration requirements are needed to enable these environments to interact on the network. This is a good protocol choice in situations where Windows for Workgroups and NT are the only operating environments on the network.

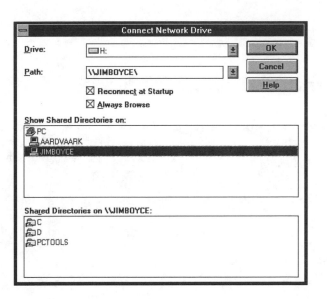

Figure 31.2
A remote shared resource viewed in Windows for Workgroups.

In addition to NetBEUI, both Windows for Workgroups and NT support the IPX/SPX with NetBIOS protocol (which is examined in Chapter 32, "Integrating Windows and Novell NetWare"). The IPX/SPX protocol is a good choice if you want workstations on the network to communicate through an IPX router, such as a Novell NetWare server. The support for NetBIOS also enables you to support applications that rely on NetBIOS, such as Lotus Notes.

The choice of a protocol for Windows for Workgroups under NT essentially revolves around one consideration: whether the network must provide communication with other environments such as Novell NetWare or UNIX. If the network consists only of Windows for Workgroups and NT environments, the native NetBEUI support is the best choice. If you are integrating these two environments with NetWare servers, add support for IPX/SPX. For integration with UNIX systems, add support for TCP/IP protocol.

The IPX/SPX protocol and NetBIOS issues are examined in Chapters 32, "Integrating Windows and Novell NetWare," and 33, "Using Multiple Protocols." The TCP/IP protocol is examined in Chapter 33.

Sharing Resources between WFWG and NT Nodes

Windows for Workgroups nodes can share their disk and printer resources, making them available to other users on the network. Chapter 28, "Sharing Resources in Windows," explains ways you can share these types of resources on a Windows for Workgroups node. In addition, NT nodes can share their disk and printer resources in much the same way.

This makes it possible for Windows for Workgroups nodes to access resources on NT nodes and vice versa.

Sharing Directories on an NT Node

To share directories on an NT node, your user account must have the necessary permission to do so. By default, members of the Administrators group and the Power Users group can share disk and printer resources. The first step is to ensure that your user account has those privileges. If you do not have the necessary privileges, consult your network administrator for help.

To share a disk resource on an NT node, open File Manager and choose the directory to be shared from the directory tree window. Choose Disk, then Share As (see fig. 31.3), or click on the Share As button from File Manager's toolbar. The New Share dialog box then appears, as shown in figure 31.4.

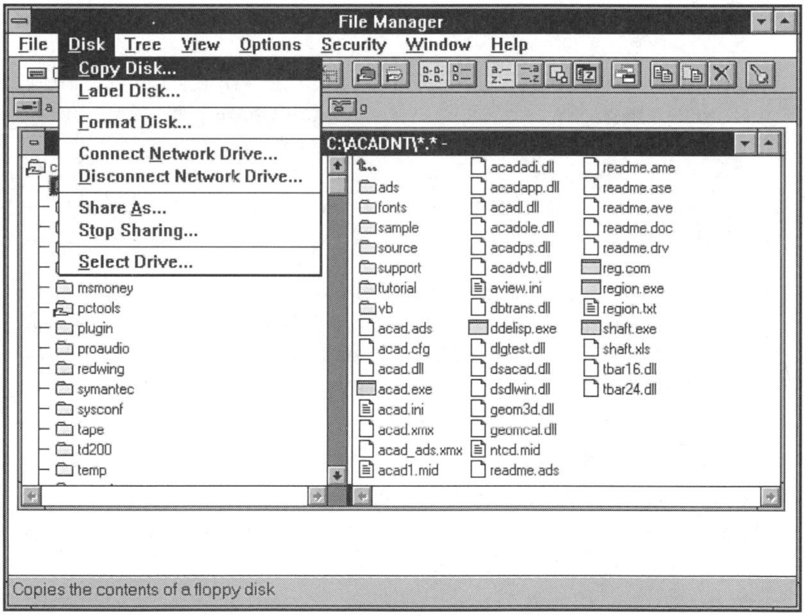

Figure 31.3
The Disk menu in File Manager.

The Share Name edit box defines the name by which the shared resource is seen by other users on the network. The Share Name edit box automatically contains the name of the selected directory; if you prefer, you can change the name. The Path edit box by default contains the path to the selected directory. If you have made a mistake by choosing the wrong directory, type the correct directory path in the Path edit box.

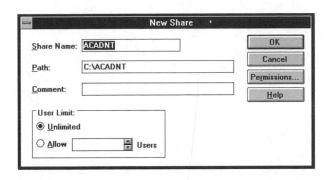

Figure 31.4
The New Share dialog box.

Networking and Windows

The controls in the User Limit group box determine the number of users who can access the shared directory at any one time. If you choose the Unlimited option button, an unlimited number of users can be connected to the shared directory at the same time. You can choose the Allow option button and use the corresponding spin control to set a specific limit on the maximum number of users who can be connected to the shared directory at one time.

To set access permissions on the shared directory, choose the Permissions button. This displays the Access Through Share Permissions dialog box shown in figure 31.5.

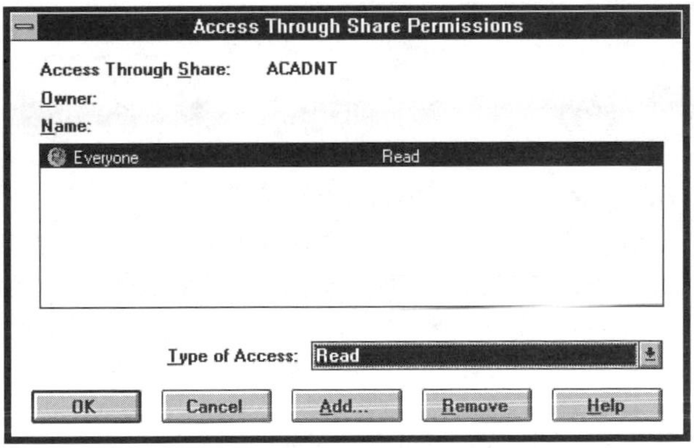

Figure 31.5
The Access Through Share Permissions dialog box.

The Name list box contains a list of all the groups to which you can assign access privileges in the shared directory. To modify the list of groups that can access the shared directory, choose the Add button to display the Add Users and Groups dialog box shown in figure 31.6. Use the controls provided by this dialog box to add or remove groups from the list and to view the names of users who are members of specific groups. Select a group name and choose the Add button to add the group to the list of users who are able to access the shared directory. When you have selected all the groups and users you want to have access to the directory, click on OK.

Figure 31.6
The Add Users
and Groups
dialog box.

The Type of Access drop-down list box in the Access Through Share Permissions dialog box provides four options for controlling access to the shared directory. Each group or user in the Name list can have its own setting. These four options are explained in the following list:

- ✔ **No Access.** This permission setting prevents any access to the shared directory, its subdirectories, and its files by the selected group or user.

- ✔ **Read.** This permission setting enables the selected user or group to view file names and subdirectory names, change to the shared directory's subdirectories, view data in document files, and run applications from the shared directory (and its subdirectories).

- ✔ **Change.** This permission setting gives the selected user or group all the rights offered by the Read setting. In addition, users or groups who have Change permission also can add files and subdirectories to the shared directory, change data in files, and delete subdirectories and files.

- ✔ **Full Control.** This permission setting gives the selected user or group all the rights offered by the Change setting. In addition, users or groups who have Full Control permission also can change permissions of NTFS files and directories and take ownership of NTFS files and directories.

You can use a number of methods to control the access permissions of Windows for Workgroups users working with resources on an NT node. The first method is to provide access to the shared directory for the group Everyone, then set the access rights accordingly. This method, however, uses something of a "shotgun method" of providing user access because it grants all users the same access privileges to the shared directory. Even if this is your desired intent, the method is not a good choice.

If you want to maintain as much control as possible over the resources on the NT node, you should use a different method. One such method is to add the NETWORK group to the list of users and groups who can access the shared resource, then set the privileges for this group accordingly. The NETWORK group consists of all users who attempt to access the shared directory over the network. This includes all Windows for Workgroups nodes.

Using the NETWORK group to enable access by Windows for Workgroups nodes to the resource is still something of a shotgun method, however. To provide the best control, create one or more groups containing the user names of each Windows for Workgroups user who accesses the shared resource. Add these users individually or as part of a group to the Names list. Then, set access permissions on the individual user names or groups as desired.

 Connecting from a Windows for Workgroups node to a resource shared on an NT node is no different from connecting to a shared resource on another Windows for Workgroups node. Refer to Chapter 28, "Sharing Resources in Windows," for information on sharing and accessing shared resources from a Windows for Workgroups node.

NT Connections to WFWG Disk Resources

Connecting from an NT node to a shared disk resource on a Windows for Workgroups node is very similar to a WFWG-to-NT connection. From the NT node, open File Manager and choose the Connect Network Drive button from the toolbar, or choose Disk, Connect Network Drive. The Connect Network Drive dialog box appears, as shown in figure 31.7.

The NT and WFWG nodes appear in their respective workgroups without any indication of the type of operating environment running on each node. In other words, you cannot tell which nodes are running Windows for Workgroups and which are running NT (nor is there generally a need to know).

To connect to a shared resource on a Windows for Workgroups node, first choose from the Drive drop-down list the drive ID with which you want to associate the remote shared directory. Next, choose from the Shared Directories list the node containing the desired resource. The list expands to display the shared resources on that node. Select the desired shared resource, then click on OK.

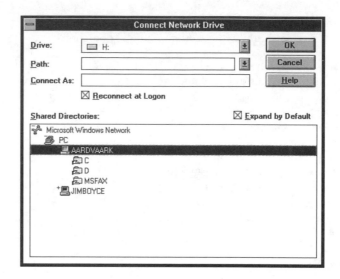

Figure 31.7
The NT Connect
Network Drive
dialog box.

Printer Sharing from NT

NT nodes can share printers just like Windows for Workgroups nodes. When an NT node shares a printer that is connected to it, other users, whether NT nodes or Windows for Workgroups nodes, can access the printer. NT nodes, however, have much greater control over access permissions for the printers they are sharing than WFWG nodes do.

To share a printer from an NT node, your user account must have the necessary permission levels. By default, members of the Administrators group and Power Users group can share printers. If you do not have the necessary security permission to share a printer connected to your NT node, consult your network administrator for help.

To share a printer from an NT node, open Print Manager (located in the Main group). If the printer has not yet been created, choose Printer, then Create Printer to display the Create Printer dialog box (see fig. 31.8).

Figure 31.8
The NT Create
Printer dialog box.

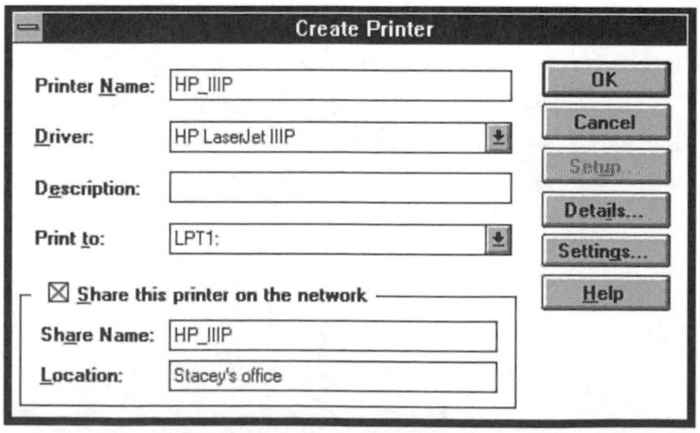

In the Printer <u>N</u>ame edit box, type the name by which you want the printer to appear in Print Manager. From the <u>D</u>river list, choose the driver for the appropriate printer. If you want to add an optional description to the printer, type the description in the De<u>s</u>cription edit box. From the Print <u>t</u>o drop-down list, choose the port to which the printer is connected on the local NT node.

To make the printer available on the network, place a check in the check box labeled <u>S</u>hare this printer on the network. In the Sh<u>a</u>re Name edit box, type the name by which you want the printer to be known on the network. Use the <u>L</u>ocation edit box to add a comment to the printer share name, such as its physical location in the building. After specifying these options, click on OK. If the driver is not yet installed, Print Manager prompts you for the location of the driver file. Supply the network path or path to the distribution CD containing the printer driver files. After the driver is installed, Print Manager displays a Printer Setup dialog box (see fig. 31.9). Specify any necessary options, then click on OK.

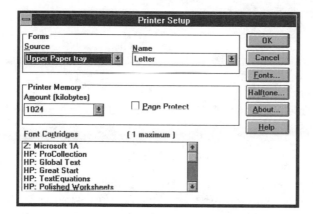

Figure 31.9
A typical Printer Setup dialog box.

As with disk resources, connecting from a WFWG node to a shared printer on an NT node is no different than connecting a printer on a WFWG node. Refer to Chapter 28, "Sharing Resources in Windows," for information on connecting to a shared printer from Windows for Workgroups.

NT Connections to WFWG Printer Resources

An NT node can connect to a shared printer on a Windows for Workgroups node just as it can connect to shared printer resources on NT nodes. The process used to connect to a shared printer on a WFWG node is identical to connecting to a shared printer on an NT node. Open Print Manager and verify that a printer has been created that references the correct type of driver for the printer you are accessing across the network. (Refer to the preceding section for information on creating a printer under NT.)

Select the printer object you want to associate with the remote network printer and choose Printer, Connect to Printer. The Connect to Printer dialog box shown in figure 31.10 appears.

Figure 31.10
The Connect to Printer dialog box.

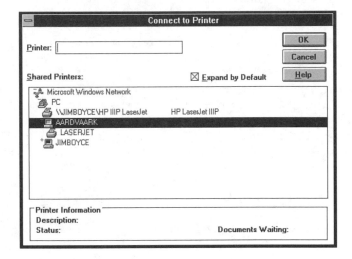

From the Shared Printers list, choose the machine that controls the printer to which you want to connect. Its printers appear in the list underneath the machine name. Select the printer you want to use. Its status and the number of documents waiting to be printed appears in the Printer Information group box at the bottom of the dialog box. When you are sure you have selected the proper printer, click on OK.

If the remote machine does not have a printer driver installed that is suitable for your workstation, and the proper printer driver has not yet been installed on your NT node, Print Manager displays the Connect to Printer dialog box shown in figure 31.11.

Figure 31.11
Print Manager displays this Connect to Printer dialog box if the proper driver is not available.

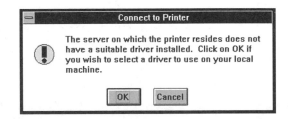

A WFWG printer driver generally does not work for the NT node. For this reason, you must install a local NT printer driver for the remote printer and associate it with the remote printer.

If you click on OK in the Connect to Printer dialog box that asks whether you want to install a printer driver, the Select Driver dialog box shown in figure 31.12 appears. From the Driver drop-down list, select the appropriate printer driver, then click on OK. Print Manager displays the Printer Setup dialog box, enabling you to set options for the printer. Set any necessary options, then click on OK. The printer driver then is associated with the remote printer, and you can print to it as if it were a local printer.

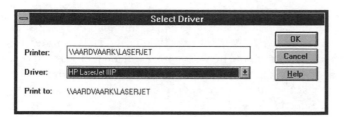

Figure 31.12
The Select Driver dialog box.

Examining Security Concerns

In some companies, security is not a critical issue. Companies using NT, however, often rely on NT's built-in security features to protect sensitive data and control access to system resources such as file services, applications, and printer services. To these companies, security is a prime consideration.

Windows for Workgroups offers *share-level security* for shared resources. This means each shared resource can be protected by password. A shared disk, for example, can be protected using different combinations of read-only and read-write access under Windows for Workgroups. As figure 31.13 shows, a disk resource can have two different passwords: one for read-only access and another for full (read-write) access. This enables some users to read from the disk but not modify it, and other users to have full access to the disk. Both types of access can be protected by password.

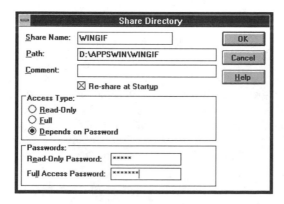

Figure 31.13
Disk resources can have various share-level security options.

Any new user can create his own user account under Windows for Workgroups, and this can create security problems if the network resources are not protected by password. If a resource is not protected by a password, any user can log in to the network and gain access to that resource. Sharing a resource without a password presents a potentially grave security risk.

Windows NT and NT Advanced Server support user-level security. *User-level security* requires each user to have a predefined user name and password. This predefined user name and password are validated by the server to determine whether a user can access a specific resource. To a certain extent, Windows for Workgroups also provides user-level security because each user logs in to the network with a specific user name and password. The primary difference is that in an NT environment, the Administrator account on a particular workstation has full control over creation of user names and passwords affecting that workstation's resources.

You can use the security model in Windows for Workgroups to control access to peer resources of other Windows for Workgroups nodes. This means resources shared by a Windows for Workgroups node rely on the security features in Windows for Workgroups to protect them from unauthorized access. To protect resources shared by an NT server or workstation, you must rely on the security features inherent in NT. This is an advantage, though, because NT provides much more control over who can access a resource, and what types of access users can have to that resource.

Workgroups and Domains

A *workgroup* is a logical grouping of computers. Members of a workgroup can share peer resources and access a common post office. A member of a workgroup also can access resources shared by other workgroups. All Windows for Workgroups nodes belong to a specific workgroup. Windows NT nodes also can belong to workgroups.

 Although a WFWG or NT node can belong to as many workgroups as desired, it can belong to only one workgroup at a time.

A *domain* is similar to a workgroup, but adds a higher level of security. A domain is a group of nodes (including servers and workstations) grouped together just like the nodes in a workgroup. In a domain, however, a single security system controls access to each of the elements in the domain. The use of domains requires NT Advanced Server, because an NT Advanced Server node must act as the domain controller.

Note An NT Advanced Server node must be either a member of a domain or a domain controller.

Windows for Workgroups nodes and NT nodes can join domains. To join a domain on an NT node, open the Control Panel and choose the Network icon. This displays the Network Settings dialog box shown in figure 31.14.

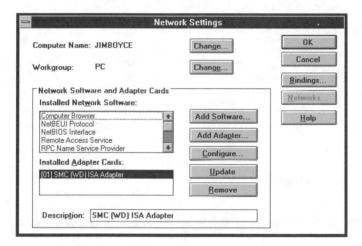

Figure 31.14
The NT Network Settings dialog box.

The current workgroup is shown near the top of the dialog box. To join a domain, choose the Change button beside the Workgroup label. The Control Panel then displays the Domain/Workgroup Settings dialog box shown in figure 31.15.

Figure 31.15
The Domain/Workgroup Settings dialog box.

Choose the **D**omain option button, type the name of the domain in the associated edit box, then click on OK to join the domain.

In order for a Windows for Workgroups user to join a domain, that user must have a user account and password on the domain controller. Windows for Workgroups includes an application called ADMINCFG (the program file is ADMINCFG.EXE) that enables a network administrator to control security issues for WFWG nodes, including requiring a WFWG user to log in to a domain before being granted access to the network. The following section explains the use of ADMINCFG.

Using ADMINCFG

ADMINCFG provides a single application a network administrator can use to control security features of a Windows for Workgroups network. ADMINCFG controls file and printer sharing, availability of NetDDE, control of passwords, and other security issues. ADMINCFG also controls access to NT security features by Windows for Workgroups nodes. This section of the chapter explains the ways in which you can install and use ADMINCFG.

Installing ADMINCFG

By default, Windows for Workgroups Setup does not install ADMINCFG. The compressed file ADMINCFG.EX_, located on the last Windows for Workgroups distribution floppy disk, contains ADMINCFG.EXE. To install ADMINCFG, perform the following steps:

1. Insert the last Windows for Workgroups distribution floppy disk (disk 8 of the 3½-inch distribution set) in the node's floppy drive.

2. From File Manager or Program Manager's **F**ile menu, choose **R**un.

3. In the Run dialog box, enter the following command:

   `EXPAND A:\ADMINCFG.EX_ C:\WINDOWS\ADMINCFG.EXE`

   Substitute **B:** for A: in the command line if you are using drive B. Substitute the correct destination path if Windows for Workgroups is installed in a directory other than C:\WINDOWS.

4. In Program Manager, open the group you want to contain the ADMINCFG program item.

5. In Program Manager, choose **F**ile, **N**ew. In the New Program Object dialog box, choose the Program **I**tem option button, then click on OK.

6. In the Program Item Properties dialog box, enter the information shown in figure 31.16, then click on OK. To run ADMINCFG, double-click on its icon.

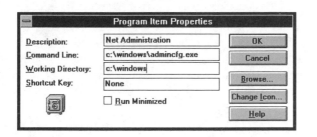

Figure 31.16
The Program Item
Properties dialog
box.

V

Networking and Windows

Sharing Options

When you run ADMINCFG, it displays a dialog box that you must use to locate and choose a security settings file. By default, the file WFWSYS.CFG, located on the node's local drive (or in its default network directory if it is a diskless workstation), contains the security settings controlled by ADMINCFG. The security settings file can reside on any drive, however, and can have a unique name. Later in this chapter you learn the ways in which you can force a node to update its settings automatically from a server at start-up. For now, assume you are using the security settings file located on the node's local disk.

After you specify which security settings file to use, the Security Settings dialog box shown in figure 31.17 appears. The Sharing Options control group in this dialog box provides control of three network-related features on the current node:

✔ **Disable File Sharing.** If this check box contains a check, users on the workstation are not able to share local disk resources with other users on the network.

✔ **Disable Print Sharing.** If this check box contains a check, users on the workstation are not able to share local printers with other users on the network.

✔ **Disable Network DDE Sharing.** If this check box contains a check, users on the workstation are not able to share data using the Clipbook Viewer. Chat, which relies on NetDDE, is disabled. Other applications relying on NetDDE also are disabled.

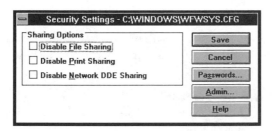

Figure 31.17
The Security
Settings dialog
box.

Password Settings

In addition to controlling sharing, ADMINCFG enables you to control the way passwords are maintained and validated. Choosing the Passwords button in the Security Settings dialog box displays the Password Settings dialog box shown in figure 31.18.

Figure 31.18

The Password
Settings dialog
box.

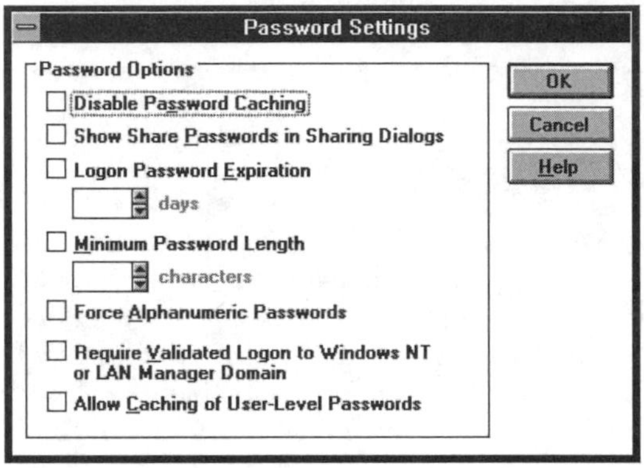

The controls in the Password Settings dialog box control a variety of password-related options. These options are explained in the following list:

✔ **Disable Password Caching.** This option controls whether passwords for shared resources are maintained from session to session. If this option is disabled, passwords are not retained in a password cache file. The user has to supply a password each time he connects to a shared resource, even if he has used that resource in the past.

✔ **Show Share Passwords in Sharing Dialogs.** If this option is enabled, passwords are displayed as text in the File Sharing and Printer Sharing dialog boxes.

✔ **Logon Password Expiration.** Use this option to force a user to change his password periodically. The password is in effect for the number of days specified by the associated spin control.

✔ **Minimum Password Length.** Use this option to require that passwords consist of the minimum number of characters specified by the associated spin control.

✔ **Force Alphanumeric Passwords.** Enable this option to require passwords to contain both letters and numbers. If this option is disabled, passwords do not have to consist of a combination of letters and numbers.

✔ **Require Validated Logon to Windows NT or LAN Manager Domain.**
If this option is enabled, the user is prompted at login to provide a password
validated by an NT or LAN Manager domain controller. If the user does not have
an account and a valid password on the domain, he is not given access to network
resources. Use this option to integrate Windows for Workgroups nodes into an NT
domain.

✔ **Allow Caching of User-Level Passwords.** This option controls whether
passwords for user-level servers (NT and LAN Manager servers) are stored for
future sessions. For greatest security, leave this check box cleared.

If you are integrating Windows for Workgroups nodes into an NT Advanced Server
environment, use the Require Validated Logon to Windows NT or LAN Manager Domain
option to ensure security of the network resources in the domain. If you want a user's
passwords for shared resources on the domain to be cached between sessions, place a
check in the Allow Caching of User-Level Passwords check box. For greatest security,
however, consider leaving this option disabled.

Using Administrator Settings

Choosing the Admin button in ADMINCFG's Security Settings dialog box displays the
Administrator Settings dialog box shown in figure 31.19. This dialog box enables you to
force the security settings to update from a network server each time Windows for
Workgroups is started on the node. The dialog box also enables you to create a custom
message that is displayed when the user logs in.

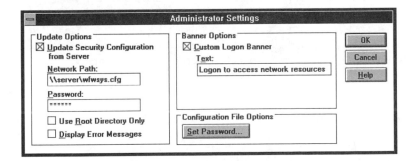

Figure 31.19
The Administrator
Settings dialog
box.

The controls in the Update Options group enable you to cause the workstation's security
options to be updated from a network server each time the user logs in to the network. In
essence, this option redirects Windows for Workgroups to load the security settings from
a file on a network server rather than from a local WFWSYS.CFG. Specify the path and
security file name for the desired security settings file. You can use a UNC name format
(such as \\SERVER\WFWSYS.CFG), if desired.

The Banner Options group enables you to specify a custom login message that is displayed in the title bar of the login dialog box in place of the default title, "Welcome to Windows for Workgroups." This option is useful for displaying short login messages such as "Login required for network access."

Troubleshooting NT and WFWG Problems

This section provides a list of problems you might experience when integrating Windows for Workgroups into NT and NT Advanced Server environments.

NT Server Does Not Validate Login

NT Advanced Server does not validate the login of a Windows for Workgroups 3.11 workstation if the WFWG machine name contains a space. The machine name must consist of valid characters and cannot contain a space. Substitute a dash (-) or underscore (_) in place of the space to retain readability of the machine name. Change the user account on the domain if necessary, then change the node's machine name and reboot it for the change to take effect.

Lowercase Extended Characters in Passwords

Although a Windows for Workgroups node can use lowercase extended characters in passwords to access resources shared by other Windows for Workgroups nodes, you cannot use lowercase extended characters in passwords when connecting to an NT server. This error occurs because the password is converted to uppercase before being sent to the NT server. Because some of the international characters do not have uppercase equivalents, an error occurs.

International Characters in NT Share Name

If you attempt to connect to a shared resource on an NT server and the share name contains international characters, an error occurs.

Empty Server Browse List

You might receive the error "Empty server list" when browsing for network resources from a Windows for Workgroups node in an NT Advanced Server domain. This error occurs only if the WFWG node is serving as a backup browse master. To overcome the problem, change (or add) the `MaintainServerList` to read **MaintainServerList=No**. This setting belongs in the [network] section of the node's SYSTEM.INI file.

Chapter Snapshot

Although Windows for Workgroups itself is a powerful network operating system, many users want to use its enhanced network interface to augment their current networking environment. To address these users' needs, Microsoft designed Windows for Workgroups so that it can peacefully coexist with, and in many cases extend the functionality of, existing network operating systems.

By far, Novell NetWare is the most common network operating system in use today. This chapter covers the integration of Windows for Workgroups with Novell NetWare by discussing the following topics:

In addition to providing a discussion of general topics, this chapter provides specific tips for troubleshooting problems that can occur when using Windows for Workgroups in conjunction with NetWare.

CHAPTER

Integrating Windows and Novell NetWare

R ight out of the box, Windows for Workgroups provides support for Novell
NetWare and other networks. With this secondary network support installed, you
can seamlessly access shared resources on file servers running NetWare. This
enables you to enjoy the peer-to-peer benefits in Windows for Workgroups without losing
the security and administration features in NetWare. Windows for Workgroups extends
the basic functionality of the networked Windows environment by adding benefits that
NetWare does not provide.

This chapter assumes you are using Windows for Workgroups 3.11 in a NetWare environment. Windows for Workgroups 3.11 provides much better integration with NetWare than Windows for Workgroups 3.1.

When used in conjunction with NetWare, Windows for Workgroups is the primary network, and NetWare is a secondary network. The concept of primary and secondary networks becomes clearer as you read about how secondary network support is installed and configured for Windows for Workgroups.

Installing NetWare Support for Windows for Workgroups

By default, Windows for Workgroups installs only its own network support during installation. If you are upgrading from Windows for Workgroups 3.1 to version 3.11, however, Setup also installs the IPX/SPX Compatible Transport with NetBIOS driver. Two options exist for installing NetWare support for Windows for Workgroups. The first option is to install NetWare support during Windows Setup.

NetWare Support through Setup

If NetWare support is installed and operating on a PC when you install Windows for Workgroups 3.11, Setup automatically detects NetWare and installs support for it. The simplest method for installing NetWare support for Windows for Workgroups is to ensure that NetWare is functioning on the node when you install Windows for Workgroups. An additional advantage of configuring and running NetWare before running Windows Setup is that you can install a full copy of the Windows for Workgroups files on a server and install Windows across the network. This eliminates the need to use the Windows distribution disks to install Windows on the local node.

For Setup to automatically detect NetWare and correctly configure support for it, the node must be configured with either an IPX driver (IPX.COM) or an ODI driver. In addition, a NetWare 3.x or 4.x shell must be configured to enable the node to access disk and printer resources.

If you have the choice of using either IPX or ODI drivers, choose an ODI driver. Novell recommends the use of ODI drivers over IPX, and using the ODI driver offers greater flexibility for configuring network services and protocols.

If at all possible, ensure that NetWare is properly installed and configured on the node before attempting to install Windows for Workgroups. This ensures that Setup properly installs network support for NetWare.

NetWare Support through Network Setup

If you install Windows for Workgroups as a stand-alone network and later decide you want to add NetWare support, or if NetWare is not running on the machine when you install Windows for Workgroups, you can add NetWare support through the Network Setup item in the Network group.

First, open the Network group in Program Manager and choose the Network Setup icon to display the Network Setup dialog box (see fig. 32.1). Next, click on the Networks button to display the Networks dialog box (see fig. 32.2).

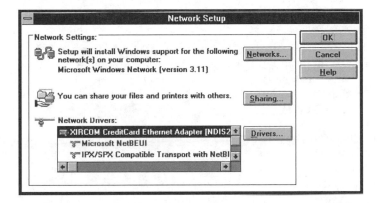

Figure 32.1
Use the Network Setup dialog box to change network options.

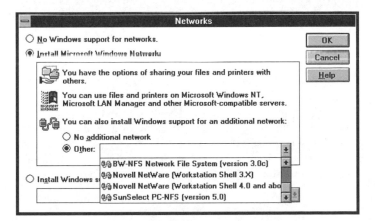

Figure 32.2
Use the Networks dialog box to add support for other networks.

To add NetWare support, click on the **O**ther option button, then choose the appropriate Novell NetWare entry in the list box. If you are running version 3.*x* of the network shell, choose the Novell NetWare entry with the 3.*x* shell designation beside it. If you are using version 4.0 or higher of the network shell, choose the Novell NetWare entry with the version 4.0 shell designation beside it. Next, click on OK. Network Setup attempts to detect the driver model you are using. If Network Setup for some reason cannot detect the driver model (you have not started the NetWare client software, for example), Network Setup then displays the Novell NetWare dialog box shown in figure 32.3.

Figure 32.3
Choose a network driver using the Novell NetWare dialog box.

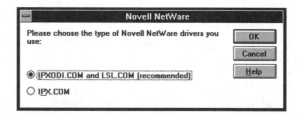

From the Novell NetWare dialog box, choose either the IPXODI.COM and LSL.COM driver (for use with ODI drivers) or the IPX.COM driver (for use with the monolithic IPX driver). If possible, you should use the IPXODI.COM and LSL.COM driver for added flexibility in configuring your network. Using this driver, for example, makes it possible for you to use multiple protocols.

After selecting the driver you want to use, click on OK to close the Novell NetWare dialog box, then click on OK in the Network Setup dialog box. Network Setup then prompts you to specify the location of the NetWare driver, which can be found on the Windows distribution disks or on a shared Windows installation on the server. Follow the prompts to install the necessary drivers. Network Setup prompts you to reboot the system for the changes to take place. After rebooting the system, make sure that NetWare is functioning on the workstation, then start Windows and test the node's network capabilities to verify it is working properly.

ODI Driver Support

The Open Datalink Interface (ODI) driver model, developed by Novell and Apple, offers advantages over the IPX driver model used in many NetWare installations. The ODI driver model provides a protocol and consistent application programming interface (API) that make it possible to support multiple protocols on a single network adapter. If you plan to use additional protocols, you should use the ODI driver model, rather than the IPX driver model, with Windows for Workgroups 3.11.

The ODI driver model consists of three primary components, which are shown in figure 32.4 and described in the following list:

✔ **MLID (Multiple-Link Interface Driver).** The MLID forms the lowest level in the driver model. The MLID driver is hardware-dependent; it is provided by the network adapter manufacturer.

✔ **LSL (Link Support Layer).** The LSL provides a bridge between the MLID driver and the protocol driver (such as IPXODI.COM), enabling the protocol driver and MLID to communicate.

✔ **IPXODI.COM.** This is the ODI-compliant version of the IPX/SPX protocol. It serves as the communications protocol between a NetWare server and NetWare client.

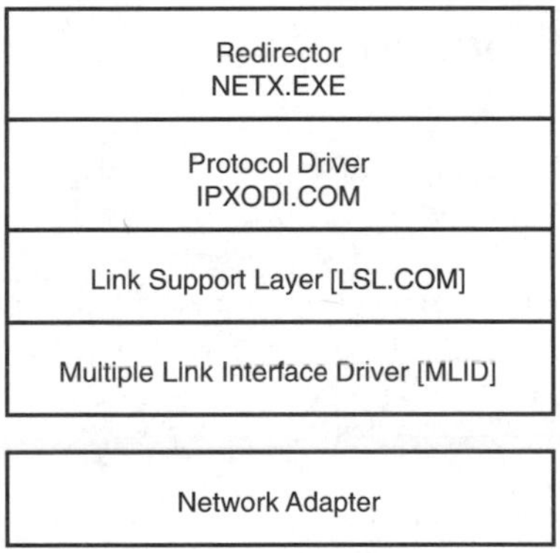

Redirector NETX.EXE
Protocol Driver IPXODI.COM
Link Support Layer [LSL.COM]
Multiple Link Interface Driver [MLID]

Network Adapter

Figure 32.4
The ODI driver model.

In order for ODI support to function properly under Windows for Workgroups, all components of ODI must be in place and functioning prior to installing NetWare support for Windows for Workgroups on the node. The node should be able to boot and initialize LSL.COM, IPXODI.COM, the MLID, and NETX.EXE without errors. If the ODI drivers are properly installed and functioning when you install Windows for Workgroups NetWare support, Network Setup recognizes the ODI drivers and automatically configures support for them in Windows for Workgroups.

When using an ODI driver, the file NET.CFG is used to configure the network environment on the node. In addition, the workstation might contain a SHELL.CFG file. If both of these files exist on the node, they are processed during network initialization (first SHELL.CFG, then NET.CFG). The NET.CFG and SHELL.CFG files configure parameters for NETX, IPX, NetBIOS, and other general network parameters. Any entries that are duplicated in NET.CFG and SHELL.CFG are ignored when NET.CFG is processed.

To simplify administration, consider combining the settings in SHELL.CFG into NET.CFG. Also ensure that the correct NET.CFG file is used if more than one is available to the system. When LSL.COM executes, it looks in the current directory for NET.CFG, then in the directory containing LSL.COM if different from the current directory. NETX.EXE by default checks the directory containing NETX.EXE for the NET.CFG file. You can use the /C=*path* switch with the LSL.COM and NETX.EXE command lines to direct each to look for NET.CFG in a different directory. The following example shows the use of the /C switch with NETX.EXE to load the driver NET.CFG from the \NETWARE directory on drive C:

```
NETX.EXE /C=C:\NETWARE\NET.CFG
```

For additional information on ODI support, consult the Microsoft Windows for Workgroups 3.11 Resource Kit.

The LASTDRIVE Setting

One of the settings Network Setup alters is the LASTDRIVE variable in CONFIG.SYS. If the workstation is running version 3.*x* of the NetWare shell, Network Setup sets the value of LASTDRIVE to the letter P. NetWare 3.*x* maps network drives beginning with the drive letter after the setting of LASTDRIVE. Using a setting of LASTDRIVE=P might cause problems with login scripts on your system, because changing the LASTDRIVE setting changes the drive ID at which redirected network drives are mapped. A script that is referencing drive F, for example, no longer works because the logical drive mapping no longer is F.

When installing NetWare 3.*x* support under Windows for Workgroups, you must verify that the LASTDRIVE setting in CONFIG.SYS is set properly for your workstation. If your scripts rely on a specific drive mapping, omit the LASTDRIVE setting from CONFIG.SYS. This enables NetWare to assign its drive letters properly.

NetWare 4.*x* uses the same drive mapping scheme as Windows for Workgroups: drives are mapped up to the value of LASTDRIVE, and not beyond. When installing support for NetWare 4.*x*, Network Setup sets LASTDRIVE=Z. To control the drive letter at which NetWare begins mapping redirected drives, change the value of the First Network Drive= entry in NET.CFG.

NetWare Drivers

NetWare secondary network support is implemented through a series of DOS-based device drivers and through Windows-based virtual device drivers (VxDs). Table 32.1 contains a list of these drivers and their corresponding functions. The files listed in Table 32.1 are not shipped with Windows for Workgroups 3.11; you must acquire these files from Novell. The files are available from a Novell representative or from the NOVFILES and NOVLIB forums on CompuServe.

Table 32.1
Device Drivers and VxDs

Component	Function
VIPX.386	Windows device driver that virtualizes the IPX protocol, supporting multiple virtual DOS machines
VNETWARE.386	Windows virtual device driver that virtualizes the NetWare shell (NETX.COM) and also provides some NetWare Core Protocol (NCP) buffering to support multiple DOS virtual machines
NETWARE.DRV	NetWare Windows driver
NETWARE.HLP	Help file for the NetWare Windows driver
NWPOPUP.COM	Windows utility that provides user interface for NetWare's messaging functions

Integrating Windows for Workgroups with NetWare's Login

NetWare has long been praised for its robust scripting capabilities. Login scripts for both the overall system and for individual users provide a powerful mechanism for creating custom login environments for each user. The entire workstation environment can be configured based on user name and password. This includes network drive mappings, environment variables, and external program execution.

Similarly, Windows for Workgroups provides resharing options that enable you to reestablish the desired network environment automatically whenever Windows is started. In addition, the WIN.INI file LOAD and RUN lines, in conjunction with the StartUp group in Program Manager, enable you to restore much of your working environment automatically.

Most important, each of these systems enables you to perform this reconnection without relying upon DOS. Novell enables you to store these settings in individual login script files. Windows for Workgroups maintains a list of connections in the CONNECT.DAT file located in the main Windows subdirectory. Connections kept from session to session are called *persistent connections.*

With all this configuration power on-hand, it is important to define which function does what and why. This section examines the various functions in detail and lays out a step-by-step plan to configure a flexible, consistent, and easy-to-diagnose network environment.

Examining the AUTOEXEC.BAT File

DOS itself provides an automated scripting facility in the form of the AUTOEXEC.BAT file. In a networked environment, however, it usually is best to keep AUTOEXEC.BAT as generic as possible, and to use the network-supplied facilities (such as NET.CFG) for customizing the user-environment. This helps reduce support costs by creating a consistent environment at the DOS level and making it easier for network support personnel to diagnose and isolate problems.

The following generic AUTOEXEC.BAT file automates the network connection, login, and Windows start-up functions when using the MSIPX driver configuration:

```
ECHO OFF
CLS
SET TEMP=C:\WINDOWS\TEMP
PATH=C:\;C:\DOS;C:\WINDOWS
C:\WINDOWS\NET START
C:\WINDOWS\MSIPX
C:\WINDOWS\NETX
F:
LOGIN
C:
CD\WINDOWS
PAUSE
WIN
```

The `F:` entry in the preceding AUTOEXEC.BAT file depends on the `LASTDRIVE=` setting in the CONFIG.SYS file. Windows for Workgroups defaults to `LASTDRIVE=P` and the login drive becomes `Q` if a version 3.*x* NetWare shell is used. Notice the `PAUSE` statement just before the Windows execution command, `WIN`. This is optional, but can prove convenient for users who need quick access to their systems. This simple addition enables you to break out of AUTOEXEC.BAT before Windows is started, and thus avoids the often time-consuming loading process when all you want to do is copy a file to a floppy disk or perform a similar task.

By keeping AUTOEXEC.BAT as generic as possible, you make the system easier to diagnose and more accessible to other users who might need to use the system at some point. This is a common scenario in educational institutions wherein many users often share a limited number of systems.

Drive Mapping

After you simplify your AUTOEXEC.BAT files, the next step is to decide how to implement drive mappings. Because both NetWare and Windows for Workgroups provide facilities for creating persistent network connections, you must define which mappings need to be implemented system-wide, and which ones are isolated to individuals or small groups.

The simplest approach is to use the NetWare system login script functions to implement all system-wide mappings. This includes drive mappings that point to important subdirectories such as SYS:PUBLIC, as well as those that point to shared applications and data files. These mappings are not subject to frequent changes, and as such, can be implemented in a more permanent manner.

Login scripts are accessed through the NetWare SYSCON utility and are subject to the security scheme of NetWare. Users typically have access to their own individual login scripts, but only the Supervisor (or a Supervisor-equivalent) can modify the System Login Script. Figure 32.5 shows the SYSCON utility's System Login Script editing screen, complete with sample drive mapping commands.

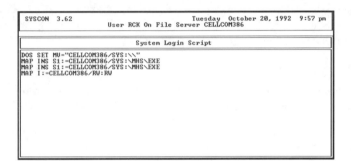

Figure 32.5
A sample system login script in the NetWare SYSCON utility.

For more information on the NetWare MAP command and use of the SYSCON utility, refer to your NetWare documentation.

Individual or group mappings can be more difficult to organize. If central management of individual mappings is important, you are better off using individual login scripts because they can be accessed centrally through the SYSCON utility. If user convenience is more important than centralized management, enabling the individual users to map drives through the Windows for Workgroups File Manager and other network dialog boxes makes more sense.

The main point is that the combination of Windows for Workgroups and NetWare provides a broad and flexible set of mechanisms for configuring your network environment. The NetWare environment is unchanged by Windows for Workgroups, enabling network administrators and users to design a system balancing the need for consistency with the desire for individual flexibility.

Configuration Settings for NetWare

You might need to add two settings to your NET.CFG file when using NetWare and Windows for Workgroups. By default, NetWare file servers do not include current and parent directory entries specified by dot (.) and double-dot (..) in a directory listing. If you have problems listing directories or simply want to include these entries in directory lists, add the SHOW DOTS setting to NET.CFG as follows:

    SHOW DOTS = ON

The FILE HANDLES setting is another configuration setting you should consider adding to NET.CFG. By default, NetWare enables you to access up to 40 files. In Windows, it is easy to quickly exceed that number of open files. You can increase the number of files that can be open by adding the FILE HANDLES setting to NET.CFG. The following statement increases the number of possible open files to 60:

    FILE HANDLES = 60

In addition to setting FILE HANDLES in NET.CFG, you also should set FILES=60 (or whatever value you have assigned to FILE HANDLES in NET.CFG) in the node's CONFIG.SYS file.

Configuring NetWare Security

After you have streamlined your login process, the final step is to analyze the ways to integrate Windows for Workgroups into the NetWare security scheme.

NetWare itself provides some of the most robust and comprehensive security mechanisms in the networking industry. Data can be protected at the volume, subdirectory, file, and even attribute levels. NetWare security is so tight that even passwords are encrypted as they are sent over the network cable from workstation to server.

In contrast, Windows for Workgroups' security is much less robust and is primarily intended to protect sensitive data from casual browsing. Windows for Workgroups' security also is much less flexible in the way it arbitrates access to nested subdirectories. Under NetWare, users can be restricted from accessing nested subdirectories even though they have access to the parent subdirectory.

In Windows for Workgroups, access to the parent subdirectory also gives the user access to any nested files or subdirectories. Windows for Workgroups also does not provide for file-level or attribute security. These limitations are partially imposed by DOS itself. The NetWare file system is designed from the ground up to support multiple users, and as a result it features more extensive security.

As in the decision about login scripts, you must analyze the ways the various resources are to be used and then come up with a flexible, useful plan to implement them.

The simplest approach is to place sensitive data on the NetWare server because it provides a much more secure environment. This can include accounting data, sensitive documents, or financial worksheets. You then can use the sharing functions of Windows for Workgroups to set up application servers. *Application servers* are systems that share application software but do not necessarily store any data.

By separating the data and applications in this manner, you also are enhancing network performance by distributing the workload between network resources. Instead of a single server acting as the primary network resource (and also the primary network failure point), the processing power of the entire network is shared, increasing performance and productivity.

Unfortunately, this kind of distributed processing also has its drawbacks. First, any time you rely on a peer workstation to provide a key network service, you run the risk of losing that resource due to user error or application failure. If your workstation functions as a primary workgroup mail server and contains the WGPO subdirectory structure, for instance, accidentally bumping your power switch and turning off your system can have disastrous repercussions, especially in a larger network. The same is true if an application crashes your system.

Again, as with network mappings, you must analyze what resources need to be accessed, how critical consistent access to those resources is, and how secure the data associated with those resources must remain. Fortunately, the combination of Windows for Workgroups and NetWare provides a broad variety of options to implement a sound network architecture.

Examining IPX Protocol Support for NetWare

Under Windows for Workgroups, NetWare is implemented as a secondary network. Windows for Workgroups is considered the primary network and uses the NetBEUI transport protocol along with the Server Message Block (SMB) API to communicate with other workstations. Because of its use of NetBEUI, Windows for Workgroups can coexist with and directly integrate into a wide variety of existing NetBEUI-based network operating systems. These include Microsoft NT and NT Advanced Server, Microsoft LAN Manager, 3Com 3+ Open, IBM PC LAN, MS-NET, DEC Pathworks, and many other SMB/NetBEUI supporting systems. To share resources under these environments is relatively straightforward because all the systems use the same transport protocol.

NetWare, on the other hand, uses Novell's own Internetwork Packet Exchange (IPX) protocol for communication between workstations and servers. IPX and NetBEUI are not directly compatible, and as a result Windows for Workgroups incorporates its own IPX-compatible drivers to provide integration with NetWare.

NDIS and Microsoft IPX/SPX

To circumvent the problems of NetBEUI/IPX incompatibility, Windows for Workgroups relies on the Network Driver Interface Specification (NDIS) to integrate multiple protocol stacks onto a single network interface card (NIC). This process of attaching multiple protocol stacks to a single NIC is referred to as binding the protocol to the network card. By binding both the NetBEUI and IPX protocol stacks to the network card, Windows for Workgroups provides simultaneous access to NetWare and NetBEUI-based servers.

NDIS is an industry standard technique that vendors can use to bind multiple stacks to a single network card. Any NDIS-compatible transport protocol can be used with Windows for Workgroups to provide a system of dual-redirection. Using dual-redirection, network requests are routed to the appropriate transport protocol stack by the NDIS protocol manager. The protocol stacks then encapsulate the data and transmit the network packets to their appropriate destinations.

Unfortunately, the IPX protocol stack in Novell NetWare is not NDIS-compliant. This is due to the monolithic design of the NetWare protocol stack. A *monolithic protocol stack* takes all the network card–specific information provided in the card's driver and incorporates it into a single protocol stack and driver entity. Although this combination has excellent performance characteristics, it makes supporting multiple protocol stacks impossible for a network card. The NetWare stack is in control from top to bottom.

With the limitations of the IPX stack in mind, Microsoft chose to modify the standard NetWare stack, breaking it down into its various components: protocol (including NetWare Core Protocol components), network driver, and any necessary translation code. Microsoft then wrote a translation-layer driver to convert calls from the newly encapsulated IPX driver into NDIS-compatible commands. The result was MSIPX, a fully NetWare-compatible, NDIS-compliant protocol stack suitable for use in a dual-redirection environment.

32-Bit IPX/SPX Protocol with NetBIOS

Windows for Workgroups 3.11 includes a new 32-bit IPX/SPX NDIS 3.0-compatible protocol called NWLink. This protocol provides better performance than real-mode IPX protocol and enables Windows for Workgroups 3.11 nodes to communicate using a routable IPX-compatible protocol. This new 32-bit implementation of IPX/SPX offers a number of advantages over the previous real-mode implementation of the IPX/SPX protocol. Because the NWLink driver handles all virtualization of IPX protocol, the Novell VIPX.386 driver is no longer required. In addition, Windows for Workgroups 3.11 includes a 32-bit NetBIOS provider called NWNBLink. This provider performs the same functions as the Novell NetBIOS driver, but improves performance virtualizing NetBIOS support. With NWNBLink installed, the Novell NETBIOS.EXE driver is no longer required. The move to protected-mode drivers from real-mode not only improves overall performance, but also eliminates the need to load real-mode drivers (such as NETBIOS.EXE), conserving conventional memory.

NWLink handles all non-NCP (NetWare Core Protocol) IPX traffic. Windows for Workgroups does not process NCP traffic used by the NetWare redirector to communicate with NetWare servers for file and printer services. If you intend to access file and printer services on a NetWare server, you must configure the real-mode IPX protocol on the node (which is accomplished by configuring the node to access the server from DOS using the monolithic IPX or ODI drivers).

You can use the 32-bit IPX/SPX support with or without NetBIOS support. If you require support for NetBIOS on your node, configure Windows for Workgroups to use the IPX/SPX Compatible Transport with NetBIOS driver. If you do not require NetBIOS support, configure Windows for Workgroups to use the IPX/SPX Compatible Transport (without NetBIOS support). To install either of these protocols, choose the Network Setup icon in the Network group in Program Manager. Choose the Drivers button, then the Add Protocol button to display the Add Network Protocol dialog box (see fig. 32.6). Choose the appropriate IPX/SPX driver from the list, then click on OK. Follow Network Setup's prompts to supply the disk containing the appropriate driver. Network Setup reconfigures your network options and prompts you to reboot the node for changes to take effect.

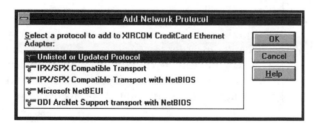

Figure 32.6
The Add Network Protocol dialog box.

NWNBLink is Windows for Workgroups' 32-bit implementation of NetBIOS services for IPX. As mentioned previously, NWNBLink is compatible (and replaces) Novell's NetBIOS provider, NETBIOS.EXE. NetBIOS is necessary to support NetDDE services over an IPX protocol. It also is necessary if you plan to use any NetBIOS applications (such as Lotus Notes) on a NetWare server.

Chapter Snapshot

Windows for Workgroups directly supports many other network operating systems. In addition, Windows for Workgroups can be configured to operate with multiple network protocols, making possible communications with multiple network environments from a single workstation. This chapter examines many issues related to supporting multiple protocols under Windows for Workgroups, including the following topics:

Although it is not necessary to understand the inner workings of a protocol stack to use it on your system, this chapter provides some background information about how protocol stacks are configured and how they function. This background information helps you understand the ways to configure and to use multiple protocols in your network environment.

CHAPTER

Using Multiple Protocols

W indows for Workgroups can coexist with many protocols by using a standardized protocol stack support mechanism designed by 3Com and Microsoft, and supported by a number of network vendors. This mechanism is known as the Network Driver Interface Specification (NDIS). Windows for Workgroups also supports a similar specification, called ODI, which is supported by Novell. If you understand the purpose and operation of protocol stacks, skip the following section and go straight to the section titled "Examining NDIS."

Understanding Protocol Stacks

Modern protocols are layered protocols that often are divided into seven defined layers. Each layer provides services to the layers above it and uses services from the layer below it. These services are defined clearly for a particular protocol stack. One layer of a protocol can change without affecting the other layers because the interfaces between layers are (or should be) well defined.

Examining the OSI Layered Protocol Model

The International Standards Organization (ISO) created the Open System Interconnection (OSI) standards, which state that computer communication protocols should be layered into seven distinct parts. Although many protocols in use today have a slightly different layering system than the one presented by the ISO, the basic model is widely respected. To better understand NDIS discussion, you should be familiar with at least the first three layers.

 When you read the following sections about protocol layers, keep in mind that although the ISO and the Institute of Electrical and Electronic Engineers (IEEE) defined the layers and the services each layer provides, the two organizations did not attempt to define the implementation on specific systems.

Layer 1: The Physical Layer

The physical layer, the lowest layer of the OSI stack, is the interface to the physical media over which computer bits are transmitted. At this layer, the physical media is specified. Physical media can include the number of wires used, the purpose of each wire if the network uses copper cable, or the fiber type used in fiber-optic links. Link synchronization also is done at this layer. Higher layers regard layer 1 as a bit pipe—no error correction is performed, and no guarantee exists that bits put into the pipe emerge from the other end.

Layer 2: The Data Link Layer

The second layer, the data link layer, offers valuable services such as error detection and correction, and the capability to activate, deactivate, and maintain a particular link. When the IEEE examined the ISO protocol stack, they decided to split the ISO second layer into a Media Access Control (MAC) layer and a Logical Link Control (LLC) layer. This is where NDIS fits in, as you see in the next section. The series of standards that define these layers are denoted series 802 (see fig. 33.1). This series is divided into 802.1, which defines how LAN protocols interface with layers 3 and higher; 802.2, which is the LLC standard; and the series 802.3 through 802.5, which define the MAC for CSMA/CD (Ethernet), Token Bus, and Token Ring, respectively.

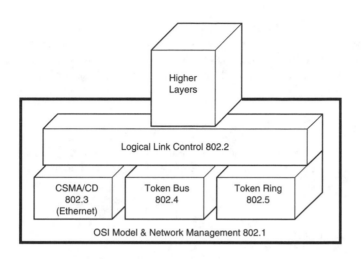

Figure 33.1
IEEE 802 series standards.

Layer 3: The Network Layer

The network layer provides the following services:

- ✔ **Routing.** Decides how a packet of information should get from one computer to another.

- ✔ **Addressing.** Converts a logical address into a physical address.

- ✔ **Flow control.** Delays the transmission of a packet of information when the network is busy.

In certain instances, the actual use of protocol software violates the intention of these definitions. The X.25 protocol, for example, extends through layer 3, but often is used to connect LANs together. Because LANs have their own end-to-end error recovery and flow-control protocols, these services are duplicated in the X.25 transport.

Layers 4–7: The Upper Layers

The remaining layers—transport, session, presentation, and application—are important to computer protocols, but are unimportant when trying to understand how multiple protocol stacks work together on a single computer.

If you would like to learn more about OSI layers 4–7, read *NetWare: The Professional Reference,* published by New Riders Publishing.

The most common implementation of the flexibility offered in a layered protocol is the capability of a single network operating system to operate over various physical media, such as copper, fiber, or radio. In addition, a layered protocol enables a network operating system to operate over a variety of low-level network protocols, such as Ethernet, Token Ring, ARCnet, x.25, and ISDN. Until recently, most network operating system vendors grouped all the lower layers together to form a monolithic protocol stack supporting their particular networks. In the last few years, a number of proposals, such as NDIS, have been offered that more closely model the IEEE standard, and have been opened to the public. NDIS is an open standard that provides a definitive interface at the Media Access Control layer, enabling upper levels of a protocol to be unaware of data transport mechanisms.

Examining NDIS

To promote an open protocol standard, Microsoft and 3Com collaborated in 1989 to write a specification that defined fully the interface between the IEEE-defined Media Access Control (MAC) and the Logical Link Control (LLC) layers. This specification is known as the Network Driver Interface Specification (NDIS). Figure 33.2 illustrates how the NDIS interface operates over various physical layer cable types. By conforming to this specification, any network interface card that has an NDIS driver can communicate with any protocol driver that also conforms to the NDIS specification.

Figure 33.2
NDIS: standard interface at the MAC protocol layer.

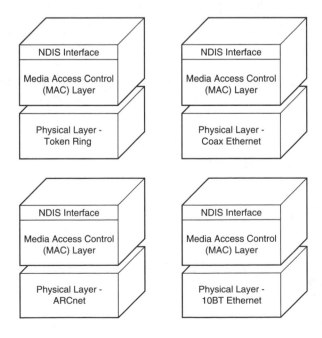

Windows for Workgroups 3.11 supports 16-bit NDIS 2.0 network adapter drivers as well as 32-bit NDIS 3.0 network adapter drivers. The following list explains some characteristics of NDIS 2.0 drivers:

✔ The file names of NDIS 2.0 network adapter drivers typically have a DOS file extension.

✔ NDIS 2.0 drivers are written as 16-bit real-mode drivers and operate in conventional memory.

✔ An NDIS 2.0 driver can support only one adapter. In a system containing multiple NICs, multiple instances of the driver must be loaded to support the NICs (one instance for each adapter).

✔ NDIS 2.0 protocols must use an NDIS 2.0 driver, but NDIS 3.0 protocols also can use the NDIS 2.0 driver (with support from the real-mode mapping layer, as described next).

The NetBEUI and NWLink protocols used in Windows for Workgroups are NDIS 3.0 protocols. These protocols can bind to an NDIS 2.0 driver only if the NDIS 2.0 mapping layer, NDIS2SUP.386, and the real-mode stub, NDISHLP.SYS, are installed. The NDIS 3.0 protocol also relies on the NDIS 3.0 support layer, provided by NDIS.386. Because the NDIS 2.0 mapper and driver must operate in real mode and use conventional memory rather than extended memory, performance using the NDIS 2.0 driver model suffers compared to an NDIS 3.0-only model.

NDIS 3.0

Full support for NDIS 3.0 network drivers is new in Windows for Workgroups 3.11. *NDIS 3.0 network drivers* are 32-bit, protected-mode drivers that provide enhanced performance and improved memory management over NDIS 2.0 drivers. Two primary advantages of NDIS 3.0 are the following:

✔ NDIS 3.0 resides in extended memory and operates in protected mode. This reduces the driver footprint in conventional memory and offers better performance by eliminating the need for the processor to switch from protected mode to real mode when servicing the driver.

✔ NDIS 3.0 drivers are 32-bit drivers written in C using common APIs, making NDIS 3.0 drivers easily portable between environments (such as NT and Windows for Workgroups).

The use of an NDIS 3.0 driver simplifies network configuration and improves memory management. Rather than loading network drivers prior to starting Windows for Workgroups, the NDIS 3.0 drivers enable Windows to load the network virtual device drivers after Windows starts.

If your network adapter supports an NDIS 3.0 driver (check with the vendor or manufacturer to receive the latest drivers), you should use the NDIS 3.0 drivers exclusively and eliminate the NDIS 2.0 drivers. The method for installing an NDIS 3.0 driver varies from adapter to adapter. Consult the installation documentation for the network adapter for specific steps to follow when installing and using the driver.

Understanding the PROTOCOL.INI File

The PROTOCOL.INI file is important to the process of creating protocol stacks on your PC. When you install Windows for Workgroups, the Setup program creates this file and places the correct entries in it for your network interface card, the NetBEUI protocol, and perhaps the support for the IPX/SPX protocol if you are using Novell NetWare. A line similar to the following was added to your CONFIG.SYS file with your system's specific path names:

```
DEVICE=C:\WIN31\PROTMAN.DOS /i:C:\WIN31
```

If you are adding support for other protocols not directly supported by Windows for Workgroups, you might need to place additional entries into the PROTOCOL.INI file manually. Even if you work with your vendor to modify the file, it is helpful to know what you are doing and what the various sections of the file are for.

Examining Structure and Settings

The basic format of the PROTOCOL.INI file is similar to every other INI file used in Windows:

```
[section-name]
setting-name=setting-value
setting-name=setting-value
...
```

The section-name parameter is always in brackets and can be any combination of upper- and lowercase alphanumeric characters. The order of the sections is unimportant, just as in the Windows INI files. Nevertheless, they usually appear in the order presented in the following sections.

[network.setup]

The PROTOCOL.INI [network.setup] section contains information about the protocols in use for your specific installation. A typical entry might look like this:

```
[network.setup]
version=0x3110
netcard=ms$smc270,1,MS$SMC270
```

```
transport=ms$netbeui,MS$NETBEUI
lana0=ms$smc270,1,ms$netbeui
```

These settings perform the following functions:

- ✔ `version=` Specifies the current version of Windows for Workgroups. The version is assigned by the setup program.

- ✔ `netcard=` Specifies the name of the network card you are using as found in the NETWORK.INF file in the Windows' system directory. If you look at that file, you can see the entire selection of network cards supported by Windows for Workgroups. If you use a card not listed in the NETWORK.INF file and manually edit this entry, no description appears in the Adapter dialog box (accessed by choosing Networks in the Control Panel). In the preceding example, the entry refers to a Standard Microsystems P270E network adapter.

- ✔ `transport=` Specifies the name of the protocol driver used by Windows for Workgroups.

- ✔ `lana#=` Each combination of network interface card and protocol driver forms a LANA. LANAs start at 0 and, in this example, LANA0 is the combination of the P270E card and the Microsoft NetBEUI protocol. If you also want to add the Microsoft TCP/IP protocol, you would need to add a second LANA entry:

```
lana=ms$smc270,1,ms$tcp
```

You would, of course, use the name for your network interface card in the preceding line.

[protman]

This short section provides basic information to the protocol manager.

```
[protman]
DriverName=PROTMAN$
PRIORITY=MS$NETBEUI
```

These settings perform the following functions:

- ✔ `drivername=` Preset by the setup program, the name of the protocol manager is PROTMAN$. You should not need to change this.

- ✔ `priority=` Incoming frames of information are processed in a particular priority determined by this list. Names of protocols not on this list are processed in a default priority determined by the protocol manager. You might never need to worry about this unless you have a busy PC that is handling a lot of traffic over different protocol stacks.

[protocol]

The protocol sections are used to describe each protocol driver individually. In the following example, the protocol driver is NetBEUI, the default protocol for Windows for Workgroups. A [protocol] section exists for each protocol driver in use. The name in brackets is the name for the protocol.

```
[NETBEUI]
DriverName=netbeui$
SESSIONS=10
NCBS=12
BINDINGS=XIRMAC,ASYMAC,SDIALIN$
LANABASE=0
```

These settings perform the following functions:

- ✔ drivername=   A required entry in every protocol driver section. The name is dependent on the protocol driver, and you should use the name provided in the documentation for the protocol you are using. You should not need to change this.

- ✔ bindings=   Another entry required by every protocol driver. This setting tells the protocol driver which network NDIS interface to connect to. In this example, the protocol manager tells the protocol driver to bind to the XIRMAC, ASYMAC, and SDIALIN$ card drivers. The card driver entries follow this section.

- ✔ lanabase=   Many protocols can be told the lowest LANA number they are used with. This should agree with the LANA number specified in the [network.setup] section.

- ✔ SESSIONS= and NCBS=   Protocols might need additional information, such as the parameters used by these two settings, to initialize properly and to provide the capability to tune for specific installations.

[netcard]

Every installed network card has a section in the PROTOCOL.INI file dedicated to it. The section name is the name of the network card. In the following example an SMC P270E card is specified. You might notice that no bindings entry exists. This is because it is the lowest-level driver, and has no lower-level protocol to bind to.

```
[MS$SMC270]
DriverName=SMC_ARC$
interrupt=7
iobase=0x300
memorybase=0xD800
```

These settings perform the following functions:

✔ `drivername=` This is a required entry in every network card section. This setting is preset in the card driver software, which means you should use the name provided in the documentation for the NDIS driver you are using. You should not need to change this.

✔ `interrupt=` Also referred to as IRQ, this is the interrupt request level used by the network interface card. This must match the setting of the card.

✔ `iobase=` Also referred to as IOADDRESS, port_address, or other similar names, this is the input/output address used by the card.

✔ `memorybase=` Also referred to as membase or sharedram, this is the location of the adapter card in the normal RAM address space. Remember that you must exclude the shared RAM address space used by the network card in any expanded memory manager you might be using.

Later in this chapter, you are shown a complete PROTOCOL.INI file example for TCP/IP. Just remember that your specific settings depend on the protocol and network adapter card that you are using.

Connecting with UNIX: Combining WFWG with TCP/IP

Transmission Control Protocol/Internet Protocol (TCP/IP) is a widely used software communications protocol that became popular in the mid-1980s when the Defense Advanced Research Projects Agency (DARPA) required that all computers connected to ARPANET use the TCP/IP protocol for communication. Since then, the TCP/IP Internet, or simply Internet, has grown and become a worldwide network. Many universities and companies also use TCP/IP for internal use because it is a well-understood and well-documented protocol. UNIX systems in particular use TCP/IP to connect to each other. If you work in a UNIX shop, you undoubtedly will run into TCP/IP at some point.

Understanding the Benefits of TCP/IP

In many companies, users are demanding connectivity to the system that best meets their needs. A PC program might be the best choice for word processing, but an X Windows system program could be the only choice for computer-assisted software engineering. To use the X program, you need to connect to a UNIX host using TCP/IP. This means you need to provide TCP/IP on the workstation in addition to the Windows for Workgroups NetBEUI protocol. You also can use TCP/IP to connect to host computers outside your company, greatly extending the users' reach of the network.

Adding a New Protocol

An earlier section in this chapter, "Examining NDIS," describes how NDIS provides a common MAC layer interface to upper-level protocols. Many TCP/IP protocol stacks consist of monolithic protocol stacks that connect directly to the hardware or use non-NDIS standards. Today, many vendors are designing protocols that can connect to an NDIS driver. Microsoft, for example, supplies a TCP/IP protocol with its LAN Manager product that connects directly with the NDIS layer. Other vendors use a protocol shim that does a small translation between the NDIS layer and the upper TCP/IP layers.

This shim is called a *packet driver*. In the following paragraphs, you see the ways to add a TCP/IP protocol to Windows for Workgroups. Rather than list a step-by-step procedure for a particular vendor's protocol, the following discussion is a general approach to adding a second protocol. The example files, however, are specific to the Microsoft TCP/IP protocol as supplied with LAN Manager version 2.1.

To get started, examine the diagram in figure 33.3, which illustrates the protocol stacks of WFWG and two TCP/IP providers as separate entities. You can see each of them has a hardware interface layer, a transport layer, and a set of higher layer application protocols.

Figure 33.3
Three separate protocol stacks: Windows for Workgroups, an NDIS-compliant TCP/IP stack, and an older TCP/IP stack.

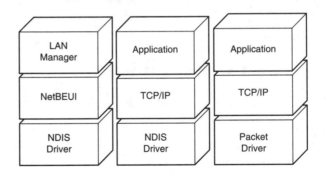

To add TCP/IP you might continue to use the hardware interface provided by the NDIS driver, but then add a shim. The shim enables a non-NDIS compliant TCP/IP protocol to get the services it needs from the NDIS driver (see fig. 33.4).

Figure 33.4
Protocols combined on NDIS, with an adapter protocol layer for the non-NDIS TCP/IP.

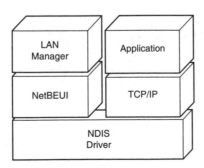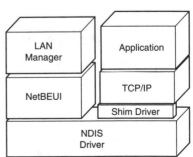

The small shim protocol layer generally can be provided by the same vendor that supplied the TCP/IP programs, or you can get it from public bulletin board systems or the Internet.

To accomplish what you see in figure 33.4, you need to follow several basic steps and understand a few concepts. First, remember that the NetBEUI protocol loaded by Windows for Workgroups is loaded dynamically when Windows starts (unless you load it yourself first with the NET START FULL command). Other protocols, however, are not built into Windows and do not have DLL libraries to run. Instead, you need to start them before you start Windows. Then tell Windows it needs to attend to another protocol in real mode. For NDIS-compliant TCP/IP stacks, you also make entries into the PROTOCOL.INI file so that the Protocol Manager can bind the protocol to the NDIS driver. For the non-NDIS TCP/IP protocol, add an entry for the packet driver shim, which is the NDIS-compliant part of the protocol stack.

In the following sections, you modify your system's CONFIG.SYS, AUTOEXEC.BAT, and PROTOCOL.INI files. Make sure you make backup copies before you begin. In addition, be sure to make an emergency boot disk so that you can recover from mistakes in the CONFIG.SYS file.

If you happen to be using the TCP/IP protocol from Microsoft, the files needed for the TCP/IP protocol can be obtained from a LAN Manager workstation that already has the TCP/IP protocol stack installed.

You should not install LAN Manager on the same workstation as Windows for Workgroups because the LAN Manager 2.1 installation program has not been updated to accommodate Windows for Workgroups. It overwrites important entries in the SYSTEM.INI and CONFIG.SYS files.

Getting the Right Files

The files you need to create a real-mode protocol stack vary from vendor to vendor. The Microsoft TCP/IP requires these files:

NEMM.DOS

TCPDRV.DOS

UMB.COM

EMSBFR.EXE

TCPTSR.EXE

TINYRFC.EXE

NMTSR.EXE

TCPUTILS.INI

PING.EXE

The last program, PING.EXE, is a utility all TCP/IP users are familiar with: PING.EXE checks for basic connectivity between your workstation and other hosts. If you are using the shim packet driver for a non-NDIS protocol, it has a name similar to DIS_PKT.DOS or DIS_PKT.GUP.

You can put the files anywhere you want on the hard disk, but for this example, they are placed in the Windows main directory.

For the TCP/IP protocol to work properly, you also create a subdirectory called ETC in the Windows main directory. The ETC directory contains several files needed by the TCP/IP protocol, including a HOSTS file that enables you to connect to TCP/IP hosts by name rather than by number. Other files in the ETC directory are used by TCP/IP—refer to your TCP/IP documentation for a description of the HOSTS file and these additional files.

Before you start the installation, you should obtain the following information from your network administrator:

✔ Your workstation's IP address

✔ Your subnet mask

✔ The address of the default gateway (if used)

✔ An address of a host you can use to test the protocol

Now you need to edit the CONFIG.SYS, AUTOEXEC.BAT, and PROTOCOL.INI system files. If you are using the Microsoft TCP/IP protocol, you also must edit the TCPUTILS.INI file.

The following examples illustrate typical system files using an SMC ARCnet adapter with an NDIS driver called SMC_ARC.DOS. You need to substitute in your own CONFIG.SYS and AUTOEXEC.BAT files the name and settings of your network interface card.

Editing the CONFIG.SYS File

Add entries to the CONFIG.SYS file to load any required TCP/IP protocols. Some newer TCP/IP protocols add only the packet driver, DIS_PKT.DOS, to the CONFIG.SYS file.

```
device=c:\qemm\qemm386.sys exclude=b000-c8ff exclude=d000-d8ff
```

You might have a different expanded memory manager, but remember to exclude any addresses used by your network interface card, and any other add-in cards you have.

```
DOS=HIGH,UMB
SHELL=C:\DOS\COMMAND.COM C:\DOS\ /E:2048 /P
FILES=30
BUFFERS=12
LASTDRIVE=Z
device=C:\WIN31\PROTMAN.DOS /i:C:\WIN31
device=C:\WIN31\NEMM.DOS
device=C:\WIN31\TCPDRV.DOS /i:C:\WIN31
```

The preceding two lines are specific to the Microsoft protocol. If you use another vendor's protocol, refer to its documentation for the appropriate entries.

If the protocol you plan to use is not NDIS-compliant, you might need to add a line similar to the following to your system's CONFIG.SYS file:

```
device=C:\WIN31\DIS_PKT.DOS
```

The preceding line is not used with Microsoft's TCP/IP.

```
device=C:\WIN31\WORKGROUP.SYS
device=C:\WIN31\SMC_ARC.DOS
```

The final two lines in this example CONFIG.SYS file load a driver required by Windows for Workgroups (WORKGROUP.SYS) and the protocol driver for the SMC ARCnet card.

Editing the AUTOEXEC.BAT File

Modify the AUTOEXEC.BAT file to load any required TSR programs.

```
C:\WIN31\UMB.COM
C:\WIN31\NET START
C:\WIN31\EMSBFR
C:\WIN31\TCPTSR
C:\WIN31\TINYRFC
C:\WIN31\NMTSR
```

Remember that the AUTOEXEC.BAT file is a list of DOS commands you can enter manually from the DOS prompt. Because the manual addition of protocols is tricky, you should type each command at the DOS prompt before you include them in the AUTOEXEC.BAT file. This way, you can check things slowly and stop when an error occurs.

Note that this is for the Microsoft TCP/IP protocol. The commands entered in the preceding sample file are used to start the protocol Microsoft under DOS. Enter the appropriate commands for the TCP/IP you are using.

Editing the PROTOCOL.INI File

You need to make only a few additions to the PROTOCOL.INI file for the packet driver to accept the TCP/IP protocol. In order to bind all the protocol modules together, you now add a few lines to the PROTOCOL.INI file.

```
[network.setup]
version=0x3100
netcard=ms$smc270,1,MS$SMC270
transport=ms$netbeui,MS$NETBEUI
transport=ms$tcp,MS$TCP
lana0=ms$smc270,1,ms$netbeui
lana1=ms$smc270,1,ms$tcp

[protman]
DriverName=PROTMAN$
PRIORITY=MS$NETBEUI

[MS$NETBEUI]
DriverName=netbeui$
SESSIONS=6
NCBS=12
BINDINGS=MS$SMC270
LANABASE=0

[MS$SMC270]
DriverName=SMC_ARC$
interrupt=7
iobase=0x300
memorybase=0xD800

[ms$tcp]
drivername=TCPIP$
```

Be sure that "TCPIP$" is in uppercase letters.

```
nbsessions=10
bindings=MS$SMC270
lanabase=1
```

Note that this is the second network, so the lanabase is not 0.

```
ipaddress0=133 5 232 123
subnetmask0=255 255 255 0
defaultgateway0=133 5 231 1
```

Note that the IP addresses for this protocol are separated by spaces instead of the more traditional periods. If you are using a packet driver shim, then you have the following entry instead of the preceding entry:

```
[PKTDRV]
drivername=PKTDRV
bindings=MS$SMC270
intvec=0x65
```

In this case, you also substitute PKTDRV for MS$TCP on the transport and lanabase= lines. You might also need the entry chainvec=0x66. The documentation from the vendor of the TCP/IP software should explain this.

Editing the SYSTEM.INI File

A few entries in the SYSTEM.INI file are needed for adding any real-mode protocol stack. If you have read the chapter on adding support for Novell NetWare, you already might be familiar with this.

Add the following entry in the [386Enh] section:

V86ModeLanas=1

This entry tells Windows that a real-mode protocol is in use on the specified LANA; the number 1 should agree with the LANA that you specified in the PROTOCOL.INI file. If you have additional real-mode protocols loaded (such as NetWare), list all the real-mode protocol LANAs on this line, separating each with a comma.

To make room for the additional protocol communications buffers, increase the netheapsize= parameter in the [386Enh] section to 60 from the default of 20. This adds buffer space for passing network data frames between real and protected modes. No good way exists for you to determine the optimal setting for this number.

If the vendor of the TCP/IP protocol has special support for Windows, or if they have uncovered other compatibility problems with Windows, you might need to add additional entries. Please check the documentation that came with the protocol.

Getting Ready To Test

Now you should be ready to reboot and try your changes. To test your changes, restart your workstation and see what happens. Be sure to write down any error messages in case you need to call Microsoft or the TCP/IP vendor for support. Do not be surprised if things do not work right at first. This is why you made the emergency boot disk and backed up your system initialization files.

Tracking Down Problems

When you attempt to add communications protocols to your workstation that are not formally supported by Microsoft, you can run into problems. The key to solving the problem is to narrow down its scope to the exact program or driver that is failing. The following guidelines can help you find the error:

✔ Start with a clean system. It is possible you have a workstation that is crammed with memory managers, drive utilities, alternate Windows drivers, and even TSRs. Save all the configuration files, then get rid of everything you do not need for the protocols. You might even need to remove hardware from the PC that could be interfering. If the protocols work, add what you removed one at a time until you uncover the culprit.

✔ Double-check the PROTOCOL.INI file. Remember that the BINDINGS= entries must reference the correct NDIS driver.

✔ Make sure you are not using the same LANA number or LANABASE for two protocols.

✔ Before you add new lines to the AUTOEXEC.BAT file (and before starting Windows), enter each line manually from the DOS prompt.

✔ Always verify that the computer you are trying to communicate with is working. It seems silly, but in many cases problems beyond your own workstation keep you from success. Use the PING utility that comes with your TCP/IP software to test the connection.

✔ Start slowly. Make sure Windows for Workgroups works by itself before you try to add additional protocols.

✔ Write down everything you do. Later you might want to go back to a particular step or discuss specific error messages or configurations with the technical support group from the company supplying the protocol.

Creating E-Mail Links with Gateways

E-mail has become a mainstay of many businesses for routine and frequent correspondence between employees and others outside the company. Windows for Workgroups supports e-mail, but the built-in programs can be used to communicate only with others on the same network using the same post office. To be able to connect e-mail to other post offices and other networks, you need to upgrade the Windows for Workgroups mail system to a full Microsoft Mail 3.*x* system.

Adding the Microsoft Mail Extensions to WFWG

Microsoft offers an add-on package to Windows for Workgroups that upgrades the built-in mail system to a full Microsoft Mail 3.*x* post office. This extension provides your users with dial-in mail capability, connections to other MS Mail 3.*x* post offices, and connections to gateways of other networks. Gateways for the following mail systems can be purchased from Microsoft:

- ✔ MCI Mail

- ✔ SNADS Mail, including IBM's DISSOS

- ✔ IBM PROFS and OfficeVision

- ✔ SMTP (UNIX mail using TCP/IP)

- ✔ X.400

- ✔ 3+Mail

- ✔ Facsimile

- ✔ MIIS and MHS-compatible systems

- ✔ Microsoft Mail for PC Networks, and Microsoft Mail for AppleTalk Networks

In addition, the File Format API module from Microsoft is available. This module enables you to write your own mail gateway program.

Installing the Post Office Extensions

The Microsoft Mail 3.*x* system has an inherent concept of a client/server LAN relationship, as opposed to the peer-to-peer concept in Windows for Workgroups. As such, the extensions package, which is mostly a Microsoft Mail 3.*x* package, assumes a server exists that contains the post office. This is not necessarily true if you are using only peer-to-peer networking. In that case, simply consider the workstation that contains the post office as the server.

The setup for Mail extensions gives you three options for installing the post office:

- ✔ Leave the post office on the existing system. The upgrade of the post office and the addition of new client software setup directories takes over 7.5 MB of disk space. For this reason, make sure you have a large amount of free hard disk space before you choose this option.

- ✔ Create a new peer workstation that is dedicated to the post office (and possibly other central functions). This becomes a de facto server.

✔ Specify a different network for the location of the post office or install a LAN Manager server. You can install the post office on the server for a NetWare network, for example, and use it from your Windows for Workgroups network. This makes sense if you are concerned about the security or reliability of a peer workstation. Every user's mail goes through the post office. As a result, make sure Mail is located on a reliable system with plenty of extra disk space.

If you decide to leave the post office on the existing system, the upgrade is transparent, and you can continue to use the post office the same way as before. The second and third installation options require you to edit the MSMAIL.INI file so that it points to the new post office location after you move the post office.

The program for upgrading the post office, called Extend, is a DOS program. If you are running Windows when you start Extend, Windows creates a DOS session for you. You should be running Windows for Workgroups because you need network access if the post office is not on your workstation. The step-by-step instructions for upgrading to a full Microsoft Mail 3.*x* post office are straightforward and come with the Extensions package.

If for any reason the installation process is interrupted and you need to start over, you must manually erase all the new files created in the post office directory structure. All the files added by the Extend program are marked as read-only. If you try to reinstall Mail, Extend fails when it tries to rewrite the new files and directories.

Upgrading Windows for Workgroups Mail Program

After you upgrade the Microsoft Mail post office, you are ready to upgrade each user's Mail program. The new end-user Microsoft Mail programs include the following features not found in the Windows for Workgroups mail package:

✔ Expanded online Help

✔ A spelling checker

✔ Online demos

You can try these new features before you upgrade other users to see if the added features are worth the effort.

The Microsoft Mail Extensions upgrade package comes with the necessary files for the users' workstations, but before the files can be accessed, you need to install them in a central location. As before, the Microsoft Mail program makes the assumption you have a central server that all users access. For Windows for Workgroups, you need to choose a particular workstation that is the central source for the Microsoft Mail users' programs. You should install the user programs on that workstation and share the directory with all users. As with the post office Extend program, the installation program for decompressing and installing the end users' files in a central location is a DOS program. Windows creates a DOS session when you run the install program.

After you install the user files, individual users can upgrade their own workstations by connecting to the common file workstation and then running the Setup program. As you add additional Windows for Workgroups users, each user can upgrade to the full Mail package on their own.

Adding the UNIX Gateway System

After the post office is upgraded, you can add a gateway system. A *gateway* is a dedicated PC that serves only as an external system link. A gateway PC requires the following hardware and software:

✔ MS-DOS 3.1 or later

✔ A designated SMTP host for message routing

✔ A network interface card that connects to the Windows for Workgroups LAN

✔ A network interface card that connects to the TCP/IP network; this could be the same as the Windows for Workgroups LAN card with both protocols running it if you are sharing a common network for both TCP/IP and Windows NetBEUI

✔ A TCP/IP protocol stack compatible with the gateway software (contact Microsoft for the most current list)

✔ The Microsoft Mail Gateway to SMTP software for the local post office

✔ A copy of Microsoft Mail Gateway Access for SMTP software for each Microsoft Mail post office reached through the local post office

The gateway system offers access with the following major standards:

✔ RFC 821 Simple Mail Transfer Protocol (SMTP) over TCP/IP

✔ RFC 822 ARPA Internet text messaging standard

✔ Both incoming and outgoing UUENCODED attachments

✔ RFC 1154 Encoding Header Field for Internet Messages

In addition to enabling mail connectivity to UNIX hosts and users, the SMTP mail gateway also can be configured to use a TCP/IP backbone as a long-distance mail carrier between Microsoft Mail systems. Because the mail messages sent this way are fully encapsulated, you can send a single text message with multimedia and binary attachments across the TCP/IP network.

Chapter Snapshot

Using the Remote Access Services (RAS) server built into
Windows NT and NT Advanced Server, Windows for
Workgroups users can connect to an NT and NT Advanced
Server environment and gain access to the network's shared
resources over a phone line or null modem connection. In
addition, Windows for Workgroups nodes can function as
point-to-point servers through RAS, enabling a user to
connect to a WFWG node to use its shared resources. This
chapter examines issues relating to RAS on NT and Windows for Workgroups systems, including the following
topics:

To understand the benefits of RAS, you first should have a
basic understanding of the capabilities that RAS provides.

CHAPTER

Using Remote Access Services

Windows NT and NT Advanced Server both offer built-in Remote Access Services (RAS). Remote users who have user accounts on a Windows NT server or in an NT Advanced Server domain can connect to the network by dial-in connection (phone lines) or by null modem connection and gain access to network resources such as file and printer services and e-mail. This connection can be accomplished if the remote user is running Windows NT or Windows for Workgroups 3.11.

NT Advanced Server's RAS supports dial-in connections for up to 64 users simultaneously. Windows NT's RAS supports only a single dial-in connection at a time. After a user has connected to the system through RAS, all remote network resources that normally are available to him as a local user become available transparently over the dial-in connection. The user can connect to shared directories, use shared printers, and perform other actions with shared resources that can be accomplished by local users.

The Remote Access Services on NT Advanced Server provide support for named pipes, Remote Procedure Call (RPC), and the LAN Manager API. NT Advanced Server RAS also provides remote access to SQL Server, SNA Server for Windows NT, and Lotus Notes. Connection capabilities include standard public phone lines, X.25, and ISDN.

Windows for Workgroups 3.11 includes the necessary client software to enable remote WFWG nodes to dial into the Windows NT and NT Advanced Server RAS to access network resources. In addition, a Point-to-Point server is available to enable Windows for Workgroups nodes to share their local resources through dial-in connections. This Point-to-Point server supports only a single connection at a time. In addition, only resources on the WFWG node that is acting as a server are available to dial-in users. For security reasons, any other network resources that are available to the WFWG server are not made available to dial-in users.

If you need to have full network access through RAS, one option is to install Windows NT or NT Advanced Server to provide that capability. Another option is to use a product—such as Shiva's NetModem for Windows for Workgroups—that provides access to network resources.

The Windows for Workgroups Point-to-Point server software is available free of charge on CompuServe, from the Microsoft Download Service, and from other online sources (see the section "Using Microsoft's Point-to-Point Server" in this chapter). The Point-to-Point server is an excellent option to provide access to a user's primary office system from remote locations (such as home or a hotel).

If security and access to other network resources is a primary concern, consider installing NT Advanced Server and using its RAS to provide these features.

Installing and Configuring the RAS Client Software

By default, the RAS client software is not installed by Setup when you install Windows for Workgroups. To install the RAS client software, open the Network group in Program Manager and choose the Remote Access icon. Windows displays the dialog box shown in figure 34.1. To install the RAS client software, choose the Install button.

Figure 34.1
The Remote Access dialog box indicating the RAS client software is not installed.

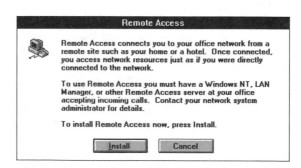

After you choose the Install button, Windows begins copying driver files and configuring the RAS client software. Windows displays the dialog box shown in figure 34.2 if the Enhanced Mode Protocol Manager is already installed on the system. You can choose No to continue working with the existing protocol manager. If you want to replace it with a later version, choose the Yes button. To have Remote Access install all new drivers, choose the Yes to All button.

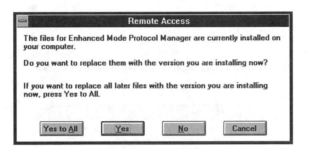

Figure 34.2
The Remote Access dialog box indicating that the Enhanced Mode Protocol Manager is already installed.

It is unlikely that you will need to update this file. As of this writing, the Enhanced Mode Protocol Manager that ships with Windows for Workgroups 3.11 is the latest version.

After Remote Access has installed the necessary software on your system, it will prompt you to specify the modem and communications port you will be using for remote access (see fig. 34.3). Select from the Port list the COM port to which the modem is connected. Select from the Device list the modem brand and model you will be using. If your modem is not listed, you might be able to use one of the modems included in the list if your modem is compatible with it; many modems are compatible with the Hayes line of modems, for example. If you are unsure which modem to use, refer to your modem manual for a list of compatible modems or contact your modem vendor's technical support staff for assistance.

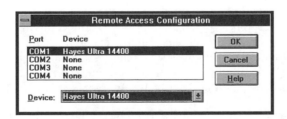

Figure 34.3
Use the Remote Access Configuration dialog box to select a COM port and modem.

After you have selected a port and modem, Remote Access modifies your SYSTEM.INI and PROTOCOL.INI files. The original files are backed up using new file names (see fig. 34.4). Remote Access then prompts you to reboot the computer for the changes to take effect (see fig. 34.5). If you want to continue working and reboot the system later, choose the Continue button (you will not be able to use Remote Access until the system is rebooted). To reboot the system immediately, choose the Restart Computer button.

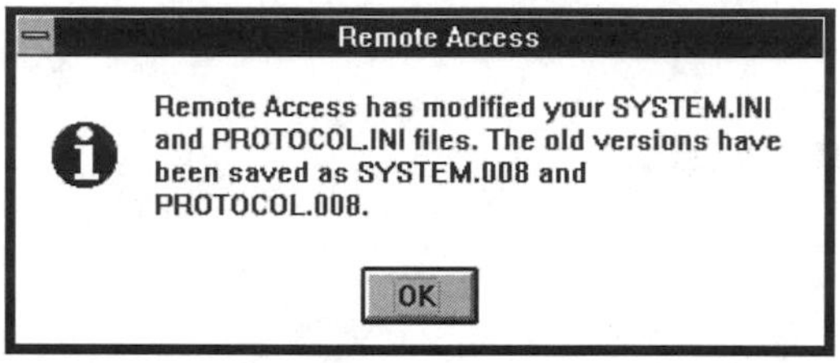

Figure 34.4
Remote Access backs up your existing SYSTEM.INI and PROTOCOL.INI files.

Figure 34.5
You must reboot the computer before you can use Remote Access.

Configuring the RAS Client Software

After the RAS client software is installed, you must set configuration options such as the phone number for the dial-in connection. To start the RAS client and configure it, open the Network group and choose the Remote Access icon. The Remote Access program window shown in figure 34.6 appears.

If there are no existing dial-in entries, Remote Access automatically prompts you to create an entry when the program starts. If you have an existing entry and want to add a new one, choose the Add button to display the Add Phone Book Entry dialog box shown in figure 34.7.

In the Entry Name text box, type a descriptive name for the phone book entry you are creating. This entry name will appear in the list of possible connections in the main Remote Access program window. In the Phone Number text box, enter the phone number of the remote system. If your phone system requires a dialing prefix (such as 9 to get an outside line), include it with the phone number. In the Description field, enter a description or comments that more fully describe the remote system.

You also might need to set additional options, depending on the type of connection you are making to the remote system. Choose the Advanced button to expand the dialog box to include the additional controls shown in figure 34.8.

The Port drop-down list enables you to select the port associated with the current phone book entry. If necessary, you can use the Remote Access Configuration dialog box (refer to figure 34.3) to configure a different device for each of your available COM ports. If you are using a modem for remote access to one or more systems and a null modem connection to a local system, for example, configure each of these using the Remote Access Configuration dialog box (choose Setup, then Configuration).

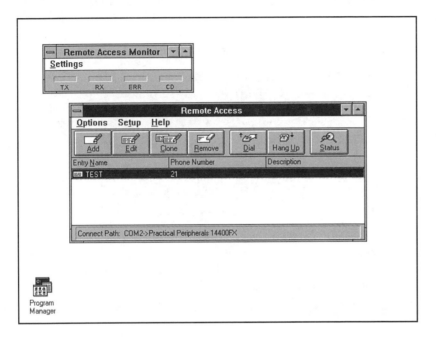

Figure 34.6
The Remote Access program window and Remote Access Monitor window.

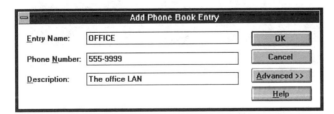

Figure 34.7
Use the Add Phone Book Entry dialog box to create dialing entries for remote systems.

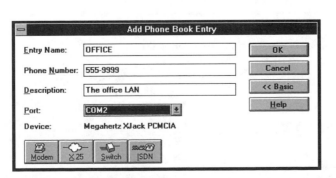

Figure 34.8
The Add Phone Book Entry dialog box expanded to show advanced options.

Tip

The entries in the **P**ort drop-down list in the Add Phone Book Entry dialog box enable you to select from the port configurations you previously configured. If you have not assigned a device to a particular port, that port will not appear in the drop-down list.

In addition to displaying configured COM ports, the **P**ort drop-down list also displays other entries. The following list explains these additional port entries:

✔ **Any modem port.** This selection causes Remote Access to attempt a connection on each of the possible modem ports until a connection succeeds.

✔ **Any X.25 port.** This selection causes Remote Access to attempt a connection on each of the possible X.25 ports until a connection succeeds.

✔ **Any ISDN port.** This selection causes Remote Access to attempt a connection on each of the possible ISDN ports until a connection succeeds.

When you select a port, the device type that is associated with the selected port appears below the **P**ort drop-down list.

The **M**odem button displays the Modem Settings dialog box (see fig. 34.9), which you can use to set options for a modem connection. Use the **I**nitial Speed drop-down list to specify the speed at which the modem will first attempt a connection to the remote server. Depending on the capabilities of the remote modem, line quality, and other issues, the actual speed can vary during the session.

Figure 34.9

Setting modem connection options in the Modem Settings dialog box.

Modem Settings	
Modem: Megahertz XJack PCMCIA	OK
Initial speed (bps): 19200	Cancel
Hardware Features	Help
⊠ Enable hardware flow control	
⊠ Enable modem error control	
☐ Enable modem compression	
☐ Enter modem commands manually	

The Hardware Features group box provides a set of check boxes you can use to manage flow control, error correction, and compression. In most situations, the flow control and error correction check boxes should be enabled. The compression option, however, usually should be turned off because your system probably provides compression using software, which produces better performance than hardware compression by the modem.

Attempting to send a compressed file with hardware compression enabled actually increases transmission time and the number of bytes to be transferred. Leave hardware compression turned off if you are transmitting or receiving compressed files.

The last of the options in the Modem Settings dialog box—Enter modem commands manually—enables you to send commands to the modem manually when dialing. In most situations, you do not need to enable this option. This option is useful primarily for testing new modem configurations before adding them to the MODEM.INF file (which defines modem scripts). You do not need to enable this option if you intend to dial manually using a telephone keypad. Instead, use the Operator Assisted or Manual Dialing command in the Options menu.

For information on configuring X.25 and ISDN connections, consult the Remote Access Help file. The Remote Access Help file also covers methods for integrating remote access with modem pool switches and security servers. Because these options do not apply in the majority of cases, *Inside Windows, Platinum Edition* does not cover them.

After you have selected and configured a modem and set the other configuration options described previously, you are ready to use RAS to connect to a remote system.

The Remote Access Monitor

By default, Remote Access starts the Remote Access Monitor as soon as the program starts. The Remote Access Monitor is a separate window (refer to figure 34.6) that displays connection information and mimics the function of modem front-panel lights. The RX and TX lights indicate reception and transmission of data. The ERR light indicates error conditions. The CD light indicates the status of Carrier Detect. If you do not want to use the monitor, select the Options menu in the Remote Access window and clear the Launch Monitor at Start Up command.

Using RAS To Access Remote Resources

As explained earlier in this chapter, you can use the RAS client software provided with Windows for Workgroups 3.11 to connect to remote systems running NT, NT Advanced Server, or other systems providing remote access services (including a Windows for Workgroups node, as explained later in this chapter in the section titled "Configuring RAS on NT").

Using RAS to connect to remote resources is relatively simple. After you have configured RAS on your system and created a phone book entry in the Remote Access program, dial the remote system. To do so, double-click on its entry in the phone book list or select an entry and choose the Dial button. Remote Access then displays the Authentication dialog box shown in figure 34.10.

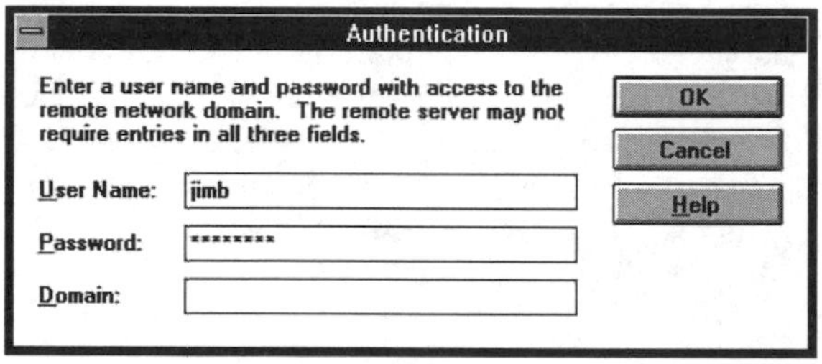

Figure 34.10
The Authentication dialog box prompts you for user information for the remote system.

Authentication
Enter a user name and password with access to the remote network domain. The remote server may not require entries in all three fields.
User Name: jimb
Password: ********
Domain:

OK Cancel Help

Remote Access does not use the information in the Authentication dialog box to actually log you in to the remote system. Instead, it uses the information to determine if you have the necessary rights to access the system. Therefore, you also have to log in after Remote Access connects to the remote system.

Generally, the information you supply in the Authentication dialog box matches your user name and password on the remote system. It might or might not be the same as your local user name and password, depending on the configuration of the remote system.

Tip

If you are joining a domain on the remote system, the domain name that you specify in the Domain text box must be the same domain on which your remote access account is located.

After you have entered the appropriate information in the Authentication dialog box, click on OK. Remote Access will dial the remote system and initiate a connection. When the connection is established, Remote Access displays the dialog box shown in figure 34.11.

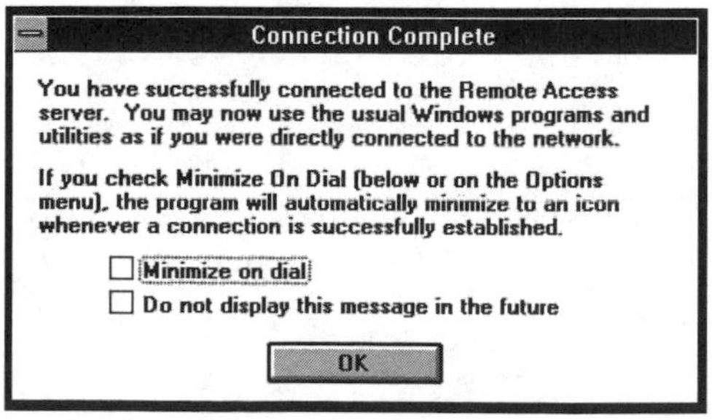

Figure 34.11
This dialog box appears when a connection is first established.

Connection Complete
You have successfully connected to the Remote Access server. You may now use the usual Windows programs and utilities as if you were directly connected to the network.
If you check Minimize On Dial (below or on the Options menu), the program will automatically minimize to an icon whenever a connection is successfully established.
☐ Minimize on dial
☐ Do not display this message in the future
OK

If you place a check in the box labeled Minimize on dial, the Remote Access program window automatically shrinks to an icon as soon as the connection is established. If you do not want to view this dialog box in future sessions, place a check in the box labeled Do not display this message in the future.

You can configure Remote Access to minimize as soon as you dial, and also have Remote Access minimize when it hangs up the connection. To set either of these options, choose **O**ptions, then either Minimize on **D**ial or Minimize on **H**ang Up, or both.

Using Network Resources

Once your system is connected by Remote Access to the remote system, you are able to access resources on the remote system. The level of access you have depends on the operating environment of the remote system. If the remote system is running Windows NT or NT Advanced Server, you can gain access to any network-wide resources for which you have user-level access rights (determined by the remote system administrator). If you are a member of a domain, and you have specified a domain name in Remote Access's Authentication dialog box, you have access to resources in your domain.

If you are connecting to a remote Windows for Workgroups system that is running Microsoft's Point-to-Point server (see the section "Using Microsoft's Point-to-Point Server" in this chapter), you can access only those shared resources on the remote node for which you have access permission.

To use a shared resource on a remote system to which you are connected by Remote Access, employ the same procedure you would use to access a resource if you were connected to the LAN locally. To connect to and use a disk resource, for example, open File Manager and choose **D**isk, **C**onnect Network Drive.

If you experience the error message dialog box shown in figure 34.12 when browsing for resources on a Windows for Workgroups node that is running the Point-to-Point server, add the setting `MaintainServerList=Yes` to the `[Network]` section of the remote node's SYSTEM.INI file.

If the remote server does not appear in the Connect Network Drive dialog box, enter the name of the remote machine and the share name in the **P**ath text box (see fig. 34.13).

To connect to a remote network printer, use the same process you would use to connect to a printer located on your LAN. For information on connecting to and using network printers, refer to Chapter 28, "Sharing Resources in Windows."

Figure 34.12
The Windows for Workgroups dialog box indicating that the remote system is not maintaining the server list.

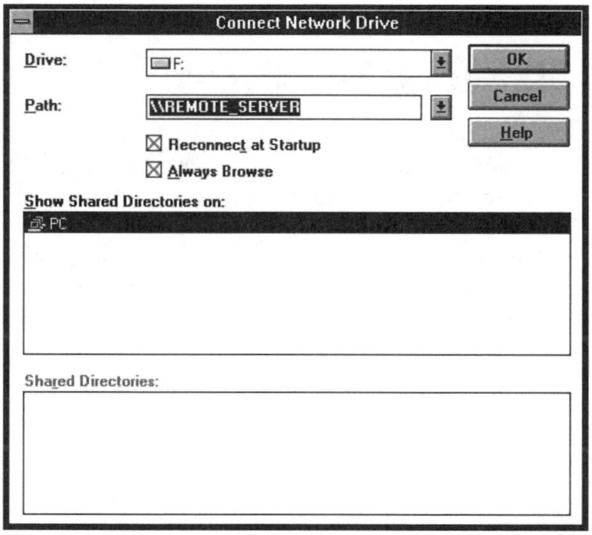

Figure 34.13
The Connect Network Drive dialog box.

Configuring RAS on NT

Before you can dial into an NT environment using Windows for Workgroups (or any other RAS client, including an NT client), you must install and configure Remote Access Services on NT. To install RAS on NT, first log on to the NT node as an administrator. Then open the Control Panel in the Main program group and choose the Network icon. The Network Settings dialog box shown in figure 34.14 appears.

Verify that RAS is not already installed on the node. Browse through the Installed Network Software list box. If you do not find Remote Access Services listed, RAS has not yet been installed. To install RAS, choose the Add Software button. This displays the Add Network Software dialog box shown in figure 34.15.

From the Network Software drop-down list, choose Remote Access Service, then click on the Continue button. NT prompts you to specify the location of the NT distribution files (see fig. 34.16). Specify the proper path, then click on the Continue button. After NT copies the necessary drivers, it displays the Add Port dialog box shown in figure 34.17. From the Port drop-down list, choose the port to which the modem (or null modem cable) is connected, then click on OK.

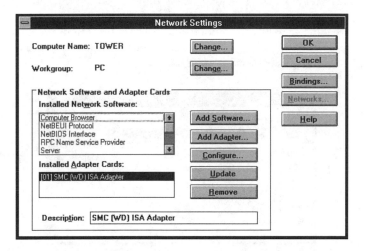

Figure 34.14
The Network Settings dialog box enables you to install RAS under NT.

Figure 34.15
The Add Network Software dialog box.

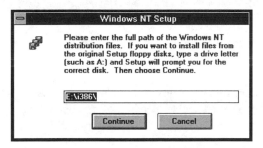

Figure 34.16
NT Setup prompts you for the location of the NT distribution files.

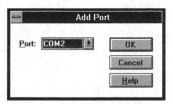

Figure 34.17
The Add Port dialog box.

NT then displays the Configure Port dialog box shown in figure 34.18. From the Attached Device list box, choose the type of modem being used to provide remote access. In the Port Usage group box, choose the option button that specifies the type of RAS configuration you want for the node. If you choose the Dial out only option button, you will only be able to dial out—other users will not be able to dial into this NT node. If you want to restrict the node to dial-in access only, and not enable users to dial out using the specified port, choose the Receive calls only option button. To enable both services for the selected port, choose the Dial out and Receive calls option button.

Figure 34.18
Use the Configure Port dialog box to specify modem type and access options.

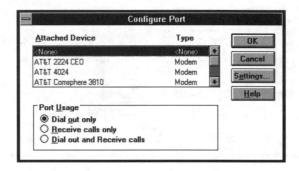

Choosing the Settings button in the Configure Port dialog box displays the Settings dialog box (see fig. 34.19), which enables you to specify various options for the selected port. Set the options according to your preferences and to the requirements of your modem, then click on OK.

Figure 34.19
Use the Settings dialog box to control modem preferences.

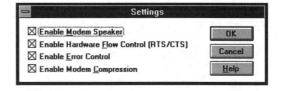

Note

As when configuring the Windows for Workgroups RAS client software, clear the check box labeled Enable Modem Compression and use software compression.

After you have configured the port and modem, the Remote Access Setup dialog box appears (see fig. 34.20). If you have other modems or ports to configure, choose the Add or Clone buttons to create the new port settings. Use the Add button if you need to specify different settings for the next port, and use the Clone button to copy settings from one port to another.

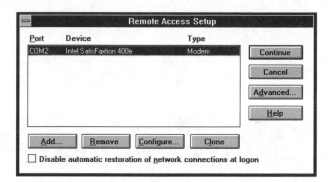

Figure 34.20
The Remote Access Setup dialog box.

When you have completed adding each necessary port, choose the Advanced button to display the Advanced Configuration dialog box (see fig. 34.21). This dialog box enables you to control the type of access that dial-in users will have to the network. To provide access to only the current NT node, choose the option button labeled This computer only. Users dialing in to the system will not be able to access any other shared resources. To provide access to resources across the network, choose the option labeled Entire network.

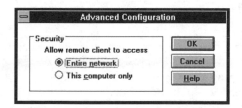

Figure 34.21
The Advanced Configuration dialog box enables you to control access to resources.

Even if you choose the Entire network option button, dial-in users are not able to access resources on the LAN unless they have the proper user accounts and passwords.

After you set the desired access type, click on the OK button to close the Advanced Configuration dialog box, then click on the Continue button in the Remote Access Setup dialog box to complete the configuration process. NT then displays a simple dialog box informing you that you must use the Remote Access Admin program to assign access permissions. Click on OK in this dialog box, then choose Yes when NT prompts you to restart the computer for the changes to take effect.

Access Permissions

After you have installed and configured RAS on the NT node, open the new Remote Access Service group (created automatically by Setup during the configuration process) and choose the Remote Access Admin icon. This opens the Remote Access Admin program shown in figure 34.22.

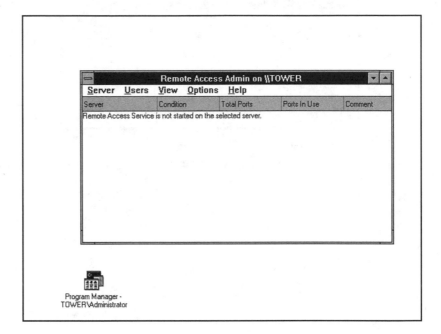

To start RAS, choose Server, Start Remote Access. The Start Remote Access Service dialog box shown in figure 34.23 appears. In the Server text box, enter the machine name of the NT server that provides remote access services, and click on OK to start the service. The status in the Condition field of the Remote Access Admin window changes to read "Running", indicating that RAS is now running on the associated server.

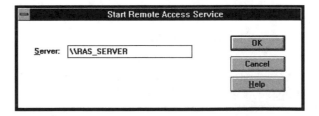

Next, set permissions for dial-in users. To do so, choose Users, Permissions. In the Remote Access Permissions dialog box (see fig. 34.24), select the existing user account to which you want to provide dial-in access. Place a check in the check box labeled Grant dialin permission to user.

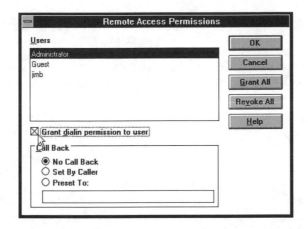

Figure 34.24
The Remote
Access
Permissions dialog
box.

Networking and Windows

In the **C**all Back group box, specify whether the selected user requires call-back. If call-back is used, NT performs the authentication process when the user dials in. If authentication is verified, NT hangs up the connection and dials the user back according to the options set in the **C**all Back group box. The following list explains the options in the **C**all Back group box:

- ✔ **No Call Back.** If this option is selected, the user is given access to the shared resources without being called back.

- ✔ **Set By Caller.** If this option is selected, NT prompts the dial-in user for a number at which NT can call the user back. NT then hangs up the connection and calls the user back.

- ✔ **Preset To.** If this option is selected, the call back number specified in the associated text box is used. You can associate a different call-back number with each user.

For the best security, avoid using the Set By Caller option unless the user is dialing in from various locations. If the user dials in from the same number each time, use the Preset To option to define the number at which the user will be called back to make the connection.

When you finish assigning user permissions, click on OK to close the Remote Access Permissions dialog box. If you prefer, you can close the Remote Access Admin program—it does not need to be running for NT to provide remote access services.

Using Microsoft's Point-to-Point Server

The Microsoft Point-to-Point Server is a free add-on for Windows for Workgroups that enables a Windows for Workgroups node to act as a remote access server. Users dial into the WFWG node and access locally shared resources. You cannot, however, connect to a WFWG node using RAS and gain access to resources that are not located on that node. In other words, you cannot gain access to a LAN by dialing into a WFWG node on the LAN. Even with this limitation, the Point-to-Point Server offers an excellent means for users to connect from home or other sites to their main office computer. To provide LAN-wide remote access, use NT or NT Advanced Server to provide RAS on the network.

The Microsoft Point-to-Point Server is available from the Microsoft Download Service at (206) 936-6735 in the Windows for Workgroups Appnotes section as WFWPTP.EXE. The Point-to-Point Server also is available on CompuServe in the MSWRKGRP forum.

The Point-to-Point Server is contained in a self-extracting archive named WFWPTP.EXE. To install the Point-to-Point Server, first install and configure Remote Access on the Windows for Workgroups workstation that will be acting as a server. Then use the following steps to install the Point-to-Point Server:

1. Create a directory or format a 1.44 MB or 1.2 MB floppy disk to contain the Point-to-Point Server source files. These steps assume that you are formatting a floppy disk and using it in drive A.

2. Exit Windows, and at the DOS prompt change to the directory containing WFWPTP.EXE, type **WFWPTP A:**, and press Enter. This will expand the archive to the floppy.

3. Change to the drive containing the Point-to-Point Server files (such as drive A) and type **COPYPTP C:\WINDOWS**, then press Enter. If Windows for Workgroups is located on a path other than C:\WINDOWS, specify the appropriate directory in place of C:\WINDOWS.

4. Restart Windows.

At this point, the Point-to-Point Server is installed. Next, you must open Remote Access and configure it to accept incoming calls. To do so, open the Network group and choose the Remote Access icon. Choose Se*t*up, *C*onfigure to display the Remote Access Configuration dialog box (see fig. 34.25). This dialog box now contains additional options for configuring dial-in capability.

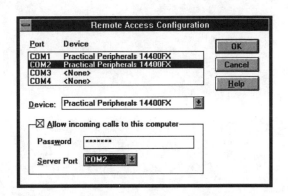

To enable incoming calls, place a check in the box labeled Allow incoming calls to this computer. In the Password text box type a password to protect access to the system. If you are configuring your own workstation as a server and will be dialing into it yourself, consider using a password that is different from your normal LAN password for extra security. To complete dial-in configuration, choose the port to be used for dial-in from the Server Port drop-down list box. When your settings are complete, click on OK.

After you have configured Remote Access to enable incoming calls, you must set it to monitor the port for incoming calls (essentially, place the modem in auto-answer mode). Choose the Answer button in the toolbar to cause Remote Access to monitor for incoming calls.

Part Six

Applying Multimedia

Chapter Snapshot

Multimedia has been slow to gain widespread acceptance, partly because so much confusion still exists about what multimedia really is. This chapter gives you an overview of multimedia and helps you with the following issues:

This chapter—along with Chapters 36 and 37—examines the different aspects of Windows multimedia. In them you will learn what multimedia really is, why it is an important new technology, and how you can take advantage of it.

35
CHAPTER

Working with Multimedia in Windows

Nothing is new about multimedia. Much of it, in fact, is relatively old technology that is being used in new ways. Essentially, *multimedia* is the merging of different kinds of media (and thus the term *multimedia*). Multimedia brings together sound, full-motion video, and still images to the computer environment. This merging of data formats is not very useful in itself, but like all tools, with proper application it can be useful.

Exploring Multimedia's Possibilities

Multimedia represents a fundamental change in the way you deal with computers and with the data you create on a computer. Multimedia capabilities enable you to make computer data mimic the real world more closely. You can, for example, embed a voice annotation in a letter. Assuming the recipients of the letter have the necessary hardware in their computer, they can double-click on the embedded annotation and hear your voice commenting about the document. Figure 35.1 shows a sound being recorded for embedding in a Word for Windows document.

Figure 35.1
A sound being recorded for embedding in a document.

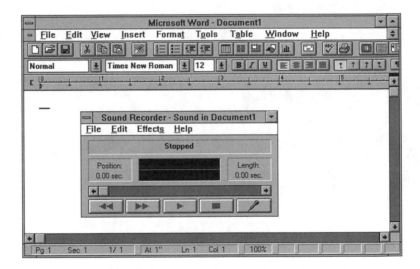

Suppose you want to develop a presentation to help you sell a new product. Ideally, the presentation should include sound, still images, and video. How do you bring those things together? By using multimedia authoring tools, you can create a single presentation that includes all the components you can play back on your computer.

Like any technology, multimedia can be applied in a nearly endless number of ways; it is more than just the capability to embed a sound in a document or create presentations. One of the most important uses for multimedia, for example, is in education. Multimedia brings together a wealth of data in different formats, potentially making the learning experience much richer. What better way to learn about windsurfing, for example, than to view a video of it and see an expert's techniques (see fig. 35.2)?

Generally, most users who are familiar with multimedia break it into four basic categories:

✔ **Information.** This category takes in a wide range of uses, including most business uses. Some examples include information kiosks, such as those found in shopping malls; business presentations to illustrate a product's design characteristics; general business presentations to market a product or provide an overview of a project; and office-communication functions such as embedding voice and video annotations in e-mail.

✔ **Education.** Multimedia presents many new ways for people to learn. Examples of multimedia learning tools include electronic encyclopedias and other online references such as books of quotations and dictionaries that contain video and sound clips; learning games that incorporate digitized sound and audio; and musical references that include detailed information about the composer and the work as well as the work itself.

✔ **Training.** Many companies are using multimedia for hands-on training. These multimedia training courses cover everything from learning to use a software application to troubleshooting and assembling electronic and other types of devices.

✔ **Entertainment.** Many computer games now include digitized sound and high-quality graphics. In Microsoft's Flight Simulator, for example, you actually hear a digitized voice speaking to you from the airport control tower as you fly.

Figure 35.2
A multimedia video clip being played back on a PC.

The combination of multimedia and the computer's capability to organize and process information provide a more free-form learning experience. After listening to and watching the windsurfing video, you might want to read a synopsis of early windsurfing designs and aborted ventures, or learn about some other person or event related to windsurfing. Because the computer can cross-link information, you can jump around the information provided, free-associating data and learning in the way that most interests you.

Multimedia, therefore, covers a wide range of capabilities. The following activities are just some of the things you can do with multimedia in Windows:

- ✔ Embed digitized sounds, such as voice annotations, in a document

- ✔ Assign sounds to different Windows events so that the sound is played when the event occurs

- ✔ Browse through an encyclopedia on CD and view text, hear recordings, and view video clips of each topic

- ✔ Develop presentations that combine video, still images, and sounds

- ✔ Listen to audio CDs on your computer

- ✔ Look up quotations and cross-reference the source of the quotation, and perhaps even hear it spoken by the original speaker

- ✔ Thoroughly explore musical works by hearing the piece, seeing the composer's image, reading about the composer's life, and learning about the themes behind the music

- ✔ Capture video clips from tape, laser disc, television, video camera, or other video sources and using those video clips in presentations or embedding them in documents

- ✔ Run or install software from CD-ROM, eliminating numerous floppy disks or saving a large amount of your hard disk's free space

- ✔ Play games that include stereo sound effects, realistic 3D images, and lifelike graphics

To play sounds included with multimedia applications (such as an online encyclopedia), your system must contain a sound adapter. Later sections of this chapter and Chapter 36 examine multimedia audio and sound adapters in more detail.

Determining Your Hardware and Software Needs

Of course, before you start working with multimedia, you have to make sure that you have the right hardware and software. Your hardware and software choices depend on how you plan to use multimedia. If you want to create basic multimedia documents by adding sound to your text files, you need a sound card and a CD-ROM drive. If you want to take advantage of other multimedia capabilities, such as video capture, you need to add other kinds of hardware and software to your PC.

Before you go on a hardware shopping spree, you need to identify the multimedia tasks you want to perform on your PC. Then decide which items of hardware and software you need to accomplish those tasks. Table 35.1 lists some of the most common multimedia capabilities and defines the hardware and software they require.

Table 35.1
Defining Your Multimedia Requirements

If You Want To Do This	You Need This
Play audio CDs	A CD-ROM drive, a host adapter for the CD-ROM drive (usually a SCSI adapter), speakers or head-phones, a sound card (optional), an MCI Audio CD driver (included with Windows 3.1), and Media Player (included with Windows 3.1) or some other audio-playback program
Embed sound in a document	A sound card and a microphone; sound cards usually supply the appropriate drivers
Play an embedded sound	A sound card and speakers or headphones
Watch TV on the computer	A TV adapter board, speakers, and a sound card
Capture video clips	A video adapter board and video editing software
Create multimedia presentations	Multimedia authoring software and multimedia data sources (a video source, a sound source, and more)
Assign sounds to system events	A sound card and speakers
View multimedia references such as encyclopedias	A CD-ROM drive with a host adapter and a sound card

If you want to experiment with sound without buying a sound adapter, you can install an optional speaker driver for Windows that will enable sounds to be played back on your PC's standard speaker. This driver is available on CompuServe and from the Microsoft BBS as a self-extracting archive named SPEAK.EXE.

VI

Applying Multimedia

The most common uses for multimedia require a CD-ROM drive, a host adapter for the CD-ROM, a sound card, and a set of speakers. If you plan to perform extensive multimedia authoring, including output to tape, you also need additional special-purpose video and audio equipment. If you plan to produce your own CDs, you need CD mastering software and hardware. The vast majority of everyday multimedia users, however, need only a CD-ROM drive and a sound card.

The following list summarizes the primary-system hardware requirements to support multimedia under Windows:

- ✔ **CPU.** A 486-25 or better system is recommended, with a higher CPU speed or Pentium processor naturally offering better performance.

- ✔ **RAM.** 4 MB minimum, with 8 MB recommended.

- ✔ **Video.** VGA 256-color adapter and display, with SuperVGA (800×600 or better) recommended.

Exploring Multimedia Upgrade Kits

A number of vendors now offer multimedia upgrade kits for PCs. These upgrade kits usually include a CD-ROM drive, a SCSI adapter for the CD-ROM drive, a sound card, and sometimes speakers. This type of upgrade kit provides all the basic components you need to add multimedia capabilities to your Windows PC.

The following list describes some of the multimedia upgrade kits that are currently available from various vendors. This list does not represent all the available upgrade kits, but does cover some of the most popular ones.

- ✔ **Media Vision Fusion CD.** Media Vision offers a number of multimedia upgrade kits, the newest of which are the Fusion CD kits. The kits include a sound card, a CD-ROM drive and adapter, speakers, and software.

    Fusion CD 16. This kit includes a 16-bit Pro AudioSpectrum 16 sound card, a Sony internal CD-ROM drive, speakers, and a selection of CD-ROM applications.

    Fusion CD. This kit includes an 8-bit Pro AudioSpectrum Plus sound card, an NEC CD-ROM drive, and speakers.

- ✔ **Media Vision Pro 16 Multimedia System.** This kit provides a higher-performance CD-ROM drive than the Fusion kits. It includes a 16-bit Pro AudioSpectrum 16 sound card, an NEC MV8 internal CD-ROM drive, and a selection of multimedia applications including 1-2-3, Multimedia Encyclopedia, King's Quest V, ACTION!, and Where in the World is Carmen San Diego?.

✔ **Media Vision CDPC XL.** If you are looking for a system that does not require you to open your computer to install it, the Media Vision CDPC XL system is the one for you. It combines all its components into a single desktop unit that sits under your computer's monitor or beside your PC on the desk. This kit includes a Pro AudioSpectrum 16 sound card, dual-speed CD-ROM drive, 100 W amplifier, built-in speakers, multisource analog mixing, and selected multimedia applications.

✔ **NEC Multimedia Gallery.** This kit includes an NEC CDR-74 external CD-ROM, an NEC audio card and SCSI adapter, external speakers, and selected multimedia applications.

Other Features To Look For

Many vendors offer their own multimedia upgrade kits with various capabilities and at various prices. When you evaluate any multimedia upgrade kit, be sure to look for the following features:

✔ **16-bit audio.** 16-bit audio capability gives you much better sound quality than 8-bit kits.

✔ **Bundled software.** Evaluate the software that comes with the kit. You often can buy the individual hardware components for less than the cost of the kit. If you do not want the applications that come with the kit, consider buying the hardware components separately.

✔ **SCSI-2 compatible host adapter.** To ensure upward mobility for your system, the SCSI host adapter that comes with the kit should be SCSI-2 compatible.

You also should be aware that not all SCSI adapters built into the various sound cards are fully compatible with all hardware. You might experience problems when trying to attach additional SCSI devices to the adapter.

If you plan to add additional SCSI devices to the system, verify the compatibility of the host adapter that comes with the kit or purchase a separate host adapter, such as those available from Future Domain and Adaptec (both of which are supported by Windows NT).

Choosing a Multimedia-Capable PC

Many vendors now offer computers that already have the necessary multimedia hardware and drivers installed in them. These systems consist of a 486-based computer, an internal CD-ROM drive, a SCSI host adapter, a sound card, speakers, and bundled software.

When you evaluate multimedia-ready PCs, look for the most powerful CPU you can afford. The system's overall performance depends heavily on the CPU's capability. The minimum recommendation for a working multimedia system is a 386DX system. For a home system, a 386SX-20 is acceptable, but this type of system cannot play back video as smoothly as a faster system can. A 486 or Pentium system is a much better choice than a 386 system.

In addition, take into account the same factors that relate to selecting individual multimedia hardware items. Look for a multimedia PC, for example, that includes 16-bit sound rather than 8-bit sound.

To help you select a system that supports multimedia under Windows, the industry has adopted a standard for minimum hardware requirements. A PC that meets or surpasses these standards is referred to as MPC-compatible, or an MPC system. Look for the MPC reference when choosing a multimedia system for Windows.

Examining CD-ROM Drives

To understand CD-ROM (compact disc read-only memory) drives, you must first understand CDs, or compact discs. A *CD* is a data-storage device—a plastic disc coated with metal that is just under 4 ¾ inches in diameter. One side of the CD is used to store data in digital format. The data takes the form of pits in the disc's surface, which are burned in by a laser beam. When you want to read the data from the disc, your PC's CD-ROM drive bounces its own laser beam off the disc's surface. The laser can detect the pits in the surface and read them as a digital signal. Computer files, sounds, and video images can be stored on CDs.

A computer's CD-ROM drive is very much like those used in stereo systems. The primary difference is that the computer CD-ROM drives use error-correcting codes to ensure accurate playback of the data that is stored on the disc.

Looking At the Benefits of CD-ROM

Compact discs offer a number of advantages over older data-storage methods such as floppy disks. The first of these advantages is capacity. A single CD can store roughly 680 MB of data, or the equivalent of 472 high-density 3 ½-inch floppy disks. This high capacity is required by multimedia because sound and video require very large amounts of storage space per second of data.

Most data CDs use a standard that provides 525 MB of storage. This is due to the error-correcting codes taking 155 MB of space. Most vendors use the smaller amount of storage space because one bad digital bit can make a CD useless.

Many software publishers now distribute their software on compact disc as well as on floppy disk. Some manufacturers offer special versions of their products on CD, which include additional support programs, clip art, animations, sound, and more. Lotus 1-2-3 and CorelDRAW! are two examples. Other software publishers offer their software on CD only or as an optional format. Microsoft Word for Windows and Windows NT are two such examples.

Another advantage of CDs is their portability. Remember that a single CD can carry up to 680 MB of data and programs. Because the CD is an optical storage device rather than a magnetic one, it also is less likely to be damaged. You do not, for example, have to worry about carrying CDs through the X-ray machine at the airport as you do with a hard disk or floppy disk. Because CDs are made from rigid plastic, they are almost indestructible in everyday use. And they rarely wear out.

Audio CDs are virtually indestructible; CD-ROMs can be destroyed by one good scratch.

The U.S. Navy rejected CDs as a storage medium because of a phenomenon called *CD rot*. The pitted substrate is metallic, which makes it susceptible to corrosion from the air encased with it. The only solution is to use gold or other noncorrosive metal. This can become expensive.

Choosing a CD-ROM Drive

Many different CD-ROM drives currently are available, all with different performance capabilities. The capacity and format capability of CD-ROM drives are fixed; you do not have to worry about compatibility—you can use a CD in any manufacturer's drive. You should, however, take into consideration the drive's access speed, data transfer rate, and other factors.

One of the more useful standards is *CD XA,* which interleaves audio and data sectors. Older CD-ROM drives did not support CD XA.

Computer users who already have Level 1 CD-ROM drives, also known as MPC CD-ROM drives, must decide whether they want to limit themselves to their current drive or upgrade to the newer CD XA standard.

VI

Applying Multimedia

Access Speed

The speed at which the CD-ROM drive can locate a specific item of data is called its *access speed*. Today's CD-ROM drives offer access speeds of about 256–500 ms. The NEC CDR-84, for example, has an access speed of 280 ms. The lower the number, the faster the access time. Drives with faster access speeds generally are more expensive, but the performance improvement can be worth the additional cost.

Access speed depends on what you plan to do with your CD-ROM drive. If you are using CDs only to install big programs such as Windows NT, save some money and get a slow clunker CD-ROM drive.

Data Transfer Rate

The rate at which a CD-ROM drive can transfer data from the CD to the CPU is called its *data transfer rate*. The transfer rate is particularly important in video playback. A transfer rate of at least 150 KB per second is necessary to ensure smooth video performance. The higher the transfer rate (the higher the number), the better the drive performs.

Data Buffer Size

CD-ROM drives contain a buffer to store data temporarily. The drive reads the information into the buffer, which is located on the CD-ROM drive itself, and the buffered data is then moved from the buffer to the CPU. The buffer is important to performance because it enables the drive to read ahead, storing data in the buffer before it is requested by the CPU. Further, data can be transferred from a buffer more quickly than it can from a disc. Look for a data buffer size of at least 64 KB, with larger values indicating a larger (and better) buffer size.

Form Factor

You can choose from two types (or form factors) of CD-ROM drives: internal and external. You can install an internal CD-ROM drive in your system just like a floppy drive or half-height hard disk. You need a free drive bay to install the system. If you do not have a free drive bay, you have a couple of alternatives.

The first alternative is to replace your dual floppy drives (if you have dual drives) with a single two-unit drive. These drives contain a 5 ¼-inch and a 3 ½-inch drive in a single half-height drive unit. This unit frees one of your existing floppy drive bays for the internal CD-ROM drive.

The other option is to move your hard drive. If you have a tower case, additional drive bays probably are inside the case. Most cases, for example, have a drive bay at the top of the unit, above the floppy drive bays.

If neither of these options appeals to you, you can buy an external CD-ROM drive. Functionally, internal and external drives are the same. The only difference is that internal drives take their power from the computer's power supply; external drives have their own power supplies. Internal drives, therefore, are less expensive. External drives offer quick portability to other systems, and you can carry an external drive with you on the road.

Sound Capability

Virtually all CD-ROM drives support audio CDs as well as data CDs. The CD-ROM drive often has a mini-headphone jack on its front panel and a sound connector on the back of the unit. If you want to listen to audio CDs on your system or listen to other multimedia audio, you should be able to do so even without a sound card. You can connect the CD-ROM drive to a set of small amplified speakers (available at most electronics and department stores), your stereo system, or a set of headphones. Figures 35.3 and 35.4 show two typical audio connections for CD-ROM drives.

 Most CD-ROM drives require a special program for running audio music.

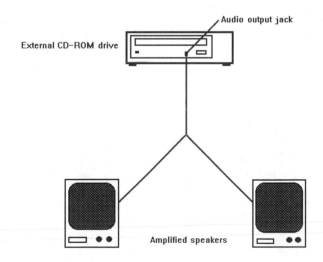

Figure 35.3
CD audio connections from the front panel jack.

VI

Applying Multimedia

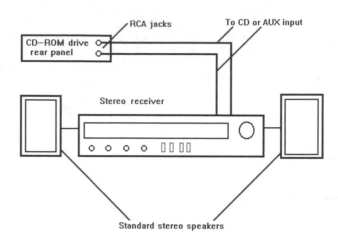

Figure 35.4
CD audio
connections
through rear jacks.

Connecting your CD-ROM to a set of external speakers or to a stereo system will give you good sound from the system, but you probably will get better sound if you connect the CD-ROM to a sound card in your system. For best performance with CD audio, choose a 16-bit audio card.

Adding Sound

Another item you might want to add to your system is a sound card. A sound card provides a wider range of sound than PC speakers and provides features such as stereo output and stereo input. In addition, sound cards include software that enables you to mix sound from different sources and output it to disk or an external recording source. Sound cards also include software that enables you to capture and edit sounds. Figure 35.5 shows one of the mixer programs that is included with the Media Vision Pro AudioSpectrum 16 sound card.

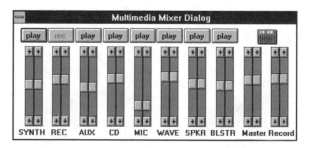

Figure 35.5
A mixer pro-
gram included
with the Pro
AudioSpectrum
16 sound card.

Sound cards now are available from many different manufacturers. The most popular are the Creative Labs Sound Blaster Pro, the Media Vision Pro AudioSpectrum 16, and the Turtle Beach Systems Multisound. A number of other manufacturers and cards are available, however, that offer similar performance.

Adding a sound card to your system not only enables you to enjoy much higher quality sound, but also captures sounds from CD, microphone, a stereo system, or virtually any audio source. You can use these digitized audio clips in multimedia presentations or embed them in documents. Chapter 36, "Using Multimedia Audio," examines sound and sound boards in more detail.

Adding Video

The second option you might want to consider for your multimedia PC is video. Video options for PCs include the following:

✔ Displaying and overlaying video with the computer's display (overlaying video on the VGA signal)

✔ Watching television in a window on the computer

✔ Capturing video clips to disk

✔ Editing video clips

✔ Outputting edited and mixed video to an external recording source

Figure 35.6 shows Microsoft Video for Windows working with video input from a Truevision Bravado video card.

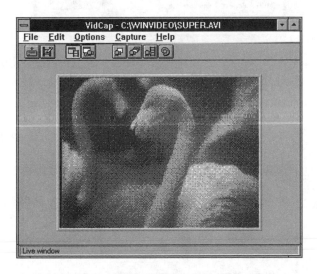

Figure 35.6
Video for Windows overlaying a video source for capture.

The capabilities for video capture and editing vary widely from card to card. As is often the case, higher price usually means better performance.

The different types of video capture boards and TV boards enable you to capture still images from video or capture live video clips to include in documents or presentations. Chapter 37, "Using Multimedia Video," examines video in more detail.

Installing and Configuring Multimedia Drivers

The Control Panel enables you to install and configure drivers for multimedia devices. The installation programs that come with some multimedia devices will install all the necessary drivers for you automatically. Many, however, direct you to the Control Panel to install drivers.

To install or configure a multimedia driver, open the Control Panel and double-click on the Drivers icon to display the Drivers dialog box shown in figure 35.7. Use this dialog box to add, remove, and configure multimedia drivers.

Figure 35.7
The Drivers dialog box in the Control Panel enables you to install multimedia drivers.

Configuring an Existing Driver

To configure a driver that already is installed, click on the driver in the list, then choose Setup. The Setup dialog box that appears for a specific driver varies with each driver. Figure 35.8 shows the Setup dialog box for the Truevision Bravado Video Capture driver.

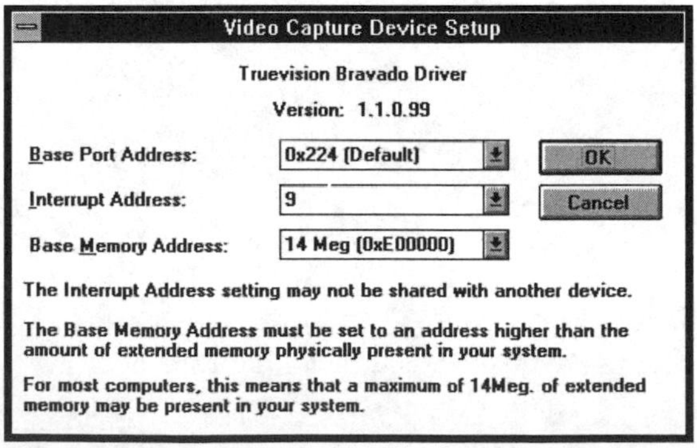

Figure 35.8
The Setup dialog box for the Truevision Bravado Video Capture driver.

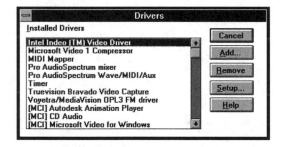

Installing a New Driver

To install a new driver, click on <u>A</u>dd in the Driver's dialog box. The Control Panel displays a dialog box that contains a list of a few common multimedia drivers. If the driver you need is listed, select it and click on OK. If the driver you need to install was shipped with the multimedia device, select the option labeled Unlisted or Updated Driver, then click on OK. The Control Panel will prompt you to insert the disk containing the driver. After installing a new driver, you might need to choose <u>S</u>etup to configure it for use.

Exploring Multimedia Authoring

By far the most common use for multimedia in business today is in presentations of one kind or another. Many companies use multimedia to create product presentations, software tutorials, and training materials. These presentations and tutorials are called *multimedia applications*. Often, these multimedia applications are interactive, enabling the user to access the material randomly in the application, jumping from topic to topic. In other cases, the multimedia application is sequential, displaying or playing one item at a time in sequence.

The capability to capture sounds, still images, and video clips is not very useful if you have no way to bring them together as a presentation. Multimedia authoring software provides that capability. One such program is HSC InterActive, from HSC Software.

HSC InterActive

HSC InterActive enables nonprogrammers to build multimedia applications by organizing icons that represent functions, such as displaying video images or playing sounds, in the multimedia application. Figure 35.9 shows HSC InterActive's main program window.

Creating a multimedia application with HSC InterActive consists of four basic kinds of tasks:

1. **Planning.** This stage consists of planning what the application will accomplish, planning how the application will appear, and gathering the multimedia sources (video clips, sounds, and so forth) for the application.

2. **Building.** This stage consists of designing the overall structure of the application. This is done by building a flowchart of icons in which each icon represents a function in the application.

3. **Adding content.** This stage includes adding content to the functions in the structure, such as assigning specific bit-map images, specifying menu options, defining text to be displayed, and generally filling in the structure of the application.

4. **Editing.** At this stage you test the application and fine-tune it by changing the structure or content.

Figure 35.9
The HSC
InterActive
program window.

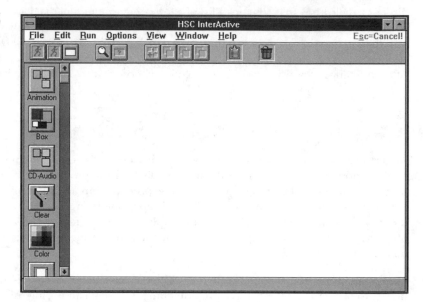

Building the Structure

After you have decided how you want to present the information in your multimedia application, you can begin building the structure. Select File, New to open a new document window containing a single icon labeled Start. This represents the beginning, or entry point, of your application (see fig. 35.10).

The next step is to build the structure of the application by adding to the flowchart icons that represent specific functions. To add a function to the application, simply drag an icon from the HSC InterActive icon bar into the application window and drop it into place. To display a bitmap as the first function (such as a logo or introductory screen), for example, drag the Display icon from the icon bar and drop it onto the Start icon (see fig. 35.11).

Next, assume that you want to make the application pause for 10 seconds to give the user time to view the image. Drag a Pause icon from the icon bar and drop it onto the Display icon. HSC InterActive automatically inserts the Pause function right after the Display function (see fig. 35.12). If you want to insert an icon between two others in the structure, you simply drop the icon onto the first of the two existing icons, and the program inserts the new function after the selected icon.

In addition to single-item functions, HSC InterActive includes composite functions. These predefined composite functions are built of multiple icons. Dragging an icon that represents a composite function from the icon bar into your application window inserts multiple icons in their correct relationship to one another in the application's structure, displaying them so in the application window. Figure 35.13 shows a Menu function that has been added after the last Pause icon. Adding a single Menu item places a total of 11 icons in the application with a single drag-drop operation.

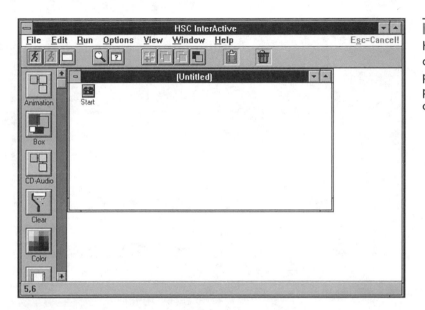

Figure 35.10
HSC InterActive automatically provides a starting point for the application.

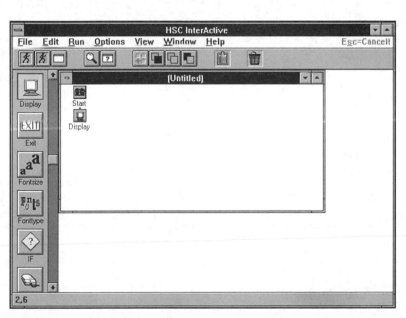

Figure 35.11
A Display icon has been dropped onto the Start icon.

Figure 35.12
A Pause function added after the Display function.

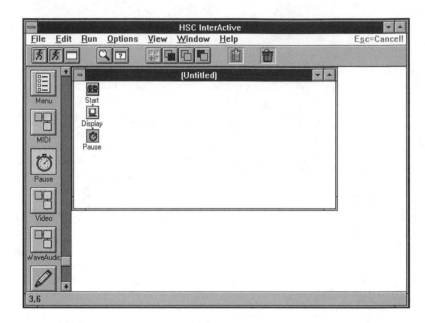

Figure 35.13
A composite Menu function added to the application.

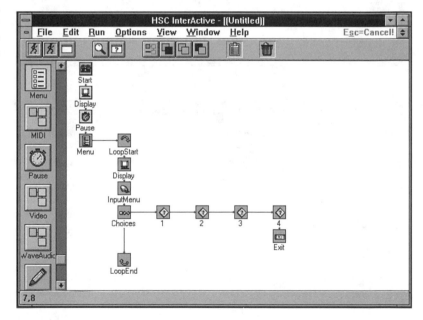

A number of predefined single and composite functions are built into HSC InterActive. The following list explains the icons in HSC InterActive's icon bar:

✔ **Animation.** Enables you to insert an animation in the multimedia presentation.

✔ **Box.** Enables you to draw a box. To specify a color for the box, you precede it with a Color icon that changes the active colors. The box might be used to mask an area of the screen or to outline important information or a picture.

✔ **CD-Audio.** Uses Multimedia Control Interface (MCI) commands to play an audio selection from CD.

✔ **Clear.** Clears the screen to a specified color. This enables you to make the transition from one display to another, such as blanking the display between graphics displays.

✔ **Color.** Specifies the current outline and fill color. Insert this icon in the structure to change the color of the next object, such as a box or text.

✔ **Display.** Displays a graphic on-screen at that flow-point in the application. The image can be a bitmap, vector drawing, or animation routine.

✔ **Exit.** Provides flow control for the application, exiting a composite function, a loop, or a nested loop in the application.

✔ **Fontsize.** Sets the height, width, and bold/normal properties of text generated by the Write icon. Use the Fontsize icon before a Write icon to specify a new font to be used by the Write icon.

✔ **Fonttype.** Sets the font name to be used by the Write icon. Precede the Write icon with a Fonttype icon to change font type.

✔ **IF.** Provides conditional execution. The IF icon tests for a condition that you specify (such as a testing the value of an input number), then branches execution of the application accordingly.

✔ **InputMenu.** Prompts for input from the user, enabling the user to choose from two or more choices. These might include menu choices, multiple-choice answers to questions, or selecting different areas of the screen.

✔ **Laserdisc.** Opens and plays a selection from a laser disc through standard MCI commands.

✔ **Menu.** Creates a menu structure that presents a menu screen to the user. Use this icon to define quickly a menu of choices from which the user of your multimedia application can choose.

✔ **MIDI.** Plays a sound from a MIDI file.

✔ **Pause.** Pauses application execution for a specified time limit.

✔ **Video.** Plays video clips using MCI commands.

✔ **WaveAudio.** Plays WAV files (sound files).

✔ **Write.** Displays text on-screen at a specified location.

Adding Content

After you have defined the general structure of your multimedia application by dragging icons into place (see fig. 35.14), you can begin adding content to each icon. Although the icon specifies a function, the content of the icon specifies the following:

✔ Data to be displayed or played by the function

✔ Text to be displayed

✔ Position the function will use on the display for input or output

✔ Other details associated with the function

Figure 35.14
A number of icons added to the application to define its structure.

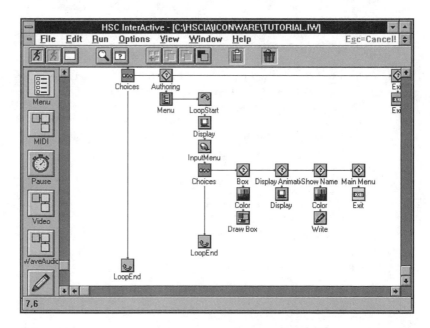

To add content to an icon, double-click on the icon. HSC InterActive opens a dialog box that you use to fill in the needed data items for the function. To fill in the content for all the icons in a composite structure, start with the uppermost icon in the structure. After you have supplied the content for the first icon, HSC InterActive automatically cycles through each of the proceeding icons, displaying dialog boxes for each one until the content of the entire substructure is fleshed out. Figures 35.15, 35.16, and 35.17 show dialog boxes used by HSC InterActive to add content to typical functions.

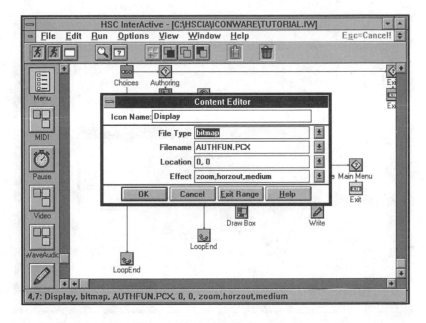

Figure 35.15
The Content Editor
dialog box for a
Display icon.

VI

Applying Multimedia

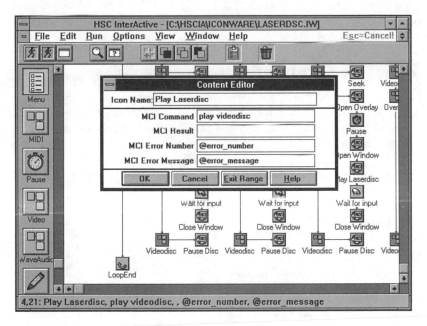

Figure 35.16
A Content Editor
dialog box for an
MCI command
function.

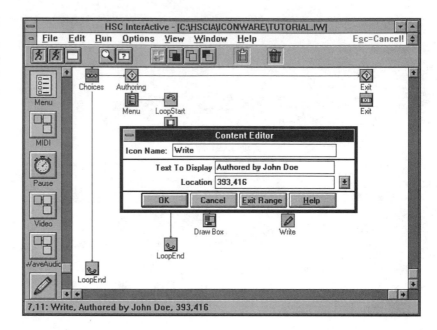

Figure 35.17
The Content Editor
for specifying text
to be displayed by
the Write icon.

Generally, to complete the contents of an icon you must specify text, an image or other file on disk, a color combination, font style, or other such information.

Editing Images and Animations

HSC InterActive includes three editors that enable you to create, capture, and edit animations and still graphics. The first of the editors is the IconAnimate editor, which enables you to create and edit animations. Figure 35.18 shows the IconAnimate window with a sample animation loaded into it.

Figure 35.18
The IconAnimate
window with a
sample animation
loaded into it.

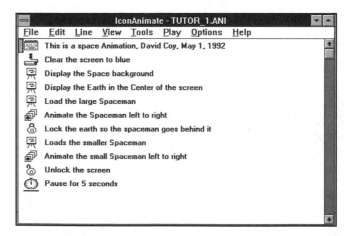

The IconAnimate editor enables you to create animations in much the same way you build a multimedia application—by dragging icons that represent different functions into a logical structure. You then fill out the structure by adding contents to each icon, just as you do with the multimedia application's icons.

Animations include the capability to move images across the screen, move images behind one another, display text, flash the display, and use special effects, such as fade-in and fade-out. After an animation is created with the IconAnimate editor, it can be added to the multimedia application with the Animation icon in the main program window.

Editing Graphics

The Graphics Editor in HSC InterActive enables you to create and edit graphic images in BMP, RLE, and PCX formats. It includes the usual range of graphics editing tools, including those used to create lines, circles, boxes, ellipses, command buttons, text, and other entities. It also includes paint tools for spray painting and filling objects, as well as erase tools. Figure 35.19 shows the Graphics Editor window with a sample image loaded into it for editing.

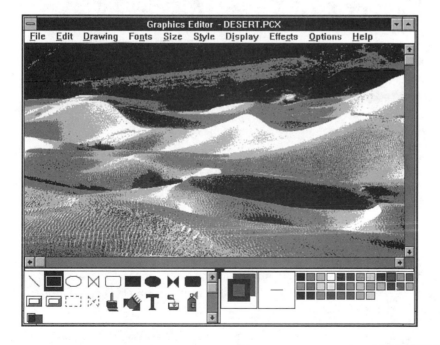

Figure 35.19
An image loaded into the Graphics Editor for editing.

In addition to providing a range of tools for creating graphical entities and text, the Graphics Editor includes special tools for creating blended backgrounds, defining custom colors, and defining the appearance of command buttons. Figure 35.20 shows a blended background created by the Screen Blends Editor.

Figure 35.20
A blended
background
created by the
Screen Blends
Editor.

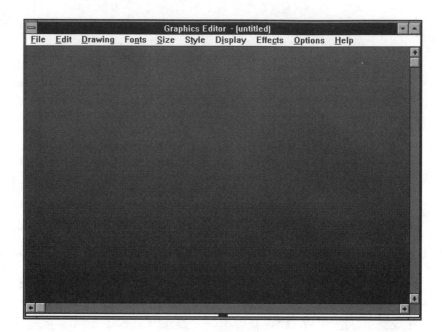

Running and Editing the Application

After you have defined the application by building its structure and filling in the contents of its icons, you can run the application to test it. The program provides options such as running the application from the top or starting with a specific icon. The program displays error messages to help you detect and fix problems with the application.

To edit the contents of an icon, double-click on it. To add icons to the structure, drag the icons from the icon bar. To delete icons from the structure, select the icons and press Del. If you need to move an icon or composite structure from one location in the application to another, you can cut it to the Clipboard and paste it into the desired location.

When it comes time to distribute the application, you can copy it to disk, complete with all support files (graphics files and more) with a single command. Other HSC InterActive users then can install the application on their systems and run it. HSC InterActive also includes a run-time module that enables you to distribute your multimedia applications to users who do not have the HSC InterActive software.

For more information about HSC InterActive, contact HSC Software at the following:

HSC Software
1661 Lincoln Blvd., Suite 101
Santa Monica, CA 90404
(310) 392-8441

IconAuthor

IconAuthor, from AimTech Corp., is a superset of the programs provided with HSC InterActive. It uses the same method of structuring a multimedia application with icons and even provides the same graphics editors as HSC InterActive. IconAuthor provides a much wider range of functions, however, and adds the capability to read and use dBASE database files in multimedia applications. IconAuthor also supports dynamic data exchange (DDE), enabling your multimedia application to communicate and interact with other Windows applications that support DDE, such as Microsoft Excel or Word for Windows. Figure 35.21 shows the IconAuthor program window with a sample application loaded for editing.

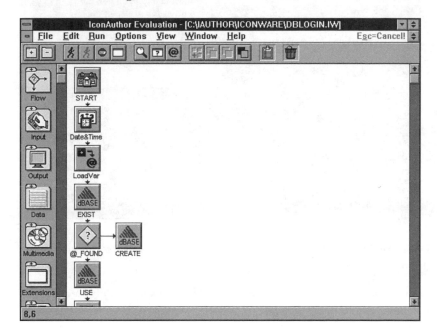

Figure 35.21
The IconAuthor program is a superset of HSC InterActive, offering many additional features.

VI

Applying Multimedia

In addition to the icon function types provided with HSC InterActive, IconAuthor includes added conditional branching functions, 11 database functions, added video and audio functions, and DDE and other communications functions. It also provides additional input and output functions, including dialog box output, and supports multiple application and text windows in the multimedia application, and a wider range of video and audio sources.

Other Programs Included with IconAuthor

In addition to the Graphics Editor, Animation Editor, and RezSolution programs included with HSC InterActive, IconAuthor includes a program for creating run-time data objects (SmartObject Editor), a debugger (IAScope) and a video editing program (Video Editor).

The SmartObject Editor, shown in figure 35.22, enables you to create files that contain display-only or interactive objects. The SmartObject Editor enables you to create forms and dialog boxes, for example, that can be displayed by your multimedia application. You can create a dialog box to prompt for input from the user, for example.

Figure 35.22
The SmartObject
Editor with a
sample file.

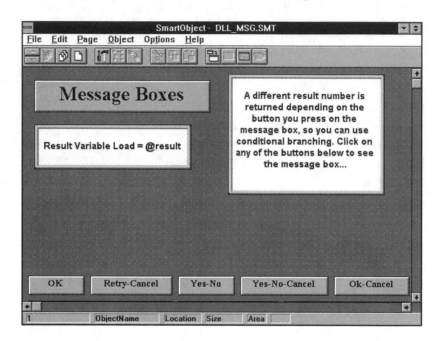

You can use the SmartObject Editor to create interface components for user input that mirror the look and feel of a typical Windows application.

The IAScope program provides a debugger for your multimedia applications and enables you to control program execution during testing with stop points. You can use IAScope to view the stack and variables, and to monitor other information about the multimedia application as you test it.

The Video Editor enables you to view video from videodisc, videotape, or a digital video file. You can use it to browse an entire video clip or selected frames. You also can use the Video Editor to import frame numbers into an object for display in your application.

For more information about IconAuthor, contact AimTech Corporation at the following:

AimTech Corporation
20 Trafalgar Square
Nashua, NH 03063
(603) 883-0220

Other Multimedia Authoring Software

HSC InterActive and IconAuthor are just two of the applications available for multimedia authoring. The following sections list and explain some of the other multimedia authoring tools that are available for Windows.

Authorware Professional

Authorware Professional uses icon-based development to enable nonprogrammers to create multimedia applications. A run-time module enables you to distribute multimedia applications developed with Authorware Professional. For more information about Authorware Professional, contact:

>Authorware, Inc.
>600 Townsend Suite 310 West
>San Francisco, CA 94103
>(800) 288-4797

Multimedia Development Kit

The MDK from Microsoft includes tools that enable nonprogrammers to create multimedia applications, and provides extensive support for multimedia application development in the C programming language. For more information on the MDK, contact:

>Microsoft Corporation
>One Microsoft Way
>Redmond, WA 98052
>(800) 541-1261

Multimedia ToolBook and Multimedia Resource Kit

ToolBook provides a complete set of tools and programming support for creating object-oriented multimedia applications. The Multimedia Resource Kit provides additional controls for various multimedia hardware, including CD ROM, laserdisc, MIDI, audio cards, video adapters, and more. For more information about ToolBook, contact:

>Asymetrix Corporation
>110-110th Ave. N.E. Suite 700
>Bellevue, WA 98004
>(800) 448-6543

VI

Applying Multimedia

ObjectVision for Windows

ObjectVision for Windows is a multimedia programming environment from Borland International. Its visual programming tools enable even nonprogrammers to create multimedia Windows applications, and it supports DDE, OLE, and remote calls to DLLs. For more information, contact:

Borland International
1800 Green Hills Road
Scotts Valley, CA 95067
(800) 331-0877

Chapter Snapshot

Chapter 35 provided an overview of Windows-based multimedia to give you an idea of what multimedia includes and how you can take advantage of it. This chapter teaches you about new audio technologies and how you can use them with Windows. This chapter covers the following topics:

If you are thinking about investing in a sound card for your system or want to use a card that you already have, this chapter gives you a good overview of how you can use audio in Windows.

36

CHAPTER

Using Multimedia Audio

S ound capability has been a main component of Macintosh and Amiga computers for quite some time. Even so, sound has found its way onto the PC and into Windows only recently. Windows 3.1 includes a few utilities that let you add sound to the Windows environment and play, edit, and record sounds.

There are a number of reasons to add sound capability to your Windows system. You may simply want to be able to listen to CDs while you work. Or you may want to take advantage of the many disk based educational programs that include sound. Many games also can take advantage of an audio board, giving them much more realistic sound. Whatever your desires for sound in Windows, you can find a solution to fit your budget.

Understanding Audio Hardware and Software

If you want to take advantage of Windows' sound capabilities, you need to have a PC with a sound card (or audio card) installed in it. These cards are available from companies such as Media Vision and Creative Labs. You can install a sound card in your computer in much the same way you install a hard disk controller or video card. A sound card usually contains different types of input and output jacks, including stereo input and output lines, a microphone jack, and a MIDI port.

Many sound pros listen to their PC's sounds through headphones, but you may instead want to use external speakers. (Anything but that little speaker that's built into your computer!) If you do not have stand-alone speakers for your PC, you can connect the sound card to the auxiliary line-in of your stereo. If you want to record from live sources (such as voice recordings), you need a microphone. If you want to create your own musical compositions, you need a MIDI-capable electronic keyboard.

If you are serious about composition on your computer, you may also want to buy a sequencer software package. A *sequencer* enables you to create, annotate, mix, and play back music that you create by using MIDI musical devices (such as electronic keyboards) or MIDI files. Also available are drum machines, synthesizers, Analog/Digital (A/D) converters, and much more.

Of course, very few pieces of hardware can work without some sort of software. Although Windows 3.1 and the Windows Multimedia Extensions include sound applications, audio cards also generally include their own DOS and Windows software for playing, recording, and editing sounds. Figures 36.1 and 36.2 show some of the applications that are included with the Pro AudioSpectrum 16 card.

Windows also includes software that enables you to add sound to the Windows environment. The Music Box program, shown in figure 36.3, was originally included with the Windows Multimedia Extensions. Figure 36.4 shows the Media Player, which is included with Windows 3.1. Music Box enables you to play audio CDs in Windows. Media Player enables you to play audio CDs as well as other multimedia sources, including WAV, MIDI, video, and other types of multimedia files.

There are many different applications, both commercial and shareware, that enable you to record, edit, and play back audio on your audio card.

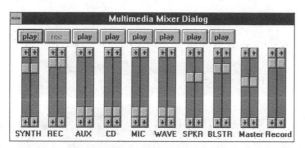

Figure 36.1
The ProMixer
and Fade Mixer
programs.

Figure 36.2
The Pocket
Recorder and
Pocket Mixer
programs.

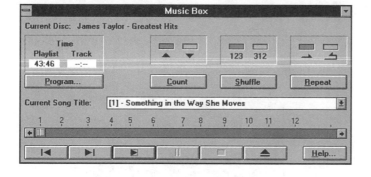

Figure 36.3
Music Box lets you
play audio CDs in
Windows.

Figure 36.4
Media Player
can play many
different types
of multimedia
devices and files.

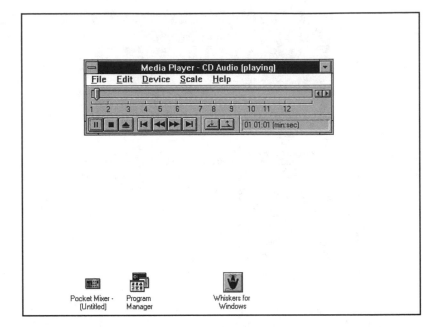

Figure 36.4
Media Player
can play many
different types
of multimedia
devices and files.

Understanding Sound File Types

Windows uses two basic types of sound files: waveform (WAV) files and MIDI (MID) files. Each type of file stores sounds in a different way, and each is suited to different applications.

Waveform (WAV) Files

A *waveform* file stores the data that is necessary to duplicate the waveform that defines a sound. Windows stores waveform files with the WAV file-name extension. Figure 36.5 shows the Windows Sound Recorder with a WAV file loaded for playing and editing.

Figure 36.5
A WAV file
loaded into the
Sound Recorder.

WAVs work on the basic concept that a sound is the ear's interpretation of waves that move the air and create differences of pressure in the ear. A sound is defined by its wave's shape, size, frequency, and so on. By capturing the wave's components and storing the definition in a file, we can reproduce the sound by reproducing the wave that makes the sound.

Sounds are recorded digitally and stored in WAV files through a technique called *sampling*. The sound is sampled at a certain frequency, meaning that the sound is sampled *x* number of times per second. If 22 KHz sampling is used, for example, the sound is sampled 22,000 times per second. The higher the sampling frequency, the truer the sound reproduction will be (sampling frequency and the actual frequency of the sound wave are not related in any way). WAV files typically are very large, because it takes a lot of data to represent a second of sound. A 30-second sound sampled at 22 KHz requires well over 600 KB to store on disk.

Files with a WAV file extension are generic Windows waveform files. Specific sound adapters work with their own waveform file formats, which have different file formats with their own specific file extensions. Common waveform file formats use the VOC, SND, and MOD file extensions. You can use these types of waveform files in Windows, but you must convert them to the WAV file format. You can use shareware applications (such as Makin' Waves) as well as commercial software to convert waveform files to WAV format.

MIDI (MID) Files

Another type of sound file is the MIDI file, which has a MID extension. MIDI stands for *Musical Instrument Digital Interface*. Unlike WAV files, which store sounds as waveforms, MID files store notes, duration, and other information needed to reproduce a sound, rather than the sound itself. MID files therefore rely on a MIDI synthesizer to reproduce the sounds based on the information in the file.

The synthesizer that reproduces the sound from a MID file can be contained on your system's sound adapter, or the sound adapter may communicate with an external MIDI synthesizer, which reproduces the sound.

Examining Sound Adapters

Only a few years ago, you could find only one or two sound cards for use in a PC. Now several different manufacturers offer a number of sound cards at all levels of sophistication. Even Microsoft now offers its own sound system, called appropriately the Microsoft Sound System.

The following sections introduce the Microsoft Sound System and several other popular sound cards.

Microsoft Sound System

The Microsoft Sound System is a hardware/software package aimed at business users, although it also supports CD audio and game audio. The system includes an 8/16-bit sound card, headphones, a microphone, and software. The package includes the following Windows utilities (note that some are enhancements to existing Windows components):

- ✔ **Volume Control.** This utility enables you to control the card's overall output volume, adjust left/right balance, turn the mute control on and off, and control and balance sound for individual sound sources.

- ✔ **Recording Control.** This utility specifies the recording source to be used (microphone or line-in), and controls recording input levels.

- ✔ **Quick Recorder.** This utility enables you to record, edit, and play sounds. The Quick Recorder also supports OLE, so that you can attach sounds to a document and play sounds attached to a document.

- ✔ **Sound Finder.** This file-management tool helps you locate, play, and edit sound files.

- ✔ **ProofReader.** This utility reads data from Microsoft Excel or Lotus 1-2-3 spreadsheets as if you had a person reading the spreadsheet to you.

- ✔ **Voice Pilot.** This utility enables you to record and store voice commands, which you then can use to control the computer.

- ✔ **Sound.** An enhanced Sound tool (in the Windows Control Panel) enables you to create sound schemes for your system in much the same way you create a color scheme for the desktop. A sound scheme associates specific sounds with Windows events.

- ✔ **Desktop.** An enhanced Desktop tool (in the Control Panel) enables you to set up an audio screen saver that blanks the display and plays different sounds. Like a visual screen saver, the audio screen saver can be password-protected.

- ✔ **Music Box.** This utility enables you to play audio CDs on your computer.

If you are interested in experimenting with voice commands, or have a disability that prevents you from using other traditional forms of input, you will find the Microsoft Sound System a useful tool. You might want to consider the Microsoft Sound System if you want to have the computer read spreadsheets "out loud" while you visually check your data.

If you are interested in using MIDI devices or in achieving the highest-quality sound possible, you might prefer one of the many other sound cards that are available. The Microsoft Sound System does not provide a MIDI connection, and although it does support high-fidelity recording, other (although more expensive) audio cards offer better sound resolution.

For more information on the Microsoft Sound System, contact:

> Microsoft Corporation
> One Microsoft Way
> Redmond, WA 98052
> 206-882-8080

Pro AudioSpectrum 16

The Pro AudioSpectrum 16 (PAS-16) sound adapter from Media Vision is a hardware/software combination aimed at general and business users. The kit includes a 16-bit sound card, software, and manuals. An option kit provides a SCSI cable, audio cable, and drivers for connecting a CD-ROM drive to the sound card's on-board SCSI port.

The PAS-16 sound adapter supports recording and playback at up to 44 KHz, which is the frequency supported by audio CD. Thus, the PAS-16 provides excellent sound recording fidelity. In addition to on-board SCSI, the board includes Sound Blaster and AdLib compatibility and contains a 20-voice stereo FM synthesizer, MIDI port, and multiple inputs and outputs.

The PAS-16 includes the following Windows-based software:

- ✔ **Pocket Mixer.** A mini-mixer that controls input and output levels for headphones, MIDI, WAV, CD, microphone, speaker, and an auxiliary source (see fig. 36.6).

- ✔ **Pocket Recorder.** The Pocket Recorder enables you to record, play, and edit sounds in WAV format (see fig. 36.7). It supports recording in mono or stereo, sampling at 8 bits or 16 bits, and six sampling rates from 8 KHz to 44.1 KHz. Pocket Recorder also enables you to add special effects to the sound, slow it down, speed it up, and change its voice.

- ✔ **Pocket CD.** The Pocket CD program plays audio CDs on your computer. It provides functions for storing information about a CD, including the CD's name, artist, track titles, track playlist, and other information (see fig. 36.8).

- ✔ **Pro Mixer.** The Pro Mixer provides an expanded version of the mixer, with slide controls for setting record and play levels for all of the input and output sources supported by the PAS-16 (see fig. 36.9). It also includes a Fade Mixer, analog WAV meter, and an equalizer.

VI

Applying Multimedia

Figure 36.6
The Pocket Mixer.

Figure 36.7
The Pocket
Recorder.

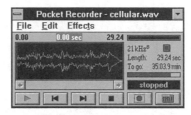

Figure 36.8
The Pocket CD
program.

Figure 36.9
The Pro Mixer.

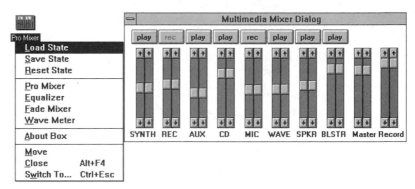

For more information on the Pro AudioSpectrum 16, contact:

Media Vision
3185 Laurelview Court
Fremont, CA 94538
800-845-5870

Sound Blaster Pro

The Sound Blaster Pro is one of the best-selling sound cards because its predecessor, the Sound Blaster, was one of the few sound cards available when audio first became popular in PCs. The Sound Blaster Pro includes an on-board SCSI adapter that can drive a limited number of CD-ROM drives. Many applications, particularly games, support the Sound Blaster and Sound Blaster Pro sound cards.

For more information on the Sound Blaster Pro, contact:

> Creative Labs
> 1901 McCarthy Blvd.
> Milpitas, CA 95035
> 408-428-6600

Pro AudioSpectrum Plus

The Pro AudioSpectrum Plus is an 8-bit sound card, a predecessor to Media Vision's Pro AudioSpectrum 16. It supports playback and sampling at 22 KHz, and is compatible with Sound Blaster and AdLib. It is less expensive than the PAS-16, but does not offer the same quality of sound reproduction and recording. For more information, contact Media Vision at the address and phone number listed previously.

MultiSound

The MultiSound is a sound card for serious music enthusiasts. It is a 16-bit card that supports three sampling rates from 11.025 KHz up to 44.1 KHz. Instead of using a synthesizer to reproduce various instrument sounds, the MultiSound uses on-board ROM chips that store digitized samples from real instruments. This provides a much more realistic sound.

If you are using MIDI instruments for music composition or performance, check out the MultiSound card. For more information, contact:

> Turtle Beach Systems
> Cyber Center, Unit 33
> 1600 Pennsylvania Ave.
> York, PA 17404
> 717-843-6916

Built-In SCSI Support

Many sound cards include a built-in SCSI host adapter, which you can use to connect a CD-ROM drive to your computer. Sound cards also usually have a plug into which you can connect an audio cable from the CD drive.

SCSI stands for *Small Computer System Interface,* and is pronounced "scuzzy." Check the documentation and specifications for your sound card to determine if it includes a SCSI adapter. Refer to Chapter 35 for more information about integrating SCSI devices with your system.

If you want to use your sound card's SCSI adapter with a CD-ROM drive, you need a SCSI CD-ROM device driver. Such a driver should be included with the audio card—if not, it should be available as an option. Media Vision, for example, offers an optional CD-ROM cable kit for its Pro AudioSpectrum 16 card. The kit includes a SCSI cable, audio cable, and software driver.

Even if your audio adapter includes a built-in SCSI host adapter, you might want to think about buying a dedicated SCSI host adapter. Often, the sound card's SCSI adapter does not provide the same level of performance as a dedicated SCSI adapter. Further, you can more likely get drivers for a dedicated card for Windows NT and other operating environments than you can for the SCSI host adapter on an audio card.

Adding Sound Hardware to Windows

The way you install a sound card varies according to the type of card you have. Usually, installation includes setting jumpers on the adapter to specify the IRQ and DMA channel to be used by the adapter. The audio adapter's manual should explain the process for setting the jumpers; just remember that the card must use a unique IRQ. You may need to check the documentation of the other adapters in your system, or even check the adapters themselves, to determine which IRQs already are in use. This will help you identify a free IRQ, which you can assign to the audio adapter. Table 36.1 identifies some of the common IRQ assignments.

Table 36.1
Common IRQ Assignments

IRQ	Device
NMI	Non-Maskable Interrupt, reports parity errors
0	System timer
1	Keyboard
2	EGA/VGA, and cascade interrupt for second IRQ controller

IRQ	Device
3	COM2, COM4
4	COM1, COM3
5	LPT2
6	Floppy disk, or hard disk/floppy disk controller
7	LPT1
8	Real-time clock interrupt
9	Software redirected to IRQ2
10	Available
11	Available
12	Available
13	Coprocessor (FPU)
14	Hard disk controller
15	Available, or hard disk controller

Internal Connections

If you also are installing a CD-ROM drive, you need to make some connections between the sound card and the CD-ROM drive. If the sound card includes a built-in SCSI host adapter that will be used to drive the CD-ROM drive, you must connect a SCSI cable between the CD-ROM drive and the sound card.

The sound adapter will probably include a SCSI connector on the card itself. If the CD-ROM drive is internal, a standard SCSI ribbon cable connects the drive and the adapter. If the CD-ROM drive is external, a short cable and bracket assembly are often used to connect the SCSI port on the sound card to a SCSI connector that mounts in one of the available bracket slots in the back of the computer. An external SCSI cable then connects the CD-ROM drive to the back of the computer. This cable and bracket assembly is usually included with the sound card or is available as an option.

If you want the CD-ROM drive's audio to be played through the sound card, you must connect an audio cable between the two devices. If the sound card does not include such an audio cable, you should be able to purchase one as an option for the board.

External Connections

You can connect a sound card to your PC's built-in speaker, but the speaker in a typical PC is not capable of very good sound reproduction. Also, the speaker is not capable of very high output. If you do not want the sound card to play through your system's PC speaker, you need to connect the sound card to a set of speakers or to a stereo system. Many cards can drive a set of standard stereo speakers without additional amplification. If you prefer a set of small speakers for your desk or bookshelf, you should be able to find a set of amplified desktop speakers in nearly any electronics, sound, or department store. Even if the card does not require amplified speakers, the amplification will provide greater output and also will enable you to use the speakers with a portable radio or CD player.

Playing Audio CDs

After you have installed a CD-ROM drive and audio card in your system, you probably will want to play audio CDs on your computer. You may want to listen to music while you work, or record part of a song to disk and then assign it to a Windows event.

The installation software that comes with your sound card (or CD-ROM drive) may automatically configure Windows to support audio CD. If it does not, however, it is a simple matter to add CD audio support to Windows. The process varies according to the application you will be using to play the CD; the following sections show you how to add support for your CD-ROM drive.

Hardware Drivers

The first step in getting audio CD support under Windows is to install the CD-ROM device driver for your SCSI host adapter. If you are using an on-board SCSI adapter on your sound card, the device driver should be included with the sound card or should be available as an option. If you are using a dedicated SCSI host adapter, such as the Future Domain or Adaptec adapters, the CD-ROM driver should be included with the SCSI host adapter. Follow the directions that came with the audio card's SCSI kit or the SCSI host adapter to install the CD-ROM device driver in CONFIG.SYS.

Adding MSCDEX to AUTOEXEC.BAT

The next step in playing audio CDs is to add the Microsoft CD Extension to your system. The CD-extension file MSCDEX.EXE is included with Windows 3.1 and MS-DOS 6, and is available from the Microsoft BBS or MSL forum on CompuServe. MSCDEX enables you to access the CD-ROM drive from DOS and from Windows. It is necessary for data CDs as well as for audio CDs.

The MSCDEX entry in AUTOEXEC.BAT varies according to the drive designation set up by your system's CD-ROM driver in CONFIG.SYS. Here is the format of the MSCDEX command line:

```
MSCDEX /D:driver1 /D:driver2... /E /K /S /V /L:letter /M:number
```

The /D switch defines the name of the driver(s) with which MSCDEX is associated. This driver is loading in CONFIG.SYS. If you have more than one CD-ROM device in your system, you need to add more than one /D switch to the MSCDEX entry (and to the device driver entry in CONFIG.SYS). For single-CD device systems, only one /D switch is required.

Although the MSCDEX command line most often appears in AUTOEXEC.BAT to load the driver automatically at system boot time, you can load the driver from the DOS command line at any time outside of Windows. Simply type the command at the DOS prompt.

The following example shows the entries for a Future Domain driver entry in CONFIG.SYS and a corresponding entry in AUTOEXEC.BAT for MSCDEX:

```
CONFIG.SYS entry for Future Domain CD driver:
DEVICE=C:\FDCD.SYS /D:MSCD000

AUTOEXEC.BAT entry for MSCDEX:
C:\WINWORK\MSCDEX.EXE /D:MSCD000 /M:20 /S
```

The /D:MSCD000 portion of the MSCDEX command line associates MSCDEX with the device that is identified by the device driver command line in CONFIG.SYS.

MSCDEX Command-Line Switches

You can use the following command-line switches with the MSCDEX command:

- ✔ **/D:*drive_signature*.** Specifies the name of a driver association set up with the CD-ROM device driver in CONFIG.SYS. The MSCDEX line must contain at least one /D specification, and may contain multiple entries if multiple drives are present in the system.

- ✔ **/E.** Specifies that the CD-ROM driver can use expanded memory to store sector buffers if expanded memory is available.

- ✔ **/K.** Causes MS-DOS to recognize CD-ROM volumes that are encoded in Kanji.

- ✔ **/S.** Enables the drive to be shared on MS-NET and Windows for Workgroups network servers.

- ✔ **/V.** (Verbose) Causes MSCDEX to display memory statistics on start-up.

VI

Applying Multimedia

✔ **/L:letter.** Specifies the drive letter that is assigned to the first CD-ROM (which is specified by the first /D switch, usually as MSCD0000). If other /D switches are used with MSCDEX to define other CD-ROM drives, these drives take the next available drive letter after the one specified by the /L parameter. If the first drive is defined as drive E by specifying /L:E, for example, the second CD-ROM drive is drive F.

✔ **/M:number.** Specifies the number of buffers MSCDEX uses to buffer CD-ROM sectors.

Installing the MCI CD Audio Driver

If you plan to use a program to play audio CDs that uses the Windows MCI (Multimedia Command Interface) command set, such as the Windows accessory Media Player (MPLAYER.EXE), you must install the MCI CD Audio device driver.

If the MCI driver is not yet installed on your system, follow these steps to install it:

1. Open the Control Panel and choose the Drivers icon. The Drivers dialog box appears, as shown in figure 36.10.

Figure 36.10

The Drivers dialog box lists installed multimedia drivers.

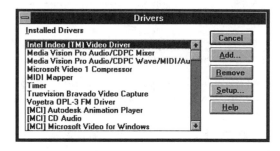

2. Verify that the MCI CD Audio driver is not yet listed in the Installed Drivers list. If it is, you do not need to complete the remaining steps; the driver is already installed on your system.

3. Choose the Add button.

4. From the List of Drivers list box, choose MCI CD Audio, and then choose OK.

5. In the Drivers dialog box, choose the Setup button. Windows should display the dialog box shown in figure 36.11. If it displays an error dialog box, your CD-ROM is not being detected by Windows. Make sure that your hardware is installed properly and that you have installed the necessary drivers in CONFIG.SYS and are running MSCDEX.

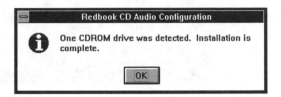

Figure 36.11
This dialog box indicates successful installation of the MCI CD Audio driver.

6. Exit from the confirmation dialog box and choose the Close button from the Drivers dialog box.

Playing CDs—Software Options

You may have more than one option for playing audio CDs in Windows. If your sound card or CD-ROM drive does not include a program for playing audio CDs, you can use the Media Player, which is included with Windows 3.1, to play CDs.

Using Media Player To Play Audio CDs

Media Player is located in the Accessories group, and is located in your Windows directory as MPLAYER.EXE. When you start Media Player, its window appears as shown in figure 36.12. Media Player lets you play and edit the different types of multimedia files that are supported by your system's hardware.

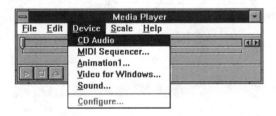

Figure 36.12
Using the Media Player.

To play an audio CD, first insert the CD into the CD-ROM's disc cartridge and place it in the CD-ROM drive, or place the disc in the player's sliding tray. Then, in Media Player, select the Device menu and choose CD Audio. If the CD Audio option does not appear in the Device menu, the MCI CD Audio device driver is not properly installed. When you select CD Audio, Media Player examines the CD that is in the drive and displays information about the number of tracks or length of the disc, depending on how Media Player is configured. By default, Media Player shows the length of the disk, in minutes and seconds.

To switch Media Player from displaying time information to displaying track information for the CD, choose Scale, then Tracks. To start the CD playing at the first track, click on the Play button (see fig. 36.13). To play a specific track, either click on the Track Forward or Track Reverse buttons.

VI

Applying Multimedia

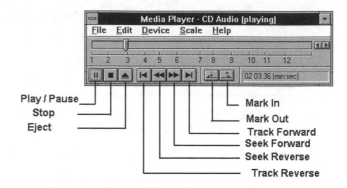

If your CD-ROM drive is connected to your system's sound card (if there is one), you should hear the CD begin to play through the sound card's speakers. If you do not have a sound card installed in the system, connect headphones to the CD-ROM drive to hear the audio CD.

Although Media Player does a fine job of playing audio CDs in Windows, it does not enable you to store disc or track information or define a play list for a CD. There are many CD-player shareware programs available in the WINADV forum on CompuServe. Also, most sound cards include a Windows program to play audio CDs. These programs, such as Music Box, which is shown in figure 36.14, enable you to store disc and track information about each disc, and to program a playlist for each CD.

Music Box is included with the Microsoft Sound System and the Microsoft Multimedia Extensions for Windows.

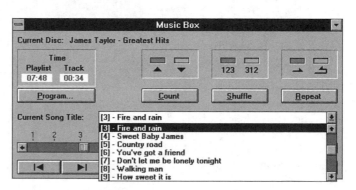

Media Player enables you to play other types of multimedia files besides audio CDs. Media Player is discussed in greater depth in other sections that relate to other types of multimedia sources.

Assigning Sounds to System Events

If your system has a sound card installed, you can assign sounds to be played when certain Windows events occur. You can program the system to play the TADA.WAV file ("Tah Dah!") when Windows starts. If you want to get creative, you can load a WAV file of Porky Pig saying "That's all folks!" and have it play when you exit Windows. (You can download this WAV file and many others from bulletin board services such as CompuServe.)

To assign a WAV sound to a Windows event, open the Control Panel and choose the Sound icon. The Sound dialog box appears, as shown in figure 36.15.

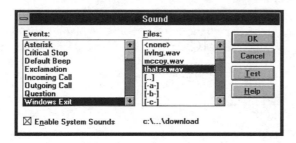

Figure 36.15
The Sound dialog box.

The Events list box contains a list of predefined Windows events. To associate a WAV file with an event, first click on the event in the Events list. Then use the Files list box to locate the WAV file that you want to play when the associated Windows event occurs. To test a sound (that is, to hear it play), click on the sound in the Files list and choose the Test button. When you have associated as many sounds as you want, choose the OK button to exit from the Sound dialog box.

If all the controls in the Sound dialog box are dimmed, your system is not capable of playing WAV files (it does not have a sound card or the optional speaker driver).

If you want to turn off temporarily sounds associated with system events, clear the check box marked Enable System Sounds in the Sound dialog box. To turn sounds back on, check the Enable System Sounds check box.

Embedding Sound Objects in Documents

If you use Windows 3.1, you can use Windows' OLE (object linking and embedding) to embed a sound in a document. You can, for example, record a voice notation and embed it into a Word for Windows document or an Excel spreadsheet. You or someone else then can double-click on the sound object and hear it played back, assuming that the system on which the document is being viewed has sound capability. Or, you may want to include a short voice note in an e-mail message.

Embedding a Sound Object in a Document

There are a number of ways to embed an OLE object into a document, as Chapter 22 explains. If you want to record a sound and embed it in a document, the easiest method is to use the document application's Insert menu (the menu name and technique may vary from one application to another, but the concept and overall procedure are the same).

First, you must have a sound card and microphone installed in the system on which you want to embed the sound in the document. In order for a recipient of the document to be able to play back the sound, he or she must also have a sound card in his system.

To embed a sound object in a Word for Windows document, take the following steps:

1. From Word's Insert menu, choose Object. The Object dialog box appears, as shown in figure 36.16.

Figure 36.16
The Object dialog box in Word for Windows.

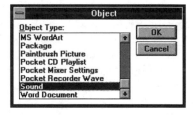

2. Scroll through the list of objects in the Object dialog box and locate the Sound entry.

3. Click on the Sound entry, then choose the OK button. The Sound Recorder appears on the desktop.

4. When you are ready to record your annotation, click on the microphone button. The screen pointer changes to an hourglass as the Sound Recorder sets up the recording.

5. When the arrow pointer reappears, the Sound Recorder is recording. Speak your message into the microphone, then click on the Stop button when you are finished. (The Stop button has a filled rectangle on it.)

6. From the Sound Recorder's File menu, choose Exit. Sound Recorder asks whether you want to update the object in the document. Choose Yes to embed the sound in the document.

For other methods on embedding objects in a document, refer to Chapter 22.

Embedding Voice Annotation in an E-Mail Message

If you want to embed a sound recording in an e-mail message, you must first record the sound and store it in a file. Then you can attach the sound recording to the e-mail message by using the appropriate command for your e-mail software.

For most mail programs you begin by composing the note, and then locating the cursor where you want the sound icon to appear in the message. Next, choose the mail program's Attach command (or whatever command enables you to attach files to a message). If you are using Microsoft Mail, for example, choose the Attach button. Mail then prompts you with a dialog box to choose the file(s) to be attached (see fig. 36.17).

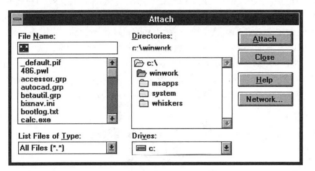

Figure 36.17
Microsoft Mail's Attach dialog box.

After you have attached the sound file to the message, transmit it as you normally transmit e-mail messages on your system. Bear in mind, however, that the recipient must have sound capability in his or her system to play back the sound.

Exploring MIDI

As you read earlier in this chapter, MIDI (which stands for Musical Instrument Digital Interface) stores the notes, duration, and other information needed to reproduce sounds. There are a number of different types of MIDI instruments, the most common of which is the electronic keyboard.

To play MIDI files and work with MIDI devices on your Windows PC, you must have a sound card that contains a MIDI synthesizer. The MIDI synthesizer is responsible for converting the MIDI instructions into sound. You also need a program to play MIDI files. If your sound card does not include a program to play MIDI files in Windows, you can use the Media Player. First, however, you must install the necessary MIDI drivers.

Installing MIDI Drivers

Your sound card's installation software probably will set up Windows for playing MIDI files by installing a few device drivers for you. If you need to install them manually, however, you can do so by using the Drivers icon in Control Panel.

To install MIDI drivers, open the Control Panel and double-click on the Drivers icon. In the Drivers dialog box, choose the Add button. Then select the MIDI drivers that are required by your sound card. If your sound card is not listed, choose the Unlisted or Updated Driver option to install the necessary MIDI drivers from your sound card's software disks. Refer to the card's manual for more information on installing these drivers.

In addition to one or more drivers specific to your sound card, you also need to install the MIDI Mapper and MCI MIDI Sequencer drivers. These drivers are listed in the List of Drivers list box in the Add dialog box. Add these drivers as described earlier in this chapter. Depending on your sound card's driver, you may need to use the Setup button in the Drivers dialog box to configure the driver for your card. There are no setup options necessary for the MCI MIDI Sequencer or MIDI Mapper drivers. Refer to your sound card's manual for help configuring the sound card's MIDI driver.

Playing MIDI Files with Media Player

After you have installed and configured the necessary drivers, you can use the Media Player to play MIDI files. Open the Accessories group and start the Media Player. It appears on your desktop, as shown in figure 36.18.

Figure 36.18
The Media Player enables you to play MIDI files.

From the Media Player's Device menu, choose MIDI Sequencer. Media Player then displays a dialog box that you can use to locate the MIDI file that you want to play. Locate and select the file, and then choose OK to load it. To play the file, click on the Play button.

Chapter Snapshot

Chapter 36 examined one aspect of multimedia—audio—in detail. In this chapter, you learn how video has become a big part of multimedia in Windows and how you can take advantage of it. You learn to display video in a window, capture video clips, and capture still images from video. You also learn about technology that enables you to watch TV in a window on your PC.

This chapter covers the following multimedia video topics:

If you are wondering what multimedia video options are available to you for Windows, this chapter will help you understand these capabilities. If you already have identified a need for multimedia video capability, this chapter provides information about specific hardware and software choices.

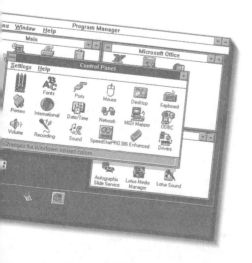

37

CHAPTER

Using Multimedia Video

Until recently, computer video in Windows meant a typical VGA or Super VGA display—nothing beyond the standard Windows interface. No one considered that the term "video" referred to moving video. Today, multimedia video and Windows give you the capability to view video in a window on your PC. You can view video from sources such as VCRs, cameras, and cable TV side-by-side with your spreadsheet, database, or word processing applications. You also can capture video to disk and edit it.

Understanding Multimedia Video

The capability to view and capture video in Windows enables you to use recorded or live video in your multimedia applications. You might have a video database on CD of real estate for sale, a video catalog of vacation spots, training courses, or other video collections. You could build a multimedia application that enables a user to choose video clips for viewing. Perhaps you want to develop a security system that uses Windows as a front end. The capability to open windows and view different video sources could become a central part of your security application.

Displaying Video

To display video in Windows, you do not need any special hardware. You do, however, need some software, such as Microsoft's Video for Windows.

Displaying Captured Video

Microsoft Video for Windows, which is discussed in detail later in this chapter, enables you to display video clips that have been captured and stored on your system's hard disk or on a CD. You do not need any special hardware to view captured video with Video for Windows. Video for Windows provides the necessary drivers to enable the standard Windows Media Player to play back captured video files. Figure 37.1 shows a video clip loaded into the Media Player for display. Later in this chapter you learn how video clips can be captured and stored on disk.

Figure 37.1
A video clip in the
Media Player.

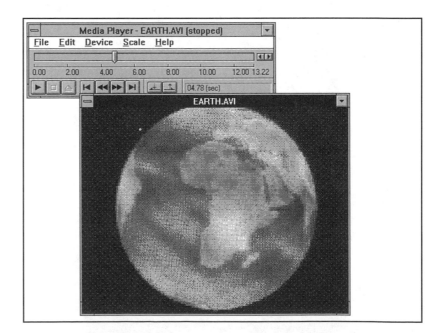

Video for Windows includes a run-time module that you can distribute with any multimedia applications that you create. This module enables your application's users to view video clips that are a part of your multimedia application. The run-time module can be distributed royalty-free as part of your application.

Video for Windows also supports hardware based on the Intel Indeo Video Technology and other i760-based video compression hardware. You can add video cards based on this technology to improve video capture and display.

Displaying Live Video

In addition to displaying captured video that is stored on disk or CD, you can display live video in Windows. To do so, you must have a video capture card or a television adapter in your system. The cost of this type of hardware varies according to the adapter's capabilities. Adapters are available in a wide range of prices. Some adapters provide only television, only video, or a combination of the two. All, however, provide a means for capturing a still image from the live video source.

Figure 37.2 shows video displayed in Windows by the Truevision Bravado 16 video adapter.

Figure 37.2
Live video displayed by the Truevision Bravado 16 video adapter.

TV cards for Windows include an on-board television tuner that essentially makes your PC "cable-ready." You can plug a standard cable TV lead into the card and have access to all the channels you can view on your TV. Video cards that do not include TV support can display TV, but the signal must be routed through a VCR or other device to convert the signal to the proper format. The cable connects to the VCR, for example, and the VCR connects to the video card. Figure 37.3 shows a TV transmission through the Hauppauge Win/TV adapter.

Figure 37.3
Hauppauge Win/TV adapter used to display TV in Windows.

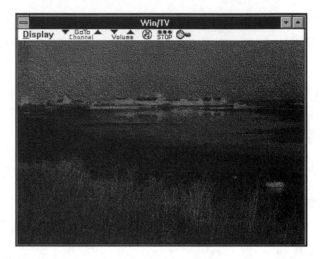

Later sections of this chapter examine a variety of video and TV cards for Windows.

Capturing Video

To capture video from a video source (a VCR or cable TV), you must have a board that supports video capture, such as the Truevision Bravado 16 or New Media Graphics SuperVideo Windows. You also need a video source that the card supports (usually any source that can output NTSC or PAL video signals).

NTSC is the standard television transmission signal used in the United States. PAL is the equivalent standard used in Europe.

When you buy a video capture card, it should include software that lets you capture video in various formats. The software included with the Truevision Bravado 16 card, for example, enables you to capture a still image from a video source and save it in any one of 14 file formats, including PostScript, Targa (TGA), and GIF.

Editing Video

The level of editing you can perform on captured video depends on the capabilities of the card you are using and the software. Many cards include software that lets you view captured single frames and convert files to various graphics-file formats.

Video for Windows enables you to edit video clips, selectively adding, deleting, and overwriting video frames, even if you do not have video capture hardware installed on your system. Figure 37.4 shows the VidEdit program that is included with Video for Windows. Video for Windows also includes a sophisticated bitmap editor that you can use to modify individual frames in your video, then paste them back into the video sequence.

Figure 37.4
VidEdit enables you to edit video clips in Windows.

Some software, particularly the software bundled with most video capture cards, can perform only simple editing tasks, such as converting a captured still image from one format to another or selectively editing the frames in a video clip. Video for Windows, however, offers more extensive editing capabilities.

Storing Video

Video files, like WAV audio files, consume a great deal of disk space. A sample file included with Video for Windows consists of just 81 frames (just over five seconds of video) but takes up over 1 MB of disk space—even in its compressed state.

A large hard disk is acceptable for storing video clips as you are working on them, but you probably need to put them on a CD if you want to distribute them. Although you are working with video on your hard disk, remember that disk fragmentation has a significant effect not only on playback speed, but also on the capability to capture video without dropping any frames. For the best performance, you should defragment the hard disk before beginning a video capture sequence. You also may want to defragment the disk before playing back video from the hard disk.

Video for Windows

Microsoft's Video for Windows enables you to capture, play, and edit video. Video for Windows is a software-only product, but it supports Intel Indeo-based hardware and other i760-based video hardware products (the Intel processor used in Intel's Indeo products) for better capture and playback performance.

Video for Windows includes five new applications and an enhanced Media Player. The applications enable you to display and capture video and to edit video, WAV files, color palettes, and bitmaps (such as single-frame images). Figures 37.5 through 37.9 show the applications that are bundled with Video for Windows.

Figure 37.5
VidEdit lets you play and edit video clips.

Figure 37.6
VidCap lets you preview and capture video to disk.

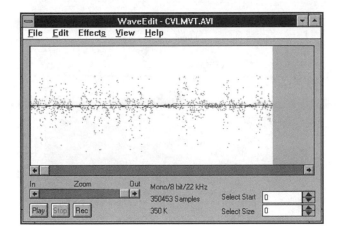

Figure 37.7
WaveEdit lets you edit the audio portion of a video clip.

Figure 37.8
PalEdit provides a color palette editor for controlling a video's color palette.

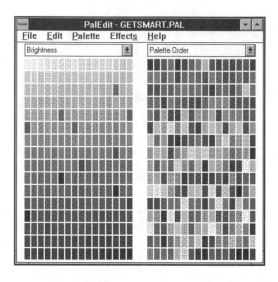

Figure 37.9
BitEdit lets you edit bitmaps, such as individual video frames.

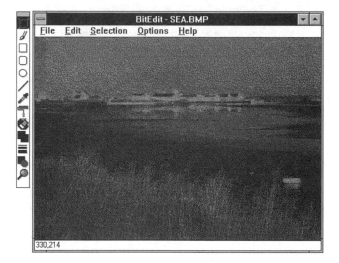

Using VidEdit To Display Video

Video for Windows enables you to play and edit video without a video capture card—but you do need a CD-ROM drive. Video for Windows comes with a large selection of video clip samples (stored on CD) that you can display and edit.

To play a video clip in Video for Windows, you can use either the VidEdit application or the Media Player. To play a video with the Media Player, start the Media Player and select <u>D</u>evice, <u>V</u>ideo for Windows. Media Player displays a standard file dialog box, which you can use to locate the desired AVI file. (AVI is the Video for Windows file format.) Figure 37.10 shows the Media Player playing a video clip in a window.

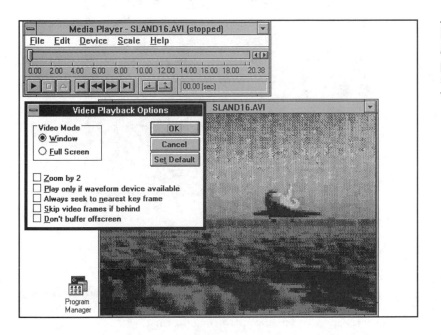

Figure 37.10
Media Player can play video full-screen or in a window.

Video for Windows uses a standard data file format called Audio/Video Interleaved format (AVI). AVI files store video and audio in the same file, interleaved in much the same way that audio is stored with images on movie film (although the technology and actual storage method are completely different). A single frame of the video consists of an audio portion and a video portion that reside side-by-side in the file. Both Video for Windows and the Media Player can play back AVI files.

You also can use the VidEdit application to display video clips. To do so, first open the AVI file, and then click on the Play button. VidEdit offers options to play video and audio, video only, or audio only. Figure 37.11 shows VidEdit playing a sample video clip that is included with Video for Windows.

Figure 37.11
VidEdit playing a
sample video clip.

Capturing Video

The VidCap application supplied with Video for Windows enables you to capture video clips to disk if you have a supported video capture card. You also need a video source, such as a VCR or cable TV input. Depending on the card, you may need a VCR or other device to convert the cable signal into the proper format for the card.

VidCap provides four options for capturing video. You can capture a single frame, selection of frames, continuous video sequence, or a video color palette. Single frames, frame selections, and palettes are captured to disk. Video sequences can be captured either to memory or to disk. If you capture video to memory, you can save it to disk when the capture is complete.

Capturing Single Frames

You can use VidCap to capture a single frame of video and store it to disk as a Windows Device-Independent Bitmap (DIB). You then can load it into the BitEdit application to edit the frame and import it into a video sequence.

Capturing a Selection of Frames

VidCap also lets you capture selected frames to an AVI file on disk. You first specify the file into which the frames will be stored, and then select Capture, Frames. VidCap displays the Capture Frames dialog box, as shown in figure 37.12. Click on the Capture button to capture the current frame to the specified AVI file.

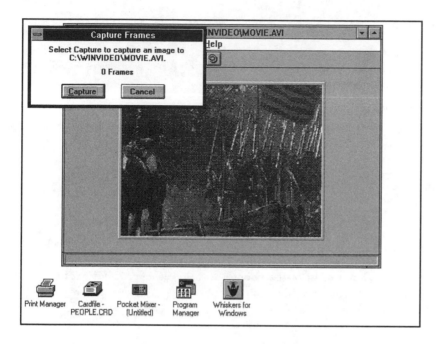

Figure 37.12
VidCap lets you capture selected frames to an AVI file.

Capturing Video Sequences

VidCap supports a number of options for capturing a video sequence to an AVI file or to memory. If captured to memory, a video clip can be saved to disk after the capture is complete. VidCap supports the following four video size modes (based on a full size of 640×480):

- ✔ 1/8: 80×60
- ✔ 1/4: 160×120
- ✔ 1/2: 320×240
- ✔ Full: 640×480

The larger the video mode selected, the more memory and disk space is required to capture a video sequence. In addition, the ratio of dropped frames increases as the image size increases. Capturing full-screen video without losing over half of the video's frames requires special high-speed (and expensive) video capture equipment.

In addition to these different video sizes, VidCap supports the following color modes:

✔ **8-bit palettized.** Stores the video in 8-bit color depth with a single palette. The default palette is a 64-shade, grayscale palette, but you can capture a color palette and assign it to the video clip.

✔ **16-bit RGB.** Captures the video using 16-bit color depth, without a palette. Color information is stored with each frame, doubling the amount of video data in each frame.

✔ **24-bit RGB.** Captures the video using 24-bit color depth, without a palette. Color information is stored with each frame, tripling the amount of video data in each frame.

As with video mode, higher color resolution results in more dropped frames, because more information must be captured for each frame. Even so, you do not have to have a 24-bit video adapter in your system to capture in 24-bit RGB mode. You may not be able to edit 24-bit images without a 24-bit video adapter, however.

Figure 37.13 shows the dialog box used in VidCap to specify the video mode for a video sequence capture.

Figure 37.13
Setting the size and color options for a video sequence.

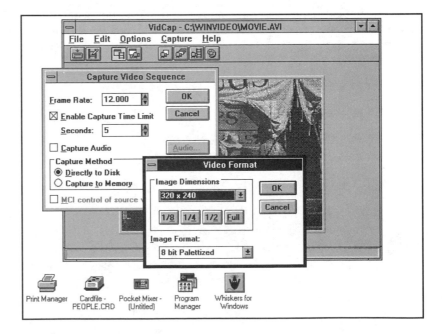

If you capture a video clip with the 8-bit palettized option and the default palette, the resulting video clip is grayscale. An alternative is to capture a color palette from the video source (explained later), and then capture the video sequence by using the 8-bit palettized option. When played back, the video uses the captured color palette rather than the default grayscale palette. For the best color reproduction, you can use either the 16-bit RGB or 24-bit RGB options.

Your success in capturing video sequences with VidCap depends on the video mode in which you capture the frames (8-bit palettized, 16-bit RGB, 24-bit RGB, and image size). As you increase the capture size (to one-half, for example), you also increase the likelihood that frames will be missed during capture. Also, both of the RGB modes increase the number of frames that are dropped from the sequence because VidCap must handle a much higher volume of data.

Figure 37.14 shows the Capture Video Sequence dialog box that enables you to control video sequence capture options. You can use this dialog box to specify the frame rate, time limit, capture method, and other video sequence options. If an MCI-controllable VCR or other device is used as the video source, you also can use the Capture Video Sequence dialog box to control the device, specifying start and stop points, for example.

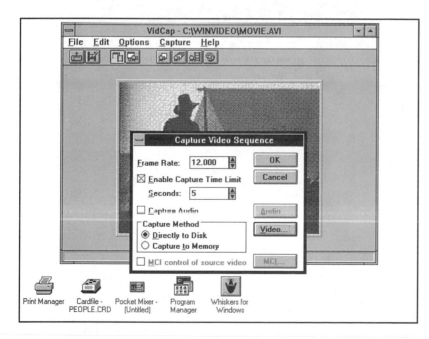

Figure 37.14
The Capture Video Sequence dialog box controls capture options.

Capturing a Palette

If you want to capture video using the 8-bit palettized option, but want the video to appear in color, you first must capture a palette from the video source. The palette is stored on disk as a sampling of colors. The video then can be sampled in grayscale and the palette applied later for playback. The advantage to this method is that sampling in grayscale generates the fewest dropped frames. If, however, the colors vary widely in the captured video, the single color palette is applied to the entire clip, potentially making portions of the video look different from the original (because a different range of colors is being used).

VidCap offers a handful of options for capturing a palette; you control those options through the Capture Palette dialog box, which appears in figure 37.15. You can specify the number of colors to include in the palette, for example. The more colors in the palette, the better the color resolution.

Figure 37.15
Capturing a color palette from the video source.

Reducing the number of colors can help provide smaller video files after the video is compressed.

You also can capture a palette from a single frame of video or create a palette from a series of frames. You can improve the color resolution of the captured video sequence by sampling a selection of frames, thus building a palette from a wider selection of colors. After you have captured a palette, the video sequence you later capture with the 8-bit palettized option will use the captured palette automatically. You also can use the PalEdit application to save a palette to a file for editing.

Editing Video

The VidEdit application supplied with Video for Windows enables you to edit AVI video sequence files, as well as DIB sequence files and Autodesk Animation files (FLI and FLC files). VidEdit enables you to play back a sequence, cut and insert frames, synchronize video and audio, and perform many other editing operations on the video. Figure 37.16 shows VidEdit with an AVI file loaded for editing.

Figure 37.16
VidEdit with an AVI file loaded for editing.

VI

Applying Multimedia

VidEdit lets you specify the following characteristics for the video sequence:

✔ **Compression options.** You can specify the compression method to be used, which enables you to optimize compression for specific devices, such as hard disk and CD-ROM at various data-transfer rates. You also can specify the video-compression technique to be used, such as Full Frames, Microsoft Video 1, or Intel Indeo Video. You can use predefined settings or create custom settings.

✔ **Adjust frame rate.** You can adjust the number of frames per second without affecting the duration of the sequence or its synchronization with the audio track. Changing the frame rate adds or deletes frames from the sequence.

✔ **Synchronize audio and video.** You can fine-tune the synchronization between the audio and video tracks, changing the frame rate and audio offset to achieve synchronization between the two.

✔ **Change audio format.** You can control the characteristics of the audio track, including mono/stereo, sampling size (8-bit/16-bit), and sampling frequency.

✔ **Change video format.** You can select from the 8-bit, 16-bit, and 24-bit video options.

You also can create a palette from a loaded video sequence, crop and resize frames, and control other frame selection and playback options.

VidEdit enables you to export frames to a variety of file formats, enabling you to load them into other applications or into BitEdit for editing.

Editing Bitmaps

The BitEdit application enables you to edit bitmaps. You can, for example, export a frame to a bitmap file, perform extensive editing on the frame, and then insert it back into the video by using the VidEdit application. Figure 37.17 shows the BitEdit application with a bitmap that has been copied from a video sequence to a bitmap file.

Figure 37.17
A video frame displayed in BitEdit for editing.

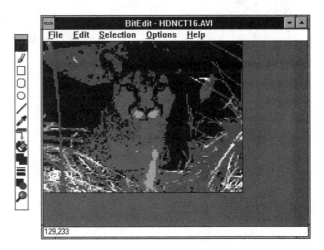

BitEdit provides all the graphics tools found in a typical graphics paint program. In addition, it provides specialized tools for color reduction, scaling, and palette manipulation. It also supports a wide variety of file formats, so you can import files from and export them to virtually any source. BitEdit is an excellent tool for editing frames, developing title frames, adding captions to your video sequence, and adding special effects to the video.

Editing Color Palettes

The PalEdit application lets you edit a palette file that you have captured from a video source or a palette contained in a bitmap or AVI file. Figure 37.18 shows the PalEdit application.

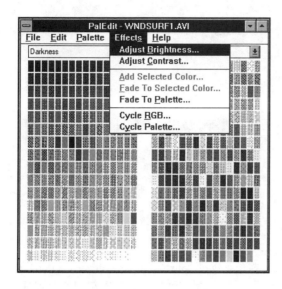

Figure 37.18
The PalEdit
application is used
to edit palette files.

You can use PalEdit to perform the following functions:

✔ Modify a color in a palette

✔ Change the color tint, brightness, and contrast of the entire palette

✔ Reduce the number of colors in the palette

✔ Copy colors from one palette to another

✔ Create a single palette that can be used by multiple video sequences or bitmap files

Editing Audio (WAV)

The WaveEdit application enables you to edit WAV files. You can use WaveEdit to edit a WAV file, the WAV track from an AVI file, an Apple AIFF file, or a Microsoft PCM waveform file. You can pull the audio track from a video sequence, for example, and modify it. Figure 37.19 shows the WaveEdit application with the WAV track from an AVI file loaded for editing.

WaveEdit does not offer a broad range of audio editing effects, but it does enable you to fade selections of the audio track up and down, insert silence, amplify a selection, and use the Clipboard to cut and paste audio.

Figure 37.19
WaveEdit editing
the audio track
from an AVI file.

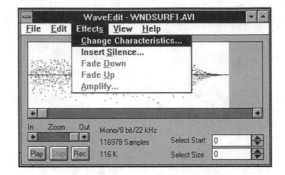

Viewing Television in Windows

You can choose from a number of add-in video boards that let you watch TV in a window. These boards include TV tuners that essentially make your Windows PC "cable-ready." In addition to supporting input from cable TV, these video boards also support input from other composite video sources, such as a VCR, video camera, or laser disc player. This section briefly examines two Windows TV cards: the Hauppauge Win/TV and the New Media Graphics WatchIt! cards.

Hauppauge Win/TV

The Hauppauge Win/TV card is a 16-bit TV adapter for Windows. You can install up to three Win/TV cards in a system, providing input from three simultaneous sources. This card supports these video sources:

- ✔ NSTC-M
- ✔ NTSC-N
- ✔ PAL-B
- ✔ PAL-G
- ✔ PAL-H
- ✔ PAL-I
- ✔ PAL-M
- ✔ PAL-N
- ✔ SECAM
- ✔ S-Video

You can connect cable TV, a VCR, a laser disc player, or a camcorder to the Win/TV card. The card's tuner supports up to 122 channels. The card supports 640×480 and 800×600 video non-interlaced modes and 1,024×768 interlaced modes. The audio output on the Win/TV card can drive unamplified speakers.

The Win/TV board's software displays the video input in a fully resizeable window. When reduced to an icon, the Win/TV application displays the video in the icon. Figure 37.20 shows the Win/TV application.

Figure 37.20
The Hauppauge Win/TV application.

With the Win/TV application, you can control all aspects of the Win/TV card. You can set and choose channels, control audio, and set video options for brightness, contrast, saturation, and color. The Win/TV application also enables you to capture and save an image in a variety of graphics file formats.

New Media Graphics WatchIT!

The New Media Graphics WatchIT! is an 8-bit TV adapter for Windows. The WatchIT! card supports up to 99 channels and accepts input from cable TV, a VCR, or a video camera. Unlike the Win/TV board, however, WatchIT! works only at 640×480 resolution. The WatchIT! card cannot drive unamplified speakers, but it includes a pair of mini-headphones.

The WatchIT! software supports three window sizes at $\frac{1}{16}$, $\frac{1}{4}$, and full-screen (640×480). When reduced to an icon, the icon does not continue to display video. The software lets you capture and save a video frame in a variety of graphic-file formats. Figure 37.21 shows the WatchIT! application.

Figure 37.21
The WatchIT! TV
application and
remote control.

The WatchIT! card also includes a DOS application that you can use to watch TV while working in the DOS environment outside of Windows.

INDEX

INDEX

INDEX

INDEX

INDEX

INDEX

INDEX

INDEX

INDEX

INDEX

INDEX

INDEX

INDEX

INDEX

INDEX

INDEX

INDEX

INDEX

INDEX

INDEX

INDEX

INDEX

INDEX

INDEX

INDEX

INDEX

INDEX

INDEX

INDEX

INDEX

INDEX

INDEX

INDEX

INDEX

INDEX

INDEX

Inside Windows, Platinum Edition
REGISTRATION CARD

Fill out this card to receive information about future Windows books and other New Riders titles!

Name _____ **Title** _____

Company _____

Address _____

City/State/ZIP _____

I bought this book because: _____

_____

I purchased this book from:

☐ A bookstore (Name _____)

☐ A software or electronics store (Name _____)

☐ A mail order (Name of Catalog _____)

I purchase this many computer books each year:

☐ 1–5 ☐ 6 or more

I currently use these applications: _____

_____

_____

_____

I found these chapters to be the most informative: _____

_____

I found these chapters to be the least informative: _____

_____

Additional comments: _____

_____

☐ I would like to see my name in print! You may use my name and quote me in future New Riders products and promotions. My daytime phone number is:_____

New Riders Publishing 201 West 103rd Street • Indianapolis, Indiana 46290 USA

Fold Here

PLACE
STAMP
HERE

New Riders Publishing
201 West 103rd Street
Indianapolis, Indiana 46290
USA

Fold Here

- -

PLACE
STAMP
HERE

New Riders Publishing
201 West 103rd Street
Indianapolis, Indiana 46290
USA